LEEDS TRANSPORT

VOLUME 4 1953 to 1974

By

J.Soper Dipl.T.P., Dipl. Arch.

Published by the Leeds Transport Historical Society 2007

A Society for the study and preservation of local passenger transport
Registered Charity No. 501642
Registered Address: 4 Maplewood Paddock, York YO24 3LB

Printed by Amadeus Press, Cleckheaton BD19 4TQ

To my wife, Valerie, again for continuing patience and understanding.

Contents

First published 2007

ISBN 978-0-9510280-2-5

Introduction

Volume 4 of Leeds Transport carries forward the story of the trams and buses from 1953 when the tramways were at the beginning of a modernisation programme. However, in that year a decision was made to abandon the tramways system. The story then continues to 1974 when the Leeds City Transport undertaking ceased to exist. It became incorporated into the West Yorkshire Passenger Transport Executive, which also included the local municipal transport undertakings of Bradford, Halifax and Huddersfield.

At the request of a number of readers, the L.T.H.S. has decided to produce a Volume 5 and carry forward the Leeds transport story into the WYPTE years and also include details of all known preserved Leeds City Transport and WYPTE vehicles. It is also intended to include some of the many photographs for which space was not available in the previous volumes. An index for all five volumes will be provided in Volume 5. However, for readers requiring an index for Volumes 1 to 4, this will be available free of charge from the Honorary Secretary of the L.T.H.S. at 4 Maplewood Paddock, York, YO24 3LB.

We apologise if we have overlooked any contributors to this volume, and would like to thank Messrs. B.Donald, I.M.Dougill, P.Malone, J.B.Parkin, B.Pickup, J.N.D. Proudlock and A.K.Terry for helping in the research and checking the script. The Appendix on the bus fleet and tickets chapter would have been impossible without the expertise of Mr. Parkin. Similarly that on the bus destination blinds would not exist without the help of Mr. Terry.

Special thanks are due to the late W.D.Wilson who allowed copies to be made of his very detailed diaries and notes on both trams and buses. E.Smith, son of Councillor T.W.Smith, Deputy Chairman of the Transport Committee, helped by allowing his father's records to be consulted.

We would like to thank the following who have helped with this volume in various ways: R.Benton, C.Bogg, A.W.Bond, R.Brook, D.Broughton, A.Cowell, M.Gilks, P.Groves, H.Heyworth, M.Hindes, P.D.Johnson, J.G.Kaye, J. Lambert, W.M.Lloyd, G.Lumb, J.D.Markham, Miss J.Newiss, Messrs. K.Plant, B.Render, E.Snart, Mrs. H.M.Spencer, R.Syms, Dr. C.C.Thornburn, Messrs. C.Wales, D.Watson, B.Wilkinson, C.Withey, G.Wilton, C.Wright, A.D.Young and the staff of the National Tramway Museum Library, Leeds Reference Library, the West Yorkshire Archives Department, Leeds Corporation, Leeds City Transport Department, West Yorkshire Passenger Transport Executive and Yorkshire Rider Ltd.

The principal source of information was the 'Leeds Tramway News', later the 'Leeds and District Transport News' and currently the Metro Transport News'. These were edited from 1952 to 1958 by A.K.Terry and from 1958 to date by J.B.Parkin. As far as is known this is the only detailed and accurate source of information on Leeds transport after the late 1950's. It mainly gives information on rolling stock, routes and fare collection. It also gives details of alterations to the roads used by buses. Apart from occasional references in the local newspapers, this information does not appear to be recorded elsewhere.

In 1967 a new Conservative Council was elected and from the historian's point of view this was a retrograde step. The new administration embarked on an extensive "cost cutting exercise". The Transport Committee was combined with three other committees. Council documentation was "simplified". Minutes of committees, which had been printed were now typed and the information was sparse. If there were any queries the lack of detail rendered both Council officials and Councillors less accountable. The admirable annual reports of Committees, which gave important statistical information on the Corporation's activities were discontinued. Hence after 1969 there is little statistical detail on Leeds transport. Passenger numbers, mileage run by buses etc. are rarely officially recorded and much information, including financial details, became very generalised and of little use to researchers.

Information found has been supplemented by the local newspapers, 'The Yorkshire Post', 'Yorkshire Evening Post' and 'Yorkshire Evening News'. All issues covering the period in question have been consulted.

The City Council minutes, the General Manager's and Transport Committee annual reports and reports of other committees, the City Council annual accounts, most of the above at the Leeds Reference Library, were checked. The traffic records or "Guard Books" and tramcar and motor bus drawings and photographs at the West Yorkshire Archives Department, Wakefield, have been inspected.

Articles in the Leeds Transport Historical Society's news sheets have provided information, as also have contemporary publications such as 'Modern Tramway,' Buses Illustrated', 'Tramway Review' and the 'Tramway Museum Society Journal'.

Technical publications, 'Transport World', 'Passenger Transport'. 'The Journal of the Institute of Transport', and minutes of the National Joint Industrial Council for the Transport industry were seen at the National Tramway Museum Library.

Modern publications consulted were 'Leeds Trams, 1939-1959', by Andrew D.Young; 'Leeds, A History of its Tramways', by Noel Proudlock; 'Leeds Trams, A Penny Ride to Town, 1933 to 1950' by Brian Render; 'The Felthams', by K.C. Blacker; 'Charles Roe, Coachbuilders, Vol.1' by R.Marshall; 'Charles H. Roe, includes Optare'. by Geoff Lumb and 'Leeds Cinemas Remembered' by R.E.Preedy.

All known sources of information have been checked, but there are contradictions between some sources and any further details or photographs would be welcome. Photographs not credited are in the Society collection.

In its publications the aim of the Leeds Transport Historical Society is to try and obtain 100% accuracy. When many different topics are discussed, some very specialised, this is difficult to achieve. Subsequent research has shown that some inaccuracies crept into Volumes 1 to 3 and we are very grateful to those who have kindly pointed them out. Addenda to Volumes 1 to 3 are included at the end of this volume, which incorporate corrections and additional information that has since come to light.

Since the publication of Volume 3 the L.T.H.S. has acquired the Leeds photographic collection of the late W.D.Wilson. The Society is also preparing a digital archive of all known black and white Leeds transport photographs taken prior to 1953 and all known Leeds tramway and early bus colour photographs. In conjunction with the National Tramway Museum Archive it is hoped that these will be available to all through the Internet.

In addition to its interest in the history of Leeds transport, the L.T.H.S., founded in February 1959, assists with the restoration and maintenance of the Leeds tramcars at the National Tramway Museum, Crich, Derbyshire, and Leeds buses at the Keighley Bus Museum. It also owns the body of Leeds, 1898-built, Milnes double deck horse tram No.107. A start has recently been made on this vehicle's restoration.

J.Soper, Leeds Transport Historical Society,
2 Eastbrook Court, Bramham, Wetherby, West Yorkshire, LS23 6ZA.
April 2007.

For a period of over 25 years the Leeds tramway scene was dominated by the 1926-1927 built 185 Chamberlain cars. They were the largest series of trams in the Leeds fleet. Car 49 was photographed on the double bend on the picturesque Temple Newsam route on 19 April 1954. This route and that to Cross Gates, were the final tram routes to be abandoned on 7 November 1959. *Author.*

The Tramways: the Beginning of the End

In early 1953 the Leeds tramways system was at the start of an extensive modernisation programme. The Transport Committee of the Conservative-controlled City Council was under the chairmanship of Alderman Donald G. Cowling. Also on the Committee was Councillor Bertrand Mather who had chaired a Special Investigation Sub-Committee, which had spent "hundreds of hours" trying to make economies on the tramways system in retiming and modifying services. It had, however, been thwarted by ever increasing costs in labour and materials.

The tramways had always had a very frequent service with a low fares culture. For a period of 50 years from 1894 to 1944 fares had remained virtually static. The average fare paid per passenger in 1894 had been 1·290d. and in 1944 1·577d. By 1953 it had increased by about one penny to 2·667d. Bus fares were higher than tram fares, sometimes by as much as 100% for the same distance. Buses were less frequent and there were fewer stops per mile.

As an economy, Mather's Sub-Committee had recommended that the short, lightly used, Half Mile Lane to Stanningley section be abandoned and this had taken place on 2 January 1953. Also recommended for closure was route number 4, the Kirkstall Abbey tramway. The rails were in urgent need of renewal and the trams were facing severe competition from not only the Corporation's number 71 bus route to Guiseley, but parallel services operated by Samuel Ledgard Ltd. and the West Yorkshire Road Car Company. No operator on the route was making a profit.

Services making a loss were the remainder of the number 14 Half Mile Lane route and the 1, 2 and 3 routes (Lawnswood to Moortown and Roundhay circulars). The 1, 2 and 3's accounted for half the loss on the tramways. Both the Half Mile Lane and Lawnswood services suffered from bus competition. The Lawnswood, Moortown and Roundhay areas were the most affluent in the city and the trams were suffering due to the recent abolition of petrol rationing. Passengers were deserting public transport in favour of the motor car.

On order from local coach builders, Charles H. Roe Ltd., were two experimental single deck rail cars. If successful, it was hoped that these would be the prototypes of a new fleet of tramcars to replace the existing fleet, nearly all of which was over twenty years old.

The Transport Committee had enjoyed the tacit support of the Labour party opposition under Councillor John Rafferty, (from May 1952 an Alderman), but it had always been lukewarm. The far-sighted proposals of the war time Conservative Reconstruction Committee to institute a system of underground tramways in the city centre to the design of the Transport General Manager, William Vane Morland and the City Engineer, Colonel W.S. Cameron, had not been liked by the Socialists and when they took over control of the City Council in November 1945 the plans were "put on ice."

One of the local newspapers, the now defunct 'Yorkshire Evening News', had been editorially opposed to the tramways, and from the abandonment of the decrepit tramway system in Manchester in 1949, it had conducted a virulent campaign in Leeds and blamed all the financial and other problems on the tramways. It ignored the very low tram fares and the fact that on most routes the trams were running at four-minute intervals. In 1950 the Leeds trams and buses had carried 252 million passengers, the highest number ever achieved.

The newspaper campaign reached a crescendo in January and February 1953 with full page articles week

Briggate barriers during Coronation week 1953 with Chamberlain 58 in the blue livery. For the Coronation, the Transport Department decorated the roof of the barriers with red, white and blue bunting. The date: 31 May 1953. *Author.*

after week in an effort to influence the City Council elections due to be held in May. There were headlines such as "Trams are museum pieces with no economic future," and the newspaper rejected the proposed experiments with railcars as they "merely complicated the situation."

The Conservatives wished to continue with tramway modernisation, but the Socialists had been out of power for two years and succumbed to the propaganda of the 'Yorkshire Evening News'. The Liberal party was also in favour of tramway abandonment.

Alderman Rafferty made his famous remark to a young newspaper reporter, Keith Waterhouse, some two months before the official announcement that the Socialists were to abandon the tramways. Pointing to some trams in Park Row he remarked, "Tha sees yon trams lad? We're getting shot o' the buggers." The announcement came on 6 March 1953 stating that if elected, the Socialist party would embark on a policy of tramway abandonment. The trams were to be replaced by motor buses.

In an article Councillor Mather condemned the Socialist "facile arguments" and their proposals as "loose thinking." He pointed out the very low tram fares and that the changeover from trams to buses was almost entirely confined to cities in Great Britain. In virtually every other country tramways were being modernised and extended. Mather said that in other towns the changeover from trams to buses had not resulted in less congestion, faster journeys and huge profits. He compared the four minute

In 1952 the Kirkstall Abbey tramway had been recommended for closure by Councillor Bertrand Mather's Special Investigation Sub-Committee. On 11 October 1953 Horsfield car 251 is at the Cardigan Square tram stop at Kirkstall Library in Abbey Road. It is heading for Kirkstall Abbey. *Author.*

It was hoped that the new railcars would be a prototype to replace the existing tramway fleet. 602 is in Duncan Street on 14 June 1953. The decorations for the Coronation of Queen Elizabeth II are still in place. *Author.*

It was rare to see two trams passing in Bishopgate Street. The street was used by trams running to and from Swinegate Depot and by the peak hour service from Belle Isle to Hyde Park. The trams are 119 and 408 and the photograph was taken at 5.40 p.m. on Wednesday 1 July 1953. The City Station is in the background. *Author.*

tram service to the Belle Isle Estate with the fifteen minute bus service to the housing estate at Moortown. "Is it surprising that this bus has a better chance of paying than the tram, which has to spread its income over nearly four times as many vehicles?"

Mather said he could name a road in Leeds, which had been adapted for buses by minor alterations, and had cost more than providing the same length of tram route. This item did not appear in the "cost per mile" for the buses, but would have been included in the tram costs. He said that major assets would be destroyed, such as the long stretches of reserved track, which segregated the trams from other road traffic. He queried the long-term effects of relying on imported fuel oil rather than coal-produced electricity. He advised that the matter be "very carefully" studied before a decision was made.

Alderman David Beevers, leader of the Socialist group, said that the trams were at a great disadvantage economically. Beevers said that the city was losing money on the trams while the buses were making a slight profit. The transport undertaking expected to have a deficit at the end of the financial year of £53,340 and a deficit of £107,210 at 31 March 1954, bringing the accumulated deficit to £478,000.

"The recently announced rise in the price of coal will lead to a further increase in the price of electricity and this will add a further burden to the running of tramways, " said Beevers. He optimistically stated that there was a possibility that tax on fuel oil would be reduced. He admitted that the cost of maintaining the highways would be transferred from the tramways to the highways authorities, but thought that this would be less costly. "This does not mean that trams will disappear from Leeds in the next few months if we are returned to power," he said. "But a start will be made on the changeover immediately we are in power. It will be a slow process taking possibly from 10

to 15 years with old and unserviceable tracks going first."

....There is no question of the city keeping old crocks of trams for use on the last routes to be abolished, for it is our intention to purchase modern railcars of the type now undergoing tests in Leeds," said Alderman Beevers. "This will ensure that the standard of comfort is maintained on the tramways to the end."

'Yorkshire Evening News', 6 March 1953.

One of the promises of the Socialists in the municipal election campaign of 1945 was a pledge to introduce penny fares on the trams. This they had been unable to do. However, immediately after the Socialist tramway abandonment statement of 6 March, the Conservative-controlled Transport Committee announced that, "in an effort to attract more passengers," it would reintroduce penny fares. The concession was aimed primarily at housewives and the elderly, custom that had been driven away by fare increases.

The proposal, which did not include bus services, was for the introduction of one, two or three penny fare stages from all tram termini. The penny journeys would be about half a mile. This was about half the pre-war distance. Alderman Cowling commented:

"We feel that the proposal will benefit the public and substantially increase the department's revenue. The additional revenue will be more or less net profit, because the vehicles will still be running in the normal way. At present they are less than half full at many parts of the day."

'The Yorkshire Post', 11 March 1953.

Councillor Mather said that what the Committee was doing was to reduce the price to attract custom without any additional expense to the department.

At its meeting on 16 March the scheme to introduce 33 penny fare stages on the outer sections of the tram routes was approved by the Transport Committee. The proposal was opposed by the Socialists, but came into effect on Sunday, 12 April. Although stated to be a "big success" the number of additional passengers attracted in the first two weeks was 10,248 with an increased income of about £21 weekly, hardly likely to have much effect on reducing the department's large deficit.

The City Council elections resulted in the Socialist being returned to power with a majority of 12 seats. At the Transport Committee on 19 May Alderman Rafferty was elected Chairman.

From the inception of the Tramways Committee in the 1890's, it had been customary for a member of the opposition party to occupy the post of deputy chairman. This changed in 1953. Despite protestations from Councillor Mather and the other Conservatives, Rafferty appointed Socialist, Councillor T.W. Smith, as his deputy. Smith was of a completely different character to Rafferty – a "very quiet man," to quote his son, Eric. A deputy chairman had access to confidential information on the Department's activities. This was denied to the Conservatives under the Rafferty administration.

Alderman Cowling left the Transport Committee and was Lord Mayor of Leeds for the years 1953-54. He later retired to Carlton Husthwaite, near Thirsk, where he died on 30 January 1975 at the age of 70. Councillor Mather became spokesman for the Conservatives on the new Transport Committee.

At the following Committee meeting on 15 June there was a resolution to scrap the penny fares scheme and begin a programme of tramway abandonment. The first route to be closed was the number 14 route from Corn Exchange to Half Mile Lane. A scheme was to be prepared for the closure of route 4 to Kirkstall Abbey and 10 to Compton Road and the substitution of a bus service between the two points. Upon the closure of the Compton Road service, the Dewsbury Road trams were to be linked with the Harehills and Roundhay services, The 14 route had received major consideration by the Special Investigation Sub-Committee a year or so before. A.B.Findlay, the General Manager, had said in a report of September 1951, that this area was "in the most need of examination." The tram route was paralleled by the number 54, 65 and 72 bus services for much of its length. One of the proposals of the Sub-Committee had been to re-route the 65 Pudsey bus service via Kirkstall to avoid competition with the trams. The timetable of the cross-city 44 bus route was to be revised to co-ordinate with that of the altered 65 service. On 16 February 1953 the proposals had been agreed by the Transport Committee, and an application for approval was made to the Yorkshire Traffic Commissioners. The alterations, however, had not been put into effect. The decision to abandon the Half Mile Lane trams resulted in the proposed bus route modifications being thrown out by the new Transport Committee.

The reason why the Half Mile Lane route was the first to be selected for abandonment was not stated. The track was in serviceable condition and had several years of life. Over a mile of the tramway was on a central reserved track. At the City Council meeting on 1 July, Rafferty said

Evening sunlight in Chapeltown Road at Sheepscar on 18 January 1953 with Chamberlain car 64. The rails of the Roundhay tram route can be seen in the foreground. Although Chapeltown Road exists in name, everything on this photograph has disappeared: the tram, buildings and even St. Clement's Church in the misty background. The church was demolished in April and May 1976. *Author.*

At the beginning of 1953 Leeds-built car 396 was still running, but not for long. It was photographed in Call Lane at the Corn Exchange on 4 February 1953 on route 14 to Half Mile Lane. *Author*.

Horsfield car 221 at Half Mile Lane on 12 September 1953.   The number 14 route to Half Mile Lane was the first tramway route to be abandoned under the new Socialist administration. *Author*.

the decision was based on a desire to reduce as quickly as possible the loss now being incurred. He made no reference to the new railcars, which had just entered service, nor were they, except on one brief occasion, subsequently mentioned by Rafferty.

The proposals were bitterly opposed by the Conservatives. Councillor Bennett said most of the trams were 25 years old and comparison with buses was being made against a ridiculous background. Had any city solved its transport problems by scrapping its trams and electric transport on heavy routes? Everywhere, one found greater congestion, added chaos and inability to get home. Returns showed that buses had not decreased losses. The tram service, which it was proposed to scrap was one of the most important in the city and about one third of the track was up to date and enclosed.

Councillor Mather described the proposal to substitute buses for trams as a "Leeds groundnuts scheme" and said it would appear to cost £16,000 more than the present set up. Alderman Rafferty, it seemed, had adopted the Hitler technique of relying on intuition coupled with a refusal to face facts, which might challenge these intuitive processes. Further economies could reasonably have been expected if the Conservatives had remained in control.

Mather was also upset about the decision to abolish penny fares saying it had not been a fair trial.

"The main disadvantage of the penny fares scheme is that it was a Conservative idea, and must therefore be put out of operation by a Socialist administration regardless of any adverse effect on the public."

'Yorkshire Evening Post', 2 July 1953.

Alderman F.H. O'Donnell, Socialist, said that the penny fares scheme was making a daily loss. The penny fares were withdrawn on 12 July.

The decision to abandon the tramway system marked an end to the small improvements, which had taken place under the Conservatives. The last major one was the addition of a third loading track in Call Lane at the Corn Exchange. This was completed in March 1953, and is discussed in Chapter 56 of Volume 3.

One improvement suggested by the previous administration was, however, carried out. This was the change of the Cross Flatts Park short working in Dewsbury Road to a point about a quarter of a mile closer to the city centre at the Crescent Cinema, opposite Woodview Grove. There were fewer houses between the Crescent and Cross Flatts Park and the trams were usually empty. A turning point at the Crescent saved a lot of "dead" mileage. A crossover was inserted over a period of a month from 18 August to mid-September 1953.

In July 1953 plans were submitted by the City Engineer to alter the junction of Balm Road and Church Street in Hunslet on the Belle Isle and Middleton circular tram route. This would ease the curve and improve the tramway track arrangement at this location. The alteration would have necessitated the relaying of some of the tram track in Church Street and Balm Road, and was rejected by the Transport Committee.

The crossover in the middle of Belle Isle Circus was removed in late July 1953. This turning point had not been used since the tramway was extended to Middleton Road, Belle Isle, in 1946.

The original proposals of the Socialist party had been to abandon the tramway system gradually over a period of from ten to fifteen years. On his "annual tour of inspection" on 4 August 1953, Rafferty said that the policy of the Transport Committee was now to scrap the trams "as soon as possible." He appears to have been acting on his own initiative for no reference to the policy change was made in the minutes of the Transport Committee. He said that there was a scheme for a big new bus garage at Seacroft and plans were to be drawn up to convert the tram depot at Headingley into a bus garage.

"The Seacroft bus depot will be on land on the Ring Road between Wetherby Road and Wellington Hill. It will accommodate about 100 buses and will be the second largest in Leeds. Conversion of the Headingley tram depot will begin next year when the Kirkstall and Stanningley tram routes have been scrapped and replaced by buses. There is already garage accommodation for 40 buses and there will be room for a further 30 when the conversion has been carried out. The trams will be housed at other depots in the city."

'The Yorkshire Post', 25 August 1953.

In November 1953 the Transport Committee agreed to inform the Ministry of Transport that it intended "within an approximate period of ten years" to abandon the various tram routes in the city and replace them with bus services.

Application was made to the Yorkshire Traffic Commissioners for the closure of the Half Mile Lane tram service and the substitution of buses. Approval was received on 17 September, the Transport Department announcing that it was to start the new bus service on Sunday, 4 October 1953. The last tram was to run on the Saturday night. This marked the start of the tramway abandonment programme.

Horsfield car 248 leaves the Norman Grove tram stop in Abbey Road on 1 September 1953. *Author.*

A wintry scene in Harrogate Road, Chapel Allerton, on Sunday, 8 February 1953. A Chamberlain car is approaching the brow of the hill at Wood Lane. The writer recorded in his diary that the new sodium electric lighting in Harrogate Road between Stainbeck Lane and Wood Lane was switched on at 4.45 p.m. on 9 November 1953. The gas lamps were turned off for the last time at 5.30 p.m. *Author*.

Horsfield car 250 passes one of the most distinctive features in Armley Road on the number 14 tram route – the "clock school". Opened on 27 October 1878 as Armley Board School and latterly known as Armley County Primary School, it closed on 26 May 1989. It is one of the few buildings in Armley Road, existing in 1953, that still stands. It is currently used as offices. The date of the photograph: 16 August 1953. *Author*.

In 1953 there were still one or two cars running in the pre-1948 princess blue and white livery. 443 was photographed at Meanwood Terminus on 1 August 1953. *Author*.

408, the only car of its type to be repainted in the red livery, at Bramley Town End on 18 July 1953. *Author*.

CHAPTER 74

Tramway Abandonments 1953 to 1956

On that fateful day, 1 July 1953, when the City Council confirmed the tramway abandonment proposals, there were exactly 379 trams in the fleet. Of these 346 were serviceable, 10 were withdrawn from service and 22 Felthams and single deck car 600 were stored awaiting completion. 321 cars were in the red and white livery and 32 were still in the pre-1950 blue and white livery. 139 Chamberlains, five ex-Southampton and five ex-Manchester cars still existed. The two experimental railcars, 601 and 602, had entered service at the beginning of June and were running on various routes.

Cars withdrawn from service were Chamberlains 66, 97 and 432, ex-Southampton car 297 and cars which had been out of service for some time and stored for other purposes: 345, 359, 377, 399 and 446. Chamberlain car 420 was also out of service, but was awaiting conversion into an overhead rail derrick.

The number 14, Corn Exchange to Half Mile Lane tram service, was about five miles in length and its closure took place on Saturday, 3 October 1953, the last car being Horsfield 166. 166 left Half Mile Lane at about midnight and a replacement bus service, also numbered 14, began on Sunday, 4 October, from the Central Bus Station and followed the route of the 65 Pudsey bus service.

Many of the stopping places on the route were altered in a bid to speed up the bus service in comparison with the trams, the number of stops being reduced by five. The journey time by tram from the Corn Exchange had been 27 minutes. By bus from the Bus Station, about a quarter of a mile further, it was 26 minutes. Taking into account the reduction in the number of stops, the travel times by bus and tram were about the same. The buses ran at the same frequencies as the trams - about every four minutes at busy periods. After a short time the off peak service

deteriorated considerably and this was noticed by Councillor Mather at the following City Council meeting. The fares were generally about the same as on the trams, but one or two intermediate stage fares were increased. The bus fare for the full distance from the Bus Station to Half Mile Lane was 6d. compared with the 5d. tram fare from the Corn Exchange.

On the 3rd, the last tram from Bramley Town End to the Corn Exchange had been Austerity car 275 and on the Friday evening the last to reverse at the Wellington Bridge crossover and return to Half Mile Lane was Horsfield 247.

The closure of the 14 route resulted in some fairly extensive alterations at the Corn Exchange. As indicated on the map, much of the track was altered and the Elland Road and Beeston loading points were transferred to the island opposite the Corn Exchange. This alteration was effected on 1 October, but by lunchtime on the same day the stops had reverted to their former positions. The new arrangement was instituted on 4 October, the old Elland Road tram barrier being used by the 54 and 65 buses and the Beeston tram barrier by the new number 14 buses.

The first track alteration was the removal of half of the rarely used facing crossover in New Market Street (the half that connected with the centre track). This was completed by 30 September and, after the last tram had returned from Half Mile Lane, the two crossings for the No. 1 curve were removed and a bend inserted joining the centre track with the southern one near the Corn Exchange. The outer track and part of the centre track became redundant. The whole of the track alterations were completed on 25 October 1953.

At the November City Council meeting Councillor Mather "shadow chairman" of the Transport Committee, said the new Stanningley bus route confirmed the fears

There were still a few of the ex-Manchester "Pilcher" cars about in 1953. 281 is on Stanningley Road and about to enter the central reservation. The date is 12 September 1953. *Author.*

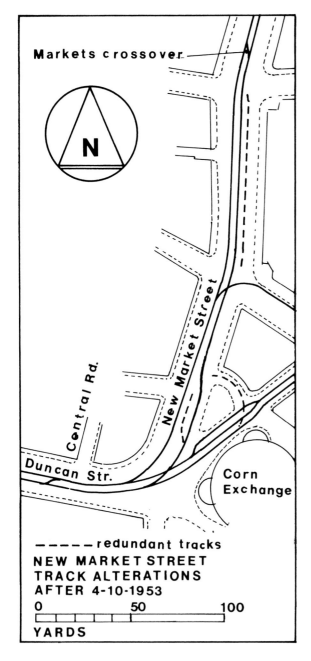

Markets crossover

Central Rd.

New Market Street

Duncan Str.

Corn Exchange

— — — — — redundant tracks

**NEW MARKET STREET
TRACK ALTERATIONS
AFTER 4-10-1953**

0   50   100

YARDS

The remaining ex-Southampton cars and two of the ex-Manchester Pilcher cars, 280 and 283, were withdrawn. The other cars taken out of service were all Chamberlains on E.M.B. Pivotal trucks. Following a scrapping session in Low Fields Road Permanent Way Yard between October and December 1953 the number of cars in the fleet was reduced to 338.

Austerity car 275 which had operated on the 14 route for the whole of its life, was transferred to the 25 Hunslet service.

The overhead wiring in Stanningley Road from Bramley Town End to the terminus was removed on Sunday, 18 October, using Bedford motor derricks MNW 857 and MUG 231. The rails on the reserved track in Stanningley Road were in good condition and recovered for reuse elsewhere. During October and November extensive rail grinding took place using rail grinders 1, 6 and trailer 3. They were observed there on 6 November and this is believed to be the last date that any trams travelled along Armley Road. Track removal on the reservation began at Cockshott Lane on 24 November and all, with the exception of road crossings, had been removed by mid-December. On 13 December the overhead wiring was removed between the White Horse junction and Branch Road. The remaining overhead was removed on 10 January 1954.

The West Riding buses operating to Wakefield and Rothwell which used the No.1 curve at the Corn Exchange, but in the opposite direction to the trams, continued to use the curve after the trams ceased running. However, after 4 October they ran in the same direction as the former trams and used the tram loading point. The Transport Committee did not like this arrangement and applied for permission to close the short section of road used by the West Riding buses.

The West Riding Company asked to relocate the bus terminal point in the Central Bus Station, but this was rejected for lack of space. Instead, in September 1954 the Leeds Town Planning Committee suggested that a new bus station be built in New York Street on the site of the former St. James' Church on the corner of New York Street and Cross York Street. The site was about 1,000 sq. yards in area and the purchase price was £11,000. This was eventually granted and the buses were removed. From 9 October 1956 the Wakefield and Rothwell buses terminated at the new location. The Corn Exchange island was then connected to the other paving, forming an enlarged pedestrian area for tram and bus loading. This work was done in early 1957, loading barriers for bus services 11, 15 and 16 were erected and the new arrangement came into use on Tuesday, 22 January.

A service reduction occurred from Saturday 6 February 1954 when the Saturday service on the Harehills 3 and Beeston 5 route was discontinued. Trams then ran from Mondays to Fridays only from the early morning to after the evening peak hour. The normal Corn Exchange-Beeston service was not affected.

On Sunday 7 February there was heavy snow in Leeds and this caused some unusual workings on the York Road routes. There were two overhead wire breakages at the Selby Road and York Road junction and railcar 602 became marooned on the inward track between the junction and Cross Gates terminus. It made at least one journey on the inward track between the two locations. Felthams 531 and 548 were stranded in Selby Road and all services from the city were turned at the Lupton Avenue crossover.

The next tram routes to be abandoned were those to Kirkstall Abbey and Compton Road. The application to the Traffic Commissioners was approved on 1 March 1954. Mr.Haselgrove, for the Corporation, said the routes were to be abandoned for three reasons: a lot of money was required for repairs on the Kirkstall Abbey route, it was another step towards the entire removal of trams from

expressed some months previously that the service would be drastically reduced. During the morning off-peak period seven trams had been replaced by four buses, and during the afternoon 12 trams by seven buses.

"This inferior service does not extend to Pudsey, where the frequency has been improved, so we now have the ridiculous situation that the transport facilities to Pudsey have been increased at the expense of Leeds ratepayers, just as all the fare increases are borne by Leeds citizens. Pudsey has had several decreases....

....These inequitable arrangements are the inevitable result of embarking on a programme without a full investigation, and support once again our suggestion that the whole policy and operation of the Transport Department under Alderman Rafferty's leadership should be made the subject of a sound financial investigation by the City Treasurer, who could give us a detailed picture from the city point of view, completely independent of departmental parochialism."

'The Yorkshire Post', 17 November 1953.

The abandonment of the Half Mile service resulted in the withdrawal of about 24 trams. The last of the cars in the blue livery were withdrawn, including cars 98 and 443, the last to run in the pre-1948 princess blue and white livery.

The redundant facing crossover in New Market Street is partly removed as Horsfield car 236 loads at the Beeston tram stop on 30 September 1953.   A red West Riding bus is on the No. 1 curve at the Corn Exchange,   Note the temporary paving of old granite setts. *Author*.

The conductor holds the rope as the bow arcs on the overhead at the Wellington Bridge crossover. Horsfield 247 is reversing for the last time for Half Mile Lane on 2 October 1953.   Motor cars are waiting to turn from Westgate into Wellington Street and the setting is Bean Ing Mill, currently the site of the Yorkshire Post Offices.   *Author*.

Wellington Street and the link-up would make a useful and economical cross-city service. The bus terminus at Kirkstall was to be at Abbey Walk to ease the turning of buses. The Burley Mills turning point was to be in the same location as the trams.

Preliminary work was required at the Burley Mills layby used by the Haddon Place trams. The layby was to be used by the replacement buses and the trams were withdrawn on Saturday 6 March 1954, the last car being Horsfield 184. On the Sunday the overhead wiring was removed and over the following days the trackwork. A new bus turning circle in tarmacadam was substituted.

The two tram routes ceased to run on Saturday night, 3 April 1954. The last tram to Kirkstall Abbey was driven by Bill Hepworth, one of the best known and "fastest" of the Leeds tram drivers.

"Earlier in the day an official of the Transport Department had been coldly matter of fact. "There won't be a ceremony," he said. To us, this is just a last tram on a Saturday night." But the people who live along the Kirkstall Road route were determined to give the last tram a good send off and when No.127 came rattling round the corner with the familiar "No.4" and the words "Kirkstall Abbey" shining in the darkness, there was quite a crowd waiting.

A ragged cheer went up as we read the notice stuck in the tram window: "Last tram to Kirkstall. 57 years service 1897-1954." This notice had not been put up by the hard-hearted Transport Department. Some young men of the

Leeds University Railway Society, who had earlier bid farewell to the last tram at Compton Road at the other end of the route, were responsible....

....The tram was not one of the sleek ex-London vehicles with leather seats and a special compartment for the driver. It was a tram of the old school and we settled ourselves on the hard, wooden-backed seats. Before we left there was a small ceremony sponsored by the Railway Society. Driver William Hepworth and Conductor Harold Jephcott were each presented with a bottle of sauce; a wreath was hung on the front of No.127; photographs were taken. Then we were off. It was 11.49 p.m."

'The Yorkshire Post', 5 April 1954.

The last tram from the Corn Exchange to Compton Road was Horsfield car 194. There were no track alterations associated with the two abandonments. Rails falling into disuse were from the Woodpecker junction to Compton Road and from Kirkstall Road tramway works to the Abbey. By the end of May 1954 all overhead wiring on the two routes had been removed.

The abandonment of the Kirkstall Abbey tramway was not as controversial as that to Half Mile Lane. The route had been recommended for closure by Councillor Bertrand Mather's Special Sub-Committee a year or so earlier. The track on the Compton Road route had been doubled during the War in anticipation of a proposed post war extension of the tramway to Seacroft. The extension had not taken place. The decision to close the route was criticised by Councillor Mather who said that the change

Austerity car 275 in its lined red livery, returning from Half Mile Lane, and Horsfield car 159 bound for Kirkstall Abbey were photographed in City Square on 21 August 1953. *Author*.

As a result of the withdrawal of the number 14 tram route the remaining trams in the blue livery were withdrawn including the last ex-Southampton trams. 294 is at Hunslet terminus on 5 September 1953. The car had run for several months with a dented dash. *Author*.

The remaining blue cars finished up like this. On 1 September 1953 Chamberlain 46 had just been overturned in Low Fields Road Permanent Way Yard and was awaiting burning. The 16 years old youth in the Roundhay High School uniform is David Packer. A scrap E.M.B. Pivotal truck is in the right foreground. *Author*.

On 7 February 1954 railcar 602 was marooned between the York Road/Selby Road junction and Cross Gates due to an overhead wire breakage at the junction. It ran a shuttle service between the two points and has just left the Cross Gates Road reservation and is entering York Road. *Author*.

New trackwork in Dewsbury Road on 20 August 1953. Permanent way workmen stop to allow Feltham 513 to pass. The two trolley devices in the left foreground were used for lifting and moving rails into position. *Author*.

The notice displayed in Chamberlain 127 on its last journey to Kirkstall Abbey, 3 April 1954. *Author.*

over was "merely because the Socialists could not think of anywhere else as a terminus for the Kirkstall buses."

Simultaneously with the closure of the two routes, the short working to Cross Flatts Park on the Dewsbury Road route was discontinued. On Friday evening, 2 April, the last scheduled car to turn at Cross Flatts Park was Chamberlain 133, but a few cars did turn there after that date. The crossover was removed in September 1954. The Crescent short working came into use on Monday, 5 April. Trams on the Dewsbury Road route, which had operated through to Compton Road were now altered to run to Harehills and Roundhay (route 3). They also continued to work through to 11 Gipton Estate. Between Dewsbury Road and Harehills or Roundhay, trams ran in both directions up and down Briggate, cars for Dewsbury Road using the former route 4 barrier In Briggate. At peak hours on Mondays to Fridays cars from Harehills, Roundhay or Gipton short worked to the new Crescent crossover.

Trams continued to show CROSS FLATTS PARK on the destination indicators, but, as this destination was two stops short of the Park, the word PARK was blacked out. It was then realised that Cross Flatts implied an area beyond the Park and following pressure from Councillor T.W.Smith, the destination indicators were altered to show CRESCENT. From 24 January 1955 the new destination was officially displayed on the trams.

It was found that at peak hours cars to Dewsbury Road were often full whereas those to the Crescent cinema were only partially occupied. There were complaints from passengers and according to Eric Smith, his father brought up the matter at a meeting of the Transport Committee. The Chairman, Alderman Rafferty, said he knew how to solve the situation saying, "We'll send all the buggers through to the terminus." And so, from then onwards at the evening peak, most trams to Dewsbury Road ran through to the terminus.

Also closed in April 1954 was Headingley tram depot. The trams were transferred to either Chapeltown or Swinegate Depots. At the time of the changeover certain tramcar running schedules were altered on the numbers 1, 3 and 11 tram routes.

The tram journey time from Briggate to Kirkstall Abbey had been 19 minutes and from the Corn Exchange to Compton Road 12 minutes. By bus via the slightly shorter route from Eastgate the times were 17 and 11 minutes respectively. Two stops on the Kirkstall Abbey section were omitted. Bus frequencies and fares at first were about the same as the trams.

Over 20 trams were withdrawn from service. These included the remaining Chamberlain cars on E.M.B. Pivotal trucks, Chamberlains damaged in collisions and the ex-Manchester Pilcher cars.

T.H.Parkinson, in charge of the tram scrapping programme, said that trams were being scrapped by type and added that they "were concentrating on retaining all usable spares that were common."

Between April and June 1954 24 passenger cars were scrapped in Low Fields Road Permanent Way Yard. These included 377, used as the towing car and still in the blue livery. In June 1954 the number of trams in the fleet had been reduced to 314.

Councillor Mather was very upset by the way in which the tramway abandonment was being progressed and at the City Council meeting on 5 May 1954 proposed a special resolution asking that the Finance and Parliamentary Committee be instructed "to undertake an investigation into the effect on city finances of the present operation and policy of the Transport Committee."

Mather said the undertaking was running at a loss of about £70,000 a year and was involved in a changeover policy which would cost at least £3,250,000, yet no details of the financial effects had been given to the City Council or Transport Committee.

"It was suggested that the Finance Committee should undertake this investigation because the ramifications of transport costs were so widespread that they affected many other committees and could have a direct and adverse effect on the rates.

The Transport Committee could always make a phoney economy by shifting some of its costs on to another committee....

...."Nobody really knows," said Coun. Mather, "whether the present policy of substituting buses for trams is good or bad, as it has never been examined, particularly from the city point of view.

Horsfield 218 viewed through the arch of the railway viaduct in Kirkstall Road, looking towards Willow Road, on 16 January 1954. *Author.*

On Sunday, 4 October 1953, the day after the abandonment of the number 14 tram route, the connecting track to the No. 1 curve at the Corn Exchange was removed.   Horsfield car 193 bound for Beeston is on the new track in New Market Street. On the left is the Tramways Department Aveling Porter steam roller E 6351. *Author*.

There was snow in Leeds in January and February 1954.   On 31 January Horsfield car 231, in wintry sunshine, is in Stoney Rock Lane, Burmantofts, bound for Compton Road terminus and passing the Beckett Street cemetery. *Author*.

Horsfield car 233 is entering Nippet Lane from Burmantofts Street on 21 March 1954. Most of the junction of the former Beckett Street tramway to Harehills Road, abandoned in 1946, is still in place. All the property on this photograph was removed in the middle 1960's. Author.

"So far three routes have been converted. The Stanningley route was converted on a false financial basis, which was exposed to this Council some months ago....

....Factors which had been ignored or skilfully kept out of public view, said Coun.Mather, included:

The loss of rates and overheads amounting to about £40,000 per year in perpetuity....

.... Road re-instatement, which together with other work, would probably cost three quarters of a million pounds.

Extra road maintenance caused by the increased wear and tear of buses.

The loss of existing tramway capital, which would appear to be about half a million pounds.

The cost of altering City Square, and providing extra bus stations and parking facilities.

The investigation would also include reduced services, reduced stopping places, rerouting and the increase in queues at rush hours....

...."Observations in the past year," said Coun. Mather, "lead to a suspicion that the Socialists are giving a good service immediately after the changeover until public interest has died down and then reducing it to far below that of the original tram service.

"There are also grounds for believing that the tramway side of the undertaking is being operated by them inefficiently in order to bolster up a case which they have not properly investigated....

'Yorkshire Evening Post', 5 May 1954.

Councillor Bernard Lyons said that whenever proper criticism had been levelled against aspects of policy there had been a complete refusal by Alderman Rafferty to consider any suggestion however helpful or constructive.

His reply to any criticism was in the form of a personal attack on the speaker.

"I must warn Alderman Rafferty," said Councillor Lyons, "that when financial disaster comes to his department as a result of present operation and policy, his reduction of present transport debates to a forum for sarcastic personal comment will not solve his problems, nor lighten the burden which he is loading on to the present oppressed ratepayer."

Alderman Rafferty in reply quoted the report of the Royal Commission on Transport of 1930, which had recommended that tramways be abandoned.

"Whereas in 1927 nearly 15,000 tramcars were in operation in this country, there were now fewer than 3,000. Only three firms were interested in tramcar construction and of these only two had done anything about tramcar development. Three firms were concerned with the provision of tram rails and only two with overhead equipment, " said Rafferty.

"Ever since 1941 trams had lost money each year except during one year, 1948, whereas since 1939 buses have shown a profit every year except two, and those followed heavy wage increases." Rafferty said that since the abandonment of the Half Mile Lane, Kirkstall Abbey and Compton Road services, £10,000 had been saved on permanent way and £17,000 on Kirkstall Road Works.

In his annual report for 1954, A.B.Findlay had said that the Leeds tram fares were the cheapest in the country, but Rafferty made no mention of the very low tram fares as compared with the buses. He also did not make reference to the reduced services and fewer stopping places on the new bus routes. Mather's comments were ignored and at the following meeting of the Transport Committee on 23 June 1954 further tramway abandonments were approved. The closures were to be on dates "to be arranged". The routes were as follows:

Route 1 Briggate-Lawnswood.
Route 5 Corn Exchange-Beeston.
Route 6 Corn Exchange-Meanwood.
Route 8 Corn Exchange-Elland Road.
Route 11 Corn Exchange- Gipton.
Route 15 Corn Exchange-Whingate.
Route 16 Corn Exchange-New Inn.

The Committee asked the General Manager to submit schemes for new bus services between Whingate and Seacroft, New Inn and Gipton, Lawnswood and Beeston, and Meanwood to Elland Road, Cottingley and Morley.

These proposals when implemented would result in about half of the tram track in the city being abandoned. There would be no trams in City Square or along Boar Lane, the only line on the west side of the city being in Wellington Street and Kirkstall Road to allow access to Kirkstall Road Tramway Works.

From Wednesday, 2 June 1954, buses replaced trams on the service to the Greyhound Stadium in Elland Road. Meetings were held at the Stadium on Wednesday and Saturday evenings and trams ran for the last time on Saturday 29 May. The overhead wiring was removed in October 1954. Unfortunately there was no prior announcement of the tramway closure and the event was not photographed.

A burst water main in Kirkgate near the junction with Harper Street on 25 October 1954 caused some major tramway diversions. Cars working the east Leeds routes turned at the Woodpecker crossover and the rarely used No.2 curve from the Cross Gates barrier in Kirkgate to Call Lane came into use for trams from west Leeds and Dewsbury Road. This curve had been disused from the early 1930s and three Felthams, 508, 511 and 538, derailed. Thereafter Felthams turning for the Tong Road routes reversed on the Markets crossover. Most other cars used the No.2 curve. A special shuttle bus service was worked from Harper Street to the Woodpecker Inn.

An identical problem with the same water main occurred three weeks later on 16 November and similar diversions took place. On this occasion no Felthams were used on the 15 Whingate and 16 New Inn services. The No.2 curve, Woodpecker crossover and shuttle bus service were again employed.

To facilitate the turning of tramcars from the York Road district following the abandonment of the 15 Whingate and 16 New Inn services, a city centre reversing point was proposed. It was to be located in Kirkgate between New Market Street and Call Lane, and on 20 September 1954 a tender from Edgar Allen Ltd. in the sum of £1,740 for the special trackwork was approved. The proposals were subject to the approval of the Divisional Road Engineer. A plan of the proposed turning point has not been discovered, but it is understood to have included a track parallel to that used by the Cross Gates trams. The new track was to enable Halton trams to reverse and is thought to have included a scissors crossover. There is no record of any approval being received from the Divisional Road Engineer.

Under the tramway abandonment programme, the Whingate and New Inn routes were to follow the Kirkstall Abbey and Compton Road services. However, the problem with the Kirkgate terminal arrangements led to the Transport Committee selecting the Gipton, Elland Road, Meanwood and Beeston routes as the next to be scrapped.

In the meantime Councillor Bertrand Mather came to the fore again with an ambitious scheme for the retention and modernisation of the remaining tramways.

In a leading article the 'Yorkshire Evening Post' said that increasing traffic congestion was resulting in "chaos" in Leeds. It said that more and more private cars were being licensed. An increasing number littered the city streets and the number of heavy vehicles was increasing.

"Many thinking people see no solution to the problem in the Socialist policy which is chiefly concerned with the scrapping of trams in favour of buses. The older streets, anyway, were never designed to accommodate a stream of big double deck buses."

''Yorkshire Evening Post', 15 February 1955.

Photographs of trams in Elland Road taken midway between the Football Ground and the Greyhound Stadium are rare. This view is of Middleton bogie 264 at Heath Mount on 23 August 1953.   It was on a private L.R.T.L. tour. The Football Ground was later rebuilt, but the Greyhound Stadium closed on 15 March 1982. *Author.*

Lance Corporal 272 was regarded as "non-standard" and was withdrawn from service a few weeks after this photograph was taken on 3 April 1955. The car is in Harrogate Road outside Chapeltown Depot. *Author*.

The newspaper said that some "big scheme" was required to ease the crush of vehicles in the city centre. It said that now was the time to plan a long way ahead. It commended Mather's scheme and said that the city planners should realise that "something big and costly would have to be done in the future."

Mather's scheme bore a resemblance to the subway plan proposed by William Vane Morland, the Leeds tramways manager, in 1944 and discussed in Chapter 54 of Volume 3.

The scheme, estimated to cost about £8,000,000, was for the removal of all public surface transport from the city centre by the construction of a subway a mile and a half long connecting eight busy traffic points.

The proposed subway, on which would run single deck rail cars, coupled in pairs, would extend from Westgate, where plans were already in hand for an exhibition hall with parking for 1,000 cars, to seven points in the central area. These were to be at the Central Railway Station in Wellington Street, City Square, The Headrow/Park Row crossing, the new Rockingham Street Bus Station, Headrow/Briggate crossing, Vicar Lane/Markets and the Central Bus Station.

Mather said that every month traffic congestion and dissatisfaction with public transport became more acute in Leeds and every other city. Road widening in the city centre was not practicable.

He said that weaknesses in the public transport system were poor off-peak frequencies (usually half hourly) on outer sections of bus routes, poor connecting facilities in the city centre, collapse of the system at peak hours when people had to queue for 20 minutes to ride for ten minutes.

Mather's suggestion as a first stage was to convert the York Road tramway into a fast railway by making the track

private from the outer termini to the Central Bus Station and then taking it to Westgate via the subway. All stops on the surface railway would have loading platforms, and fewer stops to give an express service. Rolling stock on the surface-and-subway system would be high speed single deck multiple units with power-operated doors. A one minute frequency would be possible in the subway section. Buses would feed into the railway system at Cross Gates, Westgate and other points. He proposed a park and ride system for motorists using the railway. This was a very novel idea for the time and is the first occasion on which it was suggested for Leeds.

Mather proposed that the north-south traffic be dealt with next, the services from Roundhay and Moortown entering the subway at The Headrow/Briggate point. The Belle Isle and Middleton services would enter the subway system at the Central Bus Station. He suggested that the section of tramway in the lower part of Dewsbury Road be abandoned, trams from Dewsbury Road being redirected along Moor Road and then by a new line following the disused railway to Great Wilson Street. This latter idea was not new and had been suggested in the 1920s.

"The scheme would obviously be expensive, but we are about to spend £3,000,000 on new buses, with further sums which bus operation puts on the rates. Yet with this we have no hope of having either better transport or less congestion unless we spend millions on road improvements and suffer higher fares to pay the wages of more and more crews who are forced to stay in the city centre almost motionless in the rush hours.

On the latest estimate a tunnel of the proposed type would cost about £4,000,000 a mile - about £6,000,000 in all. Add say £1,500,000 for rolling stock and £500,000 for the suggested changes on the surface, and it is reasonable to suppose that the whole cost would be about £8,000,000.

Of this, at least £3,000,000 should be treated as having the effect of a road improvement and qualify for a Government grant, leaving £3,000,000 to find on, say an 80 year loan, (for the tunnel) and £2,000,000 to find on a 25 year loan for the rolling stock....

....I would like an investigation by both parties in the Council looking into the question in detail and reaching some mutual basic policy whereby these problems could be solved to the great benefit of all citizens."

'The Yorkshire Evening Post', 15 February 1955.

Alderman Rafferty dismissed Mather's scheme as "grandiose." Mather's ideas were ignored by both the City Council and Transport Committee.

Because of large wages awards, fares were increased from 30 January 1955. The long established workmen's return fares were abolished from the same date.

Preparations were made for the abandonment of route 11, the Gipton tramway, a section of reserved track just over 600 yards long, from the Dog and Gun junction in York Road, and along Gipton Approach to Wykebeck Valley Road. This tramway had been built in 1936 as the first stage of a proposed tramway to Seacroft, which had not taken place.

The tramway ceased operation on Saturday night 23 April 1955 and was replaced by a new bus service also numbered 11. The last tram to leave Gipton Estate was Horsfield car 156 which left the terminus at 11.46 p.m.

As well as the tramway in Gipton Approach, the new siding in Call Lane, constructed in March 1953 for the

Compton Road and Gipton cars, also fell into disuse. Chapeltown Depot was closed to service cars from the same date.

The withdrawal of the Gipton Estate tramway resulted in a complete revision of the services to route 9 Dewsbury Road. Dewsbury Road cars, which had run to Gipton Estate were now directed to route 2 Moortown or Chapeltown, in addition to route 3 Harehills or Roundhay. The services were between Dewsbury Road and Chapeltown and Dewsbury Road and Harehills, but on weekday evenings (after the peak hour) and on Saturday afternoons, the service was extended to Moortown. On weekday morning and evening peak hours, throughout the evenings and on Saturdays from lunchtime, the service was extended to Roundhay Park (summer timetables were in use). During Sunday afternoons and evenings and early Saturday mornings and evenings trams operated from Dewsbury Road around the Moortown and Roundhay circular route. The services between routes 2 and 3 and route 1 were as before except that cars for route 1 no longer turned on the Stainbeck Lane spur at Chapeltown. The service to Roundhay Park only, via Moortown, ceased on 23 April with the closure of Chapeltown Depot.

From 28 March 1955, to even out rail wear, many stopping places on the Moortown route had been resited, the number of stops being reduced by one.

From 24 April, for the first time, combined tram and bus stop and fare stage signs were introduced in Leeds. In New York Street, for example, there was a stop for the number 11 buses and the tramway services in York Road. As with previous tramway closures, a number of stops

Car 377 used for towing scrap trams, spent a lot of time under Swinegate Arches.   On the right are some of the rusting Tramways Department tar boilers used for grouting granite paving setts. The date: 18 July 1953. *Author.*

1208

The oldest Leeds tramcar then in service, 408, with a Horsfield and Lance Corporal car at West Park on 8 May 1954. *Author*.

The Gipton cutting, popularly known as "Gipton Gulch", was built in 1936 for the proposed Seacroft tramway from York Road. Horsfield car 222 was photographed on 27 March 1955 four weeks before the tramway was abandoned. Another car stands at the terminus. *Author*.

The derailment of Horsfield 229 at Bentley Lane, Meanwood, the day before the tram route ceased operation, created a crowd of onlookers. However, the boy on the left was not interested. *A.D.Packer.*

were relocated. The stops between the Woodpecker Inn and Lupton Avenue, were reduced by one. The term "BUS STAGE" was new from the same date.

The journey time for the trams from the Corn Exchange to Gipton Estate had been 14 minutes. By bus from Vicar Lane (Sydney Street), about 200 yards further, but with one less stop, the journey was 13 minutes. Again the substitution of buses for trams had not resulted in any significant speeding up of the service. The 3d. fare from the city centre was unchanged. From 31 July 1955 a reduced service came into operation on the new number 11 bus route.

On the last day of service operation 32 trams were operating from Chapeltown Depot. These included 15 Chamberlain cars, 14 Horsfield cars and cars 272, 276 and 278.

After 24 April Chapeltown Depot was only used for storage purposes. The relatively modern Lance Corporal cars 273 and 274 were sent there. 272 was still in use, but was withdrawn on 18 May 1955 following an accident, and then taken to Chapeltown. Until 1949-1950 these comparatively modern cars, built in 1935, had been the most popular in Leeds with their very comfortable revolving seats. T.H. Parkinson had standardised the bus fleet into two or three basic types and was concentrating on doing the same with the trams. 272-274 were non-standard, and therefore expensive to run, as far as Parkinson was concerned. This accounted for their early withdrawal. Joining the Lance Corporals were three of the first Horsfields to be withdrawn: 211, 234 and 244. The rail grinder on a steam tram truck, No.2, was transferred from Swinegate Depot on the 25th. The other cars had been moved from storage in Kirkstall Road Works. They were later joined by Felthams, awaiting restoration, and withdrawn cars.

Chapeltown Depot remained as a morning peak hour short working for a time, cars reversing in the depot

entrance. A watchman was on duty and a spare or "fly" car was kept there as a changeover.

In May 1955 five passenger cars and three works trams were scrapped. The passenger cars included car 408, the last of the Hamilton-bodied cars, and 425, the last tram on an E.M.B. Pivotal truck. Also scrapped were Chamberlain cars 62, 114 and 439. The three works vehicles were rail grinder 2 taken from Chapeltown Depot and burned on 10 May. Also burned was a trailer rail derrick on a horse tram truck and another casualty was the trailer rail grinder No.3.

It was not long before there was another tramway closure when, on 25 June 1955, the route 6 Meanwood to 8 Elland Road services ceased operation.

An application to the Yorkshire Traffic Commissioners for the abandonment of the two routes and the integration of the services into a Meanwood-Morley bus route was approved on 15 June 1955. J.B.Gill, Chief Traffic Officer to the Transport Department, said that they were discussing with the police and other Corporation departments, the provision of an adequate bus service for football matches at Elland Road. An application for these services would shortly come before the Commissioners.

Following the usual practice when tram routes were abandoned, the stops on both routes were completely revised. On the Elland Road section the tram stops had been close together and three were removed. The stops on the Meanwood section were reduced by two. This reduction in stops enabled the replacement buses to be speeded up. In the case of Meanwood the tram journey had taken 16 minutes from the Corn Exchange. By bus it was a minute less, but the Elland Road service was improved considerably - 13 minutes by tram, ten by bus. As Councillor Bertrand Mather pointed out on a number of occasions these were not fair comparisons. If the buses had used the same stopping places as the trams it is unlikely that there would have been any increase in speed. The buses could even have been slower as the trams had quicker acceleration. Rafferty said that the department was not allowed to have the same number of stops per mile for buses as was possible with trams. He did not quote the source and it may have been a requirement of the Traffic Commissioners.

The last tram from Elland Road to Meanwood was Horsfield 249 and the last in the reverse direction, car 178. 249 left Meanwood terminus at 11.45 p.m. and 178 departed from Elland Road at 11.13 p.m. Tracks abandoned were from Sheepscar to Meanwood. Those in Elland Road were retained in order to gain access to the scrap yard in Low Fields Road.

An interesting incident occurred at Meanwood terminus on Friday, 24 June, the day before the closure. Horsfield car 229, leaving the terminus fouled the points and proceeded towards the city with the leading wheels running alongside the rails. Just before the first inward stopping place at Bentley Lane, the car slewed to the right coming to rest across the outward track. 229 was pulled back on to the rails by Horsfield 224. In the meantime cars approaching the terminus were driven back on the wrong line and reversed on the rarely used Woodhouse Ridge crossover. Five cars turned there, including Feltham 512, Horsfields 190, 216 and finally 154. It was necessary to renew the check rail at the terminus for the following day. In addition to Horsfield cars, two Chamberlains, 39 and 93, ran on the last day and also two Felthams 512 and 513.

The Beeston tram service 5, which operated to Corn Exchange, Swinegate, Meanwood or Harehills, was altered to run to the Corn Exchange only with peak hour trips to Harehills and Swinegate. This peak hour service was the only one operating on the part of Vicar Lane to the north of the Markets crossover.

Earlier, beginning on Whit Tuesday, 31 May, the football siding beyond the points leading into the scrap yard, was lifted. The overhead wiring was removed from the same date and the work was completed in about ten days. The space occupied by the tram rails was concreted over for the replacement buses.

The football siding was last used on Tuesday, 3 May, when there was a West Riding Cup Final between Leeds United and Bradford.

It had been intended to close the Beeston tramway in February or March 1956, but the date had to be brought forward to November 1955. The rails on 1 in 11 Beeston Hill were subject to excessive wear owing to the use of mechanical track brakes on the gradient and bends. These brakes were required under Ministry of Transport regulations.

"We had hoped the track would last until next year, but at this rate it will not," said Mr. Findlay, transport manager today. *"Renewing the track would have cost £4,000 only to scrap it four months later."*

'Yorkshire Evening News', 1 July 1955.

The Beeston route was the last of the hilly tram routes in Leeds. Other routes, which had required track brakes were Morley, Pudsey, Rodley and Rothwell. Track brakes were needed between Park Gates and Malvern Road and there were compulsory stops on Beeston Hill at Tempest Road and South Ridge Street. From 1950-2 when the last of the converted and Hamilton enclosed cars, some of which were fitted with track brakes, were withdrawn, the route had been operated solely with Horsfield type cars.

The last tram, Horsfield 240, left Beeston terminus for the Corn Exchange at 11.46 p.m. on Saturday, 19 November 1955.

"It will be a long time before the people of Beeston forget the trams, or Saturday night, when they gave a sentimental send-off to the last one just before midnight, Conductors and drivers always spoke of the Beeston route as the "friendly run". Nearly 200 of these "friends" turned up at the terminus on Saturday night. Many watched the last tram go by on the route. Some one had a bottle of wine for a toast, a baker sprang a surprise with a cake, and there were presents for the driver of the last tram,

Horsfield car 232 and Daimler CWD6 bus 519 (JUM 574), on the 58 Hyde Park Circular service, at the Meanwood Road and Cambridge Road junction on 5 June 1955. Car 232 is travelling towards Meanwood. *Author.*

For the last few months of their existence the Lance Corporal cars 273-274, were "relegated" to the short Hunslet route. 274 is at the Hunslet terminus on 19 March 1955. *Author.*

The most prominent feature on the Meanwood tram route was the chimney of the refuse destructor in Meanwood Road. At 258 feet it was the tallest brick chimney in Leeds and could be seen for miles around. The destructor was built from 1893 to 1895 and opened in January 1896. The chimney became disused; demolition began in January 1978 and took several months. Five miles of scaffold tube were used and among the demolition team was the well known steeple-jack Fred Dibnah. On 18 June 1955 Horsfield car 240 is heading towards Leeds with the Ridge View crossover in the foreground. *Author.*

Horsfield car 194 passes the crossover at the New Peacock Inn in Elland Road on 18 June 1955 as two people walk or run around a ladder. The New Peacock was built in 1838 by William Bradley, the former tenant of the Peacock Inn, some 200 yards to the south west. Opened as the "Prince George", it was renamed the "New Peacock" in October 1840. In January 1975 this part of Elland Road was closed to through traffic and the inn was demolished about October to allow the construction of an approach road to a roundabout serving the new M621 south west motorway. The approach road and roundabout were used for the first time on 3 June 1976. *Author*.

Horsfield car 217 in Meanwood Road near Buslingthorpe Lane, on 18 June 1955. *Author*.

Horsfield car 227 loading at the compulsory stop at Tempest Road at the top of Beeston Hill on 17 July 1955. *Author.*

Chamberlain car 1, renumbered as 9 in November 1955, at the Fenton Street tram stop in Woodhouse Lane on 27 February 1956. Blenheim Chapel is on the right. *Author.*

Mr. Wilfred Jones, Moorside Drive, Bramley, and his conductress, Mrs. Elsie Mackman, Woodview Mount, Dewsbury Road, who have been a Beeston team for three years.

'The Yorkshire Post', 21 November 1955.

Car 240 retained its "Last to Beeston" sign for a week or two after the closure of the route.

The three tram services from Beeston: Beeston-Corn Exchange, Beeston-Swinegate and Beeston-Harehills all ceased operation, the Swinegate and Harehills services on Friday 18 November. Horsfield car 188 worked the last duty from Beeston to Swinegate at 6.18 p.m. and 229 was the last Beeston-Harehills car, leaving Beeston at 6.15 p.m. 229 thus became the last "official" tram to run the full length of Vicar Lane. Two new bus services, one from the Corn Exchange and another from Swinegate, both numbered 5, replaced the trams, but there was no bus service through to Harehills. There was the usual reduction in the number of stops on the route.

The rails and overhead in Vicar Lane remained intact for a further two years, the pointwork for the outward track being removed on 29/30 June 1957. The last car to use the outward track was Horsfield 221, bound for 2 Moortown, at teatime on 21 May 1957. A fortnight later the pointwork for the inward track was removed, the last tram to traverse Vicar Lane in a southerly direction was ex-London car, 301, on 2 May 1957. The tramway in Vicar Lane remained useable as far as the markets crossover.

Simultaneously with the closure of the Beeston route, Torre Road tram depot was also closed. All trams were transferred to the one remaining depot at Swinegate.

Latterly, Torre Road Depot had been used by Feltham and Chamberlain cars, the Chamberlains being stored on the track nearest to Torre Road. This track had been difficult to access by Felthams.

Following the closure of Torre Road Depot, Felthams were to be seen on all routes except Middleton. Stored Felthams, which had been under Swinegate Arches were moved to Chapeltown Depot and the Arches used for Chamberlain cars that were still running in service.

In addition to the eleven trams stored at Torre Road, there were also 30 cars of various types at Chapeltown Depot. There were also eight cars in Torre Road Depot Yard: the three Lance Corporal cars stripped for scrap, the first Horsfield car to be stripped, 224, and four Chamberlain cars.

A scrapping session at Low Fields Road Yard in December resulted in the demise of the Lance Corporals, and Horsfield 224.

A check made on 1 January 1956 showed that the number of trams remaining in the fleet was 290. This included 69 Chamberlain cars, 103 Horsfields, the 17 Middleton bogies, cars 275-279, 301, the 89 Felthams, three railcars and cars 345, 359 and 399. Many of the Chamberlains and Horsfields were withdrawn from service and there were several Felthams, which had not yet entered service.

Over the next two months 22 trams were scrapped. These were all Chamberlains except for Horsfield car 233. Included was the last Leeds-built Chamberlain car to run in service, 423. One of the snow sweepers, No.4, was also burned. Snow sweepers, Nos.2, 3 and 5 had been in use during the snow fall of 20 December 1955. They had been joined by several Chamberlain cars temporarily fitted with snow plough equipment, including 24, 84 and 120.

During the latter part of 1955 and early 1956, the Transport Department suffered a serious staff shortage and services on all tram and bus routes were reduced. The reductions were mainly in the evenings and on Sundays. Examples were as follows:

Briggate-Dewsbury Road: evening and Sunday services reduced from five minutes to six minutes. Briggate-Moortown via Chapeltown: evening service reduced from five minutes to six minutes, Sunday service reduced from ten minutes to 12 minutes.

New wages awards to staff and rising materials costs were increasing the transport deficit and fare increases were under consideration. The tramway replacement scheme had had little or no effect on the department's finances. Councillor Mather said:

"There is no indication that the rosy picture which was presented when the Socialists came into power is being realised. Until there is some drastic overhauling of their general activities it is difficult to see how they can avoid a fare rise. Two years ago we suggested an independent financial investigation into the activities of the Transport Committee, but it was turned down by the Socialists. Subsequent events seem to indicate that we were correct in making that suggestion and that even now it may not be too late".

'The Yorkshire Post', 17 January 1956.

Passenger numbers were falling. In the year ending 31 March 1953 the number carried had been 237,576,753. Three years later it was just over 224 million. A.B.Findlay, the General Manager, said he thought that this was due to changing habits. Fewer people, he thought, were going home to lunch and at night more people were staying at home to watch TV. A further cause for the decline was "unquestionably the increase in the use of private transport." Findlay said that the decrease in passenger numbers was common throughout the country. Councillor Mather said there was a "rising tide" of criticism of the Transport Department. He listed six items that were causing dissatisfaction, including the infrequent off peak services. The mid-morning service on the Stanningley bus route was a bus every quarter of an hour, whereas three years previously there had been a tram every nine minutes. He said that there had been an overall reduction of the off-peak services on all former tram routes of 24% in the three years the Socialists had been in office. He added that the real reason for putting buses on trunk routes was to enable economies to be made by reducing the service. The reduction was caused by this policy and not by any inefficiency in the department.

Mather said that what puzzled the public was the way in which buses could be found when the chairman really wished it, and not at other times. The bus service provided at peak hours on a newly abandoned tram route had to be seen to be believed, but that standard of service rapidly deteriorated after six weeks or so. Mather also complained of the spacing of the bus stops at about quarter mile intervals, making people walk with heavy shopping. He was concerned with bad connections with the new bus services and referred to the Beeston buses. The remaining tram routes were being neglected, said Mather. It was firmly believed by many people that the chairman's and department's preoccupation with buses had caused a marked deterioration in the attention and supervision given to the remaining tram routes.

In 1953 one of the reasons given by Alderman Beevers, the leader of the Socialist party, for the abandonment of the tramways was the price of electricity. He had forecast that there was a possibility that the tax on fuel oil would be reduced. This had not happened and Rafferty bemoaned the fact that fuel tax was now costing the department £200,000 a year. He hoped that pressure by M.P.s. would persuade the Chancellor of the Exchequer to reduce the tax on diesel oil, "to save all forms of public transport from drifting further towards bankruptcy."

There had been a fare increase in January 1955 and for the year ended 31 March 1956 the Department recorded a surplus of £78,617, about £100,000 less than had been estimated. Rafferty said that the surplus was as the result of "utmost economies." He said he thought that

The section of tramway at West Park was always photogenic. Chamberlain car 113 on the 3 circular route is heading for Roundhay on 8 May 1954. In the proposed super tram scheme for the Lawnswood route, later aborted for financial reasons, the trees (which still exist) were to be felled and replaced with a central reserved track. *Author*.

Horsfield car 178 climbing Woodhouse Lane on 7 August 1955. Rowland Winn's garage is in the background. All the property and streets on the left were demolished in 1963 and 1964. *Author*.

Chamberlain car 74, newly repainted, looked very smart when it was photographed in Headingley Lane at the Original Oak Inn on 23 July 1955. *Author.*

"reasonable demands of the public had been met in the provision of new and extended services." There had been a continued staff shortage and unlimited overtime, which was expensive.

Councillor Mather said that Rafferty had failed to point out that the surplus contained certain hidden subsidies as well as the transfer of certain costs to other committees.

"He has also failed to point out that next year's loss will completely obliterate this surplus unless fares are put up again. Alderman Rafferty has been prophesying prosperity as a result of the change over from trams to buses during the past four years, but there is no evidence of any real financial benefit to the city."

'The Yorkshire Post', 1 May 1956.

Mather asked why the Socialists were intending to take £58,000 from the rate fund in the current year to bolster the Transport Department's finances. Rafferty did not reply nor comment on anticipated fare increases.

On Saturday 3 March 1956 another major tramway abandonment took place when route number 1 ceased operation. This was the Briggate to Lawnswood service, some four and a half miles long. It was the oldest tram route and had originally been opened for horse trams as far as Headingley 85 years earlier in 1871.

The spur in City Square was disused from Friday 2 March, the last car being Horsfield 247. The peak hour 27 Hyde Park-Belle Isle service ceased at the same time, the last car on the service was Feltham 519, although Horsfield 231 followed from Hyde Park afterwards, but short working to Balm Road only. There was no replacement bus service.

On the final day of operation of the number 1 route, Horsfield car 235 was the last tram to use the St. Chad's Road spur at Headingley and car 202, the last to reverse at Hyde Park.

The last tram of all, Horsfield car 222, left Lawnswood terminus at 11.56 p.m. on 3 March for City Square.

"Scenes of wild enthusiasm" greeted the car at Lawnswood terminus.

"An inspector accompanied the crew, Driver James Strickland of Prospect Street, Leeds and Conductor George Archibald, a West Indian who came to Leeds from the Leeward Islands.

The tram left Briggate precisely at 11.27 p.m. It was seen off by Alderman John Rafferty, chairman of the Leeds Corporation Transport Committee, but there was no ceremony. At City Square where many people were unable to get on, there were cheers and the sound of somebody playing the "Last Post" on a bugle....

....A large crowd cheered the tram as it arrived and there was a battery of photographers....

....As we sped for the last time along the enclosed track from Lawnswood to West Park someone struck up "Auld Lang Syne" and it was taken up fervently by the other passengers.

The tram went on its way to Swinegate Depot to the accompaniment of cheers and the plaintive note of the bugle from an open top deck window. Behind followed an escort of cars and motorcycles. Many passengers remained on the tram until it returned to Swinegate Depot, where there was finally more cheering and singing."

'The Yorkshire Post', 5 March 1956.

Regrettably on the return journey there was some vandalism and small components were removed from the car. These had to be replaced before car 222 could return to service. On the journey, waiting at the crossover at the top of Cookridge Street, was rail derrick No.2 (ex-420). It followed 222 into City Square where it joined the other rail derrick, No.1. Both derricks removed the overhead wiring, running by gravity from Park Row to Bishopgate Street.

With the closure of the route, the north bound track from Hunslet Lane along Great Wilson Street and Neville Street as far as the Sovereign Street junction fell into disuse, as did the curves from Boar Lane into Briggate. About 30 Chamberlain cars were withdrawn.

The new bus service, also numbered 1, ran from Lawnswood to Beeston, a through service recommended for the trams by Mather's sub-committee in 1952, but not implemented.

After the withdrawal of the Lawnswood trams the schedules for Middleton, Belle Isle and Hunslet cars were revised. For the first time, the Hunslet and Belle Isle routes were inter-worked by the same cars at times. For the past two years the single deck railcars had been relegated to the short Hunslet route, latterly seen at peak hours only. With the new arrangement they were used even less.

Major alterations were made to the layout of City Square. The area incorporating the tram tracks on the east and north west sides was reduced and the shelters and queuing barriers removed. The gyratory system, dating from 1937, was retained, but the number of lanes was increased from two to three, the cost of the scheme being £29,100. A casualty was the unique system of tramway traffic signals in City Square, installed in August 1939. These signals were removed on 19 February 1956.

From 11.00 p.m. on Saturday evening, 3 March, and until 6.00 a.m. on Monday the 5th, City Square was closed to traffic. 17 tons of rails and points used by the No.1 route cars were removed, and trams still running through City Square on the 15 and 16 Tong Road routes, were temporarily turned on the crossover in Wellington Street. Trams working from Cross Gates, Halton and Temple Newsam, reversed on the Duncan Street crossover.

It is interesting to note that the pointwork to the spur was removed in August 2002, during another remodelling of City Square, this time in preparation for the hopeful reintroduction of trams on the same route as that abandoned in 1956.

Routes 2 and 3 (Moortown and Roundhay), which had worked through to Headingley and Lawnswood, were now coupled with route 9 to Dewsbury Road. There was, however, no through operation from Dewsbury Road to 3 Roundhay circular. Cars ran to the Crescent short working throughout the day, but not during the evenings.

In Briggate the former Lawnswood barrier was used by the Dewsbury Road cars, queues overflowing into the old Dewsbury Road barrier.

There was heavy tram traffic on the number 1 route and some doubt at first whether buses could cope with the situation. To speed the service four stops were removed, the journey time being reduced from 24 minutes to 21 from City Square to Lawnswood.

The resiting of a fare stage in Cookridge Street led to a petition being signed by 456 people. On the trams people could travel from Headingley to The Headrow junction with Cookridge Street for 3d. They were now deposited some 300 yards away at the top of Cookridge Street, paying an extra penny if they wanted to go to The Headrow. Alderman Rafferty said that the new stops were designed to "help with the general flow of traffic." The petition was to no avail.

Despite the reduction in stops it was only possible to reduce the timing from Hyde Park to Lawnswood by one minute (14 minutes to 13). For the first week or two of bus operation inspectors were stationed at various points on the route, or were in patrol cars, and the service was "flooded" with new buses. On the first busy day, 5 March, J.B.Gill, the Chief Traffic Officer, said that the new service, in general, worked "quite well." After a short time the service deteriorated, the former peak hour two and a half minute tram service, becoming a five minute bus service. Fares were the same as the trams. It was anticipated that with the abolition of the trams, the congestion points at Hyde Park and at Headingley would disappear. This did not happen as it was found that the congestion was due to motor traffic.

From March to the closure of the next tramway routes

Chamberlain car 443 in Tong Road en route to the rarely used Whingate Junction short working. It is about to pass over the railway bridge at Thornhill Road. The date is 22 August 1953. *Author.*

The last Chamberlain car to run in service was 81 (ex-142, ex-65) during the evening peak of Friday, 20 July 1956. It was photographed at Moortown Corner on 25 February 1956. The three white bands painted on the trees in Street Lane for use in the blackout during the Second World War, are still visible. *Author*.

to Whingate and New Inn, 35 trams were scrapped. These included 16 Chamberlain cars, 18 Horsfields and 359, the former converted car, which had been used as a decorated tram from 1951 to 1955. Four of the better cars which had been regulars on the Lawnswood route, 276 and the HR/2s, cars 277-279, were now used on the through services from Roundhay and Moortown to Dewsbury Road. Austerity car 275 made a rare trip to Headingley and West Park on the last day of tramway operation in connection with football special cars.

The tram rails in Park Row were removed in late April 1956 and the road resurfaced with red tarmacadam. The remainder of the route was treated in a similar manner to other tram routes that had been abandoned. The rails were left in position, the kerbs and paving at both sides of the road raised and the whole of the road resurfaced with about three to four inches of tarmacadam.

When the Beeston tram route closed the replacement buses ran through to the Corn Exchange following the same route as the trams. However, the introduction of the Beeston-Lawnswood through bus service "changed the whole pattern of life in Beeston," said the Rev. Norman Charlton, Minister of Salem Congregational Church. Buses now ran via City Square, and the Corn Exchange and Markets were cut out, with a long walk for Beeston people. Charlton said that there had been a "very good" service to the Corn Exchange for over 50 years and many did their shopping in that area. He organised a protest campaign and on 30 May 1956 a petition bearing nearly 5,000 signatures was presented to Major F.S. Eastwood, chairman of the Yorkshire Traffic Commissioners. Charlton estimated that there was a signature from every household affected by the route alteration. The petition asked for the abandonment of the peak hour Beeston-Swinegate bus service and the institution of a new service to the Corn Exchange, following the old tram route. At the meeting of

the Transport Committee on 13 July it was decided to take no action.

The abandonment of routes 15 and 16, the Whingate and New Inn services, was scheduled for May 1956, but delayed due to poor weather. A new bus garage was under construction at Seacroft and was required for the proposed new bus services. Bad weather in January and February 1956 delayed the construction and the garage was officially opened on 13 July 1956. A week later trams were withdrawn on the New Inn and Whingate services. They were replaced by bus services operating through to Gipton and Seacroft.

Prior to the abandonment two track alterations were made in the city centre. A new crossover was put in outside the Central Bus Station in York Street, inserted between 2 and 10 June, and completed on the 13th. It was first used on 7 July when Feltham 513 reversed for Swinegate. On 10 June an overhead wire was put up in City Square in readiness for a new curve from the City Square reservation into Bishopgate Street.

On Saturday night, 21 July 1956 the last trams ran from Corn Exchange to Whingate and New Inn. These routes were the last to traverse Boar Lane, City Square and Wellington Street.

The last journey from New Inn was made by Feltham 585 which left the terminus at 11.44 p.m. The last car from Whingate was 542 which left at 11.51 p.m. and became the last car to run in both directions along Tong Road.

"From the Whingate terminus into town small crowds had gathered on the pavement to wave the tram on its way. At the terminus itself they had swarmed into the road with an enthusiasm usually confined to Royal cars. The conductress, Miss Alwyn Sutcliffe, of Kendal Drive, Leeds, had been given a small bunch of roses. It made her feel, well, you know, all funny inside, she said later. A small girl

Horsfield car 220 approaching the tram stop at Bramley Station, Stanningley Road, on 12 September 1953. *Author*.

Newly repainted Chamberlain car 93 at the St. Chad's Road spur terminus at Headingley on 23 July 1955. Headingley Bus Garage forms the setting for the photograph. The marks in the road show that there were many derailments on this sharp curve. *Author*.

Horsfield car 172 in Woodhouse Lane on 7 August 1955. This scene is relatively unchanged at the time of writing. Blenheim Chapel, converted into offices in 1981, and Blenheim Terrace on the left still exist. Compare with the photograph on page 1617 which shows a horse tram in the same location. *Author*.

put a penny in the track to be flattened and a few old women were obviously near to tears.

Old ladies were in every group on the route to town, coats thrown over their aprons, fluttering handkerchiefs and shouting to the driver. They probably remembered the good old days, fifty years ago, when trams were driven by steam engines, which trailed smoke over passengers hardy enough to weather the open top deck....

....Shortly after midnight Mr. Gilbert Towers drove 542 through City Square for the last time. The trumpeter, now armed with a relenting policeman's authority, played a shaky Last Post and in the gang of workmen already altering the track there were those who raised their caps."

'The Yorkshire Post', 23 July 1956.

On the last day of operation the routes had been worked by Feltham cars, but during the previous week a number of Chamberlains had been seen, the last being car 74 on the evening peak of 19 July. Immediately after the last tramcar had returned from Whingate the City Square junction was removed and the new curve laid from the eastbound track in City Square to the southbound track in Bishopgate Street. The curve was inserted to enable cars running between Kirkstall Road Works and Swinegate Depot to avoid Boar Lane. Previously cars had to go along Boar Lane to the Corn Exchange and reverse on either the Duncan Street or Markets crossovers.

The new curve in City Square was tested at 6.00 p.m. on 22 July by Feltham 525 which went from Swinegate Depot and reversed on the Wellington Street crossover - most probably the last car to reverse at this point - and returned to Swinegate via the new track. After the closure of the Tong Road routes, cars usually ran between the Works and Swinegate during the night.

The Whingate and New Inn services had been coupled with the Cross Gates, Halton and Temple Newsam routes. These latter services were now run through to Middleton (12) and Belle Isle (26 and 27) cars running in both directions via Briggate and Bridge End.

By July 1956 eleven of the Middleton bogie cars had been withdrawn, being regarded as non-standard. Six, 257, 261, 262, 265, 268 and 269, remained and these were used on the new through services. It was the first occasion on which this type of car had been seen on the York Road routes. Horsfield cars were also reintroduced on York Road after an absence of some five years or so. Cars 249-254 had been allocated to Torre Road Depot for a short time in 1950, but had not been used beyond the junction with Gipton Approach from that time. Except for isolated journeys when new, Felthams had not run on the Middleton and Belle Isle routes. They now ran to Middleton and Belle Isle. Two cars did trial runs the previous week to familiarise crews with the route.

With the changeover, cars on the Hunslet route were again isolated. They did not run in conjunction with the Middleton and Belle Isle cars and were now the only trams returning along Swinegate and Neville Street.

Prior to the closure of the Tong Road routes several early morning cars had run through from Whingate to Temple Newsam (22). They now ran from Middleton via Belle Isle and returned via the 26 circular. The Belle Isle (27) service operated between Belle Isle and the Corn Exchange only. During early morning peak hours and on Saturday afternoons there was a service from Harehills Lane (17) to Belle Isle (27). At other peak times extra cars ran from the new crossover at the Central Bus Station to Middleton (12) and Belle Isle (27). A regular service to the Belle Isle (26) Broom Estate, was only operated on Sunday afternoons and evenings.

Cars working into and out of Swinegate Depot for Middleton and Belle Isle were authorised to carry passengers from the depot entrance. This ruling brought the lower part of the eastbound track in Swinegate into its first service use since the abandonment of the Domestic Street tramway in 1937. During the evening peak hours extra cars were worked from Swinegate Depot to the Balm Road crossover. On one of the duties the car was returned from Balm Road to 2 Moortown.

With the new through workings the outward track in Hunslet Lane, disused from October 1939 when the terminal point for the Middleton and Hunslet cars was changed from the Corn Exchange to Swinegate, came into use again. On 22 July a little "celebration" was held for the first car, Feltham 566, that traversed Hunslet Lane. It was the first 26 Circular for that day and was followed by Horsfield car 179, the first car to go via Bridge End and Meadow Lane to Middleton 12 circular. Both cars had left Swinegate Depot and then turned at the Central Bus Station to make these journeys, They became the first trams from Middleton to Cross Gates and from Middleton via Belle Isle to Halton respectively.

The last tram from Swinegate to Middleton (12 circular) had been Middleton bogie 261 on Saturday 21 July, and from Swinegate to Middleton (26 circular), Horsfield car 156. On Friday evening 20 July, the last car from Swinegate to Balm Road had been Horsfield 191.

A new stopping place was inserted in Lower Briggate and this resulted in serious congestion on Monday evening, 23 July. Alderman Rafferty said that the ex-London Feltham cars were having difficulty in turning from Duncan Street into Lower Briggate because of the number of parked motor cars. "The congestion would be considerably relieved if parking was not allowed on Duncan Street and Lower Briggate at peak times," he said. He added that the traffic situation would improve when the West Riding buses were moved from their terminus at the Corn Exchange to New York Street. To ease the problem the Lower Briggate stop was moved back by one pole.

The removal of trams from City Square enabled road works in the Square to be completed. However, there was no improvement in traffic conditions. On 11 September 1956 members of the Town Planning and Improvements Committee visited City Square on their annual inspection.

Alderman S. Hand, Chairman of the Committee, said the Committee was "puzzled" as the withdrawal of the trams had not solved the traffic problem. The volume of traffic gyrating round the Square was getting "heavier and heavier" and the large volume of pedestrian traffic using the Square was also a cause of concern. Pedestrians were delaying the motor traffic. To improve the traffic flow, a proposal was put forward by the Traffic Advisory Committee that the central island be converted into a "cultivated roundabout" and closed to pedestrians. City Council members, however, objected and the island remained a seated refuge. Congestion worsened.

The Harehills Road spur, occasionally used during holiday times for cars working a shuttle service between Harehills Road and Roundhay Park, was disconnected between 6 and 14 October 1956. The spur formed the remains of the terminus of the former Harehills Road via Beckett Street route abandoned in 1946. Felthams 558 and 570 were the last cars to use the spur for Roundhay special duties on 8 July 1956.

With the closure of the Whingate and New Inn tramways all the remaining Chamberlain cars were taken out of service. The last Chamberlain to run was 81 (ex-142, ex-65) during the evening peak hour of Friday, 20 July. Also withdrawn from service on the same day was car 76, the oldest car still in passenger service. 76, which originally entered service on 17 July 1926, had been in service for exactly 30 years and four days.

In the months following the abandonment, 59 trams were scrapped. These included the remaining Chamberlain cars, 13 Middleton bogies, seven Feltham cars still in London Transport livery and three Felthams which had been restored for service: 552, 555 and 579. On 1 January 1957 over half of the tramcar fleet, existing in 1953 had gone. There were 170 cars left plus cars 83, 345 and 399, which were used for works purposes.

The closure of the next group of routes, 2 and 9 Moortown-Dewsbury Road, was scheduled for March 1957. In the meantime the Suez crisis intervened with a consequent shortage of fuel oil. This gave the trams a temporary reprieve. The final abandonment of the tramways is discussed in the next chapter.

Boar Lane on 30 September 1953 with two Felthams, 534 and 520, and Chamberlain 24. On the left is the Tatler Cinema, incorporated in the Royal Exchange building, demolished in March and April 1964. *Author.*

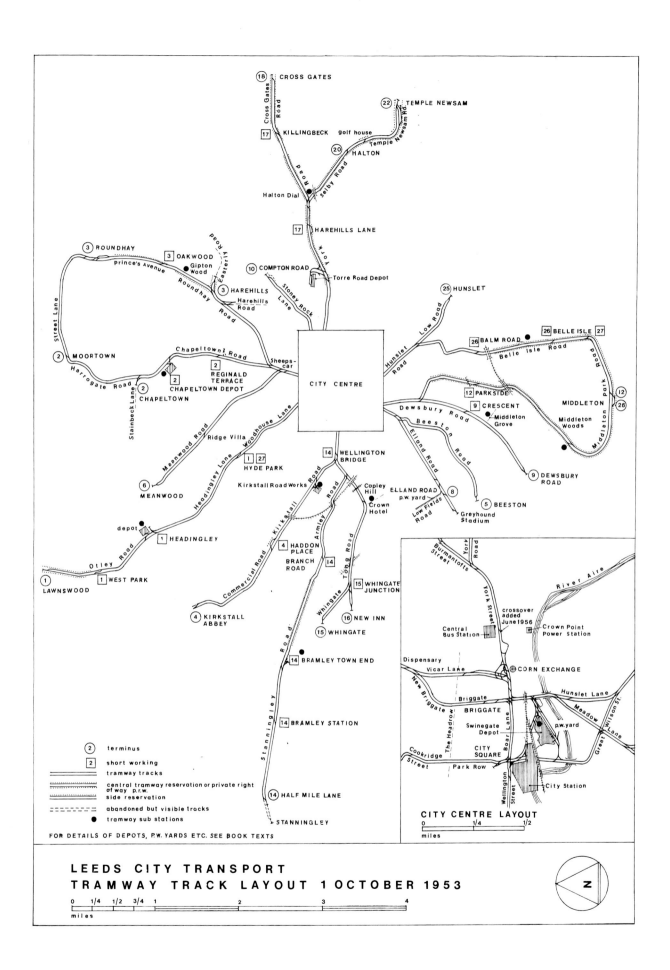

LEEDS CITY TRANSPORT
TRAMWAY TRACK LAYOUT 1 OCTOBER 1953

Passengers boarding Middleton bogie car 267 in Church Street, Hunslet. The car is about to turn into Balm Road on 17 September 1955. In 1953 the Leeds City Engineer wanted to ease the curve from Church Street into Balm Road, but the Transport Committee rejected the idea as it would involve relaying the tram track. *Author*.

Chamberlain car 7 has stopped to allow a passenger to board in Harrogate Road, Chapel Allerton. On 28 March 1955 many stopping places on the Moortown tram route were altered to even out track wear. The location is the new Wood Lane tram stop, formerly about 80 yards nearer to Moortown, and the date is 21 June 1955. *Author*.

Final Tramway Abandonments 1957 to 1959

The Suez crisis of November 1956 caused a temporary halt in the Leeds tramways abandonment programme. An increase in the price of fuel oil on 10 October and petrol rationing from 17 December 1956 led to the Leeds Labour party group asking the Transport Committee to suspend tramway closures and reintroduce the Elland Road football special trams.

A 5% cut in diesel fuel for the buses was proposed and on 30 November 1956 there was a meeting of the Transport Traffic Committee. Measures to economise in the use of fuel oil were considered. 16,000 bus miles per week had to be saved and this was to be achieved by the following:

Except on Saturdays, the departure of last buses from the city centre was to be at approximately 10.30 p.m. instead of 11.00 p.m. Private hire for social functions, weddings and funerals and late dance specials was to be suspended. Football specials were to be reduced and offset by a partial return of the tram service to Elland Road when Leeds United had home matches.

Motorists were unable to use their cars and Alderman Rafferty appealed to firms to stagger hours to relieve the peak traffic. He said the peak service would not be augmented and asked other Corporation departments and schools to alter their hours. The evening service of buses was to be reduced. Rafferty said that no more steps would be taken while the emergency lasted for any further tramway closures.

Fare increases had been under consideration by the Transport Committee for some time and the "bombshell" of an increase of 3d. per gallon plus a "temporary" surcharge of 1s. 0d. per gallon in the price of fuel oil, led to the matter being discussed at the City Council meeting on 18 December. Conservatives complained that they had not had the opportunity to discuss the proposals at the Transport Committee meeting on the previous day.

Alderman W.R.Hargrave, Conservative leader, described Rafferty as "the monolithic Canute of modern transport economics." When members of the Transport Committee received their agenda there was no mention of the proposed fare increases, no schedules and no particulars.

The original proposal had been to increase fares to raise an additional £375,000, but this was now increased by a further £125,000. Rafferty blamed the previous Conservative administration, the Chancellor of the Exchequer and Government for the financial difficulties of the Department. Hargrave said that precautionary action should have been taken "months and months ago."

"I warn the party in power, as I warn the citizens of Leeds, that unless this huge transport undertaking is released from the shackles and bedevilment of political interference and uncertainty so that those who are primarily responsible for running it efficiently as a sound and well-ordered undertaking are allowed to do so, then disaster is ahead."

'The Yorkshire Post', 18 December 1956.

Councillor Bertrand Mather said it was almost a year since the General Manager reported that the financial position of the department was very grave. Nothing was done except that a one-year direct subsidy was granted out of the rates, presumably to give the Socialists time to pluck up

Austerity car 275 was a rare visitor to Middleton. It was pictured at Middleton terminus with the prototype Middleton bogie 255 on 30 April 1955. *Author.*

Horsfield car 217, on what was left of the Low Fields Road football siding on 16 March 1957, during the fuel shortage of 1956-7. The track had remained open for access to the scrap yard. Barriers for buses have been erected over the former tram rails. *Author*.

enough courage to grasp the nettle. "In the meantime the nettle grew to gigantic proportions and ten days ago the Committee had to face the reality of a yearly loss of at least £183,000 and an accumulated deficit next March of well over half a million pounds," he said. "The whole operation of these applications," continued Mather, "indicated lack of courage, followed by panic with a final effort to unload the responsibility for the enormous rise on to the Government."

The proposal to increase fares was approved by the Socialist majority on the City Council and an application was made to the Traffic Commissioners.

In the meantime a trial run to Low Fields Road had been made with Horsfield car 246 on Thursday, 6 December, followed by 11 cars on the following Saturday. Trams were also used on 22 December (14 cars), 26 December (15 cars), 29 December (3 cars) and on all Saturdays in January, three Saturdays in February and two in March.

Diesel fuel oil was derationed in March and the 1s.0d. per gallon surcharge on the fuel price was removed on 9 April 1957. The Transport Department announced that from 7 April full bus services would be resumed. This marked the demise of the football cars.

The last Saturday on which trams were used was 16 March when 15 tramcars assisted the buses. Horsfield car 181 made the last journey from Sovereign Street to Low Fields Road and car 160 was the last to leave Low Fields Road. The former terminus in Elland Road had remained wired during the emergency, but was not used. All cars ran on to the remains of the football siding in Low Fields Road. Four-wheeled Horsfield cars, Austerity car 275 and car 276, were used throughout except on 12 January when an eight-wheeler, Feltham 583, was taken off a Park Side extra duty to work one journey to Low Fields Road.

At the Transport Committee meeting on 15 April 1957 the tramway closure scheme was revived. The Committee discussed a recommendation that the programme should be completed two years ahead of schedule. The reason, said Alderman Rafferty, was the money needed for track maintenance, overhead and vehicles. "We think it will be more economic to accelerate the abandonment programme," he said. The last services to go would be the Cross Gates and Halton routes, which it was proposed to discontinue in 1960. The original tramways abandonment scheme had been programmed to take ten years, the last tram running on 31 March 1963.

It was announced that the Dewsbury Road-Moortown via Chapeltown service, scheduled to close the previous month would now cease in September 1957.

On 7 May 1957, in a long article in the 'Yorkshire Evening Post', Councillor Mather condemned the policy of the Transport Committee saying that the city would be dependent solely on double deck buses powered by imported fuel oil. He said it became increasingly evident that the net result would be merely a change in the type of vehicle while all the original problems would still be there. He stated that the dilemma was common to all British cities for unlike on the Continent, urban transport in Britain rarely took into account the fundamental problem of moving people, but concentrated mainly on the average cost of running vehicles.

Mather said the answer to the city's problems was to get public transport off the roads and onto its own segregated tracks. He reiterated the proposals he had made some two years previously for the retention and modernisation of the remaining tramways, advocating reserved tracks wherever possible. Although there were many letters of support for Mather's proposals in the local press, his comments were again ignored by the Transport Committee.

On 19 September 1957 applications to run buses in place of trams from Dewsbury Road to Moortown and Dewsbury Road to Roundhay via Moortown were approved by the Traffic Commissioners. A.B.Findlay, the General Manager, said that trams would continue to run along Street Lane to Moortown via Roundhay. Alternate buses would run to Roundhay via Moortown "for the benefit of people living in Street Lane who wish to get to Chapeltown." In the city centre the buses would run via Vicar Lane, New Market Street and Duncan Street.

In comparison with other routes the abandonment of the Dewsbury Road-Moortown tramway "went off very quietly" according to the Leeds Transport Department. The last trams on the through service ran on Saturday night, 28 September 1957. Last cars were:

559 last Moortown 2 circular.

540 last Moortown 2.

200 last Roundhay 3 circular.

547 last Dewsbury Road 9.

154 last to use Stainbeck Lane spur.

159 last to use Crescent crossover.

With so many "last" trams it is not surprising that there was no ceremony or celebration to mark the event.

On the following morning, car 182 made the first journey on the new Moortown 3 service, trams running alternately with buses on Street Lane. In Briggate the northern half of the tram barriers was now disused, the southern half being used by passengers on route 3. The northern part was removed over the following four weeks. The new tram route was isolated from others in the city, cars for Roundhay reversing in Briggate on the southern crossover. As on earlier tram route conversions, the number of stops was reduced, but on Street Lane the buses used the tram stops. Services were speeded up; journey times from Corn Exchange to Moortown being reduced from 21 minutes to 17, Corn Exchange to Stainbeck Lane, Chapeltown, 15 minutes to 12 and from Corn Exchange to Dewsbury Road 16 minutes to 14.

On the same day as the tramway abandonment fares were increased. The $2^{1}/_{2}$d. minimum fare was raised to 3d. except that passengers could now travel for one stage for 2d. An average stage length was 0·56 miles. There was a child's half fare of 1d.

The application to raise fares had been approved by the Traffic Commissioners on 19 September. It was said that the increases were intended to keep ahead of costs and hopefully decrease the accumulated deficit. A.B.Findlay said that difficulties at peak hours were getting worse as the public had not been co-operating in spreading the load. The number of passengers continued to decrease and from April to September of the current year 3,151,000 fewer passengers had been carried, a drop of about $3^{1}/_{4}$%. Recent wages awards had cost £105,047 and the undertaking's budget was "entirely out of gear."

Findlay said that there would be fares resistance and attributed the reduction in passenger numbers to the "terrific impact" of television. The increased use of push- bikes and scooters was also a factor, he said.

Coincidental with the closure of the Moortown-Dewsbury Road tramway, the Tramway Rolling Stock Engineer, Victor J. Matterface, resigned. He left his post on 30 September for a new job as Electric Traction Engineer on the Tyneside Electric Railway of British Railways. He came to Leeds from the London Passenger Transport Board in 1948 and had a big influence on the tramway rolling stock in the period up to 1952. In that year Tom Parkinson was promoted over Matterface at Kirkstall Road Works and Matterface's activities were severely curtailed.

Horsfield car 166 in Harrogate Road below Moortown Corner. The new bus stop, made from a former tramway overhead bracket arm, indicates that this was the last day of tramway operation, 28 September 1957. *Author.*

580 was one of the Felthams that entered service in 1955. It was in the lined livery, but only ran for 19 months. It was in a collision on 16 September 1956 and had the shortest period in service of any of the Felthams in Leeds. It was photographed in Dewsbury Road on 9 August 1956. *Author.*

Horsfield car 155 at Dewsbury Road terminus on 9 August 1956. *Author.*

Horsfield car 180 waits at the Barrack Road traffic lights near the bottom of Chapeltown Road on 12 August 1956. Almost all the property on this photograph was removed over a period from 1963 to 1972. *Author.*

With the closure of the Moortown-Dewsbury Road services six routes remained, all in the north, east or south of the city, the services being:

3 Briggate-Moortown via Harehills and Roundhay.

12 and 12 circular. Corn Exchange-Middleton via Park Side.

17 Corn Exchange-Harehills Lane via York Road.

18 Corn Exchange-Cross Gates.

20 Corn Exchange-Halton.

22 Corn Exchange-Temple Newsam.

25 Swinegate-Hunslet.

26 circular. Corn Exchange-Middleton via Belle Isle.

26 Corn Exchange-Belle Isle (Broom Estate).

27 Corn Exchange-Belle Isle (Middleton Ring Road).

Three of the services, 3, 22 and 25, were generally operated on their own, but the others were worked across the city in the following manner:

18 Cross Gates-12 circular Middleton-20 Halton-26 circular Middleton-18 Cross Gates and so on.

17 Harehills Lane or 20 Halton-27 Belle Isle (peak periods and Saturdays).

Certain cars worked at various times between Middleton or Belle Isle and Temple Newsam and to Balm Road or 26 Belle Isle from the city or Halton. There was also a service between Cross Gates, or the city and 12 Middleton at certain times.

A number of Horsfield cars of the 205-254 series, some Feltham cars, Austerity Car 275, the 1948-built car 276, HR/2s 277-279 and the remaining Middleton bogies were withdrawn and scrapped. The three railcars, 600-602, were withdrawn and put in storage. Only Horsfield and Feltham cars were left for the remaining tram routes.

In June 1957, in anticipation of the abandonment of the Moortown-Dewsbury Road tramway, 41 redundant tramcars were sold to George Cohen Sons & Co. Ltd. for £7,101. Although the tender was for 41 cars, 42 were scrapped from 31 July to 5 November 1957 in Low Fields Road Yard. On Saturday evening, 26 October, there was

a final procession of cars to Low Fields Road. It was headed by Horsfield car 152 towing Feltham 545, damaged in a collision, followed by 185 towing car 276 and at the rear Horsfield 198. On the return journey the order of cars was 198, 185 and 152, 152 being the last car to return from Low Fields Road. On 5 November car 559 was the last to be burned there. Within a fortnight a start had been made with the removal of overhead wiring and the covering of tracks in Elland Road.

On 1 January 1958 the number of passenger cars remaining in the fleet had been reduced to 127. Of these 74 were Horsfields, 50 Felthams and the three railcars. In addition there were 15 works cars including cars 83, 345 and 399. All the B.T-H. Horsfields of the series 151-204 were still in use and operated the basic services, with Felthams also working the York Road-Middleton routes. The Peters Horsfields (205-254 series) were used on all routes mainly at peak periods, but were employed on all day duties on the Hunslet service. Felthams were now rarely used on the Moortown route except on certain morning duties working from York Road or Hunslet Road.

At its meeting on 15 July 1957 the Transport Committee had authorised the Town Clerk to terminate the lease of the Arches under the Leeds City Railway Station. The Arches, which were at the rear of Swinegate Depot, were leased from British Railways and used for the storage of cars. The Arches ceased to be used after 27 September when Feltham 562 left. However, the rails remained intact and they came into use again after the final closure of the tramways in 1959. They were used for the temporary storage of preserved cars.

Also abandoned in November 1957 was the tramway works in Kirkstall Road and the connecting tracks through City Square and along Wellington Street and Kirkstall Road. On Monday night, 4 November, two of the remaining three tramcars still at Kirkstall Road Works, Horsfield car 159 and the towing car, 399, were transferred to Swinegate Depot. This was the first time that 399 had traversed the streets of Leeds since the night of 4/5 September 1952, when it had been used at Harehills in connection with the runaway accident involving cars 507 and 92. Feltham 511, which had been the last car to go from Swinegate to Kirkstall Works on 1 November remained there until the night of the 7th when it returned to Swinegate. It was thus the last tram to travel along Wellington Street and through City Square. The temporary curve inserted in City Square on the abandonment of the Tong Road services in 1956, became disused. Car maintenance was transferred to Swinegate Depot.

During February 1958 there were severe snow storms in Leeds which caused some disruption to tram services. There was snow on the night of 7-8 February and the tram service had to be suspended between Halton and Temple Newsam. On Saturday morning, 8 February, snow blade 7 (ex-Chamberlain car 83), and Horsfield car 229 were in use and normal services were resumed at Temple Newsam from about 11.00 a.m. There was also heavy snow on 25-26 February.

The tram versus bus controversy came to the fore again in March 1958 with bitter correspondence in the local press between Alderman Rafferty and Councillor Mather. Rafferty had said on 7 March that the tramways were being scrapped on "overwhelming economic grounds" and the public of Leeds "refused to become Continental-minded" about the railcars.

Mather replied that the "economic grounds" had never been placed before either the Transport Committee or City Council and must be in some "secret file" at the Labour Party offices. Certainly the writer has never found any detailed economic justification for the scrapping of the tramways in either the Leeds City Transport, City Council records or in any of the local newspapers.

In regard to the railcars, Mather said that the Leeds public had never had the chance of becoming "Continental-minded". For most of their short life in Leeds the railcars had been confined to the two mile lightly used Hunslet route, entirely on street track, and had not been allowed to demonstrate their capabilities. Mather said there had never been any equipment, schedules or operating practices anything like those in Europe. £24,000 had been spent on experimental equipment - the railcars - but the results had been decided before doing the experiments.

"This remarkable conception of scientific experimentation was far more 'overwhelming' than any economic grounds that were produced, because the policy came first and the 'supporting evidence' later."...

....It is now six years since I said in the Leeds City Council that, when the trams have gone, all the old problems will still remain but in a more acute form. This is now coming true, and the only solution is to have a sound long term policy in place of struggling along daily with a diesel bus system which by its very nature cannot increase its capacity or its speed and this condemns everybody to excessive delays at the rush hours.

'The Yorkshire Evening Post', 12 March 1958.

Rafferty countered Mather's statement by saying that ten German and one French city had adopted a tramway abandonment policy. "I prefer to listen to, and act on, the advice of experts who have spent, and who are spending, their lives in modern transport, whereas Councillor Mather appears to prefer giving them advice," said Rafferty.

One expert that Rafferty was referring to was Tom Parkinson, the engineer in charge of the transport undertaking. As discussed in Volume 3 Parkinson had been put in charge of the tramway rolling stock in May 1952 and had been seconded to the Transport Committee. He considered tramways entirely out of date and was well known for his "anti-tram" views. Of similar opinion to Parkinson was J.B.Gill, the Chief Traffic Officer.

For people like Parkinson and Gill who were

On 4 November 1957 the last tram from Kirkstall Works ran along Wellington Street and through City Square. This view shows Horsfield 215 and Feltham 540 in Wellington Street passing the end of Britannia Street. The Central Station is on the left and the date is 30 August 1953. *Author.*

One had to be selective when photographing last trams on 28 September 1957 and the writer chose his local terminus at Stainbeck Lane, Chapeltown. At 11.06 p.m. Horsfield car 154 became the last tram to turn at Stainbeck Lane. *Author.*

responsible for the day to day running of the transport system, buses were easier to control than tramcars. This was confirmed by E.R.L.Fitzpayne, the Glasgow Tramways Manager, who said in his annual report for 1948 that from the management point of view the operation of motor buses involved "less anxiety and responsibility" than the running of electric vehicles whether rail bound or trackless, "yet the railed vehicle on reserved track was almost completely free from accidents."

Mather said that no city in the world had replaced a segregated railcar system with double deck buses. Where old tramways on the Continent had been replaced, it was usually by an underground system. Mather queried the function of Rafferty, all councillors and M.P.s if they merely rubber-stamped the advice of their employees. He said the duty of any public representative was to listen to, but not automatically action such advice, which was "necessarily departmental." Local officials were concerned with immediate problems and rarely looked at the broader long-term view.

Torre Road Depot had been closed to trams from November 1955, but the yard adjacent to the depot remained wired and was used for the storage of cars. On 27 and 28 July 1958 all wires in the yard were removed leaving the trams stored there: works cars 2, 8A, snow sweepers 2 and 5, water car 5 and a wire carrying bogie, stranded. The spur into Lupton Avenue from York Road remained useable.

In 1958 and 1959 maintenance of the tramcar fleet was minimal and there were breakdowns and minor fires, which caused delays to traffic and corresponding

complaints from the public. The Felthams were prone to fires and in a number of cases buses were used to give temporary assistance to the tram services.

As early as 1944, the closure of the tramway to Hunslet had been suggested by former General Manager, W.Vane Morland. The abandonment had not taken place because a turning point for the replacement bus service could not be found. In June 1958 the Coghlan Forge and Rolling Mills Ltd., whose premises were near to the tram terminus at Thwaite Gate, was approached. The intention was to turn buses in the entrance to the firm's works, but permission could not be obtained. Following at least six visits to Hunslet, the Transport Committee eventually managed to obtain police approval as a "temporary expedient" for a loading, unloading and turning point in Spring Grove Street, Thwaite Gate.

In the meantime steps had been taken to abandon the Briggate-Roundhay and the Middleton circular routes. A roundabout was proposed at Roundhay Park to enable buses to be turned and an application made to the Town Planning and Improvements Committee. The roundabout was not, however, constructed.

The withdrawal of the two services took place on Saturday night, 28 March 1959. A through bus service between Moortown, Roundhay and Middleton and Belle Isle was substituted. Tram services abandoned were:
Route 3 Briggate to Moortown via Roundhay.
Routes 12 and 12 circular Corn Exchange and Middleton via Park Side and the Middleton Light Railway.
Routes 26 and 27 Corn Exchange and Belle Isle via Hunslet Road.

Route 26 circular Corn Exchange and Middleton via Belle Isle.

The final service car to Moortown and back to Briggate was Horsfield car 160, preceded by an extra car 171. A special car, 192, reserved for members of the Transport Committee, City Council and guests, followed 160 and was the last car on the route. On its previous journey 160 had been the last car to use the Easterly Road siding and earlier in the evening 172 had worked the last journey to Roundhay only.

On the Middleton circular route the last journeys were made by Horsfield car 167 working the final 12 circular and Feltham 512 was the last 26 circular. Car 512 was thus the last tram to run over the Middleton Light Railway, acknowledged to be one of the finest stretches of tramway ever constructed in Great Britain. Much of both the 12 circular and 26 circular routes were on their own private right of way.

Working from the Central Bus Station crossover, Feltham 538 made the final journey to the Belle Isle (27) terminus, while on the 26 March Horsfield 161 had been the last Belle Isle (26) car.

Tracks abandoned were from Briggate (north of Boar Lane) to Roundhay and Moortown, Swan Junction at Waterloo Road to Middleton, Meadow Lane to Middleton, Bridge End and Hunslet Lane (southbound tracks only), New Market Street, Vicar Lane, part of Kirkgate, the curve from Swinegate to Bridge End and the two tracks joining Bridge End and Briggate.

Following the abandonment of the Beeston route in 1955 the rails in Vicar Lane had remained in place as far as the Markets crossover, but had been little used. The crossover was last used on Sunday afternoon, 22 March, on a private tour with Feltham 517. What remained of the tram barriers in Briggate was removed overnight 28/29 March.

From Sunday 29 March the Cross Gates, Halton and Temple Newsam services were altered to terminate at the Corn Exchange, all services using the Yorkshire Penny Bank curve between Kirkgate and New York Street. Cars unloaded passengers in Kirkgate, those for Cross Gates loading at the same point before turning into New York Street. Cars for Halton, Temple Newsam and the few cars running to the Harehills Lane siding loaded in New York Street as formerly.

There were the usual stop reductions, the journey time from Kirkgate to Middleton via Belle Isle being reduced from 23 minutes by tram to 20 by bus. There was a saving of two minutes - 22 to 20 minutes on the new bus route to Middleton via Dewsbury Road and the Ring Road.

Three weeks after the abandonment of the Moortown-Middleton services, the short Hunslet tramway succumbed to the motor bus. It ran for the last time on Saturday, 18 April, and was the last tramway to run in south Leeds. It was replaced the following day by a new bus service numbered 7. Four trams operated the service on the last day, Horsfields 170, 187, 189 and 195. Car 189 made the last journey from Hunslet at 11.38 p.m.

Tracks falling into disuse were from Swinegate Depot to Hunslet Lane via Neville Street (the outward track), Hunslet Road, Low Road and Thwaite Gate (both tracks), and the inward rails in Hunslet Lane and Bridge End.

From 22 April there was a big service reduction on the Halton and Cross Gates routes during the evening peak period from Mondays to Fridays. Six trams were taken off. This meant that the maximum number in use during the evening peak was reduced to 26. A further reduction occurred from 25 May when the frequency of cars between 8.30 a.m. to 4.00 p.m. on Mondays to Fridays was reduced from 7½ to ten minutes.

As a result of the tramway closures of March and April 1959 a large number of cars was withdrawn from service. During March, 17 trams were sold for scrap and removed by road from Swinegate Depot. The bodies of nine went to a yard in South Accommodation Road owned by Joseph Standish Ltd., the trucks going to a yard in Dewsbury Road owned by the same firm. The other eight cars and their trucks were taken to a yard at Churwell

The writer lived at 160 Harrogate Road, Chapel Allerton, from February 1939 to November 1957 and this view of Horsfield car 161, framed with flowers, was taken from his garden on 7 August 1955. Most of the flowers were in the garden next door at number 162. *Author*.

The three ex-London HR/2 cars, 277-279, were heavy and solidly built and lasted until 1957. Although in good condition they were taken out of service as "non-standard". 277 was photographed in Chapeltown Road at Reginald Terrace on 17 August 1956. *Author*.

There were three cinemas on the Moortown tram route: the Forum, Dominion and Kingsway. Horsfield car 235 is passing the Kingsway on the last day of tramway operation, 28 September 1957. The Kingsway closed on 23 August 1958 and was converted into the New Vilna Synagogue. It was subsequently demolished. *Author*.

Felthams 522, 554 (ex-517), 561 (ex-587), 581 and 564 (ex-557) in the yard of Joseph Standish Ltd., South Accommodation Road, Leeds, on 26 March 1959. *Author.*

Horsfield car 189 (ex-180) in York Street on 28 March 1959. The crossover outside the Central Bus Station was inserted in June 1956. Lloyds Arms on the right was demolished for road improvements in February and March 1995, but the building on the left still stands. *Author.*

After the closure of the Tong Road tram routes in July 1956, the remaining Middleton bogie cars appeared on the York Road routes. 268 and 262 are seen at Cross Gates terminus on 4 August 1956. The Regal Cinema, on the left, closed on 11 January 1964 and immediately made way for a Gem supermarket. *Author.*

owned by a Mr.Johnson. These were the first trams to be removed by road for scrap. Most trams had been scrapped in the Transport Department's Low Fields Road Permanent Way Yard, but this was now impossible.

In June a further 60 cars were sold for scrap, this time to Messrs. G. Cohen & Son Ltd. The cars were partially stripped in Swinegate Depot and were then removed on a low trailer and taken to a yard off Brown Lane in Holbeck, Leeds. Immediately on their arrival at the yard, the cars were pulled off the trailer and on to their sides and then burned. This was a relatively quick method of scrapping trams and the 60 cars were all incinerated between 2 June and 12 August 1959.

The disposal of these cars, plus the 17 scrapped a month or two earlier, left a total of exactly 50 trams in the fleet, of which 28 were Horsfield cars, 19 Felthams and the three railcars. The Horsfields were all of the 151-204 series and the Felthams of the 501-550 batch, except for 517 (ex-554).

Meanwhile an application was made to the Traffic Commissioners for the abandonment of the remaining York Road tram routes. The trams were to be replaced by bus services between Cross Gates and the Fleece Hotel, Horsforth, between Halton and Half Mile Lane, Stanningley, and between the Central Bus Station and Temple Newsam.

There were objections from the British Transport Commission and Samuel Ledgard Ltd in regard to the Cross Gates-Horsforth section. These were in competition with their rail and bus services respectively, but the objections were overruled.

Arnold Stone, Deputy Chief Traffic Officer, said it was intended to restore the link that Cross Gates people previously had with City Square and the railway stations before the abandonment of the Tong Road tramways in 1956. On the Horsforth side it gave back the service

existing along Wellington Street before the closure of the Kirkstall tramway service in 1954. He said that Kirkstall people had been anxious for years to get back that facility, but it had not been possible until now. The proposal would give people living between Kirkstall Road and Burley Road the choice of a service along The Headrow or on Wellington Street past the stations and City Square.

The abandonment had been scheduled for January 1960, but was brought forward two months, as the replacement buses were delivered earlier than originally anticipated. The new date fixed was Saturday, 7 November 1959.

During the last week of September work began on the removal of the third track at Temple Newsam terminus. The rails had been inserted during the war for the dispersal of trams. This work was required in preparation for the construction of a bus turning circle at Temple Newsam and rerouting the road over the tram tracks from the Lawn Pond to the tram terminus.

Unlike most earlier abandonments, there was an official celebration for the final closure of the tramways. Two cars, Horsfields, 160 and 178, were selected to be decorated and illuminated for the final procession.

The last day of tramway operation, Saturday, 7 November 1959, was a damp, miserable and foggy day perhaps befitting the occasion. The remaining tramway services were withdrawn:

Route 17 Corn Exchange-Harehills Lane.
Route 18 Corn Exchange-Cross Gates.
Route 20 Corn Exchange-Halton.
Route 22 Corn Exchange-Temple Newsam.

Twenty two service trams ran as follows: 156, 158, 165, 177, 181, 186, 187, 192, 195, 200, 501, 505, 512, 514, 523, 526, 528, 529, 531, 532, 538 and 542.

The services ceased in the late afternoon. Horsfield car 200 worked the last official service journey from Harehills Lane at 2.40 p.m., but was not the last tram to turn there as Feltham 505 running late to Halton was worked short to Harehills Lane shortly after 3.00 p.m. Feltham 531 was the last service car to leave Temple Newsam at 4.37 p.m. and Horsfield 158 the last Halton at 4.58 p.m. Horsfield 181 left Cross Gates terminus at 5.02 p.m. and was thus the last tram to run in normal service in Leeds. The last Feltham to run was 512, preceding 181, and the last Feltham to be seen at Halton was 529 (two cars before the final one). The duties, immediately following the last tramcars, were worked by buses.

The final procession was made up of ten Horsfield cars specially cleaned up for the occasion and numbered 1 to 10, the numbers appearing in the side destination boxes. The destination blinds were removed for the purpose. The procession left Swinegate Depot at 6.15 p.m. The first and last cars were decorated and the cars used were 178 (1), 173 (2), 176 (3), 189 (4), 175 (5), 191 (6), 198 (7), 171 (8), 172 (9) and 160 (10) which left the depot in that order.

All ten cars proceeded to the Selby Road junction where 1-5 went to Cross Gates and 6-10 to Temple Newsam. On arrival at Cross Gates car 178 went to the end of the terminal stub allowing the other four cars to return before it. 178 finally followed the other cars to the Selby Road junction where they awaited the cars from Temple Newsam.

Meanwhile cars 6-10 proceeded to Temple Newsam, where all five cars ran on to the long terminal stub, the wheels of 160 just clearing the points. The five cars returned to the Selby Road junction with 160 leading the procession back to Selby Road with in the rear car 6 (191), the last car from Temple Newsam. The five cars from Cross Gates followed with 178, the last tram, in the rear. The last trams over the various stretches of route were as follows:

Swinegate Depot to Temple Newsam.	Car 160.
Selby Road junction to Cross Gates.	Car 175.
Temple Newsam to Selby Road junction.	Car 191.
Cross Gates to Swinegate Depot.	Car 178.

On arrival in Swinegate Depot, the two decorated cars which had carried the Lord Mayor, Lady Mayoress, Transport Committee and other members of the City Council and their guests, proceeded through the depot to where A.E.C. Regent 839, the 1956 Commercial Motor Show exhibit, was waiting to take them to the Swinegate Head Office for a celebration dinner. The other eight cars carrying members of the public ran on to track 1 in the depot where their passengers alighted.

"No royal procession could have attracted more cameras; photographers were as thick as dandelions in spring. Even children, perched on their fathers' shoulders, sensed that this was a solemn moment as they stared at the tram shed's open mouth where, bedecked in jewel-coloured lights, stood the "hearse," the official "last tram," itself 30 years old, in which the Lord Mayor of Leeds (Alderman Mrs. G. Stevenson) accompanied by the mayors of Morley and Pudsey, the chairman of Leeds transport committee (Alderman J. Rafferty) and his committee, Mr. A.B. Findlay, the Leeds transport manager, and other officials were to make the last trip with Mr. A.H. Aisthorpe, a driver with 39 years' service, at the controls.

Through the barrier at the depot filed the "official mourning party" - the ten oldest drivers, the ten oldest inspectors, and the successful few in the ballot for seats in one of the ten trams of the "cortege"....

....As the procession of trams moved slowly through the streets the initial atmosphere of mourning was replaced by excitement. The first and last cars, both illuminated, had a police escort. Periodically, the procession halted or slowed as, successively, the Lord Mayor and other officials took over the controls of the first car. Gradually, too, the escorting fleet of motor cars, motor-cycles and bicycles, grew from a trickle to a stream and then to a river,

Post-war (1948-built) car 276 in Otley Road, Headingley, on 23 July 1955. In 1963 and 1964 the stone wall and fine trees that form the setting were replaced with the Arndale Centre. *Author.*

The Middleton bogie cars were regarded as "non-standard" and all were withdrawn in 1955 to 1957. 263 is passing the water tower at the top of Middleton Woods on 16 April 1955. The Ring Road is on the right. *Author*.

The shale slag heaps of Middleton Pit provide a colourful backdrop to Feltham 531 on the final day of tramway operation, 28 March 1959. 531 has just emerged from the bottom of Middleton Woods. *Author*.

1237

Passengers board Horsfield car 185 at the Spencer Place tram stop in Roundhay Road on the final day of tramway operation of route number 3, Saturday, 28 March 1959. *Author*.

Feltham car 589 in Waterloo Road, Hunslet, on 16 March 1959. Waterloo Road was permanently closed on 10 October 1976 and traffic diverted to a widened Church Street. Although all the other property has gone, the historic faience Garden Gate pub on the right hand side has been preserved. *Author*.

In tramway days York Road, adjacent to Seacroft Hospital, was a picturesque country lane and there was no pavement on one side. Fortunately there was little motor traffic. Almost immediately after the trams finished running, this section of York Road was converted into a dual carriageway by encroaching on to Killingbeck Cemetery on the left. Railcar 602 was photographed on the narrow section on 11 July 1954. *Author*.

headed by an open flivver, itself of even greater age than the tram it was tailing....

....Slowly the triumphal procession swung back into the city centre to the music of rattles and car horns. It was a fitting ride to Valhalla for a service that, at its peak in 1933, controlled a fleet of 476 cars."

'The Guardian', 9 November 1959.

A Transport Exhibition telling the story of the Leeds City Transport Department, was held to coincide with the tramway abandonment. It took place the following week in the City Art Gallery. There were photographs, models and other exhibits and evening lectures were given. Nearly 6,000 visitors saw the Exhibition, which was reported to be one of the most popular ever held in the Art Gallery.

The 50 remaining passenger and works cars in the fleet were sold to J.W. Hinchliffe Ltd., scrap merchants of Kirkstall Road, Leeds. They were broken up in Swinegate Depot from 23 November 1959 to 22 February 1960. The works cars were the first to be scrapped followed by the Horsfields and finally the Felthams. The works cars and Horsfields were broken up, but the Felthams were cut into six large sections and then transported by lorry to a yard owned by Dohm Ltd., Pollard Lane, Newlay, near Horsforth railway station. There the remains were burned. The remaining crane in Sovereign Street Yard was broken up in the yard on 27 February.

Ex-Hull works car 6 was towed from Sovereign Street Yard to Swinegate Depot on the morning of 8 December 1959. It thus had the honour of being the last tram to run on the streets of Leeds. This tram and a number of other cars were saved for preservation.

The replacement buses covered the journey from the Corn Exchange to Halton and Cross Gates in two minutes less than the journey had taken by tram. In the case of the Temple Newsam route there was a four minutes saving in time, buses taking 19 minutes by the shorter distance from the Bus Station as opposed to 23 minutes by tram from the Corn Exchange.

Most of the overhead wiring had been removed by the end of December 1959 and the tracks were either covered or removed soon afterwards.

At the time of writing, some 47 years after the last tram ran, very little remains of the massive infrastructure that was the Leeds City Tramways undertaking. Although probably 90% of the original street tramway tracks still exist, buried under tarmacadam. Rails still visible are a few in Kirkstall Road Works, the main works for First West Yorkshire Ltd. in Leeds and the rails at the entrance to the old Morley tram depot, closed in 1935, can still be seen. They include a short length of Holt's patent guard rail of 1920 vintage, possibly the only section still extant in the whole country.

With the exception of Kirkstall Road Works, Morley Depot, and the monumental stone building at Guiseley, a listed building, all the original tramway depots have been demolished or rebuilt.

In November 1960 Swinegate Depot became an exhibition hall. It is discussed further in Chapter 90. Sovereign Street Permanent Way Yard became a parking place for buses until the closure of the blister hangar garage in Sovereign Street in 1991. The site is now occupied by an office block.

The segregated reserved tracks in various parts of the city were appropriated by the Town Planning and Improvements Committee Committee, and some also went to the Parks Committee. The rails in Princes' Avenue were removed and the area turfed over and reserved as a "Rotten Row' - an area for horse riding.

The roundabout at the junction of Roundhay Road and Easterly Road was built in February 1950 and in 1955 the Corporation Parks Department created a fine display of tulips. On 7 May 1955 Chamberlain car 112 had just left the side reservation in Roundhay Road. The Clock Cinema features prominently in the background. The building still stands, but closed as a cinema on 26 February 1976. *Author*.

Horsfield car 175 in Low Road, at the junction with New Pepper Road, Hunslet, on 23 March 1957. Very little of the property in Low Road and Hunslet Road that existed in 1959, still remains. *Author*.

Horsfield car 176 at the Woodpecker at the bottom of York Road on 1 November 1959 a week before the tramway ceased operation. The Ebor Gardens Housing Estate is under construction on the right hand side. *W.D.Wilson/L.T.H.S.*

The last day of tramway operation in Leeds was very damp and dismal. Horsfield car 187 was photographed in Kirkgate on 7 November 1959. *K. Plant.*

A problem frequently encountered by tram drivers in York Street was cattle, sheep and pigs being driven to the nearby abattoir. Feltham 546 on its way to Halton is fortunately going in the opposite direction. Quarry Hill Flats and the Central Bus Station are in the background. The date is 31 March 1954. *S.G.Pickford.*

Riders had a run of about three quarters of a mile in "pleasant open country", but it was, however, rarely used for this purpose. The reserved track sections from Harehills to Oakwood and West Park to Lawnswood were turfed over whereas that in Stanningley Road was planted with trees.

The trackwork set in concrete on the Middleton route, in Belle Isle Road and the Gipton cutting was removed in 1960-1. Many of the tramway reservations remained in an untidy state for years after the trams finished running. It was not until late 1969 that the reservation in Belle Isle Road was turfed. Roundhay Road from the Clock Cinema to Oakwood was grassed in the early 'seventies. Most of the reservations, all devoid of their tramway tracks, still exist, although those in York Road and part of Selby Road have guided bus lanes.

Some of the original substations are still recognisable. A portion of the yard at Crown Point Power Station, which had been used by the Overhead Lines Department for the parking of motor derricks, was leased from July 1961 to a firm of glass merchants, Alfred Arnold (Glass) Ltd. Another part of the yard was leased to Thorp of Leeds, a firm of haulage contractors. Later other contractors leased the premises. The Transport Committee disposed of the building in 1969 and it was later demolished. The Edwardian stone substation at Hawksworth was appropriated in July 1955 as a storage depot for portable polling stations and ancillary equipment. It still exists. The Halton Dial substation was appropriated by the Street Lighting Department in March 1960 and in the late 1980s became "City Lights", a pub. The building exists, and is currently the "Wild, Wild West" - a children's play area. Copley Hill substation was appropriated by the City Museums Department in September 1956, on payment of

£1,250 and, heavily shuttered, is still in use as a Museum store. The shell of the Middleton Grove, Dewsbury Road, substation, considerably modified, remains recognisable. It is currently called Matrix Court. Headingley Depot substation was demolished in 1958. That at Belle Isle was appropriated for housing purposes in December 1959. The substation at Gipton Wood was demolished in April 1961 and the one at Middleton about the same time. The substation at Kirkstall Road Works was removed during the latter part of 1961.

Most of the tramway standards were taken over by the Street Lighting Department, the Department paying the Transport Department £8 per standard for the privilege. With the exception of one rusting pole at Whingate Junction, all the original standards have now disappeared, the penultimate three being sited in Roundhay Road near to Gathorne Terrace. They were removed in September 2002. All the wall rosettes that were used to support the overhead wiring have gone, the last being on a building in Central Road, off Duncan Street. It had been sideways fixed to a building and this probably accounted for its long survival.

A.H. Aisworth, the driver of the last tram in Leeds, was made redundant and left the service of the Transport Department on 6 March 1960. Also redundant was W.M. Forbes, the Permanent Way Engineer. In May 1960 he was transferred to the Highways Department becoming a clerk of works. Forbes' assistant, T. Jewison, who had been with the Permanent Way Department for 40 years, retired on 2 March 1960. Both were followed soon afterwards by the General Manager, A.B. Findlay.

In June 1960 Findlay intimated his intention to retire on the grounds of ill health. In 1958 he had had a major operation and another in early 1960. He officially retired on 11 October 1960 and was away from work for much of the early part of the year. Findlay's daughter related that her father had been very upset by the decision to scrap the tramways. Whether this contributed to his ill health is uncertain. He had been responsible for the design of new tramcars when he was in Glasgow, and the single deck railcars in Leeds. He had visited the continent and had seen the potential for tramway modernisation. A tall, quietly spoken, polite and kindly Scot, Findlay was no match for extrovert Alderman Rafferty. Findlay returned to his native Firth of Clyde and died on 25 March 1962 at the age of 59.

B.R. Miller, writing Findlay's obituary in 'Modern Tramway", knew him personally and recalled that after Findlay had come to Leeds he was still of the view, despite the ever mounting problem of costs, particularly trackwork, that trams - on private reservations on routes suited to their use - were preferable to either trolley or motor buses. When the future of local transport became a ridiculous "political shuttlecock" in Leeds, Findlay's views were unheard.

The writer said that Findlay would be long remembered for his clear thinking and his kindly charm. He mourned the passing of a "great tramway man".

Councillor Thomas William Smith had been the Socialist deputy chairman of the Transport Committee from 1953. His son, Eric, recalled that his father regarded Alderman Rafferty as "a bit of a card". Councillor Smith thought that Mather's ideas were "pie in the sky" and "far-fetched". At the time, he considered that the Transport Committee was making the right decision in abandoning the tramways. His thinking was, however, to change.

In 1960 he visited Brussells and saw the extensive tramway modernisation that was taking place in that city. He realised that the Leeds Transport Committee had made a very big mistake. By then it was too late.

During the war Bertrand Mather, a B.Sc., had been one of eight scientists selected by the Admiralty for research into mines, torpedoes and submarine attack and together they had devised effective protection from the German acoustic mine. Throughout the 'fifties Councillor Mather had fought "tooth and nail" to save the best of the tramway system, but had always been thwarted by the intransigence of Rafferty.

The tramways were scrapped for short-term financial reasons. The Government was not interested and at that time tram scrapping was "fashionable" in Britain. Other governments and cities in other countries took a different view and tramways were developed and modernised.

History has proved that Leeds transport managers R.L.Horsfield, W.Vane Morland and A.B.Findlay, City Engineers, J.E.Acfield and Colonel W.S.Cameron, and Councillor Bertrand Mather were right.

Thirty to forty years later a new tramway system was planned for Leeds, some of the lines ironically following almost exactly those of the tramways that were thrown away in the 1950s.

In 1994 the Prince of Wales described the abandonment of miles upon miles of tramways, many on segregated reserved tracks as "utter madness," and so it was.

Not long to go. Horsfield car 187 in the murky gloom of the afternoon of 7 November 1959 shortly before the tram service ceased. The location is Cross Gates terminus. *Author*

A threatening sky at Sheepscar as Horsfield 151 heads towards Kirkstall Abbey on 7 March 1954. The Meanwood Road tram rails and Midland Bank are on the left. The former bank building still exists. *Author*.

Feltham 520 on the central reservation in York Road on 26 September 1954. The Dog and Gun Inn is on the left. *Author*.

The Buses 1953 to 1956

In 1953 there were 416 buses in stock comprising A.E.C.s, Leylands, Daimlers, and Crossleys. All had diesel engines. 406 were double deck and there were ten single deckers. Of these vehicles most were relatively new, i.e. post-war, but there were still 80 pre-war vehicles - 72 double deckers and eight single deck - the TS8 of 1938.

There were exactly 50 bus routes covering over 178 miles and also a number of special services - schools, works, hospitals etc. Buses ran a total of 11,050,370 miles annually and carried 111,902,531 passengers. Daily departures from the Leeds city centre were about 2,650.

In the period from 1951 to 1953 40 new buses had been delivered. These comprised 30 A.E.C. Regent III 649-677 and 800 and ten Leyland PD2/14 buses, 301-310. The first six buses, 649-654, had all-metal Weymann bodies whereas the others had composite Roe bodies. All seated 58 passengers and had a width of 7ft. 6in. 800 had been exhibited at the Commercial Motor Show in 1952 and in June 1955 was renumbered 678.

Of the pre-war buses, the eight TS8 were shortly to be withdrawn and on 20 July 1953 the Transport Committee agreed to invite tenders for eight replacement single deck buses. The new buses were for use on route 45 Harehills-Wortley and route 73 Greenthorpe-Kirkstall.

On 16 November tenders were accepted for eight single deck bodies from Charles H. Roe Ltd. in the sum of £15,176. The chassis were to be from three different manufacturers:
A.C.V. Sales Ltd. (A.E.C.) 3 chassis. £5,310 12s.9d.
Leyland Motors Ltd. 3 chassis £5,727 10s.0d.
Guy Motors Ltd. 2 chassis £4,008.

The major Leeds transport event of 1953 was, of course, the decision in July to abandon the tramway system and replace it with a service of motor buses. The first route selected was the number 14 from Corn Exchange to Half Mile Lane, but no new buses were purchased for the replacement. The Department had sufficient vehicles in stock but these were pre-war buses, which had been in storage. They were repainted and were the "HUM" A.E.C. Regents 106-125 and six of the "GUA" Regents, 263, 273, 274, 276, 279 and 284. The following month two of the 1934-5 A.E.C. Regents, 139 and 142, and another of the "GUA's", 289, reappeared in service. Five "GUA", 265, 266, 277, 286 and 287, and one "FNW" Regent, 249, returned to service in December.

In October 1953 the Transport Committee agreed to invite tenders for 50 double deck buses for future tramway replacements. Tenders were received and on 21 December were accepted as follows:
Charles H. Roe Ltd. 40 double deck bodies £81,000.
Metropolitan-Cammell-Weymann 10 bodies £20,990.
A.C.V. Sales Ltd. 30 chassis £60,573.
Leyland Motors Ltd. 20 chassis £45,150. It was to be July 1954 when the first of these buses was delivered.

Beginning in March 1954 the Leyland PD2 buses, 340-399, were fitted with new type gear boxes. Buses 344, 346, 358, 375, 383 and 394 were the first and a notice was fixed in the cab indicating that there was no synchro-mesh on the first and second gears. Over 5 m.p.h. double declutching had to be employed.

The number 14 tram route was abandoned on Saturday night, 3 October 1953, and the following day a new bus service, also numbered 14, began to run from the Central Bus Station to Half Mile Lane. The route from the Bus Station (Platform C) was via Eastgate, Vicar Lane, New Market Street, Corn Exchange and then the former tram route to Half Mile Lane. On the outward journey buses were diverted via Aire Street and Thirsk Row. Routes 54 Rodley and 65 Pudsey were integrated with the new 14 service and were also diverted via Aire Street and Thirsk Row on outward journeys. "Limited stop" conditions

At the beginning of 1953 the latest buses in the Leeds fleet were the Leyland PD2/14, 301-310. 307 is in Queenswood Road, Headingley, on Football Special duties. The date is 16 October 1965. *W.D.Wilson/L.T.H.S.*

1934 A.E.C. Regent 139 was one of the old "piano front" buses returned to service in October 1953 for tramway replacement. 139 was on Elland Road Football Special duties at Low Fields Road when this photograph was taken on 21 November 1953. *Author.*

1938 A.E.C. Regent 289 of the 260-289 (GUA 785-814) series also returned to service in October 1953. Donald Wilson photographed it in Cardigan Road at the terminus of route 56, North Lane, on 27 June 1952. After its premature withdrawal it was reinstated and ran until January 1956. *W.D.Wilson/L.T.H.S.*

were applied during the evening peak hour.

Also from 4 October, service 70, (Central Bus Station-Moortown), was extended from Lingfield Approach via Lingfield Hill, Nursery Lane and Primley Park Crescent to a new terminus at Primley Park. The terminal point was in Primley Park Crescent (East) to the south of Primley Park Avenue.

On 1 February 1954 a revised timetable was instituted on the new 14 bus service. At peak periods certain buses turned at the Corn Exchange by circling the island (the No.2 curve).

There had been a small number of other bus route extensions or modifications in 1953.

Commencing on 10 May, the 67 (Central Bus Station-Dib Lane) service was extended along Easterly Road and Boggart Hill Drive to Kentmere Avenue on the Seacroft Estate. Limited stop conditions applied on weekday evenings and Saturday lunch times; passengers who wished to alight before Hollin Park Mount were not carried.

From 12 July the 75 service, (Infirmary Street-Beckett's Park), was given a Sunday morning service and on 10 January 1954 an extension from Woodbridge Cross, Queenswood Drive, and along Queenswood Drive to Spen Lane took place. In November 1953 a turning circle for the buses had been constructed at the top of Queenswood Drive at a cost of £435. Also on 10 January 1954 a new bus route was opened. This was service 30 (Central Bus Station-Ireland Wood). Buses from the Bus Station followed the route of the Cookridge buses (route 33) as far as the Modern School and then ran via the Ring Road, Spen Lane, Iveson Drive, Iveson Approach, Otley Old Road, Raynel Approach, Raynel Mount and Raynel Drive to a terminus near Farrar Lane. There were limited stop conditions from 3.30 p.m. to 7.00 p.m. on weekdays and from 11.30 a.m. to 11.00 p.m. on Saturdays. Revised timetables were introduced on services 33 and 76.

By 3 April 1954, the date of the next tramway abandonment, the new buses on order had not been delivered and the Transport Department was forced to resuscitate all of its remaining pre-war stored A.E.C. Regents. Most of these 15 vehicles had been out of service since 1950 and some had been temporarily stored until December 1953 in the former Stanley Road tram depot. They comprised the following: 129, 134, 152, 157, 170, 174, 179, 185, 188, 238, 267, 268, 269, 270 and 282.

The tramway abandonment was the withdrawal of routes 4 and 10, Kirkstall Abbey and Compton Road. These were replaced by a new bus route, 4, which ran between the two termini. The route was from Abbey Walk, a turning point a short distance beyond the Kirkstall Abbey tram terminus, via Abbey Road, Commercial Road, Kirkstall Road, West Street, Caroline Street, Park Lane, The Headrow, Eastgate, New York Road, Burmantofts Street, Nippet Lane, Stoney Rock Lane and Compton Road. Buses turning at Compton Road crossed Harehills Lane into Foundry Approach, turned right into Bellbrooke Place and back to the terminus via Bellbrooke Street and across Harehills Lane.

The tramway siding at the Burley Mills short working had been last used on Sunday 7 March 1954 and over the following three weeks or so a turning circle for buses was formed.

On the occasion of the Northern Command Tattoo at Roundhay Park from 28 June to 5 July 1954, in addition to the tram service, four additional bus services were operated. These ran from Infirmary Street, Vicar Lane, Swinegate and the Central Bus Station.

July 1954 saw the completion of a new temporary bus station in Rockingham Street, off Woodhouse Lane. The construction of this bus station is discussed in Chapter 90. It came into use on 11 July when services 31 New Farnley, 33 Cookridge, 54 Rodley and 65 Pudsey were transferred from the Central Bus Station to the new city location. Revised timetables were introduced on services 14, 30 and 44.

Shortly before the new bus station was opened, the

The 1938 Leyland TS8 buses, 19-26, were withdrawn in 1954-5. 20 was photographed in Armley Ridge Road on 11 August 1954. Christ Church, encased in scaffolding, is in the background. *W.D.Wilson/L.T.H.S.*

The first day of the Kirkstall Abbey bus service, 4 April 1954. 1934-built A.E.C. Regent 174 is at the terminus in Abbey Road. *Author.*

A.E.C. Regent III 730 was exhibited at the Commercial Motor Show at Earl's Court, London, in August 1954. It is seen at the new Rockingham Street temporary Bus Station on 7 August 1955. It is resplendent in its gold leaf lined livery and three shades of green. *Author.*

Of the A.E.C. Regent III of the 730-759 series, 730-754 had Roe bodies and 755-759 bodies by Weymann. The Weymann "Orion" bodies were more angular. 757 has just left Otley Old Road and is crossing the former tramway reservation in Otley Road. The date is 12 October 1963. *Author.*

sheds in the eastern part of Sovereign Street Permanent Way Yard were demolished. The area was marked out for buses and came into use on 4 July 1954. The park was initially used during the day by buses on services 54 and 65, which formerly had returned to Bramley Garage after the morning peak. All buses entered and left the yard from Concordia Street.

From 22 August 1954 buses to and from Rockingham Street Bus Station on the 54 service were experimentally rerouted inward via Wellington Street, King Street, East Parade, The Headrow and Woodhouse Lane. Outward journeys were via Woodhouse Lane, Great George Street, Cookridge Street, Park Row, City Square, Aire Street, Thirsk Row and Wellington Street. The alterations were done to give closer access to City Square and reduce congestion elsewhere in the city centre. There was a petition signed by 2,300 passengers objecting to the rerouting, but in March 1955 the experiment became permanent. It was said that many Rodley residents were now using buses operated by the West Yorkshire Road Car Company.

The beginning of July saw the delivery of the first of the batch of 30 A.E.C. Regent double deck buses, which had been ordered in December 1953. Numbered 730-759 (TNW 730-759), 731-735 were allocated to Sovereign Street, 736-754 to Torre Road and the remainder to Headingley Garage. The buses were on a type 9613E chassis and the principal difference between the new buses and earlier PUA's was the shallower saloon windows. 730 was exhibited at the Commercial Motor Show at Earl's Court, London, in August 1954. Buses 730-754 had Roe bodies, whereas 755-759 had bodies by Weymann. There were variations in the unladen weights of the Roe-bodied buses. 731-750 weighed 7 tons, 10 cwt and 2 qrs and 730 and 751-754 weighed 7 tons 7 cwt 2 qrs. 731-750 had composite bodies whereas 730 and 751-754 had metal-framed top decks. The Weymann bodies were more angular and also had metal top decks, but were lighter in weight than the Roes – 7 tons 0 cwt 2 qrs. Weymann bodies on subsequent Leeds buses were usually lighter in weight than

the Roe equivalent. Differences were mainly internal, but there were only two roof ventilators fitted along each side instead of three and they were more flush to the roof. The window ventilators had two sliding parts instead of one. Delivery of the 30 buses was completed in December 1954.

Simultaneously with the delivery of the last of the TNW's, the eight new single deckers, replacements for the pre-war TS8, 19-26, began to appear in service. 32-34 (TUA 32-34) on A.E.C. Reliance chassis entered service in December. They had underfloor engines, five-speed gear boxes and Roe central entrance bodies. There was seating for 34 passengers with 24 standing. The front driving area was partitioned and a new feature on Leeds buses was "Standee" windows. The TS8 had 36 seats and allowed eight standing passengers.

A further single decker, 36 (TUA 36) appeared in January 1955. It had the same Roe body as 32-34, but was on a Guy Arab chassis. Bus 35 followed in February and also had a Guy Arab chassis.

The Transport Department had formerly adopted a policy of limiting the number of chassis types in use and for many years had only purchased buses on either A.E.C. or Leyland chassis. The last Guys to be acquired were double deck buses 34-39 in 1934.

The last three single deckers, 29-31, (TUA 29-31), were delivered in May 1955. These had Leyland Tiger Cub PSUC1/5 chassis.

The delivery of the new single deckers resulted in the withdrawal of the old Leyland TS8, 24 being the last to be taken out of service - on 29 April 1955. The arrival of the new double deckers meant the demise of most of the pre-war buses reintroduced for tramway replacement. 1934 vintage "piano front" buses 129, 134, 139, 142, 152, 157 and 170 were withdrawn on 30 June 1954. They were followed by many of the other pre-war buses over the next few months. Buses retained in service for future tramway closures were 106-125, some of the "GUA" A.E.C. Regents and two "FNW's", 238 and 249.

It took over 18 months to complete the delivery of the

50 double deck buses that the Transport Committee had ordered in October 1953. Delivery of the final 20 vehicles began in March 1955. These were all of the Leyland PD2/11 type and were the first buses to be delivered to Leeds with pneumo-cyclic gear boxes and "mono-control". This type of control is discussed later. Numbered 201-220 (UUA 201-220), 201-215 had Roe bodies, identical to those on 730-754, whereas 216-220 had Weymann bodies of the same type fitted to 755-759. The last to enter service was 220, licensed from 23 June 1955.

In November 1953 the Transport Committee had decided to apply for permission to run a bus service from Leeds to Farsley. However, part of this service was to run outside the city boundary and would be in competition with services operated by the West Yorkshire Road Car Company and other private operators. The Committee withdrew the application.

In the meantime, in addition to the replacement of the Kirkstall Abbey and Compton Road trams by buses, there had been other extensions and modifications to the bus services in 1954.

In February 1954 application was made to the Yorkshire Traffic Commissioners for two new bus services. One was to run from the city centre to the new Swarcliffe Housing Estate in the east of the city and another to a new estate in the west at Intake Lane.

In connection with the Swarcliffe service, the 40 route (Stanks) was to be rerouted. There were strong objections from the West Yorkshire Road Car Company, which also applied for a bus service from Leeds to Swarcliffe and revisions to its Leeds-Aberford service. West Yorkshire claimed that the Corporation proposals would take traffic from its services, which passed through the Seacroft area. At the hearing of the Yorkshire Area Traffic Commissioners on 14 July 1954, J.B. Gill, Chief Traffic Officer for Leeds Transport Department, said that about a third of the 1,616 houses on the Swarcliffe Estate were now occupied.

Licences were granted for the new Intake and Swarcliffe services and both began operation on Sunday, 19 September 1954. The service to Swarcliffe, however, had been modified. Numbered 24 the route ran from the Platform C, (40 barrier), at the Central Bus Station via Eastgate, New York Road, York Road, Cross Gates Road, Austhorpe Road, Church Lane, Eastwood Lane and Swarcliffe Drive, terminating at the junction with Swarcliffe Avenue. The Corporation had asked for the service to run for a further 400 yards, but this had been refused.

The rerouting of the number 40 Stanks bus service was granted, but the terminus was curtailed to the junction of Pendas Grove and Kelmscott Lane, whereas it had previously run the full length of Pendas Way to Barwick Road. The West Yorkshire Road Car Company was, instead, granted permission to increase the frequency on its Leeds-Scholes-Aberford service, which ran along Barwick Road.

Alderman Rafferty, Chairman of the Transport Committee, was incensed at the decision of the Traffic Commissioners, as residents would have to walk over a quarter of a mile to reach the bus.

"We have to provide all services on these estates, and make roads especially prepared for them, and at the end we find we are not allowed to run over those roads because of services operated by outsiders. The public wanted us to run to the extremities of these estates. There were applications to do just that, but we have been turned down....

....We feel that these limitations are to the detriment of the citizens of Leeds, and I would like to know what people think of it".

'Yorkshire Evening Post', 24 August 1954.

After inspecting the area the Transport Committee

Leyland PD2/11 215 in Dulverton Road on the Cottingley Estate on 26 February 1966. The Cottingley Estate was one of the few "pre-fab" estates in Leeds.   The single storey pre-fabricated houses were erected in 1947 and demolished in the late 1960's.   Route 8 from Meanwood to Cottingley was opened on 26 June 1956 and was extended from Meanwood to Moortown on 31 October 1965. *Author.*

made an appeal to the Minister of Transport and Civil Aviation against the decision. This was, however, refused.

On 27 March 1955 the Department rerouted the 40 service via York Road and Cross Gates Road and the terminus was curtailed about 300 yards to the junction of Pendas Grove and Kelmscott Lane. The service 40 buses had previously ran via Selby Road, Chapel Street, Cross Green Lane, Green Lane and Station Road. Revised timetables were introduced on both the 40 and 41 services. Buses short working to Whitkirk had previously displayed the route number 39, but now showed 41. The number 39 became redundant.

Service 23 was from the new Rockingham Street Bus Station to Intake via Woodhouse Lane, Great George Street, Calverley Street, Park Lane, Burley Street, Burley Road, Kirkstall Hill, Kirkstall Lane, Bridge Road, Leeds and Bradford Road, Intake Lane and terminated at the junction with Coal Hill Lane. On the inward journey from Park Lane, buses ran via The Headrow and Woodhouse Lane to Rockingham Street.

The 23 service was worked by Leyland PD2 buses of the 340-399 series operating out of Bramley Garage. A.E.C. Regent III of the 451-500 series from Torre Road Depot worked the 24 route.

On 21 November 1954 a considerable number of depot movements of buses took place. On this date the alterations at Headingley Depot were completed. Following the closure of the depot to trams on 3 April 1954, the tramway part had been modified for use by buses. Buses moved in to about half of the building in July 1954 and the completion of the building resulted in a general garage reorganisation throughout the city. New running schedules were also adopted.

On 17 November 1954 there was a two and a half hours meeting of about 200 platform staff at Swinegate Depot to discuss the new schedules. There were "fiery" objections from some staff as they would have had to face an additional hours' walk to and from work. The new arrangements were eventually amicably solved with the General Manager, A.B.Findlay.

In addition to services already operating from Headingley Garage, buses on routes 45, 56, 73, 74, 75 and 76 were also transferred. The 56 service had formerly been worked from Torre Road Garage, and the 45 and 73 services from Bramley Garage. The 74, 75 and 76 routes were transferred from Sovereign Street.

Other services transferred from Torre Road Garage were the 52 and 53 to Sovereign Street and 72 to Bramley Garage.

A table is appended showing the garage allocation from 21 November.

Garage	Routes
Bramley	14, 23, 46, 49, 54, 65, 72, 77.
Headingley	30, 33, 44, 45, 50, 51, 56, 57, 58, 59, 60, 73, 74, 75, 76.
Hunslet	31, 63, 64, 67, 68, 71.
Sovereign Street	29, 32, 47, 48, 52, 53, 55.
Torre Road	4, 14, 24, 28, 34, 35, 36, 37, 38, 39, 40, 41, 42, 43, 61, 62, 66, 69, 70, 78, 79.

Peak hour services were usually supplemented by buses from the same garage, but there were instances of buses being used from other garages, particularly Torre Road.

From 21 November two bus route alterations also took place:

Service 43, (Central Bus Station-Carr Manor), was extended from Castle View along Stonegate Road to the roundabout at the junction with King Lane.

Service 71, (Central Bus Station-Guiseley). The city terminus was changed to the Rockingham Street Bus Station.

The alteration of the 71 service was decided upon "to alleviate some of the traffic congestion in the city centre, and remove some of the pressure on the Central Bus Station." Passengers, however, were not impressed and there were many protests. Rockingham Street was situated off Woodhouse Lane away from the main shopping areas, the railway stations and most office buildings. Buses now entered the city via Westgate, Caroline Street, The Headrow and Woodhouse Lane, whereas formerly they had traversed the busy city centre streets: Wellington Street, City Square, Boar Lane, Vicar Lane and Eastgate. The biggest complaint was the distance from the railway stations; a ten minutes walk with heavy luggage in poor weather was no joke. The off peak service was reduced from 15 minute to 20 minute which "added insult to injury." Both the Aireborough and Horsforth District Councils lodged a joint appeal with the Ministry of Transport. The Ministry called for the observations of the Licensing Authority and the next procedure was to appoint an inspector to consider an appeal.

However, as will be seen later, the problem was solved, so far as Leeds Corporation was concerned, by the abandonment of the 71 Leeds-Guiseley service.

There were also petitions and complaints from residents about the turning of the number 4 buses to Compton Road via Bellbrooke Place. To get over the problem, in November 1954 application was made to the Yorkshire Traffic Commissioners for authority to extend the terminus of service 4 from Compton Road via Foundry Approach to The Fairway Hotel at the junction with Oak Tree Drive. Bus services 78 and 79 to Seacroft were also to be rerouted via Nippet Lane, Stoney Rock Lane and Compton Road. Both applications were granted and the alterations came into effect on 30 January 1955. Buses short worked during peak hours to Hudson Road on the number 4 route. They turned round at an island at the end of Florence Street. The 78 and 79 services previously ran via Beckett Street, Ashley Road and Harehills Lane.

During the latter part of 1954 and early 1955 the Transport Department was facing a severe staff shortage and petitions for new bus services and extensions were not welcome. Describing the staff situation as "most critical," and "15% short," Alderman Rafferty said that if members of staff continued to leave at their present rate the public would have to face up to restricted services in the future.

"Residents of housing estates will have to appreciate that the committee cannot entertain petitions for extensions of existing services or make special provision for school children."

"We have had today a petition from a small housing estate for an extension of a bus service which has been in operation on another estate, although on the edge of their estate there is a tram service. They have an adequate tram service and are asking for an extension of a bus service."

"All such requests must, with reluctance, be turned down from now onwards".

'Yorkshire Evening Post', 18 October 1954.

Limited stop running during peak hours, which had been introduced on the 65 Pudsey route on 2 October 1950, was withdrawn on 27 February 1955.

Also in February 1955 application was made to the Yorkshire Area Traffic Commissioners for the substitution of the Gipton tram route by motor buses and this was granted on 29 March. Buses took over from the trams on Sunday, 24 April 1955, running from Vicar Lane (Sydney Street) to the former Gipton tram terminus. The route outward was via Vicar Lane, Kirkgate, New York Street,

Guy Arab 35 in Armley Ridge Road on 17 February 1962. Stanningley Road is in the background. *W.D.Wilson/L.T.H.S.*

The first day of the route 11 Gipton tramway replacement service on 24 April 1955. A pre-war A.E.C. Regent 115 (HUM 410) is standing at the terminus. At first the bus route was operated by old buses of this type. Buses showed the number 11 with a blank route blind. *Author.*

The last day of the route 71 bus route to Guiseley on 30 April 1955. Buses replaced the Guiseley trams in 1934 and, like the trams, had always lost money. A.E.C. Regent III 428 is at Guiseley terminus on 30 April and was the last bus to run on the service. *Author.*

York Street, Marsh Lane, York Road and Gipton Approach.

Buses returned by the same route as far as York Street and then ran via St. Peter's Street, Eastgate and Vicar Lane. The former tram route number, 11, was displayed and at first the route was operated solely by pre-war A.E.C. Regents.

A week after the abandonment of the Gipton tram service, the 71 Guiseley bus service ceased operation. The Guiseley buses were in competition with those of the West Yorkshire Road Car Company and Samuel Ledgard Ltd. and had always lost money. The route was "over-bussed" and there had been a reduced service from 6 October 1952. The closure of the service had been mooted in February 1954 when discussions were taking place in connection with the abandonment of the Kirkstall Abbey tram service. Following negotiations with the two bus companies, integration of the bus services on the route was agreed. The Corporation was to surrender its licence for the Guiseley service and curtail its buses to Horsforth. West Yorkshire and Ledgards were to jointly take over the Horsforth-Guiseley section.

The last Leeds Corporation bus, A.E.C. Regent 428, ran to Guiseley on Saturday, 30 April 1955 and a general reorganisation of bus services in the area took place.

West Yorkshire service 32 ran from the Company's Vicar Lane Bus Station to White Cross, Guiseley in co-ordination with Ledgard's King Street-Guiseley and Ilkley service, giving a 15 minute service to Guiseley. There was also West Yorkshire service 32A (formerly 32), which ran from Vicar Lane Bus Station to Yeadon and the Company's service 55, (Vicar Lane Bus Station-Bradford via Guiseley) service. The 55 service had formerly operated between Bradford and Yeadon only, but was now extended to Leeds, incorporating the former 32 and 55 services.

From 1 May the Leeds Corporation number 4 service (Compton Road-Kirkstall), was extended from Kirkstall Abbey to a new terminus at the Fleece Hotel, Horsforth. The extended route was via Abbey Road and New Road Side to the Fleece Hotel. The route number 71 fell into disuse and the A.E.C. Regents which formerly worked the service from Hunslet Garage were transferred to the Scott Hall Road group of routes: 34, 35, 37 and 43.

In the meantime application had been made to the Traffic Commissioners to abandon more tram routes and this time the casualty was the Elland Road-Meanwood service. On 15 June 1955 approval was received from the Traffic Commissioners. There were to be three new bus services: from Meanwood to Cottingley, Meanwood to Morley with termini at Fountain Street and Tingley Mill and from Infirmary Street via Holbeck Moor and Beeston to Middleton.

J.B.Gill, the Chief Traffic Officer, said it was planned to integrate the three services to give a good overall frequency. Travellers taking advantage of the new through routes, who had previously had to change, would save on fares.

"We are hoping to ensure that Morley people who are at present compelled to disembark at the Corn Exchange will be able to get up to the North Street end of The Headrow....

....Subject to your approval of these proposals, Meanwood people will be able to go into Morley instead of having to change from tram to bus, and Middleton passengers will no longer have to get off at Beeston, but will be able to go on to Infirmary Street and City Square."

'Yorkshire Evening Post', 15 June 1955.

The abandonment of the Meanwood and Elland Road tramway services took place on Saturday, 25 June, buses taking over the following day. Bus service 48 (Middleton-Beeston) was discontinued from the same day and services 29, 52 and 53 were revised.

The Morley bus services were extended northwards from the Corn Exchange via New Market Street, Vicar Lane, North Street, Meanwood Road and Green Road to a terminus at Church Avenue. This was over the former tram route, but extended for a further 200 yards. The 29 service which formerly ran between Infirmary Street and Cottingley via King Street, Park Place, Queen Street, West Street, Westgate, Wellington Street, Wellington Road, Gelderd Road, Spence Lane, (inward via Whitehall Road, Smith Street and Gelderd Road owing to the one-way arrangement at this location), Domestic Street, Top Moor Side, Elland Road, Ring Road Beeston, Cottingley Drive and terminating at Dulverton Road, was rerouted. The rerouting was from the end of Top Moor Side via Cemetery Road, Beeston Road, Old Lane, Ring Road (Beeston Park), Middleton Park Road, Sissons Road, Middleton Park Avenue, Throstle Road, Thorpe View and Thorpe Road (i.e. incorporating the former 48 service).

A new bus service, number 8, was introduced between Meanwood (Church Avenue) and Cottingley, operating through the city via the same route as services 52 and 53, and following the former route of service 29 from the junction of Elland Road and Top Moor Side. There was a peak hour short working to Elland Road Football Ground, number 8 buses turning at Heath Road, a short distance beyond the former tram terminus. There was also a short working of the 29 service to St. Matthew's Church, Holbeck.

Also from 26 June bus services 31, (Rockingham Street-New Farnley), and 36, (Central Bus Station-Gledhow), were linked to form a new service 31 running through the city centre from Whitehall Road via Thirsk Row, Wellington Street (returning via Aire Street), City Square, Boar Lane, Duncan Street, New Market Street, Vicar Lane, Eastgate, Regent Street, Cross Stamford Street, Roseville Road and then by the former 36 route to Gledhow. The old 36 route ran from the Central Bus Station via Eastgate, Mabgate, Cherry Row, Dolly Lane and Gledhow Road. This was the first Corporation bus to run regularly along Roseville Road. As a result of the alterations of 26 June bus route numbers 36 and 48 fell into disuse.

Because of a new one-way traffic system at the Swinnow Lane - Leeds & Bradford Road - Broad Lane junction from 4 July, buses running from Stanningley and Halton Moor on the 44 service were rerouted via Stanningley Town Street, Leeds & Bradford Road, Bradley Hill View, Swinnow Lane and Broad Lane at this point.

Alderman Rafferty's earlier protestations seem to have had some effect for on 2 October 1955 service 40, Central Bus Station-Stanks, was extended from Pendas Grove along Pendas Way as far as Kelmscott Green, a distance of about 300 yards. Service 79 was extended on the same date along North Parkway as far as Bailey's Lane. Revised timetables were introduced on services 40, 78 and 79.

On 6 November service 24, (Central Bus Station-Swarcliffe), was extended along Swarcliffe Drive to a new terminus at Mill Green Gardens. An improved timetable on the route was introduced.

Soon afterwards another abandonment took place when the Beeston tramway succumbed to the motor bus. Trams ran to Beeston for the last time on Saturday 19 November 1955 and the three tram services were replaced by two new bus services: Corn Exchange-Beeston and a peak hours only service from Swinegate to Beeston.

The replacement service from the Corn Exchange followed the former tram route, but operated inwards in the city via Bridge End, Call Lane, Kirkgate and New Market Street and outwards via New Market Street, Duncan Street and Briggate. Prior to the tramway closure a turning circle for buses had been constructed at Beeston terminus at a cost of £1,600. The new outer terminus was short of the former tram terminus, buses turning at Oldroyd Crescent. At peak periods a short working was introduced from Corn Exchange to Cross Flatts Park, Beeston Road, buses turning at Parkfield Avenue.

The Swinegate-Beeston bus service, which began on Monday 21 November, followed the former tram route. The Corn-Exchange-Beeston, Swinegate-Beeston and the short working to Cross Flatts Park showed route number 5, the same number as the former tram route.

From Sunday 18 December 1955 reduced evening and Sunday services were introduced on the numbers 44, 45, 50, 51, 57-60, 75 and 76 bus routes. Reductions took place on the 34 and 35, Alwoodley circular routes, from 15

January 1956 and on the 42 and 66 routes from 22 January.

With the institution of the new number 5 bus service, 15 withdrawn pre-war buses, an "FNW" A.E.C. Regent 249, 13 "GUA" Regents and Regent 400 were relicensed for service.

In November 1954 tenders were invited for 100 new buses and on 17 January the following year the following were accepted:

A.C.V. Sales Ltd. 80 chassis at £2,001 10s.0d. each.

Transport Vehicles (Daimler) Ltd. 20 chassis at £2,206 15s.0d. each.

Charles H. Roe Ltd. 80 bodies at £2,054 each.

Metropolitan-Cammell-Weymann Ltd. 20 bodies at £2,266 each.

Delivery of the buses was slow and in the meantime several of the 1945-built Utility Daimlers were "modernised." Beginning in April 1955 some of the Utility Daimlers of the series 77-98 and 504-512 were withdrawn from service and sent to Charles H. Roe Ltd. at Cross Gates for body overhauls. Others had body repairs at Donisthorpe Street Works. Of special interest was the rebodying by Roe of some of Daimlers using 1934 vintage "piano front" bodies from withdrawn A.E.C. Regents. They had a rather strange appearance on Daimler chassis and seven buses altogether received "new" bodies as follows:

Date	Bus	Body from A.E.C. Regent
9-8-1955	512	174
16-9-1955	78	157
29-9-1955	83	185
3-10-1955	88	134
2-11-1955	96	188
3-11-1955	510	129
4-11-1955	505	152

The chassis of the old A.E.C.s were cut up in the yard at the Crown Point tramway power station in October and November 1955. The Utility bodies were dismantled and scrapped. The chassis of A.E.C. Regent 280 was also cut up at Crown Point in November 1955. This was the first of the "GUA" Regents of the 260-289 series to be scrapped.

Eventually in December 1955 the first of the 100 buses ordered eleven months earlier was delivered and entered service. These were Daimler CVG6 double deck vehicles with air operated brakes and gear change. Metropolitan-Cammell "Orion" bodies incorporating the Leeds-type straight staircase and seating 33/28 were fitted. These had the largest seating capacity of any buses yet delivered to Leeds. The extra seating was provided by replacing the two front pairs of transverse seats in the lower saloon, by a single backward-facing transverse seat for five passengers. This was behind the driver's cab. The longitudinal seats over the offside and nearside rear wheel arches were lengthened to accommodate three and four persons respectively.

Three buses were delivered at first, numbered 532-534 (VUG 532-534), and on 11 December entered service on the new number 5 Beeston bus route. The buses were unlike any other buses previously supplied to Leeds and were the first "tin front" buses used by Leeds Corporation. They were the first of a series of 20 buses 532-551 (VUG 532-551), which were delivered from December 1955 to March 1956.

In January 1956, simultaneously with the delivery of the 20 Daimler CVG6 buses, the first two vehicles (760 and 764) of the batch of 80 A.E.C. Regent V buses was delivered. These buses, given the fleet numbers 760-839 (WUA 760-839) had "monocontrol" transmission or two-pedal control similar to that on the Leylands delivered some ten months earlier. There was no clutch, all gear changing being effected by a single hand control placed below the steering wheel for operation by the driver's

BEFORE: Daimler CWA6 83 (JUB 583) had a semi-utility body made by Park Royal Coachworks Ltd. in 1945. The body was of poor quality and was removed shortly after this photograph was taken. The date is 7 May 1955 and the location Hyde Park in Hyde Park Road. The bus is on route 60, the Hyde Park Circular service. *W.D.Wilson/ L.T.H.S.*

AFTER: The same bus as the above, Daimler CWA6 83, but as rebodied by Charles H. Roe Ltd. The old "piano-front" body is from A.E.C. Regent 185. Although the appearance was rather strange and old fashioned, the earlier bodies were of a much more substantial construction. 83 is in Low Fields Road on the new concrete roadway constructed over the former tram siding. It was on Elland Road Football Special duties on 15 November 1955. *W.D.Wilson/L,T.H.S.*

Roe bodied Leyland PD2/11 211 at Whingate on 16 April 1961. The redundant tram rails can be seen in the foreground. *W.D.Wilson /L.T.H.S.*

"Tin front" Daimler CVG6 536 with a M.C.C.W. body at Lower Wortley terminus on 23 April 1962. The layby, retaining wall and "shelter" were built in 1946 for tramway replacement. 536 was the first bus to be repainted in the new style livery with the lighter green lower saloon window surrounds. *W.D.Wilson/L.T.H.S.*

One of the series of 80 A.E.C. Regent V (760-839) delivered in 1956. 790 is at Whingate Junction on tramway replacement service 15. The date is 15 August 1960 and some tram rails and granite setts are still visible.
W.D.Wilson/L.T.H.S.

finger. An important feature of the system was a substantial reduction in physical effort for the driver. It was claimed that by the use of band brakes working in oil, a shock free transmission resulted which prolonged the life of the bus and hence, its earning capacity.

"Every gear change, it is maintained, proceeds at a uniform predetermined rate ensuring smooth, rapid and silent changes, irrespective of the driver's skill. A further advantage claimed for the system is that, throughout all gear changes, traction is continuous, giving improved vehicle performance and added passenger comfort.

'The Yorkshire Post', 2 March 1956.

760-839 are believed to have been the first monocontrol A.E.C.'s to be introduced in the country. They had 7·7 litre AV 470 engines and were fitted with Roe bodies seating 33/27. There were no front ventilators, but all upper saloon side windows had sliding ventilators, and similar ventilators were fitted to the middle pair of windows along either side. The bodies were well constructed and were described in an article in 'The Yorkshire Post'.

"The new buses now being made for Leeds Corporation have a lower saloon main framework of prime Burma teak with screwed exterior panels, and an upper saloon framework of aluminium alloy with extruded section pillars and riveted exterior panels. An interior finish of stove enamel gives a pleasing light and roomy impression in both saloons. The staircase is of the Roe safety type with two passing platforms.

It is worthy to note that the external painting of bus bodies at Roes is done entirely by hand, to ensure that the paint has the longest possible life in the often rigorous weather conditions in which public service vehicles are required to operate. Seven coats of paint are put on to the outside of each bus body. Lettering, including the name of the bus company on the side of the vehicle, the name of the particular transport undertaking's general manager, or coats of arms of towns and cities on Corporation buses are, in the main, put on by transfer."

'The Yorkshire Post', 2 March 1956.

Pre-war the average life of a motor bus was regarded as nine years, but some had run for much less than this, for example the A.E.C. "Q" buses of 1933 ran for four years only. The war, and difficulty in obtaining new buses in the years after, gave many of the older buses an extended life. However, most of the pre-war buses had been withdrawn by 1950, giving them a service life of about 12 or 13 years. A number of buses withdrawn in 1949 or 1950 were placed in storage and, as has been seen earlier, were reinstated for tramway replacement. The introduction of technical improvements, such as monocontrol and also improved body construction were said to prolong the life of the motor bus. The post-war A.E.C. Regent III ran for about 17 years, but the A.E.C. Regent V were to run for only 14 years or so possibly owing to their more lightly constructed bodies. In the early 1950's it was generally accepted that buses would run for 500,000 miles before withdrawal. Technical improvements in the latter part of the twentieth century prolonged bus life to 1,000,000 miles or over 20 years.

Delivery of the first of the Regent V began on 3 January 1956 and a special ceremony was held, one-legged Alderman Rafferty, Chairman of the Transport Committee, driving the bus around Torre Road Garage. Among those present were Lord Brabazon of Tara, chairman of Associated Commercial Vehicles, and W.R. Black and A.S.C. Chattey also of A.C.V. Sales. Charles H. Roe, and members of the Transport Committee were also present.

"Alderman Rafferty, who has driven the bus in practice on the Gipton Estate, told me today: " It is a big step forward in Leeds Transport Department history. It is the first bus I have ever driven in my life, but within minutes of entering the cab our official tester was able to leave me to my own devices.

"It is simplicity itself and can be a real contribution towards safer driving, the driver being free to concentrate his attention more on the road than has ever been possible in the past.

"The gear is conveniently situated for left-hand operation, the lever being no bigger than your little finger. There is no danger of a driver accidentally engaging reverse gear. as a separate knob must be drawn before the gate is open to receive the gear. It is the most simple flick of a finger."

'Yorkshire Evening News', 3 January 1956.

After 31 December 1955 many of the old buses taken out of storage for the Beeston tram service replacement were delicensed again.

The 100 new buses were purchased specifically for tramway replacements, the next major tram route to be abandoned being that from Briggate to Lawnswood. This took place on Saturday 3 March 1956, buses taking over the following day.

From 4 March the bus service between the Corn Exchange and Beeston was withdrawn, and a new service linking Lawnswood and Beeston, numbered 1, was introduced. The new service 1 followed the route of the former tram route as far as City Square, then via Bishopgate Street, Neville Street, Victoria Road, Meadow Road, and over the former Beeston bus route.

From 5 March the peak hour service No.5 from Swinegate to Beeston was altered to run outward via Victoria Road in place of via Great Wilson Street and Meadow Lane. New A.E.C. Regent V and Daimler CVG6 buses were used supplemented by pre-war A.E.C.s at peak hours.

The introduction of the new buses increased the bus fleet to about 490 vehicles.

Tramway track removal and alterations took place in City Square on Sunday, 4 March, and bus routes 14, 31, 32, 42, 47, 54 and 66 were diverted via Albion Street or King Street on that day.

On 18 March 1956 a number of bus route alterations took place. The route number 39 was reintroduced when a new bus service from the Central Bus Station to Whitkirk was started. The route from the Bus Station was via New York Road, York Road, Selby Road, Chapel Street, Cross Green Lane, Green Lane and the Ring Road to the junction of Selby Road with the Ring Road. Limited stop conditions applied on the route. At off peak, special journeys for shoppers were run from the Whitkirk terminus to Cross Gates tram terminus, via the Ring Road and Station Road.

Also from 18 March, service 67, (Central Bus Station-Seacroft), was extended from its existing terminus at Seacroft along Kentmere Avenue northwards for just over a quarter of a mile to a new terminus at Barncroft Drive. The limited stop conditions were extended on the 67 service and from the same date timetable revisions took place on the 4, 41, 45 and 68 bus services.

Over the following three months a number of minor alterations took place:

8 April 1956. Service 64 and Copper Works specials were rerouted via Duncan Street and Briggate on outward journeys.

30 April 1956. Service 5 buses rerouted via Great Wilson Street and Meadow Lane on outward journeys.

27 May 1956. Services 52 and 53 were extended along Britannia Road to form a circular service in the Morley area.

Another major tramway abandonment occurred on 22 July 1956 when the Tong Road services were withdrawn. Trams ran for the last time on Saturday, 21 July, and the following day there was a general rearrangement of services in not only Tong Road, but also in the Gipton and Seacroft areas.

The existing number 11 bus service from Vicar Lane to Gipton, the 78 (Central Bus Station-Seacroft, South Parkway), and the 79 Central Bus Station-Seacroft, North Parkway), services were withdrawn and replaced by three new cross city bus services:

11 Greenthorpe (Gamecock Inn) to Gipton. The route was extended beyond the former New Inn tram terminus via Tong Road and Pudsey Road to Greenthorpe.

15 Whingate to Seacroft (South Parkway).

16 Whingate to Seacroft (North Parkway, Bailey's :Lane).

Routes 15 and 16 were extended beyond the former Whingate tram terminus in Hill Top Road to the Traveller's Rest Hotel. Although not quite correct buses continued to show "WHINGATE" on the destination indicators.

Pre-war A.E.C. Regent 123 loading in New Market Street for Beeston on 17 December 1955.   *W.D.Wilson/L.T.H.S.*

Until the middle 1960's Leeds had a Coronation Street. A.E.C. Regent III 753 is on the 36 Tinshill service and is at the Coronation Street stop at the bottom of Woodhouse Lane. The date is 12 June 1963. *Author*.

The buses covered the routes of the former tram services, 15 and 16, and bus routes 11, 78 and 79 for the most part, with the extensions already referred to. They crossed the city via Wellington Street, City Square, Boar Lane, Duncan Street, Call Lane, New York Street, (Harper Street and Kirkgate in a westerly direction), York Street and Marsh Lane.

There were short workings at peak hours on all three services to Whingate Junction, and on Saturdays on routes 15 and 16 to Ironwood View, Seacroft. The former 78 and 79 services had also previously short worked to this point.

On 22 July bus service 67, (Central Bus Station-Seacroft via Harehills), was extended about a quarter of a mile from Barncroft Drive, Kentmere Avenue, along Kentmere Avenue and Monkswood Avenue to a new terminus at Monkswood Gate. Revised timetables were instituted on services 24, 29, 41, 43, 49, 74, 75 and 76.

These alterations were necessitated by the opening of a new garage at Seacroft, opened on 22 July simultaneously with the introduction of the new bus services. Bus routes operating from Seacroft Garage were as follows:

11 Greenthorpe and Gipton.	)
15 Whingate and Seacroft.	) New services.
16 Whingate and Seacroft.	)
24 Bus Station and Swarcliffe.	) Transferred from
39 Bus Station and Whitkirk and Whitkirk and Cross Gates.	) Torre Road) Garage.
41 Bus Station and Colton.	)
67 Bus Station and Seacroft.	) Transferred from
68 Bus Station and Foundry Lane.	) Hunslet Garage.

A.E.C. Regent III, 450-479, all the Crossleys, (701-721), and A.E.C. Regent V, 783-809, were transferred from Torre Road Garage to work the various services,

They ran on all the services with the exception of the Crossleys, which were usually confined to routes 11, 15 and 16.

From the same date (22 July), route 29, (City Square-Middleton), was transferred from Sovereign Street Garage to Hunslet Garage along with route 74, (Belle Isle-North Lane), and 76, (City Square-North Lane), both jointly worked with Headingley Garage. Route 49, (Hyde Park-Old Farnley), changed from Bramley Garage to Headingley Garage.

Three weeks after the abandonment of the 15 and 16 tram services, a new bus route was instituted from the Rockingham Street Bus Station to the Tinshill Estate, near Cookridge. The service, numbered 36, began on 12 August 1956 and ran from Rockingham Street via Woodhouse Lane, Headingley Lane, Otley Road, Otley Old Road, Tinshill Lane, Wood Nook Drive and Silk Mill Drive. Limited stop conditions were imposed on the route. The short workings to Tinshill on route 33, Cookridge, were withdrawn and an integrated timetable was operated on the two bus routes. The new service was worked from Headingley Garage. The Tinshill service proved popular and improved frequencies were introduced the following month.

In the meantime an order had been placed for a further 75 double deck buses: 55 A.E.C. Regent V and 20 Daimler CVG6 vehicles. The order was placed on 16 May 1955, and was an extension of the order for 100 buses placed in January 1955. It was to be 1957 before the 75 buses were delivered.

The Suez crisis of November 1956 and consequent problems with fuel supplies, resulted in reduced bus services. These are discussed next.

A.E.C. Regent V 839 with its gold leaf lining was the Commercial Motor Show Exhibit of 1956.   It is in Calverley Street on 12 June 1961 on the 61 East End Park Circular service.   Leeds Civic Hall and gardens form the setting for this photograph.   The gardens and most of the buildings in Portland Crescent on the right have gone and the site is currently occupied by "Millenium Square". *W.D.Wilson/L.T.H.S.*

On 22 July 1956 route 11, Vicar Lane-Gipton, was withdrawn and replaced by a new bus service 11 from Gipton to the Greenthorpe Estate.   Leyland PD2 368 is pictured at the Greenthorpe terminus on 15 June 1963.   The driver and conductor are leaning on the fence and behind 368 is a rag and bone man's horse and cart, still a familiar sight in the 1960's. The driver of the cart called out "rag bone" as he drove along. *Author*.

The Bus Services 1957 to 1959

The Suez crisis of 1956 caused serious problems for the Leeds Transport undertaking. The postponement of the tramway abandonment scheme and reintroduction of the football special trams has been discussed in an earlier chapter. The fuel shortage resulted in a number of bus services being reduced. There were no actual route curtailments as had occurred at the outbreak of the Second World War in 1939, but off peak services on most routes were cut back. Whereas in 1939 the fuel oil available for buses was reduced by 50%, in November 1956 the reduction was only 5%.

Nevertheless a 5% reduction meant that a saving of 15,000 bus miles had to be made each week. This was achieved in a number of ways.

Except on Saturdays, the departure of last buses from the city centre became approximately 10.30 p.m., instead of about 11.00 p.m.

Private hire for social functions, weddings and funerals was suspended.

Alderman Rafferty, Chairman of the Transport Committee, appealed to firms to stagger their hours as motorists, unable to use their cars, added to the already heavy peak load.

"The peak service would not be augmented. He wanted industrialists to get in touch with the department.

He was appealing to the Corporation departments to stagger hours of work and was suggesting that from Monday to Friday the hours should be 8.30 a.m. to 4.30 p.m. with half an hour for lunch and one Saturday worked in four.

If they were prepared to overcome the difficulty of half an hour for lunch, it would be a tremendous benefit to the Transport Department.

He also asked commercial houses to follow these lines.

If this were done the Transport Department could absorb those who would use the present peak hour service."

'Yorkshire Evening Post', 30 November 1956.

Rafferty also asked the Education Department to adjust school hours. He wanted schools to finish at 4.00 p.m., offices at 4.30 p.m. and industry from 5.00 p.m. to 6.00 p.m.

The remainder of the saving was to be made by reducing the frequency of buses after the teatime peak.

Bus service reductions were introduced over the following weeks beginning on 16 December 1956 when the Sunday service on the 55 route (Sovereign Street-Bruntcliffe) was discontinued. The day after, last buses on all routes from Monday to Friday and on Sunday were cut back to 10.30 p.m.

Over the following three months reduced services were introduced on various bus routes:

6 January 1957.   Services 42 and 66.

13 January 1957.   Services 23, 29, 31, 35, 43, 46, 54, 64 and 65.

20 January 1957.   Services 30, 33, 36, 44, 50, 75 and 76.

27 January 1957.   Services 11, 15, 16, 24, 67 and 68.

3 February 1957.   Services 1 and 4.

25 February 1957.   Services 8, 52 and 53.

4 March 1957.   Service 72.

The de-rationing of diesel fuel in March 1957 soon led to the restoration of services. From 10 March later buses were reintroduced on services 1, 5, 42, 54, 65, 66 and 77; 17 March 29, 30, 34-36, 43, 50, 56-60, 75 and 76; 24 March 8, 11, 14-16, 24, 39, 52, 53, 67 and 68; 31 March 4, 28 and 61. Full services on all bus routes were restored on 7 April 1957.

A.E.C. Regent V 849 was one of the buses placed in storage that entered service in October 1957 as a replacement for the trams on the Moortown and Dewsbury Road routes. It is on route 8 to Meanwood and is passing the Drysalter's public house at the Ring Road, Cottingley. The date, 16 June 1962, is prior to the dual carriageway being constructed at this point. *W.D.Wilson/L.T.H.S.*

The 1946 "JUM" Daimler CWD6 buses, 516-521, were all withdrawn at the end of September 1957. 518 is in Woodside View, off Burley Road, presumably on a diversion as the route 50 buses did not normally run along Woodside View. The photograph was taken on 4 August 1955. *W.D. Wilson/L.T.H.S.*

Caroline Street disappeared in 1957 to make way for the large roundabout at the northern end of Westgate. The roundabout came into use on 11 November 1957. Compare with the photograph on page 1401 which shows the Westgate roundabout photographed from approximately the same angle. A.E.C. Regent III 407 in Caroline Street is on route 71, short working to Horsforth on the Central Bus Station to Guiseley service, and the date is 30 April 1955, the last day of operation of the route. *W.D. Wilson/L.T.H.S.*

On 29 December 1957 a new cross-city service between Rodley and Halton Moor was introduced replacing existing services 28 and 54. Leyland PD2 357 was pictured at Rodley terminus on 21 November 1964 and is returning to Halton Moor. *Author.*

During the period of fuel shortages no new bus services had been introduced, but from 3 January 1957 a new terminus was brought into use for route 39 (Central Bus Station-Whitkirk). From that date buses reversed into newly widened Whitkirk Lane from the Ring Road. They stayed in Whitkirk Lane until departure. Previously buses had turned at the junction of the Ring Road and Selby Road, some 50 yards further on than the new terminus.

The fuel shortage delayed the introduction of the 75 new double deck buses, which had been ordered in May 1955. These comprised 55 A.E.C. Regent V and 20 Daimler CVG6 buses, similar to 532-551. The Regent V were delivered from November 1956 to February 1957, but were placed in storage. It was to be 1 March 1957 when the first 21, followed by five more later in the month, were licensed for service. Allocated fleet numbers 840-894 (XUM 840-894) the new Regent V were almost identical to 760-839, but differed slightly in that the near side front mudguards had reverted to earlier practice in not being "rounded off" to the lower saloon bulkhead. The remaining buses of the series, and the Daimlers, were retained in storage until September 1957 when the next tramway conversion took place.

Meanwhile in January 1957 one of the earlier A.E.C. Regent V buses, 765, was delicensed and returned to A.E.C. Ltd. in Southall, Middlesex. The bus was fitted with a new "Automonocontrol" transmission similar to that on the London "Routemaster" buses. It was still fitted with the two-pedal control common to all buses of the 760-839 series, but the gears now engaged automatically without the driver having to touch the gear lever. The bus entered service with its new transmission on 7 February 1957.

As a result of the introduction of the first of the "XUM" series of A.E.C. Regent V, many old buses were withdrawn. The last pre-war bus to run in service was 124

(HUM 419) withdrawn on 13 February 1957. The other buses of the "HUM" series, 106-125, (HUM 401-420) were all taken out of service some six months earlier. Five, 106, 111, 112, 115 and 116 were transferred to the learner fleet on 1 November 1956, later becoming learner buses Nos.1-5 respectively. These are discussed again in Chapter 89.

February and March 1957 also saw the withdrawal of the remaining semi-utility body Daimler CWA6 of 1945-6. These comprised buses 77-98 and 504-515 and included those that had been rebodied with 1934 bodies by Charles H. Roe Ltd in 1955. 12 of these buses were sold to A.M.C.C. Ltd., a subsidiary of Lansdowne Coaches of London, for £125 each.

1946 vintage "JUM" Daimler CWD6 buses, 516-521, (JUM 571-576) were withdrawn at the end of September 1957 when more new buses were delivered.

The major Leeds transport event of 1957 was the withdrawal of the Moortown-Dewsbury Road tram service and its replacement by buses. This took place in September, but in the meantime there had been a few bus service alterations.

Caroline Street, a short street connecting St. Paul's Street with Park Lane, partially disappeared in 1957. It was used by bus services 4 (Horsforth-Compton Road) and 65 (Rockingham Street-Pudsey) and was on the line of the proposed Headrow extension to Westgate (see map on page 797 of Volume 3). Owing to excavations by contractors it was closed on a number of occasions in early 1957 being reopened again later. It was finally closed on 20 April 1957, buses on services 4 and 65 being diverted to nearby Grace Street. In May most of Caroline Street was broken up and over the following few months a new roundabout was constructed at the northern end of Westgate. The roundabout came into use on 11 November 1957, routes 4 and 65 being diverted to run via the remains of Caroline Street instead of Grace Street. Grace Street was closed in part to allow the construction of a new approach to the roundabout from the Park Lane end. The new approach, an extension of Westgate to Park Lane and Victoria Square, was introduced from about 10,30 a.m. on Sunday, 23 February 1958. The short stretch of Park Lane between Park Street and Leighton Lane was permanently closed to traffic. Bus services 4 and 65 were redirected along the new road and a number of other bus services were also affected. Services 23, 50, 51, 57, 59, 74, 75, 76 and 77 were diverted via the new Westgate extension and the Caroline Street remnants.

In June 1957 the Beeston bus terminal was extended by a few yards when old property was demolished at the former tram terminus.

From Sunday, 7 July 1957, bus services 32 (Infirmary Street-Pudsey via Whitehall Road) and 43 (Central Bus Station-Carr Manor) were discontinued and a new through bus service opened between Pudsey and Carr Manor. Given the number 32, buses followed the former routes except between City Square and Sheepscar where they traversed Boar Lane, Duncan Street, New Market Street, Vicar Lane, and North Street. Vehicles on the new route were operated from Sovereign Street and Hunslet garages (the garages of the old routes 32 and 43 respectively). There were short workings to Potternewton Lane traffic roundabout on the Carr Manor side of the route. On the Pudsey side there was a special through works service from Troydale Mills to Carr Manor. The Troydale Mills works service was a branch from the normal Pudsey route and is discussed in Appendix XXI.

The abandonment of the Moortown and Dewsbury Road tram routes took place on Saturday, 28 September 1957, buses taking over the following day.

The new number 2 bus route, Moortown-Dewsbury Road, followed the former tram route for the most part, but in the city centre there were variations. Buses ran via the Corn Exchange instead of Briggate, working southwards

via Duncan Street and Briggate and northwards via Call Lane. The Dewsbury Road end of the route was extended to the junction with the Ring Road and at Moortown there was a short extension along Harrogate Road to the Chained Bull Hotel. Certain buses ran along Street Lane to Roundhay Park, reversing at the bus park, and running alternately with the Briggate-Moortown via Roundhay trams.

The short working to Stainbeck Lane, Chapeltown, was retained, buses turning around the island at the end of Stainbeck Lane. At the Dewsbury Road end the Crescent Cinema short working was discontinued and extended about a quarter of a mile to Cross Flatts Park. Buses on the new service were worked from Torre Road Garage.

To serve the new bus route the remainder of the "XUM" series of A.E.C. Regent V and Daimler CVG6 buses (552-571) entered service. The Daimlers were similar to 532-551, but had 60-seat Weymann "Orion" bodies. They did not have the opening bulkhead window ventilators, which were found on 532-551.

For a period of 18 months there was a pause in the tramway abandonment programme. In the meantime a number of small extensions and alterations to bus services took place.

From 29 December 1957 a new cross-city service between Rodley and Halton Moor came into operation. It replaced two existing services: 28 (Central Bus Station-Halton Moor) and 54 (Rockingham Street-Rodley). Numbered 54, the new route ran from Rodley, Town Street via Whitecote Hill, Upper Town Street, Lower Town Street, Stanningley Road, Armley Road, Wellington Road, Wellington Street, City Square, Boar Lane, Duncan Street, Call Lane, New York Street, (returning via Harper Street, Kirkgate and New Market Street), York Street, Marsh Lane, York Road, Osmondthorpe Lane, Neville Parade, Halton Moor Avenue, Neville Road and Ullswater Crescent, turning at Coronation Parade. Unlike the former route 28, inward journeys from Halton Moor ran via

A.E.C. Regent V   893   at the route 7   terminus at the bottom of   Queenswood   Drive,   Headingley,   on   7 June 1961.
W.D.Wilson/L.T.H.S.

"Tin front" Daimler CVG6 553 pictured in Stanningley Road on 15 October 1962. It is passing the end of Redcote Lane. Compare the vegetation with the photograph, taken at the same place some thirteen years later, on page 1463. *W.D.Wilson/L.T.H.S.*

Osmondthorpe Lane to join York Road at the Shaftesbury Hotel. Formerly buses had run via Ings Road and Skelton Terrace to join York Road. The new route was worked from Bramley Depot using mainly Leyland PD1 and PD2 buses.

Also from 29 December the special "shoppers" extension of the 39 service from Whitkirk to Cross Gates was extended along Cross Gates Lane and Barwick Road to the junction with the Ring Road. The extension was now officially regarded as route 39.

Timetable modifications were introduced on several routes and bus service 72 (Leeds-Bradford) was now worked from Torre Road Garage instead of Bramley.

From 19 January 1958 the Leeds terminal loading point for the 72 service was moved to the north east side of Infirmary Street (outside Post Office House). Buses arrived in Leeds from Wellington Street via King Street and Infirmary Street and departed via City Square and Wellington Street. Formerly the loading point had been by the side of the General Post Office. This point was now used by the 29 (Infirmary Street-Middleton) buses.

A week later, on 26 January, routes 15 and 16 (Whingate to South and North Parkway respectively) were rerouted. Formerly buses had run from Foundry Lane to South Parkway via Foundry Mill Drive, but were now redirected via a newly constructed road known as South Parkway Approach.

On 2 March 1958 an extension of route 45 (Wortley-Harehills) took place. At the Wortley end the route was extended from Upper Wortley Road along Dixon Lane as far as Kellett Crescent near to the junction with Whitehall Road. There had been a considerable amount of house and road building in the area and Kellett Crescent had recently been extended from Kellett Avenue to Dixon Lane. From Harehills the 45 service was extended to Seacroft (North Parkway) via Easterly Road, Boggart Hill Drive and Kentmere Avenue.

Prior to the extension six single deck buses were needed for the peak hour services – five on route 45 and one on the 73 service. As a result of the alteration, an additional bus had to be put on the 45 route at peak periods.

On 4 May 1958 the North Lane terminal point for services 74 (Belle Isle-North Lane) and 76 (Infirmary Street-North Lane) was transferred to the junction of Kirkstall Lane with Queenswood Drive. The North Lane terminus of the 56 buses (Central Bus Station-North Lane) was unchanged, A revised timetable was adopted on route 75 (Infirmary Street-Beckett's Park).

Until 1958 bus stop posts in Leeds had been tubular steel with finials and most were formerly ex-tramway overhead wire bracket arms cut down to the required length. From the beginning of February 1958 new bus stops were of reinforced concrete, the first to be used being on the new extension to Westgate. Others soon appeared elsewhere when posts were renewed.

During 1958 two small alterations were made to all the buses in the fleet. From 26 April 1958 near side driving mirrors were fitted to all buses and by mid-May the whole of the fleet had been dealt with.

On 25 November 1955 A.E.C. Reliance 33 appeared in service experimentally fitted with flashing or winking trafficators. These consisted of curved orange indicators on each side of the bus about 9 inches below the front side windows. The flashing indicator was a better solution than the old system. This had been a, sometimes not very visible, hinged illuminated arm that was fixed on each side of the bus.

Buses 32 and 34 were later similarly fitted and until 1958, 32-34 were the only buses in the fleet with flashing trafficators. However, this feature was becoming universally adopted on all motor vehicles, and on 18 November 1957 the Transport Committee agreed to fit flashing trafficators on all buses which had an estimated life of five years or more. 100 buses per year were to be dealt with. On 12 May 1958 tenders were accepted from various firms for 300 flashing trafficators for a total sum of £1,534 10s. 7d. The first bus to be fitted was A.E.C. Regent 646 in February 1958 and it was followed by most of the other buses over the next year or two.

The first of July 1958 was an important date in the

history of the motor bus in Great Britain. From this day the Ministry of Transport allowed the length of a two-axle double deck bus to be increased from the statutory 27 feet to 30 feet. The gross weight was increased from 12 tons to 14 tons. This enlargement resulted in an increase in seating capacity, which meant that fewer vehicles were needed and hence costs reduced. With the 27 feet body the bus manufacturers had managed to squeeze in a maximum of 62 seats. Soon this was to rise to over 70.

There were concerns over the ability of conductors to cope with the increased seating capacity and Leeds was rather slow in ordering the larger buses. On 17 June 1957 the Transport Committee accepted tenders for the last 27 feet long double deck buses to be supplied to the Department. These were A.E.C. Regent V with 8 feet wide Roe bodies. Apart from 600, 625-648 and 700, all Leeds buses until this time had 7ft. 6in. wide bodies. Leeds had been reluctant to order wider buses due to the width of the lanes at the Central Bus Station. Corporation buses of 8ft. 0in width were forbidden to use the bus station at first, but when other operators used wider buses without problems, the rule was relaxed.

15 A.E.C. Regent V were ordered and delivered from May to July 1958. Except for the extra six inches in width, these buses were very similar to the other 135 A.E.C. Regent V. The window on the off side by the staircase was not fitted. 760-894 had 60 seats and the extra two seats on the new buses were created by having seats for four over the wheel arches in the lower saloon. Grab bars were situated between this seat, there being room for two passengers each side of the bar. The backward facing seat for the passengers at the front of the lower saloon was reduced in width by about six inches. The new type flashing indicators were fitted at both the front and rear of the bus.

Numbered 895-909 these were the first buses in Leeds to have reversed registration numbers (1895 NW to 1909 NW). As a result of the introduction of 895-909, all the 1948 "LNW" Daimlers, 522-531, were taken out of service. These vehicles were in good and serviceable condition. Although their Brush built bodies were not of the best and had some rebuilding, it is perhaps surprising that they

were withdrawn, They were sold to W. North Ltd., dealers of Leeds, who in turn resold them to local bus proprietor, Samuel Ledgard Ltd. of Armley, Leeds. They were with Ledgard until 1963 and 1964. There was adverse comment by councillors and in the local press about their early withdrawal. It was to be another four years before any more buses were withdrawn, the Transport Department getting 13 to 14 years service out of them as opposed to the ten years for 522-531.

On 21 October 1957 tenders had been accepted for the first 30ft.0in. long buses in Leeds. These were to be Leyland PD3/5 type double deckers with Roe bodies and were ordered specifically for the replacement of the Moortown via Roundhay and Belle Isle and Middleton tram routes. 80 buses, 27 feet long, had originally been ordered, but this order was changed to 71 buses only, all of the new 30 feet. length. 71 large buses had a similar seating capacity to 80 smaller. Apart from, number 221, all entered service in 1959. 221 (5221 NW) was selected to be the L.C.T. bus for the Commercial Motor Show held at Earl's Court, London, from 26 September to 4 October 1958. It was the first 8ft.0in. wide by 30ft.0in. long double deck bus in Leeds. It had a 71-seat rear entrance body. A normal Leyland exposed radiator was fitted and the bus had a Leyland pneumocyclic gearbox and air brakes.

The Roe body was similar in style to those on A.E.C. Regent V 760-909, both in exterior design and in the interior window mountings. There was no backwards-facing transverse seat in the lower saloon. This type of seat had been fitted to all buses supplied to Leeds from late 1955, beginning with the "VUG" Daimler CVG6 buses, 532-551, but had been very unpopular with passengers. 221 was fitted with a Clayton heating and ventilating system, new to Leeds, which was incorporated in the near side cab canopy. There were ducts to both the upper and lower saloons and also in the driver's cab. Front and rear flashing trafficators were fitted and 221 was painted in the standard Leeds livery with the addition of gold leaf lining, similar to previous Show buses.

Although the other PD3/5 buses were delivered from September 1958 onwards, they were kept in storage until

A snow scene at St. Ann's Gardens in Burley Road with 1948-built Daimler CVD6 529 on 20 December 1955. The "LNW" Daimlers, 522-531, were withdrawn in 1958 when the A.E.C. Regent V, 895-909, were delivered. The "LNW" CVD6 all later ran for Ledgard. *W.D.Wilson/L.T.H.S.*

A.E.C. Regent V, 895-909, were the last buses with 27 feet long bodies to be supplied to the Leeds Transport Department. 901 is on route 6 to Belle Isle and is in Hunslet Road on 12 November 1966. Most of Hunslet Road from Waterloo Street to Hunslet Lane was closed on 7 May 1972 and occupied by an extension to Tetley's Brewery. This part forms the entrance to the Brewery Yard. Salem Congregational Institute on the left and Tunstall's building, originally a temperance hotel, (behind 901) still exist. *Author*.

the next major tramway abandonment, which was to take place in March 1959.

Apart from a number of frequency alterations (mainly reductions), timetable changes on various bus routes and the introduction of one or two new school services (discussed elsewhere)) very little happened on the Leeds bus routes during the latter part of 1958.

The visit of H.M. the Queen and Duke of Edinburgh to Leeds on Friday and Saturday 17 and 18 October 1958, necessitated the closing of many roads for varying periods of time with the consequent diversion or suspension of both bus and tram services. On some routes very long diversions were necessary on many roads not normally used by buses.

During the Royal Visit several buses were used by the police. Each bore a large card with a reference letter, and a label on the windscreen, reading "PRIORITY". The buses were used to take police to points where they were needed to control crowds. After the Royal Procession had passed by, the buses then transported the police to other locations where they were needed later in the day. Eight buses were noted carrying out these duties. Nearly every bus and tram route in Leeds was affected and as the diversions were complex, the details are felt to be outside the scope of this volume.

Owing to the introduction of a new one-way traffic system in Call Lane, buses on services 2, 8, 52, 53, 63 and 64 were rerouted on inward journeys via Lower Briggate and Duncan Street and via Call Lane on outward journeys. The alteration came into effect on 3 December 1958.

From 27 January 1959 buses on services 8, 52, and 53 were extended from Church Avenue for about 100 yards along Green Road, Meanwood, to a new terminus at Green View.

29 March 1959 marked big alterations in the bus and tram services in Leeds. On this date tram services 3 (Briggate to Moortown via Roundhay), 12 and 12 circular (Corn Exchange and Middleton via Dewsbury Road, 26 and 27 (Corn Exchange to Belle Isle via Hunslet Road) and 26 circular (Corn Exchange and Middleton via Belle Isle), were abandoned.

As a result of the tramway closures a number of new bus services and alterations to other services took place. New bus services were service 3, Middleton to Moortown via Belle Isle, Briggate and Roundhay; service 6, Belle Isle to Harehills or Roundhay and service 12, Corn Exchange to Middleton via Dewsbury Road.

In addition to these new services, service 2, Dewsbury Road to Moortown via Chapeltown, was altered and partly integrated with the new services.

Buses on the revised service 2 ran from Dewsbury Road or Cross Flatts Park via Briggate and New Briggate instead of via the Corn Exchange and Vicar Lane. In the opposite direction there was no route change. Buses running to Moortown reversed as formerly at the Chained Bull Hotel, but Roundhay buses worked a circular route via Harehills on their return to Middleton.

On the new bus service 3, the terminus at Middleton was located at the junction of Middleton Park Avenue and Thorpe Lane. The route from Middleton to Moortown was via Middleton Park Avenue, Middleton Park Road, Sharp Lane, Town Street, Belle Isle Road, Balm Road, Church Street, Waterloo Road, Hunslet Road, Bridge End, Briggate, New Briggate, North Street, Roundhay Road, Prince's Avenue and Street Lane. Buses generally operated a circular service returning to Middleton via Chapeltown, but there were short workings to Harehills and occasionally to Moortown only.

Service 6 started at the former 27 tram terminus at the top of Belle Isle Road and ran to Harehills or Roundhay via the 3 route. At peak periods there was a working from Briggate to Harehills, buses turning at Harehills by the Clock Cinema roundabout and in the city centre they went via New Briggate, The Headrow, Vicar Lane, New Market Street, Duncan Street and Briggate.

New service 12 terminated at Middleton at the same point as the number 3 buses and then ran via Middleton Park Avenue, Middleton Park Road, Ring Road, Dewsbury Road, Meadow Lane, Bridge End, Briggate, Duncan Street, and New Market Street terminating near Central Road. Buses returned to Middleton via Kirkgate and Call Lane to Bridge End and then as the inward route.

Services 2, 3 and 12 were all linked together by circular duties, the same bus travelling over all the route variations and taking seven hours in the process.

A new bus turning bay was built at Roundhay Park adjacent to the tennis courts and at the end of Middleton Park Avenue a turning circle was constructed, coming into use on 20 April 1959. A number of other bus service alterations took place on 29 March:

Service 33 Rockingham Street-Cookridge) was extended at the Cookridge end along Green Lane to Moseley Wood Lane.

Service 36 (Rockingham Street-Tinshill), ceased to make a circuit of the Tinshill Estate and buses were routed via Silk Mill Drive on both outward and inward journeys.

Service 74 (Belle Isle-North Lane). This service formerly part day was changed to an all day operation and was extended at the Belle Isle end via Broom Cross, Broom Crescent and Broom Place to the Ring Road (Raylands Lane). At the North Lane end the service was extended from North Lane along Queenswood Drive to Beckett's Park at the junction with Spen Lane.

Service 75 (City Square-Beckett's Park). Service discontinued.

Revised timetables were introduced on services 4, 11, 15, 16 and 55, operation of bus service 4 being transferred to Seacroft Garage. Several other buses were transferred between the various garages during March 1959. Not only was this attributed to the bus route alterations, but also to the introduction of the 70 new Leyland PD3/5 buses, which had been in storage.

The new Leylands seated 71 passengers and were similar to 221, which had appeared in service on 9 November 1958. Numbered 222-291 (5222 NW to 5291 NW) they all entered passenger service between 27 March and 1 April 1959.

The last tramway to run in south Leeds, the number 25, Swinegate-Hunslet service, ceased operation on Saturday 18 April 1959 and was replaced by a new bus service numbered 7.

The number 7 buses ran from North Lane, Headingley, (bottom of Queenswood Drive) to Hunslet via Kirkstall Lane, Cardigan Road, Burley Road, Burley Street, Park Lane, Caroline Street, Westgate, East Parade, Infirmary Street, City Square, Boar Lane, Lower Briggate, Bridge End, Hunslet Road, Low Road, Thwaite Gate and Spring Grove Street. At Spring Grove Street, buses reversed into Belmont View and returned to Thwaite Gate to pick up passengers. The Infirmary Street-Hunslet section replaced the tram service and the route from Infirmary Street to Headingley was a replacement for the 76 bus service (Infirmary Street-North Lane), which ceased to operate from 18 April. The new bus service was jointly worked by the Hunslet and Headingley Garages.

The route through the city centre differed considerably from the former tram service and to allow for this, two special buses were run from Swinegate. These operated on Mondays to Fridays only at 5.03 p.m. and 5.33 p.m. from Swinegate via Sovereign Street, Neville Street, Victoria Road, Great Wilson Street, and Hunslet Lane and joining the main route at Hunslet Road. Route number 7 was displayed on the special buses.

From 5 July 1959 the number 74 service, (Belle Isle-Beckett's Park), was extended from its terminus at the top of Queenswood Drive, a short distance along Spen Lane and Old Oak Drive to a new terminus at Old Oak Lawn.

The Daimler CVD6, 522-531, were all sold to Ledgard in January 1960. 530, newly painted in the Ledgard livery, is pictured in Commercial Road, Kirkstall, on 30 June of that year. *W.D.Wilson/L.T.H.S.*

Leyland PD3/5 221, the Commercial Motor Show Exhibit of September and October 1958, was the first of 71 buses ordered for the replacement of the Roundhay and Middleton tram services. It had a 30 feet long Roe body and was photographed at Moortown on 2 September 1961. *W.D.Wilson/L.T.H.S.*

Saturday the seventh of November 1959 was one of the most important dates in the history of Leeds transport for on this day the last of the trams ran in Leeds. The closure resulted in the reorganisation of several bus routes. The following bus routes ceased operation:

4 Compton Road (Fairway Hotel) to Horsforth.
14 Central Bus Station to Half Mile Lane.
50 Central Bus Station to Horsforth.
51 Central Bus Station to Hawksworth.
77 Central Bus Station to Bramley Town End.

They were replaced by a number of new services. The number 4 was replaced by a new 4 service running between Cross Gates and Horsforth. The route from Cross Gates was via Cross Gates Road, York Road, Marsh Lane, York Street, New York Street, Harper Street, Kirkgate, Call Lane, Duncan Street, Boar Lane, City Square, Wellington Street, Kirkstall Road, Commercial Road, Abbey Road, New Road Side and terminated at the Fleece Hotel, Horsforth. In the opposite direction the route was identical except between Duncan Street and New York Street when buses ran via New Market Street and Kirkgate. There were short workings throughout the day to Kirkstall Abbey and at peak hours to Burley Mills and Kirkstall Forge. The route was worked from Seacroft Garage with some vehicles at peak hours from Torre Road No.2 Garage.

The number 14 service was altered to run between Halton and Half Mile Lane. The Halton bus terminus was in Irwin Approach and the route to Half Mile Lane was via Selby Road, York Road, Marsh Lane, York Street, New York Street, Harper Street, Kirkgate, New Market Street, Duncan Street, Boar Lane, City Square, Wellington Street, Wellington Road, Armley Road and Stanningley Road. In the opposite direction buses ran from Duncan Street to New York Street via Call Lane. To enable buses to turn at Halton, they ran via Selby Road and Temple Newsam Road to Irwin Approach. There were short workings from Halton to Bramley Town End at certain times of the day.

The number 22 tram service was replaced by a new bus service, also numbered 22, which ran from the Central Bus Station (Platform C) to Temple Newsam. The route from the Bus Station was via Eastgate, New York Road, York Road, Selby Road and Temple Newsam Road. At Temple Newsam the buses turned temporarily at the cross roads near to the terminus, until a road was completed.

Services 14 and 22 were worked from Torre Road No.2 Garage.

Bus route 51 was discontinued entirely, but routes 50 and 77 continued to operate in modified form. These services, which had previously worked from the Central Bus Station, were now altered to run from Horsforth to Compton Road and Bramley Town End to Compton Road respectively. They replaced the former number 4 service, which now ran through to Cross Gates. Route 50 ran from Compton Road (Fairway Hotel) to Horsforth via Foundry Approach, Compton Road, Stoney Rock Lane. Nippet Lane, Burmantofts Street, New York Road, Eastgate, The Headrow, Westgate, Caroline Street, Burley Street, Burley Road, Kirkstall Hill, Morris Lane, Vesper Road, Broadway Circus, Hawkswood Crescent, Lea Farm Road, Butcher Hill, Low Lane and Broadgate Lane to Stanhope Drive. There were short workings to the Hawksworth Estate, buses showing route number 50 in place of the 51 formerly displayed.

Service 77 to Bramley Town End followed the same route from Compton Road as the 50 buses, but from Kirkstall Hill ran via Kirkstall Lane, Bridge Road, Leeds and Bradford Road, Broadlea Hill, Broadlea Avenue, Broadlea Crescent, Broad Lane, Waterloo Lane and Bramley Town Street. At certain times of the day buses inter-worked on the two services, the 50 service mainly from Headingley Garage and the 77 from Bramley Garage.

From 8 November, simultaneously with the introduction of the new bus services, timetable changes were introduced on services 54 and 65 "to provide a better balance of service along Stanningley Road," and also on route 6.

After the final abandonment of the Leeds tramways on 7 November 1959, there was a reorganisation of several bus services. A new service 4 from Cross Gates to Horsforth was inaugurated. A.E.C. Regent V 801 is loading in Call Lane outside the Corn Exchange and is bound for the Kirkstall short working of the Horsforth section. The date of the photograph is 11 April 1964. *Author.*

To serve the new bus services, 30 Daimler CVG6LX buses were brought into use. Numbered 502-531 (7502-7531 UA) most, (508, 509, and 512-531), came into service on 7 November. 504-7, 519 and 511 appeared at the beginning of November, whereas 502 and 503 had entered service the previous month. The new Daimlers were fitted with semi-automatic "Daimatic" transmission (i.e. two-pedal control), and all had Roe 8ft.0in. wide and 30ft.0in. long 71-seat bodies, 39 seated in the upper saloon and 32 in the lower. Heaters were fitted in both saloons. 517, 523, 526, 529, and 530 had a rubber finish to the floors to the platforms, whereas the others were wood. 505, 509 and 511 were fitted with hinged ventilators on the rear pair of opening windows in the upper saloon. The other buses in the series had the normal sliding ventilators.

On 1 November 1959 two single deck A.E.C. Reliance buses entered service. These were numbered 37 and 38 (8737 and 8738 UA). They had Roe centre entrance bodies with seating for 34 and standing for 24.

They were similar to the other under-floor engine single deckers in the bus fleet, but had a straighter front.

Unlike A.E.C. Reliance 32-34, the new buses had monocontrol. They were finished in the usual livery of Leeds permanent green and Leeds Lincoln green, but had, in addition, gold leaf lining.

As a result of the introduction of new buses some of the older vehicles were withdrawn. These included the first Crossley DD42/4, 701, and some of the Leyland PD1 of the 319-333 series. A few of the PD1 buses were later relicensed for service.

On 1 January 1960 the bus fleet comprised 636 vehicles (624 double deckers and 12 single deck buses) plus eight learners and six delicensed buses: 139, 320, 322, 327, 332 and 701. Bus route mileage was 188·29 and there were 63 routes in operation (including circulars) and occupying route numbers 1-8, 11, 12, 14-16, 22-24, 29-42, 44-47, 49, 50, 52-70. 72-74 and 77. There were also a number of school, hospital, works and night services.

On 31 March 1960 the number of passengers carried annually on the buses was recorded as 207,577,833. This was to decline considerably over the next few years.

A Change of General Managers

Alexander Black Findlay, the Leeds City Transport General Manager, had unwillingly presided over the abandonment of the Leeds tramways. In October 1960 he was forced to retire on grounds of ill health. Some months afterwards two other well known members of the Transport Department retired. R.J. or "Jim" Wade, the foreman at Swinegate Depot, retired on 14 December 1960 and he was followed three months later, on 31 March 1961, by Tom Parkinson, the Chief Engineer.

Parkinson was not immediately replaced. His position was covered by a "reorganisation of staff", unfortunately not specified. As Swinegate Depot was now closed, Jim Wade also did not have a successor.

However, in 1962 a replacement for Parkinson was found. This was Cecil B. France, the Assistant Rolling Stock Engineer. Before he joined the Leeds Transport Department, France had been rolling stock engineer at Swindon.

Advertisements for Findlay's replacement were placed and on 17 October 1960 the Transport Committee considered a short list of candidates for the post. These were:

R. Cox	General Manager.		Rochdale.
J.E. Frith	,,	,,	Derby.
T. Lord	,,	,,	Barrow.
J. Rostron	,,	,,	Grimsby.
J.C. Wake	,,	,,	St. Helens.

The Committee selected Thomas Lord, General Manager of the Barrow-in-Furness Transport undertaking. He took up his post on 1 February 1961.

Aged 44, Lord had been at Barrow for eleven years. A native of Burnley, Lancashire, Lord began his career with the Burnley Corporation Tramways Department (later known as the Burnley, Colne and Nelson Joint Transport Committee)). There he rose to become Assistant Engineer before being called to war service. During

Thomas Lord in 1973

Daimler CVG6 560 (YNW 560) in Stanningley Road at the Bramley Town End bus stop on 4 May 1964. Bramley Depot is on the right. *Author*.

Most of the 1946-built Leyland Titan PD1 buses of the 319-333 series (JUG 619-633) were withdrawn in 1959 and 1960. 321 is in Broom Cross, Belle Isle, on the 46 Belle Isle to Bramley Town End route and is about to turn into Middleton Road. The photograph was taken on 19 April 1960, ten days before the bus was taken out of service.
W.D.Wilson/L.T.H.S.

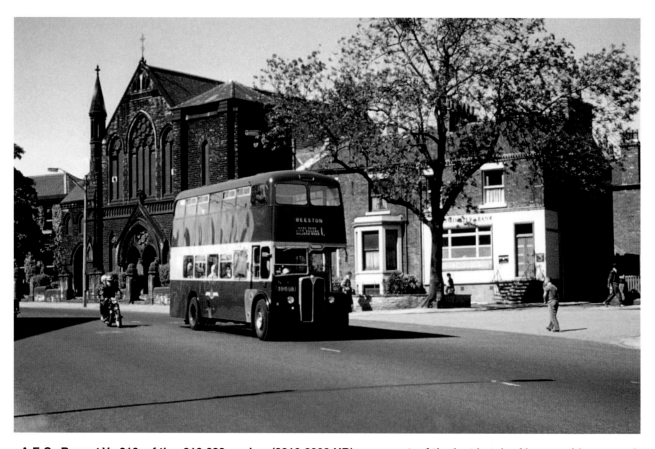

A.E.C. Regent V 910 of the 910-923 series (3910-3923 UB) was part of the last batch of buses with exposed radiators to be delivered to the Leeds City Transport undertaking. It is seen here in Woodhouse Lane on route 1 (Lawnswood to Beeston), the tramway replacement service. The date is 24 June 1962. *W.D.Wilson/L.T.H.S.*

the war he served at first with the R.A.S.C. and then with R.E.M.E. being mentioned in dispatches during the North African and Italian Campaigns. At the age of 28 he was promoted to the rank of Colonel and in 1953 was awarded the Army Emergency Reserve Decoration.

On his return to civilian life he joined Birkenhead Transport Department as Chief Engineer and in 1946 became Deputy General Manager. He moved to Barrow-in-Furness as General Manager in 1949. In Leeds, Lord was appointed at a salary of £3,315 a year, rising to £4,055.

From November 1959 to the resignation of Findlay, apart from a number of timetable alterations on various services, there had also been some modifications to bus routes. On 21 February 1960 the city terminus of service 65 (Rockingham Street-Pudsey) was transferred to the Central Bus Station. As discussed in Chapter 90, the Rockingham Street Bus Station proved to be a temporary affair, a shopping complex, the Merrion Centre being built on the site. The transfer of the 65's left three bus services, 23, 33 and 36, running from Rockingham Street. This was reduced to two when the 23 (Rockingham Street–Intake) buses were transferred to the Central Bus Station on 3 July 1960. The bus station was finally closed on 1 January 1961 when the 33 (Rockingham Street-Cookridge) and 36 (Rockingham Street-Tinshill) city terminal points were moved to the Central Bus Station.

On 20 October 1958, as well as Daimlers 502-531, fourteen A.E.C. Regent V had also been ordered. These had 30 feet long M.C.C.W. "Orion" type 71-seat bodies and were the last buses to be delivered during Findlay's managership.

The interior finish of the new buses was superior to that on previous batches of buses with "Orion" bodies. There was a new type of window surround inside the saloons, similar to that on Roe bodies delivered from 1956. There were also heaters in both saloons. Numbered 910-923 (3910-3923 UB), they were fitted

with new more powerful engines, the AV 590 9·6 litre engine with monocontrol. They had exposed radiators and were the last buses to be delivered with this feature. All subsequent buses had concealed radiators. 910-923 entered service in May and June 1960, and in September of that year the seating capacity of the upper saloon was reduced by one seat. This was in response to a directive from the N.J.I.C. or National Joint Industrial Council for the Transport Industry.

The N.J.I.C. declared that up to eight standing passengers could be carried on vehicles seating up to 70, five on 71 to 78 seaters and none on vehicles seating more than 78. From August to October 1960 all the other 71-seat buses in Leeds, (221-291 and 502-531), were converted to 70-seaters by Charles H. Roe Ltd. The first double seat on the nearside of the upper saloon was removed. It was replaced with a single seat. The double seats were retained in stock by Roe, and reused two years later on new Leeds buses.

On Tuesday morning, 19 July 1960, 922 left Leeds on loan to Aberdeen Corporation. It ran in passenger service in Aberdeen, returning to Leeds on 31 July.

Beginning in August 1960 the Leyland PD3/5 buses (221-291) were fitted with heaters. This series of buses had been provided with all the necessary fittings when built, but the actual heating units were not fitted. The buses were returned to the builders, Roe, two at a time, and the work was completed in June 1961.

In July 1960 Leyland PD3/5 249 had its Leyland 0·600 engine replaced by a new "Power Plus" engine type B600. The new engine developed 140 b.h.p. in comparison with 125 b.h.p. for the 0·600. Following the fitting of its new engine, 249 underwent fuel consumption comparative tests with Daimler CVG6LX 502.

With the introduction of the A.E.C. Regent V, 910-923, the remaining Leyland PD1 were taken out of service. An exception was 331, which had been fitted with a Leyland PD2 0·600 engine in 1948. It lasted over two years

Daimler CVG6LX/30 530 on tramway replacement service 2, Moortown to Dewsbury Road, at the Barrack Street bus stop in Chapeltown Road. The date is 25 July 1962 and St. Michael's Square, the property on the left, was demolished shortly after this photograph was taken. *Author*.

At first on weekdays the new number 9 Ring Road service was worked by double deckers working from Headingley Garage. They were usually A.E.C. Regent III buses and 744, still with its old style destination indicator, was photographed on the Ring Road at Whitkirk. The date is 29 June 1964. *Author.*

longer than the other buses of this type, being withdrawn on 31 July 1962.

In the period from Findlay's retirement to Thomas Lord taking office, there had been one or two alterations or extensions to bus services.

There was a special service to "Adel Towers", a £5,000 Show House, which was a prize in a competition organised by one of the local newspapers, the 'Yorkshire Evening News'. This was a service operated on a short period licence from the Central Bus Station to St. Helen's Lane, Adel, near to the Show House. The service began on 27 September and ran daily at approximately hourly intervals until 4 December 1960. The route was via Eastgate, The Headrow, Woodhouse Lane, Headingley Lane, Otley Road, Weetwood Lane and Long Causeway to St. Helen's Lane. Leyland PS1 28 normally worked the service and displayed a destination label "YORKSHIRE EVENING NEWS SHOW HOUSE".

A major new bus service, the longest in Leeds, began operation on Sunday, 30 October 1960. This route, service number 9, traversed the northern Ring Road of Leeds and ran from Whitkirk to Bradford Road, Pudsey.

The idea of running buses along the Ring Road was not new. There had been a pre-war service, 79, which ran from Wellington Hill, Wetherby Road, via the Ring Road, to Horsforth. It had run on Sundays only and was withdrawn on 10 September 1939, soon after the outbreak of World War II.

During 1959 work was in progress on the construction of the section of Ring Road from Rodley Lane to Swinnow and the new service was to run on part of this extension. An application to run buses on the Ring Road from Whitkirk to Rodley Lane was made to the Yorkshire Traffic Commissioners and consent was received on 22 September 1959. The consent covered 12·45 miles of the Ring Road and was said to be "only the start of what was intended would eventually be a round-city service on the Ring Road." When completed it was anticipated that the road would be about 29 miles in length. With the completion of the Rodley-Swinnow section, the Ring Road would be complete from Whitkirk in the east of the city anticlockwise to Middleton in the south. No date for the construction of the final south eastern part from Middleton to Whitkirk was given. The extension from Middleton involved the construction of an expensive viaduct and a major crossing of the River Aire. At the time of writing, 47 years later, this section has not been built. It appears to have been superseded by the A1/M1 motorway link, from Stourton to Hook Moor, which traverses part of its route. It seems unlikely that the south eastern section of the Ring Road will ever be completed.

An application for buses to run on the Ring Road from Rodley Lane and the newly completed part to Bradford Road, Pudsey, was made in March 1960 and approved soon afterwards. The total length of the route was now about 14 miles.

There had been objections to the Corporation proposals from the Farsley Omnibus Company, which operated a bus service from Rodley to Horsforth. To protect the company, passengers were not picked up on journeys to Pudsey after leaving the Stanhope Arms, Horsforth, while on journeys from Pudsey, passengers who wished to alight before this point were not carried. This was an experimental arrangement only and the restrictions were lifted on 20 August 1961.

The complete route of service 9 from Whitkirk at the junction of Selby Road with the Ring Road was as follows: Ring Road, Halton; Station Road, Ring Road, Cross Gates; Barwick Road, York Road, Ring Road, Seacroft, Shadwell, Moortown, Meanwood, Weetwood, West Park, Broadway, and the Ring Road, Pudsey, to Bradford Road. It was operated from Headingley Garage with single deck buses on Saturdays and Sundays and double deckers during the week, usually A.E.C. Regent III. The frequency was two hourly throughout the week, being altered to hourly during weekday peak hours. Much of the route was outside the city boundary and the fare for the full journey was 1s.0d. This was the highest fare on any Leeds bus service with the exception of the night buses. There was short working to and from West Park, used when buses were coming from and returning to Headingley Garage.

The Ring Road service proved popular and from 2 January 1961 two additional journeys were operated. Owing to the introduction of the new service 9, the "shopper's" section of service 39 from Selby Road and Barwick Road via the Ring Road, Halton, Station Road and Cross Gates Lane, was withdrawn after Saturday, 29 October 1960.

Beginning on Sunday, 2 January 1961, the number 16 peak period (Monday to Friday) service from City Square to North Parkway, Seacroft, was extended via Ramshead Drive, Ramshead Approach and Coal Road to a new terminus at the junction of Coal Road with the Ring Road. There had been objections from the West Yorkshire Road Car Company, which, for a number of years, had run a service from its Vicar Lane Bus Station to the same point. From 2 January the West Yorkshire buses were cut back to Stanks Lane North.

Returning now to the new General Manager, Thomas Lord, one of his first actions was to order more buses. In March tenders were invited for 25 rear-entrance, five front-entrance double deck buses and five single deckers. On 19 June 1961 tenders were accepted as follows:

A.E.C.	5 single deck chassis	£11,277 10s.0d.
Roe	5 single deck bodies	£14,075 0s. 0d.
A.E.C.	10 double deck chassis	£25,427 10s.0d.
Leyland	10 double deck chassis	£25,494 12s 6d.
Daimler	10 double deck chassis	£28,670 0s.0d.
Roe	15 double deck rear-entrance bodies	£42,570 0s. 0d.
M.C.W.	10 double deck rear-entrance bodies	£30,305 0s, 0d.
Roe	5 double deck front-entrance bodies	£16,345 0s. 0d.

The buses were to be purchased by a new method – out of revenue. It was to be 1962, however, before they were delivered.

A problem faced by many transport undertakings was loan charges. Whenever a batch of new vehicles was acquired it was customary to charge these to the capital account. Funds for the purchase were provided by the Government in the form of a loan with heavy interest charges, repayable over a period of years.

From 1959 the Transport Department tried to get over the loan problem by purchasing new buses out of revenue. The first buses to be acquired by this method were A.E.C. Reliance single deckers, 37 and 38, and the last by the old method, 910-923. From then on and for the next few years all new buses were purchased out of revenue. Thomas Lord, in his first annual report, said:

"It is hoped that the financial position of the undertaking in the future will be maintained at a level which will allow provision being made annually for replacement out of revenue."

'Annual Report of General Manager', 31 March 1961.

In 1961 the total loan debt of the undertaking was £1,279,000. Alderman Rafferty said they were hoping after a five-year period to wipe out the loan debt and then "to be able to achieve stability in fares on the city's buses."

The loan charges extended to 1981, but by the disposal of some capital assets it was hoped to clear the debt quickly. The policy was to sell Donisthorpe Street Bus Works and also Hunslet Garage.

"This would be part of a policy of cutting out waste mileage and employing staff living on the housing estates, by providing depots and garages on the perimeter of the city. After five years it is intended to meet all expenditure of the Transport Department out of revenue."

'Yorkshire Evening News', 16 October 1961.

In the meantime there had been some developments elsewhere on the transport system. On 31 May 1961 a "revolutionary" experimental system of closed-circuit television came into operation. This was to monitor congestion and traffic queues and a camera was set up in the Corn Exchange area. The idea was to make maximum

From 10 August to 20 September 1960, buses on the 45 route, Harehills-Wortley, were diverted from Dixon Lane via Lower Wortley Road, Kellett Lane and Kellett Road owing to the laying of electricity cables in Dixon Lane. A.E.C. Reliance 38 (8738 UA) was photographed in Kellett Lane, Wortley, on 21 August. *W.D.Wilson/L.T.H.S.*

On 26 February 1961 route 74 (Belle Isle-Beckett's Park) was extended from Beckett's Park to the new housing estate at Moor Grange near West Park. The 1949-built "one-off" A,E.C. Regent III 450 with its Park Royal/Roe body is at the terminus in Latchmere Crest, Moor Grange, on 15 May 1965. The bus was withdrawn from service a few weeks later on 25 June. *Author.*

use of the buses and crews available, pictures being relayed by underground cables to monitors in a central control room at he Swinegate Head Office. A new 625-line television system gave "astonishingly clear" pictures of the queues. Lord commented:

"Much of this queuing is caused when buses are delayed by traffic congestion. It is frustrating to passengers and crews.

We are always on the look out for means of saving money and increasing efficiency. I have to try to cushion the Department against an increase in the annual wage bill of £92,700, and closed-circuit television might help."

'Yorkshire Evening Post', 31 May 1961.

Lord said that the equipment was the first of its type in the country. There would be a saving of over £2,000 per annum in the wages costs of three inspectors. "If they could cut out of service just one bus, costing £2,300 a year to operate, it would have proved worthwhile."

The system was supplied by Pye Communications Ltd. After a trial, three weeks later, on 19 June, the Transport Committee agreed to hire the system from Pye for a minimum period of two years at a cost of £1,150 per annum.

Three remote-control cameras mounted on 22 feet high poles were set up in the city centre at the Corn Exchange, Briggate and City Square. The system finally came into operation on 12 January 1962.

"A traffic inspector panning by remote control a camera 200 yards away, found a lengthening queue and called for an additional bus. It arrived within two or three minutes. "And that," said the Chief Traffic Officer, Mr. J.B. Gill, " is the way to achieve passenger contentment."

'The Guardian', 13 January 1962.

There was widespread publicity on television and throughout the press. But there was concern from the trades unions and some members of the public over the Orwellian nature of the scheme. Alderman Rafferty emphatically stated that the department was not interested in being "Big Brother" or in watching courting couples propping up doorways at night. "We are interested only in running this system efficiently and economically," he said.

Prior to the adoption of closed-circuit television, the Department relied on inspectors in patrol cars and radio telephones. These had been introduced a few years earlier.

During 1961 a number of alterations and extensions to bus services took place.

From 26 February service 74 (Belle Isle-Beckett's Park) was extended from the Beckett's Park terminus at Old Oak Lawn to Latchmere Crest, Moor Grange, via a tortuous route through the new Moor Grange Housing Estate traversing Old Oak Drive, Butcher Hill, Old Farm Approach, Old Farm Drive, and Latchmere Drive. To reverse at the terminus, buses continued down Latchmere Crest and reversed at the junction with Latchmere View. From the same date a peak hour short working to the old 75 terminus at the junction of Spen Lane and Queenswood Drive was introduced.

Old Farm Drive was very narrow and, in an attempt to use a route more suitable for buses, from 25 June 1961 buses were altered to run via Old Farm Approach and Latchmere Drive instead of Old Farm Drive.

A fortnight earlier, from 11 June, service 33 (Central Bus Station-Cookridge) was extended from its terminus at Moseley Wood Lane, Cookridge. Until this time Green Lane had ended at Moseley Wood Lane, but was extended in a south westerly direction along the line of a footpath in Moseley Wood. A new private housing estate was under construction, which resulted in the destruction of most of the wood. As sections were completed the bus route was extended along the new stretch of Green Lane. The first part (two streets) was along Green Lane to a new terminus at Moseley Wood Green. A year later, on 21 June 1962, the service was further extended along the new Green Lane 80 yards to the next street, Kirkwood Drive. A much more substantial extension took place on 21 October 1962 when the 33 service was extended the full length of new Green Lane to the other end of Moseley Wood and into an existing road, Wood Hill Road, the new terminus being at Wood Hill Gardens. The frequencies were improved at peak periods on Mondays to Fridays and on Saturday mornings and afternoons. Saturday services on the 36 Tinshill route were improved at the same time. More new housing and hence increased patronage led to later journeys being introduced on Mondays to Fridays and Sundays. This improvement took place on 4 February 1963.

From 17 September 1961 two route alterations took effect. Service 31 (Gledhow-New Farnley) was extended at the Gledhow end to serve a new housing estate at Brackenwood adjacent to Lidgett Lane. The alteration led to the abandonment of the difficult section through Gledhow. The section of route abandoned was from the top of Jackson Avenue and via Gledhow Avenue, Roper Grove, Roper Avenue, James Avenue, The Drive and Lidgett Place to the terminus at St. Edmund's Church. The short section along Lidgett Park Grove and The Drive used on the inward journey was also discontinued.

The revised route from Jackson Avenue was along Gledhow Avenue, Lidgett Lane, and a new road, Brackenwood Drive, to a terminus at another new road, Lincombe Drive. At weekday peak hours there was a short working from City Square to Gledhow, buses reversing at Gledhow Avenue. However, following a petition and protests from residents in the Lidgett Place area, from 28 September the buses short-worked to the old terminus at St. Edmund's Church. Buses to St. Edmund's Church ran from Lidgett Lane via North Park Avenue in both directions.

The long standing arrangement (see pages 880 and 913 of Volume 3) whereby certain buses were extended during school term times from St. Edmund's Church to the Ring Road, was continued. Buses now ran over the new Gledhow section to St. Edmund's Church and then joined their former route at Talbot Road.

The other alteration on 17 September concerned service 47 (Central Bus Station–Old Farnley), which was rerouted to serve another new housing estate, the Cow Close Estate, sited adjacent to the Farnley Ring Road. Formerly buses had run via the Ring Road, Tong Road and Butt Lane, but were now diverted through the estate via Whincover Drive and Cross Lane.

A further alteration to service 47 took place on 28 January 1962 when the section between the Cattle Market and Ringways Service Station was changed to run via Gelderd Road and the Ring Road, Wortley, instead of Whitehall Road. From the same date an increased morning peak hour frequency was operated from the Bus Station.

From Monday, 4 December 1961, new turning arrangements were instituted at the terminus of service 68, Foundry Lane. A new roundabout had been constructed at the junction of Foundry Lane, Oakwood Lane and Amberton Road and buses now used it as a turning circle. Formerly they had proceeded to a stopping place in Oakwood Lane, but now ran to a new terminus in Amberton Road. Buses then returned to the city via Amberton Road and Oak Tree Drive before joining Oakwood Lane.

From 9 January 1962, outward buses on service 56, (Central Bus Station-North Lane), were diverted via Woodhouse Lane and Clarendon Road owing to road works in University Road. Until a short time before, this section of Clarendon Road had been named Reservoir Street. The road works were in connection with an extension of the University buildings over the Woodhouse Lane end of University Road. On Friday, 16 February 1962 University Road was permanently closed to buses

Of the 1946-built Leyland PD1 buses, 331 lasted two years longer than the other vehicles of this type. This was because it was fitted with a Leyland PD2 (0.600) engine in 1948. When withdrawn in 1962 it was the oldest bus in the fleet. It is at the bottom of Armley Road on 18 September 1960. *W.D.Wilson/L.T.H.S.*

and 56 route buses in both directions ran via Woodhouse Lane and Clarendon Road. Readers should refer to page 878 of Volume 3 for a photograph of a bus at the lower end of University Road. Running times on the route were increased by one minute to allow for the greater distance of the diversion.

A novel feature on Leeds buses was introduced experimentally in 1961. These were illuminated advertisement panels. A quotation for £155 had been accepted from Charles H. Roe in January 1961 for one bus only, and the vehicle selected was one of the Daimler CVG6LX, 503. Advertising "Typhoo Tea", it was fitted on the offside and entered service in April. The advert could not be fitted on the nearside because of likely tree damage. The experiment was successful for in September, 502 was similarly fitted, but this time advertising "Littlewoods Pools". Further buses of this type, 504-507, were later fitted. All carried "Littlewoods Pools" advertisements and were let for a minimum period of three years. From 31 March 1962, 502 was loaned to the Huddersfield Joint Omnibus Committee for trials which lasted a month. It returned to Leeds on 30 April. While at Huddersfield it ran on routes from Manchester Street Bus Station. These were routes 1 and 2 (Golcar circulars) and the 47 (Holmbridge and Holmfirth) services.

During 1961 and 1962 nearly all the buses in Leeds were fitted with rubber floors to the platforms.

No buses were withdrawn in 1961 and no new vehicles delivered. In 1962 several buses were taken out of service. 331 (JUG 631), the last of the Leyland PD1 –the oldest bus in the fleet, A.E.C. Regent 414, the first bus of the 401-415 series (JUG 634-648) and several Crossleys were withdrawn. 331 went to North's, dealers, of Leeds, being resold for use elsewhere. 414 was transferred to the Learner fleet. The Crossleys also went to North's and most were broken up soon afterwards.

The withdrawal of these buses coincided with the delivery of the first of the vehicles ordered in June 1961. These were the five front-entrance 30 feet long Daimler CVG6LX/30 buses with Roe bodies. The last buses to be delivered with front entrance bodies had been the two A.E.C. "Q" buses of 1933 and the five received a lot of publicity in the local press. This was in part due to the fact that at the same time the former Kirkstall Road Tramway Works was reopened for bus use.

The Works was officially reopened on 14 May 1962 and the five "guinea pig" buses, to quote the 'Yorkshire Evening News', were launched. The public was invited to ride in them and submit its views to the Transport Department.

"They seat 70 passengers, with eight standing. They are cosier, the doors retaining the heat better and cleaner because the doors reduce the amount of dust entering the vehicle.

They are brighter due to the fluorescent lighting and to transparent amber panels in the roof. The stairs are placed immediately opposite the entrance and behind the driver, enabling the driver to see the entrance and operate the doors.

The buses which cost £6,380 each, are being used initially on the Leeds-Bradford service to test the reaction of passengers travelling on a longer than normal city journey.

A Transport Department spokesman explained that this was necessary before similar vehicles were put into service on the busier local services. He pointed out that the public must bear in mind the suggestions must be based on a forward-entrance bus, as experience elsewhere has shown that rear-entrance doors slowed up services, because conductors had always to be at the rear at stopping places to operate the doors.

Busy local services could only be operated if the doors were placed at the front where the driver could operate them. And he added a word of advice to the public about difficulties experienced with the new type of bus. "Generally speaking, these forward-entrance buses with doors do tend to slow up operations when passengers are boarding and leaving because people automatically walk to the back of the bus."

"It would save time if passengers learned to recognise the new type of bus. We have tried to make them recognisable by placing the route number above the destination board instead of at the end of it."

'Yorkshire Evening News', 15 May 1962.

Interior panelling was mainly of Formica and the seats were in green moquette with a fawn pattern and edged with green leather. The seat backs had handrails, a new feature in Leeds. Another novel idea was the fluorescent lighting. This type of lighting had been experimentally tried in 1948 on the first 8ft.0in. wide bus in Leeds, 600, but had been unsuccessful and was soon removed.

Numbered 572-576 (572-576 CNW) the first use of the buses was on 14 May upon the reopening of Kirkstall Road Works. 572, 573 and 574 carried members of the City Council and guests from a luncheon at the Leeds Civic Hall to the Works. All entered passenger service on the 72, Leeds-Bradford route, on 27 and 28 May 1962. They were restricted to this route for most of the early part of their lives.

Inspector Henry Heyworth, in an article for 'The Leeds and District News' for May 1962, thought that from the passenger's point of view the vehicles were first class. He described the riding qualities as excellent, "the beautifully finished interior giving a ride comparable to a coach." One fault was the flywheel cover, which protruded into the lower saloon and could easily be stepped upon by anyone descending the staircase. He said that loading and unloading was slow as passengers tended to board one at a time.

During 1962 A.E.C. Regent V 910 had the distinction of being featured in a film; "The Sporting Life". The film revolved around a young rugby footballer and filming took place in Leeds and Wakefield.

The next batch of new buses appeared on 1 August 1962. These were five Daimler CVG6LX30 double deckers with Roe bodies similar to 572-576, but with rear entrances. Numbered 577-581 (577-581 CNW), the general design and finish was similar to the front entrance buses. They were fitted with the new type destination indicators, but with the destination positioned over the three-digit number blinds, at both front and rear.

There was extensive use of Formica panelling internally, but the bodies did not have all the elaborate fittings that were provided on the front entrance buses. Old type seating was fitted in place of seat frames with built-in grab rails along the top. Some second hand seating was used in the upper saloon and bell pushes were fitted in the lower saloon in place of a strip bell. More space was provided for passenger's luggage than on any other buses in the fleet. This was achieved by having one less seat in the lower saloon. The offside wheel arch seat had only three passengers, while there was an extra seat in the upper saloon. In comparison with the other 30 feet long Roe double deckers, there were only six instead of eight ventilators to the upper saloon.

Alderman Rafferty was impressed with the new buses. On the Transport Committee's annual tour of inspection on 1 August, he described the amber glass roofs and fluorescent lighting as "summer in winter." "You not only get the effect of the sunshine, but you get heating as well. You can go upstairs in these buses in winter and feel you are riding about in summer."

The new stronger seating, he hoped, would put a stop to seat slashing. "There won't be the satisfaction of bursting the upholstery," he said. "Seat slashing was a problem and was very prevalent soon after Christmas when children had been given penknives and the like as presents."

Rafferty said that in future the city's bus fleet would be known as the "Leeds Sleek Line". This prediction, however, did not happen.

Also in August 1962, six of a series of ten A.E.C. Regent V buses were delivered. Numbered 924-933 (924-933 CUG) these buses differed from earlier Regent V in having A.E.C. "new look" fronts. Until this time all Regents in Leeds had exposed radiators. The new vehicles had the radiators concealed.

The Roe bodies seated 70 passengers and were identical in deign and finish to Daimler CVG6LX30 577-581. Once again old type seats were fitted and as with 577-581, the seats to the upper saloon on the nearside were those recovered from the older 30 feet long vehicles in the fleet, 221-291, 502-531 and 910-923, when these buses had their seating capacities reduced from 71 to 70 in 1960.

The rest of the buses in the 924-933 series entered service on 1 October 1962 and were joined by a batch of five A.E.C. Reliance single deckers. These were numbered 39-43 and registered 839-843 CUM.

The single deck buses had been inspected by the Transport Committee at the Roe Works on the Committee's tour of inspection in August. One of the buses, 43, was exhibited at the Commercial Motor Show at Earl's Court from 21 to 29 September 1962. The buses were designed specifically for use on the new number 9 Ring Road service and were one-man operated. One-man operation had been a feature of the small single deck buses that had been used in Leeds in the early 1920's, but had not been employed since then.

By dispensing with bus conductors cost savings could be made and 39-43 marked the first step in this process, which was to take about 14 years to complete.

The Roe bodies were 30ft.8in. long and 8ft. 2½in. wide and seated 41 passengers. The buses were longer than normal and took advantage of a 1961 Ministry of Transport directive, which authorised an increase in the "box"

dimensions of buses of 36 feet by 8ft. 2½in. A.E.C. was the first manufacturer in Britain to adopt the new legislation, but it was to be another four years before the first 36 feet buses appeared in Leeds.

The new buses had composite bodies with front and centre entrance electrically-operated "jack knife" doors independently operated by the driver. The panelling around the windows was of beige metal with Formica imitation mahogany finish panels at the side. Other features were fluorescent lighting, two amber roof lights, two under floor heaters and a wrap round windscreen. 'The Leeds and District Transport News' thought that the bodies were of a "very smart design, with none of the rather square features of the previous buses." A detrimental feature was the rather thin seat cushions. Provision was made for a ticket issuing and change-giving machine for the driver.

Before entering service in Leeds, one, 39, was loaned to Wolverhampton Corporation from 1 October 1962 for a few weeks. The five buses entered service on route 9, the Ring Road service, on Sunday, 2 December 1962, bus 39 making the first journeys. One-man buses worked all duties on Saturdays and Sundays and also the basic mid-week service. At morning and evening peak periods the buses were supplemented by "Duplicate" double deckers usually operating short workings, arranged to coincide with the various schools and works on the route. There was heavy peak hour traffic to and from a new industrial estate at Coal Road and also at Horsforth. The service was improved and was now half hourly at peak periods and hourly at other times, including weekends.

The journey time between Whitkirk and Bradford Road was 45 minutes with a layover time of 15 minutes at either terminus. The through fare remained at 1s.0d. At first buses ran late, partly due to passengers being unfamiliar with the pay-as-you-enter system and bus drivers not being used to collecting fares. However, the teething troubles were soon overcome and the service became successful.

The ten A.E.C. Regent V, 924-933 (924-933 CUG), were the first in Leeds with the "new look" fronts. Before 1962 all Regents had exposed radiators. On 17 July 1965 930 is passing under the viaduct in Kirkstall Road. *Author.*

In 1962 the "Pride" of the Leeds bus fleet were the five front-entrance Roe-bodied Daimler CVG6LX/30 buses 572-576. They were well appointed internally and initially were used almost exclusively on the Leeds-Bradford service 72. This photograph was taken on 5 May 1971 and shows 574 in Regent Street on service 52, the Meanwood-Morley route. *W.D.Wilson/L.T.H.S.*

In June 1961 orders had been placed for ten Leyland PD3/5 chassis with exposed radiators, but in December the order was changed to the PD3A/2 type with radiators concealed. All entered service in October and December 1962. Numbered 311-320, (311-320 DUA), they were fitted with 70-seat rear entrance Weymann bodies. The new Leylands were the first of that type in the fleet with a modern front and concealed radiators. The fronts were of fibreglass and similar to Leyland lorries of the period. The Weymann bodies, which were of the "Orion" type, were finished in a better manner than previous "Orion" bodies. There was much Formica interior panelling with cream coloured window surrounds and a light green strip at roof level. The usual "Orion" front and rear roof domes were fitted, but the panelling tapered, resulting in an improved appearance. Except for the fronts, externally the bodies bore a close resemblance to A.E.C. Regent V 910-923.

Although 30 new double deck buses were delivered in 1962, only 17 buses were withdrawn. This was accounted for by the fact that certain services had recently been increased in frequency at peak periods. These included services 23, 31, 33, 36, 38, 40, 47 and 70. The buses withdrawn comprised 331 and 414, already discussed, and fifteen of the Crossleys, 702-713, 718, 719 and 721. Also delicensed at the end of December 1962 were the two Leyland PS1 single deckers 27 and 28. Until the middle of December, 28 had been in regular use on route 45 and was sold to Charles H. Roe Ltd. in February 1963 for use by the firm's sports club. Due to a shortage of buses, 27 was later reinstated.

In addition to service alterations or extensions already discussed, a number of other minor alterations took place during 1962. On 2 September service 24 (Central Bus Station-Swarcliffe) was extended from Mill Green Gardens via Stanks Lane North to a new terminus near Eastwood Drive.

A road, which did not have a bus service, was Clarendon Road in the Woodhouse district, from its junction with University Road to Great George Street. In September 1962 Councillor May Sexton asked for the number 56 service to be diverted along Clarendon Road. The Transport Committee refused the request, Alderman Rafferty said that "they did not wish to divert the best paying route in the city."

May Sexton was not happy with the decision and on 3 October 1962 the City Council received a deputation and a petition of over 600 signatures from residents. There was also support from Leeds Grammar School, the Roman Catholic College, patients and visitors attending the Leeds Maternity Hospital, two nursing homes and two hostels. The matter was referred back to the Transport Committee, but again refused. Clarendon Road was later extended through to Park Lane and buses did eventually run along the road.

The Committee also refused a request from the Jewish Housing Estate Tenant's Association at Queenshill for a bus service from the estate to Roundhay Park. Application was, however, made by the Corporation to the Traffic Commissioners for two new bus services. One was an extension of the Lawnswood bus route to Kingsley Drive, Adel. The other was to serve new housing estates in the Wigton Lane area of Alwoodley where 1,000 new houses had been constructed. In October 1962 there were some improvements in the Moortown area. From the 28th, service 32 (Pudsey-Carr Manor) was extended at the Carr Manor end via Stonegate Road to Harrogate Road, Moortown.

On the same date service 70 (Central Bus Station-Primley Park) was diverted to run via Scott Hall Road, Stainbeck Lane, Stainbeck Road, and Carr Manor Road to King Lane. An improved frequency was provided at both peak and off-peak periods.

From 13 November 1962 limited stop conditions were

Ten Weymann-bodied Leyland PD3A/2 buses, 311-320, appeared in October and December 1962. They had concealed radiators and new style fibreglass fronts similar to those on Leyland lorries of the period. 317 was photographed in Cross Gates Road on 2 June 1963. Behind the bus is the dilapidated former tramway reservation with an abandoned motor car. In the background the new dual carriageway in York Road is taking shape. *W.D.Wilson/L.T.H.S.*

The five A.E.C. Reliances, 39-43, were the first one-man operated buses in Leeds and were purchased specifically for the number 9 Ring Road bus service. They all entered passenger service on 2 December 1962. 40 was photographed about three quarters of a mile from the view of 317 above. It is on the Ring Road at the Cross Gates roundabout. *W.D.Wilson/L.T.H.S.*

introduced on service 23 (Central Bus Station-Intake) at the teatime peak period on Mondays to Fridays.

36 new buses had entered service in 1962 and on 16 April a further 40 buses were ordered. This was the start of a comprehensive scheme for bus replacement, which appears to have been initiated by the new General Manager, Thomas Lord.

On 19 November the Transport Committee approved a £1,861,000 five-year capital expenditure programme for the period from 1963 to 1968. This included provision for the purchase of 40 new buses per year over the period. Alderman Rafferty said the city would have a "sunshine bus fleet" as new vehicles would have amber tinted glazing in the roofs, fluorescent strip lighting and heaters. He said it was likely more buses would be fitted with front entrances and "they hoped to improve on bus design year by year."

Included within the capital projects were a new open parking area for buses in Sovereign Street, a new bus garage at Middleton and a three-storey canteen and social club in Sovereign Street. It was hoped that all this expenditure would be met out of revenue.

The period from 1958 to 1962 had been one of stability for the Transport Department. There had been a fare increase in 1957, which had resulted in a plunge in the number of passengers from 221 million to 208 million. From then onwards fares had been static. In 1962, in spite of a wages award, which cost the Department an extra £60,000 a year, the Transport Committee managed to defer fare increases for over a year until September 1963 when a partial fare rise took place. The Department had retained the 2d. fare for one stage only and Alderman Rafferty thought that Leeds gave an "excellent bus ride" in regard to the fare paid and distance travelled.

From 1958 to 1962 passenger numbers had declined by only two million from 208,446,621 in 1958 to 206,028,866 in 1962. Rafferty attributed this small 1% loss to the retention of the 2d. fare. He said that the loss on other transport undertakings over the same period had been 3%. In each of the four years the Department had made a small profit and the average fare paid by each passenger had risen slightly from 3·723d, to 3·990d. This stability was to last for another three years and is discussed in the next chapter.

1963 saw the last of the Crossleys in Leeds. 703 was photographed on 22 July 1956 on the first day of the route 15 Whingate bus service. It is in the car park of the Traveller's Rest public house at Hill Top Road near Whingate. At that time this was the regular turning point for the route. *W.D.Wilson/L.T.H.S.*

CHAPTER 79

The Buses 1963 to 1964

Prior to the formal decision on 19 November 1962 that 40 buses per year were to be purchased over the following five years, 40 buses had already been ordered on 16 April of that year. They comprised the following:

15 double deck A.E.C. Regent chassis £38,452 10s.
10 double deck Leyland chassis £26,470.
15 double deck Daimler chassis £43,155.
30 double deck Roe bodies £97,670.
10 double deck Weymann bodies £33,230.

Delivery of the order commenced in late August 1963. The first were the 15 Daimler CVG6LX buses with rear entrance Roe 70-seat bodies. The bodies were 30 feet long and when tenders were invited the specification had called for a width of 8ft. 2$\frac{1}{2}$in. However, the buses delivered were 8 feet wide.

The Roe bodies differed considerably in detail from the earlier 1962 deliveries. The most notable exterior difference was the destination indicators. Although new wider destination blinds along with three digit number blinds were employed, one large rectangular piece of glass was used to cover them. The space not required was masked off in the same manner as destination blind modifications then being made to the existing bus fleet. Both saloons had seats with handrails across the backs, similar to those fitted to front entrance buses, 572-576, but had slightly thicker cushions. Strip bell pushes were fitted in the lower saloons, which also had six fluorescent lights with plastic covers capable of illuminating advertisements as well as the saloon. The lights were mounted over the saloon windows and not staggered as previously. The upper saloon lights also had plastic covers and the now "standard", amber glass or "sunshine" roofs were fitted. There was extensive use of "bleached mahogany" Formica for the internal linings and seat backs. The window surrounds were of a brown material and a similar shape to those used in Roe-bodied A.E.C. Regent III from 451 upwards. The Daimlers were allocated the fleet numbers 582-596 (582-596 FUM) and 596 had been selected in connection with the reopening of the Central Bus Station on 30 September 1963. This event is discussed later.

The new vehicles were featured in a special article in the 'Yorkshire Evening News' on 27 August 1963, a few weeks before the newspaper ceased publication. The newspaper referred to bus interiors quickly becoming stained with nicotine fumes and other atmospheric pollutants. It was impressed with the white plastic finish to the ceilings, the use of melamine and amber glazing.

"This will help to maintain a brighter atmosphere for, it is hoped, the life of the bus, particularly as the material is easily cleaned."

Interior painting was now virtually eliminated and hence maintenance costs. The floors of the buses were of smooth linoleum, protected by a composition material in the gangways, platform and stairs. They were easy to clean, and a big improvement on the wooden slats that had been used on the tramcars and earlier buses.

There were by now the standard heaters, but their effectiveness was countered by the open rear platform. As was normal, there were no platform doors, the Transport Department stating that on short routes doors were a "nuisance."

However, from the passenger's comfort point of view doors were desirable. They were also cleaner as road dust was not blown into the vehicle. On city services it was not practical to leave rear platform doors under the control of the conductor. Hence came the widespread introduction of front entrance vehicles with doors operated by the driver. It was, however, to be a year or two before Leeds went over to the permanent adoption of this design.

One of the problems with the larger buses that were now appearing was that of weight. An extra ton represented an additional fuel consumption of one mile per gallon. At the time fuel tax was at the rate of 2s.9d. a gallon and this was a significant cost increase when the normal double deck bus averaged only 9 m.p.g. and often had few passengers during the day.

The ten Leyland PD3A/2 buses followed shortly after the Daimlers and all entered service during October 1963. They were numbered 321-330 (321-330 GNW) and had Weymann 70-seat rear entrance bodies and were very similar to 311-320 delivered the year before. One difference was in the seats, which had thicker cushions and handrails over the seat backs. The upper saloon heater was raised up in a similar manner to those fitted to the Roe-bodied buses. The earlier Weymann buses had heaters positioned with the warm air directed upwards towards the roof, whereas the new heaters directed the air down the gangway.

In addition to the Leylands, the new A.E.C. Regent V buses, 934-948 (934-948 GUA), also appeared in October and November 1963. The Roe rear entrance bodies were identical with those fitted on the Daimlers, 582-596.

Comparing the three new types of buses generally, the Roe buses had combined lighting for the lower saloon and illuminated advertisements, whereas the Weymann bodies did not have the latter. The Weymann had the same destination layout as the 1962 deliveries, i.e. a "T" shaped layout with the destination over the three digit number blind. The 1963 Roe-bodied A.E.C. and Daimlers had the combined rectangular glass, as already referred to. The Roe bodies all had strip bell pushes in the lower saloon whereas the Weymann did not have this feature.

As a result of the introduction of these 40 new buses, 32 old vehicles were withdrawn from service. These comprised the remaining Crossleys, 714-717 and 720, all taken out of service on 23 September 1963, "JUG" A.E.C. Regent III, 401-413 and 415 and the first of the "LUA" series of Regent III, 416-428. The oldest buses in the passenger fleet were now 429-450, all dating from 1947-1948.

In comparison with other undertakings, the principal reason that delayed the Leeds Transport Department from ordering larger buses was the Central Bus Station. The Department had just ordered new buses (discussed later), but these would be too large for the existing bus station.

On 17 September 1962 the Transport Committee passed a resolution urging the Finance and Parliamentary Committee to authorise reconstruction work. Alderman Rafferty, the Transport Committee chairman, said that the work had to be completed by the summer of 1963.

"Otherwise the new buses will not be able to operate from the bus station," he added. By that time there would be more of these buses and they wanted to avoid being forced out on to the streets for loading purposes wherever they could.

The Committee want the existing lanes at the Bus Station widening from 18 feet to 24 feet. The new buses are 8ft. 2$\frac{1}{2}$in. wide compared with the 7 feet. width of most of the existing fleet."

'The Yorkshire Post', 18 September 1962.

The bus lanes were said to be too narrow for 8 feet wide buses, although other operators were successfully working buses of this width.

The reconstruction of the Bus Station is discussed in

Daimler CVG6LX 586 was brand new when this photograph was taken on 8 September 1963. It had been in service for six days only. The location is Cross Gates terminus. *W.D.Wilson/L.T.H.S.*

When the Central Bus Station was closed for reconstruction in 1963, there were several interesting diversions along nearby streets. A.E.C. Regent V 789 on the 41 Colton service has just turned from Vicar Lane into Templar Street. The entrance to the Grand Arcade in Vicar Lane can be seen in the background. The date: 20 July 1963. *Author.*

The terminus for the 67 Seacroft service was in Bridge Street and A.E.C. Regent III 620 was photographed on 20 July 1963. The Bridge Street Pentecostal Church on the left was opened in 1930. It still exists. *Author*.

another chapter, but it is perhaps pertinent to discuss the service implications here.

The Central Bus Station closed on 1 July 1963 and was reopened in reconstructed form on 30 September of the same year. In the intervening period all services terminating at the Bus Station were diverted and transferred to nearby streets as follows:

Services 30, 33 and 36 (Otley Road routes), were diverted on inward journeys into Vicar Lane and terminated opposite the West Yorkshire Bus Station. Buses then ran outwards via New Briggate to The Headrow.

Services 34, 35, 37, 43, 69, 70, and King Lane Circus (Scott Hall Road routes) were diverted inwards via New York Road, Vicar Lane and Eastgate and terminated opposite the Yorkshire Hussar.

Services 23, 47 and 65 (Intake, Old Farnley and Pudsey) all terminated in Eastgate, turning at the roundabout at the bottom of Eastgate. Service 65 used its normal stopping place in Eastgate, but the other two services had a temporary stand by the Yorkshire Hussar.

Services 67 and 68 (Easterly Road services) were diverted inwards via New York Road, Vicar Lane and Templar Street, to a terminus in Bridge Street, and then continued outwards to their normal route in Eastgate.

Services 22, 24, 39, 40 and 41 (York Road services) were diverted inwards via New York Road, Vicar Lane, Templar Street, to a terminus in Templar Place, continuing outwards via Lady Lane to their normal routes in Eastgate.

Service 56 (North Lane) terminated outside the Central Bus Station, by the side of Millgarth Street car park.

Works and hospital special services were started in Templar Lane between Templar Street and Lady Lane.

In regard to services operated by private companies; the West Riding and Kippax Motors services, via York Road and Halton, were diverted inwards from the Bus Station via Duke Street and Kirkgate, to terminate and stand in High

Court, by the Parish Church. They then left via The Calls and other narrow streets at the rear of the Parish Church.

West Riding, South Yorkshire and Burrows' buses, which entered Leeds via Hunslet Road, were diverted into York Street, New York Street and Harper Street to Kirkgate, where they stood opposite the Parish Church. West Riding, Yorkshire Traction and Sheffield Corporation services via Dewsbury Road terminated in Sovereign Street.

During the bus station closure Lady Lane (between Templar Lane and Bridge Street) was operated as a one-way street eastbound. As a result buses terminating normally in Eastgate on services 42 and 62 also used New York Road and Vicar Lane for turning purposes.

In October 1962 an application had been made to the Yorkshire Traffic Commissioners to extend the Lawnswood bus route to Kingsley Drive, Adel, and to institute a new bus service to the Wigton Lane area of Alwoodley. Local residents had asked for the services. It had been proposed to run a 20 minute service to Adel from Lawnswood terminus via Otley Road, Holt Lane, Gainsborough Avenue, Kingsley Avenue and back to Otley Road. However, both bus routes conflicted with competing services operated by the West Yorkshire Road Car Company and, in the case of the Adel route, Samuel Ledgard buses also. Both applications had been refused.

From the beginning of 1963 to the reopening of the bus station in September of that year, there had been one or two modifications to other bus services.

From Monday, 8 April 1963 service 24 (Central Bus Station-Swarcliffe) was altered to run via Manston Drive and newly constructed Manston Approach in place of the narrow stretch of Church Lane near Manston Church.

Three weeks later, on 28 April, saw the reintroduction of service number 43, which had been formerly used by the Carr Manor buses. A new timetable and rearrangement of the 37 (Central Bus Station-Shadwell)

1285

route was introduced. A portion of the service at peak hours and on Saturdays ran via Shadwell Lane and also along the Ring Road and Birchwood Hill. Buses showed service number 37 when running along Shadwell Lane in both directions and service 43 for journeys via the Ring Road and Birchwood Hill also in both directions. Off peak, all Shadwell buses ran outward via the 37 route and inward via the 43. Before all outward journeys had operated via Shadwell Lane and inward via Birchwood Hill and the Ring Road, displaying 37 each way.

On 16 June 1963 an extension of the 11 (Gipton-Greenthorpe) service took place at the Greenthorpe end of the route. The service was extended via Pudsey Road, Ring Road, and Swinnow Road to a new terminus at Swinnow House – almost at Lowtown, Pudsey. In general, alternate buses ran through to Swinnow, the others still turning at Greenthorpe. The basic service to Swinnow was every 20 minutes on Mondays to Saturdays with a 30 minute service on Sundays.

17 June 1963 saw the start of a major road improvement in Leeds - the conversion of part of York Road into a dual carriageway. It was the section from Cross Gates Road to Barwick Road and, for the period of construction, the section of York Road as far as Cross Gates Lane was closed. At the time Corporation bus services did not use this part of York Road, but West Yorkshire Road Car Company buses had to be diverted. L.C.T. buses later used the widened section of York Road.

In the period from the reopening of the Bus Station to the end of 1963 two bus services were modified. These were services 50 and 77 both extended on 24 November at the Fairway Hotel end.

Service 50 (Horsforth-Compton Road) was extended from the Fairway Hotel, near Compton Road, via Oak Tree Drive to the Courtier Hotel, Amberton Road. Service 77 (Bramley Town End-Compton Road) was extended from the Fairway Hotel via Foundry Approach to Coldcotes Circus. Both services displayed "GIPTON" as the new terminus. At peak hours short workings were still operated to the Fairway Hotel on each route.

Two senior members of staff retired in 1963. J.B. Gill, the Chief Traffic Officer, and C.E. Grayson, the Chief Finance Officer. Gill had been Chief Traffic Officer from 1 April 1942 replacing his predecessor, H.H. Lancaster, who had been forced to retire on grounds of ill health. Gill's deputy was Arnold Stone, aged 48. Stone had been with the Transport Department from 1933 and Deputy Chief Traffic Officer from 1946. On 5 July 1963 Stone became Chief Traffic Officer. Grayson had joined the Tramways Department in 1926 and had been the Chief Accountant from 1 April 1941 replacing H. Moxon, the former Chief Accountant. Grayson retired on 20 August 1963 and was replaced by his deputy, A.S. Binns. Binns, aged 55, had been with the Department from 1923 and deputy to Grayson from April 1941. Binns retired on 19 September 1972 after 49 years service.

During the latter part of 1963 a remarkable reversal of a national trend became evident. On 31 March 1963 the number of passengers carried annually had been 203,601,298 a three million decline from the previous year. In October it was revealed that the number of passengers, in comparison with the same period the previous year, April to October, had increased by a million. Passengers had been declining steadily from the peak of nearly 253,000,000 in 1950.

"Ald. John Rafferty, chairman of the Leeds Transport Committee, told me yesterday this was contrary to the trend in other large cities. He cited Manchester where, he said, in 1962-63 there was a drop of 5·13% in passengers carried, the largest drop ever recorded in the city.

A.E.C. Regent III 600, the first 8ft. 0in. wide bus in Leeds, turning from New York Road into Vicar Lane on 28 September 1963. The 68 service was diverted during the Bus Station reconstruction. *Author.*

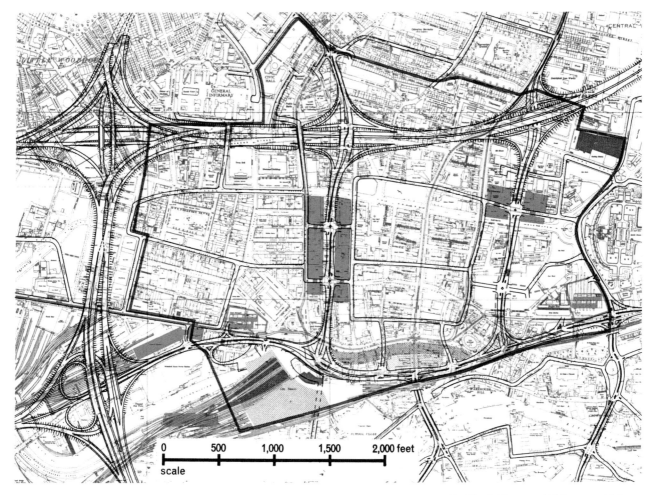

Professor Buchanan's proposals for Leeds City Centre. Buchanan Report. Traffic in Towns, 1963, page 104.

Some Leeds people to whom I spoke yesterday thought that car parking difficulties in the city centre might have something to do with the trend. Others said that the comprehensive network of bus services meant easy access to the city centre.

Ald. Rafferty put the reason down to good management and cheap fares.

"People are becoming conscious of the fact that they can travel more easily and more cheaply in Leeds on the buses than on private vehicles", he added."

'The Yorkshire Post', 22 October 1963.

There had been a major fare increase from 29 September 1957. From then onwards fares had been static and this was probably one of the reasons for the increase in passenger numbers. At the end of the financial year 1964 the passengers carried were recorded as 206,910,170. Due to staff wages increases, costs had subsequently gone up and an application was made to the Yorkshire Traffic Commissioners to increase fares. This was granted and the fare increases took effect from 22 September 1963.

THE BUCHANAN AND OTHER REPORTS

November 1963 saw the publication of an important Government document, which was to have a partial effect on transport in Leeds and on future planning developments. This was the 223-page report prepared by Professor Colin Buchanan and entitled "Traffic in Towns". Buchanan envisaged the physical separation of motor vehicle transport from pedestrian traffic. This was to be achieved by placing the two forms of traffic at different levels. Motor and other traffic would be at street level whereas pedestrians were to be on walkways at a higher level. Buildings were to be adapted to allow pedestrian access at first or even second floor level. The idea was to make the whole of a city, traffic free. One of the most important aspects of city traffic, public transport, was almost totally ignored.

The Minister of Transport, Ernest Marples, described the report as " one of the most penetrating analyses ever made into cities" and Sir Keith Joseph, Minister of Housing and Local Government, said it was a "masterly document." The report was accepted by the Government and recommended for implementation throughout the country.

Buchanan prepared a hypothetical scheme for Leeds, which included an inner ring road and pedestrian walkways in the city centre streets. He envisaged that 70 miles of motorways would be built in Leeds and estimated that the total cost of his Leeds proposals would be £90,000,000. There was to be a motorway at the rear side of the Town Hall on the line of Great George Street, Merrion Street and New York Road, and another along Basinghall Street with five storey car parks on either side. There were to be car parks adjacent to the other motorways and private motor transport was to be discouraged in the city centre. 115 acres or 48% of the central area of the city was to be demolished to make way for motorways. The city centre was to be confined within two small pedestrian areas, one bounded by Great George Street to the north, a motorway adjacent to Queen Street, a motorway on the line of Aire Street and Basinghall Street to the east. The boundaries of the other area were Basinghall Street on the west, a motorway about 50 yards to the south of Boar lane, a motorway about 40 yards from and parallel to Vicar Lane and passing through the middle of the central market, and to the north the motorway along Merrion Street. There was to be an upper level market over the motorway and a bus station underneath, adjacent to the proposed motorway and Vicar Lane.

Buchanan's report was widely praised and eulogized in a leading article in the 'Yorkshire Post'. Certainly if Buchanan's Leeds proposals had been adopted, many of the historic buildings and much of the character of the city would have been lost. A close inspection of the drawings does not indicate any provision for public transport or for servicing buildings in the pedestrian areas. From the architectural and town planning point of view, Buchanan's ideas for Leeds were horrendous. The city would indeed have been totally dominated by the motor car.

Buchanan later said that he would "rebel" at any suggestion of banning car commuters from city centres.

"I tried public transport from my house in Reading to my work in South Kensington and I also tried my car. There is no shadow of doubt that the car won every way."

'The Yorkshire Post', 30 January 1965.

Alderman Rafferty was less impressed with Buchanan's ideas.

"The idea would be to have plenty of car parks on the outer perimeter served by very adequate bus services. Ald. John Rafferty, Chairman of the Transport Committee, said that for the past two years his committee had tried to anticipate what might be the recommendations of the Buchanan report.

"We have gone in for the most modern type of bus with increased carrying capacity and the greatest comfort of passengers," he added. They hoped to convince people that it was cheaper and easier to travel to the city centre by bus than by private car.

The Yorkshire Post', 28 November 1963.

At a meeting held at the Leeds Civic Hall on 31 January 1964, Buchanan's report was criticised. Rafferty said the report "almost ignored the motor bus." He also complained that the members of the Report team had not called at the city's transport headquarters and asked the department's views. "We neither saw nor heard of any of them," he said.

Rafferty made a plea for priority to be given to the public service vehicle in future planning. He suggested that one lane of traffic should be reserved for buses so that they could deposit their passengers and then move straight on, He asserted that thousands would continue to need buses. There were people who did not own a car nor did they want one. Councillor Kavanagh optimistically looked forward "to the time when those who have cars will get rid of them; they will have a form of public transport which will be cheaper and better for them."

Alderman E.J. Loy Wooler, Lord Mayor and former Chairman of the Town Planning Committee, said that in view of the increasing traffic congestion, buses may not be the answer in 20 years time. The Council would have to think of a means of transport other than buses. He said that serious thought would have to be given to other forms of transport such as overhead rail cars or tubes.

Starting in February 1964, a pilot study into the future place of public road transport in Leeds was carried out by the Industrial Management Division of Leeds University, in conjunction with Leeds Transport Department. To be taken into account were such factors as the possible social benefits of popularising public transport to relieve traffic congestion.

"Mr. T.Lord, General Manager of Leeds City Transport, said that so far as public transport was concerned the study would start where the Buchanan report left off. This pilot study would lead to a completely objective look at urban passenger transport. The results would affect urban living and working for many years to come and may interest other large towns in this country and elsewhere. Mr .Lord also expressed the hope that the Ministry of Transport would be interested in the project".

'The Yorkshire Post', 18 February 1964.

The report entitled "The future of public transport in Leeds" appeared in June 1964 and was prepared by

A.E.C. Regent V 939 in Otley Old Road on the 36 Central Bus Station to Tinshill service. It is at the Wise Owl Hotel bus stop. The date is 3 July 1974. *W.D.Wilson/L.T.H.S.*

Leyland PD3A/2 329 at the number 15 terminus at South Parkway, Seacroft, on 16 October 1965. *J.B.Parkin.*

David Quarmby, aged 22, a lecturer at Leeds University.

The report envisaged a future where car commuters would be forced to travel all or part of the way within a city by public transport. The most significant aspect of the future transport environment, said the report, was the city's parking policy. It proposed to ban all but a small fraction of potential commuter parking in a progressively increasing area based on the city centre.

One consequence of the parking restrictions would be the decentralisation of business premises. "The primary effect," Quarmby stated, "would be to make things difficult for commuters who wish to use private cars and thus to make offices in which such people work seek sites outside the city centre."

On 15 June 1964 the Transport Committee accepted the report. In a joint statement Rafferty and Lord said they wanted to make public transport more acceptable and find a form of travel that appealed to and would be used by the city worker. To achieve this one of the recommendations was the establishment of "controlled experiments" involving express buses and a "Park and Ride" scheme.

Quarmby's report was draconian in regard to the motor car, but this was the thinking of many people at the time. Even Ernest Marples, the Minister of Transport, contradicting Buchanan's views, was considering action on Quarmby's lines. On 11 June 1964 he told the House of Commons that wider measures to restrain motor traffic might be unavoidable. "Road pricing" was suggested whereby motorists "pay directly for the use they make of congested roads." Marples, however, could not say whether such a policy would be "desirable." He said he was not "anti-motorist," but added that in all major civilised countries it was accepted new roads alone would not solve the traffic problem.

The suggested road pricing policy was to materialise in London nearly 40 years later, in 2003, but at the time of writing has not been introduced in Leeds.

Quarmby said that 125,000 people arrived in the central area of Leeds for work each day. 21,000 travelled by car, 82,000 by bus and the remainder by "walking, motor-bike, bicycle and so on." Later, although parking became more difficult and very expensive, people were not attracted to the buses. Passenger numbers were to plummet and the result was an increase in the use of motor cars and worse congestion. It was not long after Quarmby's report that parking meters and more one-way streets were introduced in Leeds.

The idea of an inner ring road with adjacent car parking was not new and had been proposed for Leeds, many years earlier. Indeed at the time the Buchanan report was published, Leeds Corporation was inviting tenders for the first £2·7 million section of an inner ring road. It was to run from Westgate roundabout to Claypit Lane and included a tunnel under University land. There was to be a multi-storey car park off Woodhouse Lane. All the property in the lower part of Woodhouse Lane was to be demolished including the rather strange two-level road, Carlton Hill, directly on the line of the new ring road. The Hyde Park circulars and 61/62 circular bus routes were to be diverted. Fortunately the Leeds inner ring road was to be located further away from the city centre than had been recommended by Buchanan.

A multi-storey car park, the first in Leeds, was already nearing completion in the new Merrion Centre, a shopping and hotel complex with pedestrian precinct, at the junction of Woodhouse Lane and Merrion Street and bounded by Wade Lane and Cobourg Street. The centre was officially opened on 26 May 1964. From Monday 11 May, bus services 28 - a new service to Long Causeway; 30 (Ireland Wood); 33 (Cookridge); 36 (Tinshill) and 56 (North Lane) were diverted from Woodhouse Lane on inward journeys via Cobourg Street and a private road through the new Centre to Woodhouse Lane. The private road was "No Entry" to motor traffic at both ends.

In June 1965, Town Centre Securities, owners of the Merrion Centre, asked that the number 1 bus route (Lawnswood-Beeston) be redirected through the Centre. The Transport Committee rejected the proposal. Buses did not run through the Centre for long as the owners wished to expand the development over the road used by the buses. They asked the Committee to discontinue the arrangement from 6 February 1966. This date, however, was delayed and did not take place until 3 May 1971.

After 1965, selected new buildings in central Leeds were constructed with high-level pedestrian walkways. This applied particularly to buildings in the Infirmary Street, City Square, East Parade, Greek Street and King Street areas. A mile of overhead walkways was planned and a pedestrian bridge was later constructed over Park Row at the City Square end, connecting the new Bond Street Centre with the walkway system in Infirmary Street. Plans were produced showing walkways around the whole of City Square and there was to be high-level pedestrian access to the Leeds City Station.

The Leeds town planners envisaged that office workers would walk over the top of podiums to new office buildings and enter their places of work on the bottom floor of tower blocks. There were to be high level piazzas in various places including one at the Briggate/Boar Lane junction. Buses and motor traffic would pass underneath. Little of this happened. The walkways were costly to build and a maintenance problem for the private companies and individuals involved. Both public and private transport, were awkward to access and there were difficulties where walkways had to pass the few remaining historic buildings. It was found in other towns where Buchanan's proposals were tested, that dirt and rubbish accumulated at the lower level and there was an increase in criminality, grafitti and vandalism. Buchanan fell out of favour and after the mid-1970's many of his ideas were ignored.

The high level walkways were rarely used in Leeds and in the late 1990's most of the experiments of 20 and 30 years earlier were removed.

Inner ring roads with adjacent car parking were constructed in most cities and motorcar traffic has subsequently been discouraged in many town centres. Pedestrian precincts have been widely adopted, but again the idea was not new. In Leeds the Lincoln Green Shopping Centre, off Beckett Street, had a pedestrian precinct as early as 1960-1. Buchanan's proposals for separating buses and motor traffic from pedestrians proved to be impractical. Much of the content of "Traffic in Towns" is now consigned to history.

One of Buchanan's predictions, however, has turned out to be reasonably accurate. In 1963 there were just under 11 million motor cars on the roads in Britain, Buchanan said that by 1980 there would be 27 million (the actual figure was rather less). By 2010 there would be 40 million cars and by then the saturation point would be reached. In November 2004 the number of motor vehicles on the road was about 31 million.

In October 1965 the Corporation said that it was to promote a Parliamentary Bill to eliminate motor traffic and convert some streets in the city into pedestrian precincts. The streets proposed were to be Commercial Street, Lands Lane and Bond Street. The Leeds Chambers of Commerce and Trade strongly objected to the proposals, but they did later become law and minibuses were to run through the precincts.

THE BEECHING "AXE"

Some six months before the appearance of the Buchanan report, another Government report prepared by a Dr.Beeching was accepted and put into effect. This was to have a more profound effect on public transport in Great Britain than that of Buchanan. It advised that any railway

From 11 May 1964 to 3 May 1971 buses ran via Cobourg Street into the Merrion Centre. A.E.C. Regent V 867 is on a private road at the Centre on 30 May 1964. The buses were removed and the Centre extended over this location. The then new building in the background in Cobourg Street was demolished about 2001. *Author*.

service that was not making a profit should be abandoned. The railways were to be almost halved in extent and be superseded by bus services. Ernest Marples, described Beeching's proposals as "honest" and that the abandonment plan would be "implemented with speed." Most local authorities and other bodies opposed the proposals.

The 'Yorkshire Post' was puzzled that Marples was considering road pricing yet was reducing the size of the rail network. "It is strange that a man who wants to take traffic off the roads should take an axe to the railways," it commented.

There were to be many closures in and around Leeds and traffic formerly carried by the railways was to be diverted to the roads either in the form of improved bus services or, as proved to be the case, mainly increased use of the motorcar.

The Leeds City Transport undertaking was not one of the main beneficiaries, but the railway closures were probably partly responsible for the stability in bus passenger numbers in the early 1960's.

This book is not intended to cover in detail the history of the railways in and around Leeds, The subject is adequately covered in other publications, but the railway lines and railway stations that were to be abandoned are listed. The closure of the stations in the municipal area obviously benefited the Leeds transport undertaking, but outside the city it was mainly the West Yorkshire Road Car Company and West Riding Automobile Company that took the traffic from the railways.

Lord Stonham, Chairman of the National Council of Inland Transport, said that under Beeching's proposals Yorkshire would become a "railway desert." Beeching's brief had been confined to the railways only and did not consider the effect on roads. Lord Stonham described Beeching's ideas as "economic lunacy."

"There were no figures on which to base any proof that this action would save money. With congestion constantly increasing on the roads variously estimated to cost the country from £500 million to £2,000 million, in a year, the very doubtful claim to save up to £40 million on the railways would be swamped."

'The Yorkshire Post', 12 October 1963.

Railway services to be closed were as follows:
Leeds Central-Castleford.
Leeds Central-Doncaster (local service).
Leeds Central-Pontefract (Baghill).
Leeds Central-Pudsey-Bradford Exchange.
Leeds City-Bradford (Forster Square)-Ilkley-Skipton.
Leeds City-Bradford (Forster Square)-Keighley-Skipton (local service).
Leeds City-Shipley-Bradford (Forster Square) (local).
Leeds City-Cudworth-Sheffield Midland (local).
Leeds City-Cross Gates-Micklefield. (local)
Leeds City-Knottingley.
Leeds City-Wetherby-Harrogate.
Leeds City-Ilkley via Arthington and Otley.

Stations to be closed within the Leeds and district area were listed as follows: Ardsley, Armley (Canal Road), Armley Moor, Arthington, Bardsey, Calverley and Rodley, Collingham, Collingham Bridge, Guiseley, Kirkstall, Newlay, Otley, Penda's Way, Pool-in-Wharfedale, Pudsey Greenside, Pudsey Lowtown, Scholes, Stanley, Thorner, Wetherby and Woodlesford.

Not listed was Leeds Central, although virtually all lines operating from the station were to be closed. There was already a £4,700,000 plan to combine the Central with the City Station. New tracks were laid and Leeds Central closed on 29 April 1967.

The closure of the two Pudsey stations resulted in protests by Leeds Corporation. At a public inquiry held in Leeds by the Yorkshire Area Transport User's Consultative

Committee, H.R.T. Shackleton representing Leeds, commented that the parking problem in Leeds was "exercising the minds of the Corporation."

"If the stations at Pudsey were closed this would increase the problem. Leeds is expanding and it felt that transport services should be improved and not curtailed. The council feels that the railways have an important part to play in the development of the city," he said."

'The Yorkshire Post', 5 November 1963.

There were similar meetings and inquiries, regarding the other railways, but all was to no avail.

The first of the local railways to be closed under the Beeching plan, was the Leeds City-Wetherby line, which ceased operation on 6 January 1964. Included were the railway stations at Penda's Way, Scholes, Thorner, Bardsey, Collingham and Wetherby. Leeds City Transport buses may have seen increased patronage from the Penda's Way station closure, but the main beneficiary was the West Yorkshire Road Car Company.

The next casualty was the Leeds Central-Pudsey (Lowtown and Greenside)-Bradford Exchange service, which closed on 15 June 1964. Passengers were diverted to the Leeds Central-Stanningley-Bradford Exchange service or, on the Leeds side of Pudsey, the Corporation 32 and 65 bus services, and the Ledgard Leeds-Pudsey (Fartown)-Bradford buses. The Ledgard route from Troydale to Calverley and that of the Farsley Omnibus Company from Pudsey to Tinshill also took some of the railway traffic. The two railway freight depots at Pudsey Greenside and Lowtown were closed on 6 July 1964.

The well-known engine shed at Copley Hill, formerly the Leeds Depot of the old Great Northern Railway Company, closed on 6 September 1964.

On 2 November the same year the closure of the Leeds Central-Castleford and Pontefract (Baghill) lines for passenger services came into effect. The West Riding Automobile Company, South Yorkshire Motors and Yorkshire Traction Company provided the replacement bus services. Ardsley and Stanley stations were closed.

There was a change of Government in October 1964. The Conservatives were ousted and replaced by Harold Wilson's Labour Government. During the election campaign the Labour party had said that the railway closures would be stopped pending a national transport inquiry. Although a number of railway closures were prevented nationally, there was only a marginal effect in the Leeds area.

The former Minister of Transport, Ernest Marples, had approved the closure of the Leeds City-Bradford, Forster Square-Ilkley-Skipton, Leeds City-Ilkley via Arthington and Otley and the services to Keighley and Skipton. On 22 March 1965 a number of closures took place. These comprised the Ilkley to Skipton section, the Leeds City-Shipley-Bradford local service and that from Leeds to Ilkley via Otley. Railway lines abandoned were from Ilkley to Skipton, and Arthington to Ilkley via Otley. The two lines remained open for goods traffic until 5 July 1965. Altered services were operated on the remaining lines in the vicinity and included was a Leeds-Skipton service. Local railway stations closed to passengers on 22 March were the little used station at Armley (Canal Road), Arthington, Calverley and Rodley, Kirkstall, Newlay, Otley and Pool-in-Wharfedale.

Leeds Corporation bus services provided a partial replacement for the closure of some of the railway stations with others catered for by the West Yorkshire Road Car Company and Samuel Ledgard.

Leeds City Council had not made formal objections to many of the railway closures, but on 27 September 1965 the Transport Committee recommended the City Council to oppose a proposal to close the stations at Armley Moor, Bramley and Laisterdyke on the Leeds-Bradford line. Stanningley station, also on the route, was to be retained.

A public inquiry by the Yorkshire Area Transport

User's Consultative Committee was held on 10 November 1965 at the Metropole Hotel in Leeds. British Railways stated that the three stations cost £7,055 a year to run, yet receipts were only £2,862. There was only one objection to the closure of Armley Moor station, and the Committee later decided that there would be "no hardship" if the three stations closed. The closure came on 4 July 1966. Bus services 11, 14,15/16, 54, 65. 72 and Hebble services 15 and 28 took over the passengers from the railway.

In the meantime, in February 1966, there were plans by Pudsey Town Council for a new railway station at Dawson's Corner, Stanningley. "Large" car parks were to be provided at the new station. It was a long-term proposal by Pudsey Council, but surprisingly on 11 September the same year British Railways began work on building the new station. On Monday, 6 March 1967 the station, known as New Pudsey, was opened. There were initially 75 car parking spaces, with facilities for increasing the number to 600 if required. Park and ride facilities, as discussed below, were offered to motorists and thus, this became the first permanent Park and Ride facility in the Leeds area. The near-by existing station at Stanningley had little car parking space and was closed to passengers on 1 January 1968.

These closures virtually completed the Beeching proposals as far as Leeds was concerned. The Leeds Central-Doncaster local service ceased in 1966. In September 1966 the Leeds City-Knottingley line was reprieved. The local service, Leeds City-Cudworth-Sheffield, closed on 1 January 1968.

PARK AND RIDE AND OTHER PROPOSALS

At a meeting of the Transport Committee on 16 December 1963 a new transport pattern for Leeds city centre was discussed. Short distance bus services from off-street car parks into the city centre were proposed.

Alderman Rafferty had referred to these in connection with the Buchanan Report and there were meetings with the Town Planning and Improvements Committee. Such a scheme would be part of a plan to ease traffic congestion in the central area. It was to be what was later referred to as a "Park and Ride" scheme. Motorists going into the city on business and for shopping would leave their cars at the fringe car parks and finish their journey by bus. There would be a combined parking fee and bus fare.

In June 1964 Thomas Lord, the Transport General Manager, announced that three Park and Ride sites were proposed. They were to be sited at Lawnswood, Roundhay and North Lane, Headingley. Express buses travelling at twice the normal bus speed of 10 or 11 m.p.h. were to be employed. An "all inclusive" fee of 1s.0d. was to be charged.

"Mr. Lord stressed that this was where a car park was within a 4d. bus ride of the city centre. The fee of 1s.0d, which they had talked about would cover the 8d. cost of taking the motorist by bus into the city centre and back to the car park.

The remaining 4d. would be the fee for leaving the car in the park and would involve a subsidy from the local authority.

It is felt that if such a car park is within a 4d. bus ride from the city centre then a 1s.0d. charge is a practical proposition."

'The Yorkshire Evening Post', 15 June 1964.

Alderman Rafferty said that the motorist would have to live a more regulated life in the future and "fit into the scheme of things in the general interest of the community."

It was to be a year or so before the first major Park and Ride scheme was adopted in Leeds. A potential candidate for the new idea was a service from the proposed Woodhouse Lane car park, adjacent to the contemplated inner ring road.

A.E.C. Regent V 963 in City Square on 4 April 1965. In the background is Priestley Hall, then 110 years old, and reduced to rubble in February 1968. Its replacement, a grey concrete structure, also named Priestley Hall, suffered the same fate in October 1995. *W.D.Wilson/L.T.H.S.*

A.E.C. Reliance 39 in Latchmere Drive at the new Moor Grange terminus on the first day of operation of route 73, Moor Grange-Greenthorpe: 1 April 1964. *Author.*

A fortnight after Lord's comments, an experimental Park and Ride scheme was adopted on the occasion of the Test Match held at Headingley from 2 to 6 July. Temporary car parks were established in Ventnor Street, off Kirkstall Road, and on Woodhouse Moor. The car parks were free and an adult fare of 3d. was charged to the cricket match. The route from Ventnor Street to the cricket match was via Burley Road and Cardigan Road, while that from Woodhouse Moor was via Headingley Lane and St. Michael's Lane. In the meantime in February 1964 a Wigan firm, N. Frankmann Ltd., applied to the Transport Committee for permission to run services of minibuses from outlying car parks to the city centre. Rafferty said that all public transport services in Leeds should be under the control of the Corporation and the private firm's application was thrown out.

In February 1964 "in order to minimise frustrating waits at bus stops," the Transport Committee agreed to experimentally fit radio-telephones in 12 buses. In 1961 Arnold Stone, the Deputy Chief Traffic Officer, had visited the United States and had seen radio-telephones in use in Buffalo. 500 buses in that town were fitted with radio-telephones and he said the system "vastly speeded up the rectification of delays, breakdowns, accidents and so forth." Gaps in services could quickly be put right. Alderman Rafferty said that if successful, the experiment, said to be the first of its kind in the country, would put Leeds "far ahead" of any other bus undertaking in the country, and would be extended to other buses.

During August 1964, 962 became the first bus in Leeds to be fitted with Pye short-wave radio equipment. 962 was used by the Committee on its annual tour of inspection on 24 August. On the same day it was featured on the B.B.C. Television programme "Look North". The radio equipment was removed within about a fortnight.

However, the experiment was reported to be "extremely successful". At the Transport Committee meeting on 21 September 1964 it was agreed to hire ten miniature pocket radio receivers for use by inspectors. These gave a distinctive "bleep" to warn them to telephone control at Swinegate.

12 buses working from Sovereign Street Garage, were fitted with radio equipment. The vehicles were Daimler CVG6 536, 538 and 540; A,E.C. Regent III 670, 672 and 674 and A.E.C. Regent V 760, 762, 764, 766, 768 and 770. The equipment was operational from 26 November.

The radio-telephones proved to be successful and in October 1965 the Transport Committee decided to install them in 25 more buses. Rafferty said that despite a shortage of drivers and conductors, the system had helped services to run more efficiently. He said that they had helped in the fight against hooliganism. Conductors faced with awkward passengers could flash details to the control room and the police were soon on the scene. The radio-telephones had enabled the control room at Swinegate to quickly sort out "traffic tangles" and had also been used to report pot holes in the road so that the Highways Department could carry out quick repairs.

A small alteration to the 69, (Central Bus Station-Moortown), service had taken place on 2 February 1964. Instead of running from Black Moor Road via Tynwald Hill, buses were altered to run from Black Moor Road via Deanswood Hill to the terminus at Cranmer Bank.

Requests from residents in the Long Causeway, Adel, area were also considered at the Transport Committee meeting in December 1963. The residents wanted a bus service from Adel to the Central Bus Station and the Committee agreed to apply to the Traffic Commissioners for a Central Bus Station-Adel service and for a change in the terminus of the 73 route, (Greenthorpe-Adel), from Adel to Moor Grange.

On 1 March 1964 a considerable number of bus route alterations took place including the new service from the Central Bus Station to Adel. Numbered 28, the hourly service ran via Eastgate, The Headrow, Woodhouse Lane, Headingley Lane, Otley Road, Weetwood Lane and Long Causeway. The Adel route was now worked by double deck buses. The previous day extensive tree lopping had taken place in Long Causeway. The Headingley to Long Causeway section of service 73 was replaced by the new 28 service. The former service 73 (Greenthorpe-Long Causeway) was altered to run to Moor Grange. From Kirkstall, the new route was via Kirkstall Lane, Morris Lane, Spen Lane, Old Oak Drive, Butcher Hill, Old Farm Approach, Latchmere Drive, Latchmere Road, Old Farm Drive, Old Farm Cross and Latchmere Drive. The last three streets listed were used as a turning circle and the terminus was close to that of the 74 buses (Moor Grange-Belle Isle). An hourly service was operated (from lunchtime only on Sundays).

In connection with the revised 73 service a new service 71 was introduced. This ran three journeys at peak periods only over the route of the 73 service from Greenthorpe to Headingley.

As referred to in the last chapter, Mrs. May Sexton had been campaigning for a considerable time for a bus service along Clarendon Road. She had organised petitions, but her approaches to the Transport Committee had always been refused. However, on 1 March 1964 a bus service was introduced along Clarendon Road. Over the previous year or two much of the property in Mount Preston and Springfield Place on the Hyde Park circular bus route (58 and 60) was demolished to make way for extensions to the University and Leeds General Infirmary. Buses were now redirected along Great George Street to Clarendon Road.

"All the residents of the area are pleased," said Mrs. Sexton, "It means that there is now direct access to the Grammar School, the Maternity Hospital and several nursing homes." Mrs. Sexton was of the opposing political party to Rafferty and he was not happy that she appeared to be taking credit for the alteration. He said that it was "obviously a publicity stunt. She wants to take all the credit for it, but it has always been part of the arrangement that buses would eventually use Clarendon Road."

At the same time as the Clarendon Road modification, all the buses on the Hyde Park circular services (57-60) were altered in the city centre to run via Vicar Lane, New Market Street, Duncan Street, Boar Lane, City Square, Infirmary Street and East Parade. Formerly they had run via The Headrow.

In May 1964 a start was made on the construction of the new Leeds Inner Ring Road and this resulted in a number of interesting road closures and alterations to bus services in the area. Great George Street was closed at the St. George's Crypt end, Fenton Street was closed and Blundell Street ceased to exist. The Hyde Park Circulars (57-60) and East End Park Circulars (61 and 62) were the bus routes affected.

The first "casualty" was the new 58 and 60 service now running from the The Headrow via Oxford Row, and Great George Street to Clarendon Road. Part of the new Inner Ring Road was being constructed in a tunnel and surfaced in a deep cutting at the end of Great George Street. The street was severed at this point and a pedestrian bridge later erected. From 6 July 1964 the 58

From October 1964 to January 1966 buses on Hyde Park Circular services 58 and 60 ran from Woodhouse Square to Park Lane via Hanover Lane. A.E.C. Regent V 893 is pictured in Hanover Lane on 14 November 1964. John Barran's clothing factory forms the setting. Benjamin Simon's premises on the right were demolished about 1976, but in 1987-8 Barran's became Joseph's Well, a suite of offices. Hanover Lane was permanently closed to through traffic when Clarendon Road was extended through to Park Lane in January 1966. *Author.*

From 1 March to 5 July 1964 buses ran from Great George Street into Clarendon Road. A deep cutting was constructed for the new Inner Ring Road and there is currently a pedestrian bridge over the Ring Road at this point. St. George's Church and crypt is in the background. The church lost its spire in 1962, but a new spire was erected in January 2006. A.E.C. Regent V 866 is leaving Great George Street and is on route 58, the Hyde Park Circular service. *Author*.

From 30 March 1927 to 1 March 1964 Leeds buses had run up and down Mount Preston. A.E.C. Regent V 888 is descending and passing Virginia Road on 27 March 1963. Mount Preston, Virginia Road and the 1860's terrace housing were removed to make way for an extension to Leeds University started in 1977. *Author*.

Beginning in May 1964 and in some following years, elderly Leeds buses were used as polling stations in the Hunslet district. A.E.C. Regent III 430 is in St Helen's Street, Hunslet, on polling day, 13 May 1965. *H. Heyworth.*

A.E.C. Reliance 45 was one week old when this photograph was taken at Raynville Approach, Bramley. The date is 8 August 1964. *W.D.Wilson/L.T.H.S.*

A.E.C. Regent V 760 was one of the buses fitted with a radio telephone in 1964.   It is in Otley Road, Lawnswood, on 12 October 1963. The former tramway reservation is on the left. *Author.*

and 60 buses were rerouted from The Headrow via Westgate, Caroline Street, Park Lane, Hanover Street, Denison Road and Woodhouse Square to Clarendon Road. Hanover Street was very narrow and from 5 October the buses ran from Woodhouse Square via the slightly wider Hanover Lane.

From midnight on Sunday, 12 July, Fenton Street was permanently closed to all traffic and the following day services 61 and 62 were rerouted as follows:

Service 61 via Woodhouse Lane and Cookridge Street, instead of Fenton Street, Calverley Street and Great George Street.

Service 62 via Portland Way and Woodhouse Lane instead of Calverley Street and Fenton Street.

From 1 March minor alterations to frequencies etc, took place on services 9, 30, 32, 33, 36 and 44.

In March 1964 an application for a bus service along Beechwood Crescent in the Burley area of Leeds was requested. A petition was presented to the Transport Committee, residents saying that they "had well over ten minutes hard walking on a very steep hill to get to the nearest bus service." The application was thrown out. Rafferty told "disgusted residents" that while the suggested diversion along Beechwood Crescent would benefit a few people it would be disadvantageous for hundreds of others. "Any advantage gained by such a diversion would be outweighed by the inconvenience caused," he said.

An alteration to the terminal arrangements of the 9 (Ring Road) and 39 (Whitkirk) services occurred on 15 May 1964 when a new loading bay and roundabout came into use. Buses stood in the new layby facing outwards and then ran to the new roundabout at the junction of Selby Road and the Ring Road to turn.

February 1964 marked the 70th "birthday" of the Leeds Transport Department. Rafferty announced plans to give the Department a "modern, streamlined look." The Department's street furniture – bus stop signs, timetable cases etc. were to be upgraded. Stationery, documents and

publicity material were also to be changed to the new style. A new house emblem or logo, "LCT" and incorporating the city coat of arms was to be adopted. Bus stop signs were to be framed by a "striking border" in green - the colour of new staff uniforms, to be introduced in May. A Leeds firm of graphic designers had designed the new logo. Timetable cases were to be made of an indestructible plastic as a protection against vandals. Thomas Lord, said that bus stops and other items would be changed gradually over the next year or so.

At an Ideal Homes Exhibition in the Queen's Hall, Leeds, held from 25 April to 9 May, the Transport Department had a stand publicising the Department's activities and introducing the new logo. There was a TV monitor linked to the three cameras in City Square, Briggate and the Corn Exchange and a mock up of the front of an A.E.C. Reliance single deck bus. The display was largely an attempt to recruit more conductors, hopefully from the exhibition visitors.

In April 1964 the Transport Committee received an unusual request for the use of an obsolescent bus as a polling station at "any polling place in the city". This was granted and on polling day, 7 May 1964, for the municipal elections, withdrawn A.E.C. Regent III, 419, was commandeered for use as a polling station on waste land off Grape Street, Hunslet Road. 419 did not appear to have been very popular and in its first two hours only two people had turned up to vote. In subsequent years in the 1960's old buses were sometimes used as polling booths in City Council elections where the electorate was tiny.

Brief reference has already been made to the new buses that were ordered in 1963. As far as Leeds Transport Department was concerned, their designs were a radical departure from the "standard" conventional Leeds bus, which had been ordered until this time.

Tenders had been accepted on 15 July 1963 and the 40 buses comprised 20 front entrance double deckers and 20 similar buses with rear entrances. Details were as follows:

On 12 July 1964 Fenton Street was permanently closed and bus services 61 and 62 rerouted. A.E.C. Regent V 818 is in Fenton Street approaching Woodhouse Lane on 16 November 1963. The property on the right was demolished in January 1964 and on the left is Harewood Barracks removed in February 1967. *Author.*

A.E.C (Sales)Ltd. 15 double deck chassis for £39,630.

Transport Vehicles (Daimler) Ltd. 5 double deck chassis for £14,480.

Transport Vehicles (Daimler) Ltd. 10 double deck chassis for £31,450.

Leyland Motors Ltd. 10 double deck chassis for £27,640.

Charles H.Roe Ltd. 20 double deck rear entrance bodies for £65,700.

Charles H.Roe Ltd. 10 double deck front entrance bodies for £36,950.

M.C.W. Ltd. 10 double deck front entrance bodies for £36,850.

As an experiment, arrangements were to be made for the installation of fully automatic air conditioning systems in one of each of the bodies to be supplied by Roe and M.C.W. The system was stated to be the first of its type.

"Alderman John Rafferty, Chairman of the Committee, said the development would bring full air conditioning for the first time in the history of the department. No other operators, private or municipal had equipment such as this. There would be a constant change of air in the buses.

Mr. Lord summed up: The passengers will breathe clean air all the time in a constant temperature."

'Yorkshire Evening Post', 15 July 1963.

In December 1963 the order with Charles Roe Ltd. was extended to include four single deck bodies. At the same time it was agreed to invite tenders for the supply of a single deck coach body.

The first buses to be delivered were 15 A.E.C. Regent V buses numbered 949-963 (949-963 JUB). They had Roe rear entrance bodies and all entered service in July 1964. They were very similar in design to 924-948, but had slightly deeper windows (about 4in.) to the lower saloon. There was a different design of seat and thicker cushions were used.

At the same time that 949-963 were delivered, the single deck buses ordered in December 1963 arrived.

These were four one-man operated buses on A.E.C. Reliance chassis with Roe 41-seat bodies. Numbered 44-47 (44-47 KUA), they all entered service in August 1964.

They were identical to the previous similar vehicles, 39-43, and were again finished with gold lining. Old type seats, with thin cushions and without grab rails were fitted, in contrast to the more luxurious seating found on the new double deck buses.

All the one-man buses, 39-47, were allocated to Headingley Garage, but following the delivery of 44-47, the spares (usually two buses) were kept at Torre Road No.2 garage, owing to a lack of room at Headingley. The buses at Torre Road were, however, changed fairly regularly.

Single deck buses were now being delivered for one-man operation, but for over three decades double deck bus design had been virtually static. It consisted of the traditional rear entrance vehicle with front engine and exposed radiator and was epitomised in Leeds by the Roe-bodied A.E.C. Regent III and V, which dominated the scene for over 20 years. There had been some modernisation of the design in the late 1950's. Buses had increased in size and there were the "tin front" Daimlers of the CVG6 design and the later type A.E.C. Regent Mark V buses. However, this was to radically change in 1964 with the introduction of the first of an entirely new type of front entrance double decker. This was the start of the policy of dispensing with conductors on all buses. Not only was the driver to drive the bus, he was also to be responsible for collecting the fares. The idea of one-man double deck buses was proposed by Manchester Corporation in September 1964 and was soon followed by Leeds and many other transport undertakings. A gradual change over to one-man operation began.

The new vehicles were Daimler Fleetlines and Leyland Atlanteans and these were to supersede the rear entrance buses over the next 12 years. These new buses are discussed in the next chapter.

CHAPTER 80

Fleetlines, Atlanteans and other matters

The 22nd International Commercial Motor Transport Exhibition was held at Earl's Court, London, from 25 September to 3 October 1964. Charles H. Roe followed its usual tradition by exhibiting one of its bodies built for the Leeds City Transport Department. There, however, tradition ended as the body of the latest exhibit was of a design new to Leeds. The front entrance body was mounted on a Daimler Fleetline CRG6 rear engine chassis, and was the first of an order for ten similar buses for Leeds.

The Fleetlne design was not new and the first bus of this type had been exhibited at the Commercial Motor Show in September 1960. It was vaguely similar to the earlier Leyland Atlantean design. Several local authorities and companies had adopted Fleetlines and Atlanteans, but Leeds clung to the traditional rear entrance bus for longer than many other undertakings.

The Leyland Atlantean originated in 1957 and slightly later there was the Guy Wulfrunian. The West Riding Automobile Company, and a number of other companies throughout the country purchased Wulfrunians. They were not very successful and never used by the Leeds City Transport undertaking and are not further discussed. At this time there were also other front entrance bus designs such as the Dennis Loline, but again these are not considered here.

The Leyland Atlantean as exhibited at the Commercial Motor Show in 1958 was of a low floor design with front entrance loading and had a rather box-like appearance. All over the world there had been many buses designed with rear engines and all had flush rear ends. However, on the Atlantean the engine was housed in a "bustle". The upper deck and engine "bustle" projected about 18 inches beyond the lower deck windows giving an unsightly cut out effect to the rear end.

A fairly orthodox bevel-driven rear axle was adopted. This involved raising the rear portion of the lower deck floor. The transmission was more complex than on the conventional bus as there was a need to take the drive from the transversely mounted engine and gear box at an angle along the vehicle to the rear axle. The angle drive box incorporated a pair of helical gears.

At first glance the layout of the Fleetline resembled closely that of the Atlantean, but there were differences. There was no change in level of the lower saloon floor and it was thus a true low-floor design.

The method of achieving the full-length low floor was found in the transmission layout. The engine was mounted transversely across the rear of the chassis with the fluid flywheel on the offside, similar to the Atlantean. The differences were in the gear box, which, although of the four-speed semi or fully automatic epicyclic type, had a hollow mainshaft construction so that the input and output shafts were at the same end, one revolving within the other. This enabled a right angle drive assembly to be fitted at the input end of the gear box and from it the propeller shaft ran almost directly forward to the rear axle which was of the dropped-centre, double-reduction type. The general body design was similar to the Atlantean, having the cut out at the rear, but the overall effect was

Daimler Fleetline 101 looked very smart with its wrap-round windscreen and gold leaf lined livery on 3 January 1965. The location is Call Lane and 101 is en route to Seacroft on service 11 Swinnow-Seacroft. *Author.*

Daimler Fleetline 101 after a year or so in service in Henconner Lane outside Bramley Depot. The date is 18 December 1966. *W.D. Wilson/L.T.H.S.*

Daimler Fleetline 104 in Wellington Street at the West Yorkshire Coach Station on 11 April 1965. A West Yorkshire dual purpose saloon is emerging from the Coach Station. *W.D.Wilson/L.T.H.S.*

Daimler CVG6LX/30 115 pictured at the Central Bus Station on 21 September 1975. It was on a private tour arranged by 'The Leeds & District Transport News' to Coventry and Birmingham. *W.D.Wilson/L.T.H.S.*

rather more refined. The Leeds vehicle exhibited in 1964 was of an improved design and had a smart wrap round one-piece windscreen, which enhanced its appearance, although the front upper saloon windows were flat.

The body by Charles H. Roe Ltd. was of metal-framed construction and had seats for 70 passengers, 41 in the upper saloon and 29 in the lower. A revised livery was adopted (discussed further in Appendix XVIII) and there was the usual gold lining used on Leeds Show buses.

Electrically operated twin jack-knife doors were fitted and controlled by the driver. The interior of the bus was very similar to those of A.E.C. Regent V, 949-963. There were the same window surrounds and thick cushioned seats with shaped back rests. Formica panelling was used extensively, although the front end panels in both saloons were of contrasting Warerite.

Ample luggage space was provided beneath and behind the staircase and over the front near side wheel. The staircase was of the straight Roe "safety" type with two passing platforms. Interior lighting consisted of six fluorescent tubes in each saloon, plus two amber Perspex panels in the roof of the upper saloon. There was a strip bell push in the lower saloon.

A negative point in the design was the absence of any opening windows. An air conditioning unit was supplied instead, consisting of a special Smith's heating and ventilation unit with individually operated "Selectavents" and demisters over each main window. This unit incorporated a thermostatically controlled valve for summer, winter, or intermediate positions. Later, in July and August 1967, Roe fitted three sliding ventilators to alternate windows of the upper saloon on both sides.

Other external features were three track digital number blinds positioned under a single destination – the new "standard" arrangement in Leeds – at both front and rear. The front blinds were changed from inside the upper saloon and the rear ones from outside. "Limited" signs were fitted

beneath the front nearside windscreen and over the entrance. There was a Park Royal type rear dome and the interior of the front and rear domes were of a single thickness whereas the remainder of the upper saloon roof was double skinned.

Twin sealed beam headlights were fitted with a combined tail light, stop light and flashing trafficator unit.

The bus was allocated the number 101 in the Leeds fleet and at the Show displayed "ROE 1964" on the number plates. 101 was the heaviest bus at the Show, having an unladen weight of 9 tons 1 cwt. It was 30 feet. long, 8 feet wide and 14 feet high. It was certainly an impressive vehicle and a complete contrast to anything that had appeared in Leeds up to that time.

On 19 October 1964 number 101 - "the omnibus of the future" - was inspected by members of the Transport Committee. Surprisingly, Alderman Rafferty, the Committee Chairman, does not appear to have made any comment, but Thomas Lord, the General Manager, discussed the air conditioning system, which he claimed was of his design. However, the 'Heating, Air Conditioning Weekly' for 13 May 1964, reporting on a similar system installed on a Manchester bus, contradicts this and said that Smith's Motor Accessory Division were the designers. Lord said that the extra cost of air conditioning equipment was not more than £100 per vehicle. The air in the bus was changed every three minutes. Lord said that the new bus and the other Fleetlines were to operate on route 11, the Gipton-Swinnow service.

All ten buses in the series, 101-110, (101-110 LNW) were licensed from 1 November 1964, but did not enter service until the following month.

102 to 110 had a different frontal design to 101 in that they were fitted with two-piece windscreens and single headlights. They were not fitted with air conditioning, having sliding ventilators and conventional heaters. In addition 102-110 had more metal internally than 101 – they did not have the Warerite panelling, and the livery was also different.

All the buses were allocated to Seacroft Garage and 101 commenced driver training on 23 November, being used for this purpose until 13 December, when it began to carry fare paying passengers for the first time.

In the meantime, a month earlier, a batch of five other buses had appeared. These were of the old rear entrance type on Daimler CVG6LX chassis with Roe 70-seat bodies. Numbered 111-115 (111-115 LNW) all entered passenger service on 2 November 1964 with the exception of 112, which appeared three days later.

The bodies of these buses were almost identical to the 15 recently delivered A.E.C. Regent V buses, 949-963. There were minor differences in the lower saloon lighting and they also had fluorescent lighting in their front and rear destination boxes.

A problem with the new Fleetlines was the throwing of mud from the rear wheels on to the lower saloon windows. As an experiment in March 1965, 109 was fitted with a piece of wood about four feet long, below the windows to obviate the nuisance. It was removed after a few days, but in late March 108 was fitted with modified mudguards on the offside. 107 followed in April, but the modifications were only partially successful in overcoming the mud problem.

As a result of the introduction of these 15 new buses and the 15 A.E.C. Regent V buses, 949-963, a few months earlier, 33 old vehicles were withdrawn. These comprised buses of five different types:

Leyland PD2: 340-349, 351-353, 356, 363, 369, 372.
A.E.C. Regent III: 429-438, 440, 445, 448.
A.E.C. Regent III: 489.
A.E.C. Regent III: 600.
Leyland PS1/1: 27.

Both 363 and 489 were withdrawn following accidents. 363 on 24 July 1964 - collision with a tree in Morris Lane, Kirkstall, and 489 prematurely taken out of service on 14 April 1964 after a collision while on night service duties.

Of special interest was 600, the first 8ft.0in.wide bus In Leeds and exhibited at the Commercial Motor Show in October 1948. It ran for almost exactly 16 years being withdrawn on 30 October 1964. At this time virtually all the buses being withdrawn had completed about 15 to 16 years in service. Also of interest was 27, the last of the two Leyland PS1/1 single deckers, withdrawn on 17 July.

It was not usual for old Leeds buses to be sold to other municipal undertakings, they were normally either scrapped or finished up with various small operators countrywide. However, five A.E.C. Regent III: 416, 420, 423, 427 and 440, sold to North's of Leeds for disposal were in turn sold to the Halifax Joint Omnibus Committee in July and November 1964. Some of the buses were renumbered in Halifax and this is detailed on pages 1130 and 1131 of Volume 3. They were withdrawn by Halifax in either May or December 1965.

The construction of a new section of the outer Ring Road was completed in 1964. The dual carriageway was 920 yards long and ran between Barwick Road and Coal Road and was the first "Buchanan style" road in Leeds and entirely free of pedestrians. It spilt in two the Swarcliffe Housing Estate and pedestrians had to cross at the roundabouts at either end or by an underpass in the middle.

The road was fenced on both sides and residents complained that an "iron curtain" had been placed through their estate. Following complaints to the City Council and an appeal to Dennis Healey, the local M.P., the objections subsided and the road was accepted. Buses on the 9 Ring Road service and School service 116 had run via Barwick Road and York Road through Seacroft village. The road opened on Tuesday, 17 November 1964 and from Friday, the 20th the two bus services were rerouted over the newly completed section of the Ring Road.

Four days earlier, on the 16th, an alteration had taken place to service 16 (City Square to Seacroft Coal Road). Buses on the peak hour extension of service 16 were extended via the Ring Road to a new terminus at

The arrival of the Daimler Fleetlines in 1964 saw the withdrawal of several of the 1949-built Leyland PD2. 344 is pictured at Greenthorpe on 15 June 1963. *Author.*

433 was one of the A.E.C. Regent III that were taken out of service in 1964.   It is seen here at the bus stop at Stanhope Place, Sheepscar Street North, on 25 July 1962.   It is on route 34, the Alwoodley Circular service.   The houses behind the bus were demolished shortly after this photograph was taken. *Author.*

Limewood Approach.   On journeys from Limewood Approach, buses ran via an un-named service road to the Ring Road.   Previously buses had turned at the junction of Coal Road and the Ring Road.

A further alteration took place to services 15 and 16 (Seacroft-Whingate) from Sunday 13 December.   They were extended from Whingate via Green Hill Road and Henconner Lane to a new terminus at Bramley Town End. A feature of the alteration was that buses on service 16 formerly terminating in City Square, now ran through to Bramley Town End. On the same day service 11 (Gipton-Greenthorpe and Swinnow) was extended at the Gipton end via Wykebeck Valley Road, South Parkway Approach and South Parkway to a new terminus at Ironwood View, Seacroft.

There was a minor alteration to service 72 (Infirmary Street-Bradford) from 1 November.   Buses now turned right into Petergate at a new roundabout at the bottom of Leeds Road, Bradford.   Passengers were dropped in Petergate and buses then turned into Forster Square before loading for their return to Leeds, on the opposite side of Petergate.

Leeds Transport Department had managed to maintain fares at a low level in comparison with other transport undertakings.   There had been a modest fare increase in September 1963, but ever increasing wages claims, which included a demand for a 40-hour week without loss of pay, was placing a strain on the department.   The number of passengers carried on the buses in the year ended 31 March 1964 had been 206,910,170, an increase of over 3,000,000 compared with the previous year.   This was contrary to the national trend and was attributed to the low

fares.   There was still an off peak minimum fare of 2d. and, during the past year, services had been increased on 25 routes in the city.

Alderman Rafferty said that in 1945 the weekly wages bill had been £17,000.   It was now £50,000.   Similarly in 1945 a new bus could be purchased for £3,000 whereas in 1964 it was £7,000.

"We can't do these things and expect to operate services at the same fare structure," Alderman Rafferty said. "What we can assure the public is that we will operate as economically as possible and include all the modern amenities associated with a progressive transport authority."

'Yorkshire Evening Post', 25 August 1964.

The 'Yorkshire Evening Post' said that this was "the writing on the wall" for the Transport Department.   "Steadily and subtly the value of money is being eroded and the unions who make the claims out of sheer self interest penalise everybody else.   The Leeds fare warning drives home the lesson."

Wages costs were partially reduced by the gradual introduction of one-man operated buses and hence the abolition of the bus conductor.   However, the gloomy predictions turned out to be accurate.   From then on passenger numbers began to fall, services were reduced and costs increased.

The proposal to increase fares was approved at the Transport Committee meeting on 21 September 1964. The short distance fares, including the 2d. minimum fare for one stage, were to be retained, but fares of 6d. and over were to be increased by one penny.   Certain concessions were also to be made to passengers.   Baby carriages, tricycles, push-chairs, wheeled shopping baskets and prams were to be carried free of charge. Until this time, 2d. had been charged and there were often arguments with bus conductors. The fare revisions were approved by the Yorkshire Traffic Commissioners on 17 November and came into effect twelve days later on the 29th.

A further blow to the Transport Department was an announcement in November 1964 of an increase of 6d. a gallon in fuel tax. This added £63,000 more per year to the running costs. Unfortunately the number of passengers carried, dropped by over 1,500,000 following the fare rise and the expected yield from increased fares did not happen. Alderman Rafferty blamed bad weather and an overtime ban by platform staff. The General Manager said that the overtime ban had led some bus passengers to use a car instead. The official view was that with the bus habit broken, they were continuing to travel by car.

It was not long before a further fare increase occurred. This was on 30 May 1965 when 4d. 5d. 6d. and 7d. fares were increased by 1d.

A novel idea for Leeds, first proposed in 1964, was the introduction of "tidal" traffic flows on the main roads leading into and out of the city. In September the following year a Leeds Corporation Order was approved making most of the main roads leading in and out of the city into clearways at peak hours and thus paving the way for new-style tidal roads. 66 roads or lengths of road were affected and it was proposed to operate the scheme from 1 November 1965. One of the worst affected roads was Headingley Lane. Ever since the abandonment of the tramways in 1956, Headingley Lane at peak periods had become increasingly congested and the plan was to create three lanes of traffic from Hyde Park Corner to Headingley village. Two lanes were to be used for traffic going into the city in the morning, and two lanes for outward traffic in the evening. This would speed up the bus services on Headingley Lane and traffic

flow generally. There was a narrow point to the north of the junction at Hyde Park and a group of shops adjacent to Wrangthorn Church were to be demolished.

Increasing motor traffic obviated any improvements and at the time of writing there is severe traffic congestion throughout the day in both directions between Hyde Park and Headingley. A two-lane system is normally operated.

The road system in Leeds was becoming difficult and on 30 October 1964 an accident in Mabgate caused most of the traffic in the city to be halted. 600 buses were halted for an hour and there was much adverse comment in the local press.

The one-way traffic system in the city centre proposed earlier in 1964 came into operation to the east of Briggate on 4 January 1965 and to the west three months later on 5 April. The idea was to speed traffic and the alterations of 4 January were major and primarily concerned Briggate and Vicar Lane, two of the major thoroughfares in the city. Briggate and New Briggate became one-way in a northerly direction and Vicar Lane one-way for south-bound traffic. Call Lane became one-way and many minor streets were also made one-way, but these had little effect on the public transport alterations. Extensive no waiting and restricted car parking areas were introduced.

Buses going south down Briggate were diverted to Vicar Lane and similarly buses travelling north along Vicar Lane now used Briggate. Services affected were as follows:

Services 3 and 3 circular (Middleton) and 6 (Belle Isle). Buses operated via Vicar Lane, New Market Street and Call Lane, instead of New Briggate and Briggate. There was no change in the other direction.

Service 4 (Kirkstall and Horsforth). Via Kirkgate and New Market Street instead of Call Lane. Buses in the other direction to Cross Gates ran via Call Lane instead of New Market Street and Kirkgate.

Services 8, 52 and 53 (Meanwood). Via Briggate and

445 was another of the A.E.C. Regent III buses withdrawn in 1964 to make way for the Daimler Fleetlines. It is in Eastgate on service 35, the Alwoodley Circular, and about to overtake it is Leyland PD2 398 on service 77 to Compton Road. The date is 20 July 1963. *Author.*

A scene in Headingley Lane on 25 April 1955 with Horsfield car 167 at the Cumberland Road tram stop. In 1965 a three-lane traffic flow system was proposed for this part of Headingley Lane. *Author*.

It was unusual for old Leeds buses to be sold to other municipal undertakings. In 1964 five A.E.C. Regent III buses, 416, 420, 423, 427 and 440, were sold to North's, dealers, of Leeds, who in turn sold them to the Halifax Joint Omnibus Committee. Halifax 49, (ex-Leeds 427) and 40 (ex-Leeds 440) and 441 (on a private 'Leeds & District Transport News' tour) are seen here in Halifax on 9 May 1965. 49 was withdrawn by Halifax on 31 May and 440 on 31 December 1965. *Author*.

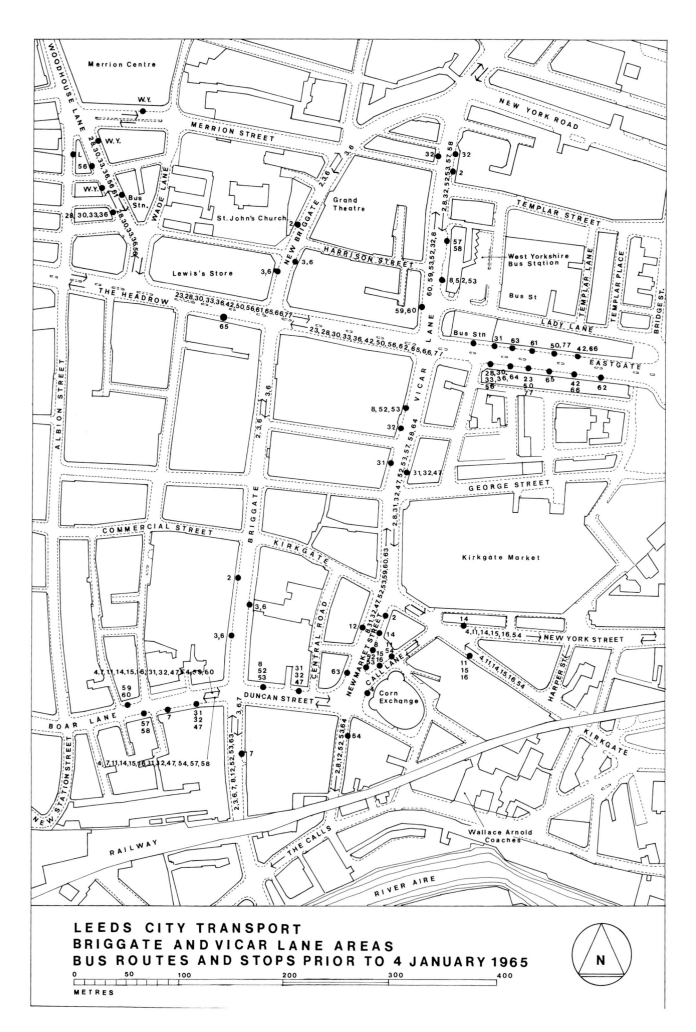

LEEDS CITY TRANSPORT
BRIGGATE AND VICAR LANE AREAS
BUS ROUTES AND STOPS PRIOR TO 4 JANUARY 1965

0   50   100   200   300   400
METRES

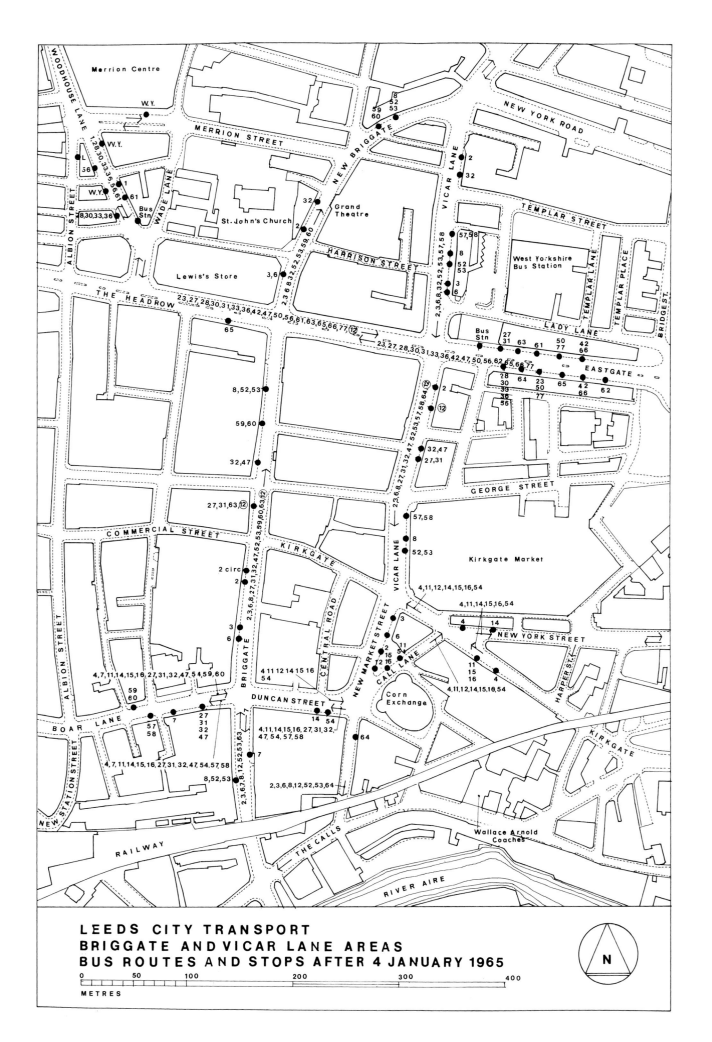

LEEDS CITY TRANSPORT
BRIGGATE AND VICAR LANE AREAS
BUS ROUTES AND STOPS AFTER 4 JANUARY 1965

"Tin front" Daimler CVG6LX/30 522, Ledgard's A.E.C. Regent V, 1954 U, and the author's new Vauxhall Viva at the bottom of Cookridge Street on Sunday 4 April 1965. After this day Cookridge Street was made one-way south to north. When the trams finished running in 1956, Boar Lane, City Square, Park Row and Cookridge Street were surfaced in red coloured tarmacadam. *Author*.

New Briggate instead of Duncan Street, New Market Street and Vicar Lane. No change in other direction, but buses working to Briggate only which had to turn before returning to Elland Road or Morley now did so via The Headrow.

Service 11 (Greenthorpe and Swinnow), 15 and 16 (Bramley Town End). Via Kirkgate and New Market Street instead of Call Lane. No change in the other direction.

Service 12 (to Corn Exchange). Buses turned at the Corn Exchange by way of Call Lane, Kirkgate and New Market Street, They continued to Middleton via Call Lane. This also applied to the 12 circular. Previously buses on this service turned at Corn Exchange by way of New Market Street, Kirkgate and Call Lane.

Service 27 (Gledhow) and 31 (Brackenwood). Via Briggate and The Headrow instead of Duncan Street, New Market Street and Vicar Lane. No change in the other direction. Service 27 was a renumbering of the 31 City Square-Gledhow (St. Edmund's Church) service, which also took place on 4 January.

Service 32 (Moortown). Via Briggate and New Briggate instead of Duncan Street, New Market Street and Vicar Lane. No change in other direction.

Service 47 (to Central Bus Station). Via Briggate and The Headrow instead of Duncan Street, New Market Street and Vicar Lane.

Services 59 and 60 Hyde Park Circulars). Via Briggate and New Briggate instead of Duncan Street, New Market Street and Vicar Lane.

Service 63 (South Accommodation Road Circular). Via Briggate and The Headrow instead of Duncan Street, New Market Street and Vicar Lane.

In addition two Works services were affected:

104 (from Yorkshire Copper Works and 137 (from Skelton Grange Power Station). Buses on these two services now proceeded to the Central Bus Station by way of Briggate and The Headrow, instead of Duncan Street, New Market Street and Vicar Lane.

There were some teething troubles at first as car users became used to the new system, but the system as a whole went "very well." Thomas Lord, the Transport General Manager, said that he was satisfied that the bus services would fit in adequately with the one-way pattern "to the benefit of the majority of the travelling public."

The alterations introduced on 5 April were more extensive and extended from Briggate in the east almost to Westgate. 50 streets were made one-way and included were Park Row (one way north to south), Cookridge Street (south to north), King Street and East Parade (south to north), and Infirmary Street (south east to north west). All these roads were used by buses, as also was the section of Albion Street from The Headrow to Woodhouse Lane. This was made one-way in a northerly direction.

A feature of the scheme in Woodhouse Lane was the provision of a special traffic lane for buses in the opposite direction to the one-way flow. From its junction with Cookridge Street to The Headrow, Woodhouse Lane became one-way south with two lanes of traffic. There was a third north-bound buses only lane, divided from the rest of the carriageway by thick white lines. L.C.T. services 28, 30. 33. 36. 56, and the joint Ledgard/West Yorkshire bus service 33 (Leeds to Rawdon via Horsforth) used the new bus lane. This was the first bus lane in Leeds.

Details of the bus route alterations were as follows:

Service 1 (Lawnswood). From City Square buses now travelled via Infirmary Street, East Parade, and The Headrow to Cookridge Street, instead of via Park Row. In the other direction buses to Beeston used Woodhouse Lane and The Headrow in place of Cookridge Street.

Service 7 (Hunslet). From Westgate buses now travelled via The Headrow, Park Row and City Square, in place of East Parade and Infirmary Street. There was no change in the other direction.

Service 29 (Middleton). Buses now ran to Middleton from Infirmary Street via East Parade and Westgate, instead of via King Street, Park Place and Queen Street. (Buses on this service had used this route on outward journeys from 4 January 1965, owing to the partial closure of Queen Street. The alteration was now permanent.

Services 42 and 66 (Harehills). Altered to run via Infirmary Street, East Parade and The Headrow instead of Park Row. No change to the route in the other direction.

Services 59 and 60 (Hyde Park circulars). Altered to run via The Headrow and Park Row instead of East Parade and Infirmary Street.

Service 61 (East End Park Circular). Altered to run via Portland Crescent, Great George Street, and Woodhouse Lane, instead of Cookridge Street and The Headrow.

Service 62 (East End Park Circular). Altered to run via The Headrow and Calverley Street in place of Cookridge Street and Great George Street.

Service 72 (Bradford). On journeys to Leeds buses continued via Wellington Street and City Square to terminate on the opposite side of Infirmary Street. Previously they turned into King Street to reach Infirmary Street. Journeys to Bradford now operated via East Parade and Westgate instead of City Square and Wellington Street.

Service 74 (Belle Isle). From Westgate buses now ran via The Headrow, Park Row and City Square in place of East Parade and Infirmary Street.

Other features introduced on 5 April 1965 and new to Leeds were "disfigurements", to quote some, in the provision of yellow lines adjacent to the kerbs. An unbroken line meant that car parking was prohibited for the whole of the working day. A broken line indicated that parking was prohibited during peak hours, motorists being allowed to park for one hour or two hours in a four-hour off peak period. Double yellow lines, prohibiting parking at any time, were introduced later. A mass of new traffic signs, traffic wardens, meter attendants and parking meters were also introduced into Leeds for the first time. Parking charges were at the rate of 6d. per hour and parking was limited to a two hour period.

The alterations were certainly beneficial to the city's bus services. Alderman Rafferty said that the buses were keeping better time schedules than for many weeks. There were some objections to buses going against the traffic flow in Woodhouse Lane. Some city councillors described the north-bound lane as "crazy," but the complaints soon subsided. Traffic generally was speeded up in the city centre, but there were complaints about dangers to pedestrians. Councillor Mather said that the problem of pedestrian flow was fast becoming as urgent as that of wheeled traffic. Most of the complaints he had heard about the new traffic scheme had, in fact been about pedestrian problems.

After a fatal accident in which the Leeds City Coroner described Briggate as a "nightmare for pedestrians at the moment." a pedestrian subway was constructed near the Boar Lane junction during the latter part of 1965. On 3 July a "push button" pedestrian-operated crossing point, the first in Leeds, came into use at the Briggate crossing at Commercial Street and Kirkgate. This included an island refuge in the centre of the road. The new crossing was a success and was soon copied in other parts of the city. Phased traffic signals were introduced elsewhere in the central area. "Green walking man" pedestrian crossing lights were first introduced in Leeds on 7 March 1967.

The alterations were reported to be the "biggest traffic changes in the city's history". Certainly, motoring in Leeds was never the same after 1965. Motorists could not leave their cars where they liked and now had to pay to park vehicles in the city. To encourage them to use public transport an experimental "Park and Ride" scheme was introduced. It was said to be the first in the country and was operated by the Transport Department from a piece of waste ground adjacent to Kirkstall Lane.

Infirmary Street on Sunday, 4 April 1965, the day before the major Stage 2 traffic alterations in Leeds. Note the new parking meters and parking bays. Front-entrance Daimler CVGLX/30 576 is at the Leeds terminus of route 72, the joint Leeds-Bradford service. On 5 April the terminal point was moved to the other side of Infirmary Street and on 31 October 1965 to the Bus Station. A year or so after this photograph was taken, all of the property on the right hand side was demolished to make way for a "Comprehensive Development" scheme. *Author.*

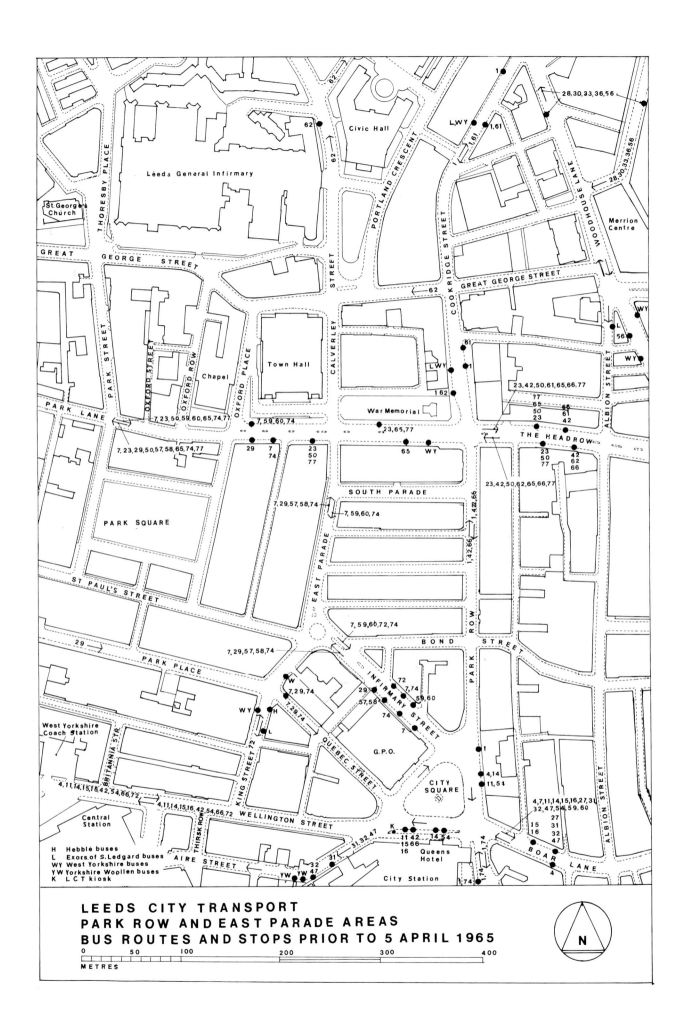

LEEDS CITY TRANSPORT
PARK ROW AND EAST PARADE AREAS
BUS ROUTES AND STOPS PRIOR TO 5 APRIL 1965

0   50   100   200   300   400
METRES

H   Hebble buses
L   Exors. of S. Ledgard buses
WY West Yorkshire buses
YW Yorkshire Woollen buses
K   LCT kiosk

N

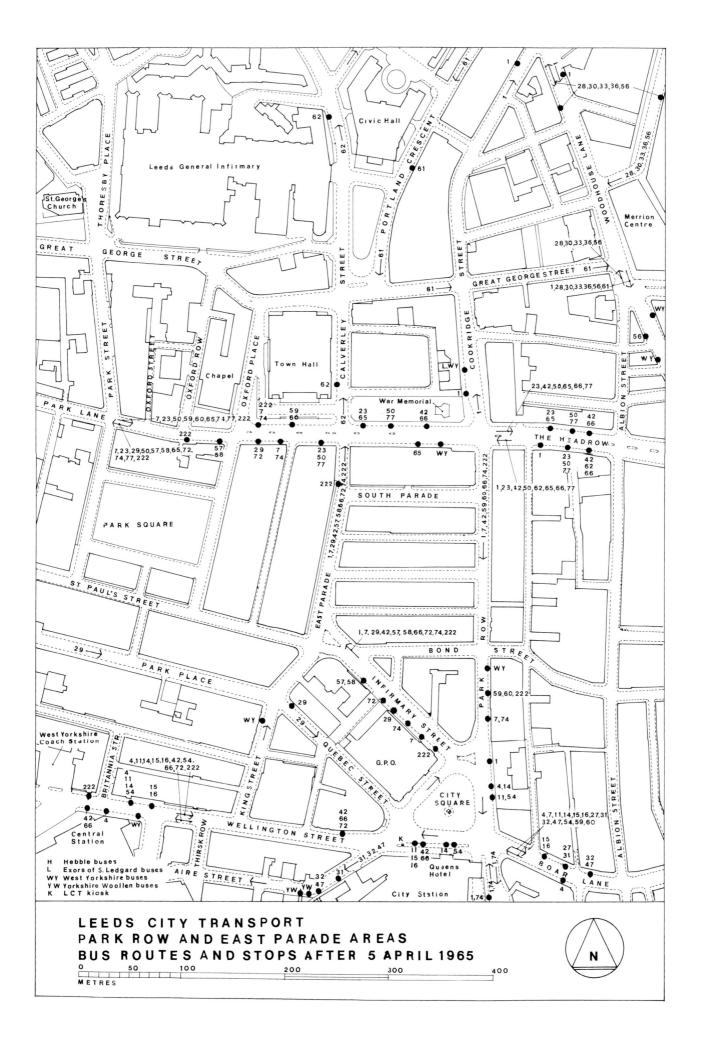

LEEDS CITY TRANSPORT
PARK ROW AND EAST PARADE AREAS
BUS ROUTES AND STOPS AFTER 5 APRIL 1965

Park and Ride Buses

The new concept of "Park and Ride" had been suggested by Councillor Bertrand Mather as early as 1955 and was briefly discussed in the last chapter.

The Kirkstall area was selected for the experiment. There was heavy traffic on Kirkstall Road and during the week beginning 7 March 1965 one of the A.E.C. Reliance buses was used for tests at peak periods to determine the best and quickest route. The route selected was from a new car park in Kirkstall Lane via Kirkstall Hill, Burley Road, Burley Street, Park Lane, Westgate, The Headrow, Park Row, City Square and Wellington Street. Passengers could alight at four stops only: Westgate, Park Row, City Square and outside the Central Station in Wellington Street. Buses then returned empty to the car park via Wellington Street, Kirkstall Road, Haddon Road, Burley Road and Kirkstall Hill.

In the evening buses left the Central Station stop and then ran via City Square, Infirmary Street, East Parade, and then followed the morning route in reverse to Kirkstall, subsequently returning empty to Wellington Street. Passengers could board the bus in Infirmary Street, East Parade and Westgate in addition to the Central Station.

In the morning, departures from Kirkstall Lane were at ten minute intervals from 7.30 a.m. to 9.30 a.m. and in the evening, from 4.30 p.m. to 6.10 p.m. The newest Leeds one-man operated single deck buses, A.E.C. Reliances, 39-47, were allocated to the service and each had "PARK AND RIDE" added to their destinations. Three buses worked the service and the fare was 1s.6d. return, which included all day parking at Kirkstall.

The route was roughly parallel to Kirkstall Road and buses took about ten minutes to cover the journey in either direction. This express bus service, numbered 222, until then the highest numbered bus service ever operated by the Department, began operation on Monday, 5 April 1965. Regrettably it was a total failure. Although well advertised, motorists ignored it. A maximum of about ten passengers used the service on any one day. On Friday, 16 April 1965, the writer and his wife used the service and were surprised to find that theirs was the only car in the Kirkstall Lane Park. They were questioned by a girl, preparing a census of passengers, offered a cup of tea by the driver of bus 41, and given a detailed description of the operation of the Solomatic ticket machine. After their return in the evening, the buses stopped running.

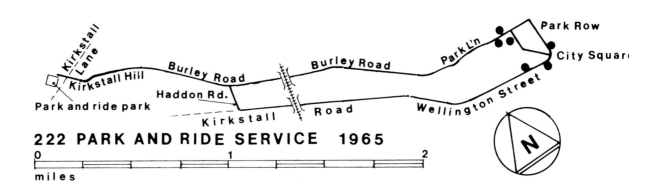

222 PARK AND RIDE SERVICE 1965

A.E.C. Reliance 43, the last 222 Park and Ride bus, seen here at the Kirkstall Lane car park waiting to depart on its final journey on 23 April 1965. There were no passengers. *Author.*

A.E.C. Reliance 42 has just left the temporary car park off Kirkstall Lane and is in Church Street, Kirkstall, and about to turn into Morris Lane to the waiting point. It is on the experimental 222 Park and Ride route from the city centre to Kirkstall. It was stated that this was the first Park and Ride service in the country. It was a total failure. The date is 16 April 1965. *Author.*

The driver, J. Calvert, poses with A.E.C. Reliance 41 at the 222 waiting point in Morris Lane, Kirkstall, on 23 April 1965, the final day of operation. There were no passengers on the bus. Behind is 43 which was the last bus to work the service. Church Street is on the left hand side. *Author.*

The local press reported that for the period, 5-16 April, only 115 passengers had been carried on 80 bus journeys inward and outward, the total receipts being less than £5. It was estimated that £8,000 per year was being lost on the service. Although motorists had complained of the new parking restrictions in the city centre they were not attracted to the Park and Ride idea.

Thomas Lord, the General Manager, said that everyone agreed with the scheme as long as someone else used it. Alderman Rafferty said that if the service continued it would cost thousands of pounds per year as well as tying up buses and personnel at peak periods.

"It seems as if motorists have been finding sufficient accommodation for themselves in the city centre in spite of what has been said about the new traffic systems driving the motorists away," he said. A special meeting of members of the Transport Committee was held on 21 April and on Friday, the 23rd, the service ceased, bus 43 running the final journey from Leeds at 6.20 p.m. It was stated that the total cost of the scheme had been £1,425 - £75 in wages and £1,350 for the preparation of the car park at Kirkstall.

This was not, however, the end of the Park and Ride idea. On the occasion of the England and New Zealand Test Match at Headingley beginning on 8 July 1965, a special bus service was operated from Hyde Park to Cardigan Road for motorists who left their cars on Woodhouse Moor car park. There was also another bus service from the Kirkstall Lane car park (formerly used by the 222 service) to the cricket ground. In subsequent years there were similar Park and Ride services on special occasions.

Other Service Alterations etc.

In addition to the Park and Ride scheme and the many alterations to bus services occasioned by the one-way alterations in the city centre, during 1965 there were other bus route extensions and alterations:

Service 12 and 12 Circular (Middleton). From 25 January these services were rerouted in the city centre: On inward journeys from Middleton. buses ran via Briggate and The Headrow to a new terminus outside Willis and Ludlow's Store in Vicar Lane. The former route was via Duncan Street, Call Lane, Kirkgate, and New Market Street to the loading point on the Corn Exchange island. On journeys to Middleton buses ran via Vicar Lane and New Market Street and then resumed their former route.

Service 38 (Whitkirk-Moortown). From 28 February, so as to enable buses to turn more easily, this service was extended about 200 yards from Moortown Corner via Harrogate Road to a new terminus at the roundabout at the junction of Harrogate Road with Stonegate Road.

Service 45 (Wortley-Meanwood only). From 10 May, buses short working from Wortley to Meanwood only were extended along Green Road to terminate at the same point as services 8, 52 and 53.

Service 4 (Horsforth-Cross Gates) and Service 24 (Central Bus Station-Swarcliffe) were withdrawn on Saturday, 17 July, and the following day replaced by two new services:

Service 24 (Horsforth-Swarcliffe) operating through the Swarcliffe Estate via Eastwood Lane, and Swarcliffe Drive, terminating at Mill Green Gardens.

Service 25 (Horsforth-Swarcliffe) operating through the Swarcliffe Estate via Eastwood Lane, Swarcliffe Drive and Swarcliffe Avenue, terminating at Stanks Drive.

In addition, at peak periods and on Saturdays, buses operated on service 24 between City Square and Cross Gates only. In the westerly direction buses on both services short worked to Kirkstall Abbey. The new terminus of the 24 service at Swarcliffe, Mill Green Gardens, was at the point where the former service 24 terminated until it was extended on 2 September 1962 via Stanks Lane North to Eastwood

Drive. The latter point was now served by the new 25 service.

An application had been made by the Transport Department to the Yorkshire Traffic Commissioners to extend the Kirkstall Abbey buses about half a mile to Kirkstall Forge as the existing turning point at Abbey Walk, Kirkstall Abbey, was considered unsafe. At the Forge there was a bus turning circle, built following the closure of the tramway in 1949, and Corporation buses turned for the Forge employees. The application had been rejected and the Corporation appealed to the Ministry of Transport. The hearing was held on 8 October 1965.

Miss E.M.Boyns, for the Corporation, said the existing turning point was not ideal because vision was restricted, due to the amount of traffic on the road, and the 'U' turn manoeuvre, which the buses had to make. It was not to increase the number of passengers, but to find a solution to a traffic problem. The West Yorkshire Road Car Company and Samuel Ledgard Ltd., whose buses ran in opposition, described it as a case of "nibbling," and said that the Corporation wanted all the traffic from the nearby housing estate. That was why they wanted to go to Kirkstall Forge. The Corporation appeal was thrown out, but the following year the Transport Department found a better excuse for abandoning the Abbey Walk turning point. Beginning on 14 February 1966, a 700 yards length of Abbey Road, an accident "black spot", was converted into a dual carriageway. This included the section passing Abbey Walk. Access was blocked and, from 1 August 1966, buses running to Kirkstall Abbey on services 24 and 25 were extended to a newly constructed turning bay at the Vesper Gate Hotel, some 150 yards past Abbey Walk. Construction of the dual carriageway took eleven months and it was opened for traffic on 12 January 1967.

On Sunday, 17 October 1965, a bus station attached to the newly built Seacroft Town Centre, came into use. Five days later, the Centre was opened by H.M. the Queen. 80,000 people were within "easy shopping distance" of the Centre and there were 120,000 in villages and townships just over the Leeds city boundary. Bus services 11, 15, 16 and 45 were all extended to the bus station from their various previous termini in the Seacroft Estate. The bus station was situated in Seacroft Avenue and is discussed further in Chapter 90.

From Monday, 18 October, buses, which formerly operated from Bramley Town End and City Square to Seacroft Coal Road (Limewood Approach) at peak hours only, on Mondays to Saturdays, as an extension to service 16, now showed route number 17.

Adjacent to the Seacroft Bus Station was the old village of Seacroft. In the nineteenth and early twentieth centuries, as Leeds expanded it absorbed the local villages and several of these still existed in the early 1960's. Leeds City Council adopted a policy of "comprehensive development" for their replacement, property and land being purchased by compulsory purchase order. In planning jargon, the authorities said that the "old engulfed village nuclei" were to be rebuilt as modern neighbourhood centres.

The centuries old village of Chapel Allerton, served by the early horse buses some one hundred years earlier, was "outdated" and obliterated in 1963-4. In spite of protests from local residents, it was replaced by anonymous local authority housing. The quaint villages of Farnley and Bramley also disappeared. In 1965 proposals were submitted for the replacement of Seacroft village. A Corporation official described the layout of Seacroft as "higgledy-piggledy" and said that many of the houses were "unfit for human habitation." Having seen what had happened at Chapel Allerton, the local residents strongly protested against the proposals and eventually won their case.

The Seacroft Town Centre was widely praised in 1965. In a glowing leading article the 'Yorkshire Evening

Post' said it "visibly expressed a new and exhilarating age."
There were suggestions that the centres of some of the nearby small towns, such as Wetherby and Otley, could be redeveloped on the same lines. Within a very short time readers of the local press were describing the new Centre as "depressing." Traders were also not happy saying that it "had not come up to expectations." The Centre was never a commercial success, was shoddily built and soon became obsolescent. 35 years or so later both it and the bus station were removed. A new bus station was later built. Most of the old village still stands.

The local opposition at Seacroft was nothing compared with the protests that attended the Corporation proposals for the comprehensive development of Headingley. A scheme was prepared by the City Architect and Engineer's Department, based on the Buchanan report, in which 32 acres of the older part of Headingley were to be replaced by a vehicle free area. It was to be similar to the Seacroft Town Centre and a major district centre serving 60,000 people. There were to be flats, service industry units, a library, clinic, shops and car parking for 300 to 400 cars. The scheme depended on the construction of a dual carriageway by-pass where bus and motor traffic on Otley Road would be diverted. This by-pass idea was not new and had been originally proposed pre-war in 1938. It had been bitterly opposed by the residents and had not been proceeded with.

The drawings show that another dual carriageway was proposed from North Lane to Shaw Lane on the western side of the village. Buses on the 44 and 45 routes were to be diverted via this new road. There was to be a bus station off St. Michael's Road. Many homes were to be demolished and there was intense opposition from the "shocked residents" at the "high handed actions" of Leeds Corporation. In July 1965 the scheme was thrown out, but a sum of £670,000 for the by-pass was included in the Ministry of Transport's 1967-68 spending programme.

Further schemes with an elevated road and the road in a cutting were submitted, but rejected by the Government. Work was scheduled to start in 1973, but was not carried out. The old part of Headingley, although heavily congested with motor and bus traffic, is still there. A similar centre for Moortown serving 28,000 people was also proposed. There was again major opposition and the scheme suffered the same fate as the Headingley proposals.

A report issued in August 1966 "Living in Leeds" announced a reversal of policy. Leeds was now to make a "determined effort" to preserve what was left of the old villages – the "quiet picturesque backwaters".

In 1965 a nationally agreed 40 hour week and service bonus scheme for bus crews had been implemented and as a result the Transport Department was again facing financial problems. Alderman Rafferty said that the cost would be in the region of £175,000. There had been fare increases in November 1964 and May 1965. In January 1966 the estimated deficit at the end of the financial year was £426,424. Rafferty said that fare increases were "inevitable."

On 6 August 1965 the then Minister of Transport, Tom Fraser, visited Leeds. He was impressed with the one-way system and said that a "special partnership" between Leeds and the Ministry of Transport was to be set up to "examine what is involved in forward-looking measures to deal with traffic in towns over the next few years." The partnership was the first of its kind. Fraser predicted that much of the city's thinking on the future development of transport was going to become of much wider application. This was to be a blueprint for similar arrangements throughout Britain. In the partnership he did not rule out anything from technical advice to financial help. He called for boldness and said that some of the things, which would have to be done might not be universally popular.

"In face of rapidly increasing car ownership, the solution of the problem lay in a concerted plan. This covered traffic management, (including measures to help the bus and restrain commuter traffic), road improvements, and comprehensive parking control, all coupled with a continuous effort to ensure that public transport services matched, to the greatest possible extent, the needs of the travelling public."

'Yorkshire Evening Post', 6 August 1965.

Daimler Fleetline 105 in the Seacroft Bus Station on 1 October 1967. *Author.*

Mr. Fraser said he was glad to see that this policy was clearly reflected in what the City Council was already doing and preparing to do. Modern ideas on traffic included an increasing need for the segregation of pedestrians and vehicles and priority for public transport would have to be taken further than had so far been done. He said that ideally public transport should be separated from other traffic by its own track, to the point of reserving lanes for buses, at any rate for parts of the day. He said that these sorts of things were not in the mind of Parliament when it passed existing legislation and it might well be that changes were needed.

A bus tour of the new one-way traffic system in the centre of the city was included in Fraser's programme.

The local press had reservations about Fraser's proposals. It hoped that Leeds would not become Whitehall's "guinea pig," and thought that traffic lanes for buses would not "commend themselves to many Leeds motorists." From Fraser's words it said that motorists were "in for a thin time."

The R.A.C. complained that the one major thing missing from the partnership was the motorist. It believed that the views of the rapidly growing number of motorists must be considered.

The first result of the partnership was the publication in December 1965 of an interim report, which said that the needs of pedestrians were to be considered. The main concern of the partnership was to deal with the potential traffic growth over the next decade and the effectiveness of possible solutions. These were to be tested in Leeds. The first priority was given to studying the future role and operational requirements for public transport. Kirkstall Road was selected for study with a view to improving traffic flows and reducing conflicts between traffic and the environment. It was to be some months before the first results of the partnership became evident.

In July 1965 the Transport Committee announced that it was to purchase 100 new buses to operate what was referred to by Alderman Rafferty, Chairman of the Transport Committee as "a three-tier wedding cake" system of public transport, which included "dumb bell" runs by some of the city's buses. Rafferty explained that the tiers of the "wedding cake" would be:

1. Stage carrying services operated by rear entrance double deck buses, as at present in use for the normal picking up and setting down of passengers.

2. Limited stop services operated by front entrance double deckers, which would speed up journeys to work and give people a later start from home.

3. Express services, almost non-stop, operated by new large capacity, single deck vehicles.

With the "wedding cake" policy in mind, on 19 July the Committee agreed to place orders for 90 new double deck buses (60 front entrance and 30 rear entrance), and ten new single deckers, for delivery over the next two years.

Alderman Rafferty said that some of the new single deck buses might be 36 feet long, compared with the 30 feet at present in use. This was with a view to introducing express-type services from estates such as Whinmoor and Seacroft into the city centre. These were to be known as "dumb bell" services with the estates at one end of them, the city centre at the other and the buses making only a few stops in between the two ends of the "dumb bell."

Under construction was the Whinmoor housing estate, on the east side of the city, adjacent to York Road. The buses would be introduced as soon as the estate was ready. The idea was to make public transport more attractive, reduce journey times, and to encourage car owners to travel on buses.

Shortly after the visit of the Minister of Transport, Rafferty expounded on the "wedding cake" idea. He looked forward to the time when nobody "need walk more than 400 yards to adequate public transport facilities."

"He argued that buses should be given a traffic lane to themselves because they carried the maximum number of people and were therefore entitled to it.

He referred to ways in which Leeds was pioneering the public transport field. The recent "park and ride" experiment had failed, only because there was no compulsion on motorists to park their cars and complete their journey to the city by bus.

But the day is not far distant when they will be glad to "park and ride" if they are going to get to the city centre in reasonable time," he added.

The possibilities of "park and ride" were still there and the car park at Kirkstall for that purpose was used at the recent Headingley Test Match when motorists were conveyed from there to the cricket ground with "tremendous success."

'The Yorkshire Post', 17 August 1965.

The 'Yorkshire Evening Post' was concerned by Rafferty's comments and said that the motor car was now an essential part of business and social life, and that it played a big part in trade and facilitated shopping. "We must watch the interests of motorists and traders. They have their rights as well as through traffic," it added.

Arnold Stone, Chief Traffic Officer of the Leeds Transport undertaking, at an inaugural address as Chairman of the Yorkshire section of the Institute of Transport, said that the bus gave the most flexible form of transport and easily fitted in with the plans of a developing city.

"To encourage the continued use of public transport we must aim at a far higher degree of reliability and efficiency." If a person could always board a bus at a particular time and reach a destination at a pre-determined time he was not likely to contemplate private transport. "He cannot, however, do so at the present time."

'The Yorkshire Post', 14 October 1965.

In September 1965 a request was received from Morley Corporation for an extension of the Leeds-Morley bus service to Thorpe and East Ardsley, but was turned down by the Transport Committee. Alderman Rafferty said "In the light of our present staff position we have had to say 'no' with regret, but we will review the position in 12 month's time."

A number of alterations to some bus services occurred during the latter part of 1965.

Service 29 (infirmary Street-Middleton) had been diverted from 4 January 1965 via Wellington Street and Queen Street to Park Place on inward journeys. This had been due to the closure of a section of Queen Street between Park Place and St. Paul's Street. Queen Street reopened to traffic in September 1965, but the 29 buses continued to use Wellington Street and Queen Street. Previously the service ran inward via Westgate, St. Paul's Street and Queen Street to Park Place.

From 31 October service 8 (Cottingley or Elland Road-Meanwood) was extended from Meanwood via Church Lane, Tongue Lane, Black Moor Road and Deanswood Hill to Cranmer Bank in the Moortown Estate. As a result service 69 (Central Bus Station to Moortown) was withdrawn on 30 October. The alterations resulted in a more frequent service to the Moortown Estate. The alterations led to a revision of services 52 and 53 (Morley to Meanwood), which had inter-worked with service 8 and also services 34/35, 37/43 and 70 which had been coordinated with the 69 buses.

Also on 31 October the long awaited extension of the joint service 72 (Infirmary Street-Bradford) was carried through to the Leeds Central Bus Station. The route from the bus station was via Eastgate, The Headrow, Westgate, Wellington Street and then as the former route. The extension was introduced due to the new one-way street

The 69 bus service, Central Bus Station-Moortown, existed for 15 years from 1 March 1950 to 30 October 1965. Leyland PD2/14 304 is at the Moortown terminus at Cranmer Bank. The date is 1 February 1964, minutes before a torrential downpour. *Author.*

Leyland Atlantean 335 at Seacroft Bus Station on 24 November 1968. *J.B.Parkin.*

system in Leeds and pressure from Bradford Corporation. The Yorkshire Traffic Commissioners granted a joint application by the Leeds and Bradford Corporations on 11 May 1965. The purpose of the extension, in the words of L. Darwin, the Bradford assistant traffic superintendent, was to "facilitate better connections with other services operating from the bus station." It marked the return of Bradford buses to the Central Bus Station after a period of 26 years. The service 72 buses had worked through to the Bus Station for a short time pre-war from 7 December 1938, but were curtailed to Infirmary Street on 11 September 1939, shortly after the outbreak of war.

In accordance with its policy of purchasing 50 new buses per year, on 15 June 1964 the Transport Committee accepted the following tenders:

A.E.C. (Sales) Ltd. 20 double deck chassis for rear entrance omnibus bodies for £54,480.

Transport Vehicles (Daimler) Ltd. 15 double deck chassis for rear entrance omnibus bodies for £43,935.

Leyland Motors Ltd. 15 double deck chassis for rear entrance omnibus bodies for £41,079 15s.0d.

Chas. H. Roe Ltd. 15 double deck rear entrance omnibus bodies (composite construction) for £51,375.

Chas. H. Roe Ltd. 20 double deck rear entrance omnibus bodies (metal framed) for £70,800.

Metropolitan-Cammell-Weymann Ltd. 15 double deck rear entrance omnibus bodies (metal framed) for £53,520.

All the chassis were subject to a delivery charge of 1s.6d. per mile.

The Transport Department did a considerable amount of private hire work using single deck buses. To assist with the private hire business, in June 1964 the Transport Committee agreed to purchase a dual-purpose coach body from Charles H. Roe Ltd. for £3,485. The coach made its appearance in February 1965 and on the 15th it was inspected by members of the Transport Committee. The Committee agreed that the coach be made available "for private hire purposes and on the occasion of annual visits by committees." The vehicle was mounted on an A.E.C. Reliance chassis, the Roe 37-seat body having, according to 'The Leeds and District Transport News', "a very pleasing appearance, strongly resembling the Roe 'Dalesman' in frontal design." The body was 30ft.6in. long and 8ft.0in. wide. The front entrance door was electrically operated and controlled by the driver. Green moquette seats were fitted. There were no opening windows, ventilation being provided by special intakes over each window. Double headlights were fitted as on Daimler Fleetline 101, and a destination blind was positioned at the front beneath the wrap round windscreen. The vehicle had a special livery, and was the first coach to be owned by the Transport Department. Numbered 10, registration ANW 710C, it made its first private hire trip from Torre Road (No.2 Garage) on 10 March 1965.

June 1965 saw the appearance of the first of the ten Leyland Atlanteans. These had been ordered almost two years earlier. Classified as Leyland Atlantean PDR/1, Mk.II they had Weymann H41/29F bodies and were numbered 331-340 (CUB 331-340C).

331 was delivered on 21 June and began driver training duties on the 28th operating on trade plates. The first to appear in service was 339 on 5 July and all had entered service by August with the exception of 340, which followed over a year later.

The bodies on the Atlanteans were similar to those on the Roe bodied Daimler Fleetlines, but with a much more square appearance at the front and rear, especially when viewed from the side. The vehicles had two-piece windscreens and engine shrouds. The Leyland Atlantean badge was carried on the engine compartment. There was no Leyland badge on the front. Internally the layout was very similar to that of the Fleetlines with ample luggage space and Roe "safety" staircases. The window surrounds

and roof were finished in a similar manner to those on the Weymann-bodied Leyland PD3A buses, 311-330. The seats were of the new standard type, complete with grab rails, now a feature of the modern Leeds bus. Initially the Atlanteans were allocated to Bramley Garage and ran on routes 11 (Gipton-Greenthorpe) and 15/16 (Bramley Town End to Seacroft South Parkway and North Parkway) respectively.

The introduction of new buses resulted in the withdrawal of more of the A.E.C. Regent III, 439, 441-444, 446, 447, 449 and 450, and four Leyland PD2 350, 371, 375 and 382. 371 and 375 were withdrawn following accidents on 24 August and 2 December 1965 respectively. 441-444, 446, 447 and 449 were notable as they were the last five-bay bodied Roe vehicles in the fleet (with the exception of 30ft. long buses). There were now no buses in the passenger fleet with wooden interior window surrounds and they were also the last in service fitted with side destination blinds.

Number 450 was an odd vehicle, being the only one of its type in the fleet. It was fitted with a Park Royal metal body constructed by Roe and was the first bus to be delivered with a sliding door to the driver's cab.

Delivery of new buses in the mid-sixties was slow and, by the end of 1965, only a few of the 1964 order had been delivered. In February 1965 the order had been modified. The rear entrance Daimlers and Leylands on order were altered to 15 Daimler Fleetlines and 15 Leyland Atlanteans. Alderman Rafferty said that the existing front entrance buses had proved "very popular" with both the passengers and crews. Points in favour of the "new-look" buses included a higher safety factor, with the virtual elimination of platform accidents, due to the driver operated doors, better luggage facilities, longer life of the vehicles, and greater passenger comfort.

The Daimlers were still to have Roe bodies and the Leylands M.C.W. Group bodies. The balance of the order for 20 A.E.C. Regent V buses with rear entrance Roe bodies was unaltered.

The acquisition of more buses and other interesting developments are discussed in the next chapter.

A.E.C. Reliance coach 10, the first coach to be owned by the Leeds Transport Department, in March 1965 before it entered passenger service.
W.D.Wilson/L.T.H.S.

CHAPTER 81

The Buses 1966 to 1967 and the end of the Rafferty Era

On 1 December 1965 the "modern" Leeds double deck front entrance bus fleet consisted of ten Daimler Fleetlines, 101-110, and nine Leyland Atlanteans, 331-339. There were 20 of the old type rear entrance A.E.C.Regent Mark V buses on order plus 15 Fleetlines and 15 Atlanteans.

In December and January the 20 rear entrance A.E.C. buses were delivered. Numbered 964-983, they all entered service from 3 December 1965 to 8 January the following year. Except for minor details, they were very similar to 949-963, delivered in 1964.

Registrations for 964-973 were DUM 964-973C and for 974-983 ENW 974-983D. Their registration numbers were positioned above the rear platform window, in a similar manner to that which had been fitted to one of the learner buses, (No.2 LUA 417) some months before. This was a new feature in Leeds, but had been seen on many buses operated by the West Riding Automobile Company for a considerable time. The rear trafficators were similar to those on the Atlanteans, being mounted above the rear and stop lights, instead of being combined with them. The front offside trafficator was mounted below cab window, instead of on the window pillar. Instead of a tungsten lamp, platform lighting was a fluorescent tube. The saloon lighting, also fluorescent, lacked the illuminated advertisement panels fitted in the lower saloons of 949-963. The amber "sunshine" roof panels were double glazed in order to avoid condensation and large type driving mirrors were supplied. 973 was fitted with an illuminated offside exterior advertisement panel.

There was a minor difference in the seating, 964-973 had seats with back cushions similar to buses 101-115, 331-339 and 949-963, i.e. with a protruding section at shoulder level. 974-983 did not have this feature, the seat backs having straight cushions.

These 20 buses were the last rear entrance buses to be purchased by Leeds Corporation, although, as will be seen, more were ordered and later cancelled. For cost reasons, the Transport Department concentrated on removing conductors from its bus operations. This could only be achieved by the use of one-man operated front entrance buses. There was already a bus service of this type in Leeds - route 9 Ring Road - and over the following years the number of one-man services increased.

It was to be another four months before the next batch of buses were delivered. These were the 15 Daimler Fleetlines, the second batch of this type of bus to be delivered to Leeds. They differed considerably in body design to the previous buses, 101-110. They were of the latest Charles Roe style very similar to some recently delivered West Riding Atlanteans. The frontal design was much improved as wrap around windscreens were fitted both upstairs and down, with the front side windows sloping downwards at the front so as to meet the upper windows. Engine shrouds were fitted at the rear, but these were of a different design to the earlier buses. On 101-110 the shrouds were flush sided and tapered in order to come level with the engine compartment. The new vehicles had the engine protruding about six inches, and various additional removable panels were fitted to the shrouds and engine compartment to give better access. Internally the finish was similar to that of the earlier buses. The new buses were numbered 116-130 (FUB 116-130D) and had Roe H41/29F bodies. They all appeared in service during May 1966.

As a result of the purchase of the 35 new buses a similar number of old buses were withdrawn. These were all of the A.E.C. Regent III or Leyland PD2 type. In January 1966 20 buses: A.E.C.Regent III, 451-465, and five Leyland PD2, 354, 355, and 357-9, were taken out of

A,E,C, Regent V 969, one of the last rear entrance buses to be supplied to Leeds, at the bottom of Churwell Hill on 3 September 1966. It is on service 53 to Meanwood and the railway viaduct is in the background. *Author.*

Daimler Fleetline 118 at Haddon Place, Kirkstall Road, on 11 July 1966. *W.D.Wilson/L.T.H.S.*

Leyland PD2 367 was one of the buses taken out of service in May and June 1966. It was photographed in Burley Road approaching the St. Ann's Gardens stop on 29 April 1966 shortly before withdrawal. It is on the 23 (Central Bus Station-Intake) service and behind is A.E.C. Regent III 743 on the 50 Horsforth service. *W.D.Wilson/L.T.H.S.*

A.E.C. Regent V 966 in Woodhouse Lane on 10 September 1971. The Central High School is in the background. The building was converted into offices in 1994. *W.D.Wilson/L.T.H.S.*

service. The withdrawals in May and June comprised 15 Leyland PD2 buses, 360-362, 364-368, 370, 373, 374 and 376-379. The only buses of this type remaining in service after June 1966 were 380, 381, and 383-399.

It was December 1966 and January 1967 when the Atlanteans were delivered and these are discussed later.

In the first six months of 1966 some route alterations took place and one or two route extensions. A big alteration was the introduction of a new service 40 from Stanks to Raynville, which began operation on 1 May. This gave residents in the Raynville Estate area of Bramley, a direct service to the city centre for the first time. It had been made possible by a road improvement at Amen Corner where the turning from Armley Ridge Road into Raynville Road had been too sharp for buses to negotiate. This had now been eased. New service 40 replaced the existing service from Stanks to the Central Bus Station. The route of the service was the same as before from Stanks (Kelmscott Green) to the Woodpecker Inn, York Road, and buses then ran via Marsh Lane, York Street, New York Street, Harper Street, Kirkgate, New Market Street, (Call Lane, New York Street in other direction), Duncan Street, Boar Lane, City Square, Wellington Street, Wellington Road, Armley Road, Stanningley Road, Armley Ridge Road, and Raynville Road as far as Outgang. The Raynville area had previously been served by the one-man services 71 and 73 from Greenthorpe to Headingley and Moor Grange respectively. Service 71 was withdrawn after Saturday 30 April 1966.

The other relatively minor route alterations and extensions in this period were as follows:

Services 61 and 62 East End Park Circulars. On 11 May 1964, East Street was closed owing to a new sewer and reopened to traffic on 6 January 1966. Services 61 and 62 were rerouted permanently over the diversion to serve the new Saxton Gardens Flats. From Duke Street, the route was Marsh Lane, Saxton Lane, Flax Place, Richmond Street and then rejoining East Street.

Service 58 and 60 Hyde Park Circulars via Clarendon Road. A permanent diversion occurred in early January 1966 when a new length of Park Lane was opened as a dual carriageway between Westgate roundabout and Belle Vue Road. Hanover Lane was closed and Hanover Way opened completely to Park Lane. Services 58 and 60 were diverted via Hanover Way.

Service 24 Horsforth-Swarcliffe. This service was extended for a short distance at Swarcliffe on 30 March 1966 when a new turning circle was brought into use. Buses now continued to the end of Swarcliffe Drive and turned into Stanks Lane North for a short distance to the new turning point.

Service 8 Cottingley-Moortown. From 1 May 1966 this service was extended at the Moortown end via Cranmer Bank to a new terminus at Cranmer Road. The extension was to be for a trial period of three months, but became permanent.

A major diversion of the 57 and 58 (Hyde Park Circulars) occurred from 29 April 1966 when buses were diverted via Woodhouse Street, Oxford Road and Meanwood Road instead of running direct from Woodhouse Street to Meanwood Road via Cambridge Road. The diversion was due to the construction of a new sewer in Cambridge Road. On 11 August the following year buses reverted to their normal route.

During the second half of 1966 there were other route alterations. One of the most interesting was the extension of the 45 service (Wortley-Seacroft Town Centre) from Seacroft to Stanks, which took place on 25 September. The route was via Seacroft Avenue, North Parkway, York Road, Stanks Lane North, Stanks Drive, Stanks Lane South, Barwick Road and Pendas Way, the terminus being at Kelmscott Green, at the same point as the terminus of service 40. Buses on this service ran through Seacroft Bus Station in both directions. Service 45 was now the longest operated by the Transport Department - 14·19 miles. The through fare was 1s.0d. for a ride lasting 66 minutes. Comparative mileages for some other long routes operated were as follows:

Service 9 Ring Road,	13·81 miles
Service 25 Horsforth to Swarcliffe	11.09 miles
Service 32 Moortown to Pudsey	12·33 miles

Service 44 Halton Moor to Stanningley   11·06 miles
Service 72 Leeds to Bradford   9·71 miles

The construction of the new Inner Ring Road had been started in July 1964. It had two 24 feet wide carriageways and by 1966 the first phase was nearing completion. On 13 March 1966 the first bridge, which carried Woodhouse Lane over the new road, came into use. Buses and other traffic had been diverted for many months via a loop road constructed to the south west of Woodhouse Lane. The first phase of the Ring Road opened in 1967, but it was not until Phase 3, which ran from the bottom of York Road, came into use that the full benefits were felt.

The lower part of Woodhouse Lane carried two-way traffic, but an alteration took place from 16 October 1966. On that day Woodhouse Lane became one-way (outward) between Portland Crescent and Blackman Lane. Buses running into Leeds via Woodhouse Lane now turned left into Blackman Lane and then right into a new road called New Woodhouse Lane, rejoining Woodhouse Lane at a point almost opposite Portland Crescent. Services affected were 1, 28, 30, 33, 36 and 56. Buses on service 61 now had to turn left into New Woodhouse Lane prior to continuing on their old route along Portland Crescent. Service 62 running in the opposite direction was not affected.

At the same time as New Woodhouse Lane was under construction, Blenheim Walk, on the northern side of Blackman Lane and leading to Woodhouse Lane, was widened. From 4 December 1966, buses running inward on services 28, 30, 33, 36 and 56 were diverted via Blenheim Walk instead of Woodhouse Lane. Service 1 (Lawnswood-Beeston) continued to run via Woodhouse Lane and Blackman Lane serving Leeds University.

An area of Leeds where there was "considerable" traffic congestion was at the junctions of Whitehall Road, Wellington Road, Spence Lane and Gelderd Road. At peak periods it was sometimes necessary to have three police constables on point duty. The one-way system in the centre of the city had eased congestion and speeded up traffic and in July 1965 the City Engineer was instructed to prepare a one-way traffic scheme for the Whitehall Road area. This came into operation on 4 December 1966 and several bus services were affected:

Service 29. On journeys from Middleton to City Square buses now ran via Wortley Lane, Gelderd Road, Spence Lane, and Wellington Road. Previously they had operated via Spence Lane, Whitehall Road, Smith Street and Gelderd Road to Wellington Road. There was no change of route in the opposite direction.

Services 31, 32 and 47. On outward journeys to New Farnley, Pudsey or Old Farnley, buses now ran via Spence Lane and Wortley Lane between Whitehall Road and Gelderd Road. Formerly they operated directly from Whitehall Road to Gelderd Road. There was no change of route in the opposite direction.

Service 46. On journeys from Middleton or Belle Isle to Bramley Town End, buses were diverted via Wortley Lane and Gelderd Road, reverting to their original route at Spence Lane. On journeys to Belle Isle or Middleton buses ran via Wellington Road, Ellis Buildings and Gelderd Road to Spence Lane.

Services 11, 15, 16, 17, 42 and 66. Outward journeys were diverted via Gelderd Road and Spence Lane instead of going directly along Wellington Road.

In Leeds some of the independent bus operators were using the continental 24-hour clock system. Leeds said it would be "out of step" if it did not conform and, from 1 April

Peak hour service 71 from Greenthorpe to Headingley was short lived and lasted from 4 March 1964 to 30 April 1966. It was one-man operated from 17 August 1964. A.E.C. Reliance 37 is seen at Bramley Town End on 4 May 1964. Bramley Depot is in the background. *Author.*

From 29 April 1966 to 11 August 1967 part of Cambridge Road was closed due to the construction of a sewer and buses on the Hyde Park Circular routes were diverted via adjacent Oxford Road. A.E.C. Regent III 604 is in Oxford Road and is passing Clayfield Place on its way to Meanwood Road. The date is 9 July 1966. The bus, Oxford Road and Clayfield Place no longer exist. There are currently fields and trees on this site. *Author.*

1966, the timing of municipal bus operation in Leeds used the 24-hour clock.

So the Transport Committee contemplates going over to the 24-hour clock system. It would be a waste of "time" for the No.67 Monkswood Gate route; the bus crews do not even keep to the 12-hour clock, but run one of their own. If the time of departure from the terminus is as printed in the official timetable, it is a coincidence.

From a letter from "Frozen Stiff".

'Yorkshire Evening Post'. 22 December 1965.

During the financial year 1965-66 the number of passengers carried on the buses decreased by 9 million. Thomas Lord, the General Manager, said the reasons were social ones accounted for by the growth in car ownership and a "greater disposition among people to stay at home in the evening and enjoy TV entertainment."

In 1966 the new Minister of Transport, Barbara Castle, made a number of proposals, which were to affect Leeds City Transport undertaking and all others throughout the country.

In March 1966 suggestions to increase bus speeds were considered. Before 1961 the maximum speed allowed for a bus was 30 m.p.h. In that year it was raised to 40 m.p.h. Improvements in bus design eventually led to the limit being later increased to 50 m.p.h.

From 1 July 1966 Government regulations were introduced permitting one-man operated double deck buses for the first time. It was stipulated that one-man buses should have an entrance at the front and doors at every entrance and exit. Standing was also allowed even if not all seats were occupied. Previously no standing was permitted if there were seats available.

The following month Mrs. Castle said she was

considering allowing an increase in length for single deck buses to the Continental length of 39ft. 4in. instead of 36ft. 0in. The bus manufacturers claimed the increase would stimulate "improved design, increase operating efficiency provide more comfort for passengers," and also assist exports. The Ministry of Transport said the change would not appreciably affect traffic movement and that no adverse affect on road safety was expected.

Of more immediate concern to the Transport Department was the imposition, announced on 20 July 1966, of a wages "freeze" and a similar freeze on bus fares. On 16 August the Department was to have applied to the Yorkshire Traffic Commissioners for authority to revise fares.

The revision would have brought in £479,000 in extra revenue in a full financial year. The increases were to cover bonuses and a 40 hour week for bus crews, which had been introduced at the end of 1965.

Rafferty said he was not responsible for the economic crisis affecting the country. "We shall have to carry the increased costs and we are likely to be well into the red by the end of the year," he commented. He said the application would be deferred "until a suitable time." It was to be heard on 21 December 1966, but was again deferred. In the meantime the deficit on the buses continued to increase. For the year ended 31 March 1967 it was estimated that it would be £388,000. Councillor Wolstenholme was concerned that the loss would have to be met out of the rates. Alderman King, Chairman of the Finance Committee, said: "The actual position is, if and when the Transport Department runs into deficit the amount will be met by bank overdraft – in the same way as any private business in a similar position." It would have no effect on rate moneys.

The proposal had been to increase most fares by an

extra penny. The Labour Government at the time was unpopular and at the City Council election the Socialists were likely to lose power. Wolstenholme said the Labour administration did not have the courage to apply for a fares increase. The increase had to await a change of Council some months later.

Rafferty had referred to possible express bus services, and at the forthcoming commercial motor show, Leeds was to have on view two of the most modern type of buses, giving "maximum comfort and speed." The Lord Mayor, Alderman J.S. Walsh, was impressed and said that public transport was "bound to replace the private car in the future."

October 1966 saw the appearance of three interesting new buses all of different types. The first was 340, ordered over two years earlier, and the final bus of the Leyland Atlantean order, originally scheduled for delivery in the 1964-65 financial year. The other two were exhibited at the Commercial Motor Show, Earl's Court, London, held from 23 September to 1 October 1966. These were a Daimler Fleetline, 131, and an A.E.C Swift, 51.

340 (CUB 340C) was a Leyland Atlantean PDR/1/1 Mk.II fitted with a H41/29F Weymann body, which had been completed by Metropolitan-Cammelll owing to the closure of the Weymann factory. 340 differed considerably from the earlier Weymann production batch, 331-339. Its frontal appearance, to quote 'The Leeds & District Transport News', was "very smart and curved, completed with a wrap-round windscreen and upper saloon front windows." The rear of the bus was of square appearance similar to 331-339. Twin headlights were fitted, like Daimler Fleetline 101, but unlike 101, it did not have a forced heating system of the same type, although this had been specified

when originally ordered. A more conventional system was fitted along with sliding windows for ventilation purposes. The interior design of the window surrounds was light green in colour and of the Metropolitan Cammell pattern. There was the usual high standard of interior finish and seating.

51 (GUM 451D) was an A.E.C. Swift fitted with a Roe B48D body and was the first rear-engine single deck bus in the fleet. It was 36ft.0in. long and 8ft. 2½ in. wide.

The Swift was a new type of single deck bus and had first appeared at the 1964 Commercial Motor Show. It had some of the features of the Leyland Panther, also a recent design, and had a new A.E.C. engine, the AH505, developed from and appreciably more powerful than the earlier AH470 type. 51 differed from the other single deckers having a wide front entrance by which two persons could enter at the same time, although the centre exit was only of single width. There were air-operated doors instead of the usual electrically worked type, those at the front being in two sections. A peaked front and rear were fitted, embracing the destination indicators, which had the route number to the left of the destination aperture instead of underneath as on most other buses that had been recently delivered. The side windows were larger than on previous single deck deliveries and in addition standee type windows were fitted, although the bus was intended for one-man operation. The interior was fitted out in the usual high Roe standard with much use of 'Formica'. A forced heating system was installed along with coach-type opening sunshine roof panels. The seating was standard and there was ample luggage space. The floor was ramped towards the rear in order to gain height over the engine. As the bus was exhibited at Earl's Court, gold lining was added to the normal style

Until 1966 the lower part of Woodhouse Lane was used for two-way traffic but from 16 October 1966 inward traffic was directed to a new road, New Woodhouse Lane. A.E.C. Regent V 976 is operating inward on the old section and was photographed outside Broadcasting House on 15 May 1966. Broadcasting House was originally a Quaker Meeting House. *W.D.Wilson/L.T.H.S.*

Leyland Atlantean 340 crossing Harehills Lane from Foundry Approach into Compton Road on 11 August 1968. Compare with the photograph on page 944 of Volume 3 which shows the same buildings in the background. *J.B. Parkin.*

Roe-bodied A.E.C. Swift 51 was a new type of bus and was the first rear-engine single deck bus in the Leeds fleet. It is seen here in Kirkstall Lane on 12 June 1967. *W.D.Wilson/L.T.H.S.*

green livery. At Earl's Court, 51 was displayed on the A.E.C. Stand and had a plate reading "A.E.C. 1967", fitted in the space occupied by the front registration number. It also had Perspex panels at the rear and on the rear side of the engine so that the power unit could be seen.

131 (HNW 131D), also painted in the green livery with gold lining, was a Daimler Fleetline CRG6LX, with a Roe H45/33F body. This bus was displayed on the Daimler Stand at Earl's Court and was the first bus of its type. It was 32ft.9in. long and 8ft.2½in. wide. The wheelbase was 18ft. 6in. and although the nominal seating capacity of the vehicle was 86, it had 78 seats only, in accordance with the L.C.T. specification. It had the usual Roe safety staircase, standard seating and ample luggage space. The frontal appearance was similar to 116-130, but on the side were only three large panoramic windows. In order to provide through ventilation, two small opening windows were positioned at either end of the large windows, along with two small ventilators in the rear emergency door, but, in addition, the sunshine roof panels to the upper saloon were of the opening type, normally fitted to coaches. Air-operated two-piece doors were fitted. 131 entered service on 28 November 1966.

340 appeared in passenger service on 7 October and, on the evenings of 4 and 6 October, had been used as a recruiting bus for staff at the new Middleton Garage.

51 was used on a demonstration for Transport Department officials and the Press on the morning of Friday 14 October, when it was driven by an A.E.C. representative. Councillor Tom Smith, Deputy chairman of the Transport Committee was a passenger, and said that 51 was the first A.E.C. rear-engined single decker to be operated by any municipality in Britain. He said that the double width entrance was to allow for automatic fare collection and ticket-issuing machines, The Transport Committee was proposing to introduce multi-journey tickets. Passengers using pre-paid multi-journey tickets were to use one half of the entrance and the other half was for those purchasing tickets from the driver.

The same afternoon 51 made an experimental journey on the 9 Ring Road service from Bradford Road to Selby Road and back. Following this duty it returned to the Cross Gates factory of Charles H. Roe for minor modifications. 340 had joined 51 on the demonstration run on 14 October. 51 eventually entered passenger service on 29 November 1966.

At the end of 1966 there were still many buses on order and deliveries continued to be very slow. In February 1965 the Transport Committee had decided to invite tenders for 100 new buses to be delivered in 1966-67 and 1967-68. These were accepted on 19 July 1965 as follows:

Leyland Motors Ltd. 30 Atlantean chassis for double deck front-entrance bodies for £91,538 7s.6d.

Transport Vehicles (Daimler) Ltd. 30 Fleetline chassis for double deck front-entrance bodies for £96,588 15s,0d.

A.E.C. Ltd. 30 Regent chassis for double deck rear-entrance bodies for £87,489.

Charles H.Roe Ltd. 60 double deck front-entrance bodies for £248,160.

Metropolitan-Cammell-Weymann Ltd. 30 double deck rear-entrance bodies (metal framed) for £110,250.

A.E.C. Ltd. 10 Reliance single deck chassis (30 ft. x 8 ft.) for £24,490 subject to an option to substitute longer chassis (36 ft.) at £2,513 per chassis.

At a meeting on 21 February 1966 the Transport Committee agreed to change the order for A.E.C. Reliances to Swifts with longer chassis. Alderman Rafferty said bigger buses, both double and single deck were to be acquired in future. The Swifts were to be all purpose vehicles. The long term policy of the Committee, said Rafferty, was aimed at seated passengers only and giving more comfortable journeys. The new single deckers would have 48 seats as compared with 40 and be 36 feet long instead of 30 feet. They were to be rear-engined, have a much lower floor height and a central exit.

Before the one-way alterations of 4 December 1966, there was bad congestion in the Gelderd Road, Whitehall Road area. A.E.C. Regent III 675 is turning from Spence Lane into Whitehall Road on 6 August 1966. *Author.*

In 1966 the five front-entrance Daimlers, although only four years old, were considered obsolete, offered for sale, but not sold. 575 is leaving East Parade and entering Infirmary Street on 27 March 1965, before the one-way alterations of a week later. It is at the roundabout that was at the junction of East Parade, Infirmary Street, King Street and St. Paul's Street. Atlas Chambers, the white faience building on the extreme left of the picture, still exists, but the other buildings which form the setting were removed between January and March 1966. *Author.*

The total cost of the ten chassis was to be £27,695. At the same time ten single deck bodies were ordered from Roe in the sum of £36,890. A further alteration to the orders was made the following month. A quotation of A.E.C. Ltd. for a further 15, 36 ft. long Swift chassis was accepted in the sum of £41,542 10s. 0d. They were to be supplied instead of 15 of the double deck Regent chassis.

Three months later the idea of purchasing any more rear entrance buses was abandoned. On 18 July 1967 the Transport Committee decided to buy 15 more Swifts in place of the remaining Regents. This would bring the single deck bus fleet up to 45. In September the cost of these 15 Swift chassis was agreed at £41,542 10s.0d.

On 19 December 1966 the order for new buses was again altered. On this occasion the Transport Committee decided to change the order for 30 Leyland Atlantean chassis for 30ft. 0in x 8ft. 0in. wide buses to a larger 78-seat size (33ft. x 8ft. 2½in.) The additional cost was to be £3,685 12s.6d. A further alteration came on 17 April 1967 when the Transport Committee decided that the order for 15 single deck A.E.C. Swifts with Roe bodies should be increased to 25 vehicles. The following month orders for new buses were again altered. The contract with Daimler for 30 Fleetline chassis for 30ft x 8ft. bodies was altered to accommodate 33ft. x 8ft 2½ in. bodies at an increased cost of £3,840.

In 1965 a special partnership between Leeds Corporation and the Ministry of Transport had been formed and in March 1966 it was stated that a new university centre was to be set up to "probe the economic and engineering aspects of transport". The first result was a survey of passengers in the Seacroft, Whinmoor and Swarcliffe areas with a view to introducing the proposed express bus services. It was said that this was the first time in Britain that residents in a suburb were to be asked to co-operate in a survey of this type. It was proposed to cut the journey time between Seacroft and Leeds by half. There would be very few stops and the new single deck high capacity buses would be used. Questionnaires were to be sent out and the answers analysed by Leeds Corporation and Ministry officials. The survey was organised by the Corporation Housing Department. Other authorities in Britain were said to be "keenly interested" in the outcome of the survey.

In October 1966 questionnaires were sent out to between 1,500 to 2,000 households in an area bounded by Barwick Road, Ring Road, York Road, the city boundary and the Whinmoor Estate area. The results of the survey were favourable and three months later Alderman Rafferty said that in May 1967 the Transport Committee hoped to start experimental express bus services to Seacroft, Swarcliffe and Whinmoor. Rafferty said that the express buses would give a quicker service and reduce traffic congestion. He also thought many private motorists would return to the buses.

In comparison with the Fleetlines and Atlanteans, the five front-entrance Daimlers, 572-576, although only four years old, were now considered obsolescent. On the same day that the Committee decided to buy no more rear entrance buses, 18 July 1966, it invited offers for 572-576. It appears that other operators also felt that the buses were out of date for there is no record of any offers being received. These buses were to remain in service in Leeds for another eight years.

Monorails - a Brief Flirtation.

In 1965 and the early part of 1966 there was much talk in the Press about the possibility of introducing overhead monorails as a means of solving the transport congestion problem in major cities. Buses were "not satisfactory" and Manchester City Council was, with Ministry of Transport financial assistance, to do a feasibility study. Councillor D.A. Wolstenholme, Conservative shadow chairman of the Transport Committee, suggested that monorails were a possibility for Leeds. There was the Safege experimental monorail in France, operating since 1962. A German Alweg monorail had been constructed between Tokyo and its airport. In 1964 a 7½ mile monorail had been proposed for Leicester. Contractors Taylor Woodrow obtained a licence to develop the French Safege system and undertake a costing exercise with Leicester Corporation. A scheme was also prepared for a projected "monorail city" near Bletchley in Buckinghamshire. Earlier Rotterdam, Frankfurt, San Francisco and Brussels had considered monorails, but all had been rejected. The monorail Wolstenholme had in mind was the new Westinghouse mass transit system, launched in January 1966, and under test at South Park, Pittsburgh, U.S.A.

In Pittsburgh local authorities and private enterprise had sponsored a two-mile demonstration "expressway". The vehicles were air-conditioned and driverless, 30 ft 6in. long, 8ft. wide and 10 ft. high, weighed 7½ tons and carried 28 passengers. They could carry up to 21,000 passengers per hour in each direction and operate singly or in trains of ten cars on an elevated, ground level or underground track. There was a round the clock service at two-minute intervals. Wolstenholme was impressed for the whole system was controlled by one person. "The computer can't put in a claim for higher wages so the fares should not need to be increased," he said.

In July 1966 the Yorkshire and Humberside Economic Planning Council said that there was a need for research into monorails. Leeds, it said, was the only place in the region where the possible use of a monorail was practicable. Dr. C.A. O'Flaherty, a member of the new Leeds University transport study group, said monorails had a "definite future." The 'Yorkshire Evening Post' said that the overhead monorail had "enormous advantages" over the bus. "its overriding appeal is speed; it also has a high safety factor. It could compete with the private car in a way the bus never could." It thought that the former express tramway tracks would be ideal for monorails.

In February 1967 C.B.Oakley, manager of Westinghouse International Transport Systems, visited Britain with a view to discussions and "selling" the system to local authorities. He described the expressway as a kind of "horizontal elevator." The capital cost of the system was said to be £500,000 per mile. Oakley stressed the "tremendous safety factor" of the expressway. "We have covered 125,000 miles and carried 100,000 passengers in our trials without a single accident," he said.

Councillor Wolstenholme was impressed and Westinghouse International exchanged letters with Leeds City Council. The driverless trains were said to resemble tube trains in appearance and appear to have been the forerunners of what was later to become the Docklands Light Railway in London. In his election manifesto for the May 1967 City Council elections, Wolstenholme advocated the introduction of the system into Leeds. Two months earlier the Conservative Political Centre had published a booklet "Get our cities moving" which proposed the introduction of monorails throughout British cities.

In May 1967 Keighley Corporation decided to do a feasibility study and shortly afterwards Blackpool toyed with the idea. Consultants for Manchester City Council completed a feasibility study and concluded that a two-rail light rail system using steel wheels on steel rails would have a lower operating cost than monorails or rubber-tyred guided vehicles. It would also be compatible with the existing British Railways network serving the Manchester

Daimler Fleetline 131 in its gold lined livery in New Woodhouse Lane on 26 November 1967. New Woodhouse Lane was opened on 16 October 1966 and, on the land behind the bus, a multi-storey car park was erected and opened on 10 August 1970. *W.D.Wilson/L.T.H.S.*

A.E.C. Regent V 948 at Middleton Circus on 25 June 1974. In November 1966 the Middleton services had been completely reorganised. *W.D.Wilson/L.T.H.S.*

area. The consultant's recommended the introduction of light railways into Manchester and their report was accepted by the City Council. A new tramway system or "Metro Link" was later constructed. In 1970 a light rail system was also proposed for Newcastle.

It was only eight years since the Leeds tramways had been abandoned and proposals for their reintroduction would cause severe embarrassment to many councillors. Nothing more was heard about monorails and the tramway/light railway proposals had to wait for a new generation of city councillors.

Back to Buses

One of the major Leeds transport events of 1966 was the opening of the new Middleton Garage and closure of the obsolete garage at Hunslet. This occurred on 13 November 1966 and is discussed in Chaper 90.

At the formal opening of the Garage on 25 November, buses on display were 51, 131, 340 and Daimler Fleetlines 122 and 128, which had carried guests. The Minister of Transport, Barbara Castle, performed the ceremony and was taken on a tour of the city in coach 10 followed by members of the Press in A.E.C. Reliance 47. In the afternoon the same two vehicles took the Minister and Press over the new Inner Ring Road, then nearing completion. Mrs Castle was also shown the new high-level pedestrian walkways under construction in the Infirmary Street area.

The Minister said that Leeds was one of the outstanding transport administrations in the country. "Leeds is showing the way.... a showpiece of what can be done.... a test bed of what would be done in the future" were among her comments.

The second interim report on the special partnership between the City Council and Ministry of Transport and Ministry of Housing and Local Government had just appeared. It proposed to establish a balance between the use of public and private transport. The aim was to give priority in access and parking for people visiting the central area to shop or transact business and encourage commuters to use buses instead of private cars.

As a result of the garage changeovers, there was a reorganisation of the Moortown and Middleton Circular services. Arnold Stone, the Chief Traffic Officer, said that the services were to be renumbered and that it was part of a plan for a simpler and more efficient pattern of operation.

Beginning on Sunday, 13 November, the Dewsbury Road/Middleton/Belle Isle/Roundhay/Moortown group of services, 2, 2 Circular, 3, 3 Circular, 6. 12 and 12 Circular were modified. These had been very complicated working arrangements and the new services, although retaining the basic plan of the circular routes, were all numbered separately in order to avoid confusion between a straight service number and a circular route. The new services were:

Service 2 Dewsbury Road-Moortown (Chained Bull Hotel). All the short workings between Cross Flatts Park or Briggate and Chapeltown or Moortown also carried this service number as before.

Service 10 Roundhay or Harehills-Middleton (Thorpe Lane) via Belle Isle Road. This service replaced service 3 to Thorpe Lane, but buses now returned to Harehills or Roundhay only, not being linked to the Moortown circulars.

Service 12 Vicar Lane-Middleton (Thorpe Lane) via Dewsbury Road. This service was unchanged from its previous form, but the first early morning buses and the last late evening buses each day ran down Middleton Park Road from Middleton Arms to the new garage in order to serve as staff buses. On arrival back at the Middleton Arms, they then continued on their normal route to the terminus at Thorpe Lane or to Vicar Lane, as appropriate.

Service 18 Vicar Lane-Middleton via Dewsbury Road. Buses on this service then continued to Harehills or Roundhay as service 19.

Service 19 Middleton Arms-Harehills or Roundhay via Belle Isle Road. This service was connected to service 18 at the Middleton Arms and formed the Middleton Circular service.

Service 20 Dewsbury Road-Moortown Corner. This was the former 2 Circular route now numbered 20 in each direction. At Moortown Corner buses changed to service 21 and continued to Belle Isle. Services 20 and 21 therefore formed the Moortown Circular service.

Service 21 Moortown Corner-Belle Isle. This was the former 3 or 3 Circular services altered to run to Belle Isle in place of Middleton (Thorpe Lane) or Middleton Arms respectively. On journeys to Moortown Corner, buses changed to Service 20 at Roundhay Park and then continued to Dewsbury Road.

As a result of the above changes the service numbers 3 and 6 along with 2, 3 and 12 circulars went out of use.

December 1966 and January of the following year saw the delivery of 15 of the Atlanteans. Numbered 341-355 (HUA 341-355D) they were of the Leyland Atlantean PDR1/1 Mk.II type and had M.C.C.W. H41/29F bodies. They were similar in appearance to 340, which had entered service some two months earlier, although they had single headlamps in place of the double ones fitted to 340. The front panels below the windscreens, which were of the wrap-round type, had large fleet numerals in the centre, filling the space where the Leyland Atlantean badge was sometimes fitted. This applied to all except 341, which had small numerals positioned below the windscreen near the offside. Curved upper saloon front windows were also fitted, but the rear end design remained the typical M.C.W. Group square pattern. Interior differences to 340 were the window panes, which were of the Weymann pattern similar to those on 331-339.

As a result of the acquisition of the 15 Atlanteans, a similar number of old buses were withdrawn. These were all of the Leyland PD2 type: 380, 381, 383-393, 395 and 399. Only four of the original 60 buses of the series were now in passenger service, 394, 396, 397 and 398.

In April 1967 nine of the A.E.C. Swifts were delivered. These were for the 45 service, (Stanks-Wortley), which was to be converted for one-man operation. The new vehicles were numbered 52-60 (JNW 952-960E) and had Roe B48D bodies. The buses were 36ft.0in. long and 8ft. 2¹/₂in. wide and identical to the earlier Swift, 51. They all entered service in the first week of April 1967, the 45 service being converted wholly to one-man operation on 30 April. Arnold Stone, the Chief Traffic Officer, said that the change over to single-manning was being done in agreement with the men's Union. The main reasons were economy and availability of staff, he said.

The introduction of the Swifts led to the rather premature withdrawal of the two Guy Arab buses 35 and 36 (TUA 35/6). These were now redundant and were the only buses of this type in the fleet. Both 35 and 36 were last used in service on the 45 route on 29 March 1967.

The Stanks-Wortley service was the second bus route in Leeds to be converted for one-man operation. After the Ring Road service, there had been the very short-lived 222 Park and Ride service. Routes 9 and 45 were now worked by the new A.E.C. Swifts, 51-60, and A.E.C. Reliances 39-47.

One-man operation resulted in a slight modification to the 45 service. The turning arrangements at Wortley were altered to avoid reversing and from 26 April buses ceased to load in the Seacroft Centre Bus Station. They now ran up and down Seacroft Avenue, stopping directly outside the bus station. Occasionally at peak hours between Wortley and King Lane, two-man buses were used, but, following the introduction of more one-man single deckers, from 3 March 1968 the route became wholly one-man.

In October 1966 there had been a request for the 42 route (Harehills-Lower Wortley) to be extended at the Lower Wortley end through the new Cow Close Estate to Old Farnley. Thomas Lord, the General Manager, said

At Hunslet Depot buses were parked on waste ground to the north east of Low Road.   A.E.C. Regent III 626 and another A.E.C. Regent behind were photographed on 14 August 1965. *Author.*

that this could not be done until roads through the new estate were completed. These were expedited over the following months, and, on 26 February 1967, the new service was opened. The route from Lower Wortley was via Lower Wortley Road, Branch Road, Ring Road (Lower Wortley), Whincover Drive and Butterbowl Drive to a new terminus at Cross Lane, Old Farnley.

Old Farnley was now served by three services, all of which terminated at different points. The 42 service served a different section of the new housing estate to the 47 service operating from the Central Bus Station, in that the 47 made a large circuit of the estate before passing the new 42 terminus at Cross Lane. This route then continued through Old Farnley village, almost as far as Troydale. The third route was service 49 operating from Hyde Park. This service did not come into contact with the 42 extension, the two termini being about 300 yards apart. However, on 30 July 1967 service 49 was extended at the Old Farnley end via Cross Lane to a new terminus at Butterbowl Drive at the same point that the recently extended 42 service terminated.

The city terminus of service 64 Circular (South Accommodation Road) service was altered from 10 March 1967. Previously situated in Eastgate, it was moved around the corner into Vicar Lane.

On 30 April 1967 there had been a few other minor route alterations:

29 (Middleton-Infirmary Street) and 46 (Belle Isle-Bramley Town End). Buses operating in the Infirmary Street and Bramley directions were altered to run from Wortley Lane left into Gelderd Road and then by way of Smithfield Street and Whitehall Road to rejoin their former route at Gelderd Road. Previously they turned right from Wortley Lane into Gelderd Road. Works service 104 (Yorkshire Copper Works) was also affected. The alteration was made for safety reasons to avoid the Gelderd Road/Whitehall Road junction.

61 and 62 (East End Park Circulars). These services had their standing point altered from Eastgate in the town centre to a point in East Park Parade adjacent to East End Park School. In addition, the peak hour and Saturday workings from Eastgate to East End Park, which formerly turned at the Park Gates, were extended to the school.

The most important road improvement in Leeds in the 1960's and 70's was undoubtedly the construction of the Inner Ring Road. When completed this was to remove much of the traffic congestion in the town centre and also enabled a number of streets to be pedestrianised. Stage 1 of the dual carriageway from Westgate roundabout to Woodhouse Lane, partly in a cutting and in a tunnel, had been started in 1964. On Saturday, 14 January 1967, it was formally opened by the Lord Mayor, Alderman J.S.Walsh. It was opened for pedestrians from 11.30 a.m. to 4.30 p.m. The official ceremony took place at 5.15 p.m. when the Lord Mayor cut a tape at the Westgate end. The official party then proceeded along the eastbound carriageway in A.E.C. Reliance coach 10, led by a police car. At the Woodhouse Lane end, another tape leading on to the west bound carriageway was cut, both vehicles returning to Westgate. Immediately afterwards, the Inner Ring Road was opened for traffic. Unfortunately it was dark at the time and the opening does not appear to have been photographed. The construction period involved the alteration and diversion of a number of bus services.

The building of the Inner Ring Road led to the planners and transport authorities modifying their future strategies. There was to be a policy to stave off the "car avalanche" and public transport was to be "revitalised." The normal bus services were to be supplemented by express buses from the suburbs, and small buses used to link the hub of the city with the railway station and fringe car parks sited adjacent to the Inner Ring Road, using the Park and Ride idea. Traffic on roads in the central area was to be restricted to three main categories: public transport, cars on their way to or from short stay car parks, and commercial vehicles delivering or collecting goods.

The scheme was to be introduced in stages, restraint on cars in the central area becoming more pronounced as the number of vehicles on the road increased. The policy of restraint had already been implemented in 1965 by the provision of 1,200 parking meters, traffic wardens and yellow lines. The Minister of Transport was expected to authorise the provision of a further 1,500 parking meters to be installed in 1967-1968.

Peter Schofield, President of the Leeds Chamber of Trade, concurred with the new proposals and thought that the Corporation was tackling the problems of the central area in "enterprising fashion." He was not sure that the Buchanan–inspired aerial walkways, then being introduced, would work. They did not. He also advocated that public transport should have its own segregated traffic lanes. "It was a pity that the old express tramway tracks had been done away with," he said.

Thomas Lord. The General Manager, said that the Department "must persuade the daily commuter to use public transport. And that means it must be made completely acceptable in every sense." The Transport Department's plans were far reaching. They included three new interchange points within the city centre, including a new bus station in Aire Street to link with the rail services. He mentioned the bigger buses then on order and said that a fleet of 20-seater minibuses "they might even be electric," was envisaged to give a quick linkage from the main interchange points in the city.

The Kirkstall Park and Ride was probably a "little ahead of its time," but Alderman Rafferty said that there was "no alternative" to the Park and Ride idea. He envisaged that many more district centres of the Seacroft type would be built. The motorist would walk from his home to the centre and then catch an express bus to the city. On the outskirts would be signs directing motorists to the nearest Park and Ride facilities. The decision to park there or chance getting in nearer to the city centre would be the motorists'.

Weekly five-day tickets, bought in advance, were to be used on the one-man express buses.

"We must allow only 2·5 seconds per passenger for boarding and ticket punching," said Mr. Lord, "or the system will lose its value." He said that the market research on the Swarcliffe Estate, done in co-operation with the Ministry of Transport, had been completed. The express buses were due to start during the summer and would be the first of many to be introduced over the next decade.

Lord said that in the matter of traffic control, Leeds was ahead of the times. In the control room at Swinegate were four closed circuit television sets manned throughout the operating period. 36 buses were fitted with radio-telephones, walkie-talkie sets were used by inspectors and the bleep pocket device was also coming into use. He said the department had reduced lost traffic mileage by a "staggering" total of 69%. Average bus speeds had been unchanged since the war. Lord said with the proposed express buses, the aim was to raise the average speed from 12 to 20 m.p.h.

At the Transport Committee meeting on 13 February 1967 a model of the proposed new South East Urban Motorway was exhibited. The new motorway was to run from the termination of the M1 motorway (then under construction) at Thwaite Gate, Hunslet, to Great Wilson Street near to the city centre. Rafferty said that when completed express buses would be introduced from the south Leeds suburbs of Middleton, Belle Isle and Hunslet via the new motorway. He envisaged an increase in the number of one-way streets and that Leeds Bridge would be made one-way outward and Victoria Bridge one-way inward. To keep the basic pattern of bus services and avoid taking people out of their way in the city centre it

Leyland Atlantean 350 in New Briggate on 18 June 1967. To make way for the new Inner Ring Road, the mock-Tudor shops which form the setting, were removed soon after this photograph was taken. *J.B.Parkin.*

A.E.C. Swift 55 at Pudsey Bus Station on 12 April 1968. *J.B.Parkin.*

Leyland PD2 393 was one of the buses withdrawn in January 1967 to make way for the 15 new Leyland Atlanteans, 341-355. 393 was photographed in Stanningley Road at Bramley Town End on 4 May 1964. *Author.*

was proposed to have "bus only" lanes against the one-way flow across the two bridges. There was already the bus lane running contra to other traffic in Woodhouse Lane and similar bus lanes were later introduced in other parts of the city. However, neither of the two bridges have been made one-way.

The Swarcliffe area of Leeds was served by bus services 24 and 25, but they did not travel direct to the Estate. This was because the West Yorkshire Road Car Company had run stage carriage services on the main York Road for many years. The 24 and 25 bus routes had to run on a circuitous route through Cross Gates.

In March 1967 an application was made to the Traffic Commissioners for authority to run express bus services between the city centre and the Swarcliffe Estate. Alderman Rafferty said the services were to be started as a result of the special partnership between Leeds City Council and the Ministry of Transport. The Ministry was regarding the services as a "demonstration project." He said there would be a non-stop journey of nearly four miles, which it was hoped would be several minutes quicker than the normal stage carriage services. Buses were to be the new one-man single deckers and there was to be a flat fare of 10d. with facilities for buying ten-journey tickets for 7s.6d. The new express bus routes were to be known as "Fastaway" services.

In addition the Transport Department said it was to introduce special shopping services to run in conjunction with the "Fastaways". One was to operate in a north-south direction and the other east-west linking Seacroft Town Centre with the outlying parts of Seacroft and Swarcliffe. Rafferty said the shopping buses would run every hour at off-peak times, and provide public transport in areas not already served. The new services, numbered 75 (Foundry Lane-Monkswood Gate) and 76 (North Parkway-Swarcliffe), were introduced on 17 July 1967.

Neither service was successful and both were withdrawn on 10 February 1968 and replaced by two new services: 75 Seacroft Town Centre-Monkswood Gate) and 76 (Seacroft Industrial Estate-Seacroft Town Centre). The

new 75 route proved successful and was renumbered 404 on 14 November 1972, The 76 service ceased on 17 May 1968.

On 19 June 1967 a trial run, was made with A.E.C. Swift 52, on the new "Fastaway" service. On board were members of the Transport Committee. Normally the journey time for the 5$\frac{1}{2}$ miles journey was 26 minutes but by the direct route 52 did the outward journey in 16 minutes 27 seconds and the inward in 17 minutes 55 seconds. More than half of the service was non-stop with a limited number of picking up points in an area bounded by York Road, Ring Road and Barwick Road. There were to be some setting down points in the city centre.

The new services began operation on 17 July 1967. Numbered 224 and 225 they corresponded to the normal services 24 and 25 respectively, although the 225 service had a short extension past the 25 terminus along Stanks Drive.

Buses operated on the two services between 6.30 and 8.30 a.m. inward and from 3.36 p.m. to 6.12 p.m. outward during the evening peak period. A 12 minute frequency was worked giving a six minute service on the combined route from Southwood Gate to the city and vice versa. Buses returned empty to Swarcliffe showing "PRIVATE" in the morning and also to the city in the evening. On Saturdays there was a 30 minute service, giving a 15 minute service to Southwood Gate.

The running times for the services was given as 18 minutes as compared with 24 minutes for service 24 and 25 minutes for the 25 buses. The service was operated by A.E.C. Swifts, assisted at certain times by A.E.C. Reliances.

The Fastaway service routes were as follows:

Service 224. From Mill Green Gardens via Swarcliffe Drive, Southwood Gate, Barwick Road, York Road, Marsh Lane, York Street, New York Street, Harper Street, Kirkgate, New Market Street, Duncan Street, Boar Lane, City Square, Infirmary Street, East Parade, and The Headrow, terminating by the Odeon Cinema. In the reverse direction, buses started at the Odeon and ran via

The Headrow, Park Row, City Square, Boar Lane, Duncan Street, Call Lane and New York Street, then continuing by the reverse of the inward route.

Service 225: From Stanks Drive (junction with Stanks Rise) via Stanks Drive, Swarcliffe Avenue and Swarcliffe Drive and then as service 224.

Both services ran express from Southwood Gate to the first dropping off place at the Woodpecker Inn, York Road. The stopping places were specially marked with red signs. There was no Sunday "Fastaway" service.

During the first two weeks of operation the number of passengers carried on the two "Fastaway" services was said to be "very encouraging." In the first week 7,404 passengers were carried and in the second week, ending 29 July, passengers were 8,409, of whom 2,650 used multi-journey tickets. There was a capacity for 14,000 passengers a week and the Department hoped to get as near 10,000 weekly as possible. It could then consider extending the express buses to other parts of the city.

Before the introduction of the Fastaways, the Transport Department had carried out an extensive publicity campaign and a coloured folder was produced. A.E.C. Swift 52 was parked at different points on the estate on the evenings of the week before the services started and an inspector on board gave information to residents. 52 carried large posters with the inscription "FASTAWAY DEMONSTRATION" on each side, positioned below the windows.

The 17th of July 1967 was a significant date in the history of Leeds transport. Not only did it mark the start of the Fastaway services, it was also the day on which Aldermen Rafferty made his last appearance as a member of the Transport Committee. At the municipal elections on 11 May 1967 the Conservatives had been re-elected to the City Council. The new Chairman of what was now re-named the Transport and Trading Services Committee, was Councillor D.A. Wolstenholme.

The Transport Department was "demoted" and lumped together with the four other trading services: the City Swimming Baths and Wash Houses, Works, Central Purchasing Department and City Markets. Alderman Mather, Rafferty's "arch opponent", also severed his links with the Transport Committee and was appointed Chairman of the Town Planning and Traffic Management Committee. One of Mather's first actions, in agreement with the Socialist party, was to ensure that the former tramway reservations were not built upon. This policy was continued with subsequent Socialist administrations. Councillor T.W. Smith, Rafferty's deputy for 14 years, retained his seat on the new Transport Sub-Committee. The new Socialist shadow chairman was Councillor Dennis Matthews.

Rafferty had first been elected to the City Council in 1933 and for most of the past 22 years had dominated the Transport Committee. A powerful personality he had been called "dictatorial" or "pig-headed" by opposition councillors on many occasions. He had been responsible for, what was soon realised to be, the very short-sighted decision to abandon the tramway system. He had refused to listen to any of the suggestions put forward by Alderman Mather.

The buses, in March 1967, were running at a loss of about £277,000 and passengers carried had declined by 3 millions over the year. Declining passenger numbers were common to most other transport undertakings. It was a nation-wide trend.

Rafferty retired from the City Council in 1968 and was Lord Mayor for the years 1968-69. He died on 13 September 1976 at the age of 77. Rafferty's deputy, Councillor Tom W. Smith, attended his last meeting of the Transport Committee on 24 March 1969. He died, aged 83 on 16 January 1981. Alderman Mather retired to Jersey in 1979 and died aged 80 on 19 February 1995. This was long enough for him to have had the satisfaction of knowing that he had been vindicated in his views.

In December 1966 the Minister of Transport produced a memorandum, which hinted at nationalisation of local transport services. There were to be Conurbation Transport Authorities or C.T.A.'s. One weakness of the existing condition of public transport, the memorandum said, was that "the day to day operation of separate undertakings is not sufficiently co-ordinated to meet the public's needs. A large number of small bus undertakings in some areas creates excessive 'joint operation and prevents economies." The C.T.A's main task would be to reorganise the structure of the bus industry as part of a public transport plan, so as to secure the best size of unit. The Leeds Chamber of Commerce viewed the proposed C.T.A.'s with "considerable caution." Malcolm Barr, chairman and managing director of the Barr and Wallace Arnold Trust Ltd., coach operators in Leeds, said there appeared to be no concern about making profits.

"The question of making profits should govern any transport undertaking as a fundamental requirement," he said. "Once you get away from the profit motive, the amount of waste can be quite fantastic."

'The Yorkshire Post', 1 February 1967.

Barr said that the local authority system was "impotent to deal with matters of profit and waste when it comes to operating a commercial transport undertaking."

Soon afterwards, the Minister of Transport announced plans for six new regional committees for improving public transport. Included among the members of the Yorkshire and Humberside Committee was Malcolm Barr. The Minister said that in the autumn of 1967 a Bill was to be introduced to decentralise the British passenger transport system. Passenger transport areas - later referred to as authorities, which would be part of local government, were to be set up and have powers to acquire any local passenger transport undertaking they required to fit into their transport plan.

Alderman Rafferty in 1956. *Leeds City Transport.*

1334

On 31 July 1967 a new body called "Voice" was launched to fight, on a national basis, Mrs. Castle's nationalisation plans. The organisation "Passenger Transport Vehicle Operators Independence Committee," claimed to represent the operators of 30,000 buses and coaches throughout the Kingdom. The Municipal Passenger Transport Association also condemned the idea of P.T.A.'s. There was opposition across the political spectrum. The 'Yorkshire Post' thought that the transport proposals were Socialist "gigantomania".

Although a Conservative-controlled Council was in power for some of this time, it was partly the result of this "gigantomania" that 1966 to 1968, saw the disappearance of four of the five remaining independent bus operators in the Leeds area. Leeds Transport Department had no involvement in the takeover of the first, but for completeness it is included. This was the service that ran between Rawmarsh and Leeds operated by T. Burrows & Sons of Wombwell, near Barnsley. It was taken over jointly by the Yorkshire Traction Company and West Riding Automobile Company. From Saturday, 22 October 1966, it became service 99 of both companies and was largely worked by Yorkshire Traction. West Riding buses took over on change overs, which occurred from time to time. The Burrows family had operated the service from March 1925 and the takeover followed the deaths in 1965 of Tom Burrows and Lewis Burrows.

Soon after Rafferty's departure, the demise of three more of the independent bus operators in Leeds, Samuel Ledgard Ltd. the Farsley Omnibus Company and Kippax and District Motors Ltd. took place. Ledgard was partly and the others wholly taken over by Leeds Corporation. This and other transport happenings in Leeds are discussed in the next chapter.

Councillor Bertrand Mather in 1954.
Yorkshire Evening News.

**Leeds Transport Committee and officials in 1961. From the left, back row Councillor J.Bissell, F.Blair (Committee Clerk), C.E.Grayson, (Finance Officer), Councillor Miss A.M.Tong, T.Lord. (General Manager), Councillor J.M. Dougary, T.H.Parkinson (Chief Engineer), J.B.Gill (Chief Traffic Officer), and Alderman H.W.Sellers. From the left, front row. Councillors S.Rostron, J.E.Hodkinson, L.Turnbull, B.Mather, Alderman J.Rafferty, Councillors T.W.Smith, D.B.Matthews, E.Atkinson and J.S.Lee. Photographed in the Transport Committee Room at Swinegate Head Office, the 1915 vintage Spanish mahogany fireplace with clock and steam tram bell has been preserved and can be seen in the Red Lion Hotel at the National Tramway Museum, Crich, Derbyshire. To mark the start of a Committee meeting the Chairman rang the bell. *Leeds City Transport.*

A Fastaway demonstration with A.E.C. Swift 52 on 14 July 1967. The location is Swarcliffe Avenue on the Swarcliffe Estate. *J.B.Parkin.*

T. Burrows & Sons bus 50 (EWW 943) leaving Duke Street and crossing York Street on 28 April 1966. It is a Bristol K6A of 1945 as rebodied with a Burlingham H61R body in 1957. Burrows' buses made their first journeys into Leeds in March 1925 and the last ran from Rawmarsh on Friday, 21 October 1966. *J.B.Parkin.*

Wolstenholme and the Ledgard, Farsley and Kippax takeovers

Alderman Rafferty's last meeting of the Transport Committee had been a stormy affair. The Socialists had refused to impose necessary fare increases, partly due to the Government policy of severe financial restraint and also for electoral reasons. The financial situation of the Department was becoming increasingly serious. The new Conservative chairman of the Committee, Councillor D.A. Wolstenholme, said that he had to grapple with a situation in which the Department was losing £10,000 a week. He said that bus fares would only be increased as a last resort. As a start an attempt was to be made to make economies elsewhere.

On 3 July 1967 the Traffic Sub-Committee approved a plan for rationalising the bus services to Halton, Temple Newsam, Whitkirk and Colton. All were losing money and the plan was to save £15,000 a year and 77,000 bus miles by merging four services into three and carrying out certain reroutings, and at the same time provide a better service to the public.

Wolstenholme said he intended to look at every route in the city with a view to rationalising them as quickly as possible. "This is the sort of way in which I feel fruitful savings can be achieved," he added.

"An amount of £540,000 additional traffic revenue was budgeted for by the Socialist administration for 1967-1968, but so far it has not been forthcoming.

"The reason the department is in this financial position is due entirely to the local council, under Labour control, co-operating with the Government on the policy of freeze and squeeze. They froze the revenue but allowed costs to rise. They withdrew an application for fares increases last August, but, when they got the green light they did not have the political courage to go ahead in January when it would have been possible."

'The Yorkshire Post,' 4 July 1967.

The Traffic Sub-Committee recommended that the 39 Whitkirk route be withdrawn; the 14 (Half Mile Lane-Halton) service should be extended to Whitkirk via Selby Road; the 22 (Central Bus Station-Temple Newsam) should be extended through to Half Mile Lane and the 41 service (Central Bus Station-Colton) should run from Half Mile Lane to Colton via Halton Ring Road instead of Hollyshaw Lane. All would run via City Square and the Corn Exchange. Each route would have a half hourly service and the growing Temple Gate private estate at Whitkirk would also be served by the route 14 buses running up Selby Road. In modified form some of these proposals were later instituted.

Wolstenholme asked Thomas Lord, the Transport Manager, and the City Architect to look into the costings of a proposed Bramley bus garage – with a view to a substantial reduction in capital cost. Work on the garage was deferred and revisions considered at the meeting of the Transport Committee on 4 September 1967. "We want a viable, vigorous transport undertaking because its future role is so important to everybody," said Wolstenholme.

At the Transport Committee meeting held on 17 July a decision was made to increase fares. In spite of the suggestions to improve efficiency, Wolstenholme said he had been "reluctantly forced to the conclusion that they could not achieve sufficient saving to avoid an increase." 3d. fares were to be increased to 4d., 5d. fares to 6d., 6d. and 7d. fares to 8d. and so on. In "modified form" the increases were approved by the Yorkshire Traffic Commissioners. As requested they would have provided £753,936 in a full year, but as granted by the Traffic Commissioners only yielded £559,500.

Wolstenholme said that he had hoped that the Department would be solvent within two years, but this would not now be possible. The fare increases took effect

New Daimler Fleetline 133 in Otley Road, West Park, on 15 October 1967. *W.D.Wilson/L.T.H.S.*

on 2 October 1967. Although a deficit was forecast for the 1967-68 financial year, a surplus of £270,000 was anticipated for 1968-69.

As might have been expected, Alderman Rafferty was bitterly opposed to the proposed fare increases and at the following City Council meeting he proposed that the increase be referred back for further consideration. His motion was rejected.

Wolstenholme claimed that the Leeds fares would still be the lowest in Yorkshire. "We intend that the city's transport shall be the most modern, efficient and courteous in the country," he said. He declared that buses would no longer be bought out of revenue. "We shall borrow the money and spread the cost of purchase over 12 years." He said that if inflation was taken into account there was not much difference in cost. The beauty of borrowing was that you could "get on and buy," he said.

Fresh modes of travel would be investigated to find the long-term system best suited to the city's development as a regional centre. Wolstenholme was presumably referring to the Westinghouse monorail system with which he had been impressed.

On 11 September 1967, at a reception given at Temple Newsam House for A.H. Grainger, the President of the International Union of Public Transport, Grainger suggested that an underground railway system be adopted for Leeds. Councillor Wolstenholme said that cities should be rebuilt around the transport network and not the network bent to fit the cities.

Of the order for 100 buses that had been placed in July 1965, by August 1967 only eleven had been delivered. The order had been amended considerably and only the ten single deckers (51-60), originally ordered as A.E.C. Reliances, but later changed to Swifts, had been supplied. Roe-bodied Daimler Fleetline, 131, had also arrived and was the first of 30 similar vehicles listed below. The amended orders were as follows:

30 Daimler Fleetline, 33 ft. long chassis. To be fitted with Roe bodies.

30 Leyland Atlanteans, 33 ft. long chassis, to be fitted with Roe bodies.

30 A.E.C. Swift rear-engine single deckers to be fitted with 48 seat M.C.W. bodies. These were in place of 30 A.E.C.Regent V rear entrance double deckers, which were also to have had M.C.W. bodies.

A further change took place on 4 September 1967 when the Transport and Trading Services Committee decided, with the agreement of Charles H. Roe Ltd., to cancel its contract to supply the bodies for 30 Atlanteans and transfer it to Park Royal Vehicles Ltd. With the exception of seven Daimlers (77-83) new in 1945, but scrapped by 1957, and bus 450, which had a Park Royal body constructed by Roe - these were the first buses with Park Royal bodies to be supplied to the Transport Department.

On 17 July 1967 the Transport Committee had agreed to invite tenders for the supply of 80 buses for delivery in 1969 and a further 80 in 1970. Half of the buses were to be double deck vehicles and the other half single deckers. They were all to be bought on the capital account.

At the end of August 1967, delivery of the first batch of the 33ft. long 78-seat Daimler Fleetlines began. 131 had been delivered some ten months earlier and the remaining 14 buses, 132-145 (LUA 132-145F) all appeared in September and October. They were of the Daimler Fleetline CRG6 type and had Roe H45/33F bodies and differing slightly from the prototype 131. The doors were of a different type, although similar in appearance, were fully air operated, whereas those on 131 were worked electro-mechanically. Air extractor fans were fitted in each saloon to aid ventilation and these were situated on the inside of the engine shrouds. 132, had white panels in the upper saloon roof, but 133-145

had what were now the standard amber panels. Most had illuminated off side advertisement panels.

No buses were withdrawn as a result of the acquisition of the 14 Fleetlines. All were needed for what was undoubtedly the most important Leeds transport event of 1967 – the disappearance of the long established Samuel Ledgard undertaking.

The Ledgard takeover

All the rolling stock and most of Ledgard's services were taken over by the West Yorkshire Road Car Company. The demise of the Company had been feared for a considerable time, but it seemed to be coping quite well in spite of the national trend of rising costs and falling passenger numbers. From the transport enthusiast's point of view the loss of Ledgard was a sad event. The Company had a big variety of 105 operational, interesting, and mainly second-hand, buses. All, with the exception of 12 fairly new buses, later operated by West Yorkshire, were lost overnight on Saturday, 14 October 1967. Leeds Corporation did not acquire any rolling stock. Rather like the last day of operation of the Leeds trams, the weather was not good and in the afternoon dismal and extremely wet. It dried up in the evening, however.

The origin of Ledgard is discussed in Volume 2 and other publications cover the history of the company. The 'Leeds and District Transport News' for November 1967, and 'Buses Illustrated' for February 1968, covered the last day of operation and the final bus fleet in great detail. It is not proposed to discuss Ledgard here, only so far as it affected the Leeds transport undertaking.

Three of the former Ledgard bus services were purchased by Leeds and these included the Leeds-Pudsey-Bradford, Leeds-Hawksworth Road-Horsforth, and the Troydale-Pudsey-Calverley services. They were purchased from the West Yorkshire Road Car Company at a cost of £29,925 and operation by the Transport Department began on Sunday, 15 October 1967. Route details were as follows:

Service 26, Leeds-Horsforth. Beginning in Park Place the route for this service was via Quebec Street, City Square, Wellington Street, Kirkstall Road, Commercial Road, Abbey Road, Hawksworth Road, Low Lane, Troy Road, Station Road, Long Row, North Broadgate Lane and Broadgate Lane, with the terminus at Stanhope Drive at the same point as existing service 50 from Gipton, both routes approaching from opposite directions. After passing along Hawksworth Road, service 26 was outside the city boundary in the Horsforth Borough. A half hourly service was operated.

Service 48, Troydale-Pudsey-Calverley. On 31 March 1957 this service had been taken over by Ledgard from Pudsey firm J.W.Kitchin & Sons and was entirely outside the city boundary in the Pudsey Borough Council area. Starting at Troydale Mills at the same point that works service 106 terminated, but running in the opposite direction, the route was via Troydale Lane, Valley Road, Littlemoor Road, Robin Lane, Lidget Hill, Cemetery Road, Marsh, Waterloo Road, Galloway Lane, Woodhall Lane, Woodhall Road, Thornhill Street and Victoria Street to Salisbury Street. At Salisbury Street buses reversed into Carr Hill Road where the picking up point was located. Again a half hourly service was operated except on evenings and all day on Sundays when it was hourly.

Service 78 Leeds-Pudsey-Bradford, operated jointly with Bradford Corporation. Starting in Park Place the route was via Quebec Street, City Square, Aire Street, Whitehall Road, Spence Lane, Wortley Lane, Gelderd Road, Smithfield Street, Whitehall Road, (Whitehall Road, Gelderd Road, Spence Lane and Whitehall Road in the reverse direction), Ring Road (Lower Wortley), Ring Road (Farnley), Pudsey Road, Hough Side Road, Lowtown, Robin Lane, Littlemoor Road, Roker Lane, Fartown,

Greenside, Upper Moor, Waterloo Road, Galloway Lane, Bradford Road, Leeds Road, Vicar Lane, Croft Street, Manchester Road and Little Horton Lane to Chester Street Bus Station (Stand 20). Buses left the Bus Station by way of Chester Street, Great Horton Road and Town Hall Square to Manchester Road, then via Croft Street etc. From Hough Side Road the route was outside the city boundary in either the Pudsey Borough or the City of Bradford. There was a half hourly service with a 15 minute service at certain times.

In addition to the above three routes, Leeds Transport Department also took over 21 school services formerly operated by Ledgard in the Leeds area,

The loss of Ledgard left only three small companies, the Farsley Omnibus Company Ltd., Kippax & District Motor Services Ltd. and South Yorkshire Motors Ltd. operating stage carriage services independently in the Leeds area. Until this time there had also been the large local independent operator, the West Riding Automobile Company. However, in October 1967, an offer had been made by the Government Transport Holding Company to add it to the Tilling Group of bus companies. This had been accepted and most services in Leeds were now either operated by the Tilling Group, B.E.T. Group, or were municipally owned. In February 1968 the B.E.T. Group was taken over by the Transport Holding Company (THC). At the time a new Transport Bill was being promoted under which the THC would disappear and all bus undertakings would come together as the National Bus Company (NBC). The NBC would co-operate with the proposed Passenger Transport Authorities in running services in their areas, and with other bus operators in the rest of the country. They would have power to acquire any bus undertakings, which fitted in with their requirements. Local authorities would be given powers to make grants to operators of loss making bus services in rural areas, and it would be made easier to obtain licenses.

Following the takeover of the West Riding Company, in February 1968 discussions took place between Leeds Transport Department and the THC regarding the co-ordination and rationalisation of services in the Greater Leeds area.

Other matters

In October 1967 the Transport Traffic Sub-Committee had agreed to apply to the Yorkshire Traffic Commissioners to divert the new 48 service via Kent Road, Crimbles Road, Lowtown, Lidget Hill, Cemetery Road and Owlcotes Road, Pudsey. At the same time the Committee decided to seek permission to extend service 2 to Middleton via the Westwood Estate.

Owing to an altered road layout at the Thornbury roundabout, Bradford, from 5 November 1967, all traffic running on Bradford Road towards Bradford was permanently diverted down Dick Lane and Gipsy Street prior to joining Leeds Road. It was part of a one-way system in this area and bus services 72 and 78 ran via the new route. In the Leeds direction buses were unaffected other than having to negotiate a slightly different road layout at the junction of the Leeds and Bradford Roads.

From 1967 to 1969 there was considerable housing development in the Camp Road area. 900 houses, including blocks of flats were built. There was no bus service along Camp Road – the lower part renamed Lovell Park Road in 1968. In June 1967 the Transport Committee applied to the Traffic Commissioners to reroute the 57 and 59 Hyde Park Circular buses via Camp Road. Thomas Lord, the General Manager, said that the rerouting would provide a link between City Square, Corn Exchange and the Markets to the Merrion Centre.

"The effects of these changes will be enormous in giving facilities to people who have previously not had

Some of Ledgard's bus services from Leeds started in Park Place. A.E.C. Regent V 1952 U is leaving Park Place for Ilkley on 27 March 1965. The building on the right hand side, which is nearing completion, is Clerical Medical House designed by Pontefract Architect, J.G.L.Poulson. The building had a life of 40 years and was removed in early 2005. *Author.*

Most of Ledgard's buses were second hand and MXX 176 was ex-London Transport RT 3661. It was a Weymann-bodied A.E.C. Regent 3RT and was pictured in Lidget Hill, Pudsey, on 30 April 1966.   It was on the Calverley to Troydale service. *Author.*

The first morning of the ex-Ledgard services with 593 and 522 in Park Place.   Daimler CVG6LX 593 was the second L.C.T. bus to operate the 78 (Leeds-Bradford via Pudsey) service and 522 behind was the first bus on the 26 (Leeds-Horsforth) route. The date is Sunday, 15 October 1967. *J.B. Parkin.*

A.E.C. Swift 1029 in York Road on Fastaway service 225.   The location is interesting for 1029 is passing Ivy Street, the location of a future underpass, formed when this part of York Road was made into a dual carriageway. The date is 5 May 1970. *J.B.Parkin.*

public transport," said Lord. The alterations came into being on 3 September and affected Hyde Park Circular services 57 to 60 and service 56 as follows:

Service 56 (Central Bus Station-North Lane). On inward journeys buses now ran past the Merrion Centre along Woodhouse Lane instead of by way of Cobourg Street and through the Merrion Centre.

Service 57 (Hyde Park Circular). Between Woodhouse Street and Vicar Lane, buses now ran via Servia Road, Camp Road, Cobourg Street, Merrion Centre, Woodhouse Lane and The Headrow.

Service 59 (Hyde Park Circular). This service, which ran in the opposite direction to the 57's, now ran from Briggate to Woodhouse Street via The Headrow, Woodhouse Lane, Merrion Street, Wade Lane, Camp Road and Servia Road.

There were revised timetables on services 58 and 60.

From Sunday, 10 September 1967, the section of Woodhouse Lane between The Headrow and Merrion Street was made one-way in a southerly direction and services 28, 30, 33, 36, 56 and 59 were diverted from The Headrow to Woodhouse Lane via Albion Street.

Construction of stage 2 of the Inner Ring Road from Claypit Lane to Regent Street began on 14 August 1967. On Saturday morning, 2 December, access to Mabgate from New York Road was permanently closed and buses on services 67 (Central Bus Station-Seacroft, Monkswood Gate) and 68 (Central Bus Station–Foundry Lane) were re-routed via Regent Street and Skinner Lane. As part of the Inner Ring Road scheme a road was to be built from Claypit Lane to Meanwood Road linking the Inner Ring Road with Sheepscar. The existing road pattern at Sheepscar was to be modified to include a one-way arrangement. North Street was to be made one-way outward and Barrack Street was to be widened and also made one-way outward.

In 1967 the financial situation of the Transport Department was grim and there was a shortage of platform staff. The year saw the start of a gradual reduction in frequencies on many bus services. The ex-Ledgard services had not been intensive and from 29 October 1967 small reductions in frequency were introduced on services 1, 7, 8, 33, 34, 35, 36, 52, 53 and 70.

At the Transport Traffic Sub-Committee meeting on 23 October the suggested withdrawal of services 63 and 64 (South Accommodation Road Circulars) on Sundays and after 6.30 p.m. was discussed, but deferred.

Until 1967 bus shelters had only been provided at exposed places in the suburbs where people had to wait probably for up to 15 minutes for a bus. In a "complete reversal of policy" the new Conservative administration decided to erect shelters in the city centre. Councillor Wolstenholme said that the Committee had the "utmost sympathy" with passengers who had to stand, even for a short time, in the rain. The former Chairman, Alderman Rafferty, said that in normal circumstances, services in the city centre were such that nobody had to wait any length of time. He thought that the Conservatives were "chasing expensive popularity." In February 1968, as an experiment, bus shelters were provided outside Mill Hill Chapel, City Square, serving routes 1, 11, 14, 24, 25, 40 and 54. Thomas Lord prepared a three year programme for installing bus shelters in the suburbs. Shelters in other parts of the city centre and outskirts soon followed.

In November 1967 a Development Review Plan for Leeds, covering the period to 1981, was revealed. It was produced by the Leeds City Engineer, C.G.Thirlwall, and was the first review of a city development plan, which had appeared in 1955. It included a new housing estate at Colton and housing at Whinmoor and Belle Isle. Motor traffic, the major road projects, in hand, or planned, pedestrian areas and public transport were also discussed.

The road plans included three urban motorways, one to the south east joining the M1 at Stourton, a south west motorway connecting with the M62 at Gildersome and a north east motorway providing a link with the A1 at Wetherby. There was also a "Woodhouse-Otley Radial". This was to be a dual carriageway starting with a connection at the new Inner Ring Road, traversing a diverted Woodhouse Lane and joining the controversial Headingley by-pass as far as Shaw Lane, The building of this new road involved the demolition of a lot of property.

Regarding public transport, the only suburban railway stations to be retained were at Cross Gates and Horsforth. All others were to be closed. It was felt that the current policy of providing express buses from the outer suburbs, supplemented by ancillary services on a more conventional basis was adequate. The "Fastaway" buses were to be "widely extended." It was proposed to close the existing Central Bus Station and have four express service terminals, one of which was to be the Vicar Lane Bus Station owned by the West Yorkshire Road Car Company. The other terminals were to be in the "redeveloped markets area", civic centre area, and in Park Square East. It was intended that city centre minibuses would link the four express terminals and percolate through the main shopping and office zones. It was hoped to provide a bus station in Aire Street for all out-of-town bus operators and form an interchange with the Leeds City Railway Station. "It would become the central terminal for all commuters from outside the city arriving by bus or train." The Review said that mass transit could be employed.

"Mass transit could take the form of suburban railway or light railway on the surface, possibly elevated or underground in part, or possibly the adaptation of such a system in the form of monorail or Hovercraft."

'The Yorkshire Post', 9 November 1967.

The Review also stated that it was proposed to provide Park and Ride facilities at selected points in outer suburban areas.

Of the major road schemes both the south east and south west motorways were later built, but the north east motorway to Wetherby and the Woodhouse-Otley radial road were not proceeded with.

It is perhaps surprising that few of the apparently laudable and straightforward proposals materialised. The express buses which in April 1968, were described by Councillor Wolstenholme as a "winner," were only extended to a limited extent, the four express bus terminals were not built, the Central Bus Station remained in the same location, minibuses were introduced in the town centre, but did not run for long, and the proposed bus station in Aire Street was not constructed. Park and Ride was adopted again, to a very limited extent, and the mass transit system in the form of a light railway or super tramway, although planned in the late 1980's was later stalled owing to financial restrictions.

Running between King Lane and Alwoodley Lane, Alwoodley, was a road, The Avenue, which did not have a bus service. In November 1967 a petition was presented from 328 residents asking for buses. There was a counter petition with 349 signatures objecting to the proposal. Councillor Wolstenholme said that no action would be taken, but a review would be made if any further housing development should take place on the south side of Alwoodley Lane.

One advantage in the introduction of front entrance buses was a reduction in the number of uncollected fares. In 1967 these had declined to 0.13% of all fares collected. Thomas Lord said that this was well below the national average. With more front entrance vehicles the problem virtually disappeared. At the Transport Traffic Sub-Committee meeting on 4 December 1967 Wolstenholme reported that by a "skilful scrutiny" of the operation of the city's buses, savings of £37,000 a year and 178,000 bus miles had been made, "without any detriment to the public". Alderman Rafferty ex-Chairman of the Transport Committee, dismissed the report.

"Regarding his statement that there had been no detriment to the public, I only wish he was as well known

Until 3 September 1967 Camp Road did not have buses, but the building of multi-storey flats justified a service. A.E.C. Regent III 613 is in Camp Road with the new flats in the background. The date is 21 September 1967. The new Inner Ring Road was to pass under Camp Road at this location. Camp Road was renamed Lovell Park Road in 1968. *Author.*

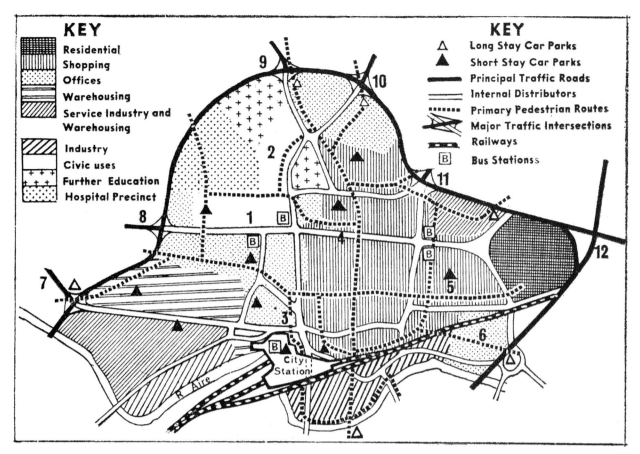

KEY

- Residential
- Shopping
- Offices
- Warehousing
- Service Industry and Warehousing
- Industry
- Civic uses
- Further Education
- Hospital Precinct

KEY

- △ Long Stay Car Parks
- ▲ Short Stay Car Parks
- ▬ Principal Traffic Roads
- Internal Distributors
- ······· Primary Pedestrian Routes
- Major Traffic Intersections
- Railways
- B Bus Stationss

MAP showing redevelopment policy for the central area of Leeds. The figures refer to: 1, Town Hall; 2, Civic Hall; 3, City Square; 4, The Headrow; 5, Markets Precinct; 6, Leeds Parish Church; 7, Kirkstall Road; 8, Burley Road; 9, Woodhouse Lane; 10, Sheepscar Continuation; 11, North Street; 12, York Road.

as myself, for during the past few weeks my telephone has hardly ceased to ring with complaints from the public of inconvenience suffered," said Rafferty.

'Yorkshire Evening Post', 5 December 1967.

At the meeting of the Transport and Trading Services Committee held on 30 October 1967 it was agreed that an order be placed for an "experimental double deck omnibus of a modified type". This was to be one of the order for 15 buses on Daimler Fleetline chassis from Charles H.Roe. Details were not specified nor were they for a chassis and special body for a minibus to be purchased out of revenue at an approximate cost of £3,500. This was also ordered.

In January 1968 there were 86 buses on order and delivery had been outstanding on some for up to two years. In spite of this, on 29 January 1968, the Transport and Trading Services Committee accepted quotations for the 160 buses for which tenders had been invited in July 1967. These were for delivery in the financial years 1969 to 1970 and comprised the following:

40 Daimler Fleetline 33ft.0in. long double deckers with Roe bodies.
40 Leyland Atlantean 33ft.0in. long double deckers with Roe bodies.
50 A.E.C. Swift 36ft. 0in. long single deckers.
15 Daimler Fleetline 36ft.0in. long single deckers.
15 Leyland Atlantean 36ft.0in. long single deckers.

Fifty five of the single deckers were to have Park Royal bodies and the remaining 25, Roe bodies.

For the first time when bulk orders were placed, Leeds did not award any to M.C.W. Ltd. Some of the buses were to be an "experimental group." These were to be the city's first buses with fully automatic transmission and power-

assisted steering. All were to be air-conditioned and fitted with front entrances.

The Transport Department did not have to wait long for the delivery of the first of the 86 buses on the earlier order. In February 1968 ten A.E.C. Swifts were delivered and they entered service from 2 to 4 March. They had Roe B48D bodies and were allocated fleet numbers 76-85, (MUG 476-485F). The buses were very similar to the ten earlier Swifts, 51-60.

A further A.E.C. Swift was delivered on 24 February. This was the first of the long awaited batch of Swifts with M.C.W. bodies. It was numbered 61 (MNW 161F) and had a M.C.W. B48D body.

The design of the body was of the same peaked design, but in other features it was considerably different to the Roe-bodied vehicles. The most obvious differences were the sloping window pillars and different depth windows, which were slightly deeper at the front half. The change on the nearside was not as obvious owing to the break caused by the centre exit door, but on the offside, there was a step down in levels in the centre. Standee type windows were not fitted nor were rear destination indicators, previously a standard feature on Leeds buses. There was also a change in the livery.

A month later the next batch of Swifts was delivered. These were 62-75 (MNW 162-175F), with M.C.W. B48D bodies. All entered service from 23 March to 12 April 1968. At the same time several of the remaining series of 15 M.C.W. bodied Swifts were being delivered. Numbered 86-100 (MUB 186-199F and MUG 100F), they were identical to 61-75 and appeared in the first two weeks of May 1968.

As a result of the purchase of the new Swifts, the Leyland Tiger Cub standee single deckers, 29-31, and

1343

Roe-bodied A.E.C. Swift 85 in Harrogate Road and about to turn into Gledhow Valley Road on 3 March 1968. It is on route 45 and destined for Stanks. *W.D.Wilson/L.T.H.S.*

A.E.C. Reliance buses, 32-34, were taken out of service. This left 37 and 38 as the only standee type single deckers still operating, but these became little used and were withdrawn on 31 May 1968. Also withdrawn was A.E.C. Regent V 787, which was involved in a spectacular accident on 14 May 1968. It received a lot of press and television coverage. The rear end of the bus was completely destroyed when a mobile pile driver overbalanced on to it. Fortunately there were few passengers on the vehicle at the time of the accident and no one was seriously injured.

There were a number of service alterations and extensions in early 1968. On 3 March a new service 3 (Moortown-Middleton) was introduced. The route from the Chained Bull Hotel was the same as former route 3 as far as the Ring Road/Dewsbury Road junction and then ran via the Ring Road (Beeson Park), Bodmin Road, Bodmin Crescent, Sissons Terrace, Acre Road and Middleton Park Avenue to the terminus in Middleton Park Avenue at the junction with Thorpe Lane. This was the same terminal point used by services 10 and 12. From 4 March the limited stop conditions on services 12 and 18 from Vicar Lane to the Rex Cinema, were removed.

The tendency of the Transport Department in 1968 was to make small reductions in frequencies, but the arrival of the new Swifts enabled an improved service to be introduced on route 9, the popular Ring Road service. On 4 March the frequency was increased to a ten minute service over the route from Whitkirk to Horsforth Woodside, with a 20 minute frequency over the whole length to Bradford Road. The basic off peak and weekend service remained hourly. Virtually all duties on this route were now one-man operated.

With the arrival of the new buses, the other single deck services, the 45, shopper's services 75, 76 and the two "Fastaway" services, 224 and 225, were worked by Swifts. The other single deck service, 73 (Moor Grange-Greenthorpe) was worked by A.E.C. Reliances, 39-47.

The end of March 1968 saw the demise of two of the remaining small independent operators in the Leeds area: The Farsley Omnibus Company and the Kippax & District Motor Company. Both companies were owned by the Barr and Wallace Arnold Trust, and were purchased by the Leeds Transport Department for the sum of £68,500. As with Burrows and most of Ledgard, all trace of the two companies vanished overnight. One day their vehicles could be seen on the streets of Leeds, the next day there

was no indication that they ever existed. The purchase of the two companies added considerably to the route mileage operated by the Transport Department outside the city boundary.

"Councillor D.A.Wolstenholme, chairman of Leeds Corporation Transport and Trading Services Committee, said he wished to stress that the acquisitions were of a purely commercial nature and the agreements had been reached "after proper bargaining and negotiation as between willing buyer and willing seller."

'Yorkshire Evening Post', 23 January 1968.

The acquisitions were approved in principle by the Ministry of Transport. Wolstenholme said that behind the Corporation's decision to expand its bus services beyond the city boundary was a "deep concern" with the possible dangers of "remote control" bus operations by the proposed Passenger Transport Authorities. There was a belief that local interests could best be served by a Corporation directly responsible to the people.

The P.T.A's as envisaged by the Government were to take over the entire finances and operations of passenger transport undertakings over a given area, bringing several undertakings under one control. Leeds was not happy and Wolstenholme said: "It would be certainly more difficult to make out a case for the imposition of a Passenger Transport Authority where a municipality such as Leeds had already achieved all rationalisation possible."

"I want to achieve all the objectives of a P.T.A, without having to have one. I want Leeds to continue to operate its own buses. Those who run public transport should always have the electors breathing down their necks."

'Yorkshire Evening Post.' 24 April 1968.

Wolstenholme said it was vital that passenger transport undertakings should be keenly susceptible to the needs and pressures of people living in its immediate area. The Leeds Corporation-Kippax-Farsley merger was only one aspect of a large scale rationlisation of bus services throughout the West Riding, he said.

The Farsley Omnibus Company

This Company was wholly taken over by the Leeds City Transport undertaking and the early history of the Company is briefly discussed in Volume 2.

Started in November 1924 by E. & W. Lawson,garage proprietors, of Bramley, was a bus service, under two

There were a lot of differences between the M.C.W. bodied A.E.C. Swifts in comparison with those with Roe bodies. 62-75 and 86-100 were identical to 61 pictured here. No. 61 is in Pudsey Market Place and the photograph was taken on 31 March 1968, the first day of operation of route 79, the ex-Farsley Omnibus Company service from Pudsey Bus Station to Horsforth. *W.D.Wilson/L.T.H.S.*

Leyland Tiger Cub PSCU/1 29 at Greenthorpe on 15 June 1963. *Author.*

33 was one of the A.E.C. Reliances taken out of service when the A.E.C. Swifts arrived. It is seen here on service 45 in King Lane on 1 February 1964. *Author.*

The spectacular accident which befell A.E.C. Regent V 787 on 14 May 1968 created a lot of interest in the local newspapers and television. Fortunately there were few passengers on the bus when this pile driver toppled over at the roundabout at the New York Road and Regent Street Junction. The rear of the bus was totally destroyed and the conductor and a passenger were injured. The pile driver was doing work in connection with the Inner Ring Road extension and the photograph was taken from the adjacent Quarry Hill Flats. *L.T.H.S.*

miles long, from Rodley to Stanningley. At Easter 1927 a Maurice Greenwood and his wife took over the service and four small 14-seater buses, from Walter Lawson of Half Mile Lane, Stanningley. They renamed the Company the Farsley Omnibus Company. Greenwood had been brought up in the motor trade and had previously owned a number of taxis. In 1933 he applied to the Traffic Commissioners to extend his route from Rodley to Horsforth (Old Ball Hotel), but was refused. He made a second application the following year for a service over a new road, Broadway, (an extension of the Leeds Outer Ring Road), between Calverley and Horsforth. There were similar applications from Samuel Ledgard, the West Yorkshire Road Car Company and the Yorkshire Woollen District Company. Following a lengthy "battle" in the Traffic Commissioner's Court, Greenwood won. He was a cheerful, well known, and popular character and was supported by Pudsey Borough Council. There was a petition signed by 1,320 people on the route. His proposed terminus, however, was curtailed to the District Council Offices, at Horsforth. The new service began on 20 April 1934 and was said to be "well patronised." An hourly service was operated with a through fare of 5d. (8d. return). The terminus at Stanningley was in Sunfield - opposite the bottom of Richardshaw Lane and where Greenwood lived. Despite objections from Leeds City Transport, he was granted permission to extend his service to Pudsey Town Hall in direct competition with the Pudsey trams. The extended route began operation on 28 February 1937. On the insistence of Leeds Corporation, there was an onerous clause in the conditions:

"On any journey from Pudsey no passenger shall be taken up except for conveyance to points beyond the Stanningley junction and on any journey from Pudsey no passenger shall be taken up at Stanningley Junction or at any point south thereof." No one could therefore ride to Stanningley Bottom or from Stanningley Bottom to Pudsey. A minimum fare of 2½d. was imposed.

The old terminal point at Sunfield, Stanningley Bottom, was also abolished. This had been difficult to access and there was an awkward turn into the main road. The route from Stanningley was via the tram route in Richardshaw Lane and Church Lane to the Cenotaph and then via New Street, Littlemoor Road, and Robin Lane to the Town Hall.

There was provision for special workmen's buses when the local mills at Stanningley and Rodley were working overtime or at holiday times. The through fare from Pudsey to Horsforth remained at 5d. and the journey time was 20 minutes.

On the outbreak of war, as an emergency measure, from 14 September 1939 the restrictions were removed. They were not reinstated after the war.

On 11 June 1949 the route was extended at the Horsforth end to a new terminus at the Old Ball Hotel.

The Farsley buses were affectionately known as the "Farsley Fliers" and, said the 'Yorkshire Evening Post', were "friendly buses with many regulars - more like a village bus service where most people know everyone." On 1 October 1952 Maurice Greenwood sold his Company to the Barr and Wallace Arnold Trust. He said that the buses had not paid over the past three years and he thought it was time to "get out." He was proud that during the 25 years that he had owned the Company there had been only one fares increase – on 25 February 1951 when the through fare was increased from 5d. to 6d. The other fares were increased proportionally. Greenwood latterly had ten single deck buses, nine normally being used for the basic service with one bus as a spare. There was a staff of 35, and he operated from a dilapidated garage in Town Street, Stanningley. The building was not taken over by the new purchaser and later passed to a haulage contractor.

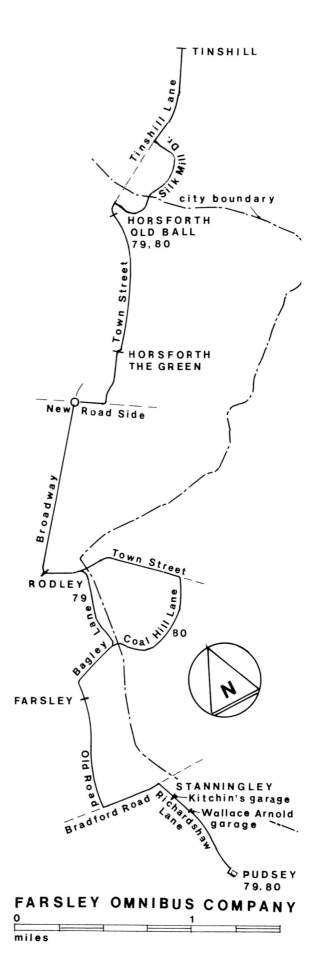

FARSLEY OMNIBUS COMPANY

Wallace Arnold had taken a foothold in the area when it purchased the motor coach firm of Aspinall's in 1945. Beginning on 27 April 1947 Wallace Arnold had operated coach tours from a garage at 63 Richardshaw Lane, Pudsey. The Farsley Company Pudsey-Horsforth bus service was worked from there. After the part takeover of another local operator and competitor on the motor coach side, J.W. Kitchin & Sons Ltd. the garage was closed and the Trust occupied Kitchin's former premises, Cavendish Garage, lower down Richardshaw Lane. In July 1965 the Farsley buses were transferred to Cavendish Garage and the old garage was sold.

After the Wallace Arnold takeover, about April 1954, peak hour workings to Smith's Crane Works at Rodley were introduced. They diverted off the main route to travel via Coal Hill Lane and Rodley Town Street. On 13 October 1956, a weekday extension of the Pudsey-Horsforth route from the Old Ball Hotel to Tinshill took place. At the same time the terminus at Pudsey was extended from the Town Hall to the new Pudsey Bus Station, which also opened on 13 October. Certain duties operated to Tinshill on Saturdays. Latterly it was impossible to work the Tinshill extension as British Railways imposed a two-ton limit on the bridge at Horsforth Railway Station. The service was suspended on 10 October 1967.

In conjunction with Wallace Arnold, the Company also ran special excursions to such places as the Blackpool illuminations, the east coast and from Pudsey to Elland Road Football Ground, Leeds.

On the final day of operation, Saturday, 30 March 1968, the service from Horsforth Old Ball, to Pudsey was worked by two Daimler CVG6 double deckers MUB 433 and MUM 459. The only other bus to be used on the last day was Daimler MUM 458, which took off duty staff from the garage in Richardshaw Lane to Pudsey Bus Station, prior to them boarding the last bus for a final ride. MUM

Buses operated by the Farsley Omnibus Company had a distinctive rear end with the Company name prominently emblazoned. KUM 849 is leaving Pudsey Market Place for Horsforth Old Ball on 30 April 1966. *Author.*

Most of the Daimler CVD6 fleet, including KUM 849, had originally been fitted with Wallace Arnold coach bodies, but were rebodied as double deckers by Charles H. Roe Ltd. In May 1957. It became part of the Farsley Omnibus Company fleet and lasted until the end of the Company. It was photographed at Pudsey Bus Station on 30 April 1966. *Author.*

Two Kippax and District buses at the Central Bus Station. Leeds, on 25 August 1964. On the left is 556 DUA, a Leyland PD3A/1, new to the Kippax fleet in 1962, and EWU 247 (ex-12), a Daimler CWA6 of 1944 vintage. *J.B.Parkin.*

459 was the last bus from Pudsey to the Old Ball and the final Farsley bus was MUB 433 which ran from Pudsey to Rodley only and then returned to the garage.

Kippax and District Motor Company Ltd.

The Kippax Company was also completely taken over by the Leeds Transport undertaking. In October 1925 the Watson bothers, Cyril and Edward, formed the Company with a Mr. Ridsdale and started a bus service from New York Road, Leeds, via Halton, Whitkirk, Swillington Common, Garforth and Kippax to Ledston Luck Colliery. Ridsdale later left the partnership. In 1934 the Company applied to the Traffic Commissioners to run a bus service between Aberford and Castleford, but was refused. The following year an application was made to run a Sundays only service from Castleford to Boston Spa via Allerton Bywater, Kippax, Garforth, Barwick-in-Elmet, Bramham and Clifford. In 1936 an application was made to run a Saturday and Sunday service between Garforth and Ulleskelf via Hook Moor, Saxton, Barkston Ash, and Church Fenton. The Company also ran a service from Castleford to Church Fenton via Kippax, Garforth, Barwick and Aberford. At the end of November 1938 takings were only 2¹/₂d. per mile and the route was cut back to operate between Castleford and Garforth only. The firm ran special works services from Kippax and Garforth to Montague Burton's Clothing Factory in Hudson Road, Leeds. There were also special footbal services from the same point to the Elland Road Football Ground.

In 1952 the undertaking was incorporated as a private company and the Barr and Wallace Arnold Trust took over on 1 June 1956 and later instituted a number of route alterations. There was much new housing in Garforth and on 4 September 1961 a service was opened between Leeds Bus Station and Garforth (Ninelands). The route from Leeds was the same as the Kippax and Ledston Luck service as far as Wakefield Road, Garforth, and then via Allendale Crescent, Kingsway, Knightsway, Poplar Avenue, Barley Hill Road, Church Lane and Ninelands Lane to a terminus by the railway bridge. The service operated on Mondays to Fridays only.

Five buses were in use on the last day of operation, Saturday, 30 March 1968. Leyland PD3/1 6237 UB and Leyland PD2/12 SUA 296 were on the Ninelands service and the latter bus worked the final duties on this route. On the main route to Ledston Luck, Daimler CVD6 MUM 461 worked the duplicate runs in the morning and early afternoon between Kippax and Garforth and Leeds. Leyland PD3A/1 buses 556 DUA and DUG 167C worked the main service. 556 DUA was the final bus over the Kippax-Ledston Luck section returning to Kippax Garage. DUG 167C, the last new bus to be delivered to the fleet, worked the last journey from Ledston Luck into Leeds from where it returned at 11.10 p.m. on the final working to Kippax.

Although both the Farsley and Kippax Companies had some modern rolling stock, none was taken over by the Leeds Transport Department. They were Roe-bodied Leyland PD3 vehicles of which Leeds already had 71 with very similar bodies. Almost the entire Leeds fleet had pre-selector or semi-automatic type gear boxes. At the time of the takeover there were only six single deckers and four double deckers fitted with "live" gear boxes and all were due for early withdrawal. The Farsley and Kippax buses had the older type "crash" gearboxes and many Leeds drivers were not trained to use them.

On 31 March 1968 several new bus routes were introduced.

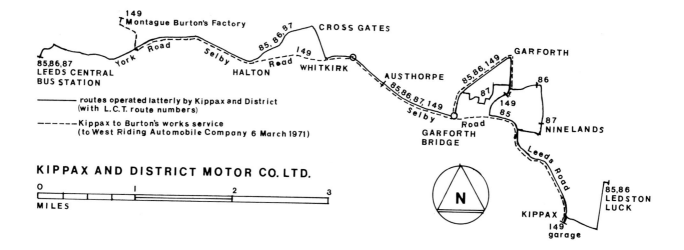

KIPPAX AND DISTRICT MOTOR CO. LTD.

0   1   2   3
MILES

Ex-Farsley Omnibus Company

Service 79, Pudsey Bus Station-Horsforth, The route from Pudsey Bus Station in the Market Place was via Church Lane, Lidget Hill, Richardshaw Lane, Bradford Road, Old Road, Town Street, (Farsley), Bagley Lane, Rodley Lane, Broadway, New Road Side, Park Side, Broadway, Fink Hill, The Green, Town Street (Horsforth), and Long Row, terminating at the Old Ball Hotel.

Service 80. Pudsey Bus Station-Horsforth.

The route for this service was the same as for service 79 to the Bagley Lane/Coal Hill Lane junction, following which buses ran to Rodley Lane by way of Coal Hill Lane and Rodley Town Street. This was a peak hour service only.

The two routes were mainly outside the Leeds city boundary in either the Pudsey or Horsforth boroughs and both were largely worked by the new one-man operated A.E.C. Swifts.

Ex-Kippax and District Motor Company Ltd.

The Kippax and District services were rather more complicated than those worked by the former Farsley Company. The main route from Leeds to Ledston Luck became service 85, while those journeys which were diverted to Garforth (Ninelands) at off peak times were given number 86. Service 87 operated from Leeds to Garforth (Ninelands) via the Kingsway Estate, without going to Garforth Town End. In addition Kippax had operated works services from Kippax and Garforth to Montague Burton's Clothing Factory in Leeds. These duties became service 149.

Service 85, Central Bus Station-Ledston Luck. From the Central Bus Station the route was via Duke Street, Eastgate, New York Road, York Road, Selby Road, Chapel Street (Halton), Cross Green Lane, Green Lane, Hollyshaw Lane and Selby Road. The latter, the A63, was followed from Whitkirk to Garforth Bridge, after which the route was via the Wakefield Road (A642) to Garforth Town End, Main Street, Garforth, Lidgett Lane, Selby Road, Leeds Road, High Street (Kippax), Longdike Lane, Barnsdale Road (A656) and Ledston Luck Villas, the terminus being at the end of this road adjacent to Ledston Luck Cottages.

Service 86, Central Bus Station-Ledston Luck. Only three journeys on a weekday operated on this route, these being the 9.09 a.m, 11.09 a.m. and 1.09 p.m. journeys from Ledston Luck to Leeds. The route from the Bus Station to Garforth Town End was the same as for service 85, buses on the 86 service then going via Main Street,

Church Lane, Ninelands Road, Ninelands Lane and Selby Road, rejoining the 85 route at the A63 junction.

Service 87 Central Bus Station-Garforth (Ninelands). This service operated on weekday peak periods and during Saturday mornings and afternoons. The route from the Bus Station to Garforth Bridge was the same as service 85. From there it was via the Wakefield Road (A642), Alandale Crescent, Kingsway, Westbourne Gardens, Westbourne Crescent, Kingsway, Knightsway, Poplar Avenue, Barleyhill Road, Main Street, Church Lane, Ninelands Road and Ninelands Lane. Buses terminated just past the railway bridge in Ninelands Lane and reversed into Hazelwood Avenue to turn. The former company used to work early morning duties directly along Kingsway, but the L.C.T. route took all buses round Westbourne Gardens and Westbourne Crescent. Limited stop conditions were imposed from the Bus Station to Halton Institute.

With the acquisition of the two companies, Leeds Corporation continued its expansion outside the city boundary and for the first time service numbers (other than works, school or other special services) were now in the 80's. The bus fleet was bigger than ever before. On 1 April 1968 the total was 708 vehicles, an increase of 19 on the previous year. There was now only one independent operator in Leeds, South Yorkshire Road Transport, which ran services from Leeds to Pontefract and Doncaster and one or two other routes in the Pontefract area. This Company was still operating into Leeds at the closure of this volume.

Other Matters

Coincidental with the takeover of the Farsley and Kippax companies, two other service alterations took place on 31 March 1968:

Service 45 (Stanks-Wortley), This route was extended from Kellett Crescent to run via Dixon Lane and Whitehall Road to a new terminus at the Ring Road by Ringways Junction.

Service 48 (Troydale-Pudsey-Calverley). This service was rerouted in two places, between Troydale Lane and Pudsey Town Hall and Cemetery Road and Galloway Lane. Buses now ran via Troydale Lane, Valley Road, Kent Road, Lowtown, (instead of Valley Road, Littlemoor Road and Robin Lane), rejoining the old route in Lidget Hill. Buses then continued via Cemetery Road, Owlcotes Road, and Galloway Lane (instead of Cemetery Road, Marsh, Waterloo Road and Galloway Lane). From Galloway Lane, the route for the remainder of the journey to Calverley was unchanged.

MUB 433, a Daimler CVD6, was formerly a Wallace Arnold coach and was rebodied by Roe in January 1957 and became part of the Farsley fleet.　It was to be the last Farsley bus and is pictured here on Saturday, 30 March 1968, at Pudsey Bus Station awaiting its final journey to Rodley. *Author.*

DUG 167C, a Leyland PD3A/1, was one of the newest of the Kippax and District buses. It was also the last Kippax bus to leave the Central Bus Station, Leeds, at 11.10 p.m. on 30 March 1968. *J.B.Parkin*

On Saturdays, from 4 May 1968, limited stop conditions were withdrawn on services 30, 33, 35, 36, 37, 43 and 70.

As a result of the purchase of the large number of A.E.C. Swifts, from 5 May 1968 two routes, Service 22 (Central Bus Station-Temple Newsam), and Service 38 (Whitkirk-Moortown) were converted to single deck operation. On the 38 route on journeys to Whitkirk, buses proceeded from Station Road via Knightsway and Selby Road to Hollyshaw Lane. Previously buses had run along Hollyshaw Lane in both directions and turned at the junction of Hollyshaw Lane and Selby Road, a very difficult and tight turn for the long one-man single deckers. There was a petition and objections to the diversion along Knightsway. There were many children in the area and on the first day of operation a demonstration was organised. A convoy of cars ran in the reverse direction to the buses, which had difficulty in getting through. On the third trip police assistance was required.

The service was to operate for a trial period of three months only. This was later extended and in February 1969 the Department applied to the Traffic Commissioners to make the route permanent. There were protests from the Knightsway Residents Committee. Arnold Stone, the Deputy General Manager, said that after the first morning there had been no further difficulties. After making a bus tour of the area, watching a ten-minute film and seeing photographs, the Commissioners agreed that the Knightsway diversion could become permanent.

On Sunday 12 May, service 48 (Troydale-Pudsey-Calverley) also went over to single deck working. It was intended that these three services be one-man operated,

but pending an agreement with the trades unions they were at first worked with two man crews. Service 46 (Belle Isle–Bramley Town End) was converted to single deck operation on 2 June 1968.

At the May 1968 elections, the Conservatives retained their majority on the City Council. Wolstenholme said that the streamlining of the City Council by combining five committees under one had brought benefits to the ratepayers. He said that each department ran its own affairs and he was only consulted on matters of policy. He thought that each department had been revitalised. "Morale stands higher today throughout the chains of command than at any time for years. It is important to understand that I am not chairman of the Transport Department. I am chairman of the Committee that decides policy," he remarked.

He did not, however, remain chairman for long. He asked to be relieved of the chairmanship because of increased business commitments. He appears to have performed well, but had been an unusual choice. He admitted that he never used public transport and must have had some difficulty relating to the problems faced by both passengers and staff. He had expressed an interest in the new automated Westinghouse electric expressway, but this may have been too forward-looking for other members of the Transport Committee. It was not referred to during his chairmanship.

Wolstenholme's successor was Alderman Colonel Lawrence Turnbull. Turnbull had been Lord Mayor for 1967-1968 and a member of the Transport Committee from 1951. He knew the "ropes". Turnbull's deputy chairman was Alderman C.S. Watson.

A.E.C. Regent V 880 at the Hyde Park terminus of service 49 in Hyde Park Road and 877 on service 57 Hyde Park Circular, photographed on 15 May 1965. The 49 cross-city service from Hyde Park to Old Farnley was the first double deck service in Leeds to became one-man operated. *Author.*

The Buses 1968 to 1969

On 27 May 1968 Alderman Turnbull chaired his first meeting of the Transport (Traffic) Sub-Committee. It was relatively uneventful. The Committee agreed to apply to the Traffic Commissioners to extend the 52 and 53 Morley services on certain journeys to the Glen Estate, Morley and to run journeys on service 48 on alternative routes along Lowtown, Crimbles Road and East Road or Valley Road, Littlemoor Road and Robin Lane, Pudsey. An application was also made for permission to alter some journeys on service 74 so as to provide a service to the new Manor Farm Estate, Middleton.

This latter application had been a long standing affair. A request for a service had been made in 1966, but a problem was a section of unmade road between Winrose Drive and Newhall Road. In May 1966 the Housing Committee had been asked to complete the road, but nothing had happened. Following complaints, in January 1968 the General Manager, Thomas Lord, was asked to come up with an alternative. A meeting was held with local councillors and they agreed that a bus service along Town Street, Middleton, would meet the needs of the Manor Farm Estate. There was no need to complete the road between Winrose Drive and Newhall Road. Authority was received from the Traffic Commissioners and the service came into operation on Sunday, 30 June 1968.

Numbered 76, the new route ran from the 74 terminus at Moor Grange, followed the 74 route to the Belle Isle/Middeton Road junction, and then ran via Belle Isle Road, Town Street (Middleton), and St, Phillip's Avenue to Middleton Park Circus, where it terminated near the Middleton Arms. A 30 minute frequency was operated with a ten minute frequency at peak periods and a 20 minute service on Saturday mornings and afternoons. Over the section from Moor Grange to Belle Isle the buses alternated with those on service 74.

The alterations on service 48 came into effect on 14 July 1968. Certain journeys reverted to the old route in Pudsey and ran via Valley Road, Littlemoor Road and Robin Lane. These became route 81 and now formed the basic service on the route. There was also rerouting of the 48 buses from Troydale to Calverley, in that from Lowtown they ran via Manor House Street to Robin Lane. Both the 48 and 81 services to Calverley could now load at the same point at Pudsey Town Hall. On 4 August 1968 the terminus at Calverley for both the 48 and 81 buses was moved from Victoria Street to Salisbury Street.

On Sunday, 28 July, another bus terminus was altered. This was the 70 service (Central Bus Station- Primley Park). Formerly buses had run from Nursery Lane into Primley Park Crescent, terminating at the junction with Primley Park Avenue by swinging round at the wide junction. The revised arrangement was for buses to run from Nursery Lane into Harrogate Road and then left into Primley Park Avenue. The new terminus was about 100 yards from the old point. Buses returned to the Central Bus Station by way of Primley Park Avenue and Primley Park Crescent to Nursery Lane and then the reverse of the outward route. This new arrangement at Primley Park cannot have been satisfactory. There were complaints and on 23 December 1968, the terminus reverted to its old position. The turning arrangements were retained.

On Monday 9 September 1968 service 27 (City Square-Gledhow) which ran on Mondays to Saturdays only was renumbered 69. The number 27 was required for future alterations to the Horsforth-Swarcliffe services.

At a meeting of the Transport (Traffic) Sub-Committee held on 22 January 1968 it had been agreed to apply to the Traffic Commissioners to merge the existing services 24, 25, and 26 into four new services numbered 24 to 27. Application was made to remove the limited stop

Daimler Fleetlines 156 and 158 were the Commercial Motor Show exhibits of September 1968. They had Roe bodies and, according to Alderman Turnbull, were "the most modern and refined double deck buses in Britain." They were in a new reversed green livery and Donald Wilson photographed 156 in Butt Lane, Old Farnley, on 13 July 1969, the first day of one-man operation on the route. *W.D.Wilson/L.T.H.S.*

A.E.C. Regent III 473 was withdrawn in August 1968. It is passing St. Luke's Street, off North Street, on 2 September 1967 travelling inward on the 32 route. This part of North Street from Sheepscar to Skinner Lane was made one-way outward from 4 May 1969. The rest of North Street followed on 5 April 1970. *Author.*

conditions on routes 12 and 18. These were granted and the revised arrangements came into effect on 13 October 1968 and were as follows:

The existing services 24 (Horsforth-Mill Green Gardens), 25 (Horsforth-Stanks Drive) and the former Ledgard service, 26 (Horsforth-Park Place, Leeds) were revised, the 26 being altered to form part of the through services to Swarcliffe. The terminal point in Park Place was discontinued and buses ran through the city centre by the same route as services 24 and 25. At Horsforth the section of service 26 from Long Row to Stanhope Drive via North Broadgate Lane and Broadgate Lane was discontinued and the buses were extended from Long Row via Town Street, The Green, Fink Hill, Broadway, and Parkside to the Fleece Hotel, terminating at the same point as the 24 and 25. On leaving the Fleece Hotel, buses used New Road Side, Sunnybank Avenue, Feather Bank Lane, Broadway, Fink Hill, The Green, Town Street, and then as previously.

The service number 26 was retained for duties, which operated over the new portion of route to Mill Green Gardens while those, which ran over this section to Stanks Drive showed 27.

The routes were, therefore, now:
Service 24. Horsforth Fleece Hotel, direct to the City and Swarcliffe, Mill Green Gardens.
Service 25, Horsforth Fleece Hotel, direct to the City and Swarcliffe, Stanks Drive.
Service 26, Horsforth Fleece Hotel, via Horsforth Town Street area to the City and Swarcliffe, Mill Green Gardens.
Service 27, Horsforth Fleece Hotel, via Horsforth Town Street area to the City and Swarcliffe, Stanks Drive.

During the evening peak period, there were short workings to the Old Ball Hotel, which showed service numbers 26 or 27.

On 8 September 1968 alterations were made at each end of the ex-Ledgard service, 78 (Leeds-Bradford). From pre-war days Ledgard had applied unsuccessfully to run buses through to the Central Bus Station, but had been thwarted on every occasion by Leeds Corporation. In Leeds the Park Place terminus was extended to the Bus Station, the route from Whitehall Road was via Thirsk Row, Wellington Street, City Square, Boar Lane, Briggate, The Headrow, Eastgate and St. Peter's Street. From the Bus Station buses ran by way of Eastgate, Vicar Lane, New Market Street, Duncan Street, Boar Lane, City Square, Aire Street and Whitehall Road. At the Bradford end the terminus was altered from Chester Street Bus Station to Hall Ings, buses running from Leeds Road into Hall Ings.

There had been protected higher fares on the former Ledgard service and these were removed on 8 September. Passengers paying 4d. for a short journey, now paid 2d. Thomas Lord said, "This is one example of the benefits passengers will receive from the policy of acquisition and rationalisation of services being actively pursued by Leeds Corporation."

The former Farsley Omnibus Company services, 79 and 80, were also extended on 9 September. Following the rebuilding of the railway bridge at Horsforth Railway Station and the removal of the 2 ton weight limit, both routes were extended from Horsforth (Old Ball Hotel) to Tinshill. The extension was in the form of a circular route around the Tinshill area. From the Old Ball the route was Station Road, Tinshill Road, Tinshill Lane, Otley Old Road, Tinshill Road and Station Road back to the Old Ball Hotel. The terminal point was at the top of Tinshill Lane near the junction with Otley Old Road.

The end of August 1968 saw two senior staff changes in the Transport Department. The Chief Traffic Officer, Arnold Stone, was promoted to the post of Deputy General Manager. Stones' replacement was his deputy, F.T. McGraw. C.B. France, the Chief Engineer, retired and he was replaced by J.M. Pearson, from 1963, Deputy Chief Engineer with the Birmingham Transport Department. Pearson continued with the Leeds Transport Department until its demise in 1974 becoming Chief Engineer with the West Yorkshire P.T.E.

In September 1968 another batch of new buses was delivered. These were the series of 30 Leyland Atlantean PDR2/1 originally ordered with Roe bodies, but changed to Park Royal a year earlier. The Park Royal bodies were

H45/33F (33ft. 0in. x 8ft. 2½in.). The buses were numbered 356-385 (PNW 356-385G) and the bodies were very similar to those on Daimler Fleetlines, 131-145, built by Roe. Minor body differences included translucent roof panels, which did not open on the Atlanteans and door operating controls. The rear fleet numerals were positioned immediately below the destination indicators instead of in the usual position on the engine compartment.

All appeared in passenger service on the first three days of September, with the exception of 383-385, which followed two to four weeks later. This series of buses was the last ordered with this type of body layout. Other double deckers on order were to have dual entrances and central staircases.

An earlier Atlantean, 355, in June 1968 was fitted with fully automatic transmission by Self Changing Gears Ltd., Coventry. It retained normal electro-magnetic gear change but was minus a first gear position. Automatic drive was obtained by putting the gear selector into the fourth gear position, which was marked "A" for automatic. Second and third gears could be engaged manually for demanding gradients etc. 355 returned to passenger service on 8 July.

Of considerable interest at the 24th International Commercial Motor Show at Earls Court, London from 20–28 September 1968, were the first two of a series of 15 dual entrance double deckers. These were of a new kind of "ultra modern" bus and the first of their type in the Leeds fleet. Numbered 156 and 158 (PUB 156/8G) they were Daimler Fleetlines, type CRG6LXB, with Roe H45/33D bodies. 156 was displayed on the Daimler stand and 158 on that of Roe.

On 10 September, Alderman Turnbull, chairman of the Transport and Trading Services Committee, had formally accepted from Charles H. Roe Ltd. 158 - "the most modern and refined double deck bus in Britain". It had "technical and passenger refinements beyond anything at present on the road," and a specially designed layout in the driver's cab reduced driving fatigue. "Driving this bus will be as easy as driving a modern private car," he added.

The 33ft,0in. long buses were fitted with the new Gardner 6LXB 10·45 litre diesel engine and "Daimatic" fully automatic transmission with power assisted steering. The Roe bodies had large "panorama" side windows, deep two-piece windscreens and front upper saloon windows, the body having a slightly peaked effect at both front and rear. Registration plates were of the reflecting type, i.e. white at the front and yellow at the rear, a new feature on Leeds buses. This was to become the national standard for all motor vehicles. A revised reversed livery of light green with a dark green centre band for one-man buses was introduced, (discussed in Appendix XIX), and the advertisement panels were slightly recessed. The front fleet numbers were positioned above the windscreen and below the destination indicators, the rear numerals being on the engine compartment. There were no rear indicators, but displays showing both route number and destination were fitted on the nearside near the entrance. There were electro-pneumatically operated jackknife doors and an interlock device so that the centre exit doors could not be opened whilst the bus was in motion.

Short wave radio equipment was fitted to both vehicles and an address system in both saloons. As the buses were intended for one-man operation, other features included a periscope, passenger-counting device in the upper saloon and a swivelling driver's seat. The standard Roe safety staircase, forward ascending, was fitted in the centre of the bus with luggage space and a conductor's locker underneath. The seating and interior finish was of the usual high Leeds standard although the lower saloon seats varied slightly.

Two similar vehicles, 159 and 160, were delivered soon afterwards. One, 159, was dispatched to Lille in France on 8 October for use during "British Shopping Week", organised by the Board of Trade and held from 11 to 19 October. 159 was accompanied by a driver and mechanic, both of whom were given a course in the French language before their visit. Both 159 and a London Transport Routemaster, RML 2760, were used on tours around Lille during the day, and in the evening carried sports teams to various local stadiums etc.

September 1968 saw the last of the buses with the old combined route number and "via" display. A.E.C. Regent III 496 on route 44 (Stanningley-Halton Moor) is at the island at the end of Stainbeck Lane, Chapel Allerton. The date is 11 May 1963. In 1964 the site behind the bus was occupied by shops and a supermarket. *Author.*

Leyland Atlantean 383 passing the Olympia Works in Roundhay Road on 24 November 1968 with the former tramway reservation in the foreground. The Works, originally occupied by the Blackburn Aeroplane Company, was demolished in August and September 1986.   No. 383 had a front entrance body and was one of the highest numbered Atlanteans in the old style livery.   The next batch of Atlanteans, 386-405, were dual door and designed for one-man operation. They were in the reversed livery.   *W.D.Wilson/L.T.H.S.*

Thomas Lord was enthusiastic about the new one-man buses, but his enthusiasm was not shared by some other General Managers.   At the annual conference of the Municipal Passenger Transport Association held on 28 August, Geoffrey Hilditch, the General Manager of the Halifax Passenger Transport undertaking was sceptical.

By the time that the cost of switching to one-man bus operation was taken into account there was going to be no saving, and it would be cheaper to go back to two-man operation, Hilditch said. One-man buses cost about £1,000 more than the older types and then there were all the various gadgets, which had to be paid for and maintained. There was increased interest on loans to pay and the new buses were slower in use.

"True, we eliminate the conductor," said Mr. Hilditch, "but we are paying 10s. a week extra to our men.... and the staffs have the promise of more cash as we make more savings, but I wonder who is pulling whose leg."

'Yorkshire Evening Post', 28 August 1968.

The arrival of 30 new double deck buses resulted in the withdrawal of 40 old vehicles. Taken out of service was A.E.C. Regent III 654, involved in a collision with a mobile crane on 21 June 1968. 654, one of a series of six Regents with Weymann bodies, was the first of its class to be withdrawn. A number of older A.E.C. Regent III were taken out of service including 466-500, all dating from 1949 and 1950. The last of the "MUG" series, 451-475, (MUG 451-475) and all the "NNW" series 476-500 (NNW 476-500) were withdrawn. Both the "MUG's" and "NNW's" had been very sound vehicles and had seen 19 years of service and used on all day duties up to their withdrawal.

Also taken out of service were, 394 and 396-398, the last four of the 60 Leyland-bodied Leyland PD2/1 buses delivered in 1949 and 1950. These were the last buses in the passenger fleet fitted with clutch transmissions and

vacuum brakes, all remaining vehicles being semi or fully automatic and with air brakes. From their introduction in 1949 and 1950 the Leyland PD2 had been worked almost exclusively from Bramley Depot and were always associated with routes operating from that Depot.

In addition, A.E.C. Regent III 618 was withdrawn following a collision on 12 September 1968.

With the withdrawal of these buses, the old type destination indicators with combined route number and "via" displays disappeared from the Leeds scene. They were also the last buses in the fleet, which did not have flashing indicators. The last of the series, 476, 481 and 498, made their final journeys on 30 September 1968.

On 24 November 1968, with one exception, the 15 Daimler Fleetline dual doorway double deckers, 146-160, entered service. The exception was 155, which appeared on 6 December. The buses were in two batches, which differed slightly. 146-155 (PUB 146-155G) were on Daimler CRG6LX chassis and had the normal Gardner 6LX engine and semi-automatic transmission. The other five buses 156-160, (PUB 156-160G) had Daimler CRG6LXB chassis, Daimatic fully automatic transmission, power steering and new Gardner 6LXB engines. Both batches had Roe H45/33D bodies. The whole batch had three sets of flashing trafficators, at the front, rear, and at the sides near the front. The new buses did not have "limited stop" signs and these also had not been fitted to the M.C.W. bodied A.E.C. Swifts, 61-75 and 86-100. The introduction of one-man buses led to the discontinuance of limited stop facilities on certain routes.

The delivery of the Fleetlines resulted in the withdrawal of several buses, mainly A.E.C. Regent III of the "NUB" series. 618 was already out of service and other Regents withdrawn were 601-614, 652, and 742. The latter was involved in an accident in Otley Old Road on 22 January 1969. It was the first of the 30 A.E.C. Regent III buses delivered in 1954 (730-759) to be withdrawn. Daimler CVG6 541 (VUG 541) was withdrawn on 20 March 1969 after the roof was severely damaged in an accident. It was the first of the "Orion" bodied Daimler buses to be taken out of service.

One of Alderman Turnbull's first actions as Chairman of the Transport and Trading Services Committee had been to recommend that the Morley buses be extended to the Glen Estate. An application had been made to the Traffic Commissioners and the extension took effect on 28 October 1968 when a new service 51, from Vicar Lane to Morley Glen Estate, was introduced. The service operated during morning and evening peak periods and on Saturdays from 9.05 a.m. until the early evening. The journeys were mainly existing workings on service 52 from Vicar Lane to Morley (Fountain Inn) extended into the new estate. The route from Vicar Lane to the Fountain Inn was the same as route 52 and then continued via Town End, High Street and Glen Road - Glen Road and South Queen Street in the opposite direction. The terminus in the Glen Estate was just past Glendale House, where a new turning circle had been constructed.

At the Transport Traffic Sub-Committee meeting on 4 September 1968 a petition was received and it was agreed to apply to extend the 74 service (Moor Grange-Belle Isle) into the Raylands Estate, Belle Isle. This came into operation on 27 October 1968. The old terminus had been at the end of Broom Place by the junction with the Ring Road and the route was extended via Raylands Lane and Raylands Way to a new terminus at Cranmore Rise. On leaving the terminal point, buses continued via Raylands Way, Cranmore Rise, Cranmore Drive, Raylands Road and returned to Raylands Way, using the former roads as a turning circle in the estate.

During 1967 and 1968 a new Stanningley by-pass was constructed. It was an extension of the outer Ring Road from Bradford Road and an application was made to extend the 9 Ring Road service from Bradford Road to Middleton Garage via the new by-pass. With the new extension, the Ring Road service from Whitkirk to Middleton Garage would be 22 miles long. Described as the "friendly route" it had

been remarkably successful and, although regarded by the Transport Department as an industrial route, was popular with sightseers at weekends. In 1968 the normal weekly average was 22,000 passengers. A Transport Department spokesman said that because the service was one-man operated, the drivers soon got to know their regular passengers and "made many friends as a result."

The Stanningley by-pass from Dawson's Corner, Bradford Road, to the Leeds Ring Road near Swinnow Lane was formally opened on 31 October 1968. It was over three months later, on 19 January 1969, that the 9 Ring Road service was extended through to Middleton.

From Bradford Road the extension was via the new Ring Road (Stanningley), Ring Road (Bramley), (Farnley), (Lower Wortley), (Beeston) and (Churwell), Dewsbury Road, Ring Road (Beeston Park), Middleton Park Road and Ring Road (Middleton). The terminus was outside Middleton Bus Garage and in order to turn, buses swung round in the entrance way to the Garage. An hourly service was operated throughout the route on Saturdays and Sundays and also at off peak times on weekdays. At peak hours a half hourly service was worked over the whole length of the route. There was a short working at Bradford Road. The journey time from Whitkirk to Middleton was 1 hour and 16 minutes. Work on the second stage of the Stanningley by-pass, from Swinnow Lane to Bramley Town End, began on 1 December 1968.

During 1968 and 1969 houses were built on a piece of land separating the dual carriageway in South Parkway. This land had formerly been owned by the Transport Department and had been allocated for the proposed pre-war extension of the tramway from Gipton Estate terminus to Seacroft. In connection with the development the inward carriageway was widened and modified as far as Ironwood View where services 11,16 and 17 turned off. The outward carriageway was also widened and was used by service 15. The bus service alterations came into effect on 11 November 1968.

Also on 11 November, New York Road was closed to inward traffic because of the building of a two-deck section of the Inner Ring Road from the Woodpecker to Regent

A.E.C. Regent III 614 was one of the buses withdrawn in 1968-9 to make way for the new dual doorway Daimler Fleetlines, 146-160. No. 614 is in Otley Road after passing the end of Alma Road on 23 May 1964. The building under construction on the right hand side is the Arndale Centre. *Author*.

Many of the "tin front" Daimlers were withdrawn in 1969. No. 533 is on service 66 (Harehills-Leysholme Estate) on 19 May 1963. It is passing the fine building which stood at the corner of Bond Street and Park Row. Designed by the eminent Victorian Architect, Sir George Gilbert Scott and built 1863-7, it was demolished soon after this photograph was taken. It was replaced by an anonymous office block. *Author.*

Street. Services 22, 39, 41, 42, 50, 65, 66, 77, 85, 86, 87, 140, 148 and 162 were diverted at the Woodpecker via Marsh Lane, York Street and Duke Street to the Central Bus Station or Eastgate. These services continued to run normally outward except around the Regent Street roundabout where they continued into the old New York Road by a new slip road.

In September 1967 work started on the construction of a £145,763 scheme to divert the outer Ring Road at the junction of Smithy Mills Lane, Meanwood. There was a very awkward bend and steep hill at this point and the dual carriageway diversion was 700 yards long. From 14 November 1968 buses on the 9 Ring Road service and other motor traffic ran via the new diversion.

In September 1968, in connection with the extension of the M1 Motorway into Leeds, approval was given by the Leeds Corporation Executive Committee for the formation of a one-way gyratory system at the end of the proposed M1. This involved making Meadow Lane, Dewsbury Road, Meadow Road, Victoria Road and Great Wilson Street into a gyratory. The new arrangement came into operation on Sunday, 12 January 1969. From about 12 noon on that day, services 2, 3, 5, 8, 12, 18, 20, 51, 52 and 53 on inward journeys ran via Victoria Road and Great Wilson Street to Meadow Lane, instead of going directly along Meadow Lane. Services 1, 55, 74 and 76 running outward used Great Wilson Street and Meadow Lane in place of Victoria Road. The M1 was opened as far as Stourton in October 1968 and the immediate result was excessive traffic congestion in the Hunslet area. Although L.C.T. buses were little affected, West Riding and other buses running from Pontefract, Castleford and Wakefield into Leeds were subject to delays at peak hours. Delays of 15 to 90 minutes were complained of and the opening of the gyratory eased the problem to some extent.

An extension to the gyratory took place on 22 June 1969 when Dewsbury Road, between Meadow Lane and Jack Lane, became one-way inward. There had been wholesale demolition in the area to make way for the extension of the M1 motorway and Jack Lane between Dewsbury Road and Meadow Road had disappeared, being replaced by a partially completed motorway intersection.

Bus services 1, 5, 8, 51, 52, 53 and 102 outward were altered to run from Meadow Lane via Dewsbury Road and the new intersection to Meadow Road. On the inward journey services 2, 3, 12, 18, 20, 55, 74, 76 and 145 were diverted from Jack Lane (services 74, 76 and 145) or Dewsbury Road (the remainder) via the new intersection and Meadow Road to Victoria Road.

In a further effort to reduce congestion, from Sunday, 16 March 1969, a new one-way system was introduced in Hunslet Road, Forster Street, Atkinson Street, Donisthorpe Street and South Accommodation Road. Bus services affected were the 63 Circular and works services 104, 109 and 137. The 63 buses were diverted from South Accommodation Road via Atkinson Street, Goodman Street, Forster Street and Hunslet Road.

From 27 January 1969 New York Road between Regent Street and North Street was closed to through traffic owing to the Inner Ring Road construction. As a result, buses on services 42, 62 and 64 terminating in Eastgate, which formerly used New York Road and Vicar Lane as a turning point now went direct into Eastgate.

From 30 March 1969 a slight alteration occurred at the terminus of the 46 bus route at Belle Isle. To ease turning, all buses to Belle Isle turned from Middleton Road into Windmill Road, and up Belle Isle Road to Middleton Road, thus forming a turning loop.

There had been talk of introducing minibuses into the central area of Leeds from shortly after the appearance of the 1963 Buchanan Report. Thomas Lord, the General Manager, had hinted at electric minibuses in 1966 and on 28 October 1968 he submitted a report for consideration by the Transport and Trading Services Committee. His report, however, had been pre-empted by a Mr. P.A. Lingard, of the Electricity Council.

On 22 October Lingard told the National Society for Clean Air, in a meeting at Harrogate, that Leeds was to take an "exciting and adventurous step," by introducing battery-operated electric minibuses from car parks on the perimeter of the city centre to the main shopping and business areas. The idea was to have a high frequency service linking the park and ride points to the central area. The buses would also serve the railway station, bus station and the new pedestrian precincts. Lingard said that electric vehicles would be ideal for the purpose. They would not admit pollution and their silence made them highly acceptable in city centres. The Electricity Council believed that they would pay their way.

Alderman Turnbull said that the proposals were a result of the special partnership between Leeds City Council and the Ministry of Transport. He said that authority had been given for a chassis and special body for a minibus to be bought for £3,500 and Thomas Lord had been carrying out research in conjunction with manufacturers. Specifications were produced and a prototype battery-operated minibus was to be built. Turnbull added:

"This is part of the future role of public transport in the city to provide a suitable alternative to the use of the private car for the daily commuter. One of these small buses might well be able to enter a precinct where other forms of transport could be restricted."

'The Yorkshire Post,' 23 October 1968.

The idea of creating four express bus terminals in the city centre was still in vogue and the minibuses were to connect these and "percolate through the main shopping and office zones." The city's Development Plan Review said that minibuses would give "manoeuvrability and speed" and would be "especially valuable for the elderly and those laden with children, luggage and purchases."

At its meeting on 16 December 1968, the Transport and Trading Services Committee agreed "in principle" to the purchase of minibuses. They would be Britain's first experimental municipal minibuses operating through shopping streets, said the 'Yorkshire Post'.

The minibuses were to be part of the city's long-term plan to ease motor traffic for the shoppers and pedestrians. The prototype electric minibus was to be supplemented by six more conventional diesel-powered minibuses which would link the Leeds City Railway Station with the Central Bus Station, the West Yorkshire Vicar Lane Bus Station and the central shopping area, It was planned to make Commercial Street and Bond Street into pedestrian areas for several hours a day with road access limited to minibuses and essential traffic for loading and unloading. Thomas Lord envisaged an eventual fleet of about 20 electric minibuses. A decision had not been made about fares, Lord said that either a flat rate could be introduced, or that fares should be free and subsidised from existing services or from parking meter revenue. Writing in the 'Municipal Review', Lord said that a good frequency was essential. He said the old concept of the tramway era had to be re-established – that if one had just missed a tram another could be seen to be coming.

"If the travelling public is expected to use public transport in future, some new bold thinking about its provision needs to be taken. The shabby unreliable vehicles and services, and inadequate interchange facilities are just not good enough for the 1970's.

"There is a place for the private car, the public service vehicle, and, indeed, the pedestrian, and the social balance of use needs to be found in the planning, development, design, layout, and traffic management in our cities."

'Municipal Review', January 1969.

Earlier, Lord had discussed one-man buses.

"The key to the success of the one-man operated double deck buses in Leeds will be in the fare collection system," said Lord in September 1968. In Leeds, experiments were being made with pre-purchased multi-journey tickets and these had proved very successful on the new Fastaway service. They relieved the driver of sales and saved time.

Besides the Fastaway service, there were already one-man single deck services on other routes in the city – 9, 45, 73, shopper's services 75/76 and 79/80. As soon as the dispute with the Trade Union was resolved it was intended to extend one-man operation on 12 other services: 22 (Central Bus Station-Temple Newsam), 34 and 35 (Central Bus Station-Alwoodley), 37 and 43 (Central Bus Station-Shadwell), 38 (Moortown-Whitkirk), 46 (Bramley Town End-Belle Isle), 57, 58, 59 and 60 (Hyde Park circulars) and 70 (Central Bus Station-Primley Park). Following the resolution of the Trade Union problems, on 17 March 1969 the Transport (Traffic) Sub-Committee agreed to apply for permission to convert services, 34, 35, 37, 43 and 70 to one-man operation and this was granted. It was also proposed to divert the Shadwell buses, 37 and 43, along Wigton Lane through the new High Ash Housing Estate. The housing on this estate had been completed about four years earlier, but was just outside the city boundary in the Wetherby Rural District Council area. The Committee agreed "in principle" to adopt one-man working on all night services.

In May and June 1968 services 22, 38, 46, 48, and 81 had been converted to single deck operation. From 19 January 1969 they became wholly one-man operated.

The Transport Department launched a publicity drive to "educate" the public in the use of one-man buses. There was the need to signal the driver to stop in good time, pay the driver on entering the bus, have the exact fare ready, signal in good time on alighting and remember that passengers boarded the bus at the front and alighted through the centre door.

In November 1968 there were 155 front entrance buses in the fleet and the Transport Department said that by 1970 it was confident that half the services in Leeds would be one-man. Some routes were already partially worked by front entrance buses. For example, by the end of 1968 route 1 (Lawnswood-Beeston) was almost entirely worked by buses of this type.

In December 1968 it was announced that the Government pay freeze for busmen was to end. The 2,000 busmen in Leeds were to receive a £1 per week pay rise back-dated for 12 months. The Trade Union agreed to implement an extension of one-man operation on single deck buses in Leeds as soon as the £1 rise was paid. The immediate result was an application to the Traffic Commissioners to increase fares. The proposed fares increase was intended to yield an additional £750,000 income per year. There were objections from the Labour party, which thought that the fares "were indiscriminate and too high." It said that the policy of buying buses by borrowing capital, at a time of high interest charges, was partly to blame. This would, however, have had little effect. Alderman Turnbull said that with the introduction of one-man buses and automatic ticket collection, it was "absolutely essential" that fares should be in multiples of 2d. with a 2d. minimum. The increases were approved and introduced on 9 February 1969. The fare structure was now between 2d and 2s.0d. on day services and from 4d. to 3s.0d. on night services. The fares had been deliberately simplified bearing in mind that decimalisation of the currency was due to take place in 1971.

The Whinmoor "Fastaway" service had proved popular and the Ministry of Transport said it was to publish a "demonstration document." Thomas Lord said it was proposed to extend the service to the northwest perimeter of the city and in the east "when road improvements allow, and as soon as circumstances permit."

"We have got to be able to run on roads which allow a certain average speed to be maintained. We have in mind introducing this service on the Cookridge route when road

BEFORE: In the late 'sixties there was massive demolition in the Dewsbury Road, Meadow Road, Meadow Lane and Jack Lane area to make way for the M1 Motorway extension into Leeds. Horsfield car 197 is in Dewsbury Road at the Jack Lane tram stop on 6 August 1956. Meadow Lane Gas Works is in the rear. *Author.*

AFTER: The bus stop in Dewsbury Road at roughly the same location as the above, but nearer to the town centre. The date is 21 September 1969 and Daimler Fleetline 126 is in the new reversed colour scheme. The setting is the Meadow Lane Gas Works and the "hi-tech" installation behind the bus is the high pressure North Sea Gas H.T.R. Reforming Plant. The Plant was built in phases from 1963 and closed In January 1976, shortly before the Gas Works itself was demolished. *W.D.Wilson/L.T.H.S.*

A.E.C. Reliance 41 in the new reversed livery turning at Middleton on the 9 Ring Road service. Middleton Bus Garage is in the background. The date is 13 July 1969. *W.D.Wilson/L.T.H.S.*

improvements in the Headingley area are carried out, and also from Garforth to Leeds."

'Yorkshire Evening Post', 15 January 1969.

On 29 October 1968, the Transport Act, 1968, received the Royal Assent. This Act, in effect nationalised public road transport in Britain. The National Bus Company came into being on 1 January 1969 and the local independent operators, West Riding Automobile Company, Yorkshire Woollen District Company and West Yorkshire Road Car Company and other undertakings throughout the country came under one control. The Act authorised the setting up of Passenger Transport Authorities. Initially four PTAs were proposed: West Midlands, Tyneside, South East Lancashire and Merseyside. The bus services of the various local authorities in the areas were merged under one authority.

Richard Marsh, the Minister of Transport, speaking at the annual luncheon of the Public Transport Association deprecated any suggestion that there was little point in bothering about public transport when it was going to be ousted by the private car. In the United States it had been admitted that one third of the urban population suffered serious disadvantage due to a lack of public transport.

"Turning to the setting up of the passenger transport authorities, the Minister remarked that whatever might have been said about them, the thinking underlying the concept of them and the National Bus Company was really quite simple. It assumed as a matter of course the need to strengthen public transport in the best interests of the country as a whole and that this could only be brought about through genuine co-operation between operators.

In the PTA areas this had been underlined by giving the executive and the National Bus Company a statutory duty to co-operate with each other. This implied a partnership between the two and with this in mind there would be formal built-in agreements between the PTA's and the NBC."

'Buses', January 1969.

The four PTA's were inaugurated on 1 April 1969. It was to be another five years before the West Yorkshire Passenger Transport Authority came into being.

Passenger numbers in Leeds stabilised at about 192 million annually from 1967 to 1969. This was not due to any improved management abilities by the new Conservative administration and passengers had continued to desert to the motorcar. It was largely due to a big increase in route mileage. Services had been acquired from Ledgard, the Farsley Omnibus Company, Kippax and District Motors and there had been route extensions. During the three years street mileage had increased from 225·45 to 260·85 and route mileage by more than this figure. The number of buses had also increased by 16. Passengers carried for the year ended 31 March 1969 had increased by 200,000 which was against the national trend. Thomas Lord contended that the increase was due to the fares, which were low compared with other places, and the quality of the service. Fares had indeed been "frozen" on Government instructions for over a year. The last fares rise had been in October 1967.

The reaction to the fares increase of February 1969 was not good. The local press said that many passengers were "irate." There was passenger resistance and numbers began to fall again.

A "great coup" for Leeds in March 1969 was the offer from a firm of advertising contractors to build 300 bus shelters worth £60,000 free of charge. In return the contractors would have limited advertising space on the shelters, Alderman Turnbull said the shelters were to be built at the rate of 100 per year. There were already 150 shelters erected by the Transport Department and the first shelter under the new scheme was put up at the end of March in Street Lane, near the junction with Talbot Road.

1361

£60,000 was to be released for other purposes and the scheme was said to be the first of its type in the country.

From about 7.30 a.m. on Sunday, 4 May 1969, a new one-way system came into use in the Sheepscar area, much of the property in the vicinity being demolished. North Street (between Skinner Lane and Sheepscar Junction), and Meanwood Road (between North Street and Barrack Street), became one-way outward, while Sheepscar Street North and Chapeltown Road (between Barrack Street and Sheepscar) and Sheepscar Street South became one-way inward. A considerable number of bus services were affected:

Services 2, 3 and 20 on journeys outward towards Moortown now used North Street, Meanwood Road, Barrack Street and Chapeltown Road.

Services 10, 19 and 21 on journeys to Roundhay ran via North Street, Meanwood Road, Barrack Street, Chapeltown Road and Roundhay Road.

The six services ran inward from Chapeltown Road or Roundhay Road ran via Sheepscar Street South, Regent Street, Gower Street, Bridge Street, and Templar Street to Vicar Lane.

Services 8, 52, 53, 58 (inward only) from Meanwood Road via Barrack Street, Chapeltown Road and then as services 2, 3 etc. to Vicar Lane.

Service 32 outward from North Street via Meanwood Road and Barrack Street, to Sheepscar Street North. Inward from Sheepscar Street North via Barrack Street, Chapeltown Road, then as services 2, 3 etc. to Vicar Lane.

Services 34, 35, 37, 43, 70, 100, 110 and 116 from Regent Street via Skinner Lane, North Street, Meanwood Road, Barrack Street, to Sheepscar Street North. Inward from Sheepscar Street North via Barrack Street and Chapeltown Road to Sheepscar Street South.

Service 61 from Barrack Road, via Chapeltown Road, new link road and Meanwood Road in place of Buslingthorpe Lane and Sackville Street.

Service 62 from Meanwood Road via Barrack Street to Barrack Road instead of Sackville Street and Buslingthorpe Lane.

From 21 July 1969 buses on service 61 were diverted via North Street and Meanwood Road, instead of using the link road from Chapeltown Road to Meanwood Road.

A problem road in Leeds was North Parkway, Seacroft. It was an isolated dual carriageway about a mile long leading nowhere. It was popular with the Transport Department as a training road for bus drivers and also a test road for buses, which had undergone repair. However, it was a long walk for residents living at the west end and there had been requests for a bus service over a period of many years. An unsuccessful shopper's service, 76, ran for about six months in 1967 to 1968. A request for a bus service was made again in May 1969, the Transport Department in replying said that the "amount of passenger traffic would not justify the service."

On 17 March 1969 a successful shoppers bus was introduced to the Manor Farm Estate at Belle Isle. Following complaints from housewives a service was instituted for an experimental period of three months. The route from the Central Bus Station was via Eastgate, Vicar Lane, service 10 route to Town Street, Middleton, then Newhall Road, Manor Farm Drive and Manor Farm Grove. On the return buses ran via Manor Farm Grove, Manor Farm Road, Newhall Crescent, Newhall Road and then the 10 route to Briggate, The Headrow, Eastgate and St, Peter's Street. The service, 82, became a normal stage carriage route.

On 6 July 1969 an extension was made to services 37 and 43 (Central Bus Station-Shadwell), It ran from Gateland Lane to a new terminus at Ash Hill Lane where a turning circle was built. The extension meant that buses could turn without reversing, as the two Shadwell routes were soon to become one-man operated.

Alderman Turnbull indicated that it was intended to introduce 12 more one-man services during 1969-70. He also announced plans for eight more Fastaway services and another 12 in the following three years – including joint services with the West Riding and West Yorkshire Companies. The experiments with pre-purchased reduced price multi-journey tickets would ease the work load of the drivers on the one-man buses.

From Sunday, 8 June 1969, one-man service 45 (Stanks-Wortley) began to use multi-journey tickets and was followed by the 49 (Hyde Park-Old Farnley) on 13 July. On this day, service 49 became the first route in Leeds to be converted to one-man double deck operation. Daimler Fleetline 156 had the honour of being the first bus. In June Alderman Turnbull had announced that agreement with the trade unions had been finalised. Also on 13 July, all night bus services were converted to one-man operation using single deck vehicles.

During the first week of operation of the multi-journey tickets on the 45 route, Thomas Lord said that there had been a "most encouraging" response from passengers.

On Sunday, 27 July 1969, one-man single deck operation was introduced on services, 34/35 (Alwoodley Circulars), 37/43 (Shadwell) and 70 (Primley Park). These had previously been operated by double deckers, At first there were complaints from residents in Shadwell due to the increased length of the buses. The complaints soon subsided. In June the Transport Committee had applied to the Traffic Commissioners to extend the Fastaway system to Alwoodley and Shadwell. Thomas Lord said that the Swarcliffe Fastaways introduced two years before, had proved "so popular with passengers" that extra buses had to be put on. He said that there would be some reduction in journey times between the two suburbs and the city centre, but did not commit himself to a figure. It was realised that because of traffic congestion the Fastaways were not very much quicker than the normal service buses. Lord said that when the Inner Ring Road was completed there would be "an enormous improvement" in timing. Fastaways were principally designed to cater for the needs of the daily commuter, said Lord. On Monday, 28 July, the two new one-man operated Fastaway services were introduced:

Service 235 (Alwoodley-Leeds).

Commencing in Alwoodley Lane at Sandmoor Drive, the route was Alwoodley Lane, King Lane (with a final pick up point at the Ring Road), Scott Hall Road, Sheepscar Street North, Barrack Street, Chapeltown Road, Inner Ring Road Sheepscar link, Claypit Lane, Woodhouse Lane, The Headrow, Park Row, Infirmary Street, and East Parade. There were dropping off points in the three latter streets. On the return journey the reverse route was followed with three pick up points only in Park Row, Infirmary Street and East Parade. Five journeys were operated at the morning peak period and seven in the evenings.

Service 237 (Shadwell-Leeds).

Beginning at the new turning circle at Shadwell, the route was Main Street, Shadwell Lane, Ring Road (Moortown), Scott Hall Road, and then as Service 235 with the same stopping places and return route. In the morning there were four journeys at half hour intervals, the last pick up point being near the Shadwell Lane/Ring Road junction. There were four evening return journeys.

On each of the services the fare was 1s.2d. with a reduction if multi-journey tickets were purchased.

On Sunday, 14 December 1969, a new section of the Inner Ring Road was opened as far as Claypit Lane and the following day the two Fastaways were rerouted from the Sheepscar link road of the Inner Ring Road via the newly opened section and Westgate to Park Row, Infirmary Street and East Parade on inward journeys, and by the reverse route on outward journeys. From 15 November 1971 services 235 and 237 were rerouted on

From 6 April 1927 to 4 May 1969 Corporation buses had run between Chapeltown Road and Meanwood Road via Buslingthorpe Lane and Sackville Street. A new one-way arrangement at Sheepscar closed the road and the buses were rerouted. A.E.C. Regent V 837 on service 62 (East End Park Circular) is in Buslingthorpe Lane and approaching the junction with Chapeltown Road on 23 July 1962. This part of Buslingthorpe Lane, Stanhope Terrace, Tetley's Wellington Inn, lamp post and bus no longer exist. However, some of the granite paving setts can be seen in "Tramway Street" at the National Tramway Museum, Crich, Derbyshire. *Author.*

outward journeys from Park Row via Infirmary Street, East Parade, Calverley Street, Great George Street, Cookridge Street, Claypit Lane and the Inner Ring Road Sheepscar link.

To work the new one-man Scott Hall Road group of services a further batch of 50 A.E.C. Swifts was in the process of delivery. The first appeared at the beginning of July and all had entered service by November 1969.

The new Swifts were numbered 1001-1050, the first time that four figure fleet numbers had appeared on Leeds buses. Registration numbers were SUB 401-450G and they had Park Royal B48D bodies, similar to the earlier Roe-bodied Swifts, although they did not have standee windows. There were side indicators, but none at the rear. The centre exit was of double width, but to allow for this, the luggage rack fitted to earlier models was sacrificed. In its place, the first nearside seat in front of the centre exit was of the tip up type, so that luggage, pushchairs, etc. could be accommodated. To improve vision the driving seat was positioned higher than on earlier vehicles. Mechanically the new vehicles differed considerably from the earlier examples in that they had C.A.V. automatic transmission and the latest AH 691 type engines, in place of the AH 505 type fitted to 51-100.

As a result of the introduction of the new single deckers, 36 older double deck buses were withdrawn. The Transport Department adopted a new policy in regard to withdrawals. Until July 1969 vehicles had been withdrawn, usually in batches, according to age. Buses were now withdrawn upon expiry of their certificates of fitness. Buses withdrawn in June, July and August were: 533, 534, 626,

628-631, 637, 638, 640-643, 645, 646, 649-651, 653, 656-668, 670. 676, 678 and 700.

The withdrawals included the first of the "VUG" series of Daimlers, 532-551, (with the exception of 541 – earlier accident damage). Also the first Roe-bodied "PUA" series of A.E.C. Regent III were taken out of service, (other than 675, another accident victim). There were also the first of the 8ft.0in. wide "ONW" series of A.E.C Regent III and 700, the only one of its type - the 1950 Commercial Motor Show exhibit. 678 was the 1952 Commercial Motor Show bus, numbered 800 at the time. The last of the Weymann-bodied "PUA" A.E.C. Regent III of the 649-654 series were now withdrawn.

Simultaneously with the delivery of the new Swifts a further batch of 20 Daimler Fleetline double deckers was delivered. These were of the Fleetline CRG6LXB type numbered 161-180 (UNW 161-180H) and were fitted with Roe bodies H45/33D as 146-160. The chassis and engines were similar to those of 156-160 delivered in 1968, but had semi-automatic transmission, like 146-155. The bodies were similar to 146-160, but a slight difference was a recessed section below the windscreen. This did not appear on the 1968 buses. Inside, the passenger counter in the lower saloon was moved to the staircase below the mirror. All 20 buses entered service from September to November 1969.

In October and November, 26 old double deck buses were withdrawn: 219, 532, 535-540, 542-547, 627, 632-636, 638, 639, 644, 647, 648, 731 and 812. Three of these were premature withdrawals. 219 was the first of the Leyland PD2/11 buses of the 201-220 series to be taken

A brand new A.E.C. Swift 1002 in Henconner Lane, Bramley Town End, on 10 July 1969. It is on route 46 (Bramley to Belle Isle) and the newly cleared site of the former Bramley Bus Garage is on the right hand side.
W.D.Wilson/L.T.H.S.

out of service. Its roof was damaged in a low bridge accident on 17 October 1969. A.E.C. Regent V 812 was withdrawn following a much more serious accident which occurred a few days later on 24 October. The bus overturned in Stoney Rock Lane, Burmantofts, hit a house and caused injury to 52 passengers. The vehicle was extensively damaged. The accident occurred at 7.00 a.m. and Stoney Rock Lane was blocked for two and a half hours. 812 was lifted by the two L.C.T. "wreckers" or breakdown wagons, UB 7931 and MUB 647. On 20 November 731 suffered damage to its roof in an accident. All the A.E.C. Regent III "ONW" series, 626-648 - the first production batch of 8ft.0in. wide buses - were now out of service. 626-648, with 600 and 700, had been the only buses of this width until 1958.

In August 1969 preliminary talks were held between Morley Corporation and Leeds City Transport Department over the introduction of Leeds buses to Gildersome to the south west of Leeds. Buses of the Yorkshire Woollen District Transport Company served the area. These were through services and at peak periods buses were full by the time they reached Gildersome. The idea was to extend the 31 service by about three quarters of a mile from its terminus at Farnley Moor Top to Gildersome.

Gildersome was in the West Riding county area and Alderman Watson, deputy chairman of the Traffic Sub-Committee, said that Leeds had no running rights over the route. He said that the Corporation was willing to extend the service subject to an agreement with the National Bus Company as part of the rationalisation policy for public transport in the Greater Leeds area.

"We are trying to make public transport easy and attractive from the dormitory areas of Leeds to help people travelling to work," he said. Watson also referred to the proposal to run a bus service through the High Ash Estate in the Wetherby Rural District Council area. He said the sub-committee was willing to run bus service 17 through the estate if asked to do so by the residents. Discussions were held with the West Yorkshire Road Car Company and Wetherby Rural District Council.

During the latter part of 1969, further conversion of bus routes to one-man operation occurred. In September the Transport Traffic Sub-Committee agreed to apply to convert services 5, 56, 57 to 60 and 63 and 64 to one-man operation. However, not all the routes were converted immediately. On 26 October service 56 (Central Bus Station-North Lane) became double deck one-man operated and services 57-60 (Hyde Park Circulars) became one-man single deck. On the same date services 63 and 64 (South Accommodation Road Circulars) became single deck operated, but worked with two-man crews. On 27 October, service 5 (Swinegate-Beeston) became single deck operated but had two-man crews.

Application was also made to introduce an express bus service from Seacroft via South Parkway and from Seacroft via North Parkway to the city centre. Authority was also sought to extend service 56 from North Lane to a new terminal point in Queenswood Drive.

On Friday, 17 October 1969, the new Minister of Transport, Fred Mulley, visited Leeds for the publication of "Planning and Transport – the Leeds Approach" This document was a report of the special partnership between Leeds City Council and the Ministry of Transport, The report and other events are discussed in the next chapter.

CHAPTER 84

The Leeds Approach and the First Minibuses

On 4 October 1969 Fred Mulley succeeded Richard Marsh as Minister of Transport and his first provincial engagement as Minister was to visit Leeds. The trip was to launch the publication, 'Planning and Transport – the Leeds Approach'. This was an important document and was to be the basis of Leeds transport policy for the remainder of the undertaking's existence and also for the first year or so of its successor, the West Yorkshire Metropolitan Transport Executive. Published by H.M. Stationery Office, the document was a report of the special partnership between Leeds City Council, the Ministry of Transport and Ministry of Housing and Local Government.

The report was published on Friday, 17 October 1969, on which day Mulley arrived in Leeds. It was held as "a stimulus to thought and action" to all planning authorities. The report was about what Leeds was doing under the "special partnership" set up in 1965. It said that the three bodies undertook a joint study "to consider the application of integrated parking, traffic management and public transport policies within the framework of land-use planning." It also covered the design and improvement of environmental areas.

"It has been shaped by the city's topography, history and general character. In preparing their traffic and transport plans we recognise that other towns and cities will need to seek solutions to their own special problems, but we think that this report will be of interest to all local planning authorities as a stimulus to thought and action."

'Planning and Transport – the Leeds Approach, 1969'

It said that Leeds faced a problem of urban renewal affecting residential, industrial and commercial areas. This problem also involved a new road system to meet modern traffic requirements. It added that the city's complete road network would have to be finished for the plan to be effective. 11,400 car parking spaces were to provide for the central business area and 7,200 spaces for the main industrial area. Drawings show three large multi-storey car parks on Stage 2 of the Inner Ring Road at Woodhouse Lane, Clay Pit Lane and in New York Road. "This quantity limits the growth in use of private car transport at about 20% of work journeys. The balance of commuting would be by public road transport and other means," the report said. "The decision which is taken must leave a sufficient residual demand for public transport to make it possible to operate an effective service," it added.

The limit of 20% put on car journeys turned out to be wildly inaccurate. The completion of the road network, while it certainly eased public transport problems in the centre of the city, also vastly increased the number of car commuters. The compilers of the report could not have foreseen the catastrophic decline that was to take place in the use of public transport over the following years. By the 1990's the number of passengers carried on the Leeds buses was to drop to about a quarter of the number carried in 1969. Of the multi-storey car parks, the Woodhouse Lane car park (opened 10 August 1970) was under construction at the time of Mulley's visit, but the other two car parks were not built.

Fred Mulley was "very impressed indeed" with the Fastaway service from the city centre to Swarcliffe. Thomas Lord, the General Manager, told the Minister that about 11,000 passengers weekly were carried on the Fastaways and that a third of those who previously drove their own cars to work from the Swarcliffe area now used the express buses. Afterwards Mulley saw the various types of buses in the Leeds fleet and visited the control centre at Swinegate. He inspected the partially completed Inner Ring Road, and inaugurated an environmental

A line up of L.C.T. buses on hire to Wallace Arnold Ltd. on 21 August 1971. The location is the Wallace Arnold Coach Station in The Calls and from the left are Leyland Atlantean 380, Daimler Fleetline 161 and Leyland Atlantean 369. All the buses are in the reversed green livery. *J.B.Parkin.*

In 1969 the last of the "ONW" series of A.E.C. Regents (626-648), the first production batch of 8 feet wide buses in Leeds, were withdrawn.   No. 634 is pictured at Hanover Lane in Park Lane on 30 May 1964 on route 74 to Moor Grange. Soon afterwards this part of Park Lane was converted into a dual carriageway. Benjamin Simon's "high grade" clothing factory. Tetleys "Three Horse Shoes" public house in Princess Street and all the other buildings on this photograph have been long gone. *Author.*

improvement scheme in the Burley Lodge Road area. Mulley commented:

"In terms of public transport the days of 'laissez faire' have gone – if they ever existed. The choice now is whether we opt for drift, with every man his own traffic snarl or whether we plan our way out of trouble. Really, its no choice at all, we must plan for survival."

'Journal of the Municipal Passenger Transport Association', p.337. September 1969.

The "Leeds approach" to public transport had been partly implemented and was a variation on what Alderman Rafferty, in 1965, had called the "three tier wedding cake" plan.   In accordance with Buchanan's ideas, the plan was road-based. It comprised, in addition to the normal inter-district bus services, three other forms of passenger service:

1. Express Bus services using the primary road network and providing non-stop fast runs between home and working areas.

2. City centre buses. These were to be small vehicles providing short movements within the central business area. These would include the proposed electric minibuses, each carrying about 24 passengers.

3. Park and ride services from outer suburban interchange points to the central areas.

Leeds also intended to run separate express bus services to and from the industrial belt to by-pass the central area.

In 1968 and 1969 there had been two fare increases on the Leeds buses. Unfortunately the projected income had not materialised owing to wages rises and passenger resistance. In October 1969 it was stated that the Department was faced with a possible deficit of £1,500,000 by the end of 1971. On 2 December 1969 a further application to increase fares was made to the Yorkshire Traffic Commissioners. At the hearing Leeds was declared to be "probably the most efficiently operated municipal undertaking in the country," but the City Council had "no

option" but to make the fares application. It was also claimed that Leeds had the lowest figures for revenue per mile and lowest costs per mile of all large municipal transport undertakings. It was said this position would be the same even if the application was granted in full.

Alderman Turnbull blamed the Socialists for refusing to raise fares in 1966-67 and letting the situation get out of hand. The opposition described the increases as "vicious." There had been a number of frequency reductions on some routes and the Socialists said that the Conservatives had tended to discourage passengers with high fares and a deteriorating service.

The 2d. minimum fare was abolished and increased to 3d. for a distance of just over half a mile for one stage. The 2d. fare was retained for children and old age pensioners. There were rises of from 1d. to 4d. in other fares and the maximum fare became 2s.3d. for 34 stages or over. On 4 January 1970 the new fare scales came into effect. The increase was expected to bring in an additional £836,000 income annually, but the deficit would still be £692,000 at the end of the financial year.

Shortly before Mulley's visit the Transport and Trading Services Committee ordered new buses. It must have had some doubt as to the financial viability of the proposed city centre minibuses for the Bond Street/Commercial Street/Lands Lane area. On 26 September 1969 it passed a resolution authorising tenders to be obtained for six minibuses "subject to a grant of 50% being obtained from the Ministry of Transport, and that the Finance and Parliamentary Committee be informed that in the opinion of this Committee any operational losses should not be met by the Transport undertaking."

The Ministry of Transport agreed to share the cost of the minibus experiment and gave Leeds a "bus priority grant". It offered to buy three of the minibuses, estimated to cost about £4,000 each and these would be leased to the Corporation for an experimental period.   The period was to be not less than six months and not more than two years depending on results. On 9 January 1970, the Ministry's offer was accepted. It was stated that Leeds would be the first authority in the country to operate minibuses. Alderman Frank Marshall, Chairman of the Committee, said it was hoped that the pedestrian precinct would be completed and the minibus service in operation by Christmas 1970. If successful, the Ministry would sell the minibuses to Leeds at their then value.

The Transport and Trading Services Committee did not have any qualms about accepting tenders for 60 new buses. These comprised 40 double deck and 20 single deck vehicles. All were to be one-man operated and were as follows:
A.E.C. Ltd. 20 Swift single deck motor bus chassis £82,035.
Leyland Motors Ltd. 40 Atlantean double deck bus chassis £160,938 6s.8d.
Park Royal Vehicles Ltd. 20 single deck motor bus bodies £90,360.
Park Royal Vehicles Ltd. 40 double deck motor bus bodies £238,480.

Prior to Mulley's visit there had been a tendency to reduce the frequency of buses on some services, but in January 1970 both services 9 (Ring Road) and 70 (Central Bus Station-Primley Park) had frequencies increased at certain times of the day.

The first day of 1970 saw a batch of new buses enter service. These were 20 of a series of 40 Leyland Atlantean double deck buses, 386-425 and a batch of 30 Daimler Fleetline single deckers, 1201-1230. The chassis of the single deckers had been delivered in December 1968, but the buses had taken a year to appear.

The 20 Leyland Atlanteans, 386-405 (UNW 386-405H) were of the PDR2/1 type and fitted with Roe H45/33D bodies. The bodies were identical with those on Daimler Fleetlines 161-180 and were the first Leylands in Leeds with front entrance and centre exit bodies. Although built at Roe's the buses carried plates to the effect that they had "Park Royal – Roe" bodies. All entered service in January and February 1970. The last six of the buses, 400-405, differed from the remainder in that they were fitted with spring brakes in place of the normal hand brakes.

The single deckers, 1201-1230 (UNW 201-230H), were of the Daimler Fleetline SRG6LXB–36 type and had Park Royal B48D bodies. They were the first single deck Fleetlines to enter service in Leeds. All had semi-automatic transmission and their bodies were virtually identical to those on A.E.C. Swifts, 1001-1050, although the Daimlers had a more normal lower driving position. In addition they had a bell push by the rear exit and strip bell pushes down the first window pillars on each side of the bus. The rear seat for five passengers was positioned higher than on the Swifts. These buses, although built by Park Royal, also displayed plates saying built by "Park Royal – Roe". All entered service from January to March 1970.

From March to May 1970 a further batch of 20 new buses appeared. These were Daimler Fleetline CRG6LXB double deckers, 181-200 (UNW 181-200H), fitted with Roe H45/33D bodies. They were identical to the earlier Fleetlines 161-180.

In July the rest of the 20 Leyland Atlantean PDR2/1 buses, 406-425 (UNW 406-425H) entered service. They were similar to 386-405, but were fully automatic and the first of their type in the fleet, other than bus 355 which had been converted experimentally in June 1968. 355 reverted to the older type gear operation in July 1970.

In May 1970 the Transport Department said that Leeds would soon have more buses equipped with two-way VHF radio-telephones than any other city in the country. After the next batch of 50 one-man buses appeared, the total would be 364 – about half the fleet. In addition there were

16 in use on service vehicles. Drivers of buses with radio-telephones "put a high value on the security provided by instant contact with central control," it said. There were also 60 UHF "pocket-fones" used by bus inspectors and 75 public address systems in buses to allow the driver to speak to passengers. The radio-telephones were supplied by Pye Communications Ltd. In April the number of closed-circuit TV cameras at strategic points had been increased from three to six in an effort to reduce traffic delays. A new console and bank of monitor screens were installed at the Swinegate Head Office. A seventh camera was added at The Headrow/Park Row junction in October 1970. The other cameras were located in City Square (2), Briggate (2), Corn Exchange and the Vicar Lane/Eastgate junction. Thomas Lord, the General Manager, said the extra camera would complete the scanning of bus operation in the city centre. "In terms of convenience, driver safety, accident reporting and even finding lost children the system is a very great asset," he remarked. It was found that the public address systems in the double deck buses were little used and they were removed at the end of 1971.

The appearance of 90 new buses led to the withdrawal of over 80 older vehicles. These included the whole of the series of "RNW" Leyland PD2/14, 301-310, the remainder of the "VUG" Daimler CVG6, 548-551, A.E.C. Regent III 619, 730, 732-741, 743-5, 748-754, A.E.C. Regent V 760, 762, 764, 777-786, 788-799, 801-808, 820-823, 825-828, 834, 835, 839, 873, and Leyland PD2/11 201 and 208.

Buses 619, 799, 834 and 873 were all withdrawn following accident damage. 873 was the first of the series of "XUM" A.E.C. Regent V buses to be withdrawn. Both 730 and 839 were former Earls Court Commercial Motor Show exhibits. From the bus driver's point of view the A.E.C. Regent V of the 760-909 series were underpowered. They had 7·7 litre A.E.C. AV 470 engines and were very sluggish. Both the earlier and later A.E.C. Regents had 9·6 litre engines.

Of particular interest were the Leyland PD2/14 buses 301-310. Dating from 1953 these were the only ten buses of this type to be constructed. They were fitted with pre-selector gears and fluid flywheels and were similar to the large "RTL" and "RTW" classes of London Transport. The "VUG" Daimlers, 532-551, fitted with M.C.W. bodies, were slightly newer dating from 1955–56 and were the first "tin front" double deck buses in Leeds.

In December 1969 Alderman Turnbull said that application was to be made to introduce two new double deck Fastaway services. This would be the first time that double deckers had been used for the express services. One service was to travel along North Parkway, Seacroft, and the other South Parkway.

Thomas Lord remarked:
"We are anxious to experiment with double deck Fastaway services. We believe the demand from the Seacroft area is such as to justify double deckers being used."

'Yorkshire Evening Post', 8 December 1969.

The two new services brought the number of express services up to six and were introduced on 19 January 1970. They were numbered 215 and 216 and ran from Seacroft Town Centre to the Corn Exchange.

The routes for the two services from the Town Centre Bus Station were via Seacroft Avenue, North Parkway, York Road, South Parkway (Service 215) and Seacroft Avenue, North Parkway and Kentmere Avenue to South Parkway (Service 216). From South Parkway, from where both services joined, they continued via South Parkway Approach, Foundry Lane, Wykebeck Valley Road, Gipton Approach, York Road, Marsh Lane, Duke Street, St. Peter's Street, Eastgate and Vicar Lane, to the Corn Exchange (Kirkgate). The outward route began in Kirkgate and was via New York Street, York Street and Marsh Lane and then the reverse of the inward route.

Both services operated inward only in the morning and outward in the evening peak on Mondays to Fridays at 15 minute frequencies. This gave a 7½ minute frequency to the Seacroft Centre. On Saturdays there was a half hourly service. The fare was 1s.6d. with a reduction for ten-journey tickets. However, from 2 February 1970 the fare was reduced to 1s.3d. with a corresponding reduction in the price of the ten-journey tickets. The reduction was made to bring the charge into line with the differential fares between the other Fastaways and the ordinary bus services. The fare was 3d. more on services 224, 225, 235 and 237 than on the normal services, but had been 6d. extra on services 215 and 216.

From Sunday, 18 January 1970, route 11 (Swinnow to Seacroft Town Centre) was extended to Whinmoor. Following pressure and petitions from residents who lived in the newest part of the large Whinmoor Estate, in June 1969 the Transport Department applied to the Traffic Commissioners for the Whinmoor extension. There had been a delay following negotiations with the West Yorkshire Road Car Company, whose competing Wetherby buses passed the estate along Coal Road and Skelton's Lane. Arnold Stone, the deputy General Manager, said that the Department was disappointed that it had not been able to give a service earlier.

From Seacroft Town Centre the route to Whinmoor was via Seacroft Avenue, North Parkway, York Road, Baildon Drive, and Sherburn Road to a new terminus at Naburn Place. Buses turned by way of Naburn Road, a short unnamed road and Naburn Place to the terminal stop in Sherburn Road. The fare from the Town Centre to the terminus was 5d. The service was operated through from Whinmoor to Greenthorpe. In December 1969 the Transport

Traffic Sub Committee agreed to apply to introduce one-man operation on routes 44, 67 and 68. On 1 March 1970 one-man double deck operation started on services 67 (Central Bus Station-Dib Lane and Monkswood Gate) and 68 (Central Bus Station-Foundry Lane). It was 5 April when one-man buses were introduced on the 44 (Halton Moor-Stanningley), route. One-man operation with both double deck and single deck buses was used. Double deckers worked the basic service through to Stanningley, with the assistance of single deckers mainly at peak times on the Headingley short workings. These were extended from Shaw Lane to North Lane (Cardigan Road) and turned from Kirkstall Lane by way of Headingley Avenue, Canterbury Road and Headingley Mount back to Kirkstall Lane. A revised timetable was introduced, the frequency of buses being increased.

In February 1970 proposals were put forward for "reserved bus sites" in the city centre, where Duplicates and buses waiting to go into service could park. The idea was to ease congestion at peak hours and nine sites were selected in Neville Street, Quebec Street, Infirmary Street, Park Row, Briggate, Kirkgate, Vicar Lane, New Briggate and Eastgate. By arrangement with the police the stands were to be marked out as stands for waiting buses. The sites were recommended by a working party of the city's Transport Planning Group and were for an experimental period of two months. They were not successful. As another means of lessening congestion the Group was asked to look into providing buses only lanes in the city centre. It was to be a year or two before these were introduced.

Beginning on 15 March 1970 an alteration occurred to routes 57 to 60, the Hyde Park Circulars. The services were altered between Woodhouse Street and the city

1227 was one of the single deck Daimler Fleetlines in Leeds. It is heading for Wortley on route 45 in Cockshott Lane, Bramley, on 19 April 1970. *W.D.Wilson/L.T.H.S.*

Leyland Atlantean 412 was new in July 1970 and is on route 29 to Middleton and passing under the railway bridge over Spence Lane, Holbeck. The date is 18 August 1973. *W.D.Wilson/L.T.H.S.*

1970 made big inroads into the "WUA" A.E.C. Regent V buses, 760-839. 780 was one of the buses withdrawn and was photographed at Roundhay Bus Park on Bank Holiday Monday, 3 August 1964. It was on the special service 103 to Roundhay. This was the last occasion on which the 103 Roundhay service operated. *Author.*

Peak period service 5, Swinegate-Beeston, suffered falling passenger numbers and ceased operation on 1 January 1971. A.E.C. Regent V 880 is in Sovereign Street on 11 June 1965. The imposing entrance to the Leeds City Transport Head Office in Swinegate can be seen in the background. *Author.*

centre in that the route formerly covered by services 57 and 59 was now 58 and 60, while the former route of 58 and 60, which had a slightly better frequency than 57 and 59, operated over the most densely populated section of route in Lovell Park Road. The 57 and 59 buses ran along Meanwood Road.

As part of the scheme for Stage 2 of the city's Inner Ring Road, North Street became one-way for northerly outward traffic between New York Road and Skinner Lane. The new arrangement came into being on Sunday, 5 April 1970. However, there were no bus service implications as the section of North Street to the north of Skinner Lane had been made one-way for buses in May 1969, when the one-way system was introduced at Sheepscar.

The completion of Stage 2 of the Inner Ring Road on Sunday, 3 May 1970, resulted in a number of bus service alterations. It was opened in an easterly direction throughout from Westgate to New York Road and in a westerly direction from New Briggate only. The following service alterations took place:

Services 2, 3, 8, 10, 19, 20, 21, 32, 52, 53 and 57 which had been operating via Regent Street, Gower Street, Bridge Street and Templar Street to Vicar Lane since 4 May 1969, were all altered to run from Regent Street to Vicar Lane via the newly reopened New York Road, which between these points was made a one-way street in a westerly direction, running parallel with the Inner Ring Road.

Services 22, 39, 41, 42, 50, 64, 66, 77, 85, 86, 87, 140, 148 and 162 had all been diverted on inward journeys owing to the closure of New York Road on 11 November 1968. The route from the Woodpecker had been Marsh Lane and Duke Street to either the Central Bus Station or Eastgate as appropriate. From 3 May this alteration became permanent in both directions, as there was now no right turn from Eastgate into New York Road. Service 63 was also now running from Eastgate to Upper Accommodation Road via this route and the 63/64 Circulars were using Shannon Street in both directions.

On 4 May service 54 (Halton Moor-Rodley) was extended at the Rodley end to improve turning arrangements. The extension, which was just outside the city boundary, was via Town Street, Canal Road and Bridge Road where the new terminal stop was situated. Buses left the terminus via Bridge Road, Rodley Lane and Town Street. Buses turning at Rodley on services 79 and 80 also used the new arrangement.

The construction of a dual carriageway from the Woodpecker to Lupton Avenue began in April 1970 and a casualty was the long established 63/64 South Accommodation Road Circular service. The bus service had been a replacement for the tram service, which had been abandoned in 1936. The dual carriageway prohibited the right hand turn from York Road into Upper Accommodation Road and on 6 June 1970 the service was discontinued.

The loss of transport facilities in the Hunslet and Dial Street areas was now served by an amended 61/62 Circular service. To serve East Street and Cross Green a new service 63 was introduced, which also provided an all day service to the Wholesale Markets and the new Cross Green Industrial Estate.

The route of the 61 service between Eastgate and East End Park was now via St. Peter's Street, Duke Street, Crown Point Road, Black Bull Street, Hunslet Road, South Accommodation Road, Easy Road, Dial Street, Upper Accommodation Road, Lavender Walk, Pontefract Lane and East Park Road to East Park Parade.

Service 62 between these points was now East Park Road, Pontefract Lane, Lavender Walk, Upper Accommodation Road Dial Street, Easy Road, South Accommodation Road, Atkinson Street, Goodman Street, Forster Street, Hunslet Road, Crown Point Road, Duke Street and St, Peter's Street to Eastgate.

The new service 63 (Vicar Lane-Cross Green), was routed via Vicar Lane, Kirkgate, New York Street, York Street, Duke Street, Marsh Lane, Saxton Lane, Flax Place, Richmond Street, East Street, Cross Green Lane and Pontefract Lane. The return journey was the same to Duke Street and then via St. Peter's Street, and Eastgate to Vicar Lane for turning purposes.

From 4 May 1970 a slight alteration took place to the 224/225 (Swarcliffe to Leeds) Fastaway services. Instead of having their final dropping off point in The Headrow near the Odeon Cinema, buses now turned from The Headrow into New Briggate to terminate. They then returned empty to Swarcliffe by way of New Briggate, North Street, and the new Inner Ring Road to New York Road and York Road to rejoin their former route.

On Sunday, 7 June 1970, one-man operated double deckers were introduced on service 22, (Central Bus Station to Temple Newsam). On fine Sundays during the summer this service was very busy and required a lot of extra buses. The service on other days was worked by one-man single deckers.

Following the Minister of Transport's visit to Leeds in October 1969, there had been an improvement in frequency on one or two bus services. This did not last. A major blow to the Leeds transport undertaking and to all other transport undertakings, was the introduction on 15 March 1970, of new regulations imposed by the Ministry of Transport in regard to the hours worked by bus drivers. Referred to as the "Hours Act", a bus driver's maximum working day was to be cut from 14 hours to 11. This meant that Leeds Transport Department would require an increase in platform staff of 653.

While undoubtedly of benefit to the health of staff, the regulations did not help their pockets, the Transport Department or passengers. This important ruling assisted in precipitating the major decline that affected the Leeds undertaking and its successors from 1970 onwards.

There were complaints in the press about long waits for buses and in July 1970 the Transport Department proposed cuts at off-peak times. Thomas Lord said that the Department was 300 platform staff under strength and was unable to operate up to 50 buses per day. It was proposed to cut several off peak services with frequencies of 20 minutes to 30 minutes. On 4 July 1970 the off peak frequency on service 79 was reduced from 20 minute to half hourly. An application for reduced services was made to the Traffic Commissioners. Services affected were: 3, 10, 12, 14, 15/16, 18/19, 20/21, 29, 33, 36, 67, 68 and 72.

Councillor Dennis Matthews, Labour spokesman on the Transport and Trading Services Committee, said there was no shortage of conductors. Proposed cuts could be avoided if one-man operation was temporarily abandoned.

"To maintain regular services along a route, you have to use more one-man buses because of their slowness. Therefore more drivers are being used than should be necessary. If conductors were put on these buses, it would speed up the service, fewer buses would then be needed, and this might prevent a cut in the services," he said.

'The Yorkshire Evening Post,' 27 June 1970.

Matthews was ignored. Service 5 (Swinegate-Beeston) had been converted to one-man operation on 3 June 1970. This service, which operated at morning and evening peak periods, and lunchtimes on Mondays to Fridays, suffered falling numbers of passengers. It had been a tramway replacement service and was partly duplicated by service 1 to Beeston. After the evening peak on 1 January 1971, the buses were withdrawn.

Further conversions to one-man working occurred on

Route 7 (Hunslet-Beckett's Park) was converted to one-man operation on 26 July 1970. Until property demolition, the turning of buses was difficult at Hunslet. Leyland Atlantean 411 is in Spring Grove Street, Hunslet, on 11 August 1976. The Belmonts on the right hand side and all the other buildings, including the Old Red Lion pub in Low Road, in the background, were removed soon after this photograph was taken. *Author.*

The Central Bus Station crammed full of buses on Sunday, 13 September 1970. The occasion was a strike meeting by bus workers. From the left are Daimler Fleetline 150, A.E.C. Swifts 67 and 1050 and Daimler Fleetline 158. *J.B.Parkin.*

26 July 1970. Services were 7 (Hunslet-North Lane) and 74 and 76 (Belle Isle and Middleton-Moor Grange). Besides the one-man operation, the following alterations took place to these routes:

Service 7 was extended from the former North Lane terminus near Eden Drive via Queenswood Drive to Spen Lane, where buses turned at the Beckett's Park turning circle. At the other end of the route, Hunslet, new turning arrangements came into force. Buses turned into Spring Grove Street as before, but instead of reversing up a side street, they continued to the end, then into Sussex Avenue and Spring Grove Mount back to Low Road.

The terminal arrangements of services 74 and 76 were altered at Moor Grange so that they now ran from Latchmere Drive via Latchmere Road, Old Farm Drive, Old Farm Cross and back to Latchmere Drive, where the new terminal stop was at Latchmere Green.

On 13 July 1970, owing to redevelopment of the Cottingley Estate, the terminus of service 8 at Cottingley was moved a short distance from the roundabout in Dulverton Road. Buses proceeded from the Ring Road as before via Cottingley Drive, but terminated at the junction with Dulverton Road.

The proposal to run Leeds buses to Gildersome was brought up again in September 1970. It had been mooted in August 1969 and the Mayor of Morley, Alderman George Rogerson, said the request "seemed to be getting nowhere." There had been innumerable complaints about the Yorkshire Woollen District bus service in the area. Arnold Stone, the Deputy General Manager, said that talks had taken place between both Morley Corporation and the bus company. He said: "We have more recently had preliminary talks with Yorkshire and further talks are to be held." He added that the new regulations on drivers' hours did not help when considering extending a service and providing extra buses. Nothing happened and it was to be 1978 in the PTA days when Leeds buses were eventually extended into Gildersome.

On 6 September 1970 service 56 (Central Bus Station -North Lane) was extended from its former terminus at North Lane via Kirkstall Lane and terminating at the bottom of Queenswood Drive, until 25 July the old terminus of the No. 7 route.

Three special services for shoppers are now discussed.

On the day a new Morrison's supermarket at Yeadon opened - 25 February 1970 - a free shopper's service was opened from the 36 bus terminus at Tinshill to the supermarket. It was given the service number 157 and the route was via Silk Mill Drive, Wood Nook Drive, Tinshill Lane, Otley Old Road, Cookridge Lane. Green Lane, Woodhill Road, Tinshill Road, Brownberrie Lane, Layton Road, Town Street, (Rawdon), Over Lane, New Road Side, Henshaw Lane and Harper Lane. On return journeys buses ran from Harper Lane via High Street and Ivegate to the outward route. The free service operated on Tuesdays, Thursdays, Fridays and Saturdays. On 1 May the free service ceased and was replaced by a new licensed service 157 with fares of 1s.9d. for adults and 11d. for children. The service ceased on 30 May 1970.

Following requests from Horsforth Council, from 20 October 1970, a Tuesdays and Fridays experimental local shopper's service was introduced from Horsforth, (Woodside Tavern) to Horsforth (New Road Side). Given the service number 88, the route from Woodside Tavern was via Low Lane, Broadgate Lane, North Broadgate Lane, Town Street, The Green, Fink Hill, Parkside, New Road Side and Sunnybank Avenue where the terminal point was situated. In the reverse direction the bus ran from Sunnybank Avenue via Featherbank Lane and Broadway to Fink Hill. The running time was ten minutes, but the one-man service was not successful and was withdrawn on 12 February 1971.

Of more success was another shopper's service 88, this time from Colton to Cross Gates, which started on 28 June 1971. The route was from the route 41 terminus at

Colton, via Meynell Road, School Lane, Selby Road, Ring Road (Halton), and Station Road to a terminus at the Gem Supermarket in Cross Gates Road. This was formerly the site of the Regal Cinema. Two journeys were operated daily by two-man double deckers from Monday to Friday. The service was still in operation at the time of the takeover by the West Yorkshire PTE in April 1974.

On 29 December 1970, service 46 (Bramley-Belle Isle or Middleton) was modified to run via Balm Road, Woodhouse Hill Road, and Leasowe Road, in place of Church Street, Grove Road, Bower Road, New Pepper Road and Pepper Road. This alteration was caused by the permanent closure of Grove Road and Bower Road, Hunslet, for redevelopment.

There had been complaints in the press about the double deck Fastaway services, 215 and 216, from the Seacroft Town Centre. Due to traffic congestion on York Road, they were no faster than the ordinary service buses. One-man operation meant slower loading and they were more expensive. Some passengers disparagingly referred to them as the "Slow-away" buses. It is perhaps significant that the published timetables did not indicate a journey time for any of the Fastaway services. From Monday 7 September, the 215 buses were altered to operate from Whinmoor in place of Seacroft Town Centre. The route between Corn Exchange and York Road, Seacroft was unaltered, but buses now continued up York Road and via Baildon Drive and Sherburn Road to Whinmoor, where they terminated at the same point as the service 11 vehicles. The turning arrangements at Whinmoor were via Naburn Road and Naburn Place. From 2 June 1971 single deckers replaced the double deck buses on these routes.

Multi-journey tickets had been popular on the Fastaway services and on 10 January 1971 they were introduced on nine extra routes: services 34/35, 37/43, 38, 44, 46, 67, 68, 70 and 73. Other routes followed later in 1971 and subsequent years.

Minibuses

The Commercial Motor Show at Earls Court held from 18 to 26 September 1970, saw the appearance of the first of the new minibuses. There had been adverse comment in the local press, as it had been announced that they were to be Mercedes Benz buses of German manufacture.

"I hate to see local government money and Ministry of Transport grants being used to contribute to our balance of payments difficulties," said a spokesman for a firm of British minibus manufacturers.

The minibuses were to be 13-seaters, each costing £3,195. Arnold Stone, deputy general manager, said that the department had examined, with the Ministry of Transport, all the various types of minibus that were on offer and the German vehicle was the only one which gave Leeds all it was looking for. "This service is an entirely new concept of public transport operation – and no service such as this is operated anywhere in this country," he said. "The Leeds experiment would be closely watched by the Ministry, and other transport operators," he added.

Thomas Lord commented:

"I would be delighted if there was a British minibus available at half the price we are paying, but the fact is that we chose this model because of cost. Whoever says there is a British model available must be talking about a personnel carrier – that is a van that has been adapted to have seats inside. I can state emphatically that these are the cheapest minibuses available."

'Yorkshire Post,' 2 June 1970.

The minibus selected for display at the Commercial Motor Show was number 30, the first of the batch of six buses, 30-35. Registered YUA 530J, it was a Mercedes-Benz L406D/35R fitted with a Deansgate B13F body built by the Williams Motor Co. (Manchester) Ltd.

The L406D was a standard Mercedes-Benz delivery van chassis, adapted with a high roof body of steel construction. It had twin jack-knife electrically-operated folding doors, ample parcel or rack accommodation for

Mercedes Benz minibus 34 on shopper's service 401 passing W.H.Smith & Sons, newsagents and stationers, in the Commercial Street shopping precinct on 3 March 1971. In 1986-7 W.H.Smith & Sons was relocated to a partly new building at the corner of Lands Lane and Albion Place. *W.D.Wilson/L.T.H.S.*

Mercedes Benz minibus 30 was displayed at the Commercial Motor Show at Earl's Court, London, in September 1970. It is at the Leeds City Station terminus on the new 401 Shopper's service. *Leeds City Transport.*

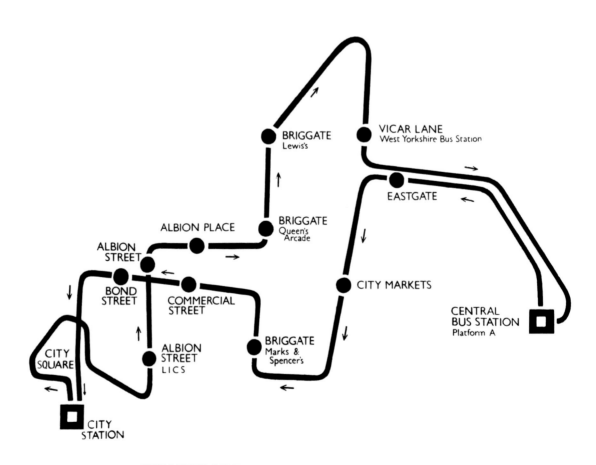

THE LEEDS CENTRAL AREA MINIBUS SERVICE

The spartan interior of Mercedes Benz minibus number 30. *Leeds City Transport.*

shoppers, fluorescent lighting and radio equipment. The interior was rather spartan with 13 seats arranged around the perimeter of the body, with standing space for nine in the centre. There were leaning rails, single-impulse Crona strip bell pushes, handrails, and an emergency exit at the rear. Built for one-man operation, a Bell Punch Autoslot machine was fitted at the Show with a change giver alongside. Standard pattern moquette was used for the seating. One long window was fitted on each side, and the front dome was modified to include a small destination indicator. The bus was in a new livery of ivory with a wide dark green band. The city coat of arms was placed in the centre of the lower panels, with the name "LEEDS" prominently displayed by the entrance.

After the Show the bus was returned to the body builders, the seats reupholstered and it subsequently made an appearance in Leeds on 1 October where it was demonstrated to L.C.T. officials. It returned to Manchester later the same day, reappearing on 3 November. From 10 November, 30 was used for driving instruction.

30-34 (YUA 530-534J) entered passenger service on Monday, 30 November 1970 on a new Central Area Shopper's Service 401. 35 had not been delivered at the time and appeared on 23 December.

Service 401 was introduced to serve the new pedestrian shopping precinct area of Commercial Street and Bond Street. On 9 September 1970 these streets, along with Lands Lane and King Charles Croft, had been closed to traffic for alterations. After completion the streets could only be used by essential service vehicles, and the new minibuses. A 7 m.p.h. speed limit was imposed on the minibuses when running through the precinct.

Beginning in the Central Bus Station, at the George Street end of Platform "A" where a new shelter had been erected, the route was via Eastgate, Vicar Lane, New Market Street, Duncan Street, Briggate, Commercial Street, Bond Street, Park Row, City Square, and the City Station concourse. Buses turned near the taxi rank and then stopped near the entrance to the main hall. The return journey was via City Square, Boar Lane, Albion Street, Albion Place, Briggate, New Briggate, Vicar Lane, Eastgate, and St, Peter's Street to the Central Bus Station. The minibuses were worked from Sovereign Street Garage and a flat fare of 3d. was charged. The service operated on Mondays to Saturdays at a six minute frequency between 10.00 a.m. and 4.00 p.m. from the Central Bus Station and between 10.03 a.m. and 4.03 p.m. from the City Station.

There were objections to the minibuses from the taxi drivers. Their cabs were not allowed into the precinct "except for weddings and funerals." This was a strange instruction as there were no churches in the precinct.

Alderman Turnbull said that the city's public transport system was being designed to operate in conditions where it would be, as far as possible, an economic alternative to the private car for work journeys. Six, big commuter car parks accommodating 11,400 cars, were proposed and they would be served by the minibuses.

There were a number of opposition councillors who were opponents of the minibus idea. Councillor Sir Karl Cohen (Labour) at the following City Council meeting said he hoped the experiment would fail quickly. He said that a pedestrian precinct should be totally reserved for pedestrians. He also said that the precinct should be extended. Alderman Bertrand Mather agreed that opinions on the merits of the service were divided in the Council and said that it was only the beginning of an experiment. "It was not expected that the scheme would be a success overnight," he said.

Although car exhaust fumes were removed from the precinct, there were still diesel fumes from the minibuses. There had been talk of a battery-operated electric minibus for over three years. In October 1969 the Leeds City Architect's Department had designed the body for a very box-like electric minibus. The drawings had been shown to Fred Mulley on his visit to Leeds and by December 1970 designs for the prototype bus were completed.

An order was placed for a 26-passenger bus to be made by Crompton Leyland Electricars of Tredegar, Monmouthshire, The bus, provided in conjunction with the Ministry of Transport, was to be tested in Leeds. It would then be decided whether to introduce improved versions in other cities.

The Department of Trade and Industry said that a contract for two vehicles had been placed with Crompton Leyland. They would have a range of about 30 miles before their traction batteries needed recharging and their top speed would be 20 m.p.h. Batteries would normally be recharged overnight or partially recharged in rest periods during the day.

Each bus was to carry 18 standing and eight seated passengers and would be about 21 feet long and weigh around nine tons. The announcement stated, "It is intended to loan the buses free of charge to transport authorities to enable them to gain first hand knowledge of the operating and technical characteristics.... As the effects of exhaust pollution are most keenly felt in city centres, there is an increasing interest in the possible use of battery electric buses." The electric minibus was due to be delivered towards the end of 1971.

More Double Deckers

In addition to minibus 30, also appearing at the Commercial Motor Show on the Roe stand, was a Leyland Atlantean double decker, 428, This bus was part of the first ten of the Leeds order for 40 Roe-bodied Atlanteans. These were 426-435 (XUM 426-435J), Leyland Atlantean PDR2/1 fitted with Roe H45/33D bodies. These buses were similar in appearance to the last series of Atlanteans 386-425, the main exterior difference being the positioning of a large digital number indicator in the first near side window. The side destination blind was omitted. The word "ATLANTEAN" now appeared on the rear in place of the usual badge. A slightly smaller type of radio aerial was fitted which was also positioned higher, and pointed upwards. They were fitted with spring parking brakes.

428 as displayed at Earl's Court differed in minor ways from 426-427 and 429-435. It did not have mudguards, simply a cut away panel of square appearance. It had continuous strip lighting in each saloon while other features were a new type of passenger counter for the upper saloon, electrically heated indicator box glass and a modified heating/ventilation system. All ten buses entered passenger service in September and October 1970.

The next series of ten Atlanteans was delivered in November 1970. Numbered 436-445 (XUM 436-445J), they were identical to 426-435. A further ten similar buses 446-455 (ANW 446-455J) were delivered in January 1971.

43 buses were withdrawn following the delivery of the Atlanteans, 426-455. These comprised the last two Roe-bodied A.E.C. Regent III of the "TNW" series, 746 and 747, and the M.C.C.W. TNW with "Orion" bodies 755-758. In addition A.E.C. Regent V 817, 824, 829-833, 836-838, Leyland PD2/11 202, 207, 209-215, 218, and 220, the latter following an accident on 27 October. A number of earlier A.E.C. Regent III were also withdrawn: 615-617, 655, 671, 673 and 677. The most surprising withdrawals were the relatively new A.E.C. Reliances, 39-43, dating from 1962 and 44-47, from 1964. These had been unpopular in operation with their single width entrance/exit at the front, and additionally there was no convenient position for a multi-journey ticket cancellor. These single deckers had under-floor

engines and after their withdrawal the only under-floor engine single decker in the fleet was coach 10. 202 and 673 had been in a collision with each other on 18 December 1970. With these withdrawals, only nine A.E.C. Regent III buses remained in service, 620-625, 669. 672 and 674. The Leyland PD2/11 buses were reduced to four with Roe bodies (203-206), and two with M.C.C.W "Orion" bodies, 216 and 217.

Decimalisation of the currency was due to begin in February 1971 and in December 1970 three withdrawn buses, 106, 664 and 750, were fitted with desks for decimal training purposes.

On 29 June 1970 the Transport and Trading Services Committee accepted tenders for 60 new double deckers for delivery in 1971 and a further 60 in 1972.

For delivery in 1971:
Leyland Motors Ltd. 30 Atlantean double deck chassis for £138,649 10s.0d.
Daimler Transport Vehicles Ltd. 30 Fleetline double deck chassis for £150,255.
Park Royal/Roe Sales Divisions (Charles H. Roe Ltd.) 60 double deck bodies £389,400.
For delivery in 1972:
Leyland Motors Ltd. 60 Atlantean double deck chassis £286,899.
Park Royal – Roe Sales Divisions (Charles H. Roe Ltd.) 60 double deck bodies £389,400.

The Transport Department said that the new buses were to be replacements for vehicles about to complete their life span within the next two years. At the time the average Leeds bus had a life of from 16 to 18 years and ran over 560,000 miles. A number of buses had reached this figure and were due for early withdrawal.

There had been a fares increase on 4 January 1970. To offset an expected loss of £260,000 on the year's working, in August a further application was made to increase fares. Increased wages were costing £350,000 in excess of the fares revenue. Alderman Turnbull said that it was with the "greatest reluctance" the Transport and Trading Services Committee was compelled to apply to the Traffic Commissioners. He said that the application had to be made before 25 August owing to the change to decimalisation on 15 February 1971. Part of the increase was to take effect in November and the remainder on 15 February. Turnbull said "soaring costs" were the problem and to get the extra revenue they "must inevitably be severe." In November, the 3d. minimum fare was to be raised to 4d., the 5d. to 6d. and so on.

There had been four fares increases in three years and there was opposition from the Socialists. Councillor Matthews said the matter had not been discussed by the Transport and Trading Services Committee and they wanted a special meeting of the Council. All the Labour party knew was what had been reported in the Press. Alderman Frank Marshall, leader of the City Council, said that the Council was "facing cost increases at an unprecedented rate," as the transport workers had submitted another substantial wages claim. Alderman Turnbull commented that the request for the fares application was as a result of a resolution of the Finance and Planning Committee.

On 15 October 1970, the application was heard by the Traffic Commissioners. There was an objection by Councillor Pepper, the deputy Labour leader, claiming that the application had not been approved by the City Council. One objector said that the time was fast approaching where it was cheaper to use a car rather than public transport. His and Pepper's intervention were to no avail and the fares increase took effect on 8 November 1970. There was, however, a concession for elderly people. The concessionary fares, which normally operated from 10 a.m. to 4.00 p.m. daily were extended to all day on Saturdays, Sundays and public holidays.   From 13

Leyland Atlantean 428 appeared on the Roe stand at the 1970 Commercial Motor Show. It differed in minor details from the earlier Atlanteans. It is at the Arndale Centre, Otley Road, Headingley, on 7 July 1971. *W.D.Wilson/L.T.H.S.*

After November 1970 the Leyland PD2/11 buses were reduced to four with Roe bodies (203-206) and two with M.C.C.W. "Orion" bodies, (216 and 217). 216 was photographed entering the Central Bus Station on 6 July 1961. It was withdrawn from service in February 1971. Quarry Hill Flats on the left were demolished in 1975-8. The brick building on the right still exists. *W.D.Wilson/L.T.H.S.*

December they were also allowed after 6.00 p.m. in the evenings.

In September and October there were a series of bus strikes not only by L.C.T. employees, but also by those of private bus operators in the area. They wanted more pay and their complaints are discussed further in Chapter 91. The dispute became bitter and the Trades Union said staff would not collect the increased fares due to come into effect on 8 November.

"People in and around Leeds were today winning the two-day bus strike battle by getting up early, giving each other lifts and walking to work.

This was the fifth consecutive Friday in which Corporation bus crews have gone on strike in support of their claim for an increased basic wage.

It appeared that most workers who normally travel by bus have now made their own alternative arrangements."

'Yorkshire Evening Post', 23 October 1970.

None of this helped the Transport Department. A considerable pay rise was eventually agreed and many of those people who had made "alternative arrangements" did not return to the bus, thus compounding the Department's difficulties.

In spite of the introduction of more express buses there was a big decline of 30 million in the number of passengers carried from 1969-1971. This approximated to 16% and was caused by higher fares and subsequent passenger resistance. There were also the strike problems and irregular running caused by the impositions of the Transport Act. The Act exacerbated the staff problem, which existed throughout the 1960's. Another major contributory factor was the slow loading one-man buses.

In November 1969 Leeds applied to the Traffic Commissioners to run a shopper's service through the new Temple Gate Estate at Halton. There were petitions from 540 people in favour of the service and 109 against. The objectors said that buses would spoil the estates' residential character. The West Riding Automobile Company also objected as its buses ran directly along Selby Road. The Commissioners deferred a decision pending the institution of a scheme to rationalise bus services in the area.

Over the following year, a scheme for the rationalisation of services in east Leeds was agreed with the West Riding Automobile Company. Several Leeds and some West Riding services were affected.

The idea was to provide better services, including non-stop express services between the city centre and the former Kippax and District Motor Company routes to Garforth and Kippax. Arnold Stone, Deputy General Manager, said several of the services would be jointly operated and the result should be better facilities for the travelling public and some economies in operation.

The proposals were approved by the Traffic Commissioners and instituted on 8 March 1971. They are discussed in the next chapter.

844 was one of the first of the "XUM" series of A.E.C. Regent V buses to be withdrawn from service. It is on route 8, the Meanwood-Cottingley service, and was photographed in New Market Street on 19 May 1963. Leyland PD3/5 286 on service 2 to Dewsbury Road is in the background. *Author.*

The Buses 1971 to 1972

There was no doubt that decimalisation resulted in a rounding up of bus fares, not only in Leeds, but on all other Yorkshire transport undertakings. In the leaflets issued indicating the fares increases, which took place on 8 November 1970, there were also details of the decimal fares to be introduced three months later.

Decimalisation day was 15 February 1971 and the new fares came into force on Sunday 21 February. From "D-Day" to the 21st. fares were charged at the old rates, but conductors gave change where possible in the new decimal currency. The 5d. fare that was operating before 8 November jumped to 7·2d. (3p) – an increase of 44%. The shilling fare was the same (5p) and surprisingly the 1s.3d. fares came down slightly to 6p. The flat fare on the new shopper's minibus service, 401, was increased from 3d. to 2p (4·8d.) Most other fares showed increases.

A further general fare rise took place on 5 December 1971 when fares were increased by about 5%. An increase also occurred on routes 39, 89, 97, 202, 203 and 204 from 5 March 1972. These services were jointly worked with the West Riding Automobile Company. They came into line with a general increase in West Riding fares. Similarly fare rises in Bradford resulted in the fares on services 72 and 78 being increased from 30 April 1972.

On Decimalisation Day there were a few A.E.C. Regent III of 1950 vintage still around. They did not last long. In March the rest of the Leyland Atlanteans, 456-465 was delivered. Registered ANW 456-465J) the buses were of the PDR2/1 type fitted with Roe H45/33D bodies and similar to 426-455.

The delivery of new buses resulted in the withdrawal of 25 older vehicles. These included 216, 217, 565, 620-625, 669, 672, 674, 840-859, 862, 874 and 887. The list comprised the last two of the M.C.C.W. bodied Leyland PD2/11 buses 216 and 217, the remaining A.E.C. Regent III, and the first of the A.E.C. Regent V of the 840-894 series, (other than 873, withdrawn earlier). 565 was the first of the 20 Weymann-bodied Daimler CVG6 buses to be taken out of service.

The A.E.C. Regent III had been one of the city's most numerous buses - 210 being operated. They had served Leeds well from 1947. The last, 624, made its final journey on 31 March 1971, after nearly 21 years service.

The rationalisation of bus services in East Leeds came into effect on 8 March 1971. The services operating in the Halton and Whitkirk areas of the city and the former Kippax and District Motor Services routes to Garforth and Kippax were revised and co-ordinated with those of the West Riding Automobile Company. L.C.T. services 14, 39, 41, 85, 86, and 87 and West Riding services 161, 162, 164 and 165 were either revised or withdrawn as follows:

Service 14 (Half Mile Lane-Halton). The existing route to Halton was extended along Selby Road to a new terminus at Barrowby Road, Austhorpe, this being a short distance from the Leeds city boundary at Bullerthorpe Lane. At the present time this point is known as Colton (Sainsbury's).

Service 41 (Central Bus Station-Colton). This long-established service - from 1935, was withdrawn and a new service from Half Mile Lane to Colton substituted. These journeys were an extension of service 14 journeys from Halton via Selby Road, School Lane and Meynell Road.

Service 39 (Central Bus Station-Whitkirk). This service now ran during peak periods and Saturdays only, the service along the Ring Road, Halton, being worked by West Riding service 162 (Leeds to Castleford). Most Monday to Friday peak services continued to work

Leyland Atlantean 461 was one of the series, 456-465, delivered in March 1971. It is in traffic-choked Wellington Street on 28 July 1976. In 1990-1 the vacant site on the left, adjacent to the Yorkshire Post building, was occupied by the Leeds Crest Hotel, later the Holiday Inn and currently named the Crowne Plaza. *Author.*

A.E.C. Regent III 624 was the last of the 210 buses of this type to run in Leeds. It ran for almost 21 years and was taken out of service on 31 March 1971.   Donald Wilson photographed 624 in Otley Road, West Park, on 21 June 1970. *W.D.Wilson/L.T.H.S.*

A.E.C. Regent V 795 at the service 41 Colton terminus on 3 May 1964. *J.B.Parkin.*

A.E.C. Regent V 979 leaving the Merrion Centre and entering Woodhouse Lane on 1 May 1971. Buses ceased to run through the Merrion Centre two days later on 3 May. *J.B.Parkin.*

between the Central Bus Station and Whitkirk, but two at tea time were extended to Swillington, which also had an hourly service on Saturday mornings and afternoons. They were a replacement for West Riding service 161 (Leeds to Swillington via Selby Road), which was withdrawn on 6 March. The new service was operated by Leeds buses only, although licensed as a joint service to both L.C.T. and West Riding. The route was as the former 39 service to Whitkirk, then via Selby Road, Swillington Lane, Neville Grove, The Drive, Wakefield Road and Church Lane where the terminal stop was situated. Buses returned via Church Lane to Neville Grove and then followed the reverse route.

Services 85/86 (Leeds-Ledston Luck) and 87 (Leeds-Garforth). These services were withdrawn along with West Riding services 164 and 165 and replaced by two new services, both jointly operated, as follows:

Service 89 (Leeds-Ledston Luck). As the former 85 service to Garforth Bridge, (Old George), then via Wakefield Road, Barley Hill Road, Main Street, Church Lane, Ninelands Lane, Selby Road, Leeds Road, High Street, Kippax, and then as before to Ledston Luck.

Service 97 (Leeds-Garforth and Kippax). As the former 87 service to Garforth Bridge, (Old George), then Wakefield Road, Alandale Crescent, Kingsway, Knightsway, Poplar Avenue, Barley Hill Road, Main Street, Church Lane and Ninelands Lane to Hazelwood Drive. The Westbourne Estate loop of the former 87 route was discontinued.

Services 89 and 97 each had an hourly frequency daily except on Sunday mornings, and buses worked alternate journeys on each service, Leeds providing two and West Riding one bus. In addition Leeds worked peak hour extras to Whitkirk Church on Service 89.

Summarising; after these alterations services 39, 89 and 97, plus West Riding 162, served Green Lane and Cross Gates, 39 and 162 then proceeded up Halton Ring Road to Whitkirk, and the 89 and 97 services up Hollyshaw Lane to Whitkirk. Services 14 and 41, plus West Riding

services 163 and 166 served the Selby Road district. Limited stop conditions were formerly imposed on the routes of both operators. These were now withdrawn except for some outward journeys from Leeds at evening peak periods.

Also from 8 March 1971, three new Fastaway services, all jointly operated with West Riding, were introduced:

Service 202 (Garforth Ninelands-Central Bus Station). Route: via Ninelands Lane, Church Lane, Lidgett Lane, Selby Road, York Road, Marsh Lane and Duke Street to the Central Bus Station.

Service 203 (Garforth Town End-Central Bus Station, Leeds). Route: via Main Street, Barley Hill Road, Wakefield Road, Selby Road, then as Service 202.

Service 204 (Kippax-Central Bus Station). From the War Memorial at Kippax via High Street, Leeds Road, Valley Road, Leeds Road, Selby Road, then as Service 202. On outward journeys, buses ran between High Street and the War Memorial by way of Gibson Lane, Cliffe Crescent and Park Avenue.

All journeys were non-stop between the Old George Inn, Garforth Bridge, and the Bus Station, except for one dropping off point at the Woodpecker Inn, York Road.

On 21 February 1971 reduced frequencies were introduced on services 1, 33 and 67 and from 27 February the frequency on the 72 Bradford service was also reduced. On 28 March reduced frequencies took effect on services 2, 3, 12, and 18 to 21.

In connection with the widening of York Road between the Woodpecker Inn and Skelton Terrace, from 11 February 1971 buses on all the York Road services were diverted on outward journeys from Leeds on to a new piece of road between Appleton Way and Lupton Avenue. There was now no way for traffic from Lupton Avenue to cross York Road and Ivy Street on the opposite side was also closed. Service 61 from East Park Road was diverted via East Park View, Welbeck Road,

Everleigh Street and the new section of York Road to the normal route at Lupton Avenue. Service 62 from Lupton Avenue turned left into York Road then Skelton Terrace and Ivy Avenue to Ivy Street. On 10 January 1972 the newly constructed roundabout under the flyover in York Road came into use. The section of Ivy Street between Ivy Avenue and York Road was reopened and buses on services 61 and 62 circulars and a number of special services reverted to their former routes.

A new bus service, 402 (Central Bus Station-Leeds Playhouse), was instituted on 15 March 1971. Only one journey was made which left the Bus Station at 7.05 p.m. and ran via Eastgate, Vicar Lane, New Market Street, Duncan Street, Boar Lane, City Square, Infirmary Street, East Parade and Calverley Street to the Playhouse car park. On the return journey after the performance the route was via Calverley Street, Portland Crescent, Woodhouse Lane, The Headrow, Park Row, City Square, Boar Lane, Briggate, The Headrow, Eastgate, St. Peter's Street and Duke Street to the Bus Station. There was a flat fare of 3p. The service was to run for an experimental period of three months, but lasted a year, and was withdrawn on 18 March 1972.

After the opening of the new Stanningley by-pass on Sunday, 21 March 1971, services 14, 41, 54, 65 and 72 were altered to run outward via the by-pass slip road and Henconner Lane back to Stanningley Road.

From 28 March 1971, services 42, (Harehills-Old Farnley) and 66 (Harehills-Leysholme Estate) became one-man operated. On 2 May service 65 (Central Bus Station-Pudsey) also became one-man. The three services used double deck buses.

On 3 May a new Fastaway service, numbered 265, from the Central Bus Station to Pudsey was introduced. Single deck one-man buses were used, leaving the 65 terminus at Chapeltown, Pudsey, via the 65 route to Richardshaw Lane, then by way of the Ring Road, Stanningley by-pass, Stanningley Road and the 65 route to the Bus Station. The by-pass cut a "considerable slice" from the 65 route, buses running every 20 minutes during the morning and evening peak periods. From 27 June a revised turning arrangement came into operation at Pudsey. Buses ran from the Cenotaph via Carlisle Road, Station Street and Greenside to the terminus in Chapeltown. There was no change to the inward route. Previously buses used Chapeltown in both directions and circled in the road at the junction with Greenside.

Also on 3 May buses on services 28, 30, 33, 36 and 58 operating inward to the Central Bus Station ceased to run via Cobourg Street and through the Merrion Centre. They now continued directly along Woodhouse Lane. The previous day reduced off peak frequencies were introduced on route 44 (Halton Moor-Stanningley). Duplicate buses on some other routes were withdrawn.

In March/April 1971 a number of minor route alterations also took place:

Service 74 (Moor Grange-Belle Isle). From Sunday, 18 April a slight rerouting took place at Belle Isle, buses continuing further up Belle Isle Road, then running by way of Nesfield View and Broom Road, instead of Middleton Road, Broom Cross and Broom Crescent.

Service 9 (Ring Road). From 8 March a new section of the Ring Road between Swinnow Lane and Hough End was opened as a dual carriageway. Buses on journeys from Middleton to Whitkirk began using the slip road to Swinnow Road. Similarly buses on service 11 (Swinnow) and 32 (Pudsey) followed the same route.

Fastaways were being introduced "thick and fast" and on 25 July 1971 two more services began. Both were operated by one-man single deckers and were as follows:

Service 233 (Cookridge-Central Bus Station). From Cookridge (Wrenbury Crescent), the route was via Tinshill Road, Wood Hill Road, Green Lane, Cookridge Lane, Otley Old Road, Spen Lane, Ring Road (West Park), and then as service 33 to the Central Bus Station. A ten minute service was worked during the morning and evening peak periods. Service 236 (Tinshill-Central Bus Station). From Tinshill terminus the route was via Silk Mill Drive, Wood Nook Drive, Tinshill Lane, Otley Old Road, Spen Lane, Ring Road (West Park), and then as service 36 to the Central Bus Station.

From the same date the limited stop conditions on services 33 and 36 were abolished.

On Saturday, 24 July, the 30 service, (Central Bus Station-Ireland Wood), was withdrawn. It was replaced by a new service 4 running between Beeston and Ireland Wood. It operated over the same route as Service 1 to Otley Road and then ran via the Ring Road (West Park) and the former 30 route to Ireland Wood.

Due to work on the extension of the M1 Motorway into Leeds, Moor Road, Hunslet, was closed from 19 July 1971. Services 46, 104 and 128 were diverted in each direction via Dewsbury Road, Tunstall Road and Beza Street.

Another Fastaway service came into being on 6 September 1971. This was service 272 (Leeds-Bradford), jointly operated by Leeds and Bradford Corporations. Each provided one A.E.C. Swift single decker, which did two return trips at peak periods. The route was one-man operated by Leeds, but Bradford was rather behind the times and had not introduced any one-man buses by this date and used two-man vehicles.

Beginning in Park Row, the outward route was by way of Infirmary Street, East Parade, Westgate, Wellington Street, Wellington Road, Armley Road, Stanningley Road, Stanningley by-pass, Ring Road (Stanningley), Ring Road (Pudsey), Bradford Road, Dick Lane, Gipsy Street and Leeds Road to Petergate. The return route from was via Leeds Road, Bradford Road, and the outward route reversed to Westgate, The Headrow and Park Row. The running time was slightly under 30 minutes.

In June and July 1971 twenty new single deck buses entered service. These were A.E.C. Swifts, 1051 to 1070 (AUB 151-170J), with Roe B48D bodies. These buses differed quite considerably from previous batches. They had splayed "V-shaped" windscreens and the lower panels at the front matched the type fitted to recent double deckers. The light green band on the new buses was not immediately below the windscreen owing to the higher driving position. A side destination, showing route number only, in large figures was positioned to the right of the entrance. Automatic transmission was fitted. The extractor fans for the forced ventilation system were also altered in position on the roof, instead of being at the rear. A different style of interior lighting was employed and the seats were of a type, which incorporated head rests, similar to buses 61-75 and 86-100. They were also fitted with the now standard radio telephones.

Twenty seven old buses were withdrawn as a result of the introduction of the new Swifts. These were all either Daimler CVG6 or A.E.C. Regent V double deckers: 563, 568, 569, 571, 860, 861, 863-872, 875-878, 881-883, 885, 886, 889, and 892. It is of interest that the number of buses taken out of service was greater than the buses that were replacing them. There were two main reasons: new double deckers had a larger seating capacity than the older vehicles; service frequencies were being gradually reduced and many "Duplicate" buses discontinued. From a peak number of around 710 in 1970, the number of buses fell rapidly in the late 'seventies and 'eighties.

In September 1971 the delivery of a new series of Leyland Atlantean double deckers began. These were 466-495 (DUA 466-495K). They were of the PDR/2 type with Roe H45/33D bodies. They were similar to the earlier dual doorway Atlanteans, but there were a few minor differences. Larger extractors were fitted for the upper saloon ventilator system. The front wheels were without

Passengers board a brand new A.E.C. Swift 1060 on Fastaway service 233 at Tinshill Road, Cookridge, in July 1971. *Leeds City Transport.*

A result of the introduction of the 233 Fastaway service to Cookridge was the withdrawal of service 30, Central Bus Station to Ireland Wood. The 30 bus service operated from 10 January 1954 to 24 July 1971. A.E.C. Regent III 488 is in Iveson Approach, Ireland Wood, and is about to turn into Iveson Drive. The date is 29 April 1966. *Author.*

A.E.C. Swift 1053 had been in service a week when this photograph was taken in Belle Isle Road on 8 July 1971. The former central tramway reservation and tramway poles can be seen in the background. *W.D.Wilson/L.T.H.S.*

wheel nut guards, which had been a standard feature on earlier Leyland vehicles. The new buses were also fitted with the later style of smaller flat flashing trafficators at the side. All thirty buses entered service in September and October 1971. There were 34 withdrawals:

Leyland PD2/11   203-206.
Daimler CVG6   552-562, 564, 566, 587, 570,
A.E.C.Regent V   765, 766, 771, 810, 811, 816, 879, 880, 884, 888, 890, 891, 893, 894. 897.

203-206 were of particular note as they were the last Leyland PD2 buses in the passenger fleet and their bodies were the last of fully composite construction. The A.E.C. Regent V were the last of the 840-894 series of buses. Also the last of the 552-571 series of Daimler CVG6 Weymann-bodied buses were withdrawn. There were now no short Daimler buses in the fleet. 897 was the first of the 895-909 series of 8ft.0in wide A.E.C. Regent V buses, new in 1958, to be taken out of service.

The much heralded minibus service in the city centre was not doing very well. In February 1971 it was stated that £426 only had been taken in fares. The Transport Department said that each of the five buses was carrying an average of 5·98 passengers per journey – 27·2 % of its carrying capacity. The cost to Leeds had been £12,500, half the cost of the £25,000 scheme, and it would take five years to recover these costs without taking into account driver's wages, running costs and depreciation. With decimalisation the fare had been increased by 60% and this had caused a drop in patronage. There were complaints from pedestrians and many people said it was quicker to walk. Sir Karl Cohen, of the Labour opposition, had been against the minibuses from the start and asked for them to be taken off. Alderman Sir Frank Marshall, leader of the City Council commented:

"This is a highly experimental venture, and the experiment is due to end quite soon. No doubt the Planning and Traffic Management Committee will then be considering what it wishes to do about it."

"It was a very original idea, and I don't think it was ever thought that it would make a profit."

'Yorkshire Evening Post', 11 February 1971.

In July 1971 a survey by the Leeds Junior Chamber of Commerce found that trade in the new precinct had increased, but the minibuses had not proved successful, either in financial or practical terms. It felt that the experiment had failed. In September 1971 the Lord Mayor, Alderman J.T.V. Watson, at an opening of a "One hundred Years of Leeds Transport" Exhibition at the City Museum, said he did not like the majority of people having the precinct spoiled for the benefit of a very small number. "I cannot bear the minibuses going across the pedestrian precinct. I would like them to go round the perimeter," he said.

The opening of the exhibition referred to, was attended by 150 guests, and had been organised by the Leeds Transport Historical Society and the Leeds City Museum. It was held at the Museum for a two-month period and proved highly successful.

Earlier, from 7 July 1971, the Transport Department in conjunction with the Ministry of Transport, carried out a survey on the minibuses. Each passenger was given a questionnaire about his travelling habits. The Transport Traffic Sub-Committee reiterated its previous appeal, that "any operational losses should not be met by the Transport Department."

However, the Department persisted with the minibus idea. On 4 October 1971, to save costs, the frequency was cut from six minutes to ten. At the same time a minibus service 403, from the recently opened Woodhouse Lane multi storey car park was introduced. The route from the car park was via New Woodhouse Lane, Woodhouse Lane, The Headrow, Park Row, City Square, Boar Lane, Briggate, The Headrow, Albion Street, Woodhouse Lane, Blackman Lane and New Woodhouse Lane. A flat fare of 2p was charged and buses ran at five minute intervals during the morning and evening peak periods and at ten minute intervals throughout the day. It was notable that this service avoided the pedestrian precinct in the Commercial Street/Bond Street area.

On 17 October 1971 two services were discontinued. These were route 41 (Colton-Half Mile Lane) and 54 (Rodley-Halton Moor). Service 14 (Austhorpe-Half Mile Lane) was curtailed at the Austhorpe end and now worked between Halton and Half Mile Lane only. The following services, all mainly operated by one-man double deckers, were introduced:

Service 6 (Halton Moor-Half Mile Lane). Route from Halton Moor via the former 54 service route to Corn Exchange and then to Half Mile Lane via the service 14 route.

Service 14 (Halton-Half Mile Lane). This service operated from Halton as formerly, (before the Austhorpe extension of March 1971). It was now a part-day service, Mondays to Fridays, with new services 83 and 84 forming the main services through Halton.

Service 83 (Rodley-Austhorpe). This ran from Rodley to Corn Exchange via the former 54 route and then from Corn Exchange to Halton as the former 14 service.

Service 84 (Rodley-Colton). This service ran from Rodley to the Corn Exchange and then as the former 54 route and from Corn Exchange to Colton as the former 41 service.

During the latter part of 1971 a number of other minor bus route alterations took place:

Services 74 and 76 (Moor Grange-Belle Isle and Middleton). From 19 August, the section of Jack Lane between Dewsbury Road and Parkfield Street was permanently closed to traffic. Buses on these services were diverted via Dewsbury Road and Parkfield Street.

Service 21 (Belle Isle-Roundhay and Moortown). From 3 October buses running towards Roundhay were altered to run from Meanwood Road to Roundhay Road directly along Barrack Road, instead of via Chapeltown Road and Roundhay Road. Services 10 and 19 to Roundhay still used the old route and there was no change on any services on journeys from Roundhay.

Service 61 (East End Park Circular) From 6 December, this service was altered to run from Hunslet Road via South Accommodation Road instead of via Forster Street and Donisthorpe Street to South Accommodation Road, Service 62 in the opposite direction was not affected.

A number of service alterations took place in the early part of 1972:

Service 45 (Wortley-Stanks). From 12 January, buses on journeys to Stanks were altered to run from York Road via Baildon Drive, Sherburn Road and Whinmoor Way to Stanks Drive. This alteration was owing to the building of an underpass under York Road from Sherburn Road to Whinmoor Way and the closing of the right turn from York Road into Stanks Lane North. There was no alteration for buses on journeys from Stanks.

Service 66 (Leysholme-Harehills). On 13 January this service was altered at the Leysholme Estate terminus. From the introduction of one-man operation, a conductor was stationed at the old terminus in Leysholme Drive, to guide drivers when reversing into a side road. A turning circle was provided at Western Flatts Park, which extended the route by one stop along Green Hill Lane.

Services 74 and 76 (Moor Grange-Belle Isle and Middleton). From 27 January buses on these routes were altered to run from Jack Lane via the new Hunslet distributor link road to Hillidge Road.

Fastaway service 224 (Swarcliffe). Following the opening

The electric minibus, CWO 516K, posed for the official photographer before it entered passenger service. *Leeds City Transport.*

of the Whinmoor Way underpass on 12 January, buses not in service running back to the 224 terminus at Swarcliffe now proceeded from York Road by way of Baildon Drive, Sherburn Road, Whinmoor Way, Stanks Drive and Stanks Lane North.

Service 62 Circular (East End Park) and Works services 104. 107, 108 and 137. From 17 February these services were rerouted to run via South Accommodation Road directly to Hunslet Road instead of via Atkinson Street and Forster Street or Goodman Street and Donisthorpe Street.

Services 48 and 81 Troydale-Pudsey-Calverley). From 6 March 1972 these services were altered to run directly via Woodhall Road to Town Gate and Carr Road to the terminus at Calverley Park. Formerly they operated from Woodhall Road via Thornhill Street, Victoria Street and Chapel Street to Carr Road. There was no alteration to the route in the opposite direction.

Service 84 (Rodley-Colton) From 3 March 1972 a new turning circle at Colton terminus was brought into use. Buses arriving at Colton dropped passengers at the same point as formerly, then continued to the circle in Colton Road, prior to picking up at the terminal stop in Meynell Road.

At all other termini on one-man routes, a turning circle or suitable loop of streets was provided.

In January 1972 the Finance and Planning Committee produced a report on the Transport Department Finances. In an effort to restore the viability of the department it made ten recommendations. It said that the policy of one-man operation should be continued and "negotiations should be undertaken to reduce ancillary labour costs where possible." It advised a comprehensive review of service levels, improvements in routing, and efforts to induce people to use buses through publicity and marketing. It did not think that a differential fare structure at peak periods and special reduced fares in off peak periods was "acceptable at the present time." There were other recommendations. A firm of consultants was appointed to advise on marketing, but in late 1972 the Transport Department appointed its own marketing staff.

The Electric Minibus, CWO 516K

One of the "major" Leeds transport events of 1972 was the arrival of the battery-operated electric bus. It received a lot of press coverage, but turned out to be something of a non-event.

The experimental bus arrived in Leeds on 13 March 1972. It was a Morrison Electricar with a Willowbrook B9F body and standing for 17 passengers. It was one of two experimentally built for the Department of Trade and Industry, whose name and arms appeared on the side of the bus, which also carried Leeds City Transport legal ownership. It was painted in an overall yellow-orange livery, relieved only by a pale grey/white front panel below the windscreen. The box-like body bore a resemblance to the drawings originally produced by the Leeds City Architect. Its front entrance was immediately behind the front wheel and perimeter seating was fitted.

The chassis was a Leyland Redline 900 FG adapted by Crompton Leyland Electricars, Tredegar, Monmouth, a firm jointly owned by the Hawker Siddeley and British Leyland Groups. The bus had a top speed of about 25 m.p.h. and could travel 35 miles under city service conditions per battery charge. This was an improvement on the specification indicated some 18 months earlier. The range rose to about 70 miles if the vehicle was driven non-stop. There were two block thermal storage heaters.

The bus was 22ft.0in. long, 8ft.1½in. wide and had an overall height of 9ft.6in. The type specification was P190/110 NP26, and Exide supplied the battery equipment. The gross weight was 9½ tons, unloaded 7¾ tons. The wheel base was 13ft. 4in. (4·1m) and the brakes were power assisted. Energy was provided by lead-acid traction type batteries 110 cells (220 volts) 376Ah capacity at the five-hour rate. These were charged overnight and could be

replaced quickly with a spare charged set to extend the daily mileage. Propulsion was by a dc series-wound motor continuously rated at 24 h.p. at 1350 rpm driving through a conventional propellor shaft and differential to the back wheels. The vehicle speed was varied by a low-loss thyristor controller.

Willowbrook used an all-metal frame construction with panelling in aluminium and glass reinforced plastic. Flaps were provided at side and rear for replacing batteries and there was a removable panel at the front which gave access to control system components.

The interior was lined with easily cleaned materials. The floor was of cork carpet with access traps to propulsion components. The front of the vehicle was a large standing area, with overhead and upright grab rails. Seating was for five across the rear and four on inward facing seats over the wheel arch. Seats were trimmed in pvc on foam rubber fillings. The driver's seat was fully adjustable and a full height partition was provided behind the seat. All main windows had sliding ventilator units, which with four roof extractor ventilators provided full ventilation. Double-folding entrance doors operated electrically and gave a clear opening of 3ft. 8in. on to an easy step. An emergency door was fitted on the offside of the vehicle. There were destination blinds at front and rear.

The bus was registered CWO 516K, and the other prototype was CAX 379K, both registered in Monmouthshire. The second vehicle was shown at an Exhibition in Brussels on 13/14 March, and both vehicles were to be tested in other areas notably the Merseyside, West Midlands and SELNEC PTE's, Bournemouth and Sheffield and the Glenrothes Development Corporation. Use in service would permit full evaluation of the vehicles and would give operating and technical data. This information was to provide a basis for future specifications. Thomas Lord, the General Manager, claimed credit and said he had put forward the idea of using battery-driven buses, free from fumes. The prototype would be the first of its kind in the world to operate for public service. He said the aim was to produce a vehicle, which would environmentally fit in with city centre pedestrian streets.

"The Government and transport undertakings want to find out about running costs and whether the advantages of electric power outweigh the problems of limited battery range.

"There is nothing like it in use anywhere so stringent tests will be necessary to prove whether it will be successful even on short distance work," Mr. Lord added."

'Yorkshire Post', 22 February 1972.

Crompton Leyland Electricity estimated that working costs would be 1p to 1·7 p per mile compared with 3p to 4p for a diesel bus. The vehicle could be modified to take more than 26 passengers. A spokesman said they would cost about £10,000 each to buy, including £2,400 for batteries and about £850 for a charger. The cost of a double deck Leyland Atlantean was about £12,000.

Following delivery on 13 March the bus had been demonstrated to the press and was also featured on television. On 12 April it was used by Keith Speed, Parliamentary Under-Secretary of State, Department of the Environment, who officially opened more traffic free shopping areas in the city.

The experimental bus entered passenger service in Leeds on Monday 10 April 1972. At first it was used only on the car park service, 403, between the multi-storey car park in Woodhouse Lane and the city centre. It was driven by one of two drivers specially trained on the vehicle. It only ran for short periods of time, but by June was running for much longer, not only on the 403 service, but also on service 401 through the shopping precinct. The bus made its last journey in Leeds on 27 July 1972, on service 401. It then went to Sheffield for a three months trial in that city and then to the West Midlands PTA for tests in Birmingham. Despite the optimism the electric bus did not return to Leeds.

A Change of Council

Alderman Turnbull had been appointed Chairman of the Transport and Trading Services Committee in May 1968 and gave way three years later to Councillor Rostron. Rostron did not last long for at the City Council elections of May 1972, a Conservative majority of two became a Labour majority of 20 seats. The Labour party abolished the Conservative idea of combining several committees, and reinstated the Transport Committee. The new Chairman was Councillor Dennis B. Matthews.

One of the first actions of the new Council was to take the minibuses out of the pedestrian precinct. Alderman Sir Karl Cohen was Chairman of the new Planning Committee and had always been opposed. He said that all traffic including the shopper's bus should be barred from the precinct between 10.00 a.m. and 6.00 p.m. every day. Labours' policy, he said, was to exclude as far as possible, private motorists from the centre of the city and to give preference to public transport.

Arnold Ziff said at a Leeds Chamber of Trade meeting that very few people used the minibuses for shopping. They merely used them to get from the railway station to the Central Bus Station. "It will be a hardship to a minority if we abolish it. We have to think about the interests of the majority," he said. From 9 September 1972 the minibuses were taken out of the precinct. They were rerouted on journeys from the Central Bus Station to the City Station

from Briggate via The Headrow to Park Row. There was no alteration in the other direction.

The Socialists had bitterly opposed the various fare increases imposed by the former Conservative administration, but one of their first actions was to make proposals for a further fares increase. The fares were to rise by about 5% and the increase took effect on 1 October 1972. Many fares were increased by 1p.

From 1970 to 1972 a new "super village" or housing estate, was built on a 127 acre site at Holt Park, about half a mile to the north west of the Lawnswood bus terminus. West Yorkshire Road Car Company buses ran along Otley Road past the Estate and consultations were held. Agreement was reached and from 7 May 1972 the number 1 bus service was extended from Lawnswood into the Estate. The route was via Otley Road and Holt Lane to a temporary new terminus at Broomfield where buses turned by reversing into the latter street. A week later this was altered to a new position beyond Broomfield. It was planned to extend the route further into the new Holt Park area as soon as the necessary roads were completed. Buses continued to short work to Lawnswood at peak times. After the construction of a new turning circle at Heathfield, Adel, on 30 June 1972 the buses were extended by way of Holt Lane to the new circle.

From 7 May, part of Hunslet Road was permanently closed to traffic. Services 7, 10, 19, 21, 82, 104 and 137 were rerouted from Bridge End by way of Meadow Lane, Great Wilson Street and Hunslet Lane to Hunslet Road.

On outward journeys, buses on these routes with outward buses on services 2, 3, 8, 12, 18, 20. 51, 52 and

A new "super village within a city" was built at Holt Park beyond the Lawnswood bus terminus in 1970-3 and was officially opened on 31 July 1973. In May 1972 the number 1 buses were extended into the estate. Daimler Fleetline 132, converted for one-man operation in November 1972 was photographed at Holt Park passing the author's then personal transport, a Ford Escort Estate car, on 2 March 1976. On the right hand side can be seen white painted horizontal softwood boarding used as fencing. It was fashionable at the time, but was almost impossible to satisfactorily maintain. *Author.*

When the northern part of Hunslet Road was closed on 7 May 1972, a new bus loading bay was opened in Meadow Lane. A.E.C. Regent V 932 on service 21 to Belle Isle is passing the loading bay on 8 May 1974. Tunstall's building is on the right hand side. *W.D.Wilson/L.T.H.S.*

53, were altered to operate via a newly built bus loading bay at the city end of Meadow Lane, also opened for the first time on 7 May. Buses on service 62 (East End Park Circular) were altered to run from Hunslet Road via Hunslet Lane and Crown Point Road, instead of directly along Hunslet Road.

From 17 April 1972 inward buses on Fastaway services 235 and 237 (Alwoodley and Shadwell) were altered to run from the Inner Ring Road by way of the slip road to Park Lane, joining Westgate at Park Street. This was because of construction work on Phase 3 of the Inner Ring Road.

Other service alterations about this time included:

Service 46 (Bramley Town End-Belle Isle or Middleton). From 26 May Burton Road between Tunstall Road and Moor Road was permanently closed due to the extension of the M1 motorway into Leeds. Buses were altered to run directly along Tunstall Road, a new section of which had been completed linking up with a new roundabout over the Motorway, near Beza Street.

Services 1, 4, 55, 74, and 76 operating from the city outwards only in a southerly direction were altered from Neville Street to use a new bus lane linking to Great Wilson Street.

Services 2, 3, 12, 18, 29, and 55 running on Dewsbury Road were affected by the closing of the section between Parkfield Street and Hunslet Hall Road due to motorway construction, from 8 June. Outward buses on these services were altered to run from Dewsbury Road via Parkfield Street and Jack Lane to a new section of Dewsbury Road, which linked to the old Dewsbury Road near Hunslet Hall Road. Inward bound buses also used this new piece of road, but joined the old road on the outward side of the railway bridge.

Service 48 (Troydale-Calverley) From 12 June, this service was rerouted from Galloway Lane to run to Calverley via Bradford Road, Ring Road (Farsley), Rodley Lane, Town

Gate and Carr Road. On journeys from Calverley, buses ran from Carr Road via Salisbury Street, Victoria Street, Rushton Street and Woodhall Road to Town Gate, then as the outward route reversed.

Changes took place at Oakwood in June 1972. Not only was the last significant section of tram track, still visible, covered over near Oakwood Clock, a new loading bay for buses was also constructed. This was for use by services 10, 19 and 21 operating outwards. They now used a new buses only loading bay and buses could filter left into Princes' Avenue thus avoiding the new traffic lights at the junction.

A mile further down Roundhay Road at the Easterly Road/Harehills Lane Junction a revision of the road layout was made. This affected service 45 (Stanks-Wortley), from 31 July. Buses from Wortley to Stanks travelled from Gledhow Valley Road via Roundhay Road to Easterly Road while in the reverse direction, they ran from Easterly Road by way of Harehills Lane and Harehills Avenue to Gledhow Valley Road. Services 10, 19, 21, 31 and 69 were diverted during the alterations and reverted to their former route when the junction was reopened in its new form on 9 August 1972.

After a successful trial with Leyland Atlantean 357 in May, on 7 July 1972, the Transport Committee agreed to convert 35 front entrance double deckers to one-man operation. 20 were to be done by Charles H. Roe Ltd. at £347 each and 15 by the Transport Department. Roe's price was later increased to £460 per bus and the Transport Committee stipulated that the Department should convert the "maximum number possible." During the latter part of 1972, several of the earlier Leyland Atlanteans were converted to one-man. These included the 356-385 series. At Kirkstall Road Works they were fitted with cash trays, fittings for ticket machines, a periscope to the upper saloon and radio equipment. In the conversion they lost their rear indicators, which were painted over. The indicator gears were substantially altered or replaced to enable both destination and digital number screens to be altered from the driver's compartment. The digital track mechanisms from the redundant rear indicators were repositioned at the front.

From 3 September 1972 service 29 (Infirmary Street-Middleton) was converted to one-man operation using Atlanteans of the 356-385 series. This was the first one-man double deck route to be worked by single doorway buses. All other double deck one-man services had buses with a central exit.

Following the conversion of 356-385 to one-man operation, in October 1972 a start was made on the Daimler Fleetlines of the 131-145 series. This was followed in 1973 by Fleetlines of the 116-130 series, later by 101-110, and Atlanteans of the 331-355 batch.

In March 1974 the last Fleetline, 110, was converted for one-man operation, but by the time of the PTE takeover on 1 April, there were still nine Atlanteans, 331-339, to be converted. These were done from April to September 1974. The whole of the Fleetline/Atlantean front entrance double deck fleet was then suitable for one-man operation.

On 7 July 1972 the Transport Committee accepted tenders from British Leyland and Daimler Transport Vehicles for 40 double deck bus chassis with an 18ft. 6in. wheelbase. The tenders were £6,388.90p and £6,866.50p each, respectively for delivery in 1973/74. 40 double deck bus bodies were ordered from Park Royal Vehicles Ltd. at £8,616 each.

The Transport Committee was thinking beyond 1974 and issued letters of intent in respect of 120 double deck buses for delivery after 1973/74. The letters were sent to British Leyland, Daimler, Park Royal and Metro Cammell Weymann Ltd. and specified that the delivery date was to be subject to negotiation between the new Passenger Transport Executive and the manufacturers. An interesting point, announced in December 1972, was that the order was to include 40 Metro Scanias, a bus type new to Leeds.

On 8 September 1972 the Committee authorised the General Manager to invite tenders for the supply of three coaches. On 20 October these were accepted as follows:

British Leyland U.K. Ltd. - three luxury coach chassis (Leyland Leopard PSU3B/4R) £13,790.55p.

Plaxtons (Scarborough) Ltd. – three luxury coach bodies (C49F) £17,682.

Besides the thirty Daimler Fleetlines, discussed next, buses on order were 35 Leyland Atlanteans with Roe bodies for delivery in January to March 1973 and 65 Leyland Atlanteans also with Roe bodies, for delivery in 1973-1974.

September 1972 saw the first of the new series of 30 Daimler Fleetline buses. They were of the Daimler/Leyland CRL6-33 type and the first Fleetlines in the Leeds fleet to have Leyland engines. They had Roe H45/33D bodies and differed from older Fleetlines in having a spring parking brake, and an electrically heated windscreen. The flooring in both saloons was completely flat, whereas the earlier buses had a series of strips down the gangway giving a planked effect. All were fitted with radio equipment and they had front covers to the ventilator slots above the bulkhead windows. Many older buses were being fitted with these covers at the time. In addition the three side windows on each side of the upper saloon had tinted green glass to avoid glare. The front and rear windows were of normal clear glass.

The earlier Fleetlines were numbered 101-110 and 116-200, but the new series was 751-780 (JUM 201-230L). It had been intended to number the buses from 201 upwards, but Leyland PD3/5 buses 221-230, still existed and would have had to be renumbered. It was unusual for Leeds buses to be delivered without the registration numbers coinciding with their fleet numbers.

Leyland Atlantean 379 was converted for one-man operation in September 1972. This photograph was taken on 10 June 1970 in Harrogate Road, Chapel Allerton, with the police station and library forming the setting. 379 is being worked with a two-man crew and is newly repainted in the reversed colour scheme. *W.D.Wilson/L.T.H.S.*

Daimler CVG6LX/30 712 (ex-512) in Roundhay Road at Oakwood on 18 March 1975. *Author.*

One of the series, 761, was exhibited on the Roe stand at the 26th International Commercial Motor Transport Exhibition, held at Earl's Court, London between 22 and 30 September 1972. It differed from the production batch in several minor ways. Opening front ventilator windows were fitted to the front bulkheads while additional aids to ventilation were louvres fitted in pairs above the three large side windows. These had external covers on the curve of the roof above the windows, there being three on each side. There was a warm air curtain at each opening door. A light coloured wood pattern melamine was fitted on the side panels, while a primrose pattern was used on the window pillars and seat backs. A new design of seating moquette of a yellow diamond pattern was employed in the lower saloon, and in the upper saloon, pale olive/amber coloured seats were fitted. At the Show the lower saloon had a carpet-like material. Electrically operated destination gear was fitted, an electrically heated windscreen and also destination indicator glasses.

It is of interest to note that while 761 was at the Show, the A.E.C. Regent V with the same fleet number was running its last days in service.

The rest of this series of Fleetlines all entered service by 9 January 1973, 757 being the last. Twenty seven withdrawals took place:

Leyland PD3/5 224, 233, 252, 268, 287, 291.

A.E.C Regent V 761, 763, 767, 768, 869 (ex-769), 870 (ex-770), 872 (ex-772), 773, 874 (ex-774), 875 (ex-775), 776, 800, 814, 819, 869 (ex-769), 898-901, 905, and 907.

291 was involved in a collision on 3 August 1972 and was the first of its type to be withdrawn.

The five remaining A.E.C. Regent V buses numbered in the 700's, 769, 770, 772, 774 and 775, were all renumbered in mid–October by the addition of 100 to their fleet numbers. Before the renumbering, some of the buses had been out of service for a few days, following the delivery of the new Daimler Fleetlines bearing the same fleet numbers. 869 (ex-769) ran for one week only with its new number.

Also renumbered from 18 November 1972 were the 30 Daimler CVG6LX/30 buses 502-531, which became 702-731. This renumbering was to enable a new batch of Leyland Atlanteans, due for delivery in early 1973, to be numbered from 496 upwards. These were to follow on from the previous Atlanteans.

The numbers 702-721 had been formerly occupied by the Crossleys, withdrawn in 1962 and 1963. Numbers 722-729 had never previously been used. The other numbers, 730 and 731, had appeared on A.E.C. Regent III buses until 1969-70.

The new buses and the "wind down" of the Leeds City Transport undertaking are discussed in the next chapter.

Leeds City Transport, the Final Year

In November 1971 came the announcement that in 1974 a West Yorkshire Passenger Transport Authority was to be formed. It was to absorb the transport undertakings of Leeds, Bradford, Halifax and Huddersfield. In the south of the county a South Yorkshire PTA was to take over the Sheffield, Doncaster and Rotherham undertakings. Until this time, Leeds, in conjunction with the Ministry of Transport, had been in the fore front of new transport ideas not only for the city, but also countrywide. After 1971 there were few new initiatives. Some of the neighbouring local authorities became involved in a "cheese-paring" exercise, by spending as little money as possible, Leeds continued to order new vehicles as usual, but councillors were concerned that they could not plan more than two years ahead.

In August 1972 the Chairman of the Transport Committee, Councillor Dennis Matthews, said that it was of great regret to him that policy on public transport was to pass to the Metropolitan County. It might have vastly different views than the City Council. He said the Council was preparing a policy of giving a much higher priority to public transport than ever before.

Both parties in the Council had been fairly consistent in supporting the then aims, which included an ultimate plan to restrict the use of cars in the city centre. Matthews said it was frustrating to be in the position of not being able to plan ahead. "If we were able to look forward indefinitely everything would be all right," he commented.

The Leeds City Transport undertaking carried on as usual. On 23 October 1972 a new experimental bus service to Holbeck was introduced. This was service 30, occupying the route number of the old Ireland Wood service. It ran at 15 minute intervals during the morning peak, lunchtimes and evening peak periods, on Mondays to Fridays. The service from Vicar Lane to Holbeck Moor began in Vicar Lane and ran via New Market Street, Call Lane, Swinegate, Sovereign Street, Neville Street, Victoria Bridge, Water Lane, Holbeck Lane, Domestic Street, Shafton Lane, and Crosby Road to a terminus in Crosby Street. The inward route was from Crosby Street via Top Moor Side, Domestic Street and the outward route reversed to Swinegate, then by way of Lower Briggate, Briggate, and The Headrow to Vicar Lane. Owing to a low bridge in Water Lane, single deckers worked the route.

On 2 April 1973 services 30 (Holbeck Moor-Vicar Lane) and 63 (Vicar Lane-Cross Green) were linked to run a through service from Holbeck Moor to Cross Green. Both service numbers were used, as the route in the Cross Green area was split to serve the Cross Green industrial area off Pontefract Lane. The joining of the two services did not cause any route alterations, the 63 being the through service. The number 30 was allocated to journeys which ran as service 63 to Pontefract Lane and then via Cross Green Approach, Cross Green Way, Knowsthorpe Gate and Pontefract Lane, approaching the terminus in New Market Approach from the opposite direction to Service 63. Service 30 continued to be a part day service and there were no through journeys on service 63 to Holbeck Moor on Saturdays or Sundays. The routes were one-man single deck operated.

On 14 November 1972 four experimental shopper's services were introduced:

405 (Hawksworth Estate-Headingley). From Broadway (Hawksworth Avenue) via Broadway, Vesper Road, Spen Lane, Queenswood Drive, Kirkstall Lane, North Lane and Otley Road, terminating at Headingley Garage.

406 (Halton Moor-Seacroft Town Centre Bus Station). From the Service 6 terminal stop via Ullswater Crescent, Neville Road, Halton Moor Avenue, Selby Avenue, Selby Road, (from Selby Road directly via Halton Moor Avenue in reverse direction), Chapel Street, Cross Green Lane, Green Lane, Station Road, Cross Gates Lane, York Road, North Parkway and Seacroft Avenue. An alteration took place on 6 March 1973 when the terminus at Halton Moor was changed to the junction of Cartmell Drive and Coronation Parade. The route to Seacroft was now Coronation Parade and Ullswater Crescent as previously. In the other direction buses ran from Ullswater Crescent via Coronation Parade into Cartmell Drive.

407 (Parkwood Estate-Dewsbury Road bottom). The route began in Parkwood Crescent, then went via Parkwood Road, Ring Road (Beeston Park) and Dewsbury Road, the link road and Meadow Road, terminating at the bottom of Dewsbury Road. In the opposite direction buses started at the bottom of Dewsbury Road and then by the inward route.

408 (Moortown Estate-Chapeltown). This route commenced at the Cranmer Bank Hotel and then via Cranmer Bank, Cranmer Road, Lingfield Approach, Lingfield Drive, Ring Road (Moortown) and Harrogate Road, terminating at Chapeltown (Stainbeck Lane). On 2 January 1973 the service was altered to start from the Ring Road and then via Black Moor Road, Deanswood Hill and Cranmer Bank to the existing terminus. This gave a complete circuit of the Moortown Estate.

From Tuesday 14 November service 75, (Seacroft Town Centre-Monkswood Gate), was renumbered 404, to bring it into line with the other shopper's services.

On Monday, 30 October 1972, when a new bridge over the new M1 motorway was opened, buses on Service 46 (Bramley Town End to Belle Isle or Middleton) were rerouted from Balm Road via Woodhouse Hill Road, Leasowe Road, and Middleton Road back to the former route higher up Middleton Road. Formerly they had gone via Belle Isle Road and East Grange Drive. On 5 February 1973 the service was altered again when it was rerouted from Balm Road via Midland Road, Pepper Road, and Middleton Road to Belle Isle.

A number of service alterations took place on 3 December 1972. On the Scott Hall Road group of services 34/35, 37/43 and 70, the single deck one-man buses were replaced by one-man double deckers. They were mainly from the conversions of front doorway only vehicles. The services were reduced in frequency and the limited stop conditions were abolished.

Services 67 and 68 (Central Bus Station-Seacroft Monkswood Gate and Foundry Lane), also had revised frequencies and the limited stop conditions on service 67 which operated during the evening peak period were withdrawn.

Limited stop arrangements had been gradually phased out, as the Fastaway services were introduced. After December 1972 the only ordinary services still operating limited stops at certain times of the day were 23 (Intake), 28 (Adel) 72 (Leeds-Bradford), joint with Bradford Corporation, and services 39, 89 and 97 (Leeds to Swillington, Ledston Luck, Garforth or Kippax), joint with West Riding.

On 4 December a new peak hour service 2 (Corn Exchange-Cross Flatts Park) was introduced. The journeys were a rerouting of certain buses on the normal 2 Dewsbury Road service. They followed the 2 route as far as the Crescent Cinema, Dewsbury Road, and then ran via Parkside Lane, Lockwood Way and Middleton Grove, terminating at the Computer House, almost back on Dewsbury Road. The service provided a link with the new Westland Trading Estate, which had been developed over the last few years.

On 14 November 1972 an experimental shopper's service was introduced to the Parkwood Estate in Dewsbury Road. A.E.C. Swift 1044 on service 407 is in Parkwood Road on 18 July 1973. On the right is the Ring Road and just visible to the right of the tree is the railway bridge over the former Great Northern Railway goods line from Beeston Junction to Park Side Junction, which closed on 3 July 1967. Tommy Wass's pub in Dewsbury Road is just discernible. The 407 bus service was not a success and was withdrawn on 31 August 1973.
W.D.Wilson/L.T.H.S.

Probably the most important road development in the history of Leeds was the extension of the M1, London to Leeds motorway, into the city centre. This took place on 15 December 1972, when the south east motorway extension was officially opened by Geoffrey Rippon, Minister for the Environment.

The motorway, which connected with the terminus of the M1 at Stourton at the Leeds city boundary, was 2½ miles long and terminated at a new interchange at the bottom of Dewsbury Road. It gave immediate relief to traffic congestion in south Leeds.

Before the official opening, the motorway was open for a public walkabout and the Transport Department ran a special bus service from the Central Bus Station to Stourton via the motorway. One-man double deckers were used and ran at ten minute intervals from 10.00 a.m. to 3.00 p.m. A flat fare of 5p (with a reduction for children) was charged. Buses travelled at a steady 10 m.p.h. in the fast lane and passengers were allowed to get off at any of four temporary stops on the motorway.

The 8th of January of the New Year saw the introduction of two new Fastaway express bus services, which used a substantial portion of the recently opened motorway:

Service 210 (Middleton-city centre). Beginning at the Thorpe Lane terminus at Middleton, the inward route was Middleton Park Avenue, Middleton Park Road, Sharp Lane, Town Street, Belle Isle Road, South East Leeds Motorway, Dewsbury Road and link road to Meadow Road, Victoria Road, Great Wilson Street, Meadow Lane, Bridge End, Lower Briggate, Briggate, The Headrow, Vicar Lane, and New Market Street to the Corn Exchange. The outward route started in Briggate and then went via The Headrow, Vicar Lane, New Market Street, Call Lane, Bridge End, Meadow Lane, Dewsbury Road, South East Leeds Motorway and the inward route reversed.

Service 221 (Belle Isle-city centre). This service commenced at the Ring Road terminus at Belle Isle and ran via Belle Isle Road, South East Leeds Motorway, and then by the same route as Service 210. Both services ran from Mondays to Fridays only, with ten minute frequencies at peak hours and were worked by A.E.C. Swift one-man single deckers.

As a result of the introduction of these two express routes, services 18 (Vicar Lane-Middleton Arms) and 19 (Roundhay-Middleton Arms) were reduced in frequency.

In January 1973 the first of a series of 35 Leyland Atlanteans was delivered. These were of a new AN68/2R type and the chassis was modified in specification, mainly to give improved serviceability. The AN68 had been launched in February 1972 and included increased width of the front passenger entrance giving easier passenger entry and exit, wider gangways, more leg room in certain areas, and improved layout of driver's controls. The bodies were of the standard design of dual doorway bus, delivered over the previous three years and similar to those fitted to the most recent Fleetlines, 751-780.

The new Atlanteans. 496-530 (JUG 496-530L), had Roe H45/33D bodies. The first 20 appeared in service in January and February and the remainder in April and May 1973. The bodies of 516-530 differed from the earlier batch in that they had front opening windows to the upper saloon bulkhead windows, as fitted to the 1972 Commercial Motor Show Fleetline, 761. 516-530 also had different sliding rear windows.

The first 20 resulted in the withdrawal of 18 buses:
Leyland PD3/5 221-2, 227, 245, 259.
A.E,C.Regent V 809, 813, 815, 818, 870, 872, 874, 875, 895, 896, 904, 906, and 908.
870, 872 and 874-5 had been numbered 770. 772, 774 and 775 respectively until October 1972. 818,

withdrawn on 30 April 1973, had the distinction of being the last 7ft. 6in. wide body bus to operate in Leeds.

From May to August 1973 a further 14 buses were withdrawn. These included:

Leyland PD3/5 225, 228-9, 235, 239, 242, 244, 246, 254, 257, 265, 272 and A.E.C.Regent V 902-3.

The Cottingley Estate, off Elland Road, had been rebuilt from 1967 to 1972. In 1970, the bus terminus had to be relocated. On 5 February 1973 new terminal turning arrangements came into operation. Buses on service 8, (Moortown-Cottingley), had terminated in Cottingley Drive, but were now altered to run into Cottingley Mount and Cottingley Vale to a new terminus in a shopping precinct. Buses left the precinct by way of another part of Cottingley Vale, then into Cottingley Mount and Cottingley Drive. The new terminus was a rather unusual arrangement, the buses running over a new paved way round the two 25 storey blocks of flats on the estate, i.e. Cottingley Towers and Cottingley Heights.

In January 1973 the Transport Committee agreed to apply to institute one-man operation on services 31, 32, 69, 72, 78 and to link services 47 and 22. A month later a request was made to convert the 28 service (Central Bus Station-Long Causeway). This was soon granted and from 26 February 1973 the terminal arrangements were altered. Instead of reversing into Wayland Drive to turn and stand, the route was extended a short distance along Long Causeway to a new turning circle on the left hand side of the road. On 4 March this service became one-man and the limited stop conditions were removed.

On 18 February 1973 the terminal standing point for service 62 (East End Park Circular) was altered from East End Park School to East Park Road.

From 1 April 1973, services 22 (Central Bus Station-Temple Newsam) and 47 (Central Bus Station-Old Farnley) were linked together to form a new through service 22. The service was double deck one-man operated. Formerly the Temple Newsam route had been worked by one-man single deckers, the 47 route had been two-man.

The route from Temple Newsam was via Temple Newsam Road, Selby Road, York Road, Marsh Lane, York Street, New York Street, Harper Street, Kirkgate, New Market Street, Duncan Street, Boar Lane, City Square, Aire Street, Whitehall Road, Spence Lane, Wortley Lane, Gelderd Road, Ring Road (Lower Wortley), Whincover Drive, Cross Lane, Hall Lane and Tong Road. In the reverse direction, the route went via Smithfield Street, Whitehall Road, Gelderd Road, Spence Lane, Whitehall Road, Thirsk Row, Wellington Street, City Square, Boar Lane, Duncan Street, Call Lane, New York Street, and the outward route reversed.

On 15 March 1973 a new turning circle came into use about one stop beyond the old terminus of service 31 (New Farnley-Brackenwood). Formerly buses had turned from Brackenwood Drive into Lincombe Drive, before reversing back into Brackenwood Drive. On 1 April this service became one-man operated using double deckers. On the same date service 32 (Pudsey-Moortown) also became one-man double deck. The day after, service 69 (City Square-Gledhow) became one-man worked with single deckers.

From 26 March 1973 the turning arrangements of service 97 (Central Bus Station-Garforth Ninelands) were altered. Formerly buses reversed into Hazelwood Avenue and then returned to the terminal stop on the other side of Ninelands Lane, but now they ran further along Ninelands Lane and then via Long Meadow Gate and Long Meadows back to Ninelands Lane.

On 20 May 1973 services 72 and 78 (Leeds-Bradford) both became one-man operated using double deck buses. Leeds used the single doorway recently modified Leyland Atlanteans. A month later, on 17 June, service 11 (Swinnow-Whinmoor) also became one-man double deck operated.

These alterations were all part of the policy of the

No. 521 was one of the new Leyland Atlanteans with front opening bulkhead windows introduced in April and May 1973. It is pictured here at Middleton on 17 May 1973. *W.D.Wilson/L.T.H.S.*

A.E.C. Regent V 818, taken out of service on 30 April 1973, was the last 7ft. 6in. wide bus to run in Leeds. It is pictured in Black Moor Road on the Moortown Estate on 23 October 1965. *Author.*

Transport Committee to convert all the bus routes in the city, as quickly as practicable to one-man operation. Reversing of buses required a conductor to be in attendance, and turning circles had to be provided where possible.

To speed up services, bus lanes were also gradually introduced. On 15 July 1973 the right turn from Neville Street into Water Lane was closed to all traffic except buses. At the same time Water Lane from Neville Street to Marshall Street became one-way westbound meaning that a buses only lane was introduced in an easterly direction.

In June 1973 the Planning Committee approved a £26,000 scheme to reduce congestion and improve the movement of buses around the Central Bus Station. There was to be a buses only lane from the Eastgate roundabout to the Bus Station. Councillor Woolmer, the Committee Chairman, said that buses were impeded by congestion at both the junction of York Street and Duke Street, and St. Peter's Street and Eastgate.

In June and July 1973 the three coaches, ordered in October 1972, were delivered. Numbered 20-22 (MUG 520-22L) they were on Leyland Leopard PSU3B/4R chassis and had C49F Plaxton Elite Express III bodies.

The bodies were standard Plaxton coach bodies built to bus grant specification with folding front doors and able to be fitted for one-man operation. They were the first vehicles in the fleet with Plaxton bodies. Interior seating was in moquette with a yellow diamond pattern of the same design as that fitted in the lower saloon of Daimler Fleetline 761. A destination indicator, comprising a name alongside a digital number blind, was placed immediately below the front windscreen. 20 was delivered on 25 June and first used on 4 July when it took a private party to Scarborough. 21 followed on 23 July and 22 on the 28th.

Although the Leeds transport undertaking had only eight months to "live", the Transport Committee was still coming up with new proposals. In July 1973 it ordered "for experimental purposes," a Commer minibus and a Leyland National single decker. The order for the Commer minibus was altered, for in November 1973, a quotation was

accepted from Seddon Motors Ltd. for the supply of a Seddon 'Pennine' 4 midi-bus in the sum of £6,248.

The experimental shopper's services, 405, 407 and 408, introduced in November 1972, had not been successful. There had been a loss of £59 a week and they were withdrawn on 31 August 1973. The Seacroft service, 406, was continued.

At the Transport Committee on 29 June 1973 it was stated that all the minibus services were losing money. The Committee asked the Finance and General Purposes Committee to adopt a policy whereby all minibus services would be financed from car parking revenues. It was also agreed to increase the flat fare on the minibuses to 3p, equivalent to 7·2d. in the old currency, an increase of 350% on the fare introduced only two years earlier. Fare increases elsewhere were also proposed.

At the West Yorkshire Metropolitan County Council elections held earlier in the year, the Labour manifesto said that public transport should be a public service rather than a commercially viable undertaking. "Fares must be kept reasonable," it said. Buses should receive the same financial support from central funds as did roads, the manifesto stated.

"There might even be coincidences in which for the benefit of the community generally, certain transport sections would be free."

The Liberals were more precise. They favoured experiments leading to the eventual introduction of "fareless public transport."

At the Transport Committee meeting, the Conservatives described the fare increases as "staggering." 1p was to be added to the adult fares, which meant an increase of 25% or more for well over half of the passengers.

The Chairman, Councillor D.B. Matthews, said that the increases would yield an extra £437,000 in the present financial year. He optimistically forecast that with the additional revenue, the estimated year-end deficit would be £195,000. "The alternative to increasing the fares would be to make a bigger subsidy than was earmarked in the accounts, or accumulate a very large deficit," he said.

At the following City Council meeting, Councillor David Austick, Liberal, proposed that public transport in Leeds should be free. He said that Leeds could not accommodate unlimited use of cars. Free public transport could replace the cars and save money on road building, he said.

Councillor Matthews said that £700,000 a year was already being spent on subsidising public transport in Leeds. Free travel would mean an increase of 50 to 60p in the pound on the rates.

Austick's motion was rejected and the City Council agreed to raise fares by a penny. The increases took place on 16 September 1973.

In September 1973 delivery began of the first twenty five of the 65 Leyland Atlantean buses on order. These were 531-555 (PUM 531-555M). They were of the AN68/2R type with Roe H45/33D bodies. They were very similar to the last series of Atlanteans, i.e. fitted with front opening windows, of the usual Leeds design. The new buses, however, had additional ventilators on the curve of the roof above the large side windows. Fleetline 761 had similar ventilators.

A point of interest with the recent bus deliveries was that, in addition to the three large side windows on both sides, the front bulkhead windows on Leyland Atlanteans from 496 upwards and Daimler Fleetlines, 751-780, had tinted green glass, known officially as Triplex Sundym glass. The opening sections fitted to the Atlanteans from 516 upwards were also fitted with this glass. On all these buses, the smaller side windows with the opening ventilators, along with the rear windows, were fitted with standard Triplex glass. There were no tinted windows in the lower saloons. 531-555 all entered service in September and October 1973. There were 20 withdrawals:

A.E.C.Reliance coach 10.
Leyland PD3/5 223, 226, 230, 238, 240-1, 243, 247-49, 251, 253, 255-6, 262, 273, 275.
A.E.C.Regent V 909. 933.

Of special interest was coach 10. This was new in 1965 and was the first coach to be owned by the Leeds Transport Department. It was one of a batch of five similar A.E.C. Reliance chassis, the other four became single deckers 44-47, withdrawn in 1971. It was originally intended that the coach be converted to a service bus, but with the withdrawal of the other Reliances because of their narrow doorways, 10 was never altered. The coach was last used in service on 24 November 1973 and was sold to W. North (P.V.) Ltd., dealers, of Sherburn-in-Elmet.

A.E.C. Regent V 909 was the last of the series of fifteen buses, 895-909. These were the only short Regent V to enter the fleet, built to a width of 8ft.0in. It was also the last 27ft.6in. long bus in the passenger fleet. 909 made its final run in service on 29 November 1973.

On 20 August 1973 the service number 41 came into use again, It had been vacant from the abandonment of the Colton-Half Mile service in October 1971. The new service 41 (Halton Moor-Stanningley) was a diversion of the long established 44 route. Alternate journeys on service 44 (Halton Moor-Stanningley) were diverted at peak periods on Monday to Fridays from Bridge Road via Broad Lane to the Leeds and Bradford Road. Service 44 operated from Bridge Road via the Leeds and Bradford Road, and Newlay Lane to Broad Lane. The rerouted journeys were numbered 41.

In September and October 1973 three new bus services were introduced:
Service 402 (Woodhouse Lane Car Park-City Centre). From 17 September, a new minibus service was introduced from Woodhouse Lane Car Park via New Woodhouse Lane, Woodhouse Lane, The Headrow, Park Row, City Square, Wellington Street, King Street, East Parade, Calverley Street, Portland Street, Woodhouse Lane, Blackman Lane

and New Woodhouse Lane. A peak period ten minute service was operated. The service was not successful, and was withdrawn on 4 January 1974.

Service 75 (Central Bus Station-Headingley). From 1 October, a new service 75 was opened to serve the new Woodsley Road Health Centre and the Beechwood Estate. From the Central Bus Station the route was via Eastgate, The Headrow, Westgate, Park Lane, Burley Street, Burley Road, Westfield Road, Hyde Park Road, Brudenell Road, Cardigan Road, Ashville Road, Beechwood Crescent, St.Ann's Drive, and St. Ann's Lane, to Queenswood Drive where the route terminated at the same point as service 56. The route was single deck operated and ran on Mondays to Saturdays only.

Service 5 (Whinmoor-Greenthorpe) From 15 October, buses, which operated on Mondays to Saturdays on service 11 from Whinmoor or Seacroft Town Centre to Greenthorpe and turned at the Gamecock Hotel, were altered to run into the Gamble Hill Estate and also the Armley Heights Estate by running through it, instead of passing by along Pudsey Road. The route was as previously to Tong Road, then via Farrow Hill, Heights Drive, Greenthorpe Road, Henconner Lane, Queensthorpe Avenue, and Gamble Hill Drive to a terminus at Gamble Hill Place. Buses left the terminus via Gamble Hill Drive, Henconner Lane, Greenthorpe Road, Heights Drive, Farrow Hill, Tong Road and then as previously. One-man operated double deck buses were used.

From 3 December the Greenthorpe terminus was slightly altered. Buses continued to terminate at Gamble Hill Drive, but at a point some 40 yards nearer the junction with Greenthorpe Avenue. Other service alterations were as follows:

Service 4 (Beeston-Ireland Wood). From 24 September, this service was extended at Ireland Wood by one stopping place. Instead of terminating at Raynel Gardens, it continued by way of Raynel Drive and Farrar Lane to a point near Holt Park School.

Service 11 (Whinmoor-Swinnow). From 15 October, a revised service was introduced, following the short workings to Greenthorpe being rerouted and renumbered as new service 5.

Services 15, 16, 17 (Bramley Town End-Seacroft). From 14 October (services 15 and 16) or 15 October (service 17), these routes became one-man operated.

Service 73 (Moor Grange-Greenthorpe). From 14 October instead of swinging round at the Gamecock Hotel terminus, buses proceeding from Bramley now ran via Henconner Lane direct to Pudsey Road.

Services 74 and 76 (Moor Grange-Belle Isle and Middleton respectively). From 17 September, these services were altered to run from Jack Lane via the Hunslet Distributor Road to Moor Road in each direction, in place of via Hillidge Road, Church Street and Beza Street.

In November 1973 the experimental Leyland National single decker, ordered in July, was delivered. The cost of the vehicle was £13,403.50p. Numbered 1301 (SUA 301M) the bus had a single front entrance whereas the other single deckers (apart from the coaches and minibuses) were standardised with dual entrance and exit doors. The Leyland National was a new type of bus and 1301 was type 1151/1R/0401 with a Leyland National B52F body. The chassis was 11 metres long and was fitted with a Leyland 510 engine and a 5-speed gearbox by Self Changing Gears Ltd. The first gear was an emergency low. When supplied it was painted in a National Bus Company poppy red livery, but was soon repainted in an experimental livery for the West Yorkshire P.T.E. This is discussed further in Appendix XIX. It was reseated with 48 standard Leeds type seats but done in a new WYPTE style, being reclassified as B48F.

An official photograph of Leyland National 1301 showing its experimental Metro livery. It had been diverted from a National Bus Company order. *Leeds City Transport*.

Until the late 1970's Colton was a pleasant farming village and Daimler Fleetline 158 is seen in Meynell Road, Colton, on 21 February 1971.   Meynell Road still exists in name but has been relocated and now forms part of a large housing estate.   *J.B.Parkin*.

Coach 10 was withdrawn in 1973 and is seen here on a Roundhay Park Tour.   It is passing the boating lake in Roundhay Park on 24 August 1966.   Behind is a Bradford Corporation bus. *J.B.Parkin.*

The seating of A.E.C. Swift 1065 had been done in a similar style in November 1973 i.e. in a fawn ambla type material complete with the PTE motif on the headrests. The bus made its first trials on 4 February 1974 and was used in passenger service on 19 February when it made a Fastaway journey to Garforth and Kippax. For a few days in February it was loaned to the Halifax Passenger Transport undertaking.

From 1 December 1973 the remaining Daimler CVG6LX/30 buses numbered in the 500's were renumbered by adding 300 to their fleet numbers. These were 572-581 (572-581 CNW), which became 872-881, and 582-596 (582-596 FUM), 882-896. Their old fleet numbers were to be occupied by new Atlanteans.

Delivered and entering service in December 1973 were the first 20 of the 40 Leyland Atlanteans on order. They were 556-575 (SUG 556-575M) and of type AN68/2R with Roe H45/33D bodies. They were very similar to the recently delivered 531-555 series other than that they had red painted wheel centres. In addition, the new series was fitted with Triplex "Sundym" glass in all upper saloon windows, including the small ones at each end of the saloon by the ventilators. All entered service between December 1973 and February 1974.

The final 20 of the Leyland Atlanteans 576-595 (SUG 576-595M) began delivery in March, but it was apparent that some would not be delivered until after the WYPTE takeover on 1 April. The new buses were the last to be supplied to the Leeds City Transport dual doorway design and were identical to 556-575.

Buses 576-580, 582-5, 590 and 591 all arrived in L.C.T. livery, although 576, 578, 583 and 590 were all delivered after the PTE takeover. On 29 March 585 and 591 became the last buses to be delivered to the Transport Department, 591 having the distinction of being the final Leeds bus to be received. 585, delivered earlier on the same day, did not enter passenger service until 2 April, whereas 591 was used by the Corporation on the day of its delivery.

Of the buses delivered after the PTE takeover, 578 and 590, on 12 April, were the last buses to come in Leeds livery, 590 being the very last. 581, 586-589, 592-595 were all delivered in the new PTE emerald (later called Verona green) and buttermilk livery.

Beginning on 20 March 1974, Daimler Fleetline buses 751-780, (JUM 201-230L), were renumbered 201-230. The fleet numbers were now the same as the registration numbers allocated to these buses.

This was not the end of the Leeds City Transport involvement in rolling stock, for 120 buses were on order and letters of intent had been sent to various manufacturers. The orders were to be modified to suit the new PTE requirements. They included 80 Leyland Atlanteans and 40 Metropolitans. The Seddon 'Pennine' midibus ordered in November 1973, also had still to be delivered.

The Leyland Atlantean chassis with modified bodies became 6001-6080 in the PTE fleet. The Metropolitans never came to Leeds and were allocated to Bradford becoming 2601-2640. Huddersfield Corporation had also ordered a Seddon 'Pennine' midibus, and both it and the Leeds order were delivered in September 1974. They became 4052 and 4053 in the Kirklees fleet.

As a result of the purchase of 41 new buses, the following older vehicles were withdrawn:

Leyland PD3/5 250, 258, 261, 263, 264, 266, 270, 271, 274, 276, 277 and A.E.C. Regent V 928 and 930.

With the withdrawal of the Leyland PD3/5 buses above, there were still 20 buses of this type left in the fleet. Numbered 231, 232, 234, 236, 237, 260, 267, 269, 278-286, and 288-290, several of these were overhauled and retained for future use by the new PTE.

A,E,C, Regent V 928, last used in service on 15 March 1974, was the final bus to be withdrawn by Leeds

City Transport. The undertaking did not sell any old buses for scrap from November 1973 until late March 1974 when ten buses were sold to Hartwood Finance Ltd. of Barnsley. These were 240, 241, 249, 253, 255-257, 273, 275 and 933. They were still in Leeds on 1 April, but were regarded as sold and were not included in the PTE stock list. On 1 April there were 24 withdrawn passenger vehicles in stock. There were also some withdrawn training buses. They all passed to the PTE for disposal.

During the last few months of its existence the Leeds Transport Department had carried out a few route alterations or modifications.

From 1 February 1974, Town Street, Horsforth, became a one-way street in a westerly direction, and a newly constructed parallel road, Church Road, now carried certain bus services, as follows:

Services 26/27 (Swarcliffe-Horsforth). These services were altered in both directions. On journeys to Horsforth (Fleece), they operated from Horsforth Town Street via Church Lane and Church Road to rejoin their former route in Fink Hill.

Services 79/80 (Tinshill/Horsforth-Pudsey). On journeys to Pudsey there was no alteration, but on journeys to Horsforth and Tinshill buses operated from Fink Hill via Church Road and Church Lane to Town Street.

From 23 January 1974 part of Phase III of the Inner Ring Road was opened. This was in the Westgate area and a large one-way scheme was brought into use. Traffic from Wellington Bridge turned left into Wellington Street, then into the remains of West Street and a new section of road to join Wellington Street at Westgate. Traffic from Kirkstall Road, the lower portion now a dual carriageway, joined the scheme at West Street. There was no alteration to bus services operating in a westbound direction. A considerable number of services were affected by the new arrangements: 5, 6, 11, 14, 15, 16, 17, 24, 25, 26, 27, 29, 40, 42, 65, 72, 83. 84, 265, 272, and night services 315, 324, 332 and 365.

From January to March 1974 a turning circle for buses was built at the Ledston Luck terminus of route 89. The new turning circle came into use by 29 March. Other service alterations took place:

Service 47 (Swinnow-Briggate). Beginning on 4 March, the peak hour duties between Swinnow and Briggate on Mondays to Fridays as duplicates on the 32 service, were rerouted in the Swinnow area and operated as service 47. The terminus at Swinnow was the same as service 11, i.e. Swinnow House, and the route was Swinnow Road, Swinnow Lane, Hough Tree Road, Pudsey Road, Ring Road (Farnley) and as service 32 to Briggate, The route in the reverse direction during the evening peak period was from Vicar Lane, New Market Street, Duncan Street, Boar Lane and then the inward route reversed.

Service 50 (Horsforth-Gipton). Beginning on 3 March, buses on this service were rerouted between Compton Road and Gipton terminus; from Compton Road via Harehills Lane, Strathmore Drive, Foundry Drive, Foundry Avenue, North Farm Road and Oak Tree Drive, to terminate at the normal terminus at the Courtier Hotel. This alteration served an area, formerly without buses. Part of route 50 which had been discontinued was covered by services 15, 16, 17 and 77.

Decisions made by the Transport Committee led to some service alterations being made after the WYPTE takeover. On 1 March 1974 the Traffic Sub-Committee had agreed that services 8, 39, 51, 52, 53, 89 and 97 be converted to one-man operation. Services 8, (renumbered 54) 51, 52 and 53 were converted on 12 May and the others later.

There had been talk of running a bus service along Wigton Lane, Alwoodley, for years. In October 1972 the Transport Committee applied for the service. As it was just outside the Leeds city boundary, there were long drawn out negotiations and objections from the West Yorkshire Road Car Company. However, from 16 June 1974, service 43, (Central Bus Station-Shadwell), was rerouted along Wigton Lane. This was the last service alteration to be initiated by the Leeds Transport Committee.

In 1973 the Transport Department was actively pursuing a bus priority scheme for City Square. The road in front of the General Post Office was to be closed to all vehicles except buses and there was also to be a buses only lane in front of the Queens Hotel. Apart from buses, vehicles would not be allowed to enter City Square along Wellington Street from the bottom of King Street to Quebec Street. In the opposite direction Wellington Street would become a one-way street. A buses only lane was to be created on one side of Infirmary Street for buses leaving City Square. It was November 1975 when the City Square alterations came into being.

Arnold Stone, deputy general manager, said that the first of the bus priority schemes – in St. Peter's Street and approved in June 1973, would be introduced about March 1974. The bus lane was to be formed in the centre of St. Peter's Street and prevent a queue at the traffic lights at the junction of St. Peter's Street and York Street. "It will be very helpful for getting buses more quickly into the bus station," said Stone. The bus lane in St. Peter's Street eventually came into use on 11 May 1975.

New road construction had dominated Leeds in the 1960s and 1970s and great changes had taken place. The Inner Ring Road and the extension of the M1 motorway into the centre transformed the city. The south west motorway, which ran along the line of Elland Road, was constructed in 1975-6, but the suggested north east motorway was not built. Planned to run from the Meadow Lane Interchange to the bottom of York Road on a 40 feet high viaduct, the road passed close to the Leeds Parish Church and would have involved the demolition of a large portion of Quarry Hill Flats. It was to have been built from 1976 to 1979, but was strongly opposed by environmentalists. They won their case.

New roads were expected to be the panacea for the city's transport problems and, undoubtedly, the developments helped bus services initially. Unfortunately the improved roads also attracted a great deal of extra motor traffic and this tended to negate the advantages. Few major road works were carried out in Leeds after the 1970s; the Corporation ran out of new road options without massive demolition and expense. If constructed, more new roads would have resulted in the complete domination of the city by the motor car. It was realised that public transport needed, if possible, to be separate from other traffic.

In 1970 Fred Mulley, the Minister of Transport, said,

"Most operators are facing severe problems. Traffic congestion causes bus services to be unreliable and people transfer to private cars. Loss of passengers means reduced revenue, which in turn necessitates fares increases and this drives away more passengers to other forms of transport, so adding to traffic congestion. Priority for buses to allow them to give a better service and win back passengers are a "must" if we are to break out of this vicious circle."

'Yorkshire Evening Post,' 22 April 1970.

Using existing roads, a city centre loop road was later formed for motor traffic. This enabled more pedestrian and public transport only areas to be created in the city centre. Motor cars were excluded from certain roads in the central area. The Fastaway or express bus services which had been introduced were in effect no different to the limited stop services in operation from the early 'fifties. By 1974 most of the limited stop services had been phased out. Traffic congestion meant no increase in speed at peak hours and unreliable buses. Fastaways ran empty in one direction, hardly economical working, and some were subsequently discontinued. Most were replaced by the "X" services in 1976 – limited stop services with an "X"

Leyland PD3/5 247 was withdrawn in November 1973. It was photographed in Chapeltown Road on 3 February 1963. The Forum Cinema is on the left hand side. The Cinema (opened 26 October 1936, closed 24 December 1959) was converted into a Bingo Hall, but it was not successful. When this photograph was taken, demolition of the building had just started. *Author.*

A.E.C. Regent V 928, last used in service on 15 March 1974, was the final bus to be withdrawn by the Leeds Transport Department. It is on route 4 in York Road on 17 July 1965 with West Yorkshire MWY 116, a Bristol Lodekka with ECW body, about to overtake. The West Yorkshire bus is on route 41, the Leeds to Wetherby via Thorner, Bramham and Boston Spa service. The former tramway reservation is on the left hand side and in 1989-90 an Asda supermarket and petrol station were built behind the wall on the right. *Author.*

Service 47 (Central Bus Station-Old Farnley) ran for nearly 26 years from 17 August 1947 to 1 April 1973. It was discontinued when the Old Farnley route was coupled with the 22 service (Central Bus Station-Temple Newsam) to form a new 22 (Old Farnley-Temple Newsam) through service. A.E.C. Regent III 735 was photographed in Hall Lane, Old Farnley, on 5 August 1969. *W.D.Wilson/L.T.H.S.*

Leyland Leopard coach 21 on Sightseeing Tour 5, a Bus and Canal Tour, on 30 August 1973. Passengers travelled by bus from the Central Bus Station and by boat on the canal from Rodley to Saltaire, then a return bus ride to Leeds. 21 is at Bridge Road, Rodley. *J.B.Parkin.*

In January 1974 part of Phase 3 of the Inner Ring Road from Westgate to Wellington Bridge was opened. The Westgate roundabout later became redundant. This view of A.E.C. Regent V 792 was taken at the roundabout on 19 September 1965. *W.D.Wilson/L.T.H.S.*

prefix to the route number. It was the introduction of bus lanes, in their infancy in 1974, and buses with more powerful engines, which were to marginally speed up bus travel.

On 1 April 1974 the new West Yorkshire Passenger Transport Executive took responsibility for the day-to-day operation and planning of public transport throughout West Yorkshire. In a statement entitled "Public Transport for West Yorkshire" it said it was to continue the Leeds philosophy as outlined in "Planning and Transport – The Leeds Approach", published in 1969. The PTE was to work in conjunction with the Ministry of Transport and other Government departments and adopt the same policies for the whole of West Yorkshire.

The PTE was headed by representatives from Leeds. The Director General was Thomas Lord, the former Leeds Transport Manager. He had been appointed in June 1973 with the later approval of the Department of the Environment. His salary was £12,055 rising to £12,775 per annum. The Chairman of the Passenger Transport Committee was Councillor Dennis B. Matthews, the former chairman of the Leeds Transport Committee.

The takeover of the Leeds City Transport undertaking by the PTE coincided with a period of severe inflation in the country as a whole. As has been seen there were many fares increases in the early 'seventies and fares continued to rise after the PTE takeover. Services, both peak time and off peak, were reduced and some lightly used services ceased altogether.

On 1 April 1974 Leeds City Council records indicate that income and expenditure on the transport undertaking for the year were the same figure i.e. £8,369,929. There was no profit or loss. This was, however, purely a book keeping exercise for some WYPTE records have survived and show that there was a loss of £1,353,406 on the Leeds undertaking. Income throughout the PTE area plummeted and considerable financial support from West Yorkshire County Council had to be provided.

There were two fare increases in 1975 and passenger resistance to the increases, estimated at 15%, turned out to be a massive 38%. County Councillor Raymond Lax accused PTE officials of not introducing service cuts early enough and making no progress with the National Bus Company on rationalisation of services and fares. A major problem was the "enormous" earnings of bus crews, he said. Staff working on Sundays were said to be earning £2.50p per hour. Many senior officers were getting far higher salaries than they would in the outside world and there was a considerable amount of duplication by officials. Lax was appalled at the extravagance and said that there should be a thorough review of the PTE's "expansive empire and expensive salary bill." The busmen disputed the £2.50p an hour figure, but in October 1975, in an attempt to save money, the PTE said that no more platform staff were to be recruited.

There was extreme concern by all councillors and at the beginning of 1976 County Councillor David Austick said that the whole of the West Yorkshire public transport system could collapse in four to five years. It was becoming very uncomfortable in the top echelons of Leeds and West Yorkshire transport. Arnold Stone had usually painted an optimistic picture, but both he and Thomas Lord immediately "got out".

Lord took early retirement. He was largely a figure-head at the WYPTE. A charismatic man, he was remarkably "quiet" during the problems of 1975 and 1976 and delegated junior officials to "take the flak" from county councillors. He was awarded a C.B.E. in the Queen's birthday honours in June 1975. However, he had also achieved notoriety in Leeds transport circles. He had a drink problem and had been arrested for being "unlawfully drunk" in Swinegate. Iain Fraser, who worked at the Swinegate Head Office at the time, said that Lord suffered from acute depression and alcoholism and "things in Swinegate could be very difficult. Each Department ran itself with only the Finance Department having any overview." There was no overall control.

Lord was aged 59 and left the service of the PTE on 30 June 1976. He died on 29 October 1988.

A former senior L.C.T. official died soon after Lord's retirement. Tom Parkinson, the chief bus engineer, died on 3 June 1977. aged 81. Victor James Matterface, his counterpart on the tramway side, passed away on 23 February 1985 at the age of 77.

Arnold Stone, aged 61, and John Rostron, 59, also took early retirement. and left on the same day as Lord. Rostron was the PTE Director of Operations and Planning and had formerly been General Manager of the Huddersfield Transport undertaking. Arnold Stone still lives in Rawdon, Leeds, but Rostron died on 26 May 2004.

G.G. Hilditch, former manager of the Halifax Transport undertaking, had been appointed Director of Engineering. He left in September 1975 to take up a post as General Manager of Leicester City Transport.

Whether Lord, Stone and Rostron left voluntarily was not officially revealed, but it is believed that there had been some "pressure" from county councillors.

Passenger numbers in Leeds continued to decline, and had more than halved from the 1970 figure to 84,585,000 in 1982. During the 1980's and 1990's passengers continued to desert the buses, the numbers "bottoming out" at between 50 and 60 million in the 1990s. Unfortunately, for commercial reasons there are no official published figures, but at the time of writing, 2005, passenger numbers in the Leeds district of the First West Yorkshire transport undertaking are believed to be about 60,000,000 annually.

Lord and Stone were the last of the "old guard" of the Leeds City Transport undertaking. It was not long before younger minds took over at the WYPTE. Seeds were sown for improvements to the buses in the form of more bus lanes and guided bus ways. The latter, in ideal circumstances a good system, but under Leeds conditions of doubtful merit. The possible reintroduction of trolley buses and tramways into the city were considered. These interesting developments are part of a continuing story.

Arnold Stone in 1973. Leeds City Transport

Leyland Atlantean 591, the last bus to be delivered to the Leeds City Transport undertaking, is in Harehills Road at the terminus of the 42 Harehills to Old Farnley service. The date is 8 March 1975. *Author.*

Note: The tables do not include the various short workings that were operated on several routes.

No.	Route	Route Length miles	Frequ- ency Mins.	No. of journeys daily	First bus	Last bus	Thro' fare	Av'ge Fare/ mile	Journey Time Mins.
1	**BEESTON to HOLT PARK**	7·59	5 and 10	Mon-Fri 128 Sat 108 Sun 71	04.45	22.48	11p	1·44p	38

Route: Town Street, Beeston, Beeston Road, Meadow Road, Victoria Road, Neville Street, Bishopgate Street, City Square, Infirmary Street, East Parade, The Headrow, Cookridge Street, Woodhouse Lane, Headingley Lane, Otley Road, and Holt Lane to Heathfield. Return from Woodhouse Lane via Blackman Lane, New Woodhouse Lane, Woodhouse Lane, The Headrow, Park Row, City Square Bishopgate Street, Neville Street, Great Wilson Street and Meadow Lane to Meadow Road. Service worked in co-ordination with service 4 at Beeston.

No.	Route	Route Length miles	Frequ- ency Mins.	No. of journeys daily	First bus	Last bus	Thro' fare	Av'ge Fare/ mile	Journey Time Mins.
2	**DEWSBURY ROAD to MOORTOWN**	6·69	20, 60 pt day	Mon-Fri 9 Sat 14	07.21	17.41	10p	1·49p	33

Route: Dewsbury Road (Waincliffe Drive), Dewsbury Road, Victoria Road, Great Wilson Street, Meadow Lane, Bridge End, Briggate, New Briggate, North Street, Meanwood Road, Barrack Street, Chapeltown Road and Harrogate Road to Chained Bull Hotel. Return journey from Chapeltown Road via Sheepscar Street South, Regent Street, New York Road, Vicar Lane, New Market Street, Call Lane, Bridge End, Meadow Lane, Dewsbury Road, Parkfield Street, Jack Lane, and Dewsbury Road. Ran in co-ordination with service 3.

No.	Route	Route Length miles	Frequ- ency Mins.	No. of journeys daily	First bus	Last bus	Thro' fare	Av'ge Fare/ mile	Journey Time Mins.
2	**CORN EXCHANGE to CROSS FLATTS PARK**	2·65	15	Mon-Fri 15 peak only	07.10	17.36	6p	2·26p	12

Route: As route 2 to Crescent Cinema, Dewsbury Road, then via Parkside Lane, Lockwood Way, and Middleton Grove, terminating at the Computer House.

No.	Route	Route Length miles	Frequ- ency Mins.	No. of journeys daily	First bus	Last bus	Thro' fare	Av'ge Fare/ mile	Journey Time Mins.
3	**MIDDLETON to MOORTOWN**	8·84	10 and 20 pt day	Mon-Fri 41 Sat 23 Sun 48	06.23	22.35	11p	1·24p	41

Route: Middleton (Thorpe Lane), Middleton Park Avenue, Acre Road, Sissons Terrace, Bodmin Crescent, Bodmin Road, Ring Road (Beeston Park) to Dewsbury Road and then as route 2 to the Chained Bull Hotel. Ran in co-ordination with service 2.

No.	Route	Route Length miles	Frequ- ency Mins.	No. of journeys daily	First bus	Last bus	Thro' fare	Av'ge Fare/ mile	Journey Time Mins.
4	**BEESTON to IRELAND WOOD**	8·18	10, 30, and 60	Mon-Fri 50 Sat 48 Sun 28	05.15	22.38	11p	1·34p	39

Route: As route 1 from Beeston to Otley Road, then via Ring Road (West Park), Spen Lane, Iveson Drive, Iveson Approach, Otley Old Road, Raynel Approach, Raynel Drive and Farrar Lane to a point near Holt Park School. Service worked in co-ordination with service 1 at Beeston.

No.	Route	Route Length miles	Frequ- ency Mins.	No. of journeys daily	First bus	Last bus	Thro' fare	Av'ge Fare/ mile	Journey Time Mins.
5	**WHINMOOR to GREENTHORPE**	9·31		Mon-Fri 6	06.11	17.41	12p	1·28p	51

Route: Whinmoor (Naburn Road), Naburn Place, Sherburn Road, Baildon Drive, York Road, North Parkway, Seacroft Avenue, Seacroft Town Centre, Seacroft Crescent, Brooklands Avenue, Kentmere Avenue, South Parkway, South Parkway Approach, Wykebeck Valley Road, Gipton Approach, York Road, Marsh Lane, York Street, Harper Street, Kirkgate, New Market Street, Duncan Street, Boar Lane, City Square, Wellington Street, Wellington Road, Gelderd Road, Spence Lane, Wellington Road, Tong Road, Farrow Hill, Heights Drive, Greenthorpe Road, Henconner Lane, Queensthorpe Avenue, and Gamble Hill Drive to a terminus at Gamble Hill Place. Return via Gamble Hill Drive, Henconner Lane, Greenthorpe Road, Heights Drive, Farrow Hill, Tong Road etc. Return from Wellington Road via new Wellington Street one-way system. There were 21 daily short workings from Seacroft Town Centre and five from New Market Street to Greenthorpe. Worked in co-ordination with Service 11.

No.	Route	Route Length miles	Frequ- ency Mins.	No. of journeys daily	First bus	Last bus	Thro' fare	Av'ge Fare/ mile	Journey Time Mins.
6	**HALF MILE LANE to HALTON MOOR**	8·92	10, 20 and 60	Mon-Fri 52 Sat 87 Sun 40	05.31	22.30	11p	1·23p	44

Route: Stanningley Road, Armley Road, Wellington Road, Wellington Street one-way system, Wellington Street, City Square, Boar Lane, Duncan Street, Call Lane, New York Street, York Street, Marsh Lane, York Road, Osmondthorpe Lane, Neville Parade, Halton Moor Avenue, Neville Road and Ullswater Crescent. Return from Stanningley Road via new slip road and Henconner Lane to Stanningley Road. Return route from York Street via Harper Street, Kirkgate and New Market Street to Duncan Street. Ran in co-ordination with service 14

No.	Route	Route Length miles	Frequ- ency Mins.	No. of journeys daily	First bus	Last bus	Thro' fare	Av'ge Fare/ mile	Journey Time Mins.
7	**HUNSLET to BECKETT PARK**	6·02	12, 15 and 30	Mon-Fri 62 Sat 53 Sun 30	05.39	22.34	10p	1·66p	34

Route: Spring Grove Street, Thwaite Gate, Low Road, Hunslet Road, Hunslet Lane, Great Wilson Street, Meadow Lane, Bridge End, Briggate, Boar Lane, City Square, Infirmary Street, East Parade, Westgate, Park Lane, Burley Street, Burley Road, Cardigan Road, Kirkstall Lane, Queenswood Drive to top of Queenswood Drive. Return route from Westgate via The Headrow and Park Row to City Square.

No.	Route	Route Length miles	Frequ- ency Mins.	No. of journeys daily	First bus	Last bus	Thro' fare	Av'ge Fare/ mile	Journey Time Mins.
8	**MOORTOWN to COTTINGLEY**	8·48	10, 15, and 20	Mon-Fri 65 Sat 62 Sun 43	05.44	22.27	11p	1·30p	38

Route: Moortown, Cranmer Bank, Deanswood Hill, Black Moor Road, Tongue Lane. Church Lane, Green Road, Meanwood Road, Barrack Street, Chapeltown Road, Sheepscar Street South, Regent Street, New York Road, Vicar Lane, New Market Street, Call Lane, Bridge End, Meadow Lane, Meadow Road, Elland Road, Ring Road (Beeston), Cottingley Drive, Cottingley Mount, Cottingley Vale to Cottingley Drive. Return from Meadow Road via Victoria Road and Great Wilson Street to Meadow Lane. Return from Bridge End via Briggate, New Briggate and North Street, to Meanwood Road.

No.	Route	Route Length miles	Frequ- ency Mins.	No. of journeys daily	First bus	Last bus	Thro' fare	Av'ge Fare/ mile	Journey Time Mins.
9	**RING ROAD Selby Road to Middleton**	22·21	15, 30, and 60,	Mon-Fri 22 Sat 28 Sun 13	07.05	22.05	15p	0·67p	76

Route: Selby Road, Ring Road (Halton), Station Road, Ring Road (Cross Gates), Ring Road (Seacroft), Ring Road (Shadwell), Ring Road (Moortown), Ring Road (Meanwood), Ring Road (Weetwood), Ring Road (West Park), Broadway, Ring Road (Farsley), Ring Road (Stanningley), Ring Road (Bramley), Ring Road (Farnley), Ring Road (Lower Wortley), Ring Road (Beeston), Ring Road (Churwell), Dewsbury Road, Ring Road (Beeston Park), Middleton Park Road to Middleton Garage.

No.	Route	Route Length miles	Frequ-ency Mins.	No. of journeys daily	First bus	Last bus	Thro' fare	Av'ge Fare/ mile	Journey Time Mins.
10	**ROUNDHAY to MIDDLETON**	8·85	10 and 20	Mon-Fri 62 Sat 49	06.58	23.00	11p	1·24p	40

Route: Roundhay Park, Prince's Avenue, Roundhay Road, Sheepscar Street South, Regent Street, New York Road, Vicar Lane, New Market Street, Call Lane, Bridge End, Meadow Lane, Great Wilson Street, Hunslet Lane, Hunslet Road, Waterloo Road, Church Street, Balm Road, Belle Isle Road, Town Street, Sharp Lane, Middleton Park Road, Middleton Park Avenue to Thorpe Lane. Return from Bridge End via Briggate, New Briggate, North Street, Meanwood Road, Barrack Street, and Chapeltown Road to Roundhay Road.

No.	Route	Route Length miles	Frequ-ency Mins.	No. of journeys daily	First bus	Last bus	Thro' fare	Av'ge Fare/ mile	Journey Time Mins.
11	**WHINMOOR to SWINNOW**	10·56	10 and 20	Mon-Fri 53 Sat 52 Sun 47	05.51	22.31	13p	1·23p	56

Route: As route 5 to Tong Road and then via Pudsey Road, Ring Road (Bramley), Stanningley By-pass, Swinnow Road to Swinnow House. Worked in co-ordination with service 5. There were three daily short workings from Seacroft Town Centre to Swinnow.

No.	Route	Route Length miles	Frequ-ency Mins.	No. of journeys daily	First bus	Last bus	Thro' fare	Av'ge Fare/ mile	Journey Time Mins.
12	**VICAR LANE to MIDDLETON** Thorpe Lane	5·03	10 20	Mon-Fri 62 Sat 57 Sun 51	04.37	23.07	9p	1·78p	23

Route: Vicar Lane, New Market Street, Call Lane, Bridge End, Meadow Lane, Dewsbury Road, Parkfield Street, Jack Lane. Dewsbury Road, Ring Road (Beeston Park), Middleton Park Avenue to Thorpe Lane. Return journey from Dewsbury Road via Victoria Road, Great Wilson Street, Meadow Lane, Bridge End, Briggate and The Headrow to Vicar Lane.

No.	Route	Route Length miles	Frequ-ency Mins.	No. of journeys daily	First bus	Last bus	Thro' fare	Av'ge Fare/ mile	Journey Time Mins.
14	**HALF MILE LANE to HALTON**	8·47	10 and 60	Mon-Fri 21	07.21	16.41	11p	1·29p	41

Route: As route 6 to York Road and then via Selby Road, Temple Newsam Road and Irwin Approach to Halton (Irwin Arms). In co-ordination with service 6.

No.	Route	Route Length miles	Frequ-ency Mins.	No. of journeys daily	First bus	Last bus	Thro' fare	Av'ge Fare/ mile	Journey Time Mins.
15	**BRAMLEY TOWN END to SEACROFT**	9·36	20 and 60	Mon-Fri 43	06.11	23.01	11p	1·14p	46

Route: Bramley Town End, Henconner Lane, Green Hill Road, Hill Top Road, Whingate, Tong Road, Wellington Road, new Wellington Street one-way system, Wellington Street, City Square, Boar Lane, Duncan Street, Call Lane, New York Street, York Street, Marsh Lane, Burmantofts Street, Nippet Lane, Stoney Rock Lane, Compton Road, Foundry Approach, Coldcotes Drive, Wykebeck Valley Road, South Parkway Approach, South Parkway, York Road and Seacroft Avenue to Seacroft Town Centre. Return from New York Street via Harper Street, Kirkgate and New Market Street to Duncan Street. Return from Wellington Road via Gelderd Road, Spence Lane, and Wellington Road, Ran alternately in co-ordination with service 16.

No.	Route	Route Length miles	Frequ-ency Mins.	No. of journeys daily	First bus	Last bus	Thro' fare	Av'ge Fare/ mile	Journey Time Mins.
16	**BRAMLEY TOWN END to SEACROFT**	9·11	20 and 60	Mon-Fri 39	06.39	22.51	11p	1·20p	46

Route: As route 15 to South Parkway then Kentmere Avenue, North Parkway, York Road and Seacroift Avenue to Seacroft Town Centre. Ran alternately in co-ordination with service 15.

No.	Route	Route Length miles	Frequ-ency Mins.	No. of journeys daily	First bus	Last bus	Thro' fare	Av'ge Fare/ mile	Journey Time Mins.
17	**BRAMLEY TOWN END to SEACROFT (Limewood Approach)**	9·60	20 and 30	Mon-Fri 4 Sat 5 peak only	05.01	07.11	11p	1·14p	48

Route: As route 16 to North Parkway then Ramshead Drive, Ramshead Approach, Ring Road (Seacroft), and Limewood Approach. Return from Limewood Approach via Limewood Road to Ramshead Approach. 15 mins. peak hour service from City Square to Limewood Approach.

No.	Route	Route Length miles	Frequ-ency Mins.	No. of journeys daily	First bus	Last bus	Thro' fare	Av'ge Fare/ mile	Journey Time Mins.
18	**VICAR LANE to MIDDLETON ARMS**	4·37	20	Mon-Fri 37 Sat 33	07.13	18.43	9p	2·05p	20

Route: Vicar Lane, New Market Street, Call Lane, Bridge End, Meadow Lane, Dewsbury Road, Parkfield Street, Jack Lane, Dewsbury Road, Ring Road, (Beeston Park), to Middleton Arms. Return from Dewsbury Road via Victoria Road, Great Wilson Street, Meadow Lane, Bridge End, Briggate and The Headrow to Vicar Lane. Worked in co-ordination with service 19, ie. Vicar Lane-Middleton Arms-Roundhay Park, and the same route in reverse.

No.	Route	Route Length miles	Frequ-ency Mins.	No. of journeys daily	First bus	Last bus	Thro' fare	Av'ge Fare/ mile	Journey Time Mins.
19	**ROUNDHAY to MIDDLETON ARMS**	8·19	20 and 40	Mon-Fri 28 Sat 34	17/43 08.48		11p	1·34p	57

No.	Route	Route Length miles	Frequ-ency Mins.	No. of journeys daily	First bus	Last bus	Thro' fare	Av'ge Fare/ mile	Journey Time Mins.
20	**DEWSBURY ROAD to MOORTOWN (Corner)**	6·69	10 and 20	Mon-Fri 84 Sat 86 Sun 44	06.13	22.53	10p	1·49p	32

Route: Dewsbury Road, Jack Lane, Parkfield Street, Dewsbury Road, Victoria Road, Great Wilson Street, Meadow Lane, Bridge End, Briggate, New Briggate, North Street, Meanwood Road, Barrack Street, Chapeltown Road, Harrogate Road, to Moortown. Return from Chapeltown Road via Sheepscar Street South, Regent Street, New York Road, Vicar Lane, New Market Street and Call Lane to Bridge End. In co-ordination with service 21.

No.	Route	Route Length miles	Frequ-ency Mins.	No. of journeys daily	First bus	Last bus	Thro' fare	Av'ge Fare/ mile	Journey Time Mins.
21	**MOORTOWN to ROUNDHAY and BELLE ISLE**	8·73	10 and 20	Mon-Fri 91 Sat 88 Sun 48	05.30	23.05	11p	1·26p	39

Route: Moortown Corner, Street Lane, Princes Avenue, Roundhay Road, Sheepscar Street South, Regent Street, New York Road, Vicar Lane, New Market Street, Call Lane, Bridge End, Meadow Lane, Great Wilson Street, Hunslet Lane, Hunslet Road, Waterloo Road, Church Street, Balm Road, Belle Isle Road. Return from Bridge End via Briggate, New Briggate, North Street, Meanwood Road, Barrack Street and Chapeltown Road to Roundhay Road. Worked in co-ordination with service 20.

No.	Route	Route Length miles	Frequ-ency Mins.	No. of journeys daily	First bus	Last bus	Thro' fare	Av'ge Fare/ mile	Journey Time Mins.
22	**TEMPLE NEWSAM to OLD FARNLEY**	9·01	30 and 60	Mon-Fri 24 Sat 21 Sun 9	06.02	22.02	11p	1·22p	45

Route: Temple Newsam Road, Selby Road, York Road, Marsh Lane, York Street, New York Street, Harper Street, Kirkgate, New Market Street, Duncan Street, Boar Lane, City Square, Aire Street, Whitehall Road, Spence Lane, Wortley Lane, Gelderd Road, Ring Road (Lower Wortley), Whincover Drive, Cross Lane, Hall Lane, and Tong Road. Return from Gelderd Road via Smithfield Street, Whitehall Road, Gelderd Road, Spence Lane, Whitehall Road, Thirsk Row, Wellington Street, City Square, Boar Lane, Duncan Street and Call Lane to New York Street.

No.	Route	Route Length miles	Frequency Mins.	No. of journeys daily	First bus	Last bus	Thro' fare	Av'ge Fare/ mile	Journey Time Mins.
23	**BUS STATION to INTAKE**	6·01	30 and 60	Mon-Fri 32 Sat 32 Sun 9	07.15	22.45	10p	1·66p	28

Route: Eastgate, The Headrow, Park Lane, Burley Street, Burley Road, Kirkstall Hill, Kirkstall Lane, Bridge Road, Leeds and Bradford Road and Intake Lane.

No.	Route	Route Length miles	Frequency Mins.	No. of journeys daily	First bus	Last bus	Thro' fare	Av'ge Fare/ mile	Journey Time Mins.
24	**HORSFORTH (Fleece) to SWARCLIFFE (Mill Green Gardens)**	10·85	10, 30, part day	Mon-Fri 19 Sat 34 Sun 15	07.06	22.36	12p	1·10p	49

Route: Horsforth (Fleece), New Road Side, Abbey Road, Commercial Road, Kirkstall Road, Wellington Street, Westgate, The Headrow, Park Row, City Square, Boar Lane, Duncan Street, Call Lane, New York Street, York Street, Marsh Lane, York Road, Cross Gates Road, Austhorpe Road, Church Lane, Eastwood Lane and Swarcliffe Drive to Mill Green Gardens. Return from New York Street via Harper Street, Kirkgate and New Market Street to Duncan Street, Worked in co-ordination with services 25, 26 and 27.

No.	Route	Route Length miles	Frequency Mins.	No. of journeys daily	First bus	Last bus	Thro' fare	Av'ge Fare/ mile	Journey Time Mins.
25	**HORSFORTH (Fleece) to SWARCLIFFE (Stanks Drive).**	11·09	15 and 3	Mon-Fri 38 Sat 10 Sun 16	05.36	23.06	13p	1·17p	50

Route: As route 24 to Swarcliffe Drive then via Swarcliffe Avenue to Stanks Drive. Ran in co-ordination with services 24, 26 and 27.

No.	Route	Route Length miles	Frequency Mins.	No. of journeys daily	First bus	Last bus	Thro' fare	Av'ge Fare/ mile	Journey Time Mins.
26	**HORSFORTH (Old Ball) to SWARCLIFFE (Mill Green Gardens)**	13·07	30 and 60	Mon-Fri 26 Sat 29 Sun 13	06.35	22.05	13p	0·99p	60

Route: Horsforth (Fleece) New Road Side, Park Side, Broadway, Fink Hill, Church Road, Church Lane, Town Street, Long Row, Station Road, Horsforth (Old Ball), Troy Road, Low Lane, Hawksworth Road, Abbey Road, and then as route 24 to Swarcliffe (Mill Green Gardens). Worked in co-ordination with services 24, 25 and 27.

No.	Route	Route Length miles	Frequency Mins.	No. of journeys daily	First bus	Last bus	Thro' fare	Av'ge Fare/ mile	Journey Time Mins.
27	**HORSFORTH (Old Ball) to SWARCLIFFE (Stanks Drive)**	13·29	60 part day	Mon-Fri 7 Sat 4 Sun 9	08.05	22.35	13p	0·98p	61

Route: As route 26 to Swarcliffe Drive then via Swarcliffe Avenue to Stanks Drive. Ran in co-ordination with services 24, 25 and 26.

No.	Route	Route Length miles	Frequency Mins.	No. of journeys daily	First bus	Last bus	Thro' fare	Av'ge Fare/ mile	Journey Time Mins.
28	**BUS STATION to LONG CAUSEWAY**	5·06	60	Mon-Fri 17 Sat 16 Sun 10	07.50	22.50	9p	1·77p	25

Route: Eastgate, The Headrow, Albion Street, Woodhouse Lane, Headingley Lane, Otley Road, Weetwood Lane and Long Causeway to a turning circle just beyond Wayland Drive. Return from Woodhouse Lane via Blackman Lane, New Woodhouse Lane and Woodhouse Lane to The Headrow.

No.	Route	Route Length miles	Frequency Mins.	No. of journeys daily	First bus	Last bus	Thro' fare	Av'ge Fare/ mile	Journey Time Mins.
29	**INFIRMARY STREET to MIDDLETON**	6·06	10, 15, 30	Mon-Fri 49	06.03	23.03	9p	1·48p	30

Route: Infirmary Street, East Parade, Westgate, Wellington Street, Wellington Road, Gelderd Road, Spence Lane, Domestic Street, Top Moor Side, Cemetery Road, Beeston Road, Old Lane, Ring Road (Beeston Park), Middleton Park Avenue, Sissons Road, Sissons Terrace and Sissons Road to Middleton (Thorpe Lane). Return from Thorpe Lane via Throstle Road, Thorpe View, Thorpe Road and Middleton Park Road to Ring Road (Beeston Park). Return from Domestic Street via Wortley Lane, Gelderd Road, Smithfield Street, Whitehall Road, Gelderd Road, Wellington Road, new Wellington Street one-way system, Wellington Street, Westgate, The Headrow and Park Row to Infirmary Street.

No.	Route	Route Length miles	Frequency Mins.	No. of journeys daily	First bus	Last bus	Thro' fare	Av'ge Fare/ mile	Journey Time Mins.
30	**HOLBECK MOOR to CROSS GREEN**	5·31	30 part day	Mon-Fri 12	07.04	17.34	9p	1·69p	25

Route: Crosby Street, Top Moor Side, Domestic Street, Holbeck Lane, Water Lane, Victoria Bridge, Neville Street, Sovereign Street, Swinegate, Briggate, The Headrow, Vicar Lane, Kirkgate, New York Street, York Street, Duke Street, Marsh Lane, Saxton Lane, Flax Place, East Street, Cross Green Lane, Pontefract Lane, Cross Green Approach, Cross Green Way, Knowsthorpe Gate, and Pontefract Lane, to New Market Approach. Return from Duke Street via St. Peter's Street, Eastgate, Vicar Lane, New Market Street and Call Lane to Swinegate and from Domestic Street via Shafton Lane and Crosby Road to Crosby Street. Worked in co-ordination with service 63.

No.	Route	Route Length miles	Frequency Mins.	No. of journeys daily	First bus	Last bus	Thro' fare	Av'ge Fare/ mile	Journey Time Mins.
31	**NEW FARNLEY to BRACKENWOOD**	9·32	10, 15, 30.	Mon-Fri 47 Sat 55 Sun 26	06.42	22.42	11p	1·18p	44

Route: New Farnley via Whitehall Road, Gelderd Road, Spence Lane, Whitehall Road, Thirsk Row, Wellington Street, City Square, Boar Lane, Briggate, New Briggate, North Street, Skinner Lane, Regent Street, Cross Stamford Street, Roseville Road, Roundhay Road, Gledhow Lane, Thorn Lane, Lidgett Walk, Jackson Avenue, Gledhow Avenue, Lidgett Lane, Brackenwood Drive, to turning circle near Lidgett Lane. Return from Regent Street via New York Road, Vicar Lane, New Market Street Duncan Street, Boar Lane, City Square, Aire Street, Whitehall Road, Spence Lane, Wortley Lane, Gelderd Road, and Smithfield Street to Whitehall Road.

No.	Route	Route Length miles	Frequency Mins.	No. of journeys daily	First bus	Last bus	Thro' fare	Av'ge Fare/ mile	Journey Time Mins.
32	**MOORTOWN to PUDSEY**	12·33	15 and 30	Mon-Fri 39 Sat 56 Sun 29	06.31	22.06	13p	1·05p	60

Route: Stonegate Road, Stainbeck Avenue, Potternewton Lane, Scott Hall Road, Sheepscar Street North, Barrack Street, Chapeltown Road, Sheepscar Street South, Regent Street, New York Road, Vicar Lane, New Market Street, Duncan Street, Boar Lane, City Square, Aire Street, Whitehall Road, Spence Lane. Wortley Lane, Gelderd Road, Smithfield Street, Whitehall Road, Ring Road (Lower Wortley), Ring Road (Farnley), Ring Road (Bramley), Swinnow Road, Lowtown, Church Lane, Chapeltown, Upper Moor, Waterloo Road to Pudsey (Waterloo). Ran in conjunction with service 47 on weekdays. Return from Boar Lane via Briggate, New Briggate, North Street, Meanwood Road and Barrack Street to Sheepscar Street North.

No.	Route	Route Length miles	Frequency Mins.	No. of journeys daily	First bus	Last bus	Thro' fare	Av'ge Fare/ mile	Journey Time Mins.
33	BUS STATION to COOKRIDGE	7·05	10, 15, 20, 60	Mon-Fri 39 Sat 29 Sun 17	06.16	23.05	10p	1·41p	30

Route: St. Peter's Street, Eastgate, The Headrow, Albion Street, Woodhouse Lane, Headingley Lane, Otley Road, Otley Old Road, Cookridge Lane, Green Lane and Wood Hill Road to Wood Hill Gardens. Return from Woodhouse Lane via Blackman Lane, New Woodhouse Lane, and Woodhouse Lane to The Headrow. Worked in co-ordination with service 36.

No.	Route	Route Length miles	Frequency Mins.	No. of journeys daily	First bus	Last bus	Thro' fare	Av'ge Fare/ mile	Journey Time Mins.
34	BUS STATION to ALWOODLEY (Circular)	11·55	15, 30 and 60	Mon-Fri 39 Sat 29 Sun 16	06.13	23.10	13p	1·12p	50

Route: Eastgate, Regent Street, Skinner Lane, North Street, Meanwood Road, Barrack Street, Sheepscar Street North, Scott Hall Road, Harrogate Road, Alwoodley Gates, Alwoodley Lane, and King Lane to Scott Hall Road and then inward route reversed to Sheepscar Street North and then Barrack Street, Chapeltown Road and Sheepscar Street South to Regent Street. Worked in co-ordination with service 35.

No.	Route	Route Length miles	Frequency Mins.	No. of journeys daily	First bus	Last bus	Thro' fare	Av'ge Fare/ mile	Journey Time Mins.
35	BUS STATION to ALWOODLEY (Circular)	11·55	15, 30 and 60	Mon-Fri 38 Sat 22 Sun 14	07.03	22.40	13p	1·12p	50

Route: As route 34 to Scott Hall Road and then via King Lane and 34 route in reverse. Ran in co-ordination with service 34. There were short workings to King Lane Circus (4 daily).

No.	Route	Route Length miles	Frequency Mins.	No. of journeys daily	First bus	Last bus	Thro' fare	Av'ge Fare/ mile	Journey Time Mins.
36	BUS STATION to TINSHILL (Silk Mill Drive)	6·35	10, 15, 20, 60	Mon-Fri 37 Sat 29 Sun 18	05.46	22.55	10p	1·57p	28

Route: As route 33 to Otley Old Road then via Tinshill Lane, Woodnook Drive and Silk Mill Drive. Ran in co-ordination with service 33.

No.	Route	Route Length miles	Frequency Mins.	No. of journeys daily	First bus	Last bus	Thro' fare	Av'ge Fare/ mile	Journey Time Mins.
37	BUS STATION to SHADWELL	6·78	30 and 60	Mon-Fri 18 Sat 18 Sun 16	06.25	23.00	10p	1·47p	30

Route: Eastgate, Regent Street, Skinner Lane, North Street, Meanwood Road, Barrack Street, Sheepscar Street North, Scott Hall Road, Street Lane, Harrogate Road, Shadwell Lane and Main Street to Ash Hill Lane. Return from Sheepscar Street North via Barrack Street, Chapeltown Road, and Sheepscar Street South to Regent Street. Worked in co-ordination with service 43. On Sundays, return from Shadwell on route 43.

No.	Route	Route Length miles	Frequency Mins.	No. of journeys daily	First bus	Last bus	Thro' fare	Av'ge Fare/ mile	Journey Time Mins.
38	MOORTOWN to WHITKIRK	5·75	30 and 60	Mon-Sat 32 Sun 24	06.50	22.00	10p	1·73p	26

Route: Moortown (Sandhill Lane), Harrogate Road, Lidgett Lane, Gledhow Lane, Oakwood Lane, Foundry Lane, Cross Gates Road, Station Road, Knightsway, Selby Road, Whitkirk Church. Return from Whitkirk Church via Hollyshaw Lane to Station Road.

No.	Route	Route Length miles	Frequency Mins.	No. of journeys daily	First bus	Last bus	Thro' fare	Av'ge Fare/ mile	Journey Time Mins.
39	BUS STATION to SWILLINGTON	5·77	60	Mon-Fri 2 Sat 10	08.08	17.08	13p	2·25p	27

Route: St. Peter's Street, York Street, Marsh Lane, York Road, Selby Road, Chapel Street, Cross Green Lane, Green Lane, Ring Road (Halton), Selby Road, Swillington Lane, Neville Grove, The Drive, Wakefield Road and Church Lane.

No.	Route	Route Length miles	Frequency Mins.	No. of journeys daily	First bus	Last bus	Thro' fare	Av'ge Fare/ mile	Journey Time Mins.
40	STANKS to RAYNVILLE	8·88	10, 20 and 30	Mon-Fri 49 Sat 45 Sun 28	05.50	22.30	12p	1·35p	43

Route: From Stanks (Kelmscott Green), Pendas Way, Manston Lane, Austhorpe Road, Station Road, Cross Gates Road, York Road, Marsh Lane, York Street, New York Street, Harper Street, Kirkgate, New Market Street, Duncan Street, Boar Lane, City Square, Wellington Street, Wellington Road, Armley Road, Stanningley Road, Armley Ridge Road, Raynville Road and terminating at Outgang. Return from Wellington Road via new Wellington Street one-way system to Wellington Street. Return from Duncan Street via Call Lane to New York Street.

No.	Route	Route Length miles	Frequency Mins.	No. of journeys daily	First bus	Last bus	Thro' fare	Av'ge Fare/ mile	Journey Time Mins.
41	HALTON MOOR to STANNINGLEY	10·94	20 peak hr	Mon-Fri 9	07.15	17.15	12p	1·09p	54

Route: As long established 44 route, but diverted from Bridge Road via Broad Lane to the Leeds and Bradford Road. Ran in co-ordination with 44 route.

No.	Route	Route Length miles	Frequency Mins.	No. of journeys daily	First bus	Last bus	Thro' fare	Av'ge Fare/ mile	Journey Time Mins.
42	HAREHILLS to OLD FARNLEY	6·17	15 and 30	Mon-Fri 74 Sat 57 Sun 43	05.15	22.45	10p	1·94p	35

Route: Harehills Road, Beckett Street, Burmantofts Street, Marsh Lane, York Street, St. Peter's Street, Eastgate, The Headrow, Park Row, City Square, Wellington Street, Wellington Road, Gelderd Road, Spence Lane, Wellington Road, Oldfield Lane, Lower Wortley Road, Branch Road, Ring Road (Lower Wortley), Whincover Drive and Butterbowl Drive to Cross Lane, Old Farnley. Return from Wellington Road via new Wellington Street one-way system to Wellington Street, Worked in co-ordination with service 66.

No.	Route	Route Length miles	Frequency Mins.	No. of journeys daily	First bus	Last bus	Thro' fare	Av'ge Fare/ mile	Journey Time Mins.
43	BUS STATION to SHADWELL	6·93	30 and 60	Mon-Fri 18 Sat 13	06.38	19.00	10p	1·44p	30

Route: As route 37 to Shadwell Lane, then via Ring Road and Birchwood Hill to Shadwell Lane.

No.	Route	Route Length miles	Frequency Mins.	No. of journeys daily	First bus	Last bus	Thro' fare	Av'ge Fare/ mile	Journey Time Mins.
44	HALTON MOOR to STANNINGLEY	11·06	10, 15 and 20	Mon-Fri 63 Sat 48 Sun 45	05.45	22.20	12p	1·08p	54

Route: Ullswater Crescent, Neville Road, Halton Moor Avenue, Neville Parade, Osmondthorpe Lane, Harehills Lane, Harrogate Road, Stainbeck Lane, Stainbeck Road, Grove Lane, Shaw Lane, Otley Road, North Lane, Kirkstall Lane, Bridge Road, Leeds and Bradford Road, Newlay Lane, Broad Lane, Town Street, Stanningley. Worked in co-ordination with service 41.

No.	Route	Route Length miles	Frequency Mins.	No. of journeys daily	First bus	Last bus	Thro' fare	Av'ge Fare/ mile	Journey Time Mins.
45	STANKS to WORTLEY	14·19	20 and 30	Mon-Fri 46 Sat 44 Sun 31	06.00	22.10	14p	0·98p	71

Route: Stanks, Pendas Way, Barwick Rd, Stanks Lane S, Stanks Drive, Stanks Lane N, York Rd, Seacroft Ave, Brooklands Ave, Bailey's Ln, North Parkway, Kentmere Ave Boggart Hill Dve, Easterly Rd, Harehills Ln, Harehills Ave, Gledhow Valley Rd, King Ln, Stonegate Rd, Monk Bridge Rd, Shaw Ln, Otley Rd, North Ln, Kirkstall Ln, Bridge Rd, Wyther Ln, Armley Ridge Rd, Cockshott Ln, Stanningley Rd, Armley Ridge Rd, Wortley Rd, Whingate, Upper Wortley Rd, Dixon Ln, Whitehall Rd. to Ring Rd. Lower Wortley. Reverse from York Rd. via Baildon Dve, Sherburn Rd. and Whinmoor Way to Stanks Drive. Reverse from Gledhow Valley Rd. via Roundhay Rd to Easterly Rd.

No.	Route	Route Length miles	Frequency Mins.	No. of journeys daily	First bus	Last bus	Thro' fare	Av'ge Fare/ mile	Journey Time Mins.
46	BRAMLEY to BELLE ISLE and MIDDLETON	7·82	10, 20 and 30	Mon-Fri 66 Sat 53 Sun 34	05.10	22.40	10p	1·27p	36 to Belle Isle

Route: Henconner Lane, Green Hill Road, Hill Top Road, Town Street, Armley, Wesley Road, Church Road, Hall Lane, Green Lane, Tong Road, Wellington Road, Gelderd Road, Spence Lane, Domestic Street, Holbeck Moor Road, Hunslet Hall Road, Dewsbury Road, Tunstall Road, Beza Street, Church Street, Balm Road, Midland Road, Pepper Road, Middleton Road, Belle Isle Road, Town Street, Middleton, Sharp Lane, Middleton Park Road to Middleton Circus. Return from Domestic Street via Wortley Lane, Gelderd Road, Smithfield Street, Whitehall Road to Gelderd Road. Note: Five journeys daily were operated to Middleton, the remainder ran to Belle Isle only.

No.	Route	Route Length miles	Frequency Mins.	No. of journeys daily	First bus	Last bus	Thro' fare	Av'ge Fare/ mile	Journey Time Mins.
47	SWINNOW HOUSE and VICAR LANE	6·22	15	Mon-Fri. 7	06.51	08,21	9p	1·44p	28

Route: From Swinnow House, Swinnow Road, Swinnow Lane, Hough Tree Road, Pudsey Road, Ring Road (Farnley), Ring Road (Lower Wortley), Whitehall Road, Gelderd Road, Spence Lane, Whitehall Road, Thirsk Row, Wellington Street, City Square, Boar Lane, Briggate and The Headrow to Vicar Lane. Worked in co-ordination with service 32 on weekdays.

No.	Route	Route Length miles	Frequency Mins.	No. of journeys daily	First bus	Last bus	Thro' fare	Av'ge Fare/ mile	Journey Time Mins.
48	TROYDALE to CALVERLEY	6·55	60	Mon-Fri 14 Sat 13	06.23	18.23	10p	1·52p	26

Route: Troydale Lane, Valley Road, Kent Road, Lowtown, Lidget Hill, Cemetery Road, Owlcotes Road, Galloway Lane, Bradford Road, Ring Road (Farsley), Rodley Lane, Town Gate, Carr Road to Calverley Park. On return from Carr Road via Salisbury Street, Victoria Street, Rushton Street and Woodhall Road to Town Gate. Worked in co-ordination with service 81.

No.	Route	Route Length miles	Frequency Mins.	No. of journeys daily	First bus	Last bus	Thro' fare	Av'ge Fare/ mile	Journey Time Mins.
49	HYDE PARK to OLD FARNLEY	3·97	10, 12 and 30	Mon-Fri 49 Sat 37 Sun 27	06.10	22.40	9p	2·26p	25

Route: Hyde Park Road, Brudenell Road, Thornville Road, Cardigan Road, Willow Road, Viaduct Road, Canal Road, Armley Road, Branch Road (outward), Crab Lane (inward), Town Street, Carr Crofts, Tong Road, Pudsey Road, Butt Lane, and Cross Lane to Old Farnley (Butterbowl Drive).

No.	Route	Route Length miles	Frequency Mins.	No. of journeys daily	First bus	Last bus	Thro' fare	Av'ge Fare/ mile	Journey Time Mins.
50	HORSFORTH to GIPTON	8·94	10, 15 and 20	Mon-Fri. 66 Sat. 80 Sun 37	05.25	22.30	11p	1·23p	40

Route: Horsforth (Stanhope Drive), Broadgate, Low Lane, Butcher Hill, Lea Farm Road, Broadway, Vesper Road, Spen Lane, Morris Lane, Kirkstall Hill, Burley Road, Burley Street, Park Lane, Westgate, The Headrow, Eastgate, St. Peter's Street, York Street, Marsh Lane, Burmantofts Street, Nippet Lane, Stoney Rock Lane, Compton Road, Harehills Lane, Strathmore Drive, Foundry Drive, Foundry Avenue, North Farm Road, and Oak Tree Drive terminating at the Courtier Hotel.

No.	Route	Route Length miles	Frequency Mins.	No. of journeys daily	First bus	Last bus	Thro' fare	Av'ge Fare/ mile	Journey Time Mins.
51	LEEDS to MORLEY, GLEN ESTATE	5·52	15, 30, 60	Mon-Fri 15 Sat 19	06.35	18.05	9p	1·63p	27

Route: Vicar Lane, New Market Street, Call Lane, Bridge End, Meadow Lane, Meadow Road, Elland Road, Victoria Road, Church Street, Chapel Hill, Queen Street, Fountain Street, High Street, Magpie Lane and Glen Road. Return from Glen Road via South Queen Street to Queen Street. Return from Meadow Road via Victoria Road, Great Wilson Street, Meadow Lane, Bridge End, Briggate and The Headrow to Vicar Lane.

No.	Route	Route Length miles	Frequency Mins.	No. of journeys daily	First bus	Last bus	Thro' fare	Av'ge Fare/ mile	Journey Time Mins.
52	MEANWOOD to MORLEY via Tingley Mill	10·29	15, 60	Mon-Fri 38 Sat 31 Sun 24	05.00	22.45	12p	1·16p	46

Route: Green Road, Meanwood Road, Barrack Street, Chapeltown Road, Sheepscar Street South, Regent Street, New York Road, Vicar Lane, New Market Street, Call Lane, Bridge End, Meadow Lane, Meadow Road, Elland Road, Victoria Road, Church Street, Chapel Hill, Queen Street, Fountain Street, High Street, Bridge Street, Tingley Mill, Britannia Road and Fountain Street to Queen Street and then inward route reversed. Return from Meadow Road via Victoria Road, Great Wilson Street, Meadow Lane, Bridge End, Briggate, New Briggate and North Street to Meanwood Road. Ran alternately in co-ordination with service 53.

No.	Route	Route Length miles	Frequency Mins.	No. of journeys daily	First bus	Last bus	Thro' fare	Av'ge Fare/ mile	Journey Time Mins.
53	MEANWOOD to MORLEY via Fountain Street	10·29	15, 60	Mon-Fri 32 Sat 26 Sun 23	06.55	22.25	12p	1·16p	46

Route: As route 52 to Fountain Street then via Britannia Road, Tingley Mill, Bridge Street, High Street and South Queen Street to Queen Street and then inward route reversed. Ran alternately in co-ordination with service 52.

No.	Route	Route Length miles	Frequency Mins.	No. of journeys daily	First bus	Last bus	Thro' fare	Av'ge Fare/ mile	Journey Time Mins.
55	SOVEREIGN STREET to BRUNTCLIFFE	7·01	20, 60	Mon-Fri 20 Sat 16 Sun 9	06.25	21.45	10p	1·42p	25

Route: Sovereign Street, Neville Street, Great Wilson Street, Meadow Lane, Dewsbury Road, Parkfield Street, Jack Lane, Dewsbury Road, Wide Lane, Middleton Road, High Street, Britannia Road. Return from Dewsbury Road via Victoria Road to Neville Street. Operated jointly with Yorkshire Woollen District Transport Co. Ltd.

No.	Route	Route Length miles	Frequency Mins.	No. of journeys daily	First bus	Last bus	Thro' fare	Av'ge Fare/ mile	Journey Time Mins.
56	BUS STATION to HEADINGLEY	3·41	8, 10, 20	Mon-Fri 86 Sat 87 Sun 40	05.45	23.10	8p	2·34p	20

Route: Eastgate, The Headrow, Albion Street, Woodhouse Lane, Clarendon Road, Moorland Road, Royal Park Road, Queen's Road, Chestnut Avenue, Victoria Road, Cardigan Road, Kirkstall Lane to Eden Drive. Return from Woodhouse Lane via Blackman Lane, New Woodhouse Lane and Woodhouse Lane to The Headrow.

No.	Route	Route Length miles	Frequency Mins.	No. of journeys daily	First bus	Last bus	Thro' fare	Av'ge Fare/ mile	Journey Time Mins.
57 59	HYDE PARK CIRCULAR via Belle Vue Road	4·31	15, 30	Mon-Fri 37 Sat 32 Sun 18	06.40	22.10	9p	2·08p	30

Route: Vicar Lane, New Market Street, Duncan Street, Boar Lane, City Square, Infirmary Street, East Parade, Westgate, Park Lane, Belle Vue Road, Moorland Road, Hyde Park Road, Hyde Park, Woodhouse Street, Cambridge Road, Meanwood Road, Barrack Street, Chapeltown Road, Sheepscar Street South, Regent Street, New York Road and Vicar Lane. **Service 59** operated in the reverse direction from Boar Lane via Briggate and North Street to Meanwood Road. Worked in coordination with services 58 and 60.

No.	Route	Route Length miles	Frequ-ency Mins.	No. of journeys daily	First bus	Last bus	Thro' fare	Av'ge Fare/ mile	Journey Time Mins.
58 60	**HYDE PARK CURCULAR** **via Clarendon Road**	4·29	15 and 30	Mon-Fri 52 Sat 50 Sun 27	06.25	22.25	9p	2·09p	30

Route: As services 57 and 59 to Park Lane then via New Hanover Lane, Clarendon Road, Woodsley Road, Belle Vue Road, Moorland Road, Hyde Park Road, Hyde Park, Woodhouse Street, Servia Road, Lovell Park Road, Wade Lane, Merrion Street, Woodhouse Lane and The Headrow to Vicar Lane. Service 60 operated in the reverse direction from Boar Lane via Briggate, The Headrow. and Albion Street to Woodhouse Lane. Worked in coordination with services 57 and 59.

No.	Route	Route Length miles	Frequ-ency Mins.	No. of journeys daily	First bus	Last bus	Thro' fare	Av'ge Fare/ mile	Journey Time Mins.
61 62	**EAST END PARK** **CIRCULAR**	6·89	11 and 15	Mon-Fri 67 Sat 65 Sun 31	05.38	22.30	10p	1·45p	45

Route: Eastgate, St. Peter's Street, Duke Street, Crown Point Road, Black Bull Street, Hunslet Road, South Accommodation Road, Easy Road, Dial Street, Upper Accommodation Road, Lavender Walk, Pontefract Lane, East Park Road, East Park Parade, Ivy Street, Lupton Avenue, Hudson Road, Compton Road, Stanley Road, Harehills Road, Bayswater Road, Roundhay Road, Barrack Road, Chapeltown Road, North Street, Meanwood Road, Oatland Road, Servia Road, Blackman Lane, New Woodhouse Lane, Woodhouse Lane, The Headrow to Eastgate. Service 62 operated in the reverse direction from Eastgate via The Headrow and Albion Street to Woodhouse Lane, from Meanwood Road via Barrack Street to Barrack Road and from Hunslet Road via Hunslet Lane to Crown Point Road.

No.	Route	Route Length miles	Frequ-ency Mins.	No. of journeys daily	First bus	Last bus	Thro' fare	Av'ge Fare/ mile	Journey Time Mins.
63	**VICAR LANE to** **CROSS GREEN**	1·69	10 30	Mon-Fri 40 Sat 56 Sun 27	05.23	22.55	6p	3·55p	11

Route: Vicar Lane, Kirkgate, New York Street, York Street, Duke Street, Marsh Lane, Saxton Lane, Flax Place, Richmond Street, East Street, Cross Green Lane and Pontefract Lane to Cross Green. Return from Duke Street via St. Peter's Street and Eastgate to Vicar Lane. Ran in co-ordination with service 30 through to Holbeck Moor via route 30 for 12 journeys on weekdays only.

No.	Route	Route Length miles	Frequ-ency Mins.	No. of journeys daily	First bus	Last bus	Thro' fare	Av'ge Fare/ mile	Journey Time Mins.
65	**BUS STATION** **to PUDSEY**	7·11	10, 15 20	Mon-Fri 62 Sat 82 Sun 42	05.20	22.50	10p	1·40p	36

Route: Eastgate, The Headrow, Westgate, Wellington Street, Wellington Road, Armley Road, Stanningley Road, slip road to new by-pass, Henconner Lane, Stanningley Road, Town Street, Richardshaw Lane, Lidget Hill, Church Lane and Chapeltown, Pudsey. Return from Wellington Road via new one-way system to Wellington Street.

No.	Route	Route Length miles	Frequ-ency Mins.	No. of journeys daily	First bus	Last bus	Thro' fare	Av'ge Fare/ mile	Journey Time Mins.
66	**HAREHILLS to** **LEYSHOLME**	4·95	20 30	Mon-Fri 35 Sat 31 Sun 24	06.45	22.25	9p	1·81p	30

Route: As route 42 to Oldfield Lane and then via Green Hill Lane to Leysholme. Worked in co-ordination with service 42.

No.	Route	Route Length miles	Frequ-ency Mins.	No. of journeys daily	First bus	Last bus	Thro' fare	Av'ge Fare/ mile	Journey Time Mins.
67	**BUS STATION to** **SEACROFT**	4·49	5, 7, 10 15, 60	Mon-Fri 63 Sat 35 Sun 26	06.05	23.20	9p	2·00p	26

Route: Eastgate, Regent Street, Skinner Lane, Cherry Row, Dolly Lane, Gledhow Road, Roundhay Road, Easterly Road, Boggart Hill Drive, Kentmere Avenue and Monkswood Avenue to Monkswood Gate. Worked in co-ordination with service 68.

No.	Route	Route Length miles	Frequ-ency Mins.	No. of journeys daily	First bus	Last bus	Thro' fare	Av'ge Fare/ mile	Journey Time Mins.
68	**BUS STATION to** **FOUNDRY LANE**	3·15	8, 15 60	Mon-Fri 51 Sat 32 Sun 20	06.27	23.10	8p	2·53p	18

Route: As route 67 to Easterly Road then via Oakwood Lane to Foundry Lane. Return from Foundry Lane via Oak Tree Drive to Oakwood Lane. Worked in co-ordination with service 67.

No.	Route	Route Length miles	Frequ-ency Mins.	No. of journeys daily	First bus	Last bus	Thro' fare	Av'ge Fare/ mile	Journey Time Mins.
69	**CITY SQUARE** **to GLEDHOW**	4·47	10, 30, and 60	Mon-Fri 21 Sat 21	07.38	17.55	9p	2·01p	23

Route: City Square, Boar Lane, Briggate, New Briggate, North Street, Skinner Lane, Regent Street, Cross Stamford Street, Roseville Road, Roundhay Road, Gledhow Lane, Thorn Lane, Lidgett Walk, Jackson Avenue, Gledhow Avenue, Lidgett Lane and North Park Avenue to St. Edmund's Church. Return from Cross Stamford Street via Regent Street, New York Road, Vicar Lane, New Market Street and Duncan Street to Boar Lane.

No.	Route	Route Length miles	Frequ-ency Mins.	No. of journeys daily	First bus	Last bus	Thro' fare	Av'ge Fare/ mile	Journey Time Mins.
70	**BUS STATION** **to PRIMLEY PARK**	5·44	10, 15 30	Mon-Fri 47 Sat 59 Sun 25	06.30	22.55	9p	1·65p	26

Route: Eastgate, Regent Street, Skinner Lane, North Street, Meanwood Road, Barrack Street, Sheepscar Street North, Scott Hall Road, Stainbeck Lane, Stainbeck Road, Carr Manor Road, King Lane, Lingfield Approach, Lingfield Hill, Nursery Lane, Harrogate Road and Primley Park Avenue to Primley Park Crescent. Return from Primley Park Avenue via Primley Park Crescent to Nursery Lane. Return from Sheepscar Street North and then Barrack Street, Chapeltown Road and Sheepscar Street South to Regent Street.

No.	Route	Route Length miles	Frequ-ency Mins.	No. of journeys daily	First bus	Last bus	Thro' fare	Av'ge Fare/ mile	Journey Time Mins.
72	**BUS STATION** **to BRADFORD**	9·71	12, 20 30	Mon-Fri 46 Sat 62 Sun 27	06.05	22.50	12p	1·23p	44

Route: Eastgate, The Headrow, Westgate, Wellington Street, Wellington Road, Armley Road, Stanningley Road, slip road to new by-pass, Henconner Lane, Stanningley Road, Town Street, Bradford Road, Dick Lane, Gipsy Street, Leeds Road and Hall Ings. Return from Leeds Road to Bradford Road and from Wellington Road via new Wellington Street one-way system to Wellington Street. Operated jointly with Bradford Corporation Transport.

No.	Route	Route Length miles	Frequ-ency Mins.	No. of journeys daily	First bus	Last bus	Thro' fare	Av'ge Fare/ mile	Journey Time Mins.
73	**MOOR GRANGE** **to GREENTHORPE**	4·54	60	Mon-Sat 17 Sun 13	06.18	23.18	8p	1·76p	23

Route: From Moor Grange (Latchmere Green), Latchmere Road, Latchmere Drive, Old Farm Approach, Butcher Hill, Spen Lane, Morris Lane, Kirkstall Lane, Bridge Road, Wyther Lane, Raynville Road, Outgang, Town Street and Henconner Lane to Pudsey Road.

No.	Route	Route Length miles	Frequency Mins.	No. of journeys daily	First bus	Last bus	Thro' fare	Av'ge Fare/ mile	Journey Time Mins.
74	BELLE ISLE to MOOR GRANGE	9·13	12 and 30	Mon-Fri 46 Sat 31 Sun 30	05.32	22.47	11p	1·20p	47

Route: From Belle Isle (Raylands Way), Cranmore Rise, Cranmore Drive, Raylands Road, Raylands Way, Raylands Lane, Broom Place, Nesfield Garth, Nesfield View, Belle Isle Road, Moor Road, Hunslet Distributor Road, Jack Lane, Parkfield Street, Dewsbury Road, Victoria Road, Neville Street, Bishopgate Street, City Square, Infirmary Street, East Parade, The Headrow, Westgate, Park Lane, Burley Street, Burley Road, Cardigan Road, Kirkstall Lane, Queenswood Drive, Spen Lane, Old Oak Drive, Butcher Hill, Old Farm Approach, Latchmere Drive to Latchmere Green. Moor Grange. Return via Latchmere Road to Latchmere Drive. Return from Neville Street via Great Wilson Street and Meadow Lane to Dewsbury Road. Worked in co-ordination with service 76.

No.	Route	Route Length miles	Frequency Mins.	No. of journeys daily	First bus	Last bus	Thro' fare	Av'ge Fare/ mile	Journey Time Mins.
75	BUS STATION to HEADINGLEY	3·47	30	Mon-Sat 26	06.35	18.35	8p	2·30p	20

Route: Eastgate, The Headrow, Westgate, Park Lane, Burley Street, Burley Road, Westfield Road, Hyde Park Road, Brudenell Road, Cardigan Road, Ashville Road, Beechwood Crescent, St. Ann's Drive and St. Ann's Lane to Queenswood Drive.

No.	Route	Route Length miles	Frequency Mins.	No. of journeys daily	First bus	Last bus	Thro' fare	Av'ge Fare/ mile	Journey Time Mins.
76	MIDDLETON to MOOR GRANGE	9·56	12 and 30	Mon-Fri 44 Sat 35 Sun 21	06.12	22.30	11p	1·15p	49

Route: Middleton Arms, St. Philip's Avenue, Town Street, Belle Isle Road and then as the 74 route to Moor Grange. Worked in co-ordination with service 74.

No.	Route	Route Length miles	Frequency Mins.	No. of journeys daily	First bus	Last bus	Thro' fare	Av'ge Fare/ mile	Journey Time Mins.
77	GIPTON to BRAMLEY TOWN END	7·53	10, 15 and 20	Mon-Fri 64 Sat 80 Sun 40	06.00	23.00	11p	1·46p	38

Route: Gipton (Coldcotes Circus), Foundry Approach, Compton Road, Stoney Rock Lane, Nippet Lane, Burmantofts Street, Marsh Lane, York Street, St. Peter's Street, Eastgate, The Headrow, Westgate, Park Lane, Burley Street, Burley Road, Kirkstall Hill, Kirkstall Lane, Bridge Road, Leeds and Bradford Road, Broadlea Hill, Broadlea Crescent, Broad Lane, Waterloo Lane, Town Street to Bramley Town End.

No.	Route	Route Length miles	Frequency Mins.	No. of journeys daily	First bus	Last bus	Thro' fare	Av'ge Fare/ mile	Journey Time Mins.
78	BUS STATION to BRADFORD	12·41	15 30	Mon-Fri 42 Sat 47 Sun 28	05.43	22.53	13p	1·04p	56

Route: Eastgate, Vicar Lane, New Market Street, Duncan Street, Boar Lane, City Square, Aire Street, Whitehall Road, Spence Lane, Wortley Lane, Gelderd Road, Smithfield Street, Whitehall Road, Ring Road, Low Wortley, Ring Road (Farnley), Pudsey Road, Hough Side Road, Lowtown, Robin Lane, Littlemoor Road, Roker Lane, Fartown, Greenside, Uppermoor, Waterloo Road, Galloway Lane, Bradford Road, Dick Lane, Gipsy Street, Leeds Road and Hall Ings. Return from Leeds Road to Bradford Road and from Whitehall Road via Gelderd Road, Spence Lane, Whitehall Road, Thirsk Row, Wellington Street, City Square, Boar Lane, Briggate, The Headrow, Eastgate and St, Peter's Street. Operated jointly with Bradford Corporation Transport Department.

No.	Route	Route Length miles	Frequency Mins.	No. of journeys daily	First bus	Last bus	Thro' fare	Av'ge Fare/ mile	Journey Time Mins.
79	PUDSEY BUS STATION to HORSFORTH (Old Ball) and TINSHILL	5·03	6·01 30	15 and Mon-Fri 42 Sat 34 Sun 24	05.45	22.30	11p 9p	1·83p 1·78p	25 31 to Tinshill

Route: Pudsey, Church Lane, Lidget Hill, Richardshaw Lane, Bradford Road, Old Road, Town Street (Farsley), Bagley Lane, Rodley Lane, Broadway, New Road Side, Park Side, Broadway, Fink Hill, Church Road, Church Lane, Town Street, Long Row to Old Ball Hotel. Two daily journeys were worked from Pudsey to Tinshill Road top plus five from Rodley to Tinshill Road top. Route from Old Ball Hotel, Horsforth via Station Road, Tinshill Road, Tinshill Lane and Otley Old Road with the return to Station Road via Tinshill Road. In co-ordination with service 80.

No.	Route	Route Length miles	Frequency Mins.	No. of journeys daily	First bus	Last bus	Thro' fare	Av'ge Fare/ mile	Journey Time Mins.
80	PUDSEY to HORSFORTH (Old Ball) via Coal Hill L'n	6·75 5·77		Mon-Fri 3 peak only	07.00	16.25	11p 9p	1·62p 1·55p	25 31 Tinshil

Route: As route 79 to the Bagley Lane/Coal Hill Lane junction and then via Coal Hill Lane and Town Street (Rodley) to Rodley Lane and then as route 79. One daily journey was operated from Tinshill to Pudsey plus one from Pudsey to Rodley. Worked in co-ordination with service 79.

No.	Route	Route Length miles	Frequency Mins.	No. of journeys daily	First bus	Last bus	Thro' fare	Av'ge Fare/ mile	Journey Time Mins.
81	TROYDALE to CALVERLEY	4·77	60	Mon-Fri 16 Sat 16 Sun 10	06.53	21.53	10p	2·09p	26

Route: As route 48 to Galloway Lane and then via Woodhall Lane, Woodhall Road, and Town Gate, From Calverley via Carr Road, Salisbury Street, Victoria Street, Thormhill Street to Woodhall Road. Worked in co-ordination with service 48.

No.	Route	Route Length miles	Frequency Mins.	No. of journeys daily	First bus	Last bus	Thro' fare	Av'ge Fare/ mile	Journey Time Mins.
82	BUS STATION to BELLE ISLE	4·31	60	Mon-Sat 10	08.33	17.33	9p	2·08p	23

Route: Eastgate, Vicar Lane, and then as route 10 to Town Street, Middleton, then Newhall Road, Manor Farm Drive and Manor Farm Grove. Return via Manor Park Grove, Manor Farm Road, Newhall Crescent, Newhall Road, and then via route 10 to Briggate, The Headrow, Eastgate, and St. Peter's Street.

No.	Route	Route Length miles	Frequency Mins.	No. of journeys daily	First bus	Last bus	Thro' fare	Av'ge Fare/ mile	Journey Time Mins.
83	RODLEY to AUSTHORPE	10·48	20 40	Mon-Fri 35 Sat 34 Sun 26	06.51	21.41	13p	1·24p	52

Route: Bridge Road, Rodley Lane, Town Street (Rodley), Whitecote Hill, Town Street (Bramley), Stanningley Road, Armley Road, Wellington Road, new Wellington Street one-way system, Wellington Street, City Square, Boar Lane, Duncan Street, Call Lane, New York Street, York Street, Marsh Lane, York Road, Selby Road to Austhorpe (Barrowby Road). There were short workings from Bramley Town End to Austhorpe (four journeys daily). Reverse direction from Stanningley Road via slip road to new by-pass and Henconner Lane to Town Street (Bramley). From Town Street (Rodley) via Canal Road to Bridge Road. Worked in co-ordination with service 84.

No.	Route	Route Length miles	Frequency Mins.	No. of journeys daily	First bus	Last bus	Thro' fare	Av'ge Fare/ mile	Journey Time Mins.
84	RODLEY to COLTON	11·09	30 60	Mon-Fri 23 Sat 28 Sun 14	06.01	22.01	13p	1·17p	57

Route: As route 83 to Selby Road and then via School Lane and Meynell Road to Colton. There were short workings from Bramley Town End to Colton (three journeys daily). Worked in co-ordination with service 83.

No.	Route	Route Length miles	Frequency Mins.	No. of journeys daily	First bus	Last bus	Thro' fare	Av'ge Fare/ mile	Journey Time Mins.
89	BUS STATION to LEDSTON LUCK	11·42	60	Mon-Fri 16 Sat 16 Sun 9	07.13	22.13	15p	1·31p	46

Route: St. Peter's Street, York Street, Marsh Lane, York Road, Selby Road, Chapel Street, Cross Green Lane, Green Lane, Hollyshaw Lane, Selby Road, Wakefield Road, Barley Hill Road, Main Street, Church Lane, Ninelands Lane, Selby Road, Leeds Road, High Street (Kippax), Longdike Lane and Ridge Road to Ledston Luck. Ran in co-ordination with service 97. Jointly operated with West Riding Automobile Company.

No.	Route	Route Length miles	Frequency Mins.	No. of journeys daily	First bus	Last bus	Thro' fare	Av'ge Fare/ mile	Journey Time Mins.
97	BUS STATION to GARFORTH (Ninelands) and KIPPAX	8·49	60	Mon-Fri 16 Sat 16 Sun 6	06.53	22.53	14p	1·64p	33 Garfth 40 Kippax

Route: As service 89 to the Old George, Garforth Bridge, Selby Road and then via Wakefield Road, Alandale Crescent, Kingsway, Knightsway, Poplar Avenue, Barley Hill Road, Main Street, Church Lane and Ninelands Lane to Long Meadow Gate. Return from Long Meadow Gate via Long Meadows to Ninelands Lane. On weekdays (one) Saturdays (nine) and Sundays (one extra journey) were extended from Ninelands via the 89 route to Kippax War Memorial. Ran in co-ordination with service 89. Jointly operated with West Riding Automobile Company.

No.	Route	Route Length miles	Frequency Mins.	No. of journeys daily	First bus	Last bus	Thro' fare	Av'ge Fare/ mile	Journey Time Mins.
202	FASTAWAY BUS STATION to GARFORTH	8·16		Mon-Fri 2 ew Sat 10	07,30	17.38	15p	1·83p	Not given

Route: As service 97 to Selby Road and then via Lidgett Lane, Garforth, Church Lane and Ninelands Lane. Jointly operated with West Riding Automobile Company, but L.C.T. provided all the journeys.

No.	Route	Route Length miles	Frequency Mins.	No. of journeys daily	First bus	Last bus	Thro' fare	Av'ge Fare/ mile	Journey Time Mins.
203	FASTAWAY BUS STATION to GARFORTH	7-75		Mon-Fri 2 each way	07.15	18-08	15p	1·93p	Not given

Route: As service 89 to Wakefield Road and then via Barley Hill Road and Main Street to Garforth Town End. Jointly operated with West Riding Automobile Company, but L.C.T. provided all journeys.

No.	Route	Route Length miles	Frequency Mins.	No. of journeys daily	First bus	Last bus	Thro' fare	Av'ge Fare/ mile	Journey Time Mins.
204	FASTAWAY BUS STATION to KIPPAX	9·00		Mon-Fri 3 each way	07.20	17.48	16p	1·77p	Not given

Route: As service 202 to Selby Road and then via Leeds Road, Valley Road, Leeds Road and High Street to Kippax War Memorial. Jointly operated with West Riding Automobile Company who provided all journeys.

No.	Route	Route Length miles	Frequency Mins.	No. of journeys daily	First bus	Last bus	Thro' fare	Av'ge Fare/ mile	Journey Time Mins.
210	FASTAWAY BRIGGATE to MIDDLETON	5·70	10	Mon-Fri 12 each way	07.00	18.00	10p	1·75p	Not given

Route: From Briggate, The Headrow, Vicar Lane, New Market Street, Call Lane, Bridge End, Meadow Lane, Dewsbury Road, South East Leeds Motorway, Belle Isle Road, Town Street, Sharp Lane, Middleton Park Road, and Middleton Park Avenue to Thorpe Lane, Middleton. Return from Dewsbury Road, link road to Meadow Road, Victoria Road, Great Wilson Street, Meadow Lane and Bridge End to Briggate,

No.	Route	Route Length miles	Frequency Mins.	No. of journeys daily	First bus	Last bus	Thro' fare	Av'ge Fare/ mile	Journey Time Mins.
215	FASTAWAY KIRKGATE to WHINMOOR	5·06	15 and 30	Mon-Fri 9 ew Sat 21 ew	06.26	18.08	11p	2·17p	Not given

Route: Kirkgate, New York Street, York Street, Marsh Lane, York Road, Gipton Approach, Wykebeck Valley Road, South Parkway Approach, South Parkway, York Road, Baildon Drive, Sherburn Road, to Naburn Place. Return from Marsh Lane via Duke Street, St, Peter's Street, Eastgate and Vicar Lane to Kirkgate.

No.	Route	Route Length miles	Frequency Mins.	No. of journeys daily	First bus	Last bus	Thro' fare	Av'ge Fare/ mile	Journey Time Mins.
216	FASTAWAY KIRKGATE to SEACROFT	4·34	15 and 30	Mon-Fri 9 ew Sat 22 ew	06.53	18.00	10p	2·30p	Not given

Route: As route 215 to South Parkway then via Kentmere Avenue, North Parkway, York Road and Seacroft Avenue to Seacroft Town Centre.

No.	Route	Route Length miles	Frequency Mins.	No. of journeys daily	First bus	Last bus	Thro' fare	Av'ge Fare/ mile	Journey Time Mins.
221	FASTAWAY BRIGGATE to BELLE ISLE	4·15	10	Mon-Fri 12 ew	07.12	17.55	9p	2·16p	Not given

Route: As service 210 to Belle Isle Road and terminating at the Ring Road.

No.	Route	Route Length miles	Frequency Mins.	No. of journeys daily	First bus	Last bus	Thro' fare	Av'ge Fare/ mile	Journey Time Mins.
224	FASTAWAY HEADROW to SWARCLIFFE	5·15	14 and 30	Mon-Fri 17ew Sat 23 ew	06.32	18.07	11p	2·13p	About 18

Route: The Headrow, Park Row, City Square, Boar Lane, Duncan Street, Call Lane, New York Street, York Street, Marsh Lane, York Road, Barwick Road, Southwood Gate, Swarcliffe Drive to Mill Green Gardens. In the reverse direction from York Street via Harper Street, Kirkgate, New Market Street, Duncan Street, Boar Lane, City Square, Infirmary Street, East Parade and The Headrow to New Briggate.

No.	Route	Route Length miles	Frequency Mins.	No. of journeys daily	First bus	Last bus	Thro' fare	Av'ge Fare/ mile	Journey Time Mins.
225	FASTAWAY HEADROW to SWARCLIFFE	5·37	14 and 30	Mon-Fri 37ew Sat 22 ew	06.36	17.00	11p	2·04p	About 18

Route: As Route 224 to Swarcliffe Drive and then via Swarcliffe Avenue to Stanks Drive (junction with Stanks Rise).

No.	Route	Route Length miles	Frequency Mins.	No. of journeys daily	First bus	Last bus	Thro' fare	Av'ge Fare/ mile	Journey Time Mins.
233	FASTAWAY BUS STATION to COOKRIDGE	7·95	8	Mon-Fri 9 each way	07.30	17.55	11p	1·38p	Not given

Route: As route 33 to Otley Road and then via Ring Road (West Park), Spen Lane, Otley Old Road, Cookridge Lane, Green Lane, Wood Hill Road and Tinshill Road to Wrenbury Crescent.

No.	Route	Route Length miles	Frequency Mins.	No. of journeys daily	First bus	Last bus	Thro' fare	Av'ge Fare/ mile	Journey Time Mins.
235	FASTAWAY PARK ROW to ALWOODLEY	6·59	10 and 15	Mon-Fri 6 +7	07.45	17.55	11p	1·66p	Not given

Route: Park Row, City Square, Infirmary Street, East Parade, Calverley Street, Great George Street, Cookridge Street, Claypit Lane, Sheepscar link road, Chapeltown Road, Barrack Street, Sheepscar Street North, Scott Hall Road, King Lane, Alwoodley Lane to Sandmoor Drive. Return from Claypit Lane via Inner Ring Road, Westgate and The Headrow to Park Row.

No.	Route	Route Length miles	Frequency Mins.	No. of journeys daily	First bus	Last bus	Thro' fare	Av'ge Fare/ mile	Journey Time Mins.
236	FASTAWAY BUS STATION to TINSHILL	6·44	15	Mon-Fri 7 each way	07.05	17.50	11p	1·70p	Not given

Route: As route 36 to Otley Road and then via Ring Road (West Park), Spen Lane, Otley Old Road, Tinshill Lane, and Wood Nook Drive to the terminus at Silk Mill Drive.

No.	Route	Route Length miles	Frequ-ency Mins.	No. of journeys daily	First bus	Last bus	Thro' fare	Av'ge Fare/ mile	Journey Time Mins.
237	**FASTAWAY PARK ROW to SHADWELL**	6·95	15 and 20	Mon-Fri 6+5	07.25	17.38	11p	1·58p	Not given

Route: As service 235 to Scott Hall Road and then Ring Road (Moortown), Shadwell Lane, Main Street to the new turning circle at Shadwell.

265	**FASTAWAY BUS STATION to PUDSEY**	6·75	15	Mon-Fri 7 each way	07.00	17.50	11p	1·62p	Not given

Route: As route 65 to Stanningley Road, new Stanningley by-pass to Richardshaw Lane, and then via the 65 route to Chapeltown (Pudsey Cenotaph), Carlisle Road, Station Street and Greenside, Chapeltown.

272	**FASTAWAY PARK ROW to BRADFORD**	9·48	30	Mon-Fri 4 each way	07.15	17.40	12p	1·26p	About 30

Route: Park Row, City Square, Infirmary Street, East Parade, Westgate, Wellington Street, Wellington Road, Armley Road, Stanningley Road, Stanningley by-pass, Ring Road (Stanningley), Ring Road (Pudsey), Bradford Road, Dick Lane, Gipsy Street, Leeds Road to Petergate. Return from Petergate via Leeds Road, Bradford Road and outward route reversed to Westgate, The Headrow and Park Row.

Leyland PD2/1 396 in Chapeltown, Pudsey, on 30 April 1966. The Cenotaph is on the right hand side and on the left are some of the 1908 vintage former tramway poles still with their R.W.Blackwell design wrought iron decoration. *Author.*

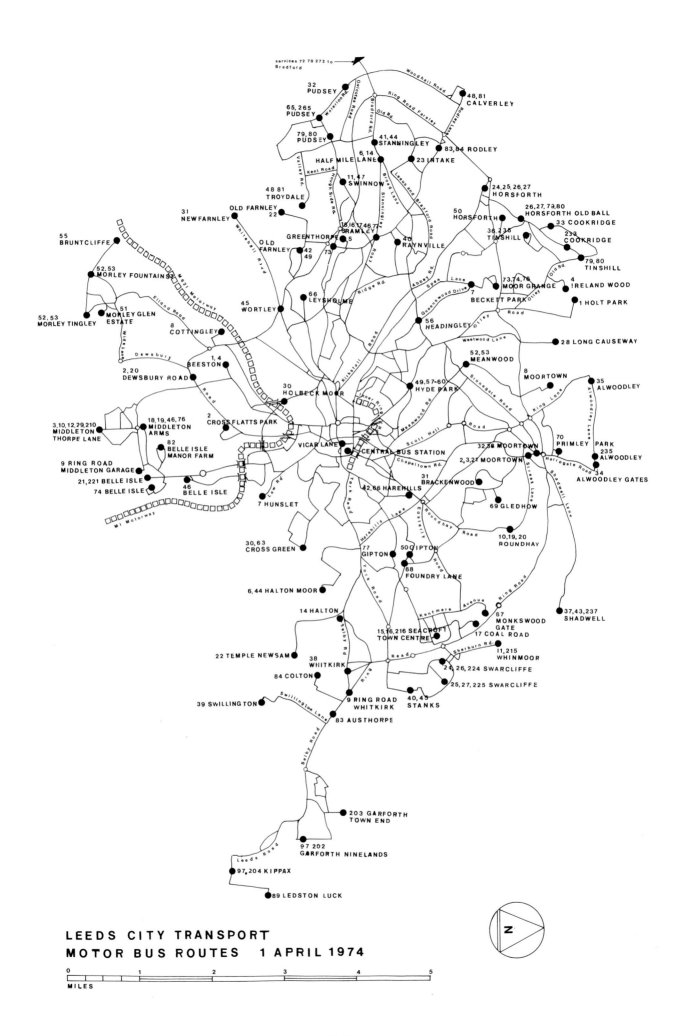

LEEDS CITY TRANSPORT
MOTOR BUS ROUTES   1 APRIL 1974

0   1   2   3   4   5
MILES

CHAPTER 87

Horsfields and Felthams 1953 to 1959

The Horsfield Cars

Before the announcement in 1953 that the tramway system was to be abandoned, some work on modernising the Horsfield cars had taken place. This is discussed in Volume 3 and had been initiated by the Tramways Rolling Stock Engineer, Victor J. Matterface. It comprised the fitting of new single blind destination boxes, Pullman sliding ventilators and electric bells and buzzers in place of Numa C air bells. Buzzers were used in the upper saloon and bells in the lower and indicated to the driver the whereabouts of the conductor. Cars not fitted with the Pullman sliding ventilators had their windows fixed to allow minimal ventilation. The ratchets, used to lower and raise the windows, at the head of the stairs were removed.

When built, the Horsfields were fitted with oval shaped cut glass lamp shades, but these had all been removed in 1949-50. The reason was stated to be so that a lower wattage lamp could be used. The redundant shades were said to have been, "sold to France." It is interesting that E.L.R.T. cars out of Lille, new in 1950, had identical shades to the Horsfield cars. Bow tubes, to guide the bow ropes, were fitted in place of pulley wheels on all Horsfields in 1953.

Work on fitting new destination indicators, Pullman sliding ventilators and electric bells and buzzers came to a halt in December 1952. After 1952 the cars fitted with G.E.C. equipment and G.D.Peters air wheel and track brakes (205-254) received little attention apart from repainting. Car 249 (17-12-1952) was the last to enter service with single blind indicators and electric bells and buzzers. Car 254 (5-12-1952) was the last to appear with Pullman type ventilators.

For a period of four years from November 1952 to the same month in 1956 only one Horsfield car, 177, (4-12-1954) received single blind destination boxes. However, the B.T-H. Horsfields were scheduled to remain until the end of the tramway system and in 1956 and 1957 no fewer than 14 cars of this type received the modification. Car 201 (5-9-1957) was the final one. This was VIctor Matterface's "last fling" on tramcar body improvements. He left his post on 30 September 1957 and after that date work on the remaining tramcar fleet was of the absolute minimum.

Similarly there had been a four years gap in the fitting of Pullman type ventilators in place of the old vertical sliding upper saloon windows. Five cars were fitted with the new ventilators in 1956-7, car 177 (10-5-1957) being the last. Six cars were fitted with electric bells and buzzers in the same period, car 175 (25-2-1957) was the final one.

The scrapping of the Horsfield cars began in December 1955 with the G.E.C. equipped cars. Apart from cars 220 and 242, which had Hoffman roller bearings, all other cars of the 205-254 series had SKF bearings to the axle boxes. Most of the B.T-H. equipped cars had Hoffman bearings but it seems that the Tramways Department had a preference for SKF. Many of these cars received SKF bearings and the scrapping of the 205-254 series resulted in more trucks with SKF bearings becoming available. From about 1952 to 1958, most of the B.T-H. cars received SKF bearings. There

Horsfield car 202 is seen here on the No.1 curve at the Corn Exchange on 22 August 1953. It was the last tram in Leeds to run under its own power and was given to Leeds City Museum, but unfortunately all the efforts of the Museum in tramway preservation ended in failure. *Author.*

Two Horsfield cars, 174 and 203, at Elland Road terminus on 18 June 1955. Both trams have the old style destination boxes. *Author.*

Horsfield car 239, with single blind destination boxes, pictured at the other end of the Elland Road tram route, Meanwood, on 25 June 1955, the last day of tramway operation. The Beckett's Arms replaced an older building of the same name in 1939 and closed its doors in 2004. The Art Deco style building was demolished in April and May 2007. *Author.*

Horsfield car 210 at the Stainbeck Lane spur, Chapeltown, on 30 May 1954. *Author.*

were also some controller alterations. In 1954-55 five Horsfields, cars 214, 229, 246, 252 and 253, were fitted with Metropolitan Vickers OK9B controllers from withdrawn Chamberlain cars. The Metropolitan Vickers controllers were very reliable and replaced the G.E.C. KA/1A controllers, which were more expensive to maintain. In April 1957 car 166 had its KA/1C controllers replaced by MVOK9Bs.

After the abandonment of the Moortown-Dewsbury Road service in September 1957, 30 Horsfields were withdrawn, all of the 205-254 series fitted with G.E.C. equipment and Peters air brakes. The B.T-H. Horsfields of the 151-204 series together with Felthams worked the basic services.

The first B.T-H. Horsfield to be withdrawn was 180 on 1 November 1957. It was, however, reinstated for service when 189 was damaged in a collision with a West Yorkshire bus on 15 March 1958. 189 exchanged numbers and trucks with car 180.

From 1955 to 1959 the practice of exchanging numbers between cars was prevalent and applied not only to the Horsfields, but also the Chamberlain and Feltham cars. Details are given in the tables. The official reason was given in reply to a letter from S. Jackson of Calverley in March 1956 and, in the words of Alderman Rafferty, briefed by tramway officials, was as follows:

"Vehicles are earmarked for scrapping over a period. During this period a minimum of expenditure is incurred on maintenance, but occasions arise where vehicles have a major failure or incur accident damage. In these cases, as the time factor is not great, substitution of vehicle numbers is made."

'The Yorkshire Evening News', 1 March 1956.

However, since the protagonists have passed on to higher places, it can perhaps now be revealed the real reason for the exchanges. It was an insurance "scam". If a car was slightly damaged in an accident and subject to an insurance claim it would not be repaired, but would exchange its number with that of a car in sound condition. The damaged car was then scrapped. The insurance money would be claimed and the insurance assessor shown the renumbered, apparently repaired, car.

The abandonment of the Middleton services and the Briggate-Moortown via Roundhay service in March 1959 resulted in the withdrawal of the remainder of the Peters, and several of the B.T-H Horsfield cars. Many Felthams were also withdrawn at this time. The Felthams had fire extinguishers and from March the remaining Horsfields in service were fitted with ex-Feltham fire extinguishers.

On the last day of tramway operation there were 28 B.T-H. Horsfield cars still in existence, 155, 156, 158, 160, 165, 169-173, 175-9, 181 186, 187, 189, 191-195, 198, and 200-202. Ten Horsfields formed the final procession of tramcars in Leeds, 178 being the ceremonial final car. Car 202 had the distinction of being the last tram in Leeds to run under its own power. This was on 26 April 1960 almost six months after the closure of the tramway system. Although the overhead wiring had been removed in Swinegate Depot, power was supplied to 202 by means of a jumper cable attached to a section box to one motor of the car. The three railcars were in Swinegate Depot at the time and 202 was used to tow them into position in order that they could be loaded for removal. In doing so it had to partly go out of the depot into Sovereign Street, a good three quarters of the car going outside.

202 had been given to Leeds City Museum by the Transport Department and was one of three Horsfield cars (160, 189 (ex-180) and 202) saved for preservation. The preservation schemes for 160 and 202 were unsuccessful and only one Horsfield, car 180, still survives. Fully restored, it runs at the National Tramway Museum, Crich, Derbyshire.

LEEDS CITY TRANSPORT HORSFIELD CARS 151-254   1950 to 1959

Double deck totally enclosed cars seating 37 up, 23 down. 90° direct staircases. 151-154 built by L.C.T., 155-254 by Brush Electrical Engineering Co. Ltd., Loughborough. 155-179, 205-229 wood slats to lower saloon floors, 180-204, 230-254 cork lower saloon floors. All had ruby glass ventilators in the lower saloon. Trucks: 151 Smith Pendulum, 152, 154-254 Peckham P35, 153 E.M.B. Flexible axle type R with SKF bearings. Motors: 151, 153, 205-254 2 x 50 h.p. G.E.C. WT 28S, 59:16 gear ratio; 152, 154-204 2 x 50 h.p. B.T-H. 509 A12, 58:15 gear ratio. Controllers: 151, 153, 205-254 G.E.C. KA/1A; 152 and 154 B.T.-H. B525A, 155-204 B.T.-H. B525C. 151, 205-254 had SKF and 152, 154-204 Hoffman roller bearings when new. Most retained trucks with their original bearings until the early 1950s; after that there were many truck exchanges. Only two cars of the 205-254 series, 220 and 242, had Hoffman bearings in place of SKF. All were fitted with folding platform doors c1934. Weight 13 tons 10 cwt. Cost £2,592 1s.6d. each.

For alterations to destination indicators, fitting of pullman sliding ventilators, electric bells and bow tubes please refer to Volume 3, Chapter 62.   HRB Hoffman Roller Bearings. SKF Skefco Roller Bearings.

No.	Date in Service	Truck bearing alterations		Mech. track brakes removed	Date last in service	Date and place scrapped	Notes
		HRB to SKF	SKF to HRB				
151	12-2-1930	---------------	---------------	---------------	28-3-1959	19-6-1959 BLN	
152	24-2-1930	---------------	---------------	---------------	2-6-1958	20-3-1959 CHL	X
153	1-7-1930	---------------	---------------	4-7-1958	28-3-1959	24-6-1959 BLN	
154	25-9-1930	12-3-1954	---------------	---------------	28-3-1959	8-6-1959 BLN	
155	14-3-1931	25-6-1957	---------------	25-6-1957	6-11-1959	20-1-1960 SD	
156	22-3-1931	c 1951	23-12-1953	---------------	7-11-1959	18-1-1960 SD	X
157	26-3-1931	19-3-1954	6-1958	---------------	15-3-1959	18-6-1959 BLN	
158	28-3-1931	17-7-1957	---------------	17-7-1957	7-11-1959	9-1-1960 SD	
159	2-4-1931	29-3-1956	---------------	---------------	15-1-1959	8-6-1959 BLN	
160	3-4-1931	25-1-1957	---------------	25-1-1957	7-11-1959	sold to M.R.P.S.	AA
161	15-4-1931	8-2-1954	---------------	12-6-1957	28-3-1959	24-6-1959 BLN	X
162	18-4-1931	---------------	---------------	---------------	28-3-1959	3-6-1959 BLN	X
163	23-4-1931	7-1956	---------------	1-3-1957	28-3-1959	4-6-1959 BLN	
164	24-4-1931	27-3-1957	---------------	27-3-1957	28-3-1959	19-6-1959 BLN	
165	28-4-1931	8-11-1952	---------------	14-3-1957	7-11-1959	29-12-1959 SD	
166	1-5-1931	1-1949	---------------	---------------	28-3-1959	18-6-1959 BLN	
167	2-5-1931	21-11-1952	---------------	28-2-1957	28-3-1959	24-6-1959 BLN	
168	7-5-1931	By 1939	---------------	7-1958	1-3-1959	8-6-1959 BLN	
169	9-5-1931	---------------	---------------	8-11-1956	5-5-1959	17-12-1959 SD	
170	12-5-1931	25-3-1953	---------------	27-12-1956	27-6-1959	22-12-1959 SD	
171	14-5-1931	10-5-1943	---------------	11-10-1956	7-11-1959	4-1-1960 SD	
172	16-5-1931	5-1957	---------------	5-1957	7-11-1959	24-12-1959 SD	
173	20-5-1931	18-5-1956	---------------	27-9-1957	7-11-1959	7-1-1960 SD	
174	22-5-1931	---------------	---------------	8-1958	28-3-1959	19-6-1959 BLN	Y
175	2-6-1931	14-11-1952	---------------	25-2-1957	7-11-1959	11-1-1960 SD	
176	29-5-1931	c 1945 22-9-1956	3-4-1953	22-9-1956	7-11-1959	8-1-1960 SD	
177	30-5-1931	1948	---------------	19-10-1956	7-11-1959	19-1-1960 SD	
178	4-6-1931	25-11-1952	---------------	1-1-1957	7-11-1959	23-1-1960 SD	
179	6-6-1931	--------------- 23-5-1958	3-3-1954	---------------	8-8-1959	12-1-1960 SD	
180	15-6-1931	1943 9-4-1958	10-10-1953 ---------------	9-4-1958	7-11-1959	sold to T.M.S.	X
181	13-6-1931	---------------	---------------	5-1957	7-11-1959	15-12-1959 SD	
182	17-6-1931	6-11-1952	---------------	8-1958	28-3-1959	26-6-1959 BLN	Y
183	20-6-1931	c 1947	---------------	---------------	27-3-1959	25-6-1959 BLN	
184	23-6-1931	1943 1954	17-12-1952 ---------------	30-11-1956	4-10-1958	21-4-1959 SAR	
185	25-6-1931	---------------	---------------	---------------	28-3-1959	26-6-1959 BLN	
186	26-6-1931	20-11-1956	---------------	20-11-1956	7-11-1959	12-12-1959 SD	
187	29-6-1931	31-1-1953	---------------	5-1957	7-11-1959	30-12-1959 SD	K
188	2-7-1931	5-12-1952	---------------	7-2-1957	28-3-1959	30-6-1959 BLN	
189	4-7-1931	5-7-1957	---------------	5-7-1957	15-3-1958	23-3-1959 CHL	
190	11-7-1931	28-11-1952	---------------	9-4-1957	26-3-1959	25-6-1959 BLN	
191	3-7-1931	18-1-1957	---------------	18-1-1957	7-11-1959	6-1-1960 SD	
192	9-7-1931	24-9-1952	---------------	28-10-1957	7-11-1959	28-12-1959 SD	
193	15-7-1931	5-12-1956	---------------	5-12-1956	6-11-1959	16-1-1960 SD	
194	17-7-1931	12-2-1954	---------------	18-4-1957	1-5-1959	13-1-1960 SD	
195	18-7-1931	1-8-1957	---------------	1-8-1957	7-11-1959	1-1-1960 SD	
196	22-7-1931	11-6-1952	13-3-1953	4-10-1956	25-3-1959	25-6-1959 BLN	
197	24-7-1931	2-1-1953	---------------	---------------	28-3-1959	26-6-1959 BLN	
198	25-7-1931	4-10-1956	---------------	---------------	7-11-1959	5-1-1960 SD	
199	28-7-1951	18-3-1953	---------------	---------------	28-3-1959	30-6-1959 BLN	
200	29-7-1931	c 1947	6-2-1954	---------------	7-11-1959	17-12-1959 SD	
201	30-7-1931	c 1947 5-9-1957	28-10-1952 ---------------	5-9-1957	29-4-1959	15-1-1960 SD	X

No.	Date in Service	Truck bearing alterations HRB to SKF	SKF to HRB	Mech. track brakes removed	Date last in service	Date and place scrapped	Notes
202	31-7-1931	30-10-1956	------------------	30-10-1956	1959	Leeds Museum	AB
203	20-8-1931	19-1-1952	9-3-1953	-----------------	28-3-1959	4-7-1959 BLN	
204	23-9-1931	4-10-1951		21-6-1945	28-3-1959	8-6-1959 BL	
205	15-8-1931	--------------	-----------------	--------------	10-2-1958	21-4-1959 SAR	
206	2-9-1931	--------------	-----------------	--------------	16-3-1957	16-9-1957 LRY	
207	9-9-1931	--------------	-----------------	--------------	24-3-1956	13-6-1956 LRY	collision
208	11-9-1931	--------------	-----------------	--------------	25-6-1955	8-8-1956 LRY	
209	28-8-1931	--------------	-----------------	--------------	28-3-1959	4-7-1959 LRY	
210	12-9-1931	--------------	-----------------	--------------	22-3-1955	4-5-1956 LRY	
211	15-9-1931	--------------	-----------------	--------------	16-3-1955	30-4-1956 LRY	
212	16-9-1931	--------------	-----------------	5-1958	28-3-1959	10-6-1959 BLN	
213	5-9-1931	--------------	-----------------	--------------	26-3-1959	1-7-1959 BLN	
214	18-9-1931	--------------	-----------------	--------------	27-3-1959	2-7-1959 BLN	
215	24-9-1931	--------------	-----------------	--------------	26-3-1959	2-7-1959 BLN	
216	19-9-1931	--------------	-----------------	8-1958	26-3-1959	1-7-1959 BLN	Y
217	23-9-1931	--------------	-----------------	--------------	5-3-1959	18-6-1959 BLN	
218	30-9-1931	--------------	-----------------	--------------	4-1955	4-5-1956 LRY	
219	25-9-1931	--------------	-----------------	8-1958	21-3-1959	30-6-1959 BLN	Y
220	30-9-1931	6-1950	c 1945	--------------	31-3-1955	8-8-1956 LRY	
221	9-1-1932	--------------	-----------------	--------------	26-3-1959	1-7-1959 BLN	
222	1-10-1931	--------------	-----------------	--------------	28-3-1959	9-6-1959 BLN	
223	3-10-1931	--------------	-----------------	--------------	17-2-1956	22-3-1956 LRY	
224	6-10-1931	--------------	-----------------	--------------	late 6-1955	15-12-1955 LRY	
225	7-10-1931	--------------	-----------------	--------------	3-1-1957	21-9-1957 LRY	
226	14-10-1931	--------------	-----------------	--------------	31-3-1955	16-8-1956 LRY	
227	10-10-1931	--------------	-----------------	--------------	10-1955	16-7-1956 LRY	
228	14-10-1931	--------------	-----------------	--------------	31-3-1955	5-7-1956 LRY	
229	21-10-1931	--------------	-----------------	--------------	28-3-1959	10-6-1959 BLN	
230	16-10-1931	--------------	-----------------	--------------	1-1955	16-8-1956 LRY	
231	17-10-1931	--------------	-----------------	--------------	27-11-1956	28-9-1957 LRY	
232	24-10-1931	--------------	-----------------	--------------	25-6-1955	8-8-1956 LRY	
233	31-10-1931	--------------	-----------------	--------------	25-6-1955	28-2-1956 LRY	
234	28-10-1931	--------------	-----------------	--------------	23-1-1955	13-6-1956 LRY	
235	31-10-1931	--------------	-----------------	--------------	9-4-1957	6-9-1957 LRY	
236	3-11-1931	--------------	-----------------	--------------	14-9-1957	21-4-1959 SAR	
237	5-11-1931	--------------	-----------------	--------------	late 3-1956	26-6-1956 LRY	
238	7-11-1931	--------------	-----------------	--------------	23-4-1956	13-6-1956 LRY	
239	13-11-1931	--------------	-----------------	--------------	25-1-1956	26-6-1956 LRY	
240	14-11-1931	--------------	-----------------	--------------	28-3-1959	10-6-1959 BLN	
241	17-11-1931	--------------	-----------------	--------------	12-1-1955	16-7-1956 LRY	
242	20-11-1931	14-5-1953	1950, 12-1956	--------------	3-3-1958	18-4-1959 CHL	
243	21-11-1931	--------------	-----------------	--------------	25-6-1955	5-7-1956 LRY	
244	23-1-1932	--------------	-----------------	--------------	24-2-1955	22-3-1956 LRY	
245	8-12-1931	--------------	-----------------	--------------	22-3-1954	5-7-1956 LRY	
246	11-12-1931	--------------	-----------------	5-1958	28-3-1959	15-6-1959 BLN	
247	12-12-1931	--------------	-----------------	8-1958	26-3-1959	15-6-1959 BLN	Y
248	15-12-1931	--------------	-----------------	--------------	3-3-1955	16-8-1956 LRY	
249	24-12-1931	--------------	-----------------	--------------	25-6-1955	13-6-1956 LRY	
250	24-12-1931	--------------	-----------------	--------------	3-5-1955	16-7-1956 LRY	
251	24-12-1931	--------------	-----------------	--------------	23-6-1956	26-6-1956 LRY	
252	2-1-1932	--------------	-----------------	9-1958	28-3-1959	8-6-1959 BLN	Y
253	2-1-1932	--------------	-----------------	--------------	28-3-1959	2-7-1959 BLN	
254	14-1-1932	--------------	-----------------	--------------	28-3-1959	4-7-1959 BLN	

NOTES

K   187 displayed with Feltham 526 and the three railcars at two "open" days at Swinegate Depot on Saturdays 15 and 29 August 1959.

X   At various times cars 152, 156, 161, 162, 180 and 201 had odd axle boxes i.e one pair of SKF bearings and one pair of Hoffman roller bearings.

Y   174, 182, 216, 219, 247 and 252 had the mechanical track brake operating wheels only removed.

AA   160 sold to the Middleton Railway Preservation Society. Left Swinegate 27-5-1961 for storage at the Middleton Railway, Leeds. After 202 was scrapped, 160 became the car allocated to Leeds City Museum. Vandalised and transferred to Armley Mills Industrial Museum, Leeds, 29-12-1973. Considered beyond restoration and burned by Museum staff 7-1981. P35 truck to Crich Tramway Museum for spares and returned to Armley Mills. Truck to Ludlam Street Museum, Bradford, 1985 and then to Beamish Open Air Museum, Durham. Truck is currently in use under Sunderland car 16.

AB   202 given to Leeds City Museum. Left Swinegate Depot 16-6-1960 for storage at the Middleton Railway, Leeds. Vandalised and dismantled 12-1963. Remains burned 11-1-1964.

LRY   Car burned in Low Fields Road Yard, Leeds.   SAR Car broken up in the yard of Joseph Standish Ltd. South Accommodation Road, Leeds.   CHL Car burned in the yard of Johnson's of Churwell, Leeds.   BLN Car burned in the Brown Lane, Holbeck, Leeds, yard of George Cohen & Son Ltd.   SD Car broken up in Swinegate Depot by J.W. Hinchliffe Ltd. scrap merchants, Kirkstall Road, Leeds.

179 was the only Horsfield with a high level destination indicator. It was photographed in Headingley Lane on 23 July 1955. *Author.*

Victor Matterface, the Tramways Rolling Stock Engineer, kept the Leeds trams looking smart in the 1950's. Horsfield car 212, newly repainted, is at Beeston terminus on 17 July 1955. The old property on the left was removed in early 1957. *Author.*

The Felthams

Of the ninety Feltham cars purchased by Leeds in 1950-1, only 68 had entered service by July 1953. Restoration of the cars had been abruptly halted in May 1952 on the instructions of Tom Parkinson, the bus rolling stock engineer.

The Felthams had not been the success predicted and when fully loaded were found to be under-powered on hills. Felthams were also being restored at Kirkstall Road Works to the detriment of the maintenance of other rolling stock. Cars 501-562, 579, 581, 583, 586, 588 and 590 were in service.

In May 1952 a number of partially restored cars were taken to the Belfast shed at Torre Road for storage. In October 1952 car 563 was moved from the Belfast shed into the main Torre Road Depot. At this time 564-570, 578, 580 and 589 were stored inside the "Belfast" shed, 571-577, 582, 584 and 585 were under the Swinegate Arches and 587 was in Kirkstall Road Works, on a temporary four-wheel truck. Of the stored cars, 563, 565, 566, 570, 580 and 589, had been repainted into the lined out Leeds red livery, but still required truck overhauls and minor work to enable them to enter service. The others, all fitted with bow collectors, were still in London Transport livery.

563 was returned to Kirkstall Road Works on 31 October 1952. Cars 565 and 567 were moved from the Belfast shed into Torre Road service depot on 17 November and on the same day 568, 569 and 578 were moved from the Belfast shed into the adjacent yard. Overnight from the 5th to Friday morning, 7 August 1953, all the stored Felthams at Torre Road were removed. The cars inside the depot and the Belfast shed were taken to Kirkstall Road Works and the ones in the yard to Swinegate Depot and Arches. The cars that had been stored in the open had suffered from exposure to the weather and vandalism.

Car 507 was out of service for, on 4 September 1952, it had been seriously damaged in a collision with car 92 at Oakwood. In August 1953 it was partly stripped and moved from Kirkstall Road Works to Swinegate Arches for storage. The car was beyond economical repair and was eventually burned in Low Fields Road Permanent Way Yard on 24 August 1955. It was the first car of its class to be scrapped.

It was rumoured in early 1954 that the stored Felthams were to be placed into service, but this was contradicted. In February 1954, the 20 or so extra staff - bodymakers, coach painters etc. - that had been employed on the restoration work at Kirkstall Road Works, were dismissed.

Many of the stored cars did eventually enter service. The first were 563, 565, 570 and 580 in February 1955. Being in the 1952 lined livery they resembled other Felthams, which had entered service at that time, except that all but 570 had painted headlamp frames. All earlier Felthams had chromium-plated headlamps. The usual alterations were made e.g. fitting of bell-strings along the lower saloon ceilings, with metal plating above the strings on the platforms, horizontal sliding windows on the interior cab doors and Leeds-type side indicators.

The ex-L.U.T. Felthams (Leeds 551-590) had Oerlikon-built G.E.C. type KB/5 AC/2 controllers. These had proved troublesome in London and were similarly a problem in Leeds. As an experiment car 563 was equipped with the Metropolitan Vickers type OK9B controllers recovered from a Chamberlain or ex-Southampton car. In being re-equipped the use of the line switch mechanism was eliminated. The MV controllers reduced skidding to a very considerable extent, but the rate of acceleration was generally reduced. The MV controllers were successful and by October 1955 all the L.U.T. Felthams in service had been fitted with this type of controller.

Felthams 535 and 548 at Whingate terminus on 19 June 1954. In the background is an L.C.T. motor derrick.
Author.

A view from another tram of the highest numbered Feltham, 590, at the Vinery Avenue tram stop in an almost traffic free York Road on 25 September 1954. In 1970-2 the section of York Road from the Woodpecker to Lupton Avenue was made into a three lane dual carriageway. At the next street, Ivy Street, a roundabout and underpass were formed under the road. Vinery Avenue and the buildings on the right still exist. *Author.*

The four trams were followed a few weeks later by the remainder of the cars, which had been partly overhauled, 564, 566, 567 and 589. Nos.564, 566 and 589 had been repainted in 1952 in the lined out red livery, but 567 was in the current unlined livery. 564, 566 and 567 had painted headlamp rims whereas those of 589 were chrome. 566 was fitted with MVOK9B controllers.

587, which had been in Kirkstall Road Works on its temporary truck for three years was the next car to appear in service. This was on 6 June 1955. It was fitted with MVOK9B controllers, but whereas all other Felthams had the interior woodwork stripped and french polished, 587 had a varnished finish. It was in the unlined red and white livery with the usual modifications and buzzer bells in addition. It was also the first to have the three-section driver's windscreen replaced with a one-piece window with a manual wiper pivoted in the bottom right-hand corner (viewed from the outside). This modification was done to most of the other Felthams over the next two years or so.

569 entered service on 15 July 1955. It had been one of the cars parked in the open in Torre Road Yard and had been extensively damaged by hooliganism. Almost every pane of glass, lamps and some other fittings were new to the car. It was finished in an identical manner to 587, but did not have the one-piece driver's windscreens.

In September 1955 eight of the Felthams still in London livery, were taken from Swinegate Arches to Chapeltown Depot for further storage. These were 572, 575-578, 582, 584 and 585. Cars 571, 573 and 574 remained under the Arches, but were moved to Chapeltown Depot in November. All the stored Felthams were now at Chapeltown Depot with the exception of 568, which, on 23 July 1955, had been transferred from Swinegate Depot to Kirkstall Road Works for overhaul. In February 1956 car 568 was joined by the other cars, which were transferred from Chapeltown Depot. 568 and also 573 entered service in April 1956. They had

the usual modifications, but the interior woodwork was not stripped to the original light oak finish. It was simply revarnished. Corroded chromium-plated handrails were not replated, but painted black.

Three further cars were renovated for service, 585 (11-6-1956), 574 (5-7-1956) and 582 (31-7-1956). They were treated in a similar manner to 568, 569 and 573, but car 574 still retained its chrome handrails. This left seven cars still unrestored: 571, 572, 575-578 and 584. They never were renovated for on 21 July 1956 the Tong Road tram services were abandoned. This left several Felthams surplus to requirements and 508, 516, 544, 551, 552, 555, 562, 579 and 580 were withdrawn and stored for scrap. The restoration of further Felthams could not be justified and from July to September 1956 cars 576, 577 and 578 were broken up in Kirkstall Road Works. The other four cars, 571, 572, 575 and 584, were taken to Low Fields Road Permanent Way Yard. There they were ignited in November 1956.

It was "downhill" for the Felthams from now on. Apart from some repainting no further modifications were done to the cars. 508, 555 and 579 had all been fitted with one-piece driver's windscreens after withdrawal from service, but never ran in this condition. 544 had had the old type windscreens removed, but new one-piece windows were never fitted. Cars 552, 555 and 579 were burned in December 1956, the first of the renovated cars (apart from 507) to be scrapped.

From 1957 to 1959, as with the Chamberlain and Horsfield cars, some Felthams exchanged numbers. The first was car 528, involved in an accident in Hunslet Road in July 1957. It exchanged numbers with 527. Others later exchanged numbers and these are listed in the tables.

A few Felthams were withdrawn from service in the first few months of 1957, some as a result of accident damage. The abandonment of the Moortown and Dewsbury Road tram services in September 1957 resulted

1420

in many more being sent to the scrap yard. In November 1957 the number of Felthams in stock had been reduced to exactly 50, some of the cars being already out of service.

During 1958 no trams were scrapped in Leeds, but the abandonment of the Middleton, Belle Isle and Moortown via Roundhay services in March 1959 resulted in 31 Felthams being taken out of service and scrapped. These included the last of the L.U.T. Felthams except for car 517 (ex-554). When the tramway system finally closed down in November 1959 the 19 Felthams still remaining were as follows: 501, 504-506, 512, 514, 515, 517, 523, 525, 526, 528, 529, 531, 532, 534, 538, 542 and 546. With the exception of cars saved for preservation, (501, 517 (ex-554) and 526.) all were broken up in January and February 1960.

Apart from cars already discussed in Chapter 66 of Volume 3 a number of cars are worthy of note. On 14 May 1952 car 503 appeared in service with experimental rubber pads over the bogie axle boxes in place of coil springs. These were not very successful and in November 1954 the car reappeared with normal bogie suspension.

On 20 January 1953, car 510 had the distinction of being the "star" in a B.B.C. Television film entitled "Tram to Temple Newsam". The film, which lasted for about three minutes, showed the car leaving the Yorkshire Penny Bank curve in Kirkgate, a view of the cab interior and two shots of the tram arriving at Temple Newsam terminus.

Other trams also appeared on the film. A television tour of the mansion followed the tram scenes.

In November 1955 car 530 was experimentally fitted with MVOK9B in place of its MVOK33B controllers. This was the only car of the M.E.T. type (501-550 series) to be fitted with MVOK9B controllers without line switch equipment. Unlike the L.U.T. cars the experiment does not appear to have been a success. On 14 November the following year 530 appeared re-equipped with MVOK33B controllers.

In April 1956, Car 523 entered service with a Horsfield Peters-type set of air-wheel brake equipment. The air-wheel brakes and quick air releases were unaltered. The air and sand pipes were lowered to accommodate the new fitting and there was a label in each cab reading "THIS CAR FITTED WITH P-35 'AIR WHEEL' CONTROL. USE HAND OPERATED BRAKE FOR PARKING ONLY". Cars 574, 582 and 585 were fitted with the same equipment when they appeared in June and July 1956. Car 301, ex-L.C.C. No.1, discussed later, had been similarly fitted in May of the same year.

Car 535 had a minor difference to the other Felthams in that the two-piece window at one end of the upper saloon was replaced with a single pane in March 1955. This followed a collision with Horsfield 246 on 23 November 1954. No other cars were similarly treated.

Feltham 588 at the tram stop in Moor Road, off Dewsbury Road, en route to Middleton on 7 September 1957. Just beyond the point where this photograph was taken the M1 Motorway (later redesignated the M621) was built across Moor Road. *Author.*

Car 301 ex-L.C.C. No.1

Before its entry into passenger service on 1 December 1951, 301 had received some minor modifications. A unitype or single blind indicator had been fitted and the lower deck side panels had been cut away at the bottom. This was done to allow the bogies to turn on the sharp curves in Kirkstall Road Works without fouling the panelling. A guard was placed between the bogies and a bow collector had been fitted. Pulley wheels to guide the bow rope had been placed at each end of the roof, but on 13 March 1953 these were replaced with bow tubes. All the Felthams had been fitted with bow tubes before they came into service.

As discussed in Volume 3, 301 had an eventful first day in service. Tom, Steward, at the time a car repairer at Chapeltown Depot, made some interesting observations.

As to the teething troubles which beset 301, the first of these was the fracturing of an air brake pipe through being fouled by one of the bogies as it swivelled when negotiating a curve, the skirt had been modified at Kirkstall Road by being cut away to allow the bogies to negotiate the tighter curves of the Leeds tracks, but it had not been foreseen that this particular air brake would foul. I forget which one it was, but I know that we fitted a new piece of pipe and put an extra link in it so that the bogie cleared it. For the first week or two after this 301 only ran on short duties whilst Oliver was supervising the drivers, and it wasn't until its first long duty that the next mishap occurred. We at Chapeltown only heard about it second hand, because apparently some cables caught fire under the platform at No.2 end, or at any rate the resistance end, and it was pushed into Swinegate Depot. They sent it to Kirkstall Road, where the cables were replaced, and we got the car back some time later. After this incident it was kept on short duties for a day or two, but it still kept blowing it's switches and even blew the line a few times. We tested the controller circuits time and time again to no avail, but eventually after going over the car with a fine tooth comb, we traced the trouble. The hand brake chain was swinging and catching the grids of the resistances thus causing a short circuit. This once again could be blamed on poor track maintenance, because 301, being lightly sprung, would roll like hell over some of the dropped joints, especially near Reginald Terrace, thus causing the hand brake chain to flap about in no uncertain manner. The only remedy was to make some "L" brackets and fasten a sheet of fibre to the underside of the platform with them between the hand brake chain and the resistances. No doubt that piece of fibre is still in place. Anyway, it was a great success, and we had no further trouble with 301. In fact some of our drivers even grew to like it."

Note: Oliver was Oliver Hamilton Anderson, the foreman at Chapeltown Depot. He died aged 84 on 1 May 1975.

From an article 'Flats snow and ice' by Tom Steward, 'Modern Tramway', February 1979.

Only one other alteration was made to 301 during its sojourn in Leeds. In May 1956 the car was fitted with Peters-type air-wheel brake operating sets recovered from a withdrawn Horsfield car, although the actual air-wheel brake mechanism was unaltered.

The former air-wheel brake operating equipment formed part of the head attachment to the controllers. It was retained, but was not now useable. This equipment had been operated in the opposite way to that on all other Leeds trams (except car 381) i.e "on" towards the driver and "off" away from him on 301. As a result the car was unpopular with drivers. After the closure of Chapeltown Depot in April 1955, 301 was transferred to Swinegate Depot and was restricted mainly to peak hour use. After the alteration it was seen on all day duties for about a week, but then reverted to peak hour working again.

301 continued to be used for peak hour only workings until the abandonment of the Moortown and Dewsbury Road tram services in September 1957. The car was donated by the Transport Department to the British Transport Commission for inclusion in the Commission's museum collection. It left Leeds for London on 26 November 1957. The vehicle was later taken to the National Tramway Museum, Crich, Derbyshire, where it still resides.

301 at Roundhay Park on 13 May 1956. *J.Pitts.*

569 looked pristine when it appeared in service in July 1955. It was photographed at New Inn terminus on 3 September 1955. *Author.*

In complete contrast to the photograph above, 583 presented a very sorry sight after being burned in Low Fields Road Yard on 7 September 1957. Unlike wooden-bodied trams, the steel framework of the Felthams remained upright and the cars were still recognisable after burning. 560 on the right hand side awaits a similar fate. The photograph was taken shortly after the flames had died down. *Author.*

LEEDS CITY TRANSPORT EX-LONDON FELTHAM CARS 501-590

Double deck totally enclosed cars seating 42 up 28 down built by the Union Construction Co. Feltham, Middlesex, in 1930-1. E.M.B. Maximum traction bogies with SKF roller bearings. Motors: 501-550 2 x 60 h.p. B.T-H. 509P1, 551-590 2 x 60 h.p. G.E.C. WT29. Controllers: 501-550 OK33B, 551-590 G.E.C. KB5. Air wheel and magnetic track and hand parking brakes. Overall length 40ft. 6in. Overall width 7ft. 1$\frac{3}{4}$in. Height to top of roof 15ft.1in.
Weight 18 tons 6 cwt. Classified UCC/1 501-550. UCC/2 551-590. Cost when new £3,420. Cost to Leeds £500 + £300 for overhaul.

No.	L.P.T.B. No.	Date in service	One-piece windscreen fitted	MVOK9B controllers fitted	Date last in service	Date and place scrapped	Notes
501	2099	17-12-1949	4-10-1955		7-11-1959	sold	A
502	2097	3-10-1950	21-11-1955		28-3-1959	13-7-1959 BLN	
503	2077	3-10-1950	5-7-1956		26-4-1957	8-8-1957 LRY	
504	2082	24-10-1950	28-10-1955		27-10-1959	10-2-1960 SD	
505	2069	24-10-1950	11-5-1956		8-8-1957	10-10-1957 LRY	B
506	2066	6-11-1950	16-12-1955		1 4-5-1959	28-1-1960 SD	
507	2070	14-11-1950	--------------		4-9-1952	24-8-1955 LRY	C
508	2073	3-1-1951	1956		3-1956	30-8-1957 LRY	D
509	2078	15-12-1950	11-8-1955		29-12-1958	23-7-1959 BLN	
510	2074	22-11-1950	13-8-1956		28-3-1959	9-7-1959 BLN	
511	2105	1-12-1950	5-6-1956		7-8-1957	12-10-1957 LRY	E
512	2088	19-1-1951	9-6-1956		7-11-1959	17-2-1960 SD	
513	2100	12-12-1950	7-6-1956		11-12-1957	20-4-1959 CHL	
514	2115	10-1-1951	9-3-1956		7-11-1959	22-2-1960 SD	
515	2093	26-1-1951	13-9-1955		30-4-1959	13-2-1960 SD	
516	2080	18-1-1951	--------------		3-1957	18-9-1957 LRY	
517	2118	24-1-1951	12-9-1955		28-1-1959	26-5-1959 SAR	G
518	2087	15-2-1951	14-1-1956		15-1-1959	24-7-1959 BLN	
519	2084	3-2-1951	21-11-1957		26-3-1959	16-7-1959 BLN	E, F
520	2081	27-1-1951	24-11-1955		7-11-1959	1-2-1960 SD	B
521	2072	24-9-1951	20-10-1955		26-3-1959	11-7-1959 BLN	
522	2108	7-2-1951	19-10-1955		28-2-1958	28-5-1959 SAR	
523	2096	18-9-1951	1956		7-11-1959	3-2-1960 SD	
524	2076	28-2-1951	19-9-1955		4-10-1958	3-4-1959 CHL	H
525	2083	6-3-1951	17-10-1955		6-11-1959	10-12-1959 SD	
526	2085	7-3-1951	13-7-1956		7-11-1959	sold to Seashore	J
527	2075	13-3-1951	4-2-1956		10-8-1957	7-10-1957 LRY	K, L
528	2086	23-3-1951	2-7-1956		1 1-7-1957	3-9-1957 LRY	K
529	2116	2-4-1951	12-9-1955		7-11-1959	12-2-1960 SD	
530	2071	30-3-1951	12-11-1955	12-11-1955	8-8-1957	19-10-1957 LRY	M
531	2106	21-4-1951	13-8-1956		7-11-1959	16-2-1960 SD	
532	2104	7-4-1951	6-3-1956		7-11-1959	20-2-1960 SD	
533	2092	19-4-1951	--------------		21-5-1957	23-8-1957 LRY	
534	2102	19-4-1951	6-10-1955		18-6-1959	8-2-1960 SD	
535	2119	1-5-1951	23-9-1955		27-3-1959	29-7-1959 BLN	
536	2110	27-6-1951	23-9-1955		12-12-1958	25-7-1959 BLN	
537	2089	15-6-1951	18-1-1956		3-5-1957	24-8-1957 LRY	
538	2094	28-5-1951	28-11-1955		7-11-1959	29-1-1960 SD	
539	2068	17-5-1951	23-3-1956		7-11-1959	19-2-1960 SD	L
540	2114	7-6-1951	--------------		28-9-1957	14-10-1957 LRY	
541	2107	1-7-1951	30-9-1955		10-1956	14-9-1957 LRY	
542	2098	21-6-1951	28-9-1955		7-11-1959	27-1-1960 SD	
543	2095	20-6-1951	19-10-1955		9-4-1957	8-8-1957 LRY	
544	2090	6-7-1951	1956		6-1956	24-9-1957 LRY	D
545	2111	16-7-1951	--------------		23-9-1957	29-10-1957 LRY	N
546	2101	30-7-1951	15-2-1956		2-5-1959	5-2-1960 SD	
547	2112	28-7-1951	4-6-1956		28-9-1957	25-10-1957 LRY	
548	2103	24-8-1951	29-12-1955		26-3-1957	20-8-1957 LRY	
549	2117	24-8-1951	22-9-1955		28-3-1959	30-7-1959 BLN	
550	2079	31-8-1951	10-5-1956		27-9-1957	28-10-1957 LRY	
551	2139	31-10-1951	--------------	12-10-1955	31-8-1956	30-9-1957 LRY	
552	2164	2-11-1951	17-5-1956	17-6-1955	7-1956	13-12-1956 LRY	
553	2150	12-11-1951	25-1-1956	9-7-1955	27-9-1957	1-11-1957 LRY	
554	2138	30-11-1951	18-5-1956	19-9-1955	30-4-1959	sold to MRPS	G
555	2131	23-11-1951	1956	18-4-1955	3-1956	11-12-1956 LRY	D
556	2152	14-12-1951	4-2-1956	13-5-1955	2-3-1959	9-7-1959 BLN	
557	2120	4-12-1951	17-11-1955	26-5-1955	26-1-1959	3-4-1959 SAR	O
558	2121	12-12-1951	29-10-1955	12-9-1955	27-9-1957	26-10-1957 LRY	
559	2137	7-1-1952	25-11-1955	28-3-1955	28-9-1957	5-11-1957 LRY	
560	2148	16-1-1952	30-5-1956	28-2-1955	27-2-1957	12-9-1957 LRY	

No.	L.P.T.B. No.	Date in service	One-piece windscreen fitted	MVOK9B controllers fitted	Date last in service	Date and place scrapped	Notes
561	2125	10-4-1952	8-10-1955	29-4-1955	20-3-1959	17-7-1959 BLN	P
562	2161	24-12-1951	-------------	29-6-1955	24-8-1956	5-10-1957 LRY	
563	2140	1-2-1955	25-8-1956	1-2-1955	10-10-1957	10-4-1959 CHL	
564	2123	5-3-1955	14-6-1956	18-10-1955	28-3-1959	28-7-1959 BLN	O
565	2126	26-2-1955	29-8-1956	10-10-1955	26-3-1959	30-7-1959 BLN	H
566	2134	18-3-1955	22-6-1956	18-3-1955	10-10-1957	4-4-1959 CHL	
567	2136	4-4-1955	22-6-1956	20-6-1955	21-10-1957	10-4-1959 CHL	
568	2127	4-4-1956	4-4-1956	4-4-1956	28-3-1959	10-8-1959 BLN	
569	2132	15-7-1955	31-8-1955	15-7-1955	28-3-1959	10-8-1959 BLN	
570	2141	12-2-1955	1-9-1956	28-10-1955	23-9-1957	23-10-1957 LRY	
571	2155	---------------	--------------	-----------	7-4-1951*	10-11-1956 LRY	
572	2128	---------------	--------------	-----------	7-4-1951*	9-11-1956 LRY	
573	2124	16-4-1956	16-4-1956	16-4-1956	17-2-1959	6-8-1959 BLN	
574	2129	5-7-1956	5-7-1956	5-7-1956	28-3-1959	11-7-1959 BLN	
575	2156	---------------	--------------	--------------	7-4-1951*	14-11-1956 LRY	
576	2151	---------------	--------------	--------------	7-4-1951*	7-1956 KW	
577	2145	---------------	--------------	--------------	7-4-1951*	8-1956 KW	
578	2142	---------------	--------------	--------------	7-4-1951*	9-1956 KW	
579	2146	21-3-1952	1956	25-6-1955	3-1956	12-12-1956 LRY	D
580	2149	18-2-1955	13-6-1956	27-5-1955	16-9-1956	31-7-1957 LRY	Q
581	2143	26-1-1952	17-5-1956	1955	1-1-1958	23-4-1959 SAR	
582	2133	31-7-1956	31-7-1956	31-7-1956	28-3-1959	10-8-1959 BLN	
583	2160	6-5-1952	31-5-1956	2-7-1955	29-3-1957	7-9-1957 LRY	
584	2135	---------------	--------------	--------------	7-4-1951*	15-11-1956 LRY	
585	2159	11-6-1956	11-6-1956	11-6-1956	27-2-1959	30-7-1959 BLN	
586	2157	5-2-1952	4-2-1956	31-10-1955	13-9-1957	7-10-1957 LRY	
587	2147	6-6-1955	6-6-1955	6-6-1955	15-1-1959	12-5-1959 SAR	P
588	2153	12-2-1952	12-6-1956	12-3-1955	9-10-1957	30-4-1959 SAR	
589	2154	28-3-1955	15-6-1956	11-6-1955	28-3-1959	18-7-1959 BLN	
590	2158	27-5-1952	10-12-1955	15-7-1955	30-8-1957	16-10-1957 LRY	

Notes

*   Car withdrawn from service in London on 7-4-1951 on the closure of the Purley and Croydon tram routes.

A   501 to British Transport Commission Museum, Clapham, London. Left Leeds 1-12-1959 arriving at Clapham two days later. Restored to its original condition as Metropolitan Electric Tramways car 355. Currently in storage at Acton.

B   505 and 520 exchanged numbers on 30-8-1957.

C   507 seriously damaged in collision with car 92 on 4-9-1952. It did not return to service.

D   Cars 508, 555 and 579 fitted with one-piece windscreens after withdrawal from service. Car 544 had the three windows at each end removed, but one-piece windscreens were not fitted.

E   Cars 519 and 511 exchanged numbers 19-8-1957.

F   In July 1952 an experiment to convert 519 into a single deck trailer car was made. It was unsuccessful.

G   517 and 554 exchanged numbers 11-2-1959. 517 (ex-554) sold to Middleton Railway Preservation Society. Left Swinegate for Middleton 26-3-1961. Vandalised and the body was burned on 20 April 1968. The bogies were saved and purchased by the Tramcar Sponsorship Organisation in January 1970. To Tramway Museum Society Clay Cross Store, then to Bonwell Street, London. Restored and now under London Transport E1 1622 at the National Tramway Museum, Crich.

H   524 and 565 exchanged numbers 24-11-1958.

J   526 withdrawn 18 April 1959, but retyred and returned to service 6 August 1959. Displayed with Horsfield 187 and the three railcars at two "open" days at Swinegate Depot 15 and 29 August 1959. Sold to the Seashore Electric Railway, Kennebunkport, Maine, U.S.A. Left Leeds 7-3-1960 and travelled via Liverpool, the United States Lines cargo vessel "American Press" to Boston and arrived at Kennebunkport 28-3-1960. Some cosmetic restoration was carried out in the 1970's. The car is currently in L.P.T.B. livery, partly dismantled and in a very poor state of repair.

K   Cars 527 and 528 exchanged numbers 25-7-1957.

L   Cars 539 and 528 (ex-527) exchanged numbers 31-8-1957.

M   530 fitted with MVOK9B controllers 12-11-1955 in place of MVOK33B. Removed and MV0K33Bs refitted 14-11-1956.

N   545 seriously damaged in a collision with a lorry in York Road on 23-9-1957 and withdrawn.

O   557 and 564 exchanged numbers 13-2-1959.

P   561 and 587 exchanged numbers 6-2-1959.

Q   580 damaged in a collision near Balm Road Railway Bridge 16-9-1956 and withdrawn.

LRY   Car burned in Low Fields Road Permanent Way Yard, Leeds.

SAR   Car broken up in the yard of Joseph Standish Ltd. South Accommodation Road, Leeds.

CHL   Car burned in the yard of Johnson's of Churwell, Leeds.

BLN   Car burned in the Brown Lane, Holbeck, Leeds, yard of George Cohen & Son Ltd.

SD   Car broken up in Swinegate Depot by J.W.Hinchliffe Ltd. scrap merchants, Kirkstall Road, Leeds.

KW   Car broken up in Kirkstall Road Works.

Feltham 573 had not been in service long when this view was taken at the Chapeltown terminus at Stainbeck Lane on 13 August 1956. Part of the Chapel Allerton Methodist Church can be seen on the left. The Church was demolished in January and February 1982. *Author.*

Car 542 loads at the Reginald Terrace tram stop, Chapeltown Road, on the final day of tramway operation on route 2, Saturday, 28 September 1957. At this period, even on a Saturday, the road was free of motor traffic. *Author.*

The Railcars

The events which led to the introduction of modern single deck railcars in Leeds are fully discussed in Volume 3. Briefly, the idea of introducing single deck cars had originated as early as 1933. The General Manager, William Vane Morland, had said that there was a vision of an underground "cut and cover" system in Leeds linked to express tram routes. Single deck cars would be required.

Vane Morland's visit to the U.S.A. in 1936 confirmed his view that the modern single deck P.C.C. car was the ideal solution to the transport problem in Leeds. His Memorandum No.2 prepared in 1944 had proposed an underground system in the city centre coupled with the tramway routes and worked by P.C.C. cars.

Unaware of Vane Morland's proposals, Bertrand Mather, an engineering scientist, had also prepared a report advocating the introduction of P.C.C. cars into the city.

During the latter part of 1944, a single deck tramcar was purchased from Sunderland Corporation for experiments in Leeds. This was Sunderland car 85 which had been out of service in Sunderland from the outbreak of war. Although it entered service after the more modern railcars, for convenience it is discussed first.

Railcar 600, ex-Sunderland 85

This car, new in 1931, was the subject of an article, which appeared in the 'Tramway & Railway World' for 12 March of that year. The car was built to the design of Charles Hopkins, the General Manager of the Sunderland Corporation Tramways Department. It was to be used to compare the operation of a modern single deck tramcar

with similar motor buses of the day. The route selected for the experiment was the Villette Road tramway, which had a low bridge in Tatham Street and was restricted to single deck vehicles.

The track on Villette Road was worn-out as also were the former antiquated 34-seat single deck tramcars, which had worked it. Before coming to a decision to abandon the tramway or reconstruct the track, the Sunderland Tramways Committee had authorised Hopkins to design the experimental car. The route had ceased to run on 27 August 1930, and it was found that with buses there had been a 20·5% increase in the number of passengers and a 14·44% mileage increase.

85 made its first trial trip on 6 March 1931 and entered passenger service a few days later on 11 March. It was an instant and sustained success. The car was fairly typical for its period having end entrances and nine windows on each side of the saloon with two hinged ventilators over each window. It was rather flat fronted and had a single headlamp. Seating 54 in comparison with the former small capacity cars, it was popular with passengers and was the first Sunderland tram to have upholstered seats. The "well appointed", transverse "comfortably sprung and upholstered" red leather seats were in a 2/2 arrangement with four passengers on short longitudinal seats at the end of the saloon. There were electric heaters on each side of the car and 3/16in. thick rubber tiling on the floor. It was said that there was a "perfect fit" at the edges of the floor trap doors, in order to "exclude truck noise." The platform steps were said to be "low".

There were six external ventilators in the roof while

Railcar 600 at Hunslet terminus on 10 March 1955. *Author.*

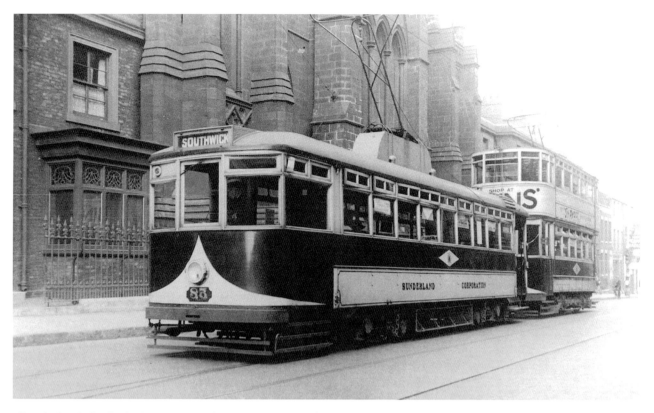

Sunderland single deck car 85 on the Villete Road to Southwick route in the late 1930's. *H.B.Priestley/National Tramway Museum.*

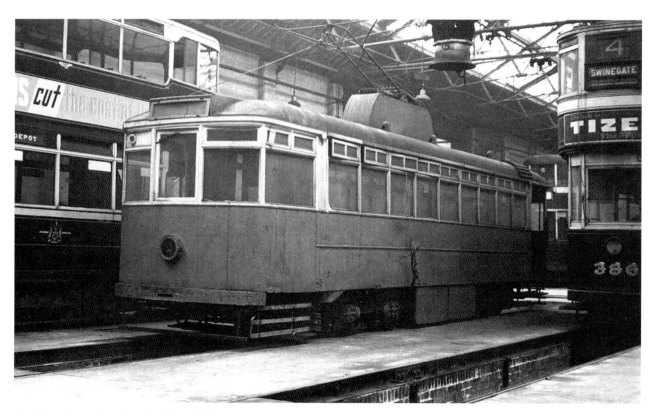

The Sunderland car looked like this for several years. It was painted in a drab grey undercoat with cream window frames and stood on a spare set of E.M.B. "Heavyweight" bogies.   The late Bob Parr photographed the car in Kirkstall Road Works on 3 October 1948. *R.B.Parr/National Tramway Museum.*

Four and a half years after the photograph on the opposite page was taken, the Sunderland car, now Leeds 600, presented a very different appearance. Rebuilding was well advanced on 7 June 1952. The tram on the right is Chamberlain car 120. *Author.*

the side ventilation above the windows was centrally operated. On each bulkhead there were two collapsible type ventilators and above the doors sliding air slots. A small, geared roller blind destination box was fixed over the driver's window, and non-geared side destination boxes were hung in the side windows on the left of the entrances. There was "brilliant illumination" provided by twelve 40 watt Silvalux lamps.

The car body was built by the Brush Electrical Engineering Co. Ltd. of Loughborough and was 41ft. 1½ in. long. Brush maximum traction bogies with Hoffman rolling bearings were employed having a 4ft.0in. wheel base and 27in. and 20in. diameter wheels. Two 50 h.p. G.E.C. type WT28ES motors were provided and were of the self ventilated inter-pole type giving "rapid acceleration" to a speed of 35 m.p.h.

The car had English Electric CDB2 controllers, E.M.B. air wheel brakes, magnetic track brakes and a conventional hand brake. The controllers must have been later replaced for when the car arrived in Leeds it was fitted with English Electric type K4 controllers.

Nick-named the "covered wagon" in Sunderland, the success of No.85 led to the tramway track being relaid. However, the alteration of the bridge in Tatham Street in 1932-33 meant that double deckers could be used on the route and 85 was used less frequently. Although it continued to run on the Villette Road-Southwick route, by the outbreak of war it was considered surplus to requirements and was placed in storage.

Unfortunately the car's date of withdrawal has not been recorded. Apart from the change of controller, the only alteration made to the car in Sunderland was the fitting of a tower on the roof to support a bow collector. This took place in late 1931 when the original roof mounted trolley was removed.

In October 1944 when the Leeds Transport Committee was considering Vane Morland's report on the future of the tramway system, it had given him authority to purchase a "tramcar bogie truck for experimental purposes." The following month, however, this had taken the form of a complete single deck bogie car, Sunderland 85. The purchase price agreed with Sunderland Corporation was £375. Probably due to wartime censorship conditions, the arrival of the car was not referred to in the press or in the minutes of the Transport Committee.

Nocturnal trips appear to have been made by the car, but the Brush maximum traction bogies were not suited to Leeds conditions. About August 1945 the bogies had been replaced with the E.M.B. L.C.C. class 6A radial axle "Heavyweight" bogies and MVOK29B controllers from ex-London HR/2 car 279. At the same time 'The Modern Tramway' had reported that a second single deck tramcar was under construction in Kirkstall Road Works, but this was simply a framework of timber, mounted on a truck, to test clearances.

As discussed in Volume 3, several night time tests took place and some of these were reported in the local press. Final major testing took place from 24 to 27 May 1946 mainly on the Middleton route. A Middleton bogie, usually 262, and a motor derrick accompanied the car. The tests were a failure. Problems were encountered with clearances on curves and there was also trouble with rotation of the bogies. Within days the equipment was removed and returned to car 279. Following a repaint 279 was returned to service in June 1946.

The body of 85, repainted in flat grey undercoat with cream window frames, was fitted with a spare pair of E.M.B. Heavyweight bogies and then remained idle in Kirkstall Road Works. During the latter part of 1946 some minor work was carried out on the body apparently as a spare time job for the body shop staff.

In December 1947 the vehicle was moved from Kirkstall Road Works to the Belfast shed in Torre Road Depot Yard for storage. There it remained until July the following year when it was returned to Kirkstall Road Works. It was prepared for further testing and in October 1948 given the fleet number 288. This was painted, in Gill Sans numerals, on the grey dashes.

Brian Render in his book, 'Leeds Tramcars, a Penny Ride to Town, 1933-1950', gives details of the testing. On the night of 12 October 1948, 288, with Middleton bogie 265, went on all routes, except Beeston, to check for overhangs on tight curves. It went out again on the night of 28 October with an accompanying Middleton bogie car to Middleton and as far as was possible on the Belle Isle extension. The two cars travelled side by side in the same direction testing track clearances and the position of the bow collector. Later a curve tester (a wooden platform on bogies fitted with a central tower and bow collector) was constructed to test clearances.

As a result of the tests it was found that it was not necessary to shorten the car, but merely to taper the ends as was being done on new cars supplied to Amsterdam and other continental cities. Plans were drawn up for rebuilding the car with centre entrances and tapered ends.

'The Modern Tramway' reported that it was hoped to provide resilient wheel bogies for the car and also to construct an experimental trailer car. Vane Morland, the General Manager, favoured trailer car operation and the two-car tram was to be tried on the new Middleton circular tram route. A trailer car was not constructed, however, but, as discussed in Volume 3, an abortive attempt had been made in July 1952 to convert Feltham car 519 into a single deck trailer car. The upper saloon was stripped down, but the experiment was not successful as it was found that the upper and lower saloon steel framework was integral.

Work began in earnest on 288 in early 1949, the body being cut in two to allow for a new drop frame to be inserted for the centre entrance. The flat body ends were removed and tapered to allow for the clearances on curves.

Following this burst of activity, work on the car ceased in December 1949. No reason appears to have been given, but it seems probable that the new General Manager, A.B. Findlay, had different ideas about the appearance of the vehicle. Certainly the finished car showed many differences from the original 1949 general arrangement drawings. Four side windows had been proposed on each side of the central entrance whereas the car finished up with five. The front of the car was simplified and less streamlined than on the original drawings. A proposed drop windscreen was omitted. The 1949 drawings do not show an advertisement panel and the bow tower was different, being of the Blackpool pattern. What is apparent is that very little of Sunderland 85 survived the alterations. The central part of the roof was original as also were part of the underframe and a few of the side windows.

The car lay idle for 18 months, work beginning again in June 1951. During this period the only item of note was the allocation, in December 1950, of the number 600 in place of 288. Work progressed rapidly during the latter part of 1951. By September the framework for the cabs had been fitted and early the following year the exterior panelling was completed and externally the car presented a "finished" appearance. Fitting out took a further two years, little work being done during 1953, before final completion in August 1954.

No record has been found of the total cost of the alterations. For much of the time the work was regarded as a spare time job in Kirkstall Road Works. Most of the equipment fitted to the car was second hand and it seems that no detailed costs were kept.

Resilient-wheeled bogies were not fitted, but a set of E.M.B. bogies was purchased from Liverpool Corporation, believed to have come from one of the trams destroyed in the Green Lane fire of 7 July 1947. They were completely overhauled and fitted under the car in May 1952. The wheels were 27in. in diameter. There were four motors each of 45 h.p. of the G.E.C. WT184 type. The gear arrangement was standard helical spur with a ratio of 71:14. Also in 1952, an experimental set of Metropolitan Vickers contactor equipment, formerly on London E/1 type semi-streamlined tram 1103, and purchased from London Transport, almost as new, was fitted in the new roof tower. The car had a normal length bow. In Sunderland an elongated bow had been employed. A pair of unused Metropolitan Vickers type AN controllers, ex-Liverpool, were also fitted to 600.

By January 1953, the tram had been almost completed. The interior bodywork had been finished in french-polished oak with Formica side panelling and white Formica ceiling panels. Saloon lighting was by four main lamps with holder covers from a Bradford Corporation tram. There were ten side lamps, five under each luggage rack, Only the seat cushioning, in red moquette with leather edging, remained to be fitted. The transverse seating was ex-Southampton, reupholstered by Messrs, Siddall & Hilton Ltd., whereas the longitudinal seating was made by the Department. Flooring was of cork and rubber and the grab handles were ex-London Transport.

The advertisement boards along the sides of the roof were fitted during 1952 and the exterior bodywork received a further coat of grey undercoat. The car now looked vaguely similar to the other railcars, which were put into service in June 1953. There were exit doors from the driver's cabs both on his right and into the car interior. New single headlamps were fitted as well as trafficators on the dashes. Standard Leeds destination boxes were fitted over the driver's cabs and entrances.

During February 1953 some testing of the car was carried out in the early mornings, but the car then lay idle for over a year. There were stirrings again in early 1954 when 600 made night-time test runs, mainly between Kirkstall Road Works and Kirkstall Abbey, between Halton and Temple Newsam and on the Middleton circular route. During the last two weeks of the Kirkstall Abbey service it made day-time tests to the Abbey. In July 1954 all work, including painting was completed.

The air-wheel, air-track and magnetic brakes were manufactured by the E.M.B. Company. Instead of the air wheel brake operating from the controller attachment, a separate E.M.B. air wheel brake operating handle, of the same type as fitted to railcar 601, was fitted to the control panel. There was a Westinghouse low pressure alarm.

The saloon capacities were 14 standing and 17 seated, with allowance for eight to stand on the platform. One of the saloons was "non-smoking". The ticket boxes were of the Feltham type. The interior labelling was covered by transparent Perspex panels - in a similar manner to railcars 601 and 602. The top half of the driver's windscreen could be opened and the car carried a portable tow bar. The unladen weight was 15 tons 15cwts.

Car 600 was finished in a red livery with white window surrounds and advertisement panels, grey roof and tower. The streamlining to the front of the car was not picked out and there was no lining, presumably for economic reasons. The bogies and lifeguards were finished in the usual brownish red. The fleet numbers, in red, were positioned over the central entrances and the cab interiors were grey.

In 1948 the car was given the classification L1, but following the withdrawal of the last of the ex-Hull cars in 1951 was reclassified G1. The class description was never painted on the vehicle.

Although "officially" designed by the General Manager, the detailed drawings were prepared by a mechanical engineering draughtsman, G.G. Hilditch. Geoff Hilditch also supervised some of the reconstruction work on the car. Hilditch worked for the Transport Department from 1950 leaving the service of the Corporation on 31 October 1953. He became well known as the General Manager of the Halifax and later the Leicester transport undertakings.

In November 1951 Hilditch also produced drawings for "modernising" the class B2 Chamberlain cars (76-150), built by the English Electric Company. Platform doors, destination boxes in the upper deck tins and more sumptuous leather upholstery were proposed. However no Chamberlains appeared with Hilditch's modifications.

On Wednesday, 4 August 1954, car 600 made its first entry into passenger service on route 25, Swinegate-Hunslet.

That is virtually the end of the story as far as 600 in Leeds is concerned, for it was confined to the two miles long Hunslet route for the whole of its short time in service. Although 600 had powerful motors and was designed for high-speed operation on reserved track routes, it was never allowed to demonstrate its capabilities. On few occasions was it seen away from Hunslet. On 22 November 1956 it was observed in Dewsbury Road on driver training duties and made occasional trips around the Moortown-Roundhay circular route on engineering test journeys.

600 was taken out of service in December 1955 and returned on 27 June 1956 following a partial bogie overhaul.

Being regarded as "non-standard", the car was last used in service on Friday, 27 September 1957, the day before the abandonment of the Moortown-Dewsbury Road tram services. No modifications were made to the vehicle between 1954 and 1957 and adverts were never painted on the advertisement panels. The car remained in storage in Swinegate Depot until the end of the tramway system and it was sold to a Maurice J. O'Connor on 11 April 1960 for £100. On 6 May 1960 No. 600 was taken to the Crich Tramway Museum, Derbyshire, and on 6 September 1964 it became the first Leeds tram to run under its own power at the Museum.

600 entered passenger service on Wednesday, 4 August 1954. This view was taken at Hunslet on the following Saturday, the 7th. In comparison with the two Roe-built railcars 601 and 602, 600 looked rather out of date with its relatively small windows and unsightly bow mounting. Internally, the French polished woodwork looked very smart, but probably rather old fashioned for a vehicle "new" in 1954. *Author.*

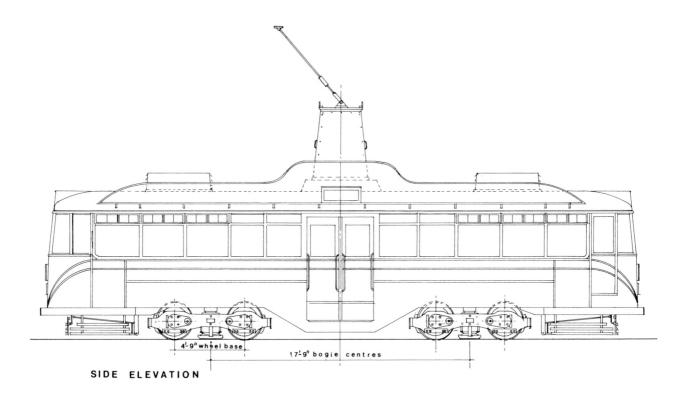

4'-9" wheel base

17'-9" bogie centres

SIDE ELEVATION

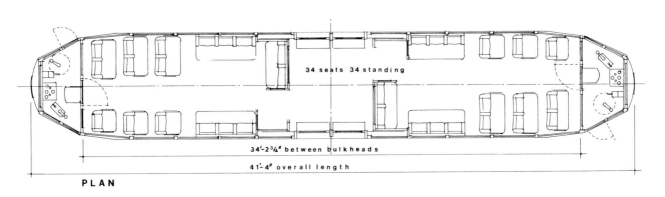

34 seats 34 standing

34'-2¾" between bulkheads

41'-4" overall length

PLAN

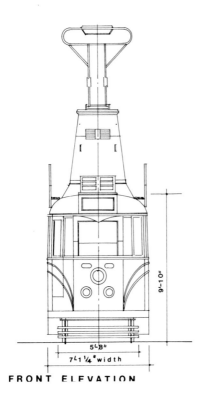

9'-10"

5'-8"

7'-1¼" width

FRONT ELEVATION

LEEDS CITY TRANSPORT
SINGLE DECK
EX-SUNDERLAND CAR NO. 600

TYPICAL DETAILS

BOGIES EX-LIVERPOOL
E.M.B. LIGHTWEIGHT

1 0 1 2 3 4 5 6 7 8 9 10 11 12
FEET

Railcars 601 and 602

There had been hints that the Leeds Transport Department wanted to acquire a modern single deck car for a number of years, but the final decision came in 1950. Work had been carried out on the ex-Sunderland car and in April 1946, the General Manager, Vane Morland, visited Blackpool. He was accompanied by four members of the L.C.T. staff and witnessed experiments with a "super-silent" Blackpool car, which had been fitted with new bogies. This was the first attempt in Britain to emulate the highly successful American P.C.C. car. Two pairs of new Maley & Taunton bogies had been acquired, inside-framed and of 6ft.0in. wheel base, and similar to those used on P.C.C. cars. For purposes of comparison, one pair had resilient rubber-sandwich wheels with a spiral bevel drive, which gave good free-wheeling performance with no gear noise. The other had conventional steel wheels and worm gear drive. One of the stream-lined single deck cars, 303, was fitted with the resilient wheels and it was in this car that the Leeds delegation was interested. Car 303 had four motors manufactured by Crompton Parkinson of Chelmsford, The four motors were intended to be operated by "VAMBAC" multi-notch controllers, but as a temporary expedient Allen West series-parallel controllers were adapted to operate the car.

'The Modern Tramway' described the experiments as "sensational" and Vane Morland appears to have been impressed.

In the meantime another single deck car, 208, was being adapted so that it could use the new equipment and the bogies from 303 were transferred. Trials were made in December 1946, 208 also being fitted with a "VAMBAC" multi-notch control system. There were a few minor problems and the bogies were returned to car 303. By the middle of 1947 the problems with the control system had been resolved, and the resilient-wheel bogies were refitted again to car 208.

The "Variable Automatic Multi-notch Braking and Acceleration Control" or "VAMBAC" system comprised in essence, a multi-notch rheostat actuated by a pilot motor. For a full technical description readers should refer to an article, which appeared in 'Engineering' for 16 April 1948. "VAMBAC" control was very impressive. There were two pedals for controller and air brake respectively On car 208 the controller gave "glideaway" acceleration to 30 m.p.h. in 17 seconds. The most modern bus of the time took 27 seconds to reach 30 m.p.h.

As a result of the success with 208, eighteen more sets of P.C.C. equipment were ordered by Blackpool, the first of the new sets being delivered in May 1949. It was was to be over a year before Leeds decided to place an order for similar equipment.

This was as a result of a visit to Blackpool on 24 June 1950 by Councillor J. Rafferty, chairman of the Transport Committee, Alderman D.G. Cowling, deputy chairman and General Manager, A.B. Findlay. By 1950 two further Blackpool cars had been fitted with "VAMBAC" equipment and resilient-wheel bogies. Both Cowling and Rafferty drove one of the cars along the Promenade. Cowling had asked if it would be possible to borrow a tram from Blackpool for experiments, but this did not take place. Maybe it was for the same reason given when an earlier request had been made two years before by the Light Railway Transport League to borrow Blackpool car 208 – that the car was too long (43 feet) and therefore "unsuitable" for use in the city.

Alderman Cowling was particularly impressed with the Blackpool cars and on 2 August 1950 the City Council had given authority for the General Manager, A.B. Findlay, to design a new type of single deck tram for Leeds. Sketch

By 5 November 1952 when this photograph was taken, work on the railcars was well advanced at Charles Roe's Works at Cross Gates. Workmen are rubbing down the paintwork on one of the cars. *L.T.H.S.*

In July 1952 an abortive attempt was made to convert Feltham 519 into a single deck trailer car. The integral steel framing of the body brought a halt to the experiment. 519 is at Gipton terminus on 23 April 1955, the final day of operation of the Gipton tram service. *Author.*

Admiring eyes from passengers waiting at the tram stop at Belle Isle as 602 passes on trial on 23 May 1953. It entered service a week later. *Author.*

Railcar 601 with Feltham 559 behind, pictured at Halton terminus on 13 June 1953 after nearly a fortnight in passenger service. *Author.*

plans were submitted to the Transport Committee on 19 March 1951 and the Committee decided to seek Ministry of Transport approval to the plans. Approval was received and estimates were prepared and in April the Leeds Corporation Finance Committee authorised the spending of £22,000 on two experimental railcars.

Although reported by the local press to be similar to the Blackpool trams in appearance, they were an advance on the Blackpool design and had features new to trams in Britain. Initially A.B.Findlay had ideas of designing one of the vehicles as a single-ended car with a large platform at the rear, on similar lines to a new single deck trolley bus that Glasgow Corporation was testing at the time. J.B. Gill, the Chief Traffic Officer, visited Glasgow on 16 and 17 April 1951 to see the trolley bus. E.R.L. Fitzpayne, the General Manager of the Glasgow Transport Department, advised against the single-ended proposal and thought that a central platform P.C.C. type car was the better solution.

The chief point about the new cars was that they would be able to move passengers quickly. Seating was to be provided for between 44 and 48 passengers. The new cars would be faster than the average Leeds tram and be able to maintain an average service speed of 12 m.p.h. as opposed to the usual speed of just over 9 m.p.h.

Detailed design work continued during the year and by November 1951 it was completed. The two cars were to have 34 seats with 36 standing and centre entrance doorways to speed loading and fare collection. Their overall length was to be 41ft. 6in. One of the cars was to have automatic acceleration, electric braking, improved springing and resilient wheels; said to reduce noise by 75%. The other car was to have resilient wheels, but with conventional equipment. Findlay was authorised to visit The Hague, Brussels and Rotterdam to gather ideas and see modern American-type single deck cars in service. E.R.L. Fitzpayne, accompanied Findlay, Also present were representatives from the Metropolitan Vickers Electrical Co. Ltd. Findlay said on his return that he was convinced that the single deck vehicle was the only type that should be considered for Leeds.

Alderman D.G. Cowling, Chairman of the Transport Committee said, before determining the future policy of the department, it would be necessary to see the two cars in operation.

"The reaction of the travelling public and the cost of any change might thus be ascertained. The City Council could then decide whether to retain tramcars or not. Two hundred of the new cars would cost about £2,000,000.

'The Yorkshire Post', 20 November 1951.

In November 1951, Charles H. Roe Ltd. of Cross Gates, Leeds, made a start on the construction of the car bodies. They were the first tramcars that Roe, well known for its motor bus and trolley bus bodies, had built and progress was slow.

In 1952, while the new railcars for Leeds were under construction, the first of an order of 25 new cars for Blackpool was completed by coach builders, Charles Roberts & Co. of Horbury, Wakefield. Roberts stated the new cars were costing about £10,000 each and that to ride in one of the 50 feet long vehicles would be "like riding in a fast car". On 27 May, the new Blackpool tram was inspected by several Yorkshire transport officials, including A.B. Findlay, T. Parkinson, and Alderman Rafferty from Leeds. In the words of Findlay:

"It is an exceedingly nice job, but will be no better than we shall have in Leeds in six months time. Ours will cost us more and will be the first all-electric-braking tram in the country."

'Yorkshire Evening Post', 27 May 1952.

In November Findlay, Alderman Cowling and Alderman Rafferty visited Blackpool to inspect one of the new cars. Findlay said that as the new Leeds railcars would be delivered soon they would like the opportunity of drawing comparisons between the Blackpool cars and the new Leeds vehicles. By this time the new cars were taking shape at Roes and Findlay estimated that with a complete fleet of these cars he could improve schedules by 25%.

"The trams will be run on all city services and if the City Council, tramway employees, and the travelling public like them the double-deckers may be scrapped and the new type used in their place.

Mr. A.B. Findlay (Leeds Traffic Manager) said today: "I hope to have the two in service by January. Leeds will get an opportunity of seeing a modern tram and of comparing them with buses and other vehicles.

"We have a number of old trams and within the next 12 months a decision will have to be made on how they are to be replaced. These two will give us our statistics."

'Yorkshire Evening Post', 5 November 1952.

By February 1953 details of the equipment to be used on the two cars began to emerge. Two firms were to be responsible: Crompton Parkinson Ltd., which had local factories at Guiseley and Doncaster, and Metropolitan Vickers Ltd., of Manchester. "Comfort, silence and speed" were promised by both firms, Crompton Parkinson adopting the latest tramway technology and Metropolitan Vickers more traditional equipment.

Dealing with the Crompton Parkinson car first, which had been allocated the fleet number 602. This was an all-electric vehicle and fitted with bogies and control equipment, similar to the American P.C.C. equivalent.

In place of orthodox tramcar bogies with the motors partly suspended from the axle and partly in the bogie, 602 had four circular, round-frame, light weight high-speed motors of 45 h.p. mounted in each bogie. Each motor drove through a carden shaft to a spiral bevel axle of high ratio reduction – the shaft drive allowing the motor to be fully spring-borne, thus increasing the smooth riding of the car and the life of the equipment.

The "VAMBAC" equipment, housed in the bow tower, gave automatic acceleration, the rate being variable and pre-selected by the driver. The control lever was moved forward and the rate pre-selected depended on the position of the lever. Full speed was always attained, the time taken depending on the acceleration rate selected.

A backward movement of the control lever brought the automatic electric braking into effect, which gave a very high rate of retardation. The system thus gave high rates of acceleration and braking combined with a very smooth vehicle motion. The car was controlled by the single control lever positioned adjacent to the seated driver's left hand and therefore very simple to drive. The controller mechanism (or accelerator) had 83 notches instead of the six to twelve notches on a conventional tramcar controller and hence acceleration and braking was in one continuous smooth sweep.

A unique feature of the car was the absence of compressed air or hydraulic brakes, thus making 602 the first British "all-electric" car. Solenoid-operated internal expanding brakes fitted to the motor brought the car to rest from 5 m.p.h., normal braking down to this speed being rheostatic. Magnetic track brakes were also fitted for emergency stopping, both track and shaft brakes being battery operated and independent of supply failure. There were indicator lamps in the driver's cab to show that all four shaft brakes were released and the track brakes applied on emergency stopping. There was an arrangement whereby, in the event of brake failure, the car could automatically be brought to a standstill. To enable the conductor to switch off the power supply and apply the shaft brake in an emergency, a switch was provided in the central entrance of the car.

The type HS44 bogies were manufactured by Maley & Taunton Ltd. of 6ft.0in. wheel base and spaced 17ft.0in. apart, centre to centre. The wheel diameter was 26⅝in. and the car weighed 16·5 tons unladen.

On the right Victor Matterface, the Tramway Rolling Stock Engineer, is describing 602's braking system to members of the press. The location is Temple Newsam terminus and the date 19 May 1953. *L.T.H.S.*

The Transport Committee inspect Railcar 602 in Sovereign Street. From the left are Councillor Stott, Alderman Webster, Councillors Horner, Miss Tong, Mr. Sowden (Committee Clerk – with bow tie), Councillors Hodkinson, Mather, Turnbull, Smith, Alderman Rafferty (with crutch), and on the car Alderman Cowling, and Councillors Stubbs and Bennett. *Yorkshire Evening News.*

The equipment on the other railcar, numbered 601, was more conventional. Metropolitan Vickers Ltd. designed the equipment to be easily maintained and for acceleration rates up to 3 m.p.h. per sec. with peak load. Rheostatic braking rates of 2·5 to 3 m.p.h. per sec. were available. Driving was made easy by the automatic control of acceleration and, if desired, braking.

There were four motors, two on each bogie of the MV109GZ type and of 50 h.p. The motors were axle hung and resiliently mounted through Silentbloc rubber bushes on a roller bearing axle tube. By this system the motor was cushioned against axle vibration caused by rail joints or other track irregularities.

To provide quiet operation the gear wheels were constructed in two main parts – the rim, which carried the teeth and the hub complete with spokes. In between the two were "Silentbloc" rubber bushes. This reduced shock on the gear teeth and motor armature, which in turn reduced wear and maintenance. To give further quiet running the gear teeth were of the helical type of 15° helix angle.

The equipment in the driving cab was kept as simple as possible. Apart from the lighting switches etc., there was a circuit breaker, and a master controller. This controller had 23 notches, which gave smooth acceleration, and there were four rates of acceleration. The driver could select any one of these after which the automatic acceleration brought the car up to the required speed.

Braking was effected by turning the controller handle back, past the zero position, and eleven brake notches gave smooth braking. Braking, however, was usually by means of an E.M.B. air wheel brake of the same type as fitted to car

600. The power switchgear was housed on the roof beneath the bow collector tower.

The E.M.B. bogies were of the lightweight type with a wheel base of 5ft.0in. with bogie centres at 26ft.9in. The 27in. diameter wheels had rubber inserts to reduce the noise from the rail. These were designed and supplied by the English Electric Co. Ltd. There were air wheel brakes operated by a separate motorman's valve and magnetic track brakes, which could also be air operated. The unladen weight of the car was 17·5 tons.

601 and 602, as far as the bodies were concerned were almost identical, the only visible difference being in the detail of the bow collector towers. Both cars had a wide central entrance, with two saloons each accommodating 17 passengers. In addition a total of 36 standing passengers could be carried on the platform and inside the saloons, making a total of 70.

Charles Roe used its patent teak/steel reinforced construction throughout and the roof over the central entrance was specially strengthened to house the control gear. The underframes were manufactured by Patchett & Co. of Leeds. There were six opening windows on each side of the saloons of the Widney double-sliding type. The doors were manually operated, and when closed the entrance step was automatically covered by a flap.

The driver had his own cab which could be entered either externally or from inside the car, There was a tip up seat on the cab side of the door leading into the saloon. The single pane windscreen slightly dropped gave excellent visibility and a windscreen wiper was fitted.

The saloons were fitted with standard tramcar throw-over seating with Dunlopillo Cushions upholstered in red and cream moquette. The timber floors were covered in cork tiles in the saloons and studded rubber on the entrance platforms.

Interior lighting was of the open reflector type, fitted below the luggage racks and running longitudinally. In addition the centre line of the ceiling of each saloon was fitted with enclosed roof lights with moonshine glass. These lamps were also fitted in the entrance.   The   roof was under-drawn with "Alhambrinal", a moulded plastic type finish supplied by the Waterproofing Co. Ltd. of Barrhead.

For the period of the Coronation of Queen Elizabeth II the cars were painted in a striking royal purple and ivory livery.   Upon repainting they were to be painted in the standard Leeds red and white colour scheme, but were never repainted in Leeds.

The delivery of the first car body, that of 602, was effected on 16 February 1953. It left the works of Charles Roe at Cross Gates at about 10.00 a.m. and was routed via Austhorpe Road, Cross Gates Road, York Road, New York Road, Eastgate, The Headrow, Park Lane, Caroline Street, West Street and Kirkstall Road to Kirkstall Road Works. According to the 'Yorkshire Evening News', the car was the "centre of attraction" all along the route. The bogies and electrical equipment were quickly fitted at the Works and on the nights of Monday, Tuesday and Wednesday, 23, 24 and 25 February the car was tested between the Works and Kirkstall Abbey.

"It was a test for the contractors responsible for the electrical equipment rather than a test for ourselves," said a member of the Transport Department. "There are certain adjustments that can only be made during running, and it was taken out for that purpose."

'Yorkshire Evening Post', 24 February 1953.

The second of the bodies to be delivered by Roes, 601, arrived at Kirkstall Road Works at 4.00 p.m. on 23 March and on the night of 25-26 March the car underwent tests.

602 made its first appearance in daylight on 8 April and went on a run from Kirkstall Road Works to Cross Gates and the following day to Temple Newsam.

The two railcars were much in the news during May as on the 12th and 13th they were inspected by Brigadier C.A. Langley on behalf of the Ministry of Transport.

For the "exhaustive" tests, part of the Middleton circular route from Park Side to Lingwell Road was closed to normal traffic from 10.00 a.m. to 4.00 p.m. on the 12th when 602 was tested, and from 10.00 a.m. to lunchtime the following day when 601 underwent trials. A special bus service was operated from Swinegate to Lingwell Road, Middleton, via Dewsbury Road.

Apart from officials of the Leeds Transport Department, aboard 602 were officials from Crompton Parkinson, Maley & Taunton and Charles Roe Ltd. The 'Yorkshire Evening Post' reported that 602 "purred like a kitten," there were no "clanks or jerks" and its silent approach was "rather startling." The car underwent 16 braking tests and as it completed each run the braking distance was measured. Tests with the lifeguard were made with a dummy.

Brigadier Langley was very impressed with the two cars and said he was "thoroughly satisfied." He said they both rode very smoothly and were a "great advance," they responded well and were easy to control. "Both promise to be excellent cars, and the workmanship is up to the high standard I expected. I think they will be a great asset to the city and I congratulate the Corporation and Transport

602 at the White Horse Junction, Wellington Road, on 28 August 1954. The pointwork of the former tracks into Armley Road, abandoned some ten months earlier, are visible. Behind 602 is a pre-war A.E.C. Regent bus.
Author.

After 13 October 1954, railcar 602 was confined to the two miles long Hunslet route. It was not seen in the city centre again and ran occasionally at peak hours. It was photographed at Hunslet terminus on 23 August 1955. By this date the bumpers had been repainted black. *Author.*

Manager," he remarked.

Although said to be capable of a maximum speed of 50 m.p.h., Brigadier Langley said the speed of the cars was limited by law and the cars were not tested above a speed of 30 m.p.h.

A.B.Findlay, the Transport Manager, said that passenger's comfort would be "a big difference from anything that Leeds has known before." The Brigadier had given permission for the cars to be used on training runs under service conditions and eight to twelve drivers were to be trained to drive the cars on all routes. Langley said that from a safety point of view he was "perfectly satisfied" with the cars. He would recommend the Ministry to give its formal approval as soon as possible. Findlay said that extensive maintenance tests had still to be carried out.

Discussing the cars, 'The Modern Tramway' said that 601 was very fast, but the motion and acoustics were "more of a tramcar character" than 602. The resilient wheels had similar characteristics to those, which had been experimentally fitted to Horsfield car 179 in 1951 and discussed in Chapter 62 of Volume 3. No. 602 had a "100% perfect performance", every bit as good as the "304" class of cars in Blackpool with absolutely no rolling. On good track there was virtually no noise in the saloon, but even resilient wheels of the latest pattern could not entirely dampen rail corrugations. 'The Modern Tramway' added that passengers noticed principally the perfectly smooth acceleration and deceleration. Drivers commented that 602 could not be simpler or easier to drive, all acceleration and deceleration being controlled by a single lever.

By 21 May approval from the Ministry of Transport had been received. This was in time for the Queen's Coronation and on Monday, 1 June 1953 the two cars entered passenger service. There was no formal ceremony, but as a "Coronation gesture" to passengers, travel on the first three days of operation was free. The cars were operated on all routes, except for route 5, Beeston. On 4 June the

two cars entered passenger service, 602 being used on the 9, 10 and 11 services, Dewsbury Road to Compton Road and Gipton Estate, and 601 on the 16 New Inn, Wortley to 20 Halton service. 601 was used on the 16/20 service until 29 June when it was transferred to routes 1, 2 and 3, Lawnswood to Moortown and Roundhay circular. 602 was transferred to the Middleton circular route. 12 and 26 circular from 11 July. Subsequent transfers were as follows:

No.601 from routes 1,2 and 3 to routes 12 and 26 circular from 7 September 1953. From 1 November it went to routes 9, 10 and 11. It remained in service on these routes until 10 December when it was involved in a collision. The car returned to service on 28 April 1954 working on 3 Roundhay, 9 Dewsbury Road and 11 Gipton. In the meantime route 10, Compton Road, had ceased operation. On 5 August 1954 the car was transferred to work on route 25, the Swinegate-Hunslet route.

No.602 was out of service for most of August 1953 due to braking problems and returned to service on 29 August on the 12 and 26 circular route, but was withdrawn again a week later. On 30 August it had suffered problems and was observed by the writer reversing at the rarely used crossover at the Middleton Woods substation.

In an effort to improve the car's performance, the control system was given an extra "crawl" notch to improve slow speed running. This resulted in extra resistances being placed on the roof, the only visible change to the car during its service in Leeds. By mid-October the car was back in service on routes 1, 2 and 3. It was transferred to Torre Road Depot on 4 January 1954 and worked on routes 15, 16, 18, 20 and 22. Except for one week when it was out of service, 602 continued to work from Torre Road until 11 September 1954, after which it was periodically used for driver training duties. It was transferred to the Hunslet route on 13 October 1954 to join railcars 600 and 601.

From then and until their withdrawal from service three years later, the most modern trams in Leeds, the railcars, were hidden away on the short Swinegate-Hunslet route and never seen on the main city centre streets. This was on the express instructions of the Chairman of the Transport Committee, Alderman Rafferty. On more than one occasion, complaints were made by the shadow chairman, Councillor Mather. The two miles long route entirely on street track, and the main A61 road to Wakefield, Barnsley and Sheffield, was often congested with motor traffic and meant that the cars could never demonstrate their full potential.

Confined to the Hunslet route, the cars made occasional trips, usually being seen only at peak hours. Following the withdrawal of the Lawnswood route and the Hyde Park short working in March 1956 the schedules on the Hunslet and Belle Isle routes were changed resulting in the same tram being used on the two routes.

"It seems to have been used as a further excuse to make even less use of the three single deck cars, Nos. 600, 601 and 602. In recent weeks No. 600 has been out of service at Kirkstall Works, and Nos. 601 and 602 have made only very rare appearances on peak hour journeys on the Hunslet route."

'The Leeds & District Transport News', March 1956.

Being regarded as non-standard, 601 and 602 ran until being officially withdrawn on 28 September 1957 upon the closure of the Moortown and Dewsbury Road tram routes. Owing to the intermittent operation of the cars during their final two years, the dates when they last ran in service have not been recorded. 600 was photographed in use on Friday evening, 27 September, and it is possible that 601 and 602 could have been used for peak hour duties during the same week. Cars 601 and 602 then remained in storage in Swinegate Depot until the closure of the tramway system in November 1959. The cars had cost a lot of money,

although initially estimated to cost £11,000 each, the final sum for the two cars came to £12,638 3s.11d. for 601 and £12,477 3s.9d. for 602. The Transport Department was hoping for a buyer. Presumably it was thinking that Blackpool Corporation or some overseas purchaser would come forward, but this was not to be. Like 600, both cars were sold privately on 11 April 1960, 601 to Dr. R. F. Youell of the Middleton Railway Preservation Society and 602 to the Railcar Preservation Society, both for £150 each.

On 6 May 1960, the same day as 600, 602 was taken to the Crich Tramway Museum in Derbyshire. 601 had a sad ending. It was moved to Middleton on 21 June 1960 and became the last tram to leave Swinegate Depot, In common with all other trams that went to Middleton, it was vandalised and on the afternoon of 24 September 1962 half of the interior of the saloon was gutted by fire. In February 1964 the Middleton Railway Preservation Society dismantled and burned the remnants.

During its time in Leeds, 601, having relatively traditional tramcar equipment never suffered any major mechanical or electrical problems. 602 on the other hand had several problems and was never entirely free from troubles for much of its service life in Leeds. It was probably rather too sophisticated for its time and one shudders to think of the maintenance difficulties that the Transport Department would have faced if 200 cars of this type had been purchased. Problems were also encountered with the Blackpool trams that were fitted with similar equipment. The equipment was removed in Blackpool after a relatively short time. However, when working properly 602, possibly the most advanced tramcar in the world in 1953, was undoubtedly the finest car ever operated by the Leeds Transport Department. Its superb qualities can still be enjoyed at the National Tramway Museum.

Railcar 601 was fitted with conventional tramcar equipment and was photographed at the Chapeltown terminus at Stainbeck Lane on 20 August 1953. 601 and 602 were the only trams ever built by Charles Roe Ltd., but the rather cramped and low seating capacity – 34 seats, with 36 standing -- did not make them very popular with the public. *Author.*

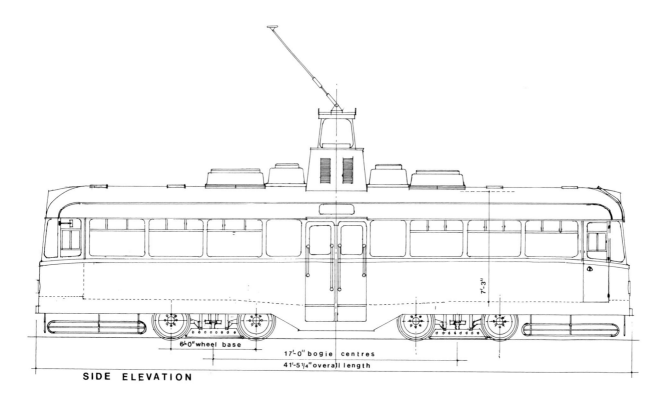

6'-0" wheel base

17'-0" bogie centres

41'-5¼" overall length

7'-3"

SIDE ELEVATION

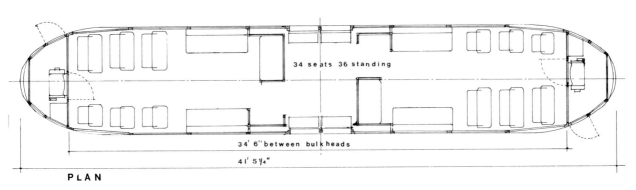

34 seats 36 standing

34' 6" between bulkheads

41' 5¼"

PLAN

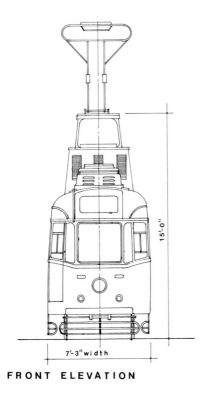

15'-0"

7'-3" width

FRONT ELEVATION

**LEEDS CITY TRANSPORT
SINGLE DECK CAR
RAILCAR NO. 602**

TYPICAL DETAILS

**BOGIES MALEY AND TAUNTON LTD.
BODY CHARLES H. ROE LTD.**

1 0 1 2 3 4 5 6 7 8 9 10 11 12
FEET

Sovereign Street Permanent Way Yard on 27 February 1953 with Works car 2 (ex-73A) and ex-Hull works car 6. Number 6 is very shabby with part of its dash in grey undercoat and still in its buff livery of 1948. The new "blister hangar" bus garage is on the left. *Author.*

8A newly repainted in Sovereign Street Yard on 6 August 1955. The platforms were fitted with vestibules in January 1954. The former Parcels Department used as a Central Cartage Garage is behind the car. *Author.*

Works Trams, Training and Works Buses

Works Trams

The tramway works rolling stock was fully discussed in Volumes 2 and 3 and the story from 1953 to 1959 was one of gradual decline and withdrawal. It is perhaps surprising that most of the works trams survived until the end of the tramway system. For clarity the same format is adopted as in Volumes 2 and 3 where the various types are discussed under separate headings.

Stores Cars

In 1953 there were three stores cars in stock numbered 2, 4A and 8A. No. 2 had been former Brush-built passenger car 73A and used as a stores car from 1937. 4A, formerly numbered 3, had been converted from Dick, Kerr car 256 in June 1936 and 8A (ex-5), also from a Dick, Kerr car, 198, in June 1927. Number 2 was in a grey livery with white numerals, whereas 4A and 8A were red with white numerals. They had received the "A" suffixes in April and May 1951 as part of a renumbering scheme, which was never finished.

Car 2 did not undergo any changes from 1953 to 1959. It entered service repainted for the last time on 5 July 1955 and became the first of the stores cars to be taken out of service. It was last used in late 1956 when it was transferred from Sovereign Street Yard to Swinegate Depot for storage and to Torre Road Depot Yard on 18 July 1957. There it remained until October 1959 when it was returned to Swinegate for scrap. The car was dismantled in Swinegate Depot on 3 December 1959.

Car 4A had appeared in service fitted with a 1,000 gallon water tank on 18 March 1953 and from then on was, strictly speaking, a water car. It was, however, used for other works purposes. It had been repainted twice in red, in April 1951 and October 1953, and appeared in a grey livery with white numerals on 22 August 1955. The car remained in use until September 1957, when following the closure of the Moortown-Dewsbury Road tram route, it was placed in storage. It was transferred to Torre Road Yard on 18 December 1957, but after five months was returned to Swinegate Depot again. It remained in occasional use until the end of the tramway system. It was dismantled in Swinegate Depot on 2 December 1959.

Car 8A had open platforms and was unpopular with the staff, especially in wet weather. However, on 27 January 1954 it entered service with its platforms enclosed. It lost its red livery and appeared in grey with white numerals on 28 July 1955, shortly after number 2, and became the last tramway stores car to be repainted. The car was used on 25 February 1958 clearing snow on the Temple Newsam route, but not much after that date. On 30 May 1958 it was taken from Swinegate to Torre Road Yard as a replacement for 4A. With 2 it returned to Swinegate Depot in October 1959 and was dismantled on 30 November of that year.

Snow Sweepers and Snow Ploughs

In 1953 all the five snow sweepers were in stock. They were of the American J.G.Brill design and were

It was rare to see the snow sweepers in daylight. 4 is outside Swinegate Depot on 26 May 1954. *Author.*

Snow sweeper 3 in use at Roundhay Park on 7 February 1954. The snow sweepers retained their war time head lamp masks until the end. *A.D.Packer.*

purpose-built and fitted with revolving brushes to clear the snow. They were very effective in clearing thick soft snow and slush.

All, except for No.2, which was defective, are believed to have been in use during the heavy snow, which fell from 7 to 10 February 1954. However, No.1, the oldest of the vehicles dating from 1900, was withdrawn immediately after the snow and stripped for scrap in Swinegate Depot. Following temporary storage in Torre Road Depot Yard it was moved to Low Fields Road Permanent Way Yard and burned on 9 April 1954. No.1 differed in design from the other snow sweepers as it had windows around the whole of the body. Cars 2 to 5 had windows at the ends only.

The four remaining snow sweepers were taken to Chapeltown Depot for storage on 21 and 22 April 1955. No.3 was already at Chapeltown and had been there for a number of years. No.2 was transferred from Torre Road Depot and 4 and 5 from Swinegate. No.2 had been the Torre Road snow sweeper for several years, and, when defective in February 1954, Chamberlain car 36 was temporarily fitted with a snow board and acted as a substitute. At the beginning of winter, 36 had been transferred from Swinegate Depot to Torre Road to be used specifically for snow plough work, and similarly cars 29 and 30 were sent respectively to Headingley and Chapeltown Depots. There is no record, however, of either 29 or 30 being fitted with snow board equipment during this period.

Snow sweeper 2 was repaired and in October 1955 No. 4 was transferred from Chapeltown Depot to Kirkstall Road Works.

There was no significant snow in Leeds again until the early hours of Tuesday, 20 December 1955. Every tram route was disrupted and snow sweepers 2, 3 and 5 were in use over the whole of the tram routes. They were assisted by Chamberlain cars 84 and 124 and stores car 4A, all of which had been temporarily fitted with snow boards. 2, 3 and 5 were also used periodically during January 1956 for snow clearance.

Number 4 was not used and became the next snow sweeper to be scrapped. It was transferred from Kirkstall Road Works to Low Fields Road Yard and burned on 8 February 1956. The car must have been defective and considered beyond repair for on 9 January a new snow plough had appeared at Swinegate in the form of Chamberlain car 83. This car had been withdrawn from passenger service on 18 November 1955 and a plough fitted at No. 1 end. The staircase and staircase handrails were removed and the dash painted in red undercoat. 83 was then returned to Kirkstall Road Works for further modification. One platform was removed and a controller and hand brake fitted inside and adjacent to the doorway of the lower saloon. During the evening of 4 September 1956 it made an experimental journey along York Road and on 30 November was transferred to Swinegate Depot renumbered "SNOW BLADE 7". On 26 October the three remaining snow sweepers were taken from Chapeltown Depot to Swinegate.

There was little snow during the winter of 1956-1957 and on 18 July 1957, with stores car 2, the three snow sweepers were taken to Torre Road Depot Yard for storage. Snow sweepers 2 and 5 were never used again after January 1956, but 3 was returned to Swinegate Depot in December 1957 and used in York Road on 20 and 21 January 1958. Snow Blade 7, ex-83, was not used on these days, but, on 7 and 8 February, it was seen for the first time clearing snow on the track between Halton and Temple Newsam.

The heavy snow and blizzards of 25 and 26 February 1958 caused widespread dislocations. Various trams were operated throughout the night on all routes, except Temple Newsam, in order to keep the lines clear, and all services were in operation early the following morning. However, high winds caused drifting and Feltham 517 became embedded in a drift near Middleton substation. The Middleton route was cleared but became blocked, reopened and blocked again. Horsfield car 197 was embedded in a 3 feet drift near Sharp Lane on Middleton

Ring Road and the tram service was curtailed at Middleton and Belle Isle (27 terminus). Wrecker UB 7931 (ex-bus 111), fitted with a snow plough, gritter UG 6308 (ex-bus 59) assisted by ex-Hull works car/rail grinder, No.6, finally released 197 at 11.25 a.m. on Thursday, 27th. Services were resumed on the Middleton circular in the late afternoon. Trams did not run to Temple Newsam until 28 February. Throughout this period there is no record of either snow sweeper 3 or Snow Blade 7 being used.

During the following winter of 1958 and 1959 there was little snow and hence February 1958 was the last occasion on which the snow clearing trams in Leeds were used. Torre Road Depot yard had been de-wired in July 1958 and on 7, 8 and 9 October 1959 the works cars stranded there, snow sweepers 2 and 5, stores cars 2 and 8A and water car 5, (discussed later), were towed out of the yard by the two wreckers, MUB 647 and UB 7931, and then by Horsfield cars to Swinegate Depot. The work was done during the night and snow sweeper 5 had the "distinction" of being the last tram to leave the yard. It was towed to Swinegate by Horsfield car 191.

Snow sweepers 2, 3 and 5 were broken up in Swinegate Depot on 7 December, 23 November and 30 November 1959 respectively and Snow Blade 7 on 7 December.

Snow blade 7 (ex-83) in use at Temple Newsam on 8 February 1958. *A.K.Terry.*

When the Torre Road snow sweeper 2 became defective, Chamberlain 36 fitted with a snow board was substituted. Unfortunately 36 could not be used as, on 7 February 1954, there were two overhead wire breakages at the York Road and Selby Road junction. All passengers were discharged at the Lupton Avenue cross over. 36 is on the track in Lupton Avenue from the depot to the outer track in York Road. A group of passengers on the right hand side is hopefully waiting for a through tram to appear. *Author.*

Rail Grinders

In 1953 the rail grinder fleet consisted of four vehicles: rail grinder 2, the original rail grinder on a steam tram truck dating from 1905, rail grinder 1 built in 1938-9, a trailer grinder 3 and ex-Hull stores car/rail grinder 6.

From 1939 to 1953 rail grinder 2 had been largely disused, but was reinstated in February 1953. 1, 3 and 6 usually worked together in tandem, but 2 normally operated on its own. It was not very effective and was subject to numerous breakdowns. After work on Street Lane in May 1954 it does not appear to have been used again and was taken to Low Fields Road Permanent Way Yard and burned on 10 May 1955.

Trailer grinder 3 was dismantled in May 1955. 6 had been used to supply the power to work trailer 3, but on 30 August 1954 appeared with its own reciprocating rail grinders, probably taken from rail grinder 2. The grinders were adjusted by a pair of mechanical track brake hand wheels inside the car. It was repainted grey with white numerals and had a brown interior. 6 became a replacement for 2 and 3.

The Tramways Department must have missed trailer 3 for in July 1956 a new trailer rail grinder was constructed in Kirkstall Road Works mounted on an ex-Chamberlain car P35 truck with 32 in. diameter wheels. In March 1957 it was painted grey with a red oxide truck. It was used in conjunction with car 6 or stores car 8A. By March 1957 rail grinder 1 had fallen into disuse. It was stored in Torre Road Yard for a time from April to July 1958 and spent the rest of its days in storage in Swinegate Depot. It was broken up in the Depot on 25 November 1959.

After the closure of the Moortown-Dewsbury Road routes in September 1957, track repairs were very minimal and generally confined to rail joints only. The remaining rail grinders, (6 and the trailer), were rarely used and

Indeed the trailer "disappeared" some time before the final abandonment of the tramways. Its fate is not known.

6 was used until the end of the tramway system mainly on general stores car duties, and on the final day of tramway operation was in Sovereign Street Yard. It was towed to Swinegate Depot on 8 December, and thus had the honour of being the last tramcar to run on the streets of Leeds. The car was not scrapped, but was purchased for private preservation.

Tower Wagons or Derricks

1953 saw a number of changes in the tramway rail derrick fleet. On 19 September 1953, one of the Leeds-built Chamberlain cars, 420, had appeared as a rail derrick numbered 2. Derrick number 1 (ex-80A) had been taken out of service in July 1953 and 2, built in 1931 on the Peckham cantilever truck of car 110A, was defective. It was thought that 2 would be scrapped, but instead it received the good Peckham cantilever truck from 80A and was overhauled and repainted. The car appeared in its new form on 28 December 1953, renumbered 1. The old 1, ex-80A, with its reversed staircase, resembled a turn of the century open top car and was burned in Low Fields Road Yard on 8 April 1954.

In addition to the above there was a trailer derrick on a horse tram truck, which had been out of use from about 1950. It was stored in Torre Road Yard for a number of years, before being burned in Low Fields Road Permanent Way Yard on 10 May 1955. Rail derricks 1 and 2 lasted until the end of the tramway system, 2 being broken up in Swinegate Depot on 25 November 1959 and 1 (ex-2) was sold privately for preservation.

The motor derrick fleet had remained unchanged from 1948-49 and comprised six vehicles, all Bedford 5 ton with towers by the Eagle Engineering Co. Ltd. The three

Rail grinder 1 at work in Street Lane on 26 May 1954. It is in its buff and red livery of 1948. Not long after the car entered service in 1939 the diagonal chain guard over the truck was modified, probably to allow for a second chain and reduction gear for the grinders. Compare with the photograph on page 1048 of Volume 3. *Author.*

Rail grinder 1 was repainted grey in late 1954.   It was photographed in Sovereign Street Permanent Way Yard on 21 January 1956.   Behind is one of the mobile mess huts on iron wheels, number 3, used by the Permanent Way Department. Rail grinder 1 was not used after March 1957. *Author.*

Rail derrick 1 was converted from a 1902 passenger car, 80A, in 1935 and much of the original tram survived including the Peckham cantilever truck and staircases.   It is in Sovereign Street on 15 April 1953.   The car was withdrawn from service in July 1953. *Author.*

When the Lawnswood tram route closed the two rail derricks were used in City Square to remove the overhead wires in the early hours of the following morning after the last tram had run. Gradually removing the wires they ran by gravity from the south end of Park Row to the junction with Boar Lane. The bright light on the top of rail derrick 1 is an acetylene flare used to illuminate the overhead wires. The "doppelganger" on the right is Geoffrey Claydon who moved during the long exposure that was required to take this photograph. *Author.*

earlier derricks, KUM 817, KUG 577 and LUA 765 had Bedford LWB OLBC chassis whereas the later derricks, MUA 309, MUG 231 and MNW 857 had chassis of the OLBX type.

As tramway abandonment proceeded the motor derricks were gradually taken out of service and sold. The first was KUG 577 in early 1954. It was sold to Bradford Corporation and was observed with its new owner on 1 April 1954 numbered 037 in the Works fleet. KUM 817 was disposed of about April 1956 following the abandonment of the Lawnswood tramway route. Where it went does not appear to have been recorded.

For major overhead breakdowns four derricks were required, and on 29 August 1956 all were in use when a lorry with an abnormally high load crashed into and brought down the wires at the Swan Junction in Hunslet Road. Both standards supporting the section breakers in Waterloo Road were broken and tramway services on the Middleton/Belle Isle circular and Hunslet route were disrupted from 6.50 p.m. on the 29th to 4.45 p.m. the following day. The two rail derricks were not brought into use on this occasion and were normally used on reserved track routes where access by motor vehicles was difficult.

In spite of this experience, it was not long before another of the motor derricks was sold. This was LUA 765, which went to an unknown purchaser during the latter part of 1956 or early 1957. Shortly before the abandonment of the Roundhay and Middleton circular routes in March 1959, MUA 309 was sold, which left two motor derricks MUG 231 and MNW 857 to deal with any eventualities on the remaining York Road tramway routes. After the abandonment of the tramway system, the newest derrick, MNW 857, was retained in stock, probably to assist the tree

lopper if required and was used during the reconstruction of the bus station in 1963. Like all the other motor derricks it was painted red, but was repainted green in May 1964. MNW 857 was still in stock in 1969, and probably remained until 1974 when the Leeds City Transport undertaking ceased to exist.

Regrettably the 'Leeds & District Transport News' recorded few details of the motor vehicle "miscellaneous" rolling stock and little is recorded elsewhere. Any further information on the motor derricks and other vehicles would be welcomed by the L.T.H.S.

Water Cars, Cranes etc.

In 1953 there were two water cars; 5, which had been converted from passenger car 126A in 1940 and stores car 4A (ex-3, ex-256A) discussed earlier. 4A had received its 1,000 gallon water tank in 1953.

Following the appearance of 4A, number 5 was used for stores car duties for a few weeks, but was then taken out of service. The car was observed in use at the end of April 1953, but there is no record of it being used after that date. Although it remained in working order, it spent the rest of its life in storage being moved from place to place. On 30 March 1954 it was moved from Sovereign Street Yard to Torre Road Yard and back to Sovereign Street again on 1 July 1955. This was for possible track-watering use on Children's Day, held at Roundhay Park on 2 July 1955. The car, however, was not used, and after two years in Sovereign Street Yard, returned to Torre Yard on 13 September 1957. There it remained until 8 October 1959 when, together with the stores cars and snow sweepers, already discussed, it was moved to Swinegate Depot for scrap and dismantled on 4 December 1959.

A sad view in Low Fields Road Permanent Way Yard of the original rail derrick 1. The track it was on was laid in September 1953 to facilitate the scrapping of trams. The photograph was taken on 7 April 1954 and the car was burned the following day. In the background is snow sweeper 1, burned on 9 April. *Author.*

Rail derrick 1 (ex-2) at the entrance to Chapeltown Depot on 2 January 1956. The depot had closed in April 1955 and shunting of cars stored in the depot was taking place. *Author.*

In 1953 Rail Derrick 2 was constructed from Chamberlain car 420. It was photographed during shunting at the western entrance to Swinegate Depot on 26 April 1954. *Author.*

An overhead linesman on Bedford Motor Derrick MUG 231 removing the overhead wires in Stanningley Road at Bramley Town End on Sunday, 18 October 1953. The wires were tied back at the section breaker at this point to enable the reserved track in Stanningley Road to be used for rail grinding purposes prior to recovery of the rails. A workman with a red flag is holding back traffic proceeding to Stanningley. *Author.*

The ex-Highways Department crane in Low Fields Road Yard on 3 September 1953, the day after it was transferred from the Highways Department in Kirkstall Road. The railway profile wheels are clearly visible, and had to be re-profiled before the crane could be used. Keith Terry is standing beside the crane. *Author.*

The fate of 4A has been discussed, and it remains now to discuss the cranes and two ex-Highways Department vehicles used by the Transport Department. Dealing with the ex-Highways Department vehicles first, the locomotive was of less use in shunting tramcars as first envisaged by Victor Matterface, the rolling stock engineer. The crane spent a period on tram jacks soon after its arrival in Low Fields Road Yard when the truck was taken away and the railway type wheels re-profiled. It was used until the end of 1955 when it appears to have become defective. Most of the shunting and overturning of trams, was done by the Dennis Lance wrecker, UB 7931. By 1955 the locomotive had fallen into disuse, but both it and the crane remained until mid-December 1957 when both were broken up. The vehicles retained their original trolleys throughout the four years they were in Low Fields Road Yard.

The two cranes in Sovereign Street Yard differed from each other in appearance. The earlier crane, which had a cab with a single row of windows, dated from 1910. The other had two rows of windows and was supplied to the Tramways Department in 1922. Both were built by Joseph Booth & Bros. of Rodley, Leeds. The cabs were made by the Department. After the ex-Highways Department crane fell into disuse, the newer crane was transferred to Low Fields Road Yard overnight on 30/31 January 1956. It was selected as it happened to be the crane nearest to the entrance to Sovereign Street Yard at the time.

Both cranes had narrow lightly constructed cabs, in comparison with the ex-Highways Department crane, and were not as stable. On 4 May the crane overturned and was righted about ten days later and returned to Kirkstall Road Works for repair. The Transport Department's mobile crane, JUG 649, a "Jones Super" crane new in September 1947, took the place of the overturned crane. The crane, apparently repaired, returned to Low Fields Road Yard the

following month, but thereafter no further mention has been found. It appears to have been broken up in Low Fields Road Yard and it seems that the ex-Highways Department crane was brought into use again.

The 1910 crane remained in Sovereign Street Yard in a very dilapidated state until the end of the tramways system. It was broken up in the yard on 27 February 1960. The mobile crane, JUG 649, was withdrawn from use, and presumably scrapped, during the latter part of 1967.

The electric cranes were painted in a light grey livery and retained their original trolleys.

A short-lived tramway vehicle appeared in March 1953. This was a "curve tester" for use in connection with the new rail cars to test clearances on the tram routes. It consisted of a wooden platform mounted on rail carrier bogies, with a central tower and bow collector, and was towed by a works car. It made night time runs from the beginning of March. At first it was kept at Sovereign Street, but was then taken to Torre Road Yard. It was scrapped in late 1953.

The "Wreckers"

Throughout the whole of the period covered by this volume the two wreckers, UB 7931 and MUB 647, were in use and both passed to the West Yorkshire Passenger Transport Executive on 1 April 1974. In addition there was HUM 211, a Bedford two-ton van, which was also classified by the Transport Department as a breakdown truck. This vehicle was withdrawn about 1956.

UB 7931, formerly painted in the standard Works fleet light grey livery, was repainted in bus type green in August 1965. Similarly in December 1965 the A.E.C. Matador MUB 647, previously light grey, also appeared in a bus green livery. In January 1973 the Matador was repainted green, but without the city coat of arms. The following

The earlier (1910) crane at the sand drying shed in Sovereign Street Permanent Way Yard on 22 August 1953. A Horsfield car is crossing Leeds Bridge in the background. *Author.*

To test clearances for the new rail cars a "curve tester" was made out of two permanent way trailer bogies. It was photographed in Torre Road Yard on 2 August 1953 and in the background is Chamberlain car 432 and ex-Southampton car 297. All the vehicles are awaiting scrap. *Author.*

The cab of the later (1922) crane had two rows of windows and was also photographed on 22 August 1953 at Sovereign Street Yard. On the left hand side is the new "blister hangar" bus garage opened in 1951. The yard is well stocked with rails and in the foreground are a pair of rail carrying bogies that were hauled by the stores cars.
Author.

month it was repainted again in an ivory livery similar to OKU 95H, below.

In December 1969 UB 7931 lost its Dennis Lance radiator, which had corroded and leaked, and was replaced by one from an A.E.C. Regent V. In February 1971 it was fitted with flashing trafficators. It was out of use for a year in 1972-3, but was repaired and was back in service again in July 1973. In the period that UB 7931 was disused, a new wrecker was purchased. This was a second hand A.E.C. Mercury lorry, registered OKU 95H. It was fitted with Holmes 600 towing and lifting equipment at Kirkstall Road Works and was painted in an ivory livery, This colour was at the time being used on the learner buses and minibuses.

After a period of driver familiarisation the vehicle entered service on 17 May 1972. It had been first registered on 19 February 1970, its original owners being Oswald Tillotson Ltd. the A.E.C. dealers of Bradford. It had always been used as a breakdown vehicle, but the Transport Department fitted heavier equipment. OKU 95H was delicensed in 1990, but UB 7931 and MUB 647 still exist, both in museums.

Tree Loppers

In order to avoid damage to vehicles, tree cutters or loppers, were required to trim overhanging branches on the various bus routes. Tree loppers originated with Manager Vane Morland, the first being Karrier JKL 46 withdrawn from passenger service in December 1932. This bus was a single deck vehicle and must have been fitted with a tower of some kind to be of any use for tree lopping. It did not last long and was withdrawn in June 1935. 46 was not replaced and, until 1950, tree trimming was carried out by the motor derricks. Due to the small area of the derrick platform there was a problem with long branches and a Transport Department lorry had also to be in attendance. A more cost effective solution was to use one vehicle only. This was achieved by converting a double deck bus into a tree cutter. The roof and upper saloon windows were removed, but the front windows were retained to afford some protection from the elements.

The first bus to receive this treatment was a 1936 built Roe bodied Leyland Titan TD4C 71, (DUB 925) which was withdrawn in December 1949. The following month it reappeared with the roof and upper deck seating removed and painted in the works overall light grey livery. 71 remained in use until March 1955 when it was replaced by

The A.E.C. Matador, MUB 647, in Torre Road Depot Yard on 21 September 1969. *H.Heyworth.*

a "new" tree lopper. 71 was cut up by the Transport Department in June 1955.

The replacement for 71 was an older vehicle, formerly bus 179 (AUM 422). This was an A.E.C. Regent of 1934 vintage with a Roe body of the early "piano front" style. No. 179, after a spell as a learner bus, was reinstated for passenger use in 1954. It ran from the closure of the Kirkstall Abbey and Compton Road tramway services on 3 April 1954 until 1 August the same year. Following a period in storage at Torre Road Depot, it appeared as a tree lopper in March 1955. Whereas 71 was in use for a period of just over five years, 179 was a tree lopper for nearly 13 years being taken out of service in February 1968. Not only was it used for trimming tree branches on all bus routes, it had extensive use on 29 February 1964 in Long Causeway, Adel. The Adel service had been used by single deck buses until this time and virtually every tree in Long Causeway had to be trimmed to allow use by double deckers.

The opportunity to replace 179 came on 12 January 1968 when one of the "PUA" A.E.C. Regent III of 1952, 675, came into collision with the low railway bridge in Sweet Street West. It lost its roof in the process and became the new tree lopper.

179, after withdrawal in February 1968, was sold on 21 September the same year, to Goodwin & Smith, breakers of Barnsley. 675 remained in use until the closure of this volume and passed to the West Yorkshire Passenger Transport Executive on 1 April 1974. It was withdrawn at the end of August 1974 and went to another breaker at Barnsley, D. Rollinson, in December of that year.

In January 1975 675 was replaced by a Leyland PD3/5 270.

Sand or Grit Wagons

Leeds City Transport Department was very self sufficient and resourceful, and many old buses were converted into works vehicles: derricks, lorries, tipping wagons, vans and also sand or grit wagons. These latter were for use in snow and icy conditions. The idea of converting buses into grit wagons originated with new Manager, William Vane Morland, in 1932.

Following withdrawal in June 1932 Dennis F number 15 (UM 873) was converted into a sand wagon and was later altered again into a derrick. Karrier JKL 68 (UM 8088) became a sand wagon in January 1935 and three of the 1929 Dennis HS buses, 91, 92 and 94 (UA 5841, 5842 and 5844), were converted in 1938-9 as replacements for 15 and 68. The Dennis HS buses lasted until 1948-9, being replaced by three A.E.C. Regents, 58, 59 and 61 (UG 6307, 6308 and 6310). 58. 59 and 61 had been withdrawn in 1946 and in sand/grit wagon form were to last another 27 or so years. Labourers in the back of the wagon shovelled salt and grit on to the road as the vehicle moved along. In October 1960 this was obviated on UG 6308 and 6310 when they were fitted with new "Spreadall" hopper bodies by Atkinson Spreaders Ltd, Clitheroe, Lancs. The grit and salt were spread automatically and the labourers were rendered redundant. In July 1962 these two gritters were painted with "dazzle" rear ends of black and yellow diagonal stripes. This was a new feature at the time. In October 1970 UG 6307, 6308 and 6310 were repainted in an overall yellow livery. The work was done by the Corporation Central Vehicle Maintenance Depot (formerly Torre Road No. 1 Garage).

UG 6307 and 6308 were delicensed on 31 January 1973. They were replaced with Bedford TK lorries formerly operated by the Cleansing Department. UG 6310 was still in occasional use working from Bramley Garage. It lasted into WYPTE days being taken out of service in April 1975. In the meantime a more modern grit wagon had been built upon the chassis of bus 170 (AUM 413) and it appeared in its new form in October 1954. The vehicle was withdrawn in 1968 and passed to Goodwin & Smith breakers of Barnsley on 21 September of that year. A fifth grit wagon was added in 1957.

After the winter of 1963-64 the grit wagons ceased to be included in the Transport Department stock lists. The vehicles and responsibility for road gritting passed to the Highways Department. However, this had been undertaken some years earlier. Following the abandonment of the Moortown-Dewsbury Road tram service in September 1957, many of the Permanent Way personnel were transferred to the Highways Department. A.B.Findlay, the Transport General Manager, said that he no longer had staff to do road gritting and it would have to be done by some other department. However, the vehicles remained on Transport Department premises. In June 1970, the L.C.T. gritters were said to be "totally out of date" and eight new gritters were ordered for the Highways and Cleansing Departments at a cost of £18,000. These never came under the control of the Transport Department and are not discussed further.

Other Miscellaneous Vehicles

In 1953 the two steam rollers, Tasker roller, JNW 299, and Aveling Porter, E 5351, were still in stock. They had been purchased second hand in 1940 and lasted about 16 years. One was withdrawn during the latter part of 1955 and the other the following year. It is not known which roller was withdrawn first.

The two Thomas Green diesel rollers (LUA 563 and LUA 834) lasted rather longer, both being withdrawn during the latter part of 1958.

1937-built FNW 664, the "Karrier Cob Senior" articulated gully cleaner, with rail carrying trailer, survived until 1956 when it was replaced by a new Karrier "Gamecock" gully cleaner. This had been ordered from Cox & Co. (Leeds) Ltd. on 19 September 1955 at a cost of £2.049 5s.0d. Its registration number was XUM 55 and it was delivered about June 1956. In February 1971 a new gully cleaner was ordered from Cox & Co. (Leeds) Ltd. for £4,027. Unfortunately details of the new vehicle have not been traced. XUM 55 was presumably withdrawn at this time.

There was another Karrier Cob in the works fleet, a cable carrier, AUA 984, new in 1935, which lasted until 1957. It was replaced by a Scammell vehicle.

There were five Scammell three-wheel mechanical horse tippers in stock in 1953. Two were taken out of service in 1955 and the rest the following year.

A former A.E.C. Regent bus 229, (DUB 949), had been converted into a lorry by the Transport Department in September 1953. It was repainted green in July 1965 and was withdrawn about June 1970.

Following the abandonment of the tramways, the miscellaneous rolling stock became less varied and not as interesting. Virtually all new works vehicles purchased after 1959 were either motor cars, small vans or the occasional lorry.

Other Vehicles

Although not strictly within the remit of this Chapter, as the vehicles were used by other departments, three former buses are included. They were a common sight in Leeds in the 1950s. One was UG 8779, formerly bus 63, which overturned in York Road on 31 March 1947. The body was scrapped and the chassis used for the construction of a musical instrument van for the newly formed Yorkshire Symphony Orchestra to carry instruments to concerts. It was often seen in Great George Street at the rear of the Town Hall when a concert was in progress. The Orchestra was disbanded at the end of July 1955 and In November UG 8779 was sold to Heavy Motor Services, Kirkstall Road, Leeds.

ANW 685, formerly A.E.C. Regent 142 was converted into a tar sprayer during the summer of 1955. It became number 209 in the Leeds Highways Department fleet. The vehicle was destroyed by fire on 23 July 1964.

Leyland Tiger TS8 number 19 was given to the Leeds Welfare Services Department in May 1955. It was

It was rare to see the tree loppers in action, but on 25 July 1973 Donald Wilson managed to find workmen on A.E.C. Regent III 675 trimming trees in Headingley Lane. 675 replaced an earlier tree lopper, ex-bus 179, in February 1968 (see overleaf). *W.D.Wilson/ L.T.H.S.*

Prior to 1950, tree lopping was usually carried out by the motor derricks, but in January of that year 1936-built Leyland Titan TD4C 71 (DUB 925) appeared with its roof removed. It was painted in the then "standard" works motor vehicle livery of grey with black mudguards and red wheel centres. It also had a black waist rail and was photographed at Roundhay Park on 26 May 1954. It ran until March the following year. *Author.*

The replacement for the Leyland Titan was ex-1934 vintage A.E.C. Regent 179. (AUM 422). It was photographed in Gledhow Valley Road on 23 July 1955. These old A.E.C. Regents were reliable vehicles and AUM 422 ran until February 1968. It would have lasted longer if A.E.C. Regent III 675 had not been "de-roofed" by the bridge in Sweet Street West. AUM 422 was painted in a more simple livery than the earlier lopper being an overall grey with black wings and grey wheel centres. The tree loppers ran intermittently, mainly during the summer months, and often ran on trade plates. *W.D.Wilson/L.T.H.S.*

Karrier Gamecock Gully Cleaner XUM 55 was a familiar sight in Sovereign Street Permanent Way Yard. It ran from 1956 to 1971 and was photographed on 5 March 1966. It was painted in a green livery. Behind is A.E.C. Regent III, 477. *Author.*

converted into a handicapped persons vehicle by Charles H. Roe Ltd. and ran until October 1960.

Training or 'Learner' buses

As with the sand/grit wagons above, the idea of using certain buses for driving instruction did not occur until 1932 and originated with Manager, Vane Morland. The first bus to be used for this purpose was a Karrier JKL of 1927 vintage, 46 (UM 6264). The vehicle doubled as the first Transport Department tree lopper, already discussed. It was used as a learner bus until 20 June 1935, when it was replaced by Dennis HS No.93, withdrawn from passenger service three weeks earlier at the end of May. 93 remained in use as a learner until April 1947 when it was scrapped.

One of the Leyland Titans of 1932, 17 (UG 1055), had been used daily during the war for the dispersal of Corporation ledgers to "safe places" each evening and returned them to Corporation offices the following morning. After the war it joined 93 as a learner bus and remained in use until 1 April 1948. Following withdrawal in 1946, Roe-bodied "piano front" A.E.C. Regents 53, 57 and 60 (UG 6302, 6306 and 6309)) joined 93 and 17. These three buses were used as "Learners" until the end of September 1949 when four other buses took their place.

The "new" buses comprised three Regents, similar to 53, 57 and 60, but of an earlier design. These were 44, 47 and 51, (UG 1031, 1034 and 1038), built in 1932, but had been extensively rebuilt after the end of the war. They had also been fitted with 7·7 litre diesel engines in February and March 1945. The fourth bus was a newer vehicle, the "one-off" 1937-built A.E.C. Regent 76 (FNW 76), which had a Weymann all-metal body. The three older buses were withdrawn in October 1951 (51) and May 1952 (44 and 47).

From 1 November 1951 the "learner" fleet was considerably expanded when seven buses were added. These were all A.E.C. Regents of the 1934 and 1935 "ANW" and "AUM" series numbered 134, 157, 169, 170, 174, 179 and 185. These all remained in use until late 1953 when,

apart from 169, they were reinstated for passenger service for tramway replacement. At this period, normally only two buses were in use at any one time for learner duties. For a short period the learner "fleet" was, for a week or two, reduced to this number for only 76 and 169 were available for use.

This was obviated by the "rescue" from Skelton Grange works duties of 1937 vintage "FNW" A.E.C. Regents 235 and 236 in January 1954. These two buses, with 76 and 169, comprised the learner fleet until 1956.

On 31 December 1955 a number of the surviving 1938 Regents of the "GUA" series (260-289) were taken out of service and four, 266, 273, 274 and 277 were selected for learner duties. 273 and 274 became learners on 16 March 1956 and 266 and 277 on 1 November the same year. On 1 November also, five of the "HUM" series of Regents, 106, 111, 112, 115 and 116 joined the learner fleet. 235 and 236 were withdrawn in March 1956 and 76, 169 and the recently introduced 273, followed on 31 October. The learner fleet, therefore, on 1 November 1956, consisted of the following eight buses: 106, 111, 112, 115, 116, 266, 274 and 277.

These eight vehicles lost their original numbers in early April 1958 being renumbered 1-8 respectively. Gill sans numerals were provided both inside and out. These were the first Leeds buses to carry these fleet numbers since 1929-30 when the Guy single deckers were withdrawn. No. 3 (ex-112) was the vehicle used as the Chief Examiner's bus in the learner fleet. The fleet remained unchanged until 1962.

In addition to the usual "elderly" buses used for learner duties, some of the newer buses were also employed for driver's instruction. A small removable window was placed behind the driver's seat and Daimler CVG6LX/30 517 had this feature almost from new. However, following an accident to 517, in September 1961, 514 took over as the Daimler Learner bus. Crossley 702 and Leyland PD2/14 301 had been fitted with removable windows in March 1955 and 379 and 380 followed in November 1956.

In July 1960 the 'Leeds & District Transport News' published a complete list of buses which had been fitted with the removable windows until that time: 20, 28, 201, 202, 245 (PD3), 301, 319, 358, 359, 377-380, 401, 402, 517, 530, 533, 702, 718, 766, 767, and 830. At the time of the listing Leyland TS8 20, Leyland PD1 319 and Daimler CVD6 530 had been withdrawn. Other buses later had the removable windows for a time.

In April 1962 an important change in driver training practice took place and thanks to the 'Leeds and District Transport News' of this date it is possible to describe it in detail. During April a new system of driving instruction was introduced. Briefly the old system of driving instruction was as follows:

Following a lecture in the "School Room" at Donisthorpe Street Garage, trainees were shown by means of an old A.E.C. Regent chassis (formerly that on bus 40 – UG 1027), fitted with a glass topped epicyclic gear box exactly what happened when the various pedals were pressed. Trainees were then allocated to an Inspector driving instructor, usually two trainees to one instructor. For the next five days, preliminary driving was carried out on one of the pre-war A.E.C. Mark I Regents, 1-8, working from Torre Road Depot and each instructor had his own school bus. On the fifth day a preliminary test was carried out over a simple course using one of the Regents. Successful candidates then passed on to training on service types of buses.

Training on vehicles fitted with semi-automatic epicyclic gear boxes was kept to a minimum and as much time as possible was spent on vehicles with the old type "live" or "crash" boxes, such as were used on the Crossleys and Leyland PD2/1 buses. After 16 days, trainees took the final driving test on a PD2/1 bus over a course, which passed through the city centre and negotiated two very steep hills, Beeston Road and Cemetery Road, also at Beeston. The trainee then had to reverse uphill from Cemetery Road into Malvern Street, by no means an easy manoeuvre.

The larger part of the training period centred on the Leyland PD2/1 buses (340-399), after the withdrawal of the PD1, probably the most difficult buses in Leeds to drive. This was where the main changes took place.

Under the new system, the preliminary training on the A.E.C. Regent was continued, but for the training on the service types, a number of experienced drivers were selected for tuition duties. The number of instructor drivers varied from garage to garage depending upon its size. Previously all instruction had been carried out at Torre Road Garage, but was now also done from the other garages.

To make things easier, training on the old type buses with clutches was kept to a minimum. Only drivers from Bramley Garage, for example, received training on the PD2/1, which were confined to that Garage. PD2/1 training was carried out by inspectors only. Although the Crossleys ran from Seacroft Garage, these were soon to be withdrawn from service and new Seacroft drivers were not taught to drive them. The final driving test was now done on an A.E.C. Regent III in place of a Leyland PD2/1.

Under the old system drivers receiving licences were able to drive all types of public service vehicle. However, only drivers from Bramley Depot received this licence. Other drivers were restricted to driving vehicles with epicyclic transmission only.

As a result of each garage doing its own training, more buses were fitted with the removable bulkhead windows behind the driver's cab. These included:

Headingley Garage.   601 and 871.
Hunslet Garage.   651 and 780.
Seacroft Garage.   631 and 781.
Sovereign Street.   731.
Torre Road Garage.   910.

In addition to the above, Bramley Garage was now using Leyland PD2/14 bus 301, which had been fitted with the removable window in 1955, but had controls similar to

In 1955 Leyland TS8 number 19 was converted into a handicapped persons vehicle for the Leeds City Welfare Department. It ran until October 1960. This photograph was taken on 15 July 1960 of the bus pulling out of Oldfield Lane into Tong Road at the Crown Hotel, New Wortley. *W.D.Wilson/L.T.H.S.*

A.E.C. Regent JUG 647 (ex-414) as Learner bus 1 appeared in October 1962. For a time it was the Chief Driving Examiner's bus. It is passing The Queen Hotel, Burley Road, on 2 March 1965. *W.D.Wilson/L.T.H.S.*

the A.E.C. Regent III type. Sovereign Street Garage had A.E.C. Regent V 770, which had been used by the Driving School at Torre Road.

The demonstration chassis and glass topped gear box from bus 40 became disused and after the closure of Donisthorpe Street Garage in June 1962, it was scrapped.

The first of the learner buses to be withdrawn was 1 (ex-106), which was used as a decorated bus for Premium Bond Week in March 1962. It was later used for similar events.

A new learner bus, numbered 1, appeared in October 1962. It was A.E.C. Regent III 414 (JUG 647), which had been withdrawn from passenger service on 31 July 1962. 414 had been extensively overhauled and modified and replaced No.3 as the Chief Driving Examiner's Bus. It was used for lecture purposes for trainee drivers and was fitted with loud speakers in both saloons. In the lower saloon, the panelling around the conductor's locker was fitted with a rack containing safe driving pamphlets etc. The only seats retained were the longitudinal seat over the near side rear wheel arch, and the front four double seats, two on each side of the gangway. The offside of the saloon was occupied by a bench, on top of which was a model fluid flywheel and photographs of vehicles damaged in accidents. A shelf pulled out from under the bench on which was a collection of flywheels and other mechanical components, which had been damaged by bad driving. The bulkhead window behind the driver's seat was removed and a loud speaker fitted on the bulkhead.

In the upper saloon all seats except the front pair on each side were retained. The backs were fitted with small wooden blocks to act as rests for note pads issued to trainees. The space provided by the removal of the two front seats was taken up by a desk over the cab, and a small swivel seat on the nearside. The front of the desk lifted up and clipped on to the ceiling to form a blackboard.

The rear panel of the bus was extended round the platform and there was a single hand-operated jack-knife door and a two-way radio.

Number 1 was finished in a recently revised livery, with light green lower saloon windows, the front destination glass being painted over and the word PRIVATE painted on. Reversible "L" plates were fitted at front and rear, a white blank being displayed when a qualified driver was at the wheel.

Alterations to the learner fleet occurred in October 1963 when the pre-war A.E.C. Regents were finally withdrawn. 4 and 7 were delicensed shortly before the end of October, but 2, 5, 6 and 8 remained until the end of the month. 1 had been out of use from early 1962 and in September 1962, 3 was withdrawn and later sold for preservation.

Taken out of passenger service in October 1963 were a number of A.E.C. Regent III and several of these became learner buses. 417 (LUA 417) and 418 (LUA 418) became 2 and 3 respectively in the Learner fleet and both entered use on 4 November 1963. They were not repainted and both retained their destination blinds. The only structural alterations were the removal of the bulkhead windows behind the driver's seat and the fitting of twin rear lights. By the end of November 3 had been repainted in the new livery with 2 following in December. Later in November and December four further buses were converted into training buses:

4 (LUA 421) formerly 421, which entered use on 1 December was repainted in the new style livery and fitted with a platform door. It had "PRIVATE" painted on the front destination window and was fitted with twin rear lights and flashing trafficators at both front and rear. It was the first learner bus to be fitted with flashing trafficators.

5 (LUA 424), formerly 424, entered service by 14 November, in the old livery but with the advertisements painted out. Destination blinds were still fitted and it had

1459

twin rear lights and provision for flashing trafficators. By early December it had been repainted in the new livery.

6 (LUA 426), formerly 426, with all the alterations as 4, but not repainted. It was in use by 27 November and was repainted in December 1963.

7 (LUA 428) formerly 428, was repainted in the new livery, but was not fitted with platform doors. It had "PRIVATE" painted on the destination window at the front and was fitted with twin rear lights and flashing trafficators at front and rear. It was in use by 1 January 1964. Platform doors were fitted a month later.

The learner fleet on 1 January 1964 consisted of seven buses, 1-7. All had been repainted in the new livery. By mid-March 1964 2, 3 and 5 had all been fitted with trafficators and "PRIVATE" had been painted on the destination windows. The buses without platform doors, 2, 3 and 5 had chains. On 4 February 1965 5 appeared in service with platform doors and a saloon heater.

From 1 April 1966 the learner fleet was increased by the addition of three more buses, 8, 9 and 11, making a total of ten vehicles, the largest it had ever been. The three newly converted buses were A.E.C. Regent III MUG 458, 456 and 460 respectively, which were originally 458, 456 and 460 in the passenger fleet. All had been withdrawn in December 1965. They had an extra rear light on the nearside and their front and rear destination glasses were painted over. Otherwise they were unaltered. The A.E.C. Reliance coach, ANW 710C, was numbered 10, hence the reason for the fleet numbers allocated to the three new learner buses.

Leyland PD2 380 was withdrawn from service on 19 December 1966 and transferred to the learner fleet. On 10 January 1967 it entered use in its new role as number 12.

On Monday, 10 February 1969, three more Learner buses appeared in use. These were the last three A.E.C.

Regent III buses of the 476-500 series and were as follows:

13 NNW 487 formerly 487.
14 NNW 494 formerly 494.
15 NNW 492 formerly 492.

All three buses had the lower dark green panels repainted, but still carried the old style insignia. The destination blind windows were painted green, the front one being lettered "PRIVATE" and at the rear, a nearside light was fitted.

The learner fleet was now the largest ever with 14 buses, of five different series of buses. All were A.E.C. Regent III except for 12, ex-380, a Leyland PD2/1.

In December 1970 the Learner fleet was further expanded by the addition of four more buses. These were recently withdrawn A.E.C. Regent V buses, 830-833. They became:

16 WUA 830, formerly 830, in service 15 December.
17 WUA 833, formerly 833, in service 28 December.
18 WUA 832, formerly 832, in service 28 December.
19 WUA 831, formerly 831, in service 16 December.

During the latter part of 1970 A.E.C. Regent III learners, 8, 9, 11, 13-15 and Leyland PD2/1 12 were all fitted with flashing trafficators at the front only.

After service on 19 March 1971, A.E.C. Regent III 9 (MUG 456) was withdrawn from service. It was replaced by a new number 9, a Leyland PD2/11 formerly 218 (UUA 218) in the passenger fleet. It was to be the first of several buses of this type, which were to replace the A.E.C. Regent III. The new 9 entered service as a Learner on 1 April 1971. It was in a new livery of ivory and dark green. The style of painting was the same as used on rear-engined double deckers with the ivory in the same position as the Lincoln green. The new style insignia was positioned at the top of the front panel, as on recently

Often seen in Great George Street at the back of the Leeds Town Hall was A.E.C. Regent UG 8779, formerly bus 63. It was used by the Yorkshire Symphony Orchestra as an instrument van and was photographed on 18 June 1955. When the Orchestra was disbanded at the end of July that year, the vehicle was sold. It was painted in a pale buff and brown livery. In addition to UG 8779, there were three other Y.S.O. vehicles: JX 3420-1, ex-Halifax Corporation A.E.C. Regals, 25 and 26, acquired in 1947 and HL 9398, a Bedford WTB, ex-West Riding 230, formerly with Bullock & Sons, acquired in 1951. All four vehicles were maintained by the Leeds Transport Department and housed at Torre Road Depot. *W.D.Wilson/L.T.H.S.*

The chassis of A.E.C. Regent 142 (ANW 685) was transferred to the Leeds Highways Department in February 1955 and fitted with tar spraying equipment. It was number 209 in the Department's fleet and painted in a green livery with black boiler. First noted in its new role on 27 August 1955, it was severely damaged by fire on 23 July 1964 and scrapped. It was photographed in Town Street, Armley, on 5 September 1957. *W.D.Wilson/ L.T.H.S.*

repainted older buses, while the usual learner markings were also carried.

A month later, on 9 April 1971, another Learner bus, 13, (NNW 487), was withdrawn and replaced by a new 13, formerly Leyland PD2/11 207 (UUA 207). This vehicle was painted in the new ivory and green Learner livery, similar to 9.

In April and July 1971 three further A.E.C. Regent III were withdrawn. These were 2, 14 and 15. Although delicensed in July, 2 appears to have been last used on 5 April and 14 and 15 on 27 July 1971. 2 was the first of the "LUA" registered buses in the learner fleet to be withdrawn, while 14 and 15 were the last two of the three "NNW" registered buses used for training purposes.

2 was replaced by a Leyland PD2/11, also numbered 2, formerly 209, (UUA 209), which entered service on 1 September 1971. It was finished in a similar manner to 9 and 13, but with a number of small differences. It had rear reflective panels, similar to those then being fitted to lorries and other commercial vehicles and also orange reflectors fitted on the sides. The cab bulkhead was partially removed to make an entrance from the saloon into the cab. The driving instructor's seat in the saloon was placed in a higher position.

On 27 August 1971 another A.E.C. Regent III, 3 (LUA 418), was taken out of service. It was replaced on 19 November 1971 when a new number 3 appeared. It was Leyland PD2/11 210, (UUA 210), finished in the ivory and dark green livery similar to the other Leyland PD2/11 tuition vehicles.

An interesting withdrawal on 31 December 1971 was Leyland PD2/1 12 (NNW 380), formerly 380 in the passenger fleet, and the last of 60 similar buses of this type, 340-399, to exist. Latterly this bus was not used very much, its purpose in the driving school being to test drivers who already held licences and who applied to become bus drivers. On 27 January 1972 A.E.C.Regent III 8 (MUG 458) was withdrawn and on 7 February a new number 8 appeared. It was Leyland PD2/11, (UUA 211), formerly 211

in the passenger fleet. It was finished in the livery of ivory and dark green.

Another A.E.C. Regent III, 11, (MUG 460), was withdrawn on 21 January 1972. The new 11 was Leyland PD2/11, (UUA 212), formerly 212. It was finished in a similar manner to the other buses of this type and was first used in its new role on 24 April 1972.

One of the four A.E.C. Regent V buses used for training purposes was withdrawn in April 1972. It was 17, (WUA 833) and had been out of use from November 1971.

The oldest A.E.C. Regent III in the Learner fleet, 1 (JUG 647) formerly 414, was withdrawn in May 1972. Leyland PD2/11, 213 (UUA 213), was its replacement, entering service on 12 June 1972. 214 (UUA 214), appeared as Learner 12 on 3 August 1972.

In August and October 1972 the last four A.E.C. Regent III, 1947-built, Learner buses were withdrawn from service:

6 (LUA 426)   last used 23 August 1972.
4 (LUA 421)   last used 25 October 1972.
5 (LUA 424)   last used 27 October 1972.
7 (LUA 428)   last used 30 October 1972.

Replacements for the four buses were two Leyland PD2/11:

4 (UUA 215), formerly 215, in service 6 November 1972.
5 (UUA 216), formerly 216, in service 17 April 1973.

A further withdrawal from the learner fleet took place on 27 March 1973 when 16, (WUA 830), was taken out of service. 19 (WUA 831) was withdrawn on 23 May 1973. This left 18 (WUA 832) as the only A.E.C, Regent V still in the tuition fleet. It retained the old style fleet name "wings" at either side of the coat of arms. It was the last bus in the fleet to show this feature and was still in use as a learner at the close of this volume.

Leyland PD3/5 buses 226, (5226 NW), and 230, (5230 NW), were withdrawn from passenger service on 12 and 26 September 1973 respectively and transferred to the Driving School on 14 and 27 September whilst still licensed for passenger use.   They were still in normal livery with their fleet numbers. They were renumbered 6 (ex-226) and 7 (ex-230) for about a fortnight only and were temporary additions to the learner fleet and last used by the driving school on 4 December, (230), and 10 December, (226). They were replaced on a permanent basis by two other Leyland PD3/5, 228, (5228 NW), and 239, (5239 NW). 228 became 6 and 239 7 and appeared on 13 and 8 November 1973 respectively. They were repainted in the now standard learner livery of ivory and green.

On 1 April 1974 there were 13 learner buses in use. 1-9, 11-13 and 18. The former 4 (LUA 421), and 19 (WUA 831) were still in stock, but out of use.

A.E.C. Regent III 428 as Learner bus 7 at Middleton Park Circus (north side) on 27 July 1971. The concrete bus stop with L.C.T. logo was of the type introduced throughout Leeds from May 1964. *W.D. Wilson/ L.T.H.S.*

A.E.C. Regent III 460 as Learner bus 11 pictured on the Ring Road, to the west of Barwick Road on 3 June 1970. *W.D.Wilson/ L.T.H.S.*

Leyland PD2/11 218 became Learner 9 in 1971 and was the first of several buses of this type to become Learners. It was photographed at Redcote Lane, Stanningley Road, on 11 June 1975 and was painted in a new learner bus livery of ivory and green. *W.D.Wilson/L.T.H.S.*

One of the last Learner buses to be introduced by the Leeds Transport Department was Leyland PD3/5 239 which became Learner bus 7 in November 1973. It was painted in the new ivory and green livery and was photographed in Wellington Road on 1 October 1975. *W.D.Wilson/ L.T.H.S.*

At 1.45 a.m. on 4 April 1954 Chamberlain car 94 became the last tram to leave Headingley Depot. It was posed for photographers in the depot entrance. *Author.*

Thomas Lord, the General Manager, described the former tram depot at Bramley as "completely out of date." Opened in 1906 it was one of the few tram depots in Leeds with any architectural merit. Access at an acute angle was easy for trams, but difficult for buses. Leyland PD2/1 347 emerges from the former front entrance of the building on 4 May 1964. *Author.*

Depots, Garages and Buildings 1953 to 1974

During the period covered by this volume there were many changes to the depots and buildings used by the Leeds Transport Department. Several of the old tram depots were closed and new garages opened. For clarity the buildings are discussed in the same order as in the previous volumes.

Headingley Depot

Headingley Tram Depot had been rebuilt in 1935 and in 1938 a bus garage added on the south eastern side of the building. Under the tramway abandonment scheme, Headingley Depot was the first to be closed. On 19 October 1953, a fortnight after the closure of the Half Mile Lane tram route, the Transport Committee agreed to the conversion of the tramway part of the building for motor bus use. The estimated cost was £23,000.

Alterations began with the removal of track 1, nearest to the existing garage, on 15 March 1954. Last used by trams in the early morning of that date, the pit was filled in and the overhead gantry removed. Preparatory work was carried out on the other tracks in the depot, but all remained in use until the closure. This coincided with the abandonment of the Kirkstall Abbey and Compton Road tram routes on Saturday, 3 April 1954. The last service car to leave the depot was Horsfield 216 at 9.40 p.m. but all the cars on evening duty returned to Headingley after service. They went to Swinegate Depot in the early hours of Sunday morning, the last being Chamberlain 94 which left track 4 at 1.45 a.m. on 4 April. By that afternoon all the overhead wiring had been removed. Conversion of the depot into a bus garage took a lot longer. The work included the filling in of the tramcar pits and re-flooring, the extension of bus repair pit facilities, increased accommodation in the traffic office and improved canteen facilities.

By July 1954 about half of the former tramway area was in use for garaging buses. The remainder of the building was completed a few weeks later. The entrance tram track to the depot was removed on 17 October 1954. During 1958 the former tramway substation at the depot was demolished and the area used for bus parking.

After a few years the garage was considered to be inadequate for the Department's needs and in 1964 proposals were considered for building a new garage at Headingley to replace the existing building. The garage was to be included in the Department's 1969–1971 capital expenditure programme, but no action was taken.

At the rear of the existing garage were 15 terrace houses originally erected in 1885 and 1887 for employees of the old Leeds Tramways Company. In February 1969 the Transport and Trading Services Committee agreed to demolish the properties and, as a short-term measure pending the building of a new garage, to use the cleared site as a bus parking area. This work was carried out during the latter part of 1969.

The Transport Committee could never make its mind up in regard to the new garage at Headingley, and the building did not materialise. The Committee's last action in relation to building developments occurred on 8 March 1974, three weeks before the takeover by the West Yorkshire Passenger Transport Executive. On that date it accepted the tender of J.B.S. Renney Ltd in the sum of £52,950 40p. for alterations and extensions to the existing garage. The work, which involved extending the garage over the site of the former houses, and building a bus park and rear entrance to the garage, took place in 1974.

There were some later modifications to the building, which finally closed on 27 June 1992. It was demolished in September 1993.

Chapeltown Depot

Chapeltown Depot was one of the former tram depots which was not converted into a bus garage. This was because of the awkward access from Harrogate Road. The building was closed to service trams from 23 April 1955, coinciding with the closure of the Gipton tram service. Chamberlain car 60 was the last service tram to leave the depot (at 12.03 p.m.), but Chamberlain 68 was left there as a standby. As it was not required again on that day 68 left about 11.35 p.m. for Swinegate with a load of sandbags and other stores. Odd service cars due to return to Chapeltown at tea time went instead to Swinegate Depot, but the evening service cars returned to Chapeltown. They were sent to Swinegate in the early hours of 24 April, the last being Horsfield car 162 at 1.34 a.m. Decorated car 359 was driven to Chapeltown the same evening to join four snow sweepers, which were already in the building. For the next year or so the depot was used for the storage of works cars and several different cars awaiting scrap. When the snow sweepers left for Swinegate on 26 October 1956, that was the end of the building as a tram depot. It was sold to the Corporation Central Purchasing Department. The overhead wiring was removed in December 1956 and the tracks later, when extensive modifications were carried out at a cost of £39,000. The building was converted into a storage depot. On 18 August 1958 it was officially opened by the Lord Mayor, Alderman Mrs. Mary Pearce.

The building was extensively altered again later and is now virtually unrecognisable as a former tram depot. It is currently used by Tech North. The house at the front of the building, originally occupied by the depot foreman, was demolished in March 1963.

Hunslet Depot

The former tram depot at Hunslet accommodated about 50 buses and had been little changed since 1935. In that year a bus washing and fuelling shed was added. The tramway tracks in the yard to the Depot were partly covered in July 1958. During the early part of 1964 a considerable amount of property on the east side of Low Road, opposite the Depot, was demolished. From May the cleared space was used at night and on Sundays for parking buses.

The depot was totally unsuitable for a modern bus fleet and access was very awkward. It was said to be "physically impossible" to get the larger buses into the building and expansion was not practicable. The construction of the new Middleton Garage gave the Transport Department an opportunity to close the building. It ceased to be operational at 8.00 p.m. on 12 November 1966, and the last bus to run into the garage was A.E.C. Regent V 792, just before eight. After that time buses returned to the new Middleton Garage. At the time of its closure, 58 buses were allocated to Hunslet Depot, some being parked on the derelict land in Low Road.

Hunslet Depot was appropriated by the Town Planning and Improvements Committee and was let to John Waddington Ltd. printers, Wakefield Road, on a 21 years lease. Waddingtons used the building as a store and when the firm vacated the premises, it was demolished in July and August 1993.

Horsfield car 162 in the entrance to Chapeltown Depot on 20 April 1955. *Author.*

On 23 April 1955, apart from four stored snow sweepers, Chapeltown Depot was empty. However, Chamberlain car 68 was retained as a standby in case of need. *Author.*

After the closure of Chapeltown Depot several service cars returned to the depot and were then driven to Swinegate. In the early hours of 24 April 1955 Horsfield car 207 heads a line of cars parked in Sovereign Street outside Swinegate Depot. *Author.*

Bramley Depot

Buses had operated from the former tram depot at Bramley from 4 December 1949. During 1955 and 1956 constructional work for an "Essex" Bus Washing Plant was carried out at the garage. The tramway substation in the building ceased to be used after October 1953 on the abandonment of the 14 tram route. It was, however, taken over by the electricity authority, the two tramway 375 kW mercury arc rectifier sets being transferred to Belle Isle substation. In 1960 a new traffic office, canteen and kitchen were built.

Following the building of the new Bramley Garage (discussed below), the depot was closed, buses leaving for the last time on 13 April 1969. The last bus to leave the depot on service appears to have been Leyland Atlantean 331.

For most of its latter existence Bramley Depot had been the home of the Leyland PD1 (319-333) and PD2 buses, (340-399), all of which, by 1969, had been withdrawn from service.

Within days of closure, demolition of the building began and was completed in June 1969.

Bramley Garage

In the early 'sixties there were proposals for the construction of a dual carriageway Stanningley by-pass road. The road was to start at the old Bramley Depot, which would be demolished to make way for the road. Thomas Lord, the General Manager, said the building was too small and described it as "completely out of date, unsatisfactory and uneconomic." A new site for a garage was required and in January 1964 the Transport Committee approved a site off Henconner Lane, Bramley. In October 1964 the land was appropriated from the Town Planning and Improvements Committee. Drawings were prepared by the City Architect's Department and the contractor was Richard Costain

(Construction) Ltd. The cost of the building was to be £611,903 plus fees of £46,750. Construction was deferred by the Conservative administration in an endeavour to save costs. Savings amounting to about £100,000 were made. Councillor D.A. Wolstenholme said the saving had been achieved by reducing the size of the parking area, there was to be echelon parking of the buses instead of block parking. One bay of the garage was deleted, reducing the covered space for buses by 25%. Building work began soon afterwards and took 18 months. The garage was modelled on the Sheffield East Bank Garage and the new Middleton Garage (opened in November 1966 and discussed later). The site was, however, much more restricted being adjacent to the new Stanningley by pass. It had facilities for the same number of administrative staff as Middleton and for servicing and housing a similar number of buses - 125. As one bay had been deleted, many of the buses had to stand in the open air. There was a perimeter road and a short section of dual carriageway at the entrance. The building became operational from 9.00 p.m. on Saturday 12 April 1969, following which buses ran into it from service. Leyland Atlantean 340 was the first, entering the garage around 10.00 pm. The entire allocation of buses from the old Bramley Depot was transferred to the new Garage on Sunday 13 April.

With the completion of the garage, the total garage capacity of the Transport Department was increased and the undertaking was "over-garaged" by about 100 vehicles. The Transport Department had ideas of expanding services and increasing the bus fleet to 800 vehicles, but this never happened. The maximum number reached was 708 in 1968. From then on the numbers declined and following service cuts from the late 'sixties onwards, levelled out at between 500 and 600 vehicles.

Seacroft Garage

Briefly mentioned in Chapter 73, the decision to build a new garage for motor buses on the Seacroft Estate was

Many buses garaged at Hunslet were parked on vacant land on the east side of Thwaite Gate, but A.E.C. Regent V 856 managed to find a space adjacent to the depot entrance. The date: 14th March 1965. *Author.*

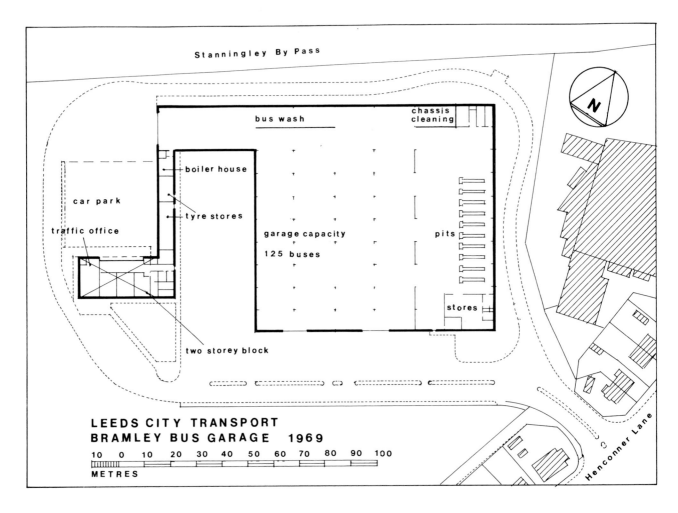

Stanningley By Pass

bus wash

chassis cleaning

boiler house

car park

tyre stores

traffic office

garage capacity

125 buses

pits

N

stores

two storey block

LEEDS CITY TRANSPORT
BRAMLEY BUS GARAGE 1969

10 0 10 20 30 40 50 60 70 80 90 100

METRES

Henconner Lane

The interior of the new Seacroft Garage in 1956 with a row of buses, mainly A.E.C. Regent V.
Leeds City Transport.

made by the Transport Committee in February 1954, the estimated cost being £160,000. The building was designed by the City Architect, R.A,H,Livett, and construction began on 10 May 1955. The contractor was Higgs & Hill Ltd. of Leeds and the garage was completed a year later. The garage was situated in Limewood Approach on the fringe of the Seacroft Estate. Alderman Rafferty, chairman of the Transport Committee, said that Seacroft would eventually have a population of 50,000. The garage location would save "thousands of miles of dead mileage," he said. The garage was 183 feet long with a single span of 100 feet and housed 50 buses. Three covered parking sheds were provided, which gave a further 48 covered spaces. Separate from the main building was a bus wash building of 1,764 sq. feet. It had a maximum capacity under winter conditions of 20 buses an hour.

It was stated that the Department's maximum garage capacity was now increased to 588 buses. The site area was 3·33 acres and the area covered by the garage and office accommodation 27,954 sq. ft.

"The main span of the garage is 100 ft. The garage has corrugated roof lights with a main colour scheme of green and buff. The airy spaciousness of the interior is enhanced by these colours. The building has ancillary rooms on two storeys finished in pastel shades. Among rooms on the second storey is an extremely attractive canteen overlooking open country with small separate tables, a contemporary style serving counter and a bright, altogether well-groomed appearance. Ultimately it is expected the canteen will provide 300 to 400 hot meals a day."

'The Yorkshire Post', 18 July 1956.

The new building also housed an oil store, traffic office, strong room, cleaner's and electrician's departments, body shop, tyre shop and refuelling section.

It was said that the completion of the garage was a "vital link" in the change over from trams to buses in the city. Until the garage was completed it was not possible to carry out the abandonment of the Whingate and New Inn tram routes.

The garage was officially opened on Friday, 13 July 1956, by the Rt. Hon. Hugh Molson M.P., the Joint Parliamentary Secretary to the Ministry of Transport and Civil Aviation. Route and vehicle operation began on Sunday, 22 July, the day after the cessation of the Whingate and New Inn tramway services.

In February 1964 proposals were made for the construction of two additional bus parking sheds adjoining the garage. The agreed cost was to be £26,050. The parking sheds were to double the capacity for vehicles at the garage. In addition the Highways Department was asked to build a garage turning circle, at an estimated cost of £2,500. The erection of the parking sheds was carried out by the Corporation Works Department during the summer of 1964. During 1965 an entrance to the garage from Limewood Approach was formed and gave direct access to and from the Ring Road. Until this time buses had reached the garage via an access road from Ramshead Drive. Also in 1965 an employees' car park was formed on the south side of the bus parking area.

There were later additions and alterations and the building remained in use as a bus garage until 3 July 1983. Extensive service reductions in the 'seventies and 'eighties rendered the building unnecessary. The garage is currently occupied by the Leeds Highways and Street Lighting Departments.

Seacroft Bus Station

During 1964 and 1965 a new civic and shopping centre was built at Seacroft. The scheme included a small bus station situated off Seacroft Avenue. Work on this started in July 1965 and on 17 October it was opened. Four bus services were extended from their termini in the Seacroft Estate to the new bus station. The route extensions were as follows:

Service 11 (Swinnow-Ironwood View) was extended from its old terminus at Ironwood View via Kentmere

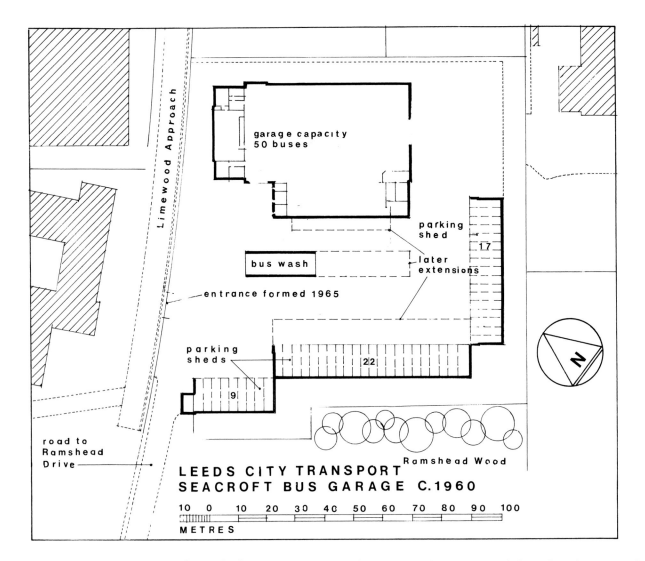

garage capacity
50 buses

parking
shed

17

later
extensions

bus wash

entrance formed 1965

parking
sheds

22

parking
sheds

9

road to
Ramshead
Drive

Ramshead Wood

N

LEEDS CITY TRANSPORT
SEACROFT BUS GARAGE C.1960

10 0 10 20 30 40 50 60 70 80 90 100
METRES

Limewood Approach

Avenue, Brooklands Avenue, Seacroft Crescent and Seacroft Avenue to the Centre.

Service 15 (Bramley Town End-South Parkway) was extended from its previous terminus at Parklands High School via South Parkway, York Road and Seacroft Avenue.

Service 16 (Bramley Town End-North Parkway) now went beyond its former terminus at Ramshead Drive via North Parkway and Seacroft Avenue to the new bus station.

Service 45 (Wortley-North Parkway) was extended to the new bus station via North Parkway.

The Ring Road service 9 which passed close to the Centre was unchanged.

The bus station had four platforms of which the 15 and 16 services used one platform and the 11 and 45 services had one each. This left one platform vacant. In December 1965 barrier rails and shelters were provided on the platforms. From 1965 to 1974 the bus station was unchanged.

Sovereign Street Yard and Garage

In June 1954 some of the single storey sheds used for tramway purposes, such as storage and drying of sand, were pulled down. The area where they stood was resurfaced and marked out with parking bays for buses. The bus parking area came into use from 4 July 1954. During the daytime, buses on the new Rockingham Street Bus Station services (see below) were parked there. Sand storage and drying was moved to Swinegate Tram Depot. Later, to save "dead mileage", buses on other services were parked in the yard.

The works trams were removed and on 25 and 26 October 1957 the overhead wiring in the eastern half of the

yard was taken down, some of the rails taken up and tarmacadam laid.

Between the morning and evening peak periods some buses from the new Seacroft Garage had been parked adjacent to platform "F" at the Central Bus Station, but from December 1957 were relocated in the extended parking area in Sovereign Street. The conversion scheme allowed off-peak parking for 40 buses.

Half of the yard remained in use until the closure of the tramway system. The overhead wiring was removed at the beginning of January 1960. The last tram in the enclosure was the 1910 vintage electric crane, dismantled in February 1960. Work on demolishing the large layout shed and machine shop began in May 1960 and was completed two and a half months later. It was a long time before Corporation buses began to use the enlarged yard. From the evening of 21 December 1961 and until 27 January the following year the yard was used by vans and lorries belonging to Billy Smart's Circus, which were using the new Queen's Hall during that period. It was not until June 1963 that the bus parking area was extended over the site of the old permanent way shed. Buses began to use the extended area in July 1963.

A number of modifications to the blister hangar garage in Sovereign Street were carried out in the summer and autumn of 1969. Torre Road No.2 Garage closed down as a running garage in October 1969 and this placed a lot of pressure on Sovereign Street Garage. From 26 October 1969 several routes were transferred between garages and Sovereign Street took over the responsibility of changing over all defective buses and attending to breakdowns. The garage also received a surplus allowance of buses to cover other garages with spares. All these tasks had formerly been done at Torre Road No.

A line of Leyland buses at the rear of the old Bramley Garage on 1 May 1966. From the left are buses 388, 324, 396, 303, 302 and 392. *W.D.Wilson/ L.T.H.S.*

A line of Leyland PD3/5 buses withdrawn for scrap and parked in the "missing bay" at the new Bramley Garage on 19 May 1974. From the left are buses 223, 243, 238, 270, 271, 276 and 250. *W.D.Wilson/L.T.H.S.*

A line of 1954-55 withdrawn single deck buses at Bramley Garage on 23 June 1968. From left to right they are 36, 31, 34, 33, 35 and 32. *W.D.Wilson/L.T.H.S.*

Garage. To cater for the new arrangements a number of modifications were done at Sovereign Street. These included new inspection pits, maintenance bays increased, and new bus washing facilities etc. The western entrance was widened and slightly repositioned to enable the wider and longer buses to enter more easily. The exit into Concordia Street had been widened earlier -in May 1969. The cost of the alterations was £10,320.

The building was unchanged until the closure of this volume and although regarded as "temporary", remained in use until 1 June 1991.

Swinegate Depot

After the removal of the sand drying plant in Sovereign Street Yard there was a delay of a few months before a start was made on 6 October 1954 on the erection of new plant in Swinegate Depot. The work involved the removal of the western-most three tracks, 28, 29 and 30, and the overhead wiring. The three tracks had been used for the storage of works cars and the latter were either removed to other parts of the depot or into Sovereign Street Permanent Way Yard.

In February 1955 track 27 was closed for most of its length to make way for a brick built coke enclosure and the new sand drying plant came into use at the end of March 1955. Also in 1955, new accommodation was provided in the depot for the Traffic Instruction School.

Owing to the impending closure of Torre Road Depot and anticipated increased use of the Swinegate Arches, in October 1955 new and improved lighting was fitted in the Depot and Arches. A gateway was formed near the exit from the main depot to the Arches. From Friday evening, 18 November 1955, Swinegate Arches came into regular use for service cars. Cars formerly stored there for overhaul or scrap, were taken to Chapeltown Depot. The use of the Arches for service cars did not last long for, with the closure of the number 1 route, Briggate to Lawnswood on 3 March the following year, the Arches reverted to storage only.

The Arches continued to be used for this purpose until 27 September 1957, the day before the abandonment of the Moortown via Chapeltown to Dewsbury Road tram services. Cars 257 and finally, Feltham 562, were the last to leave the Arches. They were moved into the main Swinegate Tram Depot.

The overhead wiring was removed on 9 October 1957 and the rails in May and June 1961.

After the closure of Kirkstall Road Works for tramcar repairs on 4 November 1957, car maintenance was carried out at Swinegate Depot. The western portion, tracks 17 to 27, was allocated for works use and tracks 1-16, remained as the running depot. Lifting equipment was transferred from Kirkstall, which enabled motor and truck changes to be effected. Body repairs, electrical work and limited painting operations were also carried out. Most of the works staff at Kirkstall was moved to Swinegate, but some workmen were retained at Kirkstall for truck maintenance.

Both the works and depot remained in use until the abandonment of the tramway system on 7 November 1959. The building was gradually vacated, car 202 being the last tram in the building. The overhead wires were removed in March 1960 and about the same time the front door of the depot was partially blocked up, leaving a small door just large enough for a van or small lorry to pass through.

There had been talk for a number of years of building an exhibition hall in Leeds and, from 1954, a six acre site had been reserved on land between Westgate and Wellington Street. Because of the large cost (£500,000 in 1954) the scheme had not been proceeded with. Swinegate Depot covered about 105,000 square feet and was considered to be a suitable and much less expensive alternative.

The City Council decided that the building be used for exhibition purposes and in November 1960 the building

The interior of the blister hangar garage in Sovereign Street with Daimler CVG6 539 and A.E.C. Regent III 753 on 28 May 1966. *Author.*

Horsfield car 202 in Swinegate Depot. It was photographed with two of the rail cars, 600 (on jacks on the left) and 601. *M.J. O'Connor/ National Tramway Museum.*

After the closure of Torre Road Depot, the Swinegate Depot Arches were occupied by service cars. The Arches were used for this purpose from 18 November 1955 to 3 March 1956, Chamberlain car 60 was photographed on 4 February 1956. *Author.*

was leased to Modern Exhibition Services Ltd. for 21 years at £4.000 per annum for use as an Exhibition Hall.

Work began on Monday, 13 February 1961, in converting the building. The rails over the pits were taken up and a new concrete floor put down. Only half of the building (tracks 1 to 15) were to be used as an exhibition hall, which was to be known as "Queen's Hall", The western half (tracks 16 to 30) was to be used for car parking. Work proceeded rapidly; a large sign reading "Queen's Hall" was erected over the front entrance and an internal entrance lobby formed. On 6 May 1961 the building opened as an Exhibition Hall, housing the Yorkshire Evening Post Ideal Homes and Food Exhibition.

Although much of the building was now used for Exhibition purposes, part of Swinegate Depot was still occupied by the Transport Department. The Traffic Superintendent's Office and Traffic Office remained in use, but, on 12 and 13 July 1961, were moved to the main transport head office in Swinegate.

In March 1969 plans were approved to redevelop the site as a £4,500,000 exhibition centre with entertainment, hotel, offices, leisure swimming pool with tropical plants, solarium, and car parking facilities for 2,000 cars. There was to be a bus station, heliport and a pedestrian walkway to the City Station. The developers were Bantam Investment Ltd. Work was to be carried out in two stages for completion by 1972 and 1978, but nothing more was heard about the project.

In June and July 1976 the remaining tram rails and pointwork at the west end of the Depot (tracks 16–30) were removed or covered with tarmacadam. As Queen's Hall, the life of the building was prolonged for 28 years. Demolition began on 8 October 1989 and took seven weeks, after which the site was used as a car park.

Torre Road Depot

The construction of Torre Road Depot, the most modern of the Leeds tram depots, is discussed in Volume 3. On 1 April 1952, 78 trams were allocated to the depot.

After the announcement that the tramways were to be abandoned, it did not remain a tram depot for long.

The first part of the complex to close to trams was the Belfast Shed in Torre Road Yard. Apart from one track (the one nearest York Road) the overhead wiring was removed during the summer of 1953 and the last car to leave was Feltham 566 about 7 August 1953. Work began immediately to make the building suitable for buses and it became part of the running garage. Earlier, a steep ramp had been constructed at the rear of what was to be the site of the Housing Shed. This gave access from the bus garage yard to the top yard. Buses entered the Belfast shed by way of a newly fitted door at the west end (opposite Walford Mount), and left at the Lupton Avenue end.

During the latter part of 1954, a new drive-through Dawson vehicle steam cleaning machine was installed in the former ambulance shed. This replaced an earlier Essex bus wash, which had been located inside the garage near to the foreman's office. Additional inspection pits were provided.

From the same day that the Beeston tram route ceased to operate, 19 November 1955, Torre Road Tram Depot closed to all service cars. The Feltham cars allocated there were transferred to Swinegate Depot, the last to leave being 562 in the early morning of the 20 November. After closure eleven Chamberlain cars were retained for storage. Work immediately began on filling the pits and removing the gantries in the depot. The Chamberlains were removed piecemeal the following month, the last to leave being cars 38 and 126 on 15 December 1955.

From an unknown post war date, the conductors' training school had been located in a single storey building in the yard close to the exit in Lupton Avenue. About November 1955 the school was transferred to Swinegate, adjacent to track 1 in the tram depot.

On 20 November 1954 the allocation at Torre Road was 205 buses and there were also four driver-training buses plus the recovery and gritting vehicles. Additionally, non-departmental vehicles garaged and maintained at Torre Road were the Electricity Board buses and the four Yorkshire Symphony Orchestra vehicles.

On 22 July 1956 Seacroft Garage had been opened and most of its allocation was transferred from Torre Road. From the same date the Belfast Shed ceased to be used for service buses and from then on housed the training fleet and stored vehicles.

It took nearly two years to convert the tram depot into a bus garage. The pits were filled in and a new concrete floor laid. Whereas the tram depot had been unheated, the buses required an oil fired heating plant and a new boiler house. The modifications increased the capacity of the garage by a further 100 buses, raising the total capacity of the garage to 230 buses. Following the abandonment of the Dewsbury Road-Moortown tram route, the garage was finally opened on 29 September 1957. It was referred to as the "Torre Road No. 2 Garage". The original bus garage was designated "Torre Road No.1 Garage". For maintenance and operational purposes the two garages were, in effect, two independent garages with their own allocations.

Before the closure of the building as a tram depot, two new outside parking sheds had been built for the buses. These were known as the "Long Shed" and the "Housing Shed". Behind the "Housing Shed" was a piece of land where badly accident damaged buses were hidden from prying eyes. The sheds came into use in August 1954. Also used for the outside storage of buses was the former extended Ambulance Shed (from 1951).

The Depot yard at Torre was used for the storage of trams long after the main building had been taken over by motor buses. Cars for scrap and latterly works cars were stored there virtually until the end of tramway operation. The overhead wires in the yard were removed on 27 and 28 July 1958 and the works cars still there, were left stranded. They were towed away between 7 and 9 October 1959.

Feltham car 538, other Felthams and two Chamberlains in Torre Road Depot on 15 October 1955. *Author.*

The yard at Torre Road Depot remained in use for storing scrap tramcars for four years after the trams were removed from the main depot. Chamberlain car 66 heads a line of cars withdrawn after the closure of the number 14 Half Mile Lane route. Behind 66 is car 35 in its odd style blue livery, the date being 18 October 1953. *Author.*

Low Fields Road Yard was used for scrapping trams until November 1957. Chamberlain 434 was photographed on 16 July 1955 and on the left is the ex-Highways Department locomotive, disused by this date. The overturned tram just visible on the right is Chamberlain car 44 and a factory chimney in Elland Road is belching smoke. Adjacent to the scrap yard was a cricket ground and cricketers can be seen to the right of the tram. Both 434 and 44 were burned on 18 July. 44 was the last tram in Leeds to have English Electric (Dick Kerr) controllers. *Author.*

With the abandonment of the last tram routes on 7 November 1959, the bus allocation reached its peak. On 1 February 1960, the official allocation at No.1 Garage was 152 and at No.2 Garage, 164, a total of 316 out of a fleet strength of 693. Also at Torre Road, were eight learner buses, the recovery and gritting vehicles as well as nine Electricity Board buses and a City Council Welfare bus. The allocation for No.2 Garage included the spare vehicles in the fleet, which covered changeovers and loans to other garages whilst their vehicles were in works.

Following the removal of the trams there was little change to the buildings in the 1960's. However, in 1963 a new steel building for housing bus chassis cleaning plant was erected and a 12 tons capacity vehicle hoist fitted. The opening of the new Middleton Garage in November 1966 resulted in many buses being transferred to Middleton. The allocation of buses to No.1 Garage dropped from 129 to 107, and No.2 Garage from 162 to 126. After 1966 the Transport Department had an excess of garage capacity.

More crews and buses moved out on 13 April 1969, when the new garage at Bramley opened. On 26 September 1969 proposals were approved by the Transport Committee for alterations to provide a "new vehicle maintenance depot and a bus garage for parking and maintenance of approximately 150 buses". This marked an important change. From 12 October 1969, the two garages were merged into one and from the same day, Sovereign Street Garage took over the responsibility of doing changeovers. As a result the spare buses and recovery vehicles moved out. Torre Road No.2 Garage (the former tram depot) temporarily closed as a running garage to enable the maintenance facilities to be extended. The pit area in No.2 Garage continued to be used for maintenance work while it also housed the driving school fleet, buses awaiting works, delicensed buses etc.

From 1956 until January 1965 stored buses had been kept in the Belfast Shed, but these were transferred to the empty, former Donisthorpe Street Bus Works, This was to make way for the vehicles from the former Central Cartage Garage in Concordia Street. From February 1965 the Belfast Shed was used for the training bus fleet together with the vehicles transferred from Concordia Street. Following the opening of Middleton Garage in November 1966, the Shed was again used mainly by buses withdrawn for scrap. There was abundant space in the main No.1 and 2 Garages and the learner buses were moved to No.2 Garage. On 24 April 1969, the Belfast shed was finally closed to buses, when withdrawn A.E.C. Regent III, 610, was moved out of the building.

In July 1969 centralisation of all the vehicles owned by the Corporation Cleansing, Highways, City Lighting, Waterworks, and Works Departments was proposed. As an economy measure the maintenance of the vehicles was to be integrated into one department. This was to be done by converting part of Torre Road Garage.

The alteration works at No.2 Garage were completed in May 1970, after which the former No.1 Garage was handed over to the Leeds City Council Central Vehicle Maintenance Department. It was then used for the overhaul of vehicles for the various Corporation Departments. At the same time, the Driver Training School was moved to Seacroft Garage, leaving 149 buses allocated to Torre Road, all in the former tram section.

In April 1970, a start was made on building the dual carriageway from Lupton Avenue to the Woodpecker Inn Junction in York Road. To make way for an underpass and roundabout at the York Road/Lupton Avenue/Ivy Street junction, the work involved the removal of a large part of Torre Road Depot Yard. Much of the tram track leading to the Belfast Shed was removed and the yard reduced in size. A slip road was constructed alongside the shed to the new underpass and, in March and April 1971, a new approach road was laid to the Belfast Shed. The old exit from the yard into Lupton Avenue was closed and a new entrance/exit formed from the new road.

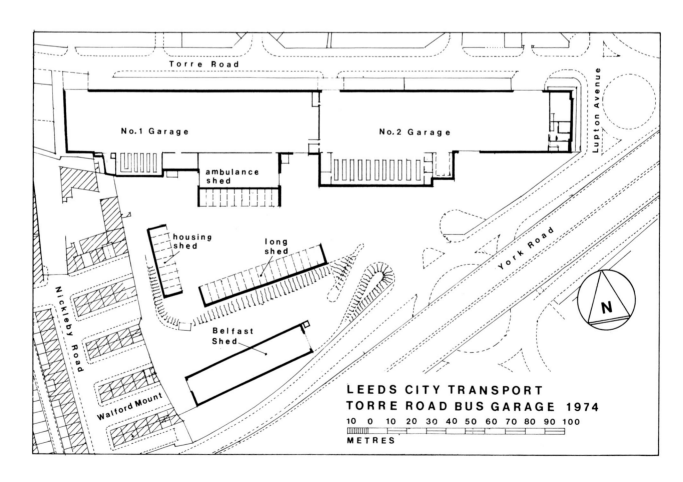

LEEDS CITY TRANSPORT
TORRE ROAD BUS GARAGE 1974

10 0 10 20 30 40 50 60 70 80 90 100

METRES

During 1971 the Belfast Shed received some minor modifications and most of the tram tracks in the interior were covered. A maintenance pit was also formed. The building was formally taken over from the Transport Department on 6 December 1971. The occupant was the Commercial Vehicle Maintenance Section at Torre Road, now looking after the vehicles used by other Corporation Departments.

The Belfast Shed was later taken over by the Corporation Hackney Carriages Department for vehicle testing and licensing, and was demolished in August 1998. It was replaced by a new building of similar size, also occupied by the Hackney Carriages Department.

In late 1973 a new traffic office was constructed at the Garage at a cost of £15,942. In later years there were two disastrous fires at the Garage causing minor alterations. The former tram depot eventually closed on 20 April 1996 and was removed. The original bus garage exists, still used by the Corporation Vehicle Maintenance Section.

Low Fields Road Permanent Way Yard

A plan of this yard and a description was included in Chapter 53 of Volume 3. The yard was unchanged from 1953 until its closure in 1957.

A track had been added in September 1953 to assist in the scrapping and burning of tramcars, and the yard was used for this purpose until 5 November 1957. Following the closure of the Elland Road tram route on 25 June 1955, the tramway had remained intact to enable trams to reach the scrap yard.

The yard was appropriated by the Town Planning and Improvements Committee and in September 1962 was let to a firm of building contractors, Messrs. J.H. Wood Ltd.

Kirkstall Road Works

A plan of Kirkstall Road Works in its final state as a tram works was shown on page 1080 of Volume 3. The Works was fairly busy until the departure of Victor Matterface, the Tramways Rolling Stock Superintendent, at the end of September 1957. It was then rapidly run down and by Monday night, 4 November, there were only three trams remaining. On 7 November the last tram left.

The Machine Shop, Truck Shop and certain ancillary services remained operational at Kirkstall for the next two years. Replacement trucks were transported by trailer to and from Swinegate Depot.

The work of converting the building into a bus repair works took an inordinately long time - nearly five years. It was to be a replacement for the Donisthorpe Street Bus Repair Works. The principal reason for the transfer to Kirkstall was that there was no room for expansion at Donisthorpe Street, which had an area of 10,697 square yards compared with 15,448 square yards at Kirkstall. It was said that due to lack of space it was not possible to give a complete bus overhaul at Donisthorpe Street. Modifications included the construction of a new boiler house, removal of the former tramway traverser, filling in of tramway pits, more dock space, 16 new interconnecting bus pits, a larger paint shop and bigger body shop. Full maintenance facilities were provided for all types of vehicles. In addition new partitions were erected, partial reroofing carried out, "temporary" offices provided, fuel oil tanks, and washing plant, etc. installed. All was finally completed in May 1962. The building was officially opened by Alderman Rafferty, Chairman of the Transport Committee. Forward-entrance Daimlers 572, 573 and 574 were used to convey the official party and guests from the Civic Hall to the Works and A.E.C. Regent V 910, newly repainted, was used to carry the Leeds Police Band to the new Works. The opening took place on 14 May, Rafferty commented:

"This marks an important milestone in the history of the Leeds Transport Department. For the first time the capacity of the central works enables us to deal not only with our own vehicles, but with the tremendous increase coming to us from other Corporation departments."

'Yorkshire Evening News' 15 May 1962

The "big move" into the new works was phased and began in June, starting with the body repair and painting sections, then part of the machine shop and later other personnel. By mid-July most of the repair work formerly carried out at Donisthorpe Street had been transferred to Kirkstall.

In front of Kirkstall Road Works was Harmer Street with a number of privately owned industrial buildings on either side. Following a Ministry of Transport inquiry on 19 August 1965, compulsory purchase powers were obtained to demolish this property. Thomas Lord said that it was "essential to extend servicing and ancillary facilities" and the only practical method was to acquire the land, which was 0·42 acres in area. In 1961 there were 638 buses, but this had increased to 664 and was increasing annually. The Transport Department urgently needed the space. It was intended to build an office block and "centralised transport workshops" on the site. Lord said the proposed building would also include a new canteen block, the present canteen facilities being "inadequate and deplorable." The City Architect prepared drawings for new offices and workshops and in October 1966, the drawings were approved by the Transport Committee. However, the following month the proposals were "deferred" for 12 months for reasons not stated. The Harmer Street property was later demolished in early 1974. The site was not, however, redeveloped, In December 1972 "in view of the urgency", the Transport Committee agreed to use the site for parking buses and employees' cars on a permanent basis. Doorways were formed in the north east wall of the works to give access for buses and the area was surfaced. It came into use as a bus and car parking area later in 1974. At the time of writing it is still used for this purpose. In the latter part of 1967 a new boiler house had been provided for the works at a cost of £48,731.

Donisthorpe Street Bus Repair Works

The bus garage and works at Donisthorpe Street had originally been opened in 1927, but with the opening of Torre Road Depot and Garage in 1937, was used solely for bus repairs and maintenance. From 1953 until its closure in July 1962 very little was done to the works. In February 1963 the building was appropriated by the Town Planning and Improvements Committee in the sum of £85,000 and was to be let to the Cleansing Department. The Cleansing Department had occupied premises in Dock Street from 1898. The Dock Street building was in an unsatisfactory condition and was in the way of a planned urban motorway. However, the Cleansing Department did not take over the Donisthorpe Street building and it reverted to the Transport Department on 17 February 1965. It was reoccupied for the storage of delicensed and withdrawn buses. It was finally vacated in late 1966 upon the opening of the new Middleton bus garage. Part of the building was later taken over for a few months by Wallace Arnold Tours as a running garage after the firm's Sayner Road Garage passed to its Sales and Service Car subsidiary. Wallace Arnold later opened a new coach station in Gelderd Road and Donisthorpe Street Garage was demolished.

Rockingham Street Bus Station

The idea of a bus station to serve the northern part of the city was formulated in 1944. It was one of the recommendations of W. Vane Morland, the General Manager in his report to the Reconstruction Committee. The site selected was at the junction of Woodhouse Lane and Merrion Street. The West Yorkshire Road Car Company had similar ideas of building a bus station in the same area, and much to the chagrin of Leeds Corporation,

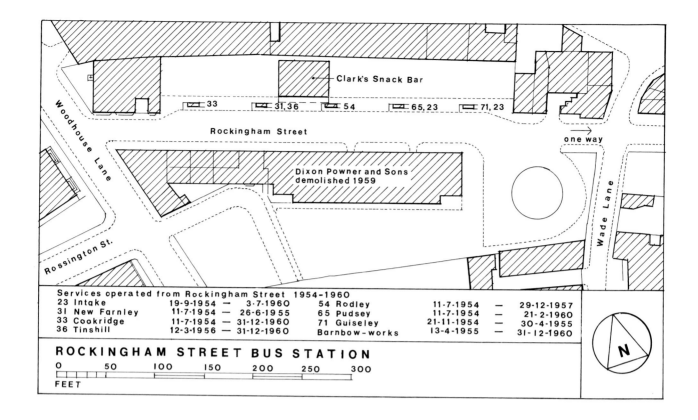

Services operated from Rockingham Street 1954-1960

23 Intake	19-9-1954 — 3-7-1960	54 Rodley	11-7-1954 —	29-12-1957
31 New Farnley	11-7-1954 — 26-6-1955	65 Pudsey	11-7-1954 —	21-2-1960
33 Cookridge	11-7-1954 — 31-12-1960	71 Guiseley	21-11-1954 —	30-4-1955
36 Tinshill	12-3-1956 — 31-12-1960	Barnbow-works	13-4-1955 —	31-12-1960

ROCKINGHAM STREET BUS STATION

0   50   100   150   200   250   300

FEET

the Company had purchased part of the site in September 1945. The Corporation in turn obtained the land by compulsory purchase order in November 1946. The Corporation proposal was to comprehensively develop the area bounded by Woodhouse Lane, Merrion Street, Wade Lane and Cobourg Street. In addition to a large, partly covered bus station to serve the north and west of the city, there was to be car parking, office and retail accommodation.

Part of the site had been occupied by the Albion Brewery, which was demolished in the 1930's. This area adjacent to Merrion Street was used for car parking. There was other old property on the site, including the factory occupied by Dixon, Powner & Sons, situated in Rockingham Street. This was a problem for the Corporation as Dixon, Powner could not find alternative premises and the Transport Department built its bus station, regarded as "temporary" on the opposite side of Rockingham Street. A permanent Merrion Street Bus Station was to be built at a later date.

Demolition of some of the property took place during the winter of 1953-54 and work began in early 1954. In April a turning circle for buses was built on the cleared site and a space provided for Dixon Powner's vehicles. A lay-by was provided on the north side of Rockingham Street, and the street resurfaced and made one way, access not being allowed from the Wade Lane end. Barriers and small bus shelters were erected at each of the five stands.

The Bus Station opened on Sunday, 11 July 1954 when services 31 New Farnley, 33 Cookridge, 54 Rodley and 65 Pudsey were transferred from the Central Bus Station. Buses entered Rockingham Street from the Woodhouse Lane end, unloaded and loaded at the barriers, turned at the new roundabout, and left via Rockingham Street into Woodhouse Lane. Only four of the five barriers were used.

From its inception the new bus station was not popular. There were many letters to the press and petitions from passengers protesting against the changes. There were no shops in the vicinity and passengers were faced with a long walk to the markets and central shopping area. The rerouting in the city centre also produced objections. The 33 service was shortened and in order to reach the new bus station services 31, 54 and 65 by passed the shops. Both services 54 and 65 had been diverted from Wellington Street via Westgate, Caroline Street, Park Lane, The Headrow and Woodhouse Lane on inward journeys. Outward via Woodhouse Lane, Great George Street Calverley Street, Park Lane and then the inward route. Only six weeks after the opening, the 54 service was rerouted to pass nearer to the railway stations, running inward from Wellington Street via King Street, East Parade, The Headrow and Woodhouse Lane.

The following month a new half hourly bus service was introduced from Rockingham Street to Intake, near Stanningley. Given the service number 23 it was routed in the same way as the Pudsey route and used the same loading barrier. On 13 April 1955 a workmen's service - one bus per day - outwards in the morning inwards in the evening, began to operate from Rockingham Street to the Barnbow Royal Ordnance Factory, near Cross Gates.

From Sunday, 21 November 1954, the fifth barrier at Rockingham Street came into use when the 71 Guiseley service was moved from the Central Bus Station. It was not occupied for long for, on 30 April 1955, the Guiseley bus service was abandoned. Shortly afterwards the vacant stand was taken over by the Intake service.

The coupling up of the 31 service with the 36 Gledhow buses forming a cross-city route in June 1955, resulted in the withdrawal of the 31 buses from Rockingham Street. However, from 12 August 1956, a new 36 bus service was introduced to the new Tinshill housing estate starting from the former 31 barrier.

Another cross-city service was introduced on 29 December 1957 when the 54 service was coupled with the 28 Halton Moor service. This marked the beginning of the

1478

end for the Bus Station. The policy of forming cross-city services rendered it superfluous.

In late 1954 "Clark's café, newsagents and tobacconists" and some toilets had been opened at the bus station, but in 1958 the café was closed. There were other partly demolished buildings in the vicinity, and the area soon took on an air of dereliction. New plans were announced for the site, which included major commercial, retail and car parking developments.

During 1960 the remaining services were removed from Rockingham Street to the Central Bus Station. The last bus from Rockingham Street was A.E.C. Regent III, 742, to 33 Cookridge which left at 11.10 p.m. on 31 December 1960. The special works service to Barnbow was withdrawn on the same day.

In its brief existence the bus station was rarely busy. In June 1962 all traces of it were removed when work began on a much more vibrant and successful enterprise – the Merrion Centre.

Central Bus Station

The Central Bus Station had been opened in 1938 and was unchanged in 1953 at the start of this Volume. It was designed for 7ft 6in. wide buses. The wider buses of the early 1950's, made it apparent that the 18 feet lanes at the Bus Station were insufficient. Although private operators ran the wider buses into the Station, it was not until later that the Transport Department allowed its own 8 feet wide vehicles to regularly use the Bus Station. The Bus Station was beginning to look rather dilapidated and the narrow lane width gave the Transport Department a strong reason for rebuilding.

In June 1962 plans for a suggested new bus station were incorporated in a big development plan for the area bounded by Vicar Lane, Eastgate, St. Peter's Street, York Street and New York Street. The site for the bus station was to be at the ground level of a building housing the City Markets and was to be built on an area partially occupied by the existing bus station and incorporating the existing wholesale meat market. There were to be seven loading platforms, running parallel with New York Street, each connected to the markets above by an escalator. There were two entrances for buses, one near the Eastgate roundabout and the other in New York Street, nearly opposite to Harper Street. The exit was to be in New York Street. The scheme came to nothing for the following year a much less ambitious scheme came to fruition.

This had been designed by the City Engineer and was approved at a meeting of the Transport Committee on 15 October 1962. The total estimated cost, including shelters, was £65,803. The 24 feet wide roadways to the new Bus Station were built by the Corporation Highways Department. The passenger shelters were supplied and fixed by Abacus Municipal Ltd. of Nottingham for the sum of £20,312. Most of the lighting, clocks and signage were carried out by the Transport Department.

The Bus Station closed on 1 July 1963 and work immediately started on its reconstruction. The bus services were moved to various nearby streets.

Strangely from its inception in 1938 financial control of the Bus Station, which had originally been regarded as "temporary", had been under, at first the Markets Committee, and then the Town Planning and Improvements Committee. However, on 1 April 1963 the responsibility was transferred to the Transport Committee, except liability for loan charges on the land, and "subject to an annual payment being made to the Town Planning and Improvements Committee."

On 30 September 1963 the rebuilt Bus Station was officially opened by the Lord Mayor, Alderman E. J. Loy Wooler. The Lord Mayor was presented with a bowl made out of an old Leeds tram gong.

The new shelters were to give protection from the weather, but many were initially unglazed. Alderman Rafferty said that the Corporation had been "unlucky," as the boat bringing the glass from Belgium "had gone down in the North Sea." The glazing was completed later, but the reconstruction work did not affect Platform A which

Daimler CVG6LX 596 and officials at the reopening of the Central Bus Station on 30 September 1963. *J.B.Parkin*

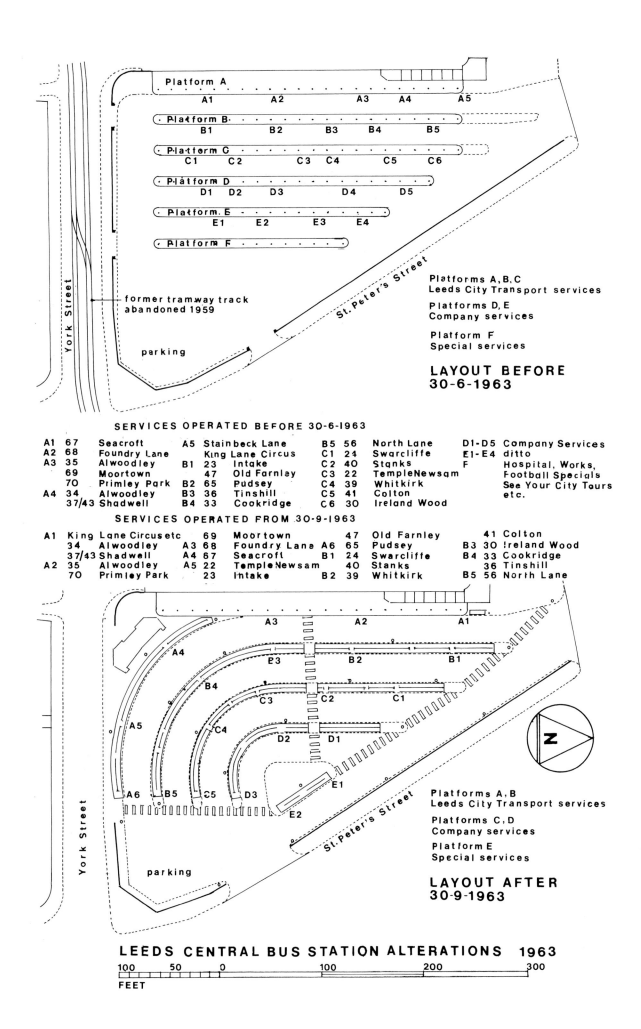

Platform A

A1　　　　A2　　　　　　A3　　A4　　　　A5

Platform B

B1　　　　B2　　　B3　　B4　　　B5

Platform C

C1　　C2　　　C3　C4　　　C5　　C6

Platform D

D1　D2　　D3　　　D4　　　D5

Platform E

E1　　E2　　　E3　　E4

Platform F

former tramway track
abandoned 1959

York Street

St. Peter's Street

parking

Platforms A, B, C
Leeds City Transport services

Platforms D, E
Company services

Platform F
Special services

**LAYOUT BEFORE
30-6-1963**

SERVICES OPERATED BEFORE 30-6-1963

A1	67	Seacroft	A5		Stainbeck Lane	B5	56	North Lane	D1-D5	Company Services
A2	68	Foundry Lane			King Lane Circus	C1	24	Swarcliffe	E1-E4	ditto
A3	35	Alwoodley	B1	23	Intake	C2	40	Stanks	F	Hospital, Works,
	69	Moortown		47	Old Farnley	C3	22	TempleNewsam		Football Specials
	70	Primley Park	B2	65	Pudsey	C4	39	Whitkirk		See Your City Tours
A4	34	Alwoodley	B3	36	Tinshill	C5	41	Colton		etc.
	37/43	Shadwell	B4	33	Cookridge	C6	30	Ireland Wood		

SERVICES OPERATED FROM 30-9-1963

A1	King Lane Circus etc		69	Moortown		47	Old Farnley		41	Colton
	34	Alwoodley	A3	68	Foundry Lane	A6	65	Pudsey	B3	30	Ireland Wood
	37/43	Shadwell	A4	67	Seacroft	B1	24	Swarcliffe	B4	33	Cookridge
A2	35	Alwoodley	A5	22	TempleNewsam		40	Stanks		36	Tinshill
	70	Primley Park		23	Intake	B2	39	Whitkirk	B5	56	North Lane

A3　　　　　　A2　　　　　A1

A4

B3　　　　B2　　　　B1

B4

C3　　C2　　C1

A5

C4

D2　　D1

A6　　B5　　C5　　D3

E1

E2

York Street

St. Peter's Street

N

parking

Platforms A, B
Leeds City Transport services

Platforms C, D
Company services

Platform E
Special services

**LAYOUT AFTER
30-9-1963**

LEEDS CENTRAL BUS STATION ALTERATIONS 1963

100　　50　　　0　　　　　100　　　　　200　　　　　300

FEET

was still open to the elements. In September 1964 the Transport Committee agreed to erect a glazed partition at a cost of £1,650. Abacus Municipal Ltd. supplied the materials to match the existing shelters. The work was completed in September 1965.

In 1969 the Leeds Chamber of Commerce suggested that the Bus Station be covered and a multi-storey car park built. Alderman Bertrand Mather, Chairman of the Planning and Traffic Management Committee, said it could be a good idea and said that if any private developer came along with proposals they would be seriously considered. Thomas Lord, General Manager, referred to a scheme already under consideration for the Bus Station area. This was the Leeds Development Plan for the period until 1981 under which the Bus Station was to be closed and two new bus stations provided, one in the area of the markets and the other to the east of Vicar Lane. Both schemes were to use both public and private finance and Commercial Union Properties Ltd. was to be responsible for the markets bus station. In the markets area the plan was to demolish existing premises between George Street and Union Street fronting on to Vicar Lane. The bus station was to have stands and parking spaces for 25 buses and also included was a 700-vehicle car park. Outline planning permission was promised on 22 September 1975, but Commercial Union withdrew the application at the last minute.

In the early seventies the economy of the country was in a serious recession and there was massive inflation. There was no local authority money available and a WYPTE spokesman said the two Leeds-initiated schemes were to be put "in the melting pot." There they remained.

Middleton Bus Garage

In June 1962 the Leeds City Engineer proposed that a site for a new garage for 120 buses be acquired at Middleton. The building was to replace the old garage at Hunslet and the site was at the junction of Middleton Park Avenue and Thorpe Lane. However, it was not long before another site was selected, situated on 6·85 acres of land near to the junction of Middleton Ring Road and Sharp Lane. On 18 November 1963, plans and estimates were approved by the Transport Committee. In May 1964 the land was appropriated from housing to transport purposes at a valuation of £30,000. The design was a copy of a new

garage recently built at East Bank, Sheffield. Sheffield Corporation allowed Leeds to use its drawings and specifications and this meant a saving to Leeds in time and fees.

An official of Leeds City Architect's Department, who was formerly at Sheffield, said this had been done through the Yorkshire Development Group and was "a further instance of close co-operation between the two cities." Thomas Lord, the Leeds Transport Manager, said the layout of the Sheffield garage was the finest he had seen. "We have modified a number of things for our own scheme, but we feel we have got the best of theirs plus a bit more of our own," he said. Tenders were invited in May 1964 and on the Transport Committee's annual tour of inspection on 24 August, Alderman Rafferty ceremoniously planted a tree on the site.

William Airey & Son (Leeds) Ltd. were the contractors for the scheme. The cost of the building was to be £536,012 5s.10d. plus fees of £43,987 14s. 2d. Construction began in October 1964 and took over two years. By May 1965 the approach roads to the building had been completed and all trace of the former tramway reservation between Sharp Lane and Belle Isle Road had vanished. A new roundabout was constructed in Belle Isle Road at the junction with the Ring Road. This became the turning point of the route 6, (Belle Isle) buses. Following the closure of Hunslet Garage, the building came into use on Sunday morning, 13 November 1966. On the 25th the Garage was formally opened by the Rt. Hon. Barbara Castle, M.P., the Minister of Transport.

The new garage was capable of accommodating 125 buses under cover although the initial allocation was 112. There was a perimeter road around the whole building and outside parking spaces for buses. The sides of the garage were largely glazed and at the front were the offices and canteen. There was a bus washing plant and the garage had its own steam cleaning plant.

As a result of the opening of the new garage 210 buses were reallocated to different garages. The Department now again had a surplus of garage capacity. Later service cuts and the reduction in the number of buses resulted in the closure of the garage. This occurred on 26 October 1986, at the time of bus deregulation. At the time of writing the building is currently occupied by the Leeds Co-op.

A.E.C. Regent III 494 in the bus wash at Middleton Garage on 1 October 1967. *Author.*

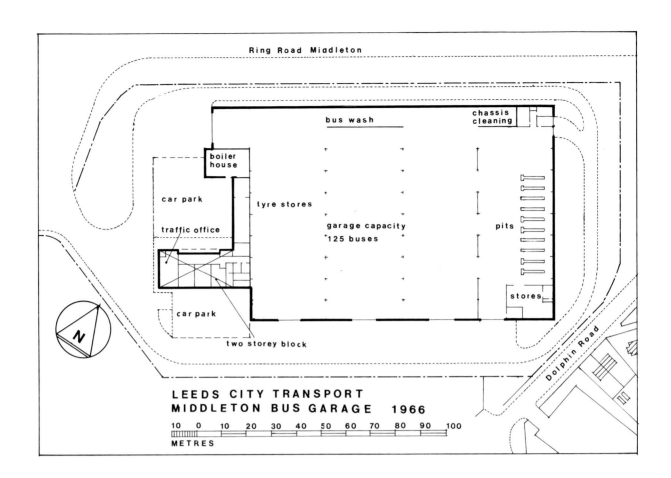

Ring Road Middleton

bus wash

chassis cleaning

boiler house

car park

tyre stores

traffic office

garage capacity
125 buses

pits

stores

car park

two storey block

Dolphin Road

**LEEDS CITY TRANSPORT
MIDDLETON BUS GARAGE 1966**

10 0 10 20 30 40 50 60 70 80 90 100
METRES

1965 to 1971 Building Programme

At its meeting on 15 November 1965 the Transport Committee approved a £2·5 million building programme for the Transport Department for the period up to 1970-71.

The programme included three new bus garages, the Middleton Garage. already under construction, a new Garage at Bramley to replace the existing building, which was affected by new road proposals, and a new garage at Headingley to replace the existing building. The new Bramley Garage was proposed for 1966-1969 and the one at Headingley for 1969-1971. New developments at Kirkstall Road Works and Torre Road Garage were also proposed. These garage developments have already been discussed.

Of particular interest was the first phase of the Department's long-term plan for redevelopment near Leeds Bridge on the banks of the River Aire, and the beginnings of a walk way alongside the river. It was known as the Concordia Street Development and it was proposed to include £36,000 in the 1965-66 and £168,000 in the 1966-67 capital programme for the first phase, the provision of a new Social Centre.

Concordia Street Social Centre

Adjacent to Sovereign Street Permanent Way Yard was the former Tramways Parcels Department Building originally erected in 1933. It was this site that was selected in 1962 for the new Social club and canteen for the employees of the Transport Department. The former Employee's Social Club had been situated on the upper floors of the offices and stores adjoining the main Swinegate Tram Depot. It had comprised a concert hall, billiard hall, changing rooms etc. By 1963 the building had been substantially vacated by the Department. The Parcels Department had closed down in 1944 and reopened as a Central Cartage Garage, for which

purpose it was used until its closure in February and demolition in April 1965.

The site was a prominent one overlooking the River Aire, but before work could commence extensive repairs to the existing river retaining wall had to be carried out. This work was done between December 1964 and February 1965.

In April 1964 Messrs Jones and Stocks, of Blenheim Terrace, Leeds, had been appointed as Architects for Phase 1 of the new Concordia Street Redevelopment Scheme.

The Social Club was to be the first stage of a larger development for the Leeds Transport Committee. A second stage was to convert the bus parking area in Concordia Street into a bus-servicing depot with a two storey car park over. The third stage linked to the Social Centre was to comprise a 12 storey office block for the Transport Department which would involve the closure of Concordia Street. Stage 4 was to be the abandonment of the Department's existing office building and redevelopment of the site for light industry. There was also to be the riverside walkway. Plans were approved and the Transport Committee agreed that the building work be carried out by the Corporation Works Department for the sum of £177,383 12s. 8d. plus fees of £24,175 1s.4d. This was more than the lowest tender received from a private contractor (Spooner's (Hull) Ltd. - £176,434 18s.8d.) and at the following City Council meeting the Transport Committee's proposal was thrown out. Spooner's got the job. The total final cost was about £213,000. Work began in March 1966 and was completed in August 1967. On 21 August, the building was opened by Councillor Thomas William Smith, the former Deputy Chairman of the Transport Committee.

"It sets the theme of a riverside walk from Leeds Bridge along the north bank at the tow path level and shows an awareness of the potential of the river as an amenity in the future development of Leeds"....

...."With the simple and robust form, together with the materials limited to brick and faced concrete, the building attempts to continue the tradition of the neighbouring buildings whilst giving a solution to its multi-purpose requirements."

From L.C.T. Brochure August 1967.

There were five floors with a car park in the basement, and on the ground floor was a new Central Cartage Garage with special facilities for the motor derrick (MNW 857). On the first floor were the kitchens and restaurant - cantilevered over the river, and there was a bridge link to the existing office building. The large and small concert rooms, billiard room, club committee room and bar were on the second floor. Above were a games room and access to the roof.

The Social Club was a typical mid-1960's building and although sturdily built soon looked shabby. It had a short life of just over 25 years and was vacated at the end of January 1993. When the Swinegate Head Office was closed in February 1994 the Social Club became redundant and was demolished soon afterwards.

The other phases of the redevelopment scheme were not carried out. In July 1966 Jones and Stocks were commissioned to produce drawings for part of Phase IV of the scheme, the riverside walkway, and the bus servicing depot. Shortly after, Phase IV was "deferred" and never resumed.

Pudsey Bus Station

Although Leeds City Transport buses only ran into Pudsey Bus Station from 1968 to 1974, for completeness it is included.

The reconstruction of Pudsey Market Place was, according to the 'Pudsey & Stanningley News', "the biggest improvement in the town for a good many years." One-way traffic was introduced and a bus station constructed, Stands and shelters were positioned at the back of the Market Place. This resulted in some criticism from passengers,

but was a deliberate policy to avoid congestion on the main road at peak periods. The total cost of the improvement was said to be in the region of £6,000.

Leeds Corporation buses on services 32 and 65 ran along Church Lane, past the Market Place, but were not directed into the new Bus Station. Neither were the Samuel Ledgard buses, which also ran into Pudsey.

On Saturday, 13 October 1956, the Farsley Omnibus Company service was extended into the Bus Station and it was on this date that it was first used. Although there does not appear to have been any public announcement, it is assumed that the Yorkshire Woollen Dewsbury buses were redirected to the Bus Station on the same day.

On 31 March 1968 the Farsley Omnibus Company was taken over by the Leeds Transport Department and from that day Leeds buses on services 79 and 80, Pudsey to Horsforth, were seen in the Bus Station. They continued to run uneventfully until the closure of this volume in 1974. The bus station still exists.

Elland Road Bus Station

A "giant" bus terminal at the Elland Football Ground was proposed in June 1970. It was designed to accommodate 80 buses taking football crowds to and from Leeds United's Elland Road ground and be situated off Low Fields Road. Arnold Stone, Deputy General Manager, said the terminal was to be "tailor-built for football crowds." The new south west motorway was to slice through Low Fields Road and vastly reduce the space available for football special buses. The Ministry of Transport said the scheme would be eligible for a 75% Government grant. A start, however, could not be made until the south west motorway was constructed. It was anticipated that this would start in 1972, but did not take place until 1974. The opening of the new terminal is just outside the scope of this volume as it occurred on 8 August at the start of the 1975 football season.

Torre Road Garage yard on 31 March 1968 with A.E.C. Regent V Welfare bus 8895 UB, the replacement for the TS8 in 1960. (see p. 1458). Alongside is Leyland Tiger Cub 31 (TUA 31) withdrawn from service. *J.B.Parkin.*

A.E.C. Regent III 411 at Rockingham Street Bus Station on 13 March 1955. It is on the 71 Guiseley service. Behind is Leyland PD2 372 on service 65 to Pudsey. Note the spartan bus station facilities and rusting former tram poles surrounded by dereliction. *W.D.Wilson/L.T.H.S.*

The interior of Middleton Garage on 1 October 1967 with a selection of different A.E.C.'s and Leylands. *Author.*

Leeds Transport Department Staff 1953 to 1974

In 1953 the average wage earned by a tram or bus driver was £7 4s. 0d. a week and a conductor £7 0s.0d. This was without overtime. It was a good wage for the time. Wages were agreed and stabilised by a national agreement formulated by the National Joint Industrial Council for the Transport Industry. The N.J.I.C. was a body on which were representatives of the Transport and General Workers Union and employer's representatives. The Leeds Transport Department, however, was facing a severe staff shortage. This was mainly due to the unsociable hours worked by transport staff. There was a large staff turnover, particularly of conductors, and following training many left after a few months. This was very costly to the Department.

A wages increase for platform staff took place on 13 December 1953 followed by another one, less than three months later, on 7 March 1954. These, however, had no effect on the staff position. By July 1954 six trams and ten buses had to be withdrawn from the morning and evening peak services. A.B.Findlay, the General Manager, submitted a special report to the Transport Committee. He blamed the six-day week and split turns that had to be worked by staff. The report said that for several years a considerable number of employees had been leaving the Department and there had been a "fairly steady drop" in the number seeking employment.

"The shrinkage of the staff in the past has been met by cutting out proved unremunerative services and by reducing spare crews," said the report.

"No large scale cutting of services can now be done and the department are still in need of 160 persons. It has been proved to be economical to work a certain amount of overtime, but the amount today is excessive.

"We have pressed for more persons, male and female, to be sent to us. Advertisements have appeared in all our vehicles and recently advertising in cinemas was again resorted to, but this time the response was very poor," the report adds."

'Yorkshire Evening News,' 19 July 1954.

There was no improvement in the staff position and in October, Alderman Rafferty, the Chairman of the Transport Committee, described the situation as "most critical."

"We are having tremendous difficulty in maintaining services owing to shortage of platform staff and we have got to warn the public that if members of the staff continue to leave at the rate they are doing the public will have to be prepared to face up to restricted services in future.

Residents of housing estates will have to appreciate that the Committee cannot entertain petitions for extensions of existing services or make special provision for school children."

'Yorkshire Evening Post', 18 October 1954.

Rafferty said that in May 1952 the platform staff had numbered 2,435. This was now 2,063. Alternative employment was available with a five-day week and without shift working. He said the services were being carried on because staff had agreed to operate a large amount of overtime. Schedules were based on a 48-hour week, but the national agreement provided for a 44-hour week. On an average the whole of the staff worked much more than 48 hours. Overtime was voluntary.

Leeds was suffering a 15% staff shortage, but this was not unusual as other cities were in similar difficulties. In Manchester there was a deficiency of drivers of 13% and conductors 17%, Nottingham 23% and 18% and so on for other transport undertakings.

"As a result of these staff shortages," said Rafferty, "one can appreciate that those in the industry are seeking a wage increase. Last week a new application was put in by the Transport and General Workers' Union for a most substantial increase in wages. If granted in full, it would mean for the city of Leeds, an additional expenditure of £200,000 a year."

The wages increase took effect on 28 November 1954, but the staff position continued to worsen. Findlay said that it was even becoming difficult to recruit and retain administrative staff in the Swinegate Head Office. He said it was apparent in days of full employment that increased wages alone were insufficient to attract labour. Shift work, imposed on a six-day week, was the "great deterrent," he reported. Many inspectors helped out by volunteering to drive and "a great deal" of overtime was worked by the platform staff," he said.

On 13 November 1955 there was another wages increase for platform staff and a conductor or conductress was now earning without overtime a minimum wage of £8 10s.0d. for a 48-hour week spread over six days. With overtime it was possible to earn between £10 and £12 a week.

The number of platform staff had dropped to 1,940 and the department announced that in an effort to maintain peak hour services it was to reduce services during other hours of the day, mainly after 7.00 p.m. on weekdays and on Sundays. Alderman Rafferty said the reductions would release 23 crews in the evenings and 45 on Sundays.

There was to be a reduction in the age for recruitment of conductors and conductresses from 19 to 18 and people who had been rejected for military service on medical grounds could also now apply to the department. The new wages were certainly an incentive, for an 18 years old girl taking a clerical job in other Corporation departments, normally received less than £4 per week.

With the shortage of staff being a nationwide problem, recruitment was carried out overseas in the British Colonies. A number of L.C.T. staff were recruited from the West Indies. As early as 1948 some employees had arrived from India, and in 1949 the first conductor from the Carribean had been employed.

By March 1956 the staff position began to slightly improve. At a public meeting held at Seacroft, Alderman Rafferty said that the difficulty was in retaining staff in a time of full employment. An encouraging sign was that six out of seven applicants for jobs in the Department were now from former employees. They had left because they thought they could do better elsewhere, but had found this not to be the case. Transport services were being maintained by the "loyalty of the staff working unlimited overtime." This was extremely expensive, said Rafferty.

During the financial year 1955-56, wages costs had risen by £120,680. In June 1956 there was another application for an increase in wages and this took place on 4 November of that year. The annual cost of this increase was about £40,000. Wages increases led to fares increases, which in turn caused more passengers to desert the trams and buses. 13 million passengers or 5·8%, were lost in the financial year 1957-58. Fares and the "downward spiral" of the Department's activities are discussed in other chapters.

Although there was a slight recession in industry at this time, there was still a staff shortage. The changeover from trams to buses resulted in some of the older tram drivers being transferred to other jobs or becoming redundant. Those under 50 years of age were trained as bus drivers.

A further wages increase for platform staff from 28 July 1957, cost the Transport Department another £90,000 annually. Increases in other sections of the undertaking brought the figure up to £123,000. There were further wages rises over the next three years. On 27 October 1958 wages increases amounted to a £75,000 cost to the Department. Further increases in 1959 and 1960 cost £208,000. The Department was still, however, suffering a shortage of about 200 in the numbers of platform staff.

On 5 June 1960 a 42-hour week came into being for all platform and depot staff. This had been arranged through the National Joint Industrial Council for the Road Passenger Transport Industry and was applied nationally. In Leeds, by agreement with the local trade union officials, every driver worked an extra five and a half hours, making 47½ in all. Overtime above this figure was worked on a voluntary basis. From 16 April 1961 more wages increases for platform and depot staff came into effect. During this period, fares increases kept pace with those of wages and for a time, in spite of falling passenger numbers, the Department was able to maintain a revenue surplus.

The Road Traffic Act of 1930 stipulated that the minimum age for a conductor should be 18, but the Transport Committee wanted this to be reduced. In June 1961 it contacted the Municipal Passenger Transport Association with a view to reducing the age limit to 17. The age for women conductors was to remain at 18. The proposed age reduction was not accepted.

In the early 'sixties the staff problem eased slightly. In spite of the hours that had to be worked, the job of a driver or conductor was now a very good one from the financial point of view. There was unemployment in other industries and a number of former staff was re-engaged.

In February 1963 Rafferty said that the Department had 2,039 drivers and conductors, but still needed more. Wages awards had taken effect from 20 May 1962, 21 April 1963, 16 February 1964 and 12 February 1965. For the year ended 31 March 1962 the extra cost to the Department was £95,941 and for the same period the following year, £65.170. The 1964 costs were £188,570 and those for 1965, £134,923. To cover the extra costs there were corresponding fares increases.

As referred to in Chapter 81, an Ideal Homes Exhibition was held at Queens Hall (formerly Swinegate Tram Depot) from 25 April to 9 May 1964. The Transport Department had a stand and there was a mock-up of the front of an A.E.C. Reliance single decker (registered LCT 2) and demonstrations of the Department's closed circuit television. The primary purpose of the display was to attract new staff. Other items on display were new green staff uniforms and an Ultimate ticket machine. There were posters encouraging people to become bus conductors.

H. McDonald of the Transport Department, who designed the stand, said: "We are very short of conductors. We are having to keep buses in the garages at peak periods just now, but we are hoping to recruit some of the exhibition visitors to help to relieve the situation." It was hoped that a modern, progressive, "with it" image would attract staff. Unfortunately the Exhibition did not have much effect on attracting new staff, and the shortage continued.

There was then a three-pronged application from the employees side of the National Joint Industrial Council for the introduction of a 40-hour week, in place of a 42-hours, with no reduction in earnings, a substantial increase in basic rates and the introduction of a bonus scheme. The bonus pay was demanded for attendance records and length of service and also for working large capacity and one-man buses. The claim was expected to cost the Transport Department an additional £300,000 per year. Speaking at the Transport Committee's annual inspection, Alderman Rafferty was concerned:

Resetting the points at Stainbeck Lane, Chapeltown, after Horsfield car 157 on 10 September 1955. The conductor is Leeds University student, Chris Thornburn. *Author.*

Tram drivers had to be careful when descending the 1 in 11 gradient of Beeston Hill. There were two compulsory stopping places and Horsfield car 223 has stopped at the lower of the stops. The date is 24 July 1955. *Author.*

"I am worried whether we can continue to retain fares at the low figure that we are operating them today," said Alderman Rafferty.

"I want to warn the public that we can't continue to face up to ever-increasing demands of this description without passing on to the public something of the increase."

'Yorkshire Evening Post', 25 August 1964.

The 'Evening Post' said that the transport staffs themselves would also have to pay the higher fares.

In an effort to cut administration costs "mechanisation without redundancy" was introduced at the Swinegate Head Office. "Mountains" of coins, nearly four tons in weight, were brought in daily by the conductors and to speed up counting and cut staff numbers, two coin counting machines, one for silver and one for copper were purchased. Mechanisation was also introduced in the ticket office. There, 47 women were employed doing waybill analysis and similar work. Punch cards and data processing machines were purchased and the number of staff was reduced to 20. The women were transferred to "more interesting" work in the Department. In May 1965 four more automatic cash counting machines were purchased. Later, in October of the same year, the Transport Committee authorised the expenditure of £14,000 on data processing equipment. The following year further coin counting machines were purchased.

The joint negotiations over the proposed 40-hour week, bonus pay for operating one-man buses and a wage increase, were protracted. Earlier, London busmen had obtained substantial increases and efficiency payments. The employers offered an increase of 7s. 0d. a week in the basic rate, but this was rejected. The talks came to a deadlock at the end of November 1964. On 1 January 1965 it was announced that the dispute was to go before an arbitration tribunal appointed by the Minister of Labour.

Many busmen countrywide objected to the delays in settling their claim. Employees of private bus companies in the Leeds area, the West Yorkshire Road Car Company, West Riding Automobile Company, Yorkshire Traction Company, Hebble, and Yorkshire Woollen District carried out token strikes or overtime bans. Leeds Corporation busmen threatened a one-day token strike on Saturday, 6 February 1965. There was also a threat of an overtime ban. The strike was to be "unofficial" and Rafferty was incensed by the attempt to carry out "guerilla warfare" within the transport industry. He said the average weekly earnings of a Leeds Corporation bus driver was at least £18 and of conductors £17. This included basic pay and overtime. Rafferty's comments were challenged by many platform staff. A bus driver earned 5s.6½d. an hour, giving a basic wage of £11 12s.9d. a week. One driver said he received £12 7s.5d. for a 46 hour week. To earn £18 he would have to work 30 hours overtime. The pay was said to be less than the Corporation paid Cleansing Department drivers for hauling refuse.

The threat to Leeds transport services was decided at a meeting on 31 January 1965.

"A spokesman for the union said today that the action proposed was unofficial and had not got the support of the union. The decisions were made after an official meeting of union members had been closed. Unofficial leaders then got support for strike action on Saturday and an immediate ban on overtime from about 300 busmen who attended a second unofficial meeting."

'Yorkshire Evening Post', 1 February 1965.

There was bitterness at the meeting and a 'Yorkshire Post' reporter was attacked and had his notebook confiscated.

The General Manager, Thomas Lord, said that the striker's action would produce no result; it would only delay negotiations with the trade union. There would be loss of pay to the individuals taking part, loss of revenue to the department and loss of goodwill of passengers. He urged all staff to carry on working normally so that negotiations could continue and be brought to a satisfactory completion with a minimum of delay.

At a following meeting of platform staff the proposed strike was rejected by a "large majority", but the overtime ban was continued for a week resulting in the loss of 90 to 140 buses at the morning and evening peak periods.

The national negotiations, for what was now an eight-month-old pay claim, were slow and became deadlocked. On 5 February pay rises of 15s.0d. per week to platform and depot staff were announced by the Industrial Court under the arbitration award. The increases took effect on Monday, 8 February. The wages increase was accepted by Corporation workers, but rejected by company employees. At the end of February, a national bus strike was called for. On 25 February, Ray Gunter, the Minister of Labour, acted and talks were held with the Ministry's chief conciliation officer on the following day. No decision was reached and the Prime Minister, Harold Wilson, was also becoming frustrated. He referred in a television broadcast to buses laid up, thousands put to inconvenience and whole factories held up by a handful, "who are too impatient to wait and see their problems settled."

On 2 March 1965 the executive council of the Transport and General Workers Union decided unanimously to back a national strike of provincial bus workers. Ray Gunter intervened and appealed to the union chiefs for a truce to allow the dispute to be investigated through arbitration or by a special committee of inquiry. The unions agreed and the threat of a national strike was averted. The company workers' pay and conditions were eventually sorted out in May 1965.

Leeds Corporation busmen had received a substantial wages rise, which resulted in a fares increase from 30 May 1965. However, there was still no agreement on the five-day 40-hour week or the proposed bonus payments. Negotiations rumbled on during 1965, eventually coming to fruition. Many drivers and conductors were "frustrated" at the slow progress of the national negotiations and on Saturday, 22 May, there was an unofficial one-day token strike by the bus workers. This was the first strike to have occurred on the Leeds transport system since 31 January 1948. Alderman Rafferty said: "This is anarchy, not trade union negotiation. The element responsible for this decision does not appear to understand the constitution of the national machinery for negotiation."

The N.J.I.C., he explained, provided an opportunity to give notice of a dispute, with a visiting committee on both sides, employers and employees, hearing the causes of a dispute. This had not happened and Rafferty said that until the bonus questioned had been resolved at national level it would not be appropriate to agree locally to something which might be completely out of line with what was agreed nationally. Rafferty said that the strike caused the public the "maximum possible inconvenience." He was a member on the employer's side of the N.J.I.C. and claimed that the strike had been directed at him personally. There had been a similar token strike at Middlesbrough where Alderman Flynn, Chairman of the town's Transport Committee, was also on the negotiating council.

"By bringing pressure on us, the unions hope to get a local bonus allowed in some places and use these examples as a lever," he claimed.

"We have resisted in this area anything that has not been nationally negotiated," Ald. Rafferty added.

'Yorkshire Post', 24 May 1965.

The city's 664 buses were out of action for the day and there was a loss in fares of about £13,000. At the time there was the continuing shortage of platform staff, which numbered about 1,870, against a "full strength" figure of 2,200. Due to service reductions and larger buses, the platform staff requirement had declined by about 250 from that of 1953.

1,850 drivers and conductors took part in the strike, the only services operating being those to the hospitals, operated by volunteer crews. There was a "rush of private cars," a "taxi bonanza," and suburban railway trains from Horsforth, Cross Gates, Stanningley, Armley Moor, Morley and Bramley were "much busier than usual." The company bus services continued to operate. Briggate was as busy as normal and some city centre stores lost trade, the worst affected being the market traders who said that it was like a "quiet weekday." Shops in the suburbs were said to have "raked it in." In the 1964-65 financial year there was a decline of 1,669,709 in the number of passengers carried on the buses. Rafferty said that the strike and overtime ban had led some bus passengers to travel instead by car. The official view was that with the bus habit broken, a number were still going by car.

At the request of Alderman A. King, Labour leader of Leeds City Council, on 27 May 1965 a "crucial" meeting of Leeds Corporation's Establishment Committee was held. This Committee, which dealt with wages, salaries and conditions of service of Corporation employees, considered the question of a local bonus scheme for bus crews. The meeting did not achieve much, but "left the door open" for local talks on an attendance bonus, and the question of a service bonus for national decision. Previously the Committee had indicated that it wanted to wait for national decisions on both bonuses. There was no discussion of extra payment for the operation of one-man buses. At a later meeting on 30 June, the Committee decided to defer consideration of the union's application until after a national meeting in London on 15 July. At that meeting the Federation of Municipal Transport Employers was to discuss pay within the industry generally.

The delay of a fortnight was not acceptable to some staff and a recommendation was made to ban voluntary overtime from Sunday, 4 July to 17 July. The local press complained that the bus workers wanted an attendance bonus for reporting for work on time for a normal working week, or overtime, and then completing these duties satisfactorily. This did not apply to any other workers. The bus workers pointed out the unsocial hours. The bonus was to amount to between 12s.0d. and £1 a week. Full employment nationally and the continuing shortage of staff put the bus workers in a strong position. In July 1965 the Transport Department advertised for staff on the local independent television station, but with little success. It was expensive and in October was dropped. Newspaper advertising was continued.

A special meeting of the Leeds branch of the Transport and General Workers Union was held on Sunday morning, 4 July. The meeting was described as "stormy", and attended by 244 employees. In a first vote 120 were in favour of imposing the ban with 124 against. In a recount 107 were for the ban and 129 against. Alderman Rafferty was "delighted". "A contrary decision would have caused great inconvenience, and this shows that when a representative meeting is called good sense prevails," he said.

On 15 July 1965 Rafferty attended a "vital" meeting of the Federation of Municipal Transport Employers. The meeting rejected the idea of local attendance bonus schemes on the ground that they made nationally agreed rates of pay and conditions of service virtually non-existent. It said that bonus schemes should be resisted. It recommended the setting up of a working party to investigate the whole pay position in the industry.

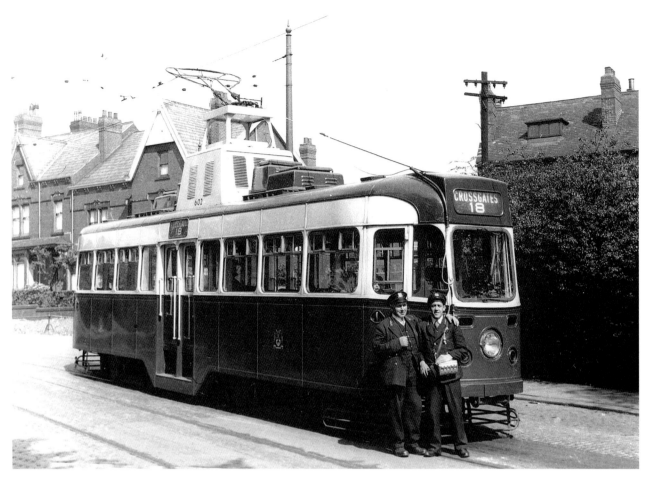

Driver and conductor pose with railcar 602 at Whingate on 8 August 1954. *W.D.Wilson/L.T.H.S.*

A meeting of the city's Establishment Committee was held on Monday, 26 July, followed by a special meeting of the Leeds branch of the trades union two days later. At the Establishment Committee meeting the local attendance bonus scheme was rejected. Councillor Waterman, chairman of the Committee said that they should await the report of the working party.

"We do think the position of pay in general in the industry needs looking at, but we want to uphold the principle of national negotiation.

"We do realise that our decision calls for patience on the part of the bus crews in Leeds, but we hope they will appreciate the reasons which have led up to that decision and be prepared to await the report of the working party."

'Yorkshire Post', 27 July 1965.

The trade union members were upset at the Committee's discussion and a letter was sent to the Leader of the Council, the Transport Committee, and the Establishment Committee. The crews decided unanimously on the letter, which expressed disgust and deplored that "despite the worsening staff position, the Leeds authority intends to continue to pay the lowest possible wages in the municipal transport industry."

The meeting also decided to request the management to review the local agreement regarding standing passengers. The existing agreement stipulated that up to 78 adult passengers could be carried.

Things then settled down for a month or two. The bonus depending on length of service, carrying capacity of buses and the 40-hour week had still to be agreed. On 9 September 1965 talks at the N.J.I.C. in London "broke up in disorder." A service bonus of between 10s.0d. and 30s.0d. a week was offered by the employers "with strings which we could not accept," said a union official. "We never even got

round to discussing the 40-hour week. We have asked them to meet us again as soon as possible," said the official.

The "strings" in the service bonus were a penalty clause under which bus crews would lose the bonus for a period in the event of an unofficial stoppage.

Eventually at a meeting of the N.J.I.C. held in London on 14 October 1965 an agreement on the 40-hour week was sorted out. It was to start at the end of the year, and in Leeds came into effect on Sunday, 2 January 1966. It was said to be the equivalent of a 5% wage increase. The working day was a minimum of 7 hours and 36 minutes. There was no agreement on the suggested bonus scheme based on length of service. In the early negotiations, the unions asked for a scheme similar to that operated in London, which was based on journeys and carrying capacity, but the employers had considered this would lead to disparities in different parts of the country.

Agreement on a bonus scheme depending on length of service was agreed by the N.J.I.C. on 19 November 1965. After consulting with a Ministry conciliation officer the Transport and General Workers Union and the General and Municipal Workers Union agreed to the 10s.0d. to 30s.0d. weekly bonus together with the contentious penalty clause. The bonus scheme began on 21 November.

The penalty was mandatory and subject to appeal to the N.J.I.C. if the employee wished. A six month loss-of-service bonus was to be imposed immediately upon any unofficial action.

Thomas Lord said the adoption of the 40-hour week would cost the department an extra £100,000 a year. The cost of the bonus scheme would be about £75,000 per annum. Alderman Rafferty said the bonus scheme was an attempt on the part of the industry to retain newcomers.

"Our turnover of platform staff is tremendous and this

is the price we have to pay to try to retain staff. The public must realise that if they want a bus service this is part of the price they have to pay. A fares rise is inevitable, " said Rafferty.

'Yorkshire Post', 23 November 1965.

In January 1966 the Transport and General Workers Union made another application for a "substantial increase" in wages for platform staff. The Union was asking for a 6·5% increase and the employers' side of the N.J.I.C. referred the claim to the Government National Board for Prices and Incomes. The employer's said that the proposed increases "would have the most serious implications for the level of fares." The Board "saw no case for the increase to exceed 3 to 3·5%" for the provincial bus workers. London bus workers were to get the full 6·5% increase (agreed some time previously) "provided there was an agreement to carry standing passengers at all times and that London's Green Line (country) bus services would accept one-man operation.

Jack Jones, General Secretary of the Transport and General Workers Union, said it was an "unwarranted interference with the Union's claims." He said:

"It seems to act in the role of an arbitration board and in some aspects makes nonsense of the tried and trusted system of Government inquiries. In that sense the report may have very harmful effects."

'Yorkshire Post', 27 May 1966.

Jones said that the union was to ignore the report and press ahead with its wage claim. The Leeds Transport Committee also said that to meet "soaring costs and a huge expected deficit," it was to apply to the Traffic Commissioners to increase bus fares.

In July 1966 the employers offered an all round wages increase of 9s.3d. per week, equivalent to 3·5 to 4% for drivers, conductors and inside staff. On 14 July, this was accepted. In addition a committee was set up to look into all aspects of increasing productivity. These were to include such matters as one-man buses, standing passengers, part-time workers and other matters.

The cost to the Transport Department of the new claim was £75,000 per year. "It is a serious situation," said Alderman Rafferty. "We got authority from the City Council only last week to apply for a fare increase, and now, even before we go to the Traffic Commissioners, there is this £75,000 extra cost." The fares application was to go before the Traffic Commissioners on 16 August.

Constant wages claims, not only in the transport industry, but also in many others were causing rapid inflation and could not be sustained. In 1966 the Government imposed its Prices and Incomes Standstill policy. This was announced by Barbara Castle, the Minister of Transport, on 20 July and put a halt to the wages claim and also the proposed fares increase. There was thus a net deficit of £271,919 for the financial year ended 31 March 1967.

The Leeds busmen were not happy with the Government action and there was "tough talking and non-co-operation." From Sunday, 28 August, a "no standing ban" was imposed on the Corporation buses. The only exception was on service 45 (Wortley-Stanks) where Standee type single deckers were employed. They carried up to ten standing passengers. The Transport Department used its largest 70-seat buses to maximum effect and said that only a few passengers were left behind on certain routes. "No great inconvenience" was caused. There had not been any complaints from passengers who were "making the best of it."

However, within a few days the local press received a "flood of letters" from passengers complaining about the ban. Elderly and infirm passengers and people visiting hospitals were left behind and one writer compared the bus workers to "overgrown spoilt children."

Alderman Rafferty said he kept receiving telephone

calls at his home and letters complaining that passengers were left at bus stops. He said that the only cities operating the no standing ban were Leeds and Dundee. Leeds had been selected by the Union for "a trial of strength." After a trade union meeting on 22 September, when the busmen decided to continue the ban, the Transport Department referred the dispute to the Federation of Municipal Passenger Transport Employers. Rafferty condemned the busmen's unilateral action and had previously warned that until normal working was resumed the busmen's service bonus would be withheld. In a letter to the Union he said the ban was a breach of discipline and gave notice that the service bonus payments would be withheld unless normal working was resumed by Friday, 23 September.

Rafferty was ignored and he advised passengers to refuse to get off the buses if there was standing room. They should stand up for their rights. There were a number of bitter confrontations and at least five physical assaults on crews. The 'Yorkshire Evening Post' said the busmen were "utterly alone" and that there was a serious rift in public and industrial relations. On the advice of their trade union, at a meeting on 5 October, the busmen decided to abandon the no standing rule. It took place the following day. The Department decision to withhold bonus payments was rescinded. That was the end of the matter.

In January 1967 there was an intensive advertising campaign in the local press by the Melbourne Tramways, Australia, for single men (aged 19-40). Wages were the equivalent of £24 a week and some of the Leeds bus conductors took up the offer. In spite of this, and the pay

Football match days were always a challenge for the Transport Department staff. Two inspectors and a policeman supervise passengers boarding Chamberlain car 122 in Sovereign Street on 23 April 1955. Swinegate Depot is on the left. *Author.*

freeze, it did not deter staff recruitment in Leeds. In other industries staff were being put on short time and there were redundancies. As a result there was an increase in L.C.T. staff numbers. On 31 March 1966 platform staff had increased from the 1965 figure of about 1,850 to 1,915. The following year the numbers were 2,049. In the period 1966-67 staff numbers increased from 2,937 to 3,074.

In November 1966 the Government announced the lifting of the pay freeze, and from 15 January 1967 a wages increase occurred nationally for all platform staff.

The extra costs to the Leeds Transport Department were £65,303. Alderman Rafferty said that the Leeds fares increase application was also unfrozen, but the Transport Committee took no action to increase fares. As discussed in Chapter 84 this was mainly for party political reasons. Under a new Conservative administration fares were increased from 2 October 1967.

In December 1966, in an a effort to achieve efficiency and a substantial saving in costs on the repair and maintenance side of the undertaking, a programme of work study was initiated at Kirkstall Road Works. A firm of consultants, Associated Industrial Consultants Ltd. of London, were engaged. The work-study had to be completed within 18 months.

"It will lead to the introduction of an incentive bonus scheme for craftsmen and semi-skilled and unskilled personnel employed on the repair and maintenance of buses.

"It will be directly concerned with productivity and in line with national policy.

"The consultants will look at all the maintenance activities such as vehicle washing and study the work from the moment a bus enters the depot," said Alderman Rafferty.

'Yorkshire Evening Post', 19 December 1966.

In September 1967 Thomas Lord said the consultants were in the middle of their report and hoped to save £33,000 a year by the introduction of work-study measures and an

incentive bonus scheme. He said, "an enormous saving in administration" had been made by computerisation.

A Work Study Officer was appointed and schemes for bus maintenance underwent trials. Work study was also applied to the Traffic Division and Lord thought that a "productivity package" could be negotiated with the trade unions. This would be self-financing and be of benefit to both crews and the Department.

By 1969 work study and the application of an incentive bonus scheme had been extended to workmen in all the garages. This produced an improvement in vehicle availability whilst, without any redundancies, there was a reduced number of employees due to natural wastage. Lord said he fully expected that with improved working methods and operating procedures at Kirkstall Road Works, there would be a big reduction in bus maintenance costs.

Developments in Sunderland were to have an effect on Leeds and other transport undertakings throughout the country. In December 1966 four bus conductresses were given the opportunity to train as bus drivers. Women had driven Leeds trams during the war and Alderman Rafferty said the city had no rule against women bus drivers. However, his view was that driving one of the new high capacity buses in heavy traffic was a man's job. It was to be several years before women bus drivers were seen on the streets of Leeds.

A problem faced by most transport undertakings in the recruitment of staff of the right type was the gap between leaving school at the age of 16 and the time when the individual could take up employment with the Traffic Department at 18. In April 1967, an experimental training period of two years was proposed. Boys would be released for further education courses to widen their general knowledge.

The training was to be divided into three-monthly periods in the garage traffic offices on census work, in the cash office, in the schedules office and in the engineering and finance divisions of the Department.

After the two-year period youths would be put on conducting duties on the buses for a year. A decision would then be made as to whether they should be transferred to duties on the administrative side, with arrangements for taking Institute of Transport examinations, or be part of the platform staff.

It was believed to be the first scheme of its kind in the country. There was an intended intake of 12 entrants in each of the next three years.

"This problem must be faced if the industry is going to get youngsters of the right type," said Ald. Rafferty.

"They are certainly not entering transport at present and this must lead to a considerable lack of experienced people in the future. The value of recruiting teenagers of the right type has been proved in various industries over many years."

'Yorkshire Evening Post', 18 May 1967.

Rules governing the employment of drivers had been in the Road Traffic Act, 1930, but were now considered out of date. In June 1967 the Minister of Transport, announced that substantial improvements were to be made. The main features of the proposals were a daily limit of nine hours on driving, limits on the working day and working week, and the introduction of a weekly rest day.

The proposed legislation was discussed on 7 August at a meeting of the Transport Traffic Sub-Committee. Councillor Wolstenholme, the new Chairman, said they were not complaining about the framework of the proposed legislation, but if implemented it would mean a 20% increase in operating costs for the transport undertaking. It was stated that the city's bus drivers were allowed to work on their rest days if they wanted to, but under the new proposals would be unable to do so.

Thomas Lord said they needed time to introduce the legislation and make it workable. He said they were introducing one-man buses because of the labour shortage, and were also increasing the efficiency of services. It was to be over two years before the new legislation was enacted.

One-man Bus Operation

With the adoption of front entrance buses, the conductor was gradually becoming superfluous to modern bus operation. In November 1965 Sir Donald Stokes, managing director of Leyland Motors, speaking at the annual conference of the Institute of Directors, said that there were 30,000 bus conductors "running round in buses all day, reading the Daily Mirror." These were enough to run a large export factory. He appealed for a change in trade union attitudes and said:

"I do not feel that we deploy our own resources with anything like intelligent skill and we must ask for a new look and approach from the trade unions.

"There are so many crazy examples to quote, but a particular one in my own industry is where you have 60,000 buses running round this country with driver and conductor when at least half of them certainly do not need a conductor, nor is one provided in countries overseas which have more up to date ideas on productivity than we have."

'Yorkshire Evening Post', 10 November 1965.

As discussed in Chapter 83, regulations permitting the use of one-man operated double deck buses came into force on 1 July 1966.

The gradual elimination of the bus conductor in Leeds had begun with the introduction of one-man single deck buses on the 9 Ring Road service in 1962. One-man operation was under consideration throughout the country. In London, in September 1966, the trades union welcomed the proposal provided that the status, pay and conditions of the busmen should be improved "far beyond that which exists today."

Discussion on the staffing of one-man buses and other matters in Leeds took place during 1967. There were also negotiations between the Union and the employer's side of the N.J.I.C. The Union was dissatisfied with progress and from 21 October 1967 imposed an overtime ban and non-co-operation on the extension of one-man operation in Leeds.

In snowy conditions it was the responsibility of the Permanent Way staff to clear the snow from the tram lines. On 10 February 1954 three workmen are brushing away the snow at Roundhay Park as a queue of trams patiently wait. *S.G.Pickford.*

Another test for the L.C.T. staff was on the occasion of the Rugby Football matches at the Hunslet Rugby League ground at Park Side on the Middleton route. An inspector is controlling the trams as Horsfield car 240 reverses on the crossover. Horsfield 163 awaits its turn to reverse. After the match on Saturday 28 March 1959, this was the last occasion on which trams turned at Park Side. *Author.*

A Union official said that his union had the right to negotiate wages and conditions with the Leeds undertaking directly. He said that the basic wage of a top-rate driver employed by Leeds Corporation was £12 17s.0d. a week and he did not have comparable working conditions with an industrial worker. On average it took him 45 hours at work to complete his 40-hour guaranteed week. The Leeds membership was making a stand to establish a fundamental principle, he said.

Thomas Lord said the ban would result in the withdrawal of 200 buses at peak periods, which would cause great inconvenience to passengers. It was in the best interests of the travelling public that pay and conditions of busmen should be agreed and ratified by the N.J.I.C. Councillor Wolstenholme commented:

"This is not really a local dispute between Leeds City Transport and the traffic staff. It is a dispute between the Transport and General Workers' Union and the Federation of Municipal Passenger Transport Employers.

"We shall await the outcome of the conciliation meeting between the union and the Federation to be held in London on November 3. Meantime I urge the resumption of normal working."

'Yorkshire Post', 28 October 1967.

The ban resulted in the withdrawal of the special bus service to Elland Road on 25 October for the Leeds United and Newcastle United football match, other matches and the big match on 7 November with Manchester United. Arrangements were made with Wallace Arnold Tours Ltd. to supply between 40 and 50 coaches.

At the morning and evening peak periods, angry passengers had to wait for up to 45 minutes, thousands were delayed for work, and there was little sympathy for the bus workers. A union official complained that conductors were "being pushed and shoved by passengers in attempts to provoke them during this difficult period." The Transport Department said that discussions could not possibly take place in "this atmosphere of duress."

National discussions were held on 3 November and a further meeting under the auspices of the Ministry of Labour on the 9th. The Leeds Transport Department said it would start discussions immediately on an incentive bonus scheme if the busmen would call off their ban. On the other issues involved – minimum wage, holidays and rates for one-man bus operation – the busmen were told that if there was no national agreement by the end of the year Leeds was prepared to negotiate locally. The overtime ban ended at midnight on 10 November 1967.

A month later agreement was reached by the N.J.I.C. on a settlement of the pay dispute. There was an immediate £1 per week increase in pay for busmen. Councillor Wolstenholme said the increased cost to the Department was more than £200,000 a year and an application for a fares increase would have to be considered.

"I sincerely hope that this national settlement will not in any way prejudice the productivity discussions which we are engaged in, because any additional savings that can be achieved can be shared between the wage element, the cost element and the fares," he said.

Unfortunately for the busmen the Government would not allow the £1 per week increase to be paid and in early December 1967 the N.J.I.C. allowed wage negotiations to be conducted directly with local authorities. Councillor Wolstenholme said the increase would be paid as soon as the Corporation was permitted. The Minister of Labour, Ray Gunter, said that if Leeds were to pay the £1 without his approval he would invoke Part Two of the Prices and Incomes Act to prevent them and, if they insisted in paying, the local authority might then be in full breach of the law.

After the N.J.I.C. national negotiations were suspended, bus branches were advised to submit pay and other claims locally. Meetings took place between the union and representatives of Leeds Corporation, but following a meeting on 22 December it was stated that the Corporation was "not in a position to give assurances which the trade union required." Another overtime ban began on 23 December and thousands of people were late for work. Thomas Lord appealed to the public to "bear with us."

The following month the Corporation said it had reached an agreement with the union to adopt one-man working on services 22, and 38. Service 48 was also to be one-man. However, when single deck operation was instituted on the three routes in May 1968 they were operated with two-man crews. They became one-man in January the following year.

On 30 January 1968, summonses, claiming £1 a week rise for the Leeds busmen, were served on the Corporation by six members of the Transport and General Workers' Union. This was a test case and the men claimed in each case £6, which represented £1 per week for six weeks from 14 December, the amount agreed between the Union and the Federation of Municipal Transport employees. The case was soon dropped and the pay rise agreement referred to the Prices and Incomes Board.

In July 1968 700 of the Leeds busmen voted to strike on 12 August in a protest against the Government's prices and incomes policy. They were bluntly told that they were "unlikely to win." Although there were bitter remarks from trade union members, the strike did not take place.

It was Christmas 1968 when the Prices and Incomes Board allowed the wages rise to take place. Members of Leeds City Council unanimously agreed to ratify the £1 per week increase. It was paid on 26 December and back-

dated to 17 December 1967. The cost to the Department was £241,200 in the financial year 1968-9. After the implementation of the award there was an increase in fares from 9 February 1969.

In 1968 the introduction of further one-man operated services had been "seriously impeded" by the unwillingness of the trade union to discuss the matter. It was said that by 1970 half of the bus fleet in Leeds would be suited to one-man operation. Thomas Lord said:

"The trade unions have accepted without reservation that the principle of one-man bus operation shall be applied throughout our industry in the future.

"But they want to be sure that their members get just reward of payment for taking part in this as a productivity element. They are arguing now not on the principle of the situation, but on the practicalities."

....."Once we have got a national agreement, the overall cost of operation will be reduced by the element of productivity involved in one-man operation," he added.

'Yorkshire Evening Post', 11 September 1968.

In December Alderman Hall, Chairman of the Leeds Corporation Establishment Committee, said the union had now agreed to implement an extension of one-man operation on single deck buses in Leeds from the date the £1 rise was paid. In January 1969 discussions on one-man operation were resumed. There were already six one-man routes and the Transport Department wanted to convert a further 12. From 16 January 1969 one-man single deck operation was introduced on services 22, 38, 46, 48, 81 and 148.

The use of one-man double deck buses had to wait for a national agreement. In May 1969 Alderman Turnbull said that Leeds had 115 double deckers capable of being used for one-man operation. They were being operated

A.E.C. Regent III 456 at Beeston terminus on 16 October 1965. The driver and conductor in their new green uniforms talk to two youths. *W.D. Wilson/ L.T.H.S.*

with two-man crews. Another 80 one-man double deckers were on order. Thomas Lord said that the question of redundancy did not arise as the Department was already 300 staff below establishment. – a shortage of 10%. Drivers of one-man buses had the benefit of additional earnings.

On 16 June 1969 a new wages increase for transport staff was announced. There was a rise of 4d. an hour for craftsmen and 14s.0d. a week for drivers and conductors. There was also, at last, an agreement on the operation of one-man double deckers. The wage rises were to cost the Transport Department about £150,000 in a full year, but an immediate fares increase was not envisaged. A fares rise did, however, take place on 4 January 1970.

Said to be the first service of its kind in Yorkshire, one-man double deck bus operation in Leeds began on 13 July 1969 on service 49 (Hyde Park-Old Farnley). More one-man routes quickly followed, but were mostly single deck operated.

The Transport Act, 1968

This Act and new regulations came into force on 15 March 1970 and there were anticipated to be serious consequences for the Leeds transport undertaking. Under the new Act a bus driver's working day was to be cut from 14 hours to 11, the maximum daily driving time being reduced from 11 hours to ten, with at least a half hour break after 5½ hours. An 11-hour rest period was to precede each working day and no driver was to be allowed to work more than a 60-hour week. In December 1969, Alderman C.S.Watson, deputy chairman of the Transport and Trading Services Committee, said that "serious disruption" to services was anticipated. To meet the requirements of the new Act the Corporation would need to increase its platform staff by 653 by 1 March.

At an emergency meeting of the Committee Alderman Watson said the Minister was entitled to grant exemptions from the provisions of the Act.

"Persistent requests have been made for consideration to be given and a letter forwarded in October 1969, to the Minister, remains unanswered," he said. The Town Clerk had telephoned the Ministry and had dictated to him a letter addressed to the Passenger Transport Association dated December 17, indicating the Minister's intention to grant some exemptions. However, no letter had reached Leeds and so far as the Corporation was aware, the letter from the Minister had not been received by the Passenger Transport Association before the Christmas holidays."

'Yorkshire Post', 30 December 1969.

The letter had asked for observations and comments by 6 January 1970 and Alderman Watson said the Corporation was being placed in an impossible situation. There would be serious disruption of the city's bus services, which would have a lasting effect, he said.

There was union co-operation and a reasonably successful recruiting campaign and the expected disruption in bus services as a result of the "Hours Act" was not quite as bad as expected. On 24 March Thomas Lord submitted a report. Alderman Turnbull, said it was "urgently necessary" to hire an extra 300 platform staff. The Department had 1,990 drivers and conductors, a loss of over 1,100 on the previous year. Alderman Turnbull said the new regulations had had an effect on the Department's ability to provide the full scheduled service at peak periods. He added: "The position has been particularly acute in the mornings, because staff previously available for overtime at this period of the day cannot now be used owing to the rest interval which must be allowed between the end of one duty and the start of the next, together with restrictions as to the total length of the working day." That prevented drivers on a late duty from working overtime in the morning peak period. Turnbull said that a "careful watch" was to be kept on the situation.

One of the first effects of the new regulations was felt at the R.L.Cup semi final at Headingley held on 21 March. Several spectators had to wait 50 minutes for a bus.

In February 1970 came the announcement of another wages award for platform staff. This was to cost £295,470 in the financial year. 1970-71. The fares rise the previous month did not take into account this new award.

The staff shortage continued throughout 1970 and there were service reductions (mainly off peak) on a number of routes. Following a hearing at the Traffic Commissioners on 15 October fares were again increased from 8 November 1970. In August the wages bill was running at £350,000 more than expected and was not helped when the transport workers submitted yet another substantial pay claim. The average basic wage for a driver was about £16 a week. There was now a national claim for a £20 a week minimum wage. To press their claim a nationwide ban on overtime and standing passengers was to be instituted from 13 September 1970.

Thomas Lord said that if granted the wages rise would cost the Department another £350,000 per year. He said it was intended to ask the meeting to support an emergency resolution to submit to Leeds Labour party. "There seems to be an opinion that busmen and manual workers are being made scapegoats by the City Council and national negotiating bodies," Lord said.

On the morning of the Sunday,13 September, buses in Leeds were halted for about three hours as Corporation busmen held a mass meeting at the Town Hall to discuss the ban and other grievances. In place of the ban on overtime and standing passengers, a regional committee of the Transport and General Workers Union recommended that a bus strike should take place every Friday in Yorkshire and North Derbyshire. It was to involve all municipal and company owned undertakings in the area. A Union spokesman said that the recommendation to replace the overtime and standing ban with a regular weekly one-day strike was made because it was felt that a one-day strike would be less inconvenient and confusing for passengers.

On the first Friday strike, on 18 September, additional trains were run from Garforth, Cross Gates, Horsforth and Headingley. Other passengers used motor cars, bicycles and even horse-drawn transport. Most firms in Leeds and the West Riding reported normal attendances, although some people had turned up late for work. The busmen were losing a day's wages each week and the strikes had no effect on their pay claim. They were becoming increasingly bitter. On 18 October nearly 2,000 Leeds busmen voted overwhelmingly to extend their Friday stoppages to include Saturday as well.

On Saturday 24 October there was a strike and Leeds city centre became a "huge free car park". Additional car parking was provided and there was car parking in the Central Bus Station and at all the bus stops. Traders were affected with takings down by about 50%.

Leeds City Council made no effort to end the strike. Alderman Frank Marshall, leader of the Council, said that the extended strike would undoubtedly cause hardship to many more people. "The average earnings for a driver working a 50-hour week on one-man operated buses is already around £37, while drivers of double deck buses are getting in the region of £28 a week, " he added. There were strikes on the following Friday and Saturday. The Union then said that the bus workers would refuse to collect the higher fares, which were to come into effect on 8 November. Alderman Turnbull said that officers of the Council were to meet the Union representatives to "clarify certain aspects."

In the meantime the employers nationally offered a 33s.0d. a week increase on basic rates from January 1971. The offer was a breach of Government policy against granting two increases within 12 months. The busmen's last rise had been in February 1970. The offer gave drivers a basic wage of £17 10s.0d. a week and conductors £17. Drivers of one-man buses were to get £21 17s.6d. for a double deck and £21 for a single deck bus. The offer was considered at a meeting of the Transport And General Workers Union in London, but rejected. At a "very stormy" meeting at Leeds Town Hall on Wednesday evening, 4 November, when the buses were suspended for three hours, the Leeds busmen "strongly criticised" the offer. They said they were "disgusted" but did agree to return to work on Friday 6 November. They said they were suspending stoppages until 2 December in the hope of having successful negotiations with the Corporation.

Under the N.J.I.C. amended conditions of service agreement, local authorities could now negotiate a settlement locally. Leeds Corporation had refused to do this maintaining that all negotiations should be done through national machinery.

Meetings were held on 13 and 25 November between Corporation and union officials and considered at a meeting of the busmen on Sunday morning 29 November. An additional 30s.0d. per week was offered on top of the national award. Alderman Turnbull said that platform staff were to be given a 25s.0d. bonus payment backdated to 8 November as a short term interim measure and 5s.0d. from 22 November as the first phase of a new comprehensive agreement. This meant that from the first pay day in January 1971 (the third) the basic rate for platform staff would in effect be £19 a week. Turnbull said the cost to the Transport Department of the national award would be £350,000 in a full year and the local award a further £150,000.

The improved offer was accepted by the busmen. A move to give greater flexibility was also agreed by the union. In future the number of men able to do driving and conducting duties would be increased from 70 to 120. Eight

standing passengers were also now allowed on one-man operated vehicles.

"There will be no more strikes – at least for the moment," said a trade union official. The Leeds busmen's dispute had lasted seven weeks and buses did not run on seven Fridays and three Saturdays. A fares increase to cover the extra costs took place on 5 December 1971.

Things were relatively quiet during 1971 on the staff side of the Department. On 13 December 1971 another wages rise was announced. The pay rise in 1971-2 was a £317,510 cost to the Department. There was another wages rise in 1972-3 and a fares increase took place from 16 September 1973.

In July 1973 the Transport and General Workers Union called for a 35-hour week for all transport workers nationally. The request however came to nothing.

A problem faced by many transport undertakings was that of late night violence, hooliganism and assaults on staff. This came to a head in Leeds in October 1973 when some youths were given lenient sentences by the courts. The busmen's union decided that after 9.00 p.m. on Fridays, Saturdays and Sundays, services would be withdrawn. The withdrawals took place over a four-week period beginning on Friday, 12 October. Councillor Dennis Matthews, Chairman of the Transport Committee, said he sympathised with the bus crews. It was "intolerable" that they should be subject to assaults, he said.

The Leeds Town Clerk was asked to write to the Association of Municipal Corporations stressing the need to impose adequate penalties on the offenders and that legislation should be promoted to increase the protection of staff. The Chairman of the Leeds Bench of Magistrates was also contacted.

During the bus curfew the taxi business in Leeds

The driver and conductor of 1934 vintage A.E.C. Regent 179 relax at the new Kirkstall Abbey terminus on 4 April 1954, the first day of operation of the tramway replacement bus service. The Abbey House is in the background.
W.D.Wilson/L.T.H.S.

L. H. Gray was one of the first bus conductresses. This photograph was taken on 22 September 1941.

"boomed." The bus ban was fully supported by bus crews in the surrounding areas. There was a similar ban in Huddersfield at the same time.

Wage claims came to the fore again and in January 1974 an offer was made by the NJIC of a £1.85 a week increase on basic rates for all platform staff with further increases for drivers of one-man buses and maintenance workers. There were also increased holiday payments for all. At a conference in London on 23 January, leaders of the 100,000 busmen in Britain accepted the pay rises, which varied from between £1.85 and £2.65 a week. The increases came within the Government's pay code and took effect from the first pay week in March. Most busmen had their incomes increased by about £3 per week. At the conclusion of this volume, therefore, the basic weekly rate for a 40-hour week was £21.75 for conductors, £22.33 for drivers, £25.08 for one-man operation and between £22.24 and £26.65 for maintenance workers. Rapid inflation in the 1970's was to result in further large rises in the wages bill and corresponding fares increases.

Staff Canteens

An important adjunct to the Corporation transport operation was the staff canteen. These were situated at all the depots and there was the main canteen at Swinegate (later at the Social club in Concordia Street). From 1953 to 1964 Councillor Aimee Muriel Tong, assisted by other councillors on occasion, was in overall charge of the canteens. She was followed in 1965 by a group of councillors who took joint responsibility.

In 1953 the average number of meals served annually was around one million. By 1960 they had declined to around 750,000 to 770,000 and remained at this level until 1965. It was found that a number of "unauthorised persons" were taking advantage of the low cost meals, and from 1965 they were banned from using the canteens. The number of meals sold dropped to under 700,000.

The canteen at Torre Road Garage had been closed in

1957 for reconstruction work. New equipment was installed and it reopened on 31 March 1958.

In October 1969 in an effort to reduce staff costs, the canteen at Seacroft Garage became fully automated. Thomas Lord said that the new style staff restaurant – "I am trying to get away from the canteen image" – was one of the first of its kind in Leeds. It was automated following a period of staffing difficulties. Dennis Noble, the Transport Department's Catering and Welfare Officer, said the selection of meals was changed to offer breakfast, lunch and tea menus. "The machines would offer a greater variety of food at all times and it would always be freshly cooked, he said." Gone was the traditional canteen and in its place was a battery of coin-operated machines. These included a new "up-to-the-minute device" known as a microwave oven. "This could sizzle a sausage sandwich in a few seconds," he said. Lord joked: "People think we run our job on bus fuel, but it's really run on cups of tea." Adequate catering at the garages was vital, he said. The automation at Seacroft was an experiment, which was to be carefully monitored.

Change of Uniform

From May 1927 to 1963 the uniform used by platform staff was of navy blue serge with red piping. There were bright nickel buttons bearing the Leeds coat of arms. The conductor's uniform was single breasted and that of the tramcar motorman or bus driver, double breasted and of the "lancer" cut. There was a cap, also in blue serge with red piping and a badge in the form of a shield and showing a side view of Chamberlain car 400 with the words "LEEDS" above on a dark blue enamel background. In August 1959 a new design of cap badge was issued to conductors. In place of the tram, a bus – a Leyland PD3/5 with Roe body – was shown. The badge retained the dark blue background.

Until March 1960 conductors and drivers showed their

The new green staff uniforms were shown at the official reopening of the Central Bus Station on 30 September 1963. Alderman E.J. Wooler, the Lord Mayor is talking to, from the left, Inspector Stanley Murphy, Driver Dermott Ferguson and his wife Margaret Ferguson. New Leyland PD3A/2 325 is in the background.

L.C.T. service numbers on the collars of their uniforms. After this date PSV badges were carried. An exception was the ex-tram drivers many of whom, after November 1959, were used on queue marshalling duties. They never had PSV badges.

In October 1962 Alderman Rafferty announced that the city's bus crews were to get "new look" uniforms to coincide with the introduction of wider and more modern buses in the city. There had been thoughts of a change of uniform in June 1961 and students at the Leeds College of Art produced various designs. None had been accepted. Rafferty said the new uniforms might be green or chocolate or some other shade. There would be consultations with union representatives and bus crews before a final decision was made.

A survey of drivers, conductors and conductresses by the 'Yorkshire Post,' revealed that none of them wanted to change the colour of the uniform. One driver remarked that the staff would look like an Afghan platoon. The dark blue was serviceable and not too conspicuous and the uniform was comfortable. The strongest cry was for more frequent issues of uniform. Only one uniform was provided and a pair of trousers had to last eight months and a jacket 18 months.

After consideration, however, on 21 January 1963, the Transport Committee decided to adopt a dark bottle green colour for the uniforms. All the new uniforms were to be single breasted and of worsted serge, of superior quality to the blue uniforms. Conductresses were to have berets and the male staff, caps. Ties were to be green. Rafferty said that the Transport Committee felt that the staff would welcome the change. The cap badge was also to change. It was of a similar design to the earlier badge, but the word "LEEDS" was on a green enamel background and the Leyland PD3/5 bus was depicted. The change of badge took place from December 1966. Many of the older staff retained their tram badges, which they regarded as a mark of "distinction" indicating seniority. Arnold Stone, the Chief Traffic Officer, said that many staff considered it an honour to wear them. The old type badge could still be seen until the demise of the transport undertaking in 1974.

The new uniforms made their appearance at the official opening of the reconstructed Central Bus Station on 30 September 1963. Beginning in May 1964 the new uniforms were issued to staff.

On 18 April 1966 Alderman Rafferty said that platform staff were to be issued with a new summer uniform, which included green shirts and collars to match with gold ties. He said that these would take the place of lightweight grey colour drill outfits and were to be worn in warm weather without tunics. They would cost more, but Rafferty said that it was hoped the smarter outfit would bring in more recruits.

Staff expressed doubts as to the suitability of the uniform, thinking that the shirts would very quickly be dirty. The conductors' bag and machine straps also cut into the shoulder.

As seen below staff numbers did increase from 1966 to 1967. Whether the improved uniform had anything to do with this is uncertain. The uniform remained standard issue for the remainder of the existence of the Leeds Transport Department. With the takeover by the West Yorkshire PTA in 1974 a new uniform was adopted.

Known Staff Numbers 1945 to 1974

Date	Platform staff	Total Staff
31-3-1945		3,779
31-3-1946		4,210
31-3-1947		4,220
31-3-1948		4,274
31-3-1949		4,313
31-3-1950		4,270
31-3-1951		4,093
31-3-1952	2,400 approx.	4,272
31-3-1953	2,040 approx.	4,036
31-3-1954	2,000 approx.	3,761
31-3-1955	1,950 approx.	3,618
31-3-1956	2,000 approx.	3,480
31-3-1957		3,389
31-3-1958		3,331
31-3-1959		3,336
31-3-1960		3,064
31-3-1961		2,962
31-3-1962		3,031
31-3-1963	2,040 approx.	3,081
31-3-1964	1,950 approx.	2,958
31-3-1965	1,850	2,903
31-3-1966	1,915	2,937
31-3-1967	2,049	3,074
31-3-1968	2,069	3,088
31-3-1969	2,112	3,128
31-3-1970	1,990	
31-3-1974		2,652

Typical tram (1927-1959), bus (1959-1966) and inspector's (pre-1950) cap badges.

Tickets and Fare Collection 1953 to 1974

By 1953 the tickets in use on the Leeds transport undertaking had been simplified and comprised five only, all of the "Ultimate" type. Trams and buses used the same type of ticket. The last of the old type Bell Punch tickets had been withdrawn on the buses on 5 November 1952.

Contract tickets, ordinary returns and workmen's returns were a loss making activity as far as the Transport Department was concerned. Contract tickets had been withdrawn on 26 June 1950 and ordinary returns on 3 September the same year. Workmen's returns were still in use and there was a special "box" on the Ultimates, which had to be marked for this purpose. There was also the 1d. Child's Park ticket which, during holiday periods, gave a reduced fare from the child's home to and from any park in Leeds. The ticket was taken out of use on 18 April 1950, but the concessionary fare was still available with the Ultimate tickets, but was not publicised after April 1951. It was not included in the "Instructions to Conductors" until the fares rise of February 1957. Conductors, however, did not suggest to passengers with youngsters that the children could travel more cheaply. Children under five years of age were carried free.

On 25 March 1952 there had been a fares increase when the 1¹/₂d. ticket was abolished. Ticket values and colours were then as follows: 1d. white, 2d. buff, 3d. orange brown, 4d. green and 5d. pink. The printer was the Glasgow Numerical Printing Company (GNP) until June 1953. The printer was then Oller Ltd. of London. Tickets by Oller were first noted on 8 June 1953, the 2d. value being the first to appear. The 1d. value soon followed.

The 4d. was issued at the beginning of August and the 3d. and 5d. at the beginning of September 1953. Printers were given a contract to supply tickets for a certain time, initially for a year, but this was later extended to three years.

As with all tickets, there was a multiplicity of ticket colour shades. There had been quite considerable shade differences on all tickets issued by Leeds Tramways and Transport Department from their introduction in 1903.

On 30 January 1955 a fares increase occurred. Workmen's returns ceased to be issued, but the Oller tickets were not modified. GNP won the contract again and on 20 June 1955 new 4d. GNP tickets came into use with "W.Ret." omitted. Within a few days there were new 3d. tickets and the other values soon followed.

Although there were only five values of Ultimate tickets, higher fares were covered by issuing multiple tickets. For example a 6d. fare was covered by two "married" - to quote the L.C.T. Traffic Records - 3d. tickets, 8d. two 4d. and so on.

From Sunday, 24 February 1957 there was a general fares increase on all tram and bus routes. All 2d. fares were increased to 2¹/₂d. and many other fares were increased by 1d. Thus the half penny unit was reintroduced into the fare structure. Maximum fares on the trams were increased from 6d. to 7d. and on the buses from 9d. to 10d. From 2 March fares on the special football service to Elland Road from Swinegate or Infirmary Street were increased from 4d. to 5d. Fares on all other special services, such as the night bus services, were also increased.

 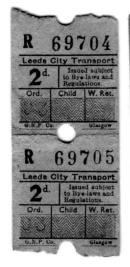   

GNP Ultimate tickets issued from 25 March 1952 to 1953.

Oller tickets issued from June 1953 to 1955. Note the Workmen's return box. Workmen's returns were discontinued from 30 January 1955. There were two slightly different printings of the Oller tickets. Note that the Oller 1d. white ticket is stamped in the Ordinary position. This indicates that it was used during the penny fares experiment from 12 April to 12 July 1953.

On the conductors' five-value Ultimate ticket machines, the 1d. and 2d. tickets were retained, but the 3d., 4d. and 5d. values were withdrawn. The five tickets now carried were 1d. white, 1¹/₂d. orange-brown, 2d. yellow, 2¹/₂d. green, and 6d. pink.

Ordinary and children's fares were now issued in accordance with the following scale:

Ordinary: 2¹/₂d. 3d. 4d. 5d. 6d. 7d. 8d. 9d.10d.

Children: 1¹/₂d. 2d. 2d. 3d. 3d. 4d. 4d. 5d. 5d.

Night service fares were 6d., 8d., 10d., 1s.0d., 1s. 2d. and 1s.4d. Children were carried at half this rate. Penny tickets were now issued only in conjunction with 6d. tickets for certain fares in excess of that figure. The following is a revised list of the ticket-issuing instructions to conductors:

1¹/₂d., 2d., 2¹/₂d., and 6d. single tickets.

3d. double 1¹/₂d.; 4d. double 2d.; 5d. double 2¹/₂d.; 7d. 6d. + 1d.; 8d. 6d. + 2 x 1d.; 9d. 6d. + 3 x 1d.; 10d. 6d. + 4 x 1d. There were issuing details for the night bus services and other information about the increased fares. These were covered in a new joint tram and bus fare book that was issued to conductors.

On trams there was a metal holder screwed to the right hand bulkhead panel in the lower saloon. This contained the fare book, which was for the reference of conductors. Although the fare book was retained on buses, from April 1957 they were not displayed on the trams. Instead, specially printed fare lists were fixed in the glazed showcases at each end of the car. These lists showed the fares for the Middleton, Hunslet and York Road routes at one end and those for the Moortown, Roundhay and Dewsbury Road services at the other end of the vehicle. The display of these fare lists brought the showcases on the Felthams into use for the first time since the cars arrived in Leeds.

In August 1957 new large fare boards were erected at the principal tram and bus stops and fare stages. The boards carried advertisements at the top.

It was not long before there was another fares increase. This took place from Sunday, 29 September 1957, fares on all Leeds routes, except Leeds-Bradford being revised. The 2¹/₂d. minimum was raised to 3d. except that passengers could now travel for one stage for 2d. The 1¹/₂d. 2¹/₂d. and 6d. tickets were discontinued and replaced by 3d. brown, 4d. green and 5d. pink tickets, thus reverting to the position before the increase of the previous February. The ¹/₂d. unit again went out and was never to return. Tickets for both day and night services were now issued as follows:

1d. white	single 1d. ticket.
2d. pale yellow	single 2d. ticket.
3d. brown	single 3d. ticket.
4d. green	single 4d. ticket.
5d. pink	single 5d. ticket.
6d.	double 3d. ticket.
7d.	5d. + 2 x 1d. tickets.
8d.	double 4d. ticket.
9d.	5d. + double 2d. ticket.
10d.	double 5d. ticket.
1s.0d.	two double 3d. tickets.
1s.2d.	three 4d. + 1 x 2d. ticket.
1s.4d.	two double 4d. tickets.

The 1s.0d. to 1s.4d. fares were used only on the night services. In September 1958 a new issue of the 3d. Ultimate tickets appeared. Oller Ltd, of London again won the contract as tickets supplier. The new issue printed by Oller was slightly darker in colour than the previous GNP Issue. 1d. 2d. and 5d. Oller tickets appeared in October and the 4d. in mid-December 1958.

Towards the end of January 1959, the colour of the 5d. Oller ticket was changed from pink to blue. This change was made because the 3d. brown/orange tickets and 5d. pink looked very similar in the electric light of the vehicles.

This was the first time that blue had been used as a ticket colour for the Ultimate tickets from their introduction in 1948.

Special Tickets issued on 7 November 1959

To mark the abandonment of the tramway system on 7 November 1959 a set of six special tickets was issued. The tickets were printed by Oller, of London, and consisted of the following values:-

1d. white, 2d. yellow, 3d. orange/brown, 4d. green, 5d. blue and 6d. pink.

The fronts and reverse of the tickets are illustrated and show that on the rear side historical data was printed. The tickets, which were in packs of 50, were carried in ticket racks, but were not punched or cancelled on issue. The size was slightly larger than a pair of Ultimate tickets, being 3in. x 1 ³/₈in.

Tickets for the last tram procession were issued by ballot, and cost 1s.0d. each for the return journey from Swinegate to either Cross Gates or Temple Newsam. They consisted of a lemon coloured card measuring 4¹/₄in. x 3in. and an example, used for the journey from Swinegate to Temple Newsam, on car 171 is illustrated.

The name of the person to whom the ticket was issued and the car on which they were to travel, was written on the ticket in Indian ink. The reverse side of the ticket was blank. A total of 600 passengers were carried on the ten cars in the procession. Some 400 other applicants for tickets were unlucky.

Tickets 1960 to 1962

The number 9 Ring Road service was opened on 30 October 1960. This was the longest bus route in Leeds and the fare from Whitkirk (Selby Road) to Bradford Road, Pudsey, was 1s.0d. A new fare of 11d. was introduced and this was covered by a double 5d. and single 1d. Ultimate ticket.

The introduction of the number 9 service and the limitations of the Ultimate machines in only being able to issue five values, resulted in the Department experimenting with two six-value machines. The new machines were used on the Ring Road service, operating from Headingley Depot, and came into use on 12 February 1961. They were used to obtain more accurate information on the number of passengers carried and the sale of higher value Ultimate tickets on this service. There were various experimental values. A 1s.0d. value was the first to appear and was used for five weeks from 12 February to 18 March 1961. An 11d. ticket took the place of the 1s.0d. ticket and was in use from 19 March to 22 April. Both tickets were printed by Oller Ltd. and were identical in design to the lower value tickets. Both were pink in colour, of the same shade as the 5d. value before it changed to blue.

The two machines were used by the same conductors all the time and only appeared on the 9 route when the conductors' normal rotas brought them on to the service. Apart from night services, the 9 was the only service on which tickets above the value of 10d. could be used. On 23 April 1961 a 10d. pink ticket came into use and was used until 27 May when it was replaced by an 8d. pink ticket the following day. That was used until 1 July when it was replaced a month later by a 9d. ticket. Once again the 9d. was pink and printed by Oller, but the value on the ticket was printed in very small lettering. The 9d. appeared on 2 July and was replaced by a 7d. ticket on 6 August.

The introduction of a 7d. value ticket completed the use of all values between 7d. and 1s.0d., all being used for a five weekly period. From 10 September 1961 a 1s.0d. pink Oller ticket appeared again and the various values were repeated again. They continued until 30 November 1962. By the time of their withdrawal, the use of the experimental values had reached 11d. on the fourth time around, working downwards from 1s.0d. to 7d. The two conductors who had the six-unit Ultimate machines, which issued these tickets, handed them in on 30 November.

The ticket contract switched to GNP again in June 1961, 2d. and 5d. values coming into use. The printing of the tickets was identical with the previous issue by GNP of three years earlier. The most notable feature of the change was that the 5d. tickets were now grey instead of blue, while the shade of yellow of the new 2d. tickets was much brighter than those of the Oller printing. The 1d., 3d. and 4d. tickets followed in July, the 1d. white and 3d. orange brown being identical in design and colour to the earlier GNP tickets. The 4d. value, however, was a much brighter grass green in place of a medium green.

Revised fares were introduced from 17 September 1961 on all services except for the 72 (Leeds to Bradford) service. The 2d. minimum fare for one stage in most cases was retained. Some fares up to 9d. were increased by 1d. The 10d., 11d. and 1s.0d. fares were unaltered. No change in the design of tickets occurred as a result of the fares increase.

In December 1961 a change to the GNP tickets occurred when the serial letters were changed to the suffix type, similar to Bell Punch Ultimates used by other transport undertakings. The 4d. value was the first to be changed, followed by the 2d. and 5d. tickets in January. The 1d. and 3d. values appeared with suffixed serial letters during March 1962. In December 1962 the five tickets appeared with a larger grained background grid to the panels.

Solomatic and other UltimateTickets

The introduction of one-man operation on the 9 Ring Road service on 2 December 1962 resulted in the introduction of a new type of ticket machine, the Solomatic, on A.E.C. Reliance buses, 39-43.

The Solomatic machine was manufactured by the Bell Punch Company and was very similar to the Ultimate machine, but was specially adapted for one-man vehicles. The machines were hired from Bell Punch at a charge of £17 each per annum.

The normal Ultimate tickets were used (1d. to 5d.), but as the Solomatic machine held six values of ticket, a 6d. red ticket was also supplied. This was similar in print to the other values in use, but the printer's imprint was slightly inset from the panel edges. There were also other very minor alterations.

The other ticket values were also soon altered in style, in a similar manner to the 6d. value, for use on both Solomatic and Ultimate machines. The revised 4d. and 5d. tickets appeared in January and the 3d. in February 1963. The revised 1d. ticket came into use in April and the 2d. in June 1963.

The new style was not to remain in use for long on the 3d. tickets. In late June 1963 the value changed slightly again. The printer's imprint was now back level with the edges of the panels, but there were other minor alterations in type setting. e.g. the words "ORD" and "CHILD" were slightly larger. The 3d. ticket reverted to the style with the printers' imprint inset in November 1963. This style was now common to all the other Ultimate and Solomatic tickets. On the new Wednesday afternoon "See Your City Tours" introduced in June 1963 conductors were supplied with special ticket boxes and machines, loaded with 1s.0d. and 6d. Ultimate tickets only. The 1s.0d. ticket was the pink Oller ticket, which had been used for statistical purposes on the Ring Road service. The adult fare of 2s.0d. was met by issuing two 1s.0d. tickets while the 1s.0d. child's fare was met by issuing two 6d. tickets of the then current type, as previously only used on the one-man buses on service 9.

A partial fares increase took place on Sunday, 22 September 1963. when fare stages were altered on several routes. The number of fare stages on most routes were now in a common series, with the main city centre stage, (the Corn Exchange or Central Bus Station) being numbered 20.

In early December 1963 several conductors at Bramley Garage were issued with rolls of GNP Ultimate tickets containing 1,000 tickets in a roll instead of the normal 500. They were printed on a slightly thinner paper than the normal issues and were of the 3d. value only. The printing style was the same as the normal 3d. They were all used up by the end of the month, but the use of 1,000 ticket rolls became standard practice for the 3d. value in late February 1964. In May 1964 the 1d. and 5d. tickets appeared in 1,000 ticket rolls and printed on thinner paper. They were identical with the thin 3d. tickets except that the printer's imprint was slightly inset from the panels; on the 3d. tickets it was level with the sides of the panels. Thin 4d. tickets appeared in July and the 2d. value in November 1964.

In February 1964 4d. tickets were appearing in a slightly different style. They had the words "ORD" and "CHILD" printed in smaller type, in a similar manner to the tickets first printed by GNP after the last issue of Oller tickets about three years previously.

Experimental T.I.M. machines.

Ticket Issuing Machine or "T.I.M." tickets had been experimentally used on Leeds trams in 1932. The tickets had been printed on flimsy paper on a machine, which had a dialling device.

"T.I.M." tickets had never "caught on" in Leeds but were used by a number of other transport undertakings. In November 1963 two experimental "T.I.M" machines came into use. They were of the latest model with fixed dials and a pointer to select the fare value. Tickets of 12 values could be issued 1d. to 1s.0d., these being marked round the dial anti-clockwise. Mechanically they were rather like a miniature adding machine and recorded how many tickets were issued of each value and also the total amount of money taken in both £.s.d. and in pence only. There was no distinction in the class of ticket shown. Both machines (serials 222 and 777) were demonstration models, the tickets bearing these initials in the position allocated for the operators name. Machine 222 was used by a conductor from Sovereign Street Garage (from 18 November 1963) on services 1, 5, 32, 42, 47, 55 and 88, whilst 777 was used from Torre Road Garage from 23 November. This machine was used on services 1 and 5 (Lawnswood-Beeston).

Both machines were used until 7 December 1963 when they were withdrawn.

Tokens

From 1904 celluloid tokens were used on the Leeds trams and later buses of the Leeds transport undertaking. These are discussed on page 711 of Volume 2. There were tokens of $\frac{1}{2}$d. (little used after 1957), 1d, 1$\frac{1}{2}$d. (also little used after 1957) and 2d. There had been a 2d. red token in the 1920's, but this appears to have fallen into disuse for, according to the L.C.T. Traffic Records, on 26 November 1951 a new 2d. red token was brought into use. In 1956 a 3d. token, green in colour, was introduced and in October 1963 a 4d. light blue token, made its appearance. The tokens remained in use until decimalisation and were withdrawn from 20 February 1971. Latterly there had been the 1d. white, 2d. red, 3d. green and 4d. light blue.

Although tokens issued by the Leeds Transport undertaking were abolished in February 1971 operators in other areas continued to use them. The SELNEC PTA used tokens in the Manchester area and they were valued

GNP Ultimate tickets issued from June 1955 to 23 February 1957 and from 29 September 1957 to late 1958.

1½d., 2½d. and 6d. GNP tickets issued from 24 February 1957 to 28 September 1957, 5d. blue Oller tickets of January 1959 and GNP 8d. pink.

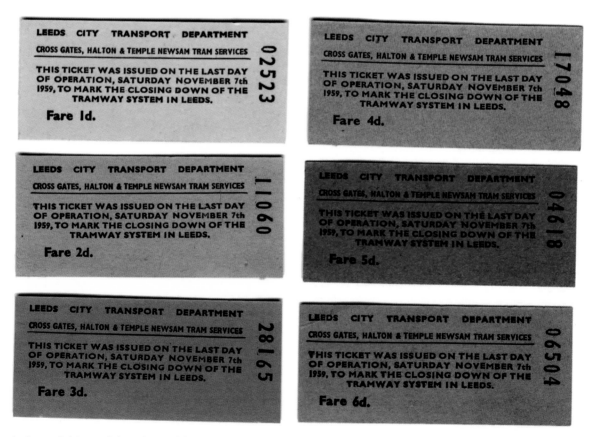

A set of special tram tickets issued for use on the last day of tramway operation. The tickets were not cancelled by the conductor. Size of tickets 76mm (3in.) x 33mm (1⁵/₁₆in.)

LEEDS CITY TRANSPORT DEPARTMENT

SEAT RESERVATION
ON
LAST TRAM
SATURDAY, 7th NOVEMBER, 1959

ISSUED TO Mr J. Soper

PASSENGERS ARE ASKED TO BE AT SWINEGATE DEPOT (MAIN GATES) AT 6.0 p.m. ADMITTANCE TO THE DEPOT TO BOARD THE LAST TRAM WILL ONLY BE GRANTED ON PRESENTATION OF THIS TICKET.

TRAM NO. 8

The reverse of one of the special tickets issued on the last day of tramway operation. It gives a "potted" history of the tramways undertaking. On the right is one of the special lemon colour tickets that were issued for use in the final tramcar procession. Size of lemon ticket 109 mm (4 5/16 in.) x 75·5 mm (3 in.)

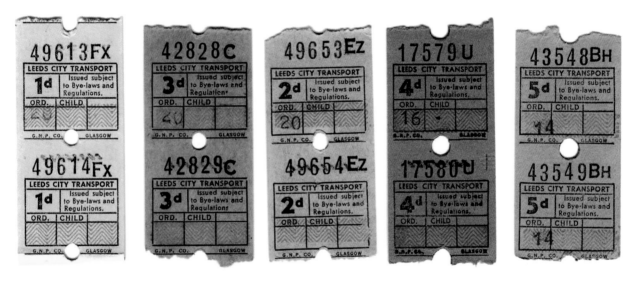

GNP Ultimates with suffix type serial letters introduced in December 1961.

Decimal Ultimate tickets introduced on 21 February 1971.

at 3p each. They were subsequently taken up by many councils, particularly in the Manchester area, and they became known as "North West Public Transport Tokens." Their use gradually spread to other areas and the name was changed to "Public Transport Tokens".

In early March 1973, Tadcaster Rural District Council issued the 3p tokens to pensioners and they became valid for use on L.C.T. buses.

More Fare Increases and Associated Matters

Beginning on 2 August 1964 a fare increase came into force on Bradford Corporation bus services. Some fares on service 72 (Leeds-Bradford) were increased. The new through fare was 11d. instead of 10d. There was no alteration to tickets.

In November 1964 a number of conductors were issued with lightweight plastic, experimental, ticket boxes. They were light green in colour and had rounded edges and corners. The old type metal boxes had sharp corners.

Another fare increase took place from Sunday, 29 November 1964. The following scale was now in use:

Adult fare	Average Distance		No. of stages
2d.	0·56	miles	1
3d.	1·11	,,	2
4d.	1·66	,,	3
5d.	2·21	,,	4
6d.	2·80	,,	5
7d.	3·36	,,	6
8d.	3·92	,,	7
8d.	4·48	,,	8
8d.	5·04	,,	9
9d.	5·60	,,	10
9d.	6·16	,,	11
9d.	6·72	,,	12
10d.	7·28	,,	13
10d.	7·84	,,	14
10d.	8·40	,,	15
11d.	8·96	,,	16
11d.	9·52	,,	17
11d.	10·08	,,	18
11d.	10·64	,,	19
11d.	11·20	,,	20
1s.0d.	13·96	,,	20 and over.

As a result of this fares rise there was no alteration in the ticket values or styles.

The introduction of the short-lived Kirkstall Park and Ride service in April 1965 employed one-man buses using Solomatic machines. The following tickets were issued:

9d. single 3 x 3d. tickets; 1s.6d. return 3 x 6d. tickets surrendered on the return journey; 5d. child single, 5d. ticket issued as "child"; 9d. child return, 3 x 3d. tickets issued as "child" and surrendered on the return journey.

The stage number indicated on the ticket was to show the date. The fare included the bus fare and all day parking.

Yet another fares increase took place from Sunday, 30 May 1965. The 2d. and 3d. fares and fares of 8d. and above were unchanged, but those of 4d., 5d., 6d. and 7d. were all increased by 1d. There was now no adult 4d. fare. Fares on night services were also increased.

There was no alteration in the tickets, but the 4d. was issued to children only. The short stages now seemed very expensive in comparison with the longer distances.

In early July 1965, the 3d. value Ultimate tickets appeared printed on a manilla type paper. This was a thin paper giving 1,000 tickets to the roll, but was stronger than the former flimsy paper. It was slightly glossy in appearance. There was a slight change in colour, the new tickets being rather more orange than the previous examples. 1d. tickets printed on manilla paper appeared in early November 1965 and the 4d. value the following month.

2d. tickets appeared on manilla paper in January 1966 and the 5d. in November of the same year.

In August 1965 a new 1s.0d. ticket, colour lilac, was introduced for use on the afternoon sightseeing tours. It was printed by GNP and was identical in printing style to the current set of Ultimate tickets. The new 1s.0d. ticket was a replacement for the Oller pink 1s.0d. tickets previously used on these tours.

On 30 April 1967 the 45 (Wortley-Stanks) service became one-man operated. Solomatic ticket machines were used and the normal GNP tickets were used except that the 6d. ticket was now coloured blue. It was produced on the current manilla paper and was a replacement for the 6d. red ticket, which was still in use on the Ring Road service. The 6d. red were the last of the old thick tickets in use.

A fares increase took place from 1 October 1967. The new scale of adult fares was now 2d., 4d., 6d., 8d., 10d., 1s.0d. and 1s.2d. Night service adult fares were 6d. minimum, then 8d. and by 4d. multiples to 2s.0d.

The tickets now carried by conductors in the Ultimate machines were of the 1d., 3d., 4d., 5d. and 1s.0d. values. The latter value was yellow in colour (unlike the lilac coloured tickets of this value used on summer sightseeing tours) and replaced the 2d. yellow ticket. On the one-man operated services, the Solomatic machines had 1d., 3d., 4d., 5d., 7d. and 1s.0d. tickets, the blue 7d. value being a replacement of the former 6d. ticket carried in these machines, which up to their withdrawal had been of both the old thick red and the later blue manilla issues.

Fare values were now made up as follows:

Fare	Ultimate machine	Solomatic machine
1d.	1d. ticket	1d. ticket
2d.	double 1d. ticket	double 1d. ticket
3d.	3d. ticket	3d. ticket
4d.	4d. ticket	4d. ticket
5d.	5d. ticket	5d. ticket
6d.	double 3d. ticket	double 3d. ticket
7d.	5d. and double 1d.	7d. ticket
8d.	double 4d. ticket	double 4d. ticket
10d.	double 5d. ticket	double 5d. ticket
1s.0d.	1s.0d. ticket	1s.0d. ticket
1s.2d.	1s.0d. + double 1d.	double 7d. ticket
1s.4d.	1s.0d. + 4d. ticket	
1s.8d.	1s.0d. + double 4d.	
2s.0d.	Two 1s.0d. tickets	

When the Ledgards' services were taken over from 15 October 1967 it was found that there were a number of other fares, not covered by the L.C.T. fare structure. There was no alteration in the tickets, but the different Ledgard fares were covered by the following tickets:

9d.	double 4d. + 1d. ticket
11d.	double 5d. + 1d. ticket
1s.1d.	1s.0d. ticket + 1d. ticket
1s.3d.	1s.0d. ticket + 3d. ticket
1s.5d.	1s.0d. ticket + 5d. ticket
1s.6d.	1s.0d. ticket + double 3d. ticket
1s.7d.	1s.0d. ticket + double 3d. and 1d. ticket.

In October 1968 some slight alterations took place in the printing of the 3d. and 4d. Ultimate tickets. Both values appeared with a large "d" of the value figure, and in addition the line between the value panel and conditions was now level with that of the line between the ordinary and child panels. Both values formerly had small thick "d" letters. There were also other very minor type setting changes in the 3d. value. The 5d. value was altered the following month in a similar manner to the 3d. and 4d. tickets, but retained the small "d".

A general fare increase took place on Sunday, 9 February 1969 with the result that the fare structure was now between 2d. and 2s.0d. on day services and 4d. and 3s.0d. on night services. On the former all fares were divisible by 2d. and on night services by 4d., the only exceptions being on services 78 and 85 to 87, where there were some 3d. 5d. and 7d. fares outside the Leeds city boundary.

With this increase the half fare rate was revised so that there were no odd pence charged (with the exception of services 85 to 87).

Tickets carried in the Ultimate and Solomatic machines were altered. Previously the range had been 1d. white, 3d. orange brown, 4d. green, 5d. grey and 1s.0d. yellow with a 7d. blue ticket in the Solomatic machines. The 1d. and 5d. values were completely withdrawn after 8 February, while in addition the 1s.0d. value came out of the Ultimate range. The 3d. and 7d. were withdrawn from the Solomatics.

The new range was 2d., 3d., 4d., 6d. and 10d. in Ultimate machines with the same tickets plus the 1s.0d. in the Solomatics. New tickets were a 2d. lilac, 6d. white, 8d. pink and 10d. grey, all printed as normal by the GNP Company. Tickets for the various fares charged were in multiples as issued previously.

From Sunday, 4 January 1970 another fares increase took place. Fare scales were now as follows. Distances travelled for the various stages were the same as indicated in the table for 29 November 1964.

Stages	Old adult fare	New fare	Old child fare	New fare
1	2d.	3d.	2d.	2d.
2	4d.	5d.	2d.	3d.
3	6d.	7d.	4d.	5d.
4	8d.	9d.	4d.	5d.
5-6	10d.	1s.0d.	6d.	6d.
7-13	1s.0d.	1s.3d.	6d.	8d.
14-17	1s.2d.	1s.6d.	8d.	9d.
18-21	1s.4d.	1s.6d.	8d.	9d.
22-25	1s.6d.	1s.9d.	10d.	11d.
26-29	1s.8d.	1s.9d.	10d.	11d.
30-33	1s.10d.	2s.0d.	1s.0d.	1s.0d.
Over 34	2s.0d.	2s.3d.	1s.0d.	1s.2d.

Night service fares were also increased, these being generally twice the daytime fare. Tickets on both the Ultimate and Solomatic machines were altered. Tickets withdrawn were the 4d. 6d. and 10d. from the Ultimates and 8d. from the Solomatics.

New values in use were 7d. green and 1s.3d. pink tickets, whilst the 5d. grey ticket was reinstated. Both Ultimates and Solomatics carried 2d., 3d., 5d., 7d. and 1s.3d. tickets with the 1s.0d. being the extra value on the Solomatics. It appears that the 5d. grey tickets were old stocks, for in early February 1970 a new 5d. white ticket was introduced. As usual the printer was GNP and of a similar printing style to the earlier tickets.

Owing to a lack of 6d. tickets in Hull, the surplus 6d. white tickets, withdrawn at the January fares increase, were acquired by Hull Corporation.

As a temporary measure, due to a shortage of orange/brown paper at the printers, a number of grey 3d. Ultimate tickets appeared in early October 1970. The grey 3d. tickets were noted with both the large and small "d" in the value section on the same ticket rolls. By the end of the month orange/brown 3d. tickets reappeared.

The new minibus service operating in the newly constructed pedestrian precinct area of Commercial Street and Bond Street began operation on 30 November 1970. A flat fare of 3d. was charged. The normal orange brown ticket was used, but it was of a thick paper and issued from a Bell Punch Autoslot machine. The "LEEDS CITY TRANSPORT" title was in larger type than on the normal Ultimates. The panel, which normally displayed the stage number carried the wording "MINI-BUS SERVICE".

On 8 November 1970 a further fares increase took place. Night bus fares were also raised, these being approximately twice the daytime fare. No new tickets were introduced, but the 7d. ticket was withdrawn from the Ultimate machines and the 1s.0d. ticket carried in its place. The 7d. ticket was retained on the Solomatics.

Decimalisation of Ultimates and Solomatics

All bus fares were charged in decimal amounts from Sunday, 21 February 1971, fares being amended accordingly. Between "D" day on Monday, 15 February and 20 February, fares were charged at the old rates, but conductors gave change where possible in the new decimal currency. The following new tickets were introduced: 1p green, 2p white, 3p lilac, 4p orange, 5p yellow and 6p red/pink. The 6p value was confined to the Solomatic machines. All were printed by GNP and were similar in design to the earlier tickets. On the green 1p ticket the pence "p" was of a much larger size than on any of the other values.

The shopper's minibus service now had a flat fare of 2p (formerly 3d.) and a white ticket of this value was issued, being in the same format as the former 3d. with the heading "MINI-BUS SERVICE". Tickets for the various fares charged were now as follows:-

Fare	Ultimate machine	Solomatic Machine
1p	1p ticket.	1p ticket
2p	2p ticket	2p ticket
3p	3p ticket	3p ticket
4p	4p ticket	4p ticket
5p	5p ticket	5p ticket
6p	2 x 3p tickets	6p ticket
7p	5p + 2 x 1p	5p + 2 x 1p
8p	2 x 4p tickets	2 x 4p tickets
9p	5p + 2 x 2p	5p + 2 x 2p
10p	2 x 5p tickets	2 x 5p tickets
11p	2 x 5p + 1p	5p + 2 x 3p
12p	2 x 5p + 2p	2 x 6p tickets
13p	------------	2 x 5p + 3p
14p	2 x 5p + 4p	2 x 5p + 4p
16p	2 x 5p + 2 x 3p	2 x 5p + 6p
18p	2 x 5p + 2 x 4p	2 x 5p + 2 x 4p
20p	4 x 5p tickets	4 x 5p tickets
22p	4 x 5p + 2p	4 x 5p + 2p
24p	4 x 5p + 4p	4 x 6p tickets

New minibus service 403 (New Woodhouse Lane Car Park-City Centre) was instituted on 4 October 1971. A flat fare of 2p was charged and the tickets were similar to the other minibus service using Autoslot machines.

A fares increase took place from 5 December 1971, but there was no change in the range of tickets. Another fares increase, on 1 October 1972, also did not result in any alteration to either the Ultimate or Solomatic tickets.

With the 1 October 1972 increase, no change was made to the 2p, 3p and 4p fares, nor to the first stage of the 5p fare, but all other adult fares were increased by 1p with corresponding increases to fares for children and elderly persons. Variations to the normal fare scale were still in force on joint services 39, 55, 72, 78, 89 and 97.

From early March 1973 a small variation to the 1p green Ultimate tickets took place. The "p" of the pence was now of the same narrow style as on other values of the tickets. On previous rolls of this ticket a rather fat "p" had been printed. There was a general fare increase from 16 September 1973 on all services, with adult fares being increased in all cases by 1p. A minimum adult fare of 3p was now in force. There was no alteration in fares for children or elderly persons with the result that half fares were now slightly under half the normal adult fares. The

Two of the experimental tickets used on the Ring Road service in 1961-62.

A 6d. Solomatic ticket issued on the experimental Kirkstall Park and Ride service. The number "16" in the stage number space indicates that the ticket was issued on 16 April 1965. Also shown is a 3d. grey.

A GNP 2d. yellow and 5d. grey of June 1961.

6d. blue and 1s.0d. lilac tickets as used on the one-man buses with Solomatic machines.

6d. red and 1s.0d. pink Solomatics.

7d. blue and 1s.0d. yellow tickets introduced on 1 October 1967.

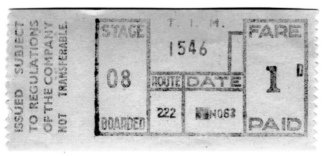

Experimental T.I.M. 1d. ticket issued in November and December 1963.

A printing oddity with the new and old styles of 3d. ticket on the same roll. The new style 4d. ticket is also illustrated.

New tickets introduced on 9 February 1969 were the 2d. lilac in two distinctive shades, the 6d. white and 10d. grey. Also shown is the special ticket issued in Lille from 11 to 19 October 1968 on Daimler Fleetline 159 for British Shopping Week.

The later style 1p green ticket with the 6p Solomatic.

fare scale differed slightly on joint routes 39, 48, 55, 72, 78, 89 and 97.

The new fares did not cause any change of the tickets used in either the Ultimate or Solomatic machines. An exception was the minibuses where the flat fare was raised from 2p to 3p. A new 3p white Autoslot ticket was introduced. It was identical to the previous minibus 2p ticket other than the fare value.

Owing to a shortage of paper, in mid-February 1974 some dark grey 2p tickets, printed as usual by GNP, appeared in use. The normal 2p tickets were white in colour and the grey tickets were used for a short time by drivers or conductors from Seacroft, Sovereign Street and Headingley Garages.

Concessionary Passes

In addition to tickets, special passes were issued to certain persons. There was the blind persons pass issued annually and enabled the blind to travel free on the Corporation's vehicles. There were also scholar's passes, which had been available since 6 September 1932. The colours of both types of pass were changed annually.

Beginning on Monday. 1 February 1965, concessionary fares came into operation for old age pensioners and certain disabled persons. They were issued with a yellow pass, approximately 3in. long x 2 1/2in. wide, entitled "Leeds City Transport", followed by the description "Elderly or Disabled Persons Permit". Also, on the front of the pass was the holder's name and address and the expiry date, which, in the case of pensioners, was the same as the date in their pension book, which had to be shown when the pass was issued or removed. Conditions of issue were on the reverse side of the pass.

On production of their passes, holders were allowed to travel at half fare on buses leaving the city centre or outer termini between 10.00 a.m. and 4.00 p.m. and after 6.00 p.m. daily, (including Saturdays and Sundays). Passes were not valid on football specials and sightseeing tours, nor could they be used on service 72 (Leeds-Bradford).

The passes were launched on 25 January 1965, in a blaze of publicity by Alderman Rafferty, the Chairman of the Transport Committee. The first recipient was Councillor Tom

Smith, the deputy chairman of the Transport Committee, who was a 67 years old retired engine driver. He was the proud owner of the first ticket, No. A000001, and it is illustrated below.

After a trial period of 12 months, the financial aspects of the pass were to be reviewed. It was expected that any loss in revenue would rank for Government grant aid.

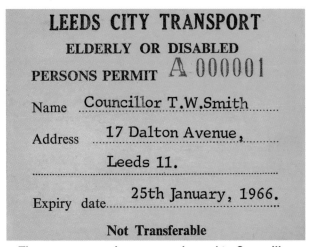

The new concessionary pass issued to Councillor Tom Smith on 25 January 1966. *E. Smith.*

From the beginning of the school term in September 1969, scholar's contract tickets became available. Lasting a term, they had to be specially purchased, and were similar in appearance to the elderly persons half fare permits. The tickets stated the points between which they were available and also the routes on which they were valid.

In December 1971 Garforth Urban District Council introduced concession vouchers for travel in its area. They were valued at 2p each and were issued to eligible persons to the value of £1. These vouchers consisted of gold coloured tickets, size 2in. x 1 1/2in. and were headed "Garforth Urban District Council Bus Travel Concession Voucher" along with a serial number on the front.

On the reverse was the value 2p, along with the wording "For travel to, from or within Garforth Urban District Council area. Exchange Vouchers for a bus ticket".

The vouchers were used on L.C.T. services 39, 89 and 97 and West Riding services, which passed through Garforth. In September 1972 the colour of the pass was changed to pale blue.

From Monday. 2 October 1972, elderly persons and disabled persons passes could be used during the evening peak periods between 4.00 p.m. and 6.00 p.m. on Mondays to Fridays.

From Sunday, 3 December 1972, Bradford City Transport Department began an elderly persons' travel concession for residents in the Pudsey area. A pre-paid ticket, printed by Williamson of Ashton-under-Lyne, was issued and holders could use them in part payment of a fare on service 78 (Leeds to Bradford via Pudsey). They were available during the hours 9.30 a.m. to 3.30 p.m. and 6.30 p.m. to 10.30 p.m. on Mondays to Fridays and Sundays. They were not valid on Saturdays. The value of the ticket was 1p which was deducted from the normal fare.

Skelton Grange Bus Tickets

On 6 May 1963 the contract service to Skelton Grange Power Station was changed to a stage carriage works service number 137 operated by the Transport Department. Special tickets were issued to staff at the power station. These were new Bell Punch type tickets of the values 3d. 4d. 5d. and 6d. all printed by the Glasgow Numerical Printing Company. The colours were the same as the current Ultimate tickets of the same value.

They were sold stapled in books of twelve tickets and were subsidised by the Central Electricity Board to the amount of 1d. per ticket, irrespective of value. The tickets were cancelled by hand clippers. Passengers who did not have the C.E.G.B. tickets to hand were issued with a normal Ultimate ticket, which was not subsidised.

As a result of the fares increase on 29 November 1964, the Skelton Grange fares were raised and an additional ticket appeared on 13 December 1964. This was a 7d. value yellow ticket identical in design to the other tickets. The fares rise six months later, on 30 May 1965, saw the appearance of an 8d. dark blue ticket about a fortnight later.

With subsequent fare increases a 9d. grey, 10d. grey. 1s.0d. yellow and 1s.3d. mauve ticket appeared. Thus at one time or another ten different Skelton Grange tickets existed.

From decimalisation of the tickets on 21 February 1971, four new tickets appeared comprising a 3p mauve, 4p red, 5p yellow and 6p lilac. They were printed by GNP to standard punch ticket design, with "To Skelton Grange" printed on the left hand side and "From Skelton Grange" on the right hand side.

The use of one-man buses on the Skelton Grange service resulted, on 25 August 1972, of multi-journey tickets being introduced. The subsidised punch type tickets gradually fell into disuse. By the time of the PTE take-over in April 1974, they had all gone.

Multi-journey Tickets

Fastaway express bus services 224 and 225, (Swarcliffe Estate to city centre), were introduced on 17 July 1967. There was a flat fare of 10d. adult, 5d. child, but passengers could buy a ten-journey ticket for specific use on this service. All concessionary fares such as scholar's passes, elderly person's half fare passes etc, could be used on the express buses.

To speed fare collection the ten-journey tickets were cancelled by the passenger in a Bell Punch Autoslot cancellor, which was a red coloured machine positioned by the right hand door on the inside of the one-man buses working the services.

The idea was that passengers who wished to pay the driver, entered through the left hand door and those with ten-journey tickets entered on the right. The tickets measured 4³/₄in. x 2in. and were headed with the City coat of arms and the L.C.T. motif. Followed by the description "10 JOURNEY TICKET" and the ticket number. Below this, it was divided into sections for each journey, with columns for the various items of information stamped by the cancelling machine, i.e. route number, journey number, day month, year and machine number. On the extreme right hand edge of the ticket, the journeys were numbered. This piece was then clipped off by the machine as each journey was used.

Conditions of issue were printed on the reverse.

The tickets were on white card with black printing, and were produced by the Bell Punch Company Ltd. There were actually two issues, one with a green arrow (pointing in the direction in which it had to be placed in the cancellor). This ticket was sold by drivers when one journey was being used at a time. The ticket then had spaces for a further nine journeys. The other ticket had ten cancelling spaces and could be purchased in advance from drivers, Head Office, Enquiry Offices or from the Estate Office at Seacroft Town Centre. Both tickets cost 7s.6d. The ten-journey tickets gave a saving of 10d. on tickets purchased at the normal rate of 10d. per single journey.

The tickets did not have any expiry date and were available for any ten journeys, irrespective of the direction travelled. They were transferable in that if stamped say three times on entering, they were valid for a journey for three people. They were not available on the normal 24 and 25 services to Swarcliffe.

Ticket holders

To publicise the Fastaway services, a coloured folder was issued giving full details, along with a specimen ten-journey ticket (slightly smaller than the actual tickets), A combined timetable/wallet was also included, the wallet being suitable for carrying a multi-journey ticket. In July 1971 a new type wallet was introduced, which did not have the timetable for individual services.

In August 1973 a new type of holder was introduced. It had a stiff plastic back on which was printed advertising for multi-journey tickets, with, on the reverse, a transparent section for holding the ticket. The former multi-journey ticket holders were made from stiff card.

As a result of the general fare increase on 9 February 1969, the flat fare on services 224 and 225 was now 1s.2d. The cost of the ten-journey tickets was increased to 10s.0d.

On 8 June 1969 ten-journey tickets were introduced on services 45 (Stanks-Wortley) and on 13 July route 49 (Hyde Park-Old Farnley). They were available from drivers where a fare of 6d. or more was charged. The driver stamped the stage number boarded, and serial number of the machine. All were made out with spaces for nine cancellations by passengers, the first journey being automatically cancelled by the sale of the ticket.

The tickets were on white card and printed by the Bell Punch Company Ltd. They were similar to those on Fastaway services 224 and 225, although the normal 10s.0d. ticket on these services was not available on the 45 and 49 services. The colour of the value was overprinted and there was an arrow showing the direction in which the ticket was to be inserted into the cancellor.

Fare	10-journey ticket	Saving	Colour overprinted
6d.	4s.0d.	1s.0d.	orange
8d.	5s.6d.	1s.2d.	dark purple
10d.	7s.0d.	1s.4d.	grey
1s.0d.	8s.6d.	1s.6d.	red
1s.2d.	10s.0d.	1s.8d.	light purple
1s.4d.	11s.6d.	1s.10d.	brown
1s.6d.	13s.0d.	2s.0d.	green
1s.8d.	14s.6d.	2s.2d.	blue

Fastaway services 235 (Alwoodley to Leeds) and 237 (Shadwell to Leeds) were introduced on 28 July 1969. The normal single fare on the buses was 1s.2d. and ten-journey tickets were available on both services at a cost of 10s.0d.

The nine and ten-journey tickets used on services 224 and 225 to Swarcliffe were withdrawn from sale from 24 August 1969 and replaced by the 1s.2d. value tickets as used on service 45. These had the fare value printed on the ticket, whereas those formerly used on the 224 and 225's had no value printed on them.

On 26 October 1969, routes 56 (Central Bus Station-North Lane) and 57 to 60 (Hyde Park circulars) became one-man operated. Multi-journey tickets were introduced.

As a result of the fare increase of 4 January 1970, several, of the tickets on services 45, 49, 56-60 and the Fastaway routes were altered. Certain of the old values were withdrawn and replaced with new ones.

The 6d., 8d., 10d., 1s.2d., 1s. 4d. and 1s. 8d. were withdrawn and new tickets of 7d., 9d., 1s.3d. and 1s.9d. values were brought into use. The only values from the former range still in use were the 1s.0d. (red) and 1s.6d. (green). All these were labelled nine-journey tickets, the tenth being automatically used when the ticket was purchased from the driver. For the Fastaway services the ten-journey ticket was still available from Offices etc.

From 19 January 1970 two additional Fastaway services, 215 and 216 were introduced between Seacroft and the Corn Exchange. A publicity leaflet was issued giving hints and advice on the multi-journey tickets, which were now available on the 45, 49, 56-60, 215, 216, 224, 225, 235 and 237 services. Tickets were of the following fares:

Fare	10-journey ticket	Saving	Colour overprinted
7d.	4s.9d.	1s.1d.	orange
9d.	6s.3d.	1s.3d.	grey
1s.0d.	8s.6d.	1s.6d.	red
1s.3d.	10s.9d.	1s.9d.	mauve
1s.6d.	13s.0d.	2s.0d.	green
1s.9d.	15s.0d.	2s.6d.	lilac

Following the fares increase of 8 November 1970, the multi-journey tickets were revised. The 7d., 9d. and 1s.6d. tickets were withdrawn and to cover replacement fares, new tickets of 8d. value (orange), 10d. grey), 1s.5d. (light green), 1s.7d. (yellow) and 2s.0d. (dark green) were introduced. The ten-journey tickets, available from enquiry offices, were withdrawn after 7 November. Multi-journey tickets were now only obtainable from drivers.

Multi-journey tickets were introduced on a considerable number of additional services from 10 January 1971:

34/35 Central Bus Station-Alwoodley.
37/43 Central Bus Station-Shadwell.
38 Whitkirk-Moortown.
44 Halton Moor-Stanningley
46 Bramley Town End – Belle Isle or Middleton.
67 Central Bus Stn-Seacroft Monkswood Gate.
68 Central Bus Station- Foundry Lane.
70 Central Bus Station-Primley Park.
73 Moor Grange-Greenthorpe.

The tickets used were the nine-journey cards where the tenth journey was automatically cancelled by the sale of the ticket.

Decimalisation of the multi-journey tickets

Following decimalisation from 21 February 1971, multi-journey tickets were available in the following values:

4p orange, 5p yellow, 6p red, 7p green, 8p purple, 9p grey, 10p blue, 11p brown, 12p light blue, 13p very dark grey.

On 28 March 1971 the number of services using ten-journey tickets was expanded as follows:-

7 Hunslet-Beckett's Park.
42 Harehills-Old Farnley.
66 Harehills-Leysholme Estate.
74 Belle Isle- Moor Grange
76 Middleton-Moor Grange

A new Fastaway service, 265, was introduced on 2 May 1970 between the Central Bus Station and Pudsey.

Ten-journey tickets were introduced and on the same day, similar tickets appeared on service 9 (Ring Road), 61/62 (East End Park Circulars), 63 (Cross Green) and 65 (Central Bus Station-Pudsey).

Further Fastaway services were started on 26 July 1971 between the Central Bus Station and Cookridge (233) and Tinshill (236). Ten-journey tickets were used. These were followed on 6 September by service 272 (Leeds-Bradford). On the Bradford service there was a flat fare of 10p for adults and 5p for children, but multi-journey tickets were not used.

From 17 September 1971 ten-journey tickets became available on services:

6 Halton Moor-Half Mile Lane.
14 Halton Moor-Half Mile Lane.
83 Rodley-Austhorpe.
84 Rodley-Colton.

Five weeks later, on 26 October, ten-journey tickets came into use on service 22 (Central Bus Station-Temple Newsam) and on 5 December, they appeared on services 48/81 (Troydale-Calverley) and 79/80 (Pudsey-Horsforth-Tinshill).

The fares increase of 5 December 1971 did not result in any change to the multi-journey tickets.

From 25 August 1972 they came into use on service 137 to Skelton Grange Power Station. On 3 September they appeared on service 29 (Infirmary Street-Middleton and a month later, on 2 October on service 75 (Seacroft Town Centre-Seacroft Monkswood Gate).

The fares increase of 1 October 1972 did not mean any alteration to the multi-journey tickets. Although a new fare of 14p was introduced on the 9 (Ring Road) service, there was no multi-journey ticket to cover it.

On 14 November 1972 four experimental shopping services numbered 405, 406, 407 and 408, came into operation. Multi-journey tickets were available on all four services.

On 8 January 1973 two new Fastaway services commenced along the recently opened south east motorway. Both services, 210 (Middleton-City Centre) and 221 (Belle Isle-City Centre) used multi-journey tickets.

From 24 May 1973 there was an increase of fares by the West Riding Automobile Company Ltd. This applied to the joint routes 39, 89, 97, and the joint Kippax/Garforth Fastaways (202, 203 and 204) - originally introduced on 8 March 1971.

To cater for the Kippax and Garforth Fastaways, new multi-journey tickets of 14p and 15p values were introduced. The new 14p tickets had green overprints while the 15p tickets were red, both being the same shades of colour as the existing 7p and 6p tickets respectively. The new values were issued to drivers in packs of twenty tickets and were unusual in having no serial letter prefixing the ticket number as on all other values in use.

Multi-journey tickets became available on works services 177 (Elida Gibbs Factory, Whinmoor) from 29 November and 105 (R.O.F. Barnbow) from 17 December 1973.

Setright "Keyspeed" Ticket Machine

From Friday, 23 June 1972, and on most days up to Saturday, 8 July, an experimental ticket machine called a Setright "Keyspeed" was used on Leyland Atlantean 357 operating on service 49 (Hyde Park-Old Farnley). 357 was a single doorway double decker, which had recently been experimentally converted for one-man operation.

The machine was the second prototype of an entirely new design, which had been used earlier by London Country Bus Services and by SELNEC PTE in the Bolton area. The machine was designed for one-man operation

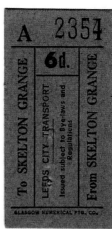

Typical tickets as issued on the Skelton Grange special works bus service.

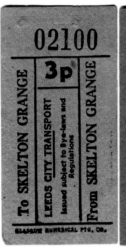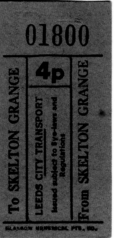

A 1s.3d., and decimal tickets issued on the Skelton Grange special works bus service from 21 February 1971.

Front and rear of the first £5 monthly ticket issued by the Leeds Transport Department.

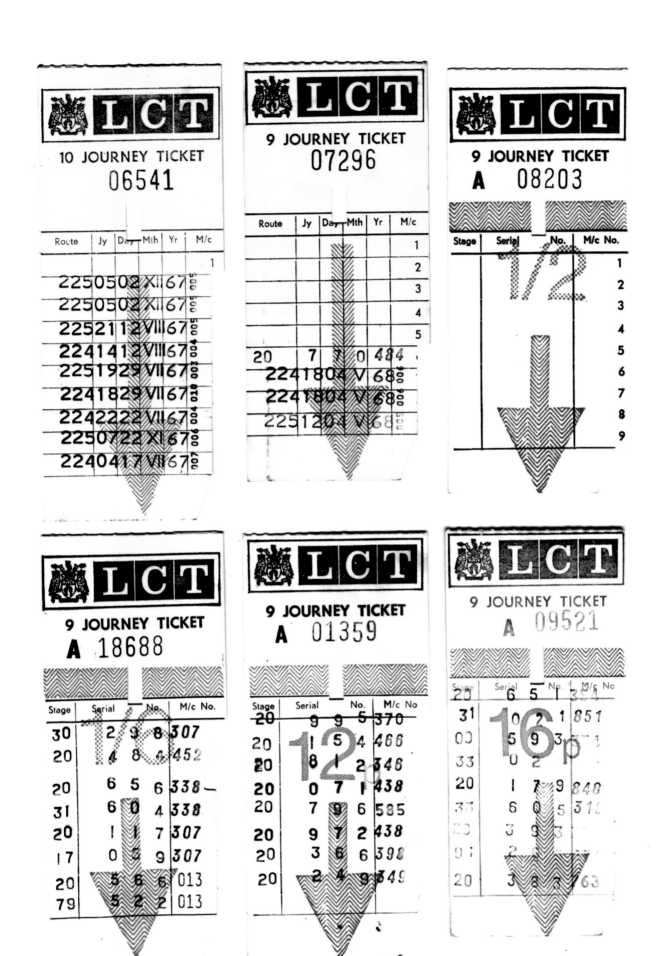

Typical multi-journey tickets issued by the Transport Department. The first two were used on the initial Fastaway services 224 and 225 to Swarcliffe from 17 July 1967 and on 235 (Alwoodley) and 237 (Shadwell) from 28 July 1969. The ten journey tickets were sold only in offices until 3 January 1970. The 1s.2d. and 1s.6d. tickets were used from 8 June 1969 and the decimal tickets from 21 February 1971.

and issued a paper ticket of a type similar to those used in supermarkets. The machine was also capable of issuing multi-journey tickets, although it did not do so while in Leeds. The machine could print the details on a blank card, and drivers would only need to carry one pack of blank cards instead of several packs.

In the conversion of further Leyland Atlanteans for one-man operation, fittings were provided for both Solomatic and Setright "Keyspeed" machines.

Two examples of the Setright "Keyspeed" machines reappeared in May 1973. Neither demonstration model bore the L.C.T. name, the tickets issued carrying the Setright Registers title. One machine was used for training purposes at Torre Road Garage, whilst the other went into use on the Scott Hall Road group of services (Alwoodley, Shadwell and Primley Park) from Monday 21 May. The machine was usually fitted to Daimler Fleetlines, 132, 133 or 134. The machine was withdrawn from use on 8 June and returned to the manufacturers for further research and modifications.

The Setright machine was in use for a further trial period from 24 to 27 July and 30 July to 3 August 1973.

The Transport Department must have been impressed for in November 1973 the Transport Committee agreed to order 50 machines for delivery at a cost of £3,850. The first five production machines were brought into use on Thursday, 3 January 1974. The machines, numbered L001-L005, were used from Torre Road Garage on converted one-man Daimler Fleetline buses, 116-145, on the 34/35 Alwoodley, 37/43 Shadwell and 70 Primley Park services.

The tickets printed by the machine bore the title "LEEDS CITY TRANSPORT", whereas the demonstration models had shown "SETRIGHT REGISTERS LTD."

The machines were also used for the issue of multi-journey tickets, by means of blank cards supplied by the Bell Punch Co. Ltd. The white tickets were longer than the usual multi-journey tickets with pre-printed values. They were validated by inserting into the machine, which printed the fare value paid on the ticket.

In case of emergency, drivers operating the new machines carried a roll of standard 1p Ultimate tickets.

Five more machines came into use on 4 February 1974 and more appeared on 19 March. Some machines were allocated to Middleton Garage for use on service 29 (infirmary Street-Middleton). On 1 April 1974 buses wired up for these machines were 116-145, 341-345, and 370-385 while in addition the new Leyland Leopard coach, 21, was partially fitted. Leyland National 1301 was also wired for Setright machines. Other buses followed later.

Monthly Tickets

From 1 January 1973 a £5 monthly ticket appeared and gave unlimited free travel on almost all L.C.T. services (including night bus routes). The limitations were services 72, 202, 203, 204 and 272, which were joint services, and on which the pass could not be used at all. On joint service 78 it was valid only on L.C.T. buses and could only be used between Leeds and Pudsey Waterloo. On services 39, 89 and 97, also joint, it was valid between Leeds and Barrowby Road only. It was available on West Riding buses on services 89 and 97 as far as Barrowby Road. The ticket used was quite large, 8in. x 1³/₄in. and was of thin card. Of this there was a section consisting of a renewal portion, which was perforated and bent under so that the ticket fitted in a wallet 5¹/₄in. x 2¹/₄in. The ticket was orange and white in colour and indicated were details of its use and restrictions. It was used in conjunction with a validation card, size 2³/₄in. x 1³/₄in., which also fitted in the plastic wallet provided with the ticket. The validation card gave the name and address of the holder and also a colour photograph of the holder, along with his or her signature. The tickets were printed by the GNP Company of Glasgow, but did not bear any imprint.

The tickets were issued from the L.C.T. Head Office in Swinegate, by personal application only. A photograph was taken for the validation card. The photographic equipment was initially hired from another Corporation Department, but in November 1973 the Transport Committee agreed to purchase its own equipment at a cost of £700. The holder of a validation card could renew his ticket at one of the Department's enquiry offices in the city centre, at Swinegate Head Office, or by post. The tickets were available to start on any date required and were not restricted to calendar months. The colour of the ticket was changed every month. That for February 1973 was green in colour, March red, April purple, May yellow, and June blue. The colour for the July 1973 issue reverted to orange and the colours were then repeated.

After 1 April 1974

The use of Leeds City Transport tickets continued for a time after 1 April. From 1 April the use of Leeds multi-journey tickets on service 78 (Leeds-Bradford) was extended from Pudsey Waterloo to Thornbury Barracks.

The use of £5 monthly tickets and elderly persons passes were also extended to Thornbury Barracks.

Although there was a fare increase on 12 May there was no alteration in Ultimate or Solomatic tickets. A 16p multi-journey ticket was introduced. The overprint value was coloured brown (similar to the 11p multi-journey ticket). The new ticket was still titled L.C.T.

From May 1974 the £5 monthly tickets issued for the Leeds district were slightly altered. They now showed a Metro Leeds title. New validation cards also now had a Metro Leeds title.

Ultimate and Solomatic tickets were still titled "Leeds City Transport" and in mid-June 1974 the colour of paper for the 4p tickets in the Ultimate and Solomatic machines was changed to pink. This was due to a shortage of orange/brown paper. The new 4p tickets, which were titled "Leeds City Transport", were very similar in appearance to the 6p tickets.

The first P.T.E. issue of Ultimate tickets appeared in late July, these being the white 2p issue. Printed as usual by the G.N.P. Co. Glasgow, the layout was altered from the style of the former Leeds City Transport tickets. The 'W.Y.' motif along with the title METRO LEEDS filled a large rectangular box on the left of the ticket, the value being positioned in a box on the right hand side. 'Issued subject to Regulations' then came underneath these items, while the bottom part of the ticket contained the usual panels headed 'ORD', 'CHILD', while one was blank.

In October 1974 the 1p green ticket, the 4p red and 5p grey (temporary printing only) and yellow changed to the new style. Following a fare increase on 1 January 1975 several ticket values were changed. The 1p, 4p and also 6p red were discontinued. The only L.C.T. Ultimate/Solomatic still in use after 1 January was the 3p. This was replaced in March 1975 by Metro Leeds tickets.

The multi-journey tickets began to appear with Metro Leeds titles in October 1974, the 9p grey and 10p blue being the first. The 6p followed in November and 8p in December. After the fares increase, the 4p, 6p, 8p and 13p tickets were withdrawn. The 7p ticket appeared with Metro Leeds headings in February 1975, and in March the 11p and 16p values followed. The 5p was changed in April.

A fares increase on 13 July 1975 marked the end of tickets headed "Leeds City Transport". The special 3p Ultimate used on the minibuses was withdrawn and the last L.C.T. headed multi-journey ticket, the 15p value, also went out of use.

The £5 monthly ticket was renamed a 'MetroCard' from 13 October 1974 and became available for use throughout the P.T.E. area. On 1 April 1975 the use of elderly persons passes was also extended over the whole of the P.T.E. area.

Leeds City Tramways/Transport Traffic Statistics 1894 to 1974

Year Ending 31 Mar	No. of trams	No. of buses	Traffic Receipts	Expenditure	Net Surplus + Deficit -	Passengers carried	Revenue Miles run	Average Fare Paid
1895	68	1	£51,013	£50,880	£133+	9,489,797	1,047,132	1·290d.
1896	68	1	£57,848	£53,099	£4,749+	10,843,457	1,105,449	1·280d.
1897	68	1	£64,225	£58,226	£5,999+	14,203,397	1,233,184	1·085d.
1898	110	1	£73,596	£73,452	£144+	15,620,985	1,477,693	1·130d.
1899	129	1	£112,071	£104,041	£8,030+	24,237,449	2,403,463	1·109d.
1900	173	1	£126,656	£120,489	£6,167+	27,634,105	2,664,754	1·099d.
1901	233	4	£180,281	£149,223	£31,058+	39,334,475	3,760,275	1·099d.
1902	249	3	£221,252	£173,011	£48,241+	48,273,300	4,726,043	1·099d.
1903	245	1	£262,443	£200,443	£62,000+	57,239,779	5,766,100	1·098d.
1904	245	1	£277,665	£225,665	£52,000+	60,739,234	6,091,437	1·097d.
1905	270	1	£294,328	£239,328	£55,000+	64,223,666	7,044,838	1·099d.
1906	270	3	£308,495	£256,995	£51,500+	68,634,126	7,126,185	1·063d.
1907	270	4	£323,912	£254,650	£69,262+	73,024,853	7,358,185	1·065d.
1908	270	4	£336,446	£272,167	£64,279+	75,734,083	7,694,989	1·066d.
1909	276	3	£338,031	£290,475	£47,556+	76,215,618	7,828,794	1·064d.
1910	282	3	£353,859	£298,542	£55,317+	78,385,015	8,152,990	1·083d.
1911	282	3	£364,927	£313,039	£51,888+	80,806,270	8,308,439	1·083d.
1912	292	2	£391,142	£329,979	£61,163+	86,021,943	8,527,957	1·089d.
1913	292	2	£407,551	£346,176	£61,375+	80,668,185	8,795,465	1·088d.
1914	315	2	£423,516	£353,512	£70,014+	93,679,774	9,204,331	1·081d.
1915	338	2	£429,902	£348,335	£81,567+	95,639,268	9,522,737	1·089d.
1916	338	2	£467,197	£395,376	£71,821+	103,453,801	9,405,121	1·103d.
1917	338	2	£507,755	£428,324	£79,431+	112,151,883	9,658,595	1·104d.
1918	338	2	£578,961	£520,961	£58,000+	124,519,119	9,547,670	1·110d.
1919	338	2	£715,532	£625,532	£90,000+	120,252,950	9.155,355	1·418d.
1920	333	2	£869,289	£785,532	£83,757+	136,567,011	9,882,737	1·515d.
1921	336	2	£989,690	£984,069	£5,621+	138,621,331	10,176,874	1·696d.
1922	348	3	£953,906	£910,640	£43,266+	129,707,972	9,326,755	1·741d.
1923	358	7	£955,586	£864,095	£91,491+	134,926,024	9,875,548	1·679d.
1924	362	8	£882,319	£833,905	£48,414+	138,642,424	10,278,031	1·511d.
1925	375	16	£919,107	£859,819	£59,288+	144,768,459	11.037,938	1·508d.
1926	378	23	£918,578	£873,684	£44,894+	148,462,619	12,363,092	1·470d.
1927	437	53	£912,913	£862,174	£50,739+	147,407,849	12,659,546	1·474d.
1928	475	54	£991,516	£924,869	£66,647+	160,825,651	13,828,632	1·466d.
1929	472	78	£995,514	£940,506	£55,008+	164,116,214	14,555,582	1·446d.
1930	458	81	£1,034,058	£977,116	£56,942+	170,307,353	15,331.572	1·452d.
1931	433	94	£1,029,267	£948,651	£80,616+	169,374,394	15,979,490	1·457d.
1932	450	94	£1,040,997	£997,587	£43,410+	168,184,589	16,231,200	1·474d.
1933	476	93	£1,015,607	£987,107	£28,500+	162,741.140	16,100,000	1·485d.
1934	476	109	£1,047,917	£1,019,417	£28,500+	167,908,571	16,450,000	1·485d.
1935	471	138	£1,089.495	£1,062,935	£26,560+	173,927,478	17,324,323	1·491d.
1936	464	180	£1,139,613	£1,115,449	£24,164+	180,259,869	18,104,880	1·534d.
1937	459	210	£1,181,432	£1,151,628	£29,804+	185,972,065	18,797,722	1·542d.
1938	456	238	£1,251,241	£1,230,181	£21,060+	196,860,770	20,093,018	1·545d.
1939	448	263	£1,275,310	£1,258,890	£16,420+	200,284,664	20,547,326	1·548d.
1940	450	262	£1,214,548	£1,210,158	£4,390+	190,480,232	18,182,367	1·550d.
1941	449	262	£1,260,665	£1,260,665	-----------	198,831,364	16,739,897	1·541d.
1942	449	262	£1,373,520	£1,306,113	£67,407+	213,500,000	16,928,687	1·560d.
1943	481	262	£1,450,402	£1,364,126	£86,276+	222,000,000	16,776,909	1·568d.
1944	479	262	£1,477,776	£1,477,776	-----------	224,849,023	16,672,621	1·577d.
1945	478	262	£1,539,062	£1,582,597	£43,535 -	232,605,776	16,872,150	1·588d.
1946	432	278	£1,534,200	£1,608,763	£74,563 -	222,276,355	16,852,780	1·656d.
1947	433	300	£1,752,946	£1,942,502	£189,556 -	244,166,331	19,543,221	1·740d.
1948	429	327	£2,058,517	£1,927,585	£130,932+	244,369,904	20,605,287	2·021d.
1949	433	368	£2,130,450	£2,092,947	£37,503+	250,057,546	21,290,195	2·044d.
1950	396	391	£2,171,716	£2,154,403	£17,313+	252,874,350	21,683,259	2·061d.
1951	394	405	£2,152,260	£2,274,340	£122,080 -	250,207,458	21,628,799	2·064d.
1952	400	385	£2,402,469	£2,581,506	£179,037 -	246,150,376	21,018,576	2·342d.

Year Ending 31 Mar	No. of trams	No. of buses	Traffic Receipts	Expenditure	Net Surplus + Deficit -	Passengers carried	Revenue Miles run	Average Fare Paid
1953	372	416	£2,640,677	£2,692,380	£51,703 -	237,576,753	20,757,841	2·667d.
1954	334	405	£2,645,515	£2,709,907	£64,392 -	237,926,450	20,681,054	2·668d.
1955	311	453	£2,674,233	£2,728,634	£54,401 -	234,136,290	20,692,135	2·741d.
1956	237	490	£2,887,825	£2,809,208	£78,617+	224,122,294	20.061,364	3·092d.
1957	170	576	£2,923,867	£2,947,835	£23,968 -	221,436,473	19,716,588	3·168d.
1958	127	563	£3,234,189	£3,107,296	£126,893+	208,446,521	20,069,318	3·723d.
1959	110	631	£3,259,537	£3,109,206	£150,331+	205.484.462	20,292,420	3·807d.
1960		650	£3,341,798	£3,175,981	£165,817+	207,577,833	20.433,128	3·810d.
1961		654	£3,358,192	£3,343,597	£14,595+	207,189,153	20,318,296	3·820d.
1962		638	£3,505,141	£3,482,427	£22,714+	206,028,866	20,579,547	3·990d.
1963		655	£3,568,784	£3,568,696	£88+	203,601,298	20,829,590	4·140d.
1964		674	£3,762,370	£3,761,075	£1,295+	206,910,170	21,231,952	4·300d.
1965		671	£3,931,227	£3,931,227	------------	205,240,461	21,346,534	4·510d.
1966		667	£4,182,168	£4,181,732	£436+	195,896,974	21,112,544	5·050d.
1967		689	£4,225,451	£4,502,262	£276,811 -	192,410,420	21,122,317	5·160d.
1968		708	£4,424,688	£4,613,401	£188,713 -	192,074,159	21,792,472	5·470d.
1969		705	£4,803,201	£5,215,477	£412,276 -	192,226,671	22,229,172	5·940d.
1970			£5,506,390	£5,037,878	£468,512+	182,221,088 estimated		
1971			£6,036,178	£5,726,461	£309,717+	172,016,085 estimated		
1972			£7,040,200	£6.396,913	£643,287+	161,610,792	21,377,970	4·356p
1973		683	£7,401,319	£7,728,197	£326,878-	162,200,846	21,291,555	4·728p
1974		702	£7,815,523	£9,168,929	£1,353,406-	158,083,200 estimated	20,824,950	

The figures include trams, trackless cars, motor and horse buses. Tramway rolling stock 1897-1902 includes horse, steam, electric cars and trailers. Bus rolling stock 1906-1911 includes horse bus (1) and motor buses. Separate trackless car statistics are included in Chapter 36 of Volume 2. Official records are not complete after 1969. The figures for the years 1973 and 1974 are from West Yorkshire Passenger Transport Executive records. Leeds City Council records for 31 March 1974 indicate that both the income and expenditure were £8,369,929 and there was no deficit/surplus.

The A.E.C. Regent III typified the Leeds bus for a period of over twenty years.   1949 built 478 was photographed in Neville Avenue, Osmondthorpe, on 11 June 1967.   It is short working to Headingley on the long established 44 Halton Moor to Stanningley service. The buses of this basic Charles Roe design, 451-500 and 600-625, are considered by some to be the best looking buses ever delivered to the Leeds City Transport undertaking. *W.D.Wilson/L.T.H.S.*

Leeds City Transport Motor Bus Fleet List 1953 to 1974

For completeness all known disposal details are included

1953

Leyland Motors Ltd. PD2/14 chassis, 0·600 engine, Wilson pre-selector gear box, air brakes.   Cost £4,220 9s.5d. each.
Charles H. Roe Ltd. H33/25R body, 7ft. 6in. wide x 27ft.0in long.   Unladen weight 7 tons 17 cwt 3 qrs.

No.	Regn. No.	Chassis No.	In Service	Withdrawn	Disposal	Notes
301	RNW 301	522432	10-1-1953	29-12-1969	a	
302	RNW 302	522433	10-1-1953	13-12-1969	a	
303	RNW 303	522434	7-2-1953	16-12-1969	a	
304	RNW 304	522435	7-2-1953	16-12-1969	a	
305	RNW 305	522436	6-2-1953	13-12-1969	a	
306	RNW 306	522437	7-2-1953	13-1-1970	b	
307	RNW 307	522438	5-2-1953	19-1-1970	b	
308	RNW 308	522439	16-2-1953	6-2-1970	b	
309	RNW 309	522440	25-3-1953	25-2-1970	b	
310	RNW 310	522441	27-3-1953	19-2-1970	b	

a   301-305 to Hartwood Finance, Barnsley, 9 to 11-2-1970. Scrapped by Dovedale Commercials, Barnsley.
b   306-310 to Auto Spares (Bingley) Ltd. breakers, 6-1970.

1954

A.E.C. Regent III chassis, A.E.C. 9·6 litre engine.   Cost £4,044 each.
Charles H. Roe Ltd. H33/25R body.   Unladen weight 7 tons 10 cwt 2 qrs (731-750), 7 tons 7 cwt 2 qrs (730, 751-4).

No.	Regn. No.	Chassis No.	In Service	Withdrawn	Disposal	Notes
730	TNW 730	9613E8138	29-10-1954	31-7-1970	a	A, B
731	TNW 731	9613E8139	1-7-1954	20-11-1969	b	Withdrawn following accident
732	TNW 732	9613E8140	1-7-1954	29-6-1970	c	
733	TNW 733	9613E8141	1-7-1954	29-6-1970	c	
734	TNW 734	9613E8142	1-7-1954	29-6-1970	c	
735	TNW 735	9613E8143	1-7-1954	28-6-1970	c	
736	TNW 736	9613E8144	1-7-1954	31-7-1970	a	
737	TNW 737	9613E8145	1-7-1954	31-7-1970	a	
738	TNW 738	9613E8146	1-8-1954	29-6-1970	c	
739	TNW 739	9613E8147	1-7-1954	31-7-1970	a	
740	TNW 740	9613E8148	1-7-1954	29-4-1970	d	
741	TNW 741	9613E8149	1-8-1954	29-6-1970	c	
742	TNW 742	9613E8150	1-8-1954	22-1-1969	e	Withdrawn following accident
743	TNW 743	9613E8151	1-7-1954	29-4-1970	d	
744	TNW 744	9613E8152	1-7-1954	28-5-1970	c	
745	TNW 745	9613E8154	1-7-1954	29-5-1970	c	
746	TNW 746	9613E8155	1-7-1954	24-9-1970	a	
747	TNW 747	9613E8157	1-8-1954	28-9-1970	a	
748	TNW 748	9613E8158	1-8-1954	12-6-1970	c	
749	TNW 749	9613E8159	1-8-1954	27-6-1970	c	
750	TNW 750	9613E8160	1-8-1954	27-6-1970	f	
751	TNW 751	9613E8156	1-9-1954	31-7-1970	a	B
752	TNW 752	9613E8161	1-9-1954	30-7-1970	a	B
753	TNW 753	9613E8162	1-9-1954	31-7-1970	a	B
754	TNW 754	9613E8163	1-9-1954	31-7-1970	a	B

A   730 was exhibited at the Commercial Motor Show, Earl's Court, London, in September 1954.
B   730, 751-754 had metal top deck framing and composite lower saloons. as compared with 731-750 (all composite).
a   730, 736-7, 739, 746-7, 751-4 to Telefilm Transport (Northern) Ltd. of Preston 11-1970, then directly to Pickersgill &
     Laverick, Barnsley, for scrap. 746 chassis and cab to Rufforth Gliding Club as a winch 12-1970.
b   731 to Hartwood Finance Ltd., Barnsley, 11-2-1970. Scrapped by Dovedale Commercials, Barnsley.
c   732-5, 738, 741, 744-5, 748-9 to Hartwood Finance, Barnsley, 9-1970. Scrapped by Dovedale Commercials.
d   740 and 743 to Auto Spares (Bingley) Ltd. breakers 6-1970.
e   742 to Ford & Fisher, breakers, Barnsley 4-6-1969. Broken up by 7-1969.
f   750 to Sovereign Street 11-1970 for decimal training purposes, then to Fisher & Ford, Carlton, Barnsley, breakers, 5-1971.

1954

A.E.C. Regent III chassis, A.E.C. 9·6 litre engine.   Cost £4.118 each.
M.C.C.W. Orion H33/25R metal body.   Unladen weight 7 tons 0 cwt 2 qrs.

No.	Regn. No.	Chassis No.	In Service	Withdrawn	Disposal	Notes
755	TNW 755	9613E8153	1-12-1954	29-10-1970	a	
756	TNW 756	9613E8164	1-12-1954	29-10-1970	a	
757	TNW 757	9613E8165	1-12-1954	29-10-1970	a	
758	TNW 758	9613E8166	1-12-1954	29-10-1970	a	
759	TNW 759	9613E8167	1-12-1954	9-1970	a	

a   All to Telefilm Transport (Northern) Ltd. 11-1970 then directly to Pickersgill & Laverick, Barnsley, for scrap.

1954

A.E.C. Reliance chassis, AH 470 7·75 litre engine, five speed gear box, air brakes. Cost £3,667 4s.3d. each.
Charles H.Roe Ltd. B34+24C metal body. "Standee" type. Unladen weight 5 tons 8 cwt 1 qr.

No.	Regn. No.	Chassis No.	In Service	Withdrawn	Disposal	Notes
32	TUA 32	MU3RA210	15-12-1954	1-3-1968	a	
33	TUA 33	MU3RA211	6-12-1954	15-3-1968	a	B,
34	TUA 34	MU3RA212	7-12-1954	3-4-1968	a	A, B

A 34 exhibited at the Commercial; Motor Show, Earl's Court, London in September 1954.

B 33 fitted with power operated doors 9.1955, 34 ditto 6 March 1956.

a 32-34 officially withdrawn 28-4-1968 although last used on dates shown. All sold to Wombwell Diesels 2 to 5-8-1968. 32 and 33 to PLC (contractor), Camden Town, London NW1 in 6-1969. Then as 31 below. Still there derelict 2007.

1955

Leyland Tiger Cub PSUC1/1 chassis, underfloor 350 95 h.p. engine, con. mesh, air brakes. Cost £3,806 3s.3d. each.
Charles H.Roe Ltd. B34+24C metal body, "Standee" type, 8ft. wide x 30ft.0in. long. Unladen weight 5 tons 18 cwt 1 qr.

No.	Regn. No.	Chassis No.	In Service	Withdrawn	Disposal	Notes
29	TUA 29	1544778	1-5-1955	15-3-1968	a	Power operated doors 15-3-1956
30	TUA 30	1544779	1-5-1955	6-3-1968	a	Power operated doors 24–3-1956
31	TUA 31	1544780	1-5-1955	25-3-1968	a	Power operated doors 30-3-1956

a 29-31 officially withdrawn 18-3-1968, 4-4-1968 and 4-4-1968 respectively but last used on dates shown. Sold to Wombwell Diesels 2 to 5-8-1968. 29 then to Orley-Dempster Ltd. Engineers, Elland, 9-1968 for use as a staff bus in South Wales by 3-1969. 31 to PLC (contractor) Camden Town, London NW1, in 5-1969. Then later to Smith, Linton, Cambridgeshire. Still there derelict, 2007, with 32-33 above.

1955

Guy Arab 5LW chassis, Gardner 5LW five cylinder engine. Cost £3,901 each.
Charles H. Roe Ltd. B34/24C metal body. "Standee" type. Unladen weight 6 tons 2 cwt 1 qr.

No.	Regn. No.	Chassis No.	In Service	Withdrawn	Disposal	Notes
35	TUA 35	LUF72311	5-2-1955	29-3-1967	a	Power operated doors 18-4-1956
36	TUA 36	LUF72312	20-1-1955	29-3-1967	a	Power operated doors 28-4-1956

a 35 and 36 sold to Wombwell Diesels 2 to 5-8-1968, then 36 to H. Cowley, dealer, Westby, Lancs, 6-1969.

1955

Leyland PD2/11 chassis, 0·600 engine, fluid coupling and pneumocyclic gear box, air brakes. Cost £4,282 10s.0d. each.
Charles H.Roe Ltd. H33/25R body, 7ft.6in. wide x 27ft.0in. long. Unladen weight 7 tons 12 cwt 2 qrs.

No.	Regn. No.	Chassis No.	In Service	Withdrawn	Disposal	Notes
201	UUA 201	542321	25-3-1955	27-1-1970	a	
202	UUA 202	542347	25-3-1955	18-12-1970	b	Withdrawn after accident.
203	UUA 203	542374	25-3-1955	30-9-1971	c	
204	UUA 204	542375	25-3-1955	30-9-1971	c	A
205	UUA 205	542388	25-3-1955	26-8-1971	c	
206	UUA 206	542389	25-3-1955	30-9-1971	c	
207	UUA 207	542403	25-3-1955	29-1-1971	d	Learner 13 from 3-5-1971. To PTE
208	UUA 208	542404	25-3-1955	23-2-1970	a	
209	UUA 209	550068	25-3-1955	29-1-1971	e	Learner 2 from 1-9-1971. ,,
210	UUA 210	550069	25-3-1955	29-1-1971	f	Learner 3 from 19-11-1971 ,,
211	UUA 211	550070	25-3-1955	29-1-1971	g	Learner 8 from 7-2-1972 ,,
212	UUA 212	550071	25-3-1955	29-1-1971	h	Learner 11 from 24-4-1972. ,,
213	UUA 213	550153	1-5-1955	29-1-1971	e	Learner 1 from 12-6-1972 ,,
214	UUA 214	550154	1-5-1955	29-1-1971	j	Learner 12 from 3-8-1972 ,,
215	UUA 215	550155	1-5-1955	29-1-1971	f	Learner 4 from 6-11-1972 ,,

201-220 were the first batch of pneumocyclic Leylands and entered service before the designations of the PD2/30 series were introduced. They were known as Leyland PD2/11 by both L.C.T. and Leyland though they were similar to the PD2/35 type.

A 204 fitted with centrifugal clutch in place of fluid flywheel c 5-1956. Removed 7-1956.

a 201 and 208 to Auto Spares (Bingley) Ltd, breakers 6-1970. Subsequently 208 to Glen Tours, Baildon, (No. 19) 7-1970, To Martin, dealer, Weaverham, 9-1970, then by 10-1970 to Pickersgill & Laverick of Barnsley for scrap.

b 202 to Fisher & Ford, Carlton, Barnsley, breakers, 5-1971.

c 203-6 to Paul Sykes, Blackerhill, Barnsley, 4-1973 for scrap.

d 13 (ex-207) transferred to (Bradford District) W.Y.P.T.E. by 5-12-1978. To Wolds Gliding Club 1981 then to R. Murray, and I. Snayde of Leeds, 8-1982 for preservation. Sole ownership later transferred to Murray. Currently operational and stored to north east of Leeds.

e Learner 1 (ex-213) withdrawn 31-5-1978. Learner 2 (ex-209) withdrawn 5-4-1978, Both sold by auction at Central Motor Auctions, Rothwell, on 21-12-1978 for scrap. 1 to Askin, breaker, Barnsley. 2 to G. Jones (Carlton Metals), near Barnsley.

f Learners 3 (ex-210) withdrawn 30-9-1975 and 4 (ex-215) withdrawn 29-9-1975. Both to Carlton Metals, breakers, Carlton Barnsley, 2-1977 for scrap.

G 8 (ex-211) withdrawn as Learner 26-1-1976 then to Paul Sykes, breaker, Barnsley, 5-1976.

h 11 (ex-212) transferred to (Kirklees District) W.Y.P.T.E. 12-12-1978. To (Bradford District) 2-1979. Renumbered A11, 5-1979. To D. Sutcliffe, Bradford, 3-1981 for preservation. To W. North, dealer, Sherburn-in-Elmet, 10-1989, then to Robson, Thornaby, Middlesbrough, 3-1991. Currently owned by Kell, County Durham.

J 12 (ex-214) withdrawn 9-1978. Sold by auction at Central Motor Auctions, Rothwell, on 21 December 1978. Purchased by N. Wilde of Shadwell and kept at Thorp Arch, then Swinegate Arches, Leeds. To Keighley Bus Museum on 6-6-1993.

1955

Leyland PD2/11 chassis, 0·600 engine, fluid coupling and pneumocyclic gear box, air brakes.   Cost £4,358 10s.0d. each.
M.C.C.W. H33/25R metal body. 7ft.6in. wide x 27ft.0in. long.   Unladen weight 7 tons 1 cwt 0 qrs.

No.	Regn. No.	Chassis No.	In Service	Withdrawn	Disposal	Notes
216	UUA 216	550193	1-6-1955	26-2-1971	a	Learner 5 from 17-4-1973. To PTE.
217	UUA 217	550194	1-6-1955	26-2-1971	b	
218	UUA 218	550195	1-6-1955	31-12-1970	a	Learner 9 from 1-4-1971. To PTE.
219	UUA 219	550196	1-6-1955	17-10-1969	c	Withdrawn after accident.
220	UUA 220	550197	23-6-1955	27-10-1970	d	Withdrawn after accident.

a   Learner 5 withdrawn 30-9-1975 and 9 17-9-1975. Both to Carlton Metals, Breakers, Carlton, Barnsley, 2-1977.
b   217 to Paul Sykes, dealer, Blackerhill, Barnsley, 4-1973 for scrap.
c   219 to Hartwood Finance, Barnsley. for scrap 9-12-1969. Used as towing vehicle by Dovedale Commercials by 3-1970 for a few months until scrapped.
d   220 to Paul Sykes, dealer and breaker, Blackerhill near Barnsley, 6-1972 for scrap.

1955-56

Daimler CVG6 chassis   Gardner 6LW 6 cylinder 8·4 litre engine.   Cost £4,631 13s,7d. each.
M.C.C.W. Orion H33/28R metal body, "tin front", 7ft.6in wide x 27ft. 0in long.   Unladen weight 6 tons 17 cwt 2 qrs.

No.	Regn. No.	Chassis No.	In Service	Withdrawn	Disposal	Notes
532	VUG 532	18805	11-12-1955	30-10-1969	a	
533	VUG 533	18806	11-12-1955	18-7-1969	b	
534	VUG 534	18807	11-12-1955	17-7-1969	b	
535	VUG 535	18808	1-1-1956	30-10-1969	a	
536	VUG 536	18809	1-1-1956	30-10-1969	a	
537	VUG 537	18810	1-1-1956	30-10-1969	a	
538	VUG 538	18811	1-1-1956	14-10-1969	a	
539	VUG 539	18812	1-1-1956	28-11-1969	c	
540	VUG 540	18813	1-1-1956	1-10-1969	c	
541	VUG 541	18814	1-1-1956	20-3-1969	d	Withdrawn following accident
542	VUG 542	18815	1-1-1956	28-11-1969	c	
543	VUG 543	18816	1-2-1956	28-11-1969	c	
544	VUG 544	18817	1-2-1956	25-11-1969	c	
545	VUG 545	18818	1-2-1956	28-11-1969	c	
546	VUG 546	18819	1-2-1956	8-12-1969	c	
547	VUG 547	18820	1-2-1956	8-12-1969	c	
548	VUG 548	18821	1-2-1956	15-12-1969	c	
549	VUG 549	18822	1-3-1956	29-12-1969	c	
550	VUG 550	18823	1-3-1956	29-12-1969	c	
551	VUG 551	18824	1-3-1956	15-12-1969	c	

a   532, 535, 537 and 538 to Hartwood Finance Ltd., Barnsey, 8-12-1969, 536 ditto 9-12-1969. Scrapped by Dovedale Commercials, Barnsley.
b   533 and 534 to Hartwood Finance Ltd., Barnsley, 28-8-1969. Scrapped by Dovedale Commercials, Barnsley.
c   538-540, 542-551 to Hartwood Finance Ltd., Barnsley, 9 to 11–2-1970. Scrapped by Dovedale Commercials.
d   541 to Ford and Fisher, breakers, Barnsley, 5-6-1969. broken up by 7-1969.

1956

A.E.C. Regent V chassis, AV 470 7·7 litre six cylinder engine, two-pedal monocontrol, air brakes. Cost £4,255 11s,6d. each.
Charles H.Roe Ltd. H33/27R metal body. 7ft. 6in. wide x 27ft.0in long.   Unladen weight 7 tons 1 cwt 2 qrs. (760-808),   6 tons 19 cwt 1 qr. (809-839)

No.	Regn. No.	Chassis No.	In Service	Withdrawn	Disposal	Notes
760	WUA 760	MD2RA066	21-1-1956	30-12-1969	a	
761	WUA 761	MD2RA067	6-2-1956	29-9-1972	b	Fitted with disc brakes 8-1960
762	WUA 762	MD2RA068	6-2-1956	24-12-1969	a	
763	WUA 763	MD2RA069	4-3-1956	29-9-1972	b	
764	WUA 764	MD2RA070	16-1-1956	30-12-1969	a	
765	WUA 765	MD2RA071	4-3-1956	8-6-1972	c	A
766	WUA 766	MD2RA072	4-3-1956	15-5-1972	c	
767	WUA 767	MD2RA073	4-3-1956	12-7-1972	c	
768	WUA 768	MD2RA074	4-3-1956	14-7-1972	c	
769	WUA 769	MD2RA075	4-3-1956	27-10-1972	b	Renumbered 869 20-10-1972
770	WUA 770	MD2RA076	4-3-1956	10-1-1973	b	Renumbered 870 16-10-1972
771	WUA 771	MD2RA077	4-3-1956	12-2-1972	d	
772	WUA 772	MD2RA078	4-3-1956	11-1-1973	b	Renumbered 872 24-10-1972
773	WUA 773	MD2RA079	4-3-1956	20-6-1972	c	
774	WUA 774	MD2RA080	4-3-1956	23-1-1973	b	Renumbered 874 24-10-1972
775	WUA 775	MD2RA081	4-3-1956	31-1-1973	b	Renumbered 875 16-10-1972
776	WUA 776	MD2RA082	4-3-1956	28-7-1972	b	
777	WUA 777	MD2RA083	4-3-1956	18-2-1970	e	
778	WUA 778	MD2RA084	12-3-1956	26-2-1970	e	
779	WUA 779	MD2RA085	4-3-1956	18-2-1970	e	
780	WUA 780	MD2RA086	12-3-1956	20-2-1970	e	
781	WUA 781	MD2RA087	26-3-1956	26-2-1970	e	
782	WUA 782	MD2RA088	4-3-1956	13-2-1970	e	

No.	Regn. No.	Chassis No.	In Service	Withdrawn	Disposal	Notes
783	WUA 783	MD2RA089	29-3-1956	27-2-1970	e	
784	WUA 784	MD2RA090	29-3-1956	27-2-1970	e	
785	WUA 785	MD2RA091	3-6-1956	30-3-1970	e	
786	WUA 786	MD2RA092	5-6-1956	26-3-1970	e	
787	WUA 787	MD2RA093	24-6-1956	14-5-1968	f	
788	WUA 788	MD2RA094	3-6-1956	29-3-1970	e	
789	WUA 789	MD2RA095	3-6-1956	29-3-1970	e	
790	WUA 790	MD2RA096	10-6-1956	28-3-1970	e	
791	WUA 791	MD2RA097	14-7-1956	29-5-1970	g	
792	WUA 792	MD2RA098	28-7-1956	29-5-1970	g	
793	WUA 793	MD2RA099	12-7-1956	27-5-1970	g	
794	WUA 794	MD2RA100	12-6-1956	26-3-1970	e	
795	WUA 795	MD2RA101	5-6-1956	26-3-1970	e	
796	WUA 796	MD2RA102	24-6-1956	26-3-1970	e	
797	WUA 797	MD2RA103	19-7-1956	28-5-1970	c	
798	WUA 798	MD2RA104	6-7-1956	28-2-1970	e	
799	WUA 799	MD2RA105	7-7-1956	4-3-1970	e	Withdrawn after accident
800	WUA 800	MD2RA106	28-7-1956	14-8-1972	b	
801	WUA 801	MD2RA107	28-7-1956	27-5-1970	g	
802	WUA 802	MD2RA108	14-7-1956	27-3-1970	e	
803	WUA 803	MD2RA109	29-7-1956	24-6-1970	g	
804	WUA 804	MD2RA110	14-7-1956	28-3-1970	e	
805	WUA 805	MD2RA111	30-6-1956	23-3-1970	e	
806	WUA 806	MD2RA112	28-7-1956	18-5-1970	g	
807	WUA 807	MD2RA113	28-7-1956	29-5-1970	g	
808	WUA 808	MD2RA114	26-7-1956	27-5-1970	g	
809	WUA 809	MD2RA115	28-7-1956	30-1-1973	b	
810	WUA 810	MD2RA116	1-9-1956	22-3-1972	d	
811	WUA 811	MD2RA117	1-9-1956	12-5-1972	c	
812	WUA 812	MD2RA118	1-9-1956	24-10-1969	a	Withdrawn after overturning.
813	WUA 813	MD2RA119	1-9-1956	19-4-1973	h	
814	WUA 814	MD2RA120	1-9-1956	30-10-1972	b	
815	WUA 815	MD2RA121	1-9-1956	9-2-1973	h	
816	WUA 816	MD2RA122	1-9-1956	12-1-1972	d	
817	WUA 817	MD2RA123	1-9-1956	23-9-1970	j	
818	WUA 818	MD2RA124	1-9-1956	30-4-1973	h	
819	WUA 819	MD2RA125	1-9-1956	20-7-1972	b	
820	WUA 820	MD2RA126	1-10-1956	31-7-1970	k	
821	WUA 821	MD2RA127	1-10-1956	30-7-1970	k	
822	WUA 822	MD2RA128	1-10-1956	31-7-1970	k	
823	WUA 823	MD2RA129	1-10-1956	31-7-1970	k	
824	WUA 824	MD2RA130	1-11-1956	17-9-1970	k	
825	WUA 825	MD2RA131	1-10-1956	24-7-1970	j	
826	WUA 826	MD2RA132	1-10-1956	31-7-1970	k	
827	WUA 827	MD2RA133	1-10-1956	31-7-1970	k	
828	WUA 828	MD2RA134	1-10-1956	31-7-1970	k	
829	WUA 829	MD2RA135	1-11-1956	26-9-1970	k	
830	WUA 830	MD2RA136	1-11-1956	30-9-1970	l	Learner bus 16 from 15-12-1970.
831	WUA 831	MD2RA137	1-10-1956	16-9-1970	m	Learner bus 19 from 16-12-1970.
832	WUA 832	MD2RA138	1-11-1956	30-9-1970	n	Learner bus 18 from 28-12-1970.
833	WUA 833	MD2RA139	1-11-1956	30-9-1970	o, d	Learner bus 17 from 28-12-1970.
834	WUA 834	MD2RA140	1-11-1956	23-2-1970	e	Withdrawn after accident.
835	WUA 835	MD2RA141	1-10-1956	31-7-1970	k	
836	WUA 836	MD2RA142	1-11-1956	16-9-1970	k	
837	WUA 837	MD2RA143	1-11-1956	24-9-1970	k	
838	WUA 838	MD2RA144	1-11-1956	30-9-1970	k	
839	WUA 839	MD2RA145	1-11-1956	17-7-1970	k	Commercial Motor Show bus 1956.

A 765 automatic gear box fitted 1-1957. Removed 1-1961.

a 760, 762, 764 and 812 to Hartwood Finance, Barnsley, 9 to 11-2-1970. Scrapped by Dovedale Commercials.

b 761, 763, 869 (ex-769), 870 (ex-770), 872 (ex-772), 874 (ex-774), 875 (ex-775), 776, 800, 809, 814 and 819 to Auto Spares, Bingley for scrap. All 4-1973.

c 765-8, 773, and 811 to Paul Sykes, dealer and breaker, Blackerhill, Barnsley, 10-1972 for scrap.

d 771, 810, 816 and 17 (ex-833) to Paul Sykes, dealer and breaker, Blackerhill, Barnsley, 6/7-1972 for scrap.

e 777-786, 788-790, 794-6, 798-9, 802, 804-5, 834 to Auto Spares (Bingley), breakers, 6 -1970. Subsequently 788 and 790 to Glen Tours, Baildon, 9-1970. 788 (Glen Tours 20) withdrawn 11-1972. 790 not used and then to W. North (P.V.) Ltd. dealers in part exchange for another vehicle by 5-1972.

f 787 withdrawn 14-5-1968 following accident with a pile driver at junction of New York Road and Regent Street. To Ford & Fisher, breakers , Barnsley, 6-6-1969. Broken up by 7-1969.

g 791-3, 797, 801, 803, 806-8 to Hartwood Finance, Barnsley, 9-1970 for scrap. Scrapped by Dovedale Commercials,.

h 813, 815 and 818 to W, North (P.V.) Ltd. 11-1973 then to breakers in Barnsley area.

j 817 to Fisher & Ford and 825 to D. Rollinson, Carlton, Barnsley, breakers, 5-1971.

k 820-4, 826-9, 835-9 to Telefilms Transport (Northern) Ltd. of Preston, then directly to Pickersgill and Laverick, Carlton, Barnsley, for scrap.

l   Learner 16 (ex-830) withdrawn 27-3-1973. To W. North, Sherburn-in-Elmet. 11-1973.
m   Learner 19 (ex-831) withdrawn 23-5-1973, To WYPTE 1-4-1974 then to Jones, Barnsley, 8-1975 for scrap.
n   Learner 18 (ex-832) To WYPTE 1-4-1974. Withdrawn 24-3-1975. To T. Williams of York 8-1982 for preservation.
o   Learner 17 (ex-833) withdrawn 11-1971. To Paul Sykes, Barnsley. 6-1972.

1957

A.E.C.Regent V chassis AV 470 7·7 litre six cylinder engine, two-pedal monocontrol, air brakes. Cost £4,368 14s,0d. each.
Charles H. Roe Ltd. H33/27R metal body, 7ft.6in. wide x 27ft.0in long bodies.   Unladen weight 6 tons 18 cwt 3 qrs.

No.	Regn. No.	Chassis No.	In Service	Withdrawn	Disposal	Notes
840	XUM 840	MD2RA324	1-10-1957	26-2-1971	a	
841	XUM 841	MD2RA325	1-10-1957	26-2-1971	a	
842	XUM 842	MD2RA326	1-10-1957	26-2-1971	a	
843	XUM 843	MD2RA327	1-10-1957	26-2-1971	a	
844	XUM 844	MD2RA328	1-10-1957	26-2-1971	a	
845	XUM 845	MD2RA329	1-10-1957	31-3-1971	a	
846	XUM 846	MD2RA330	1-10-1957	12-3-1971	a	
847	XUM 847	MD2RA331	1-10-1957	26-2-1971	b	
848	XUM 848	MD2RA332	1-10-1957	31-3-1971	a	
849	XUM 849	MD2RA333	1-10-1957	31-3-1971	a	
850	XUM 850	MD2RA334	1-10-1957	13-2-1971	c	
851	XUM 851	MD2RA335	1-10-1957	31-3-1971	a	
852	XUM 852	MD2RA336	30-9-1957	24-3-1971	a	
853	XUM 853	MD2RA337	29-9-1957	31-3-1971	a	
854	XUM 854	MD2RA338	30-9-1957	26-2-1971	a	
855	XUM 855	MD2RA339	29-9-1957	31-3-1971	a	
856	XUM 856	MD2RA340	30-9-1957	18-2-1971	a	
857	XUM 857	MD2RA341	30-9-1957	27-3-1971	a	
858	XUM 858	MD2RA342	4-9-1957	31-3-1971	a	
859	XUM 859	MD2RA343	4-9-1957	26-2-1971	a	
860	XUM 860	MD2RA344	4-9-1957	28-5-1971	b	
861	XUM 861	MD2RA345	4-9-1957	28-5-1971	b	
862	XUM 862	MD2RA346	4-9-1957	30-4-1971	a	
863	XUM 863	MD2RA347	4-9-1957	28-5-1971	b	
864	XUM 864	MD2RA348	4-9-1957	28-5-1971	b	
865	XUM 865	MD2RA349	4-9-1957	28-7-1971	b	
866	XUM 866	MD2RA350	30-9-1957	28-7-1971	b	
867	XUM 867	MD2RA351	30-9-1957	28-5-1971	b	
868	XUM 868	MD2RA352	30-9-1957	28-7-1971	b	
869	XUM 869	MD2RA353	1-3-1957	28-5-1971	b	
870	XUM 870	MD2RA354	1-3-1957	30-6-1971	b	
871	XUM 871	MD2RA355	1-3-1957	28-7-1971	b	
872	XUM 872	MD2RA356	1-3-1957	20-5-1971	a	
873	XUM 873	MD2RA357	1-3-1957	13-5-1970	d	Withdrawn after accident.
874	XUM 874	MD2RA358	1-3-1957	22-2-1971	a	
875	XUM 875	MD2RA359	1-3-1957	28-7-1971	b	
876	XUM 876	MD2RA360	1-3-1957	28-7-1971	b	
877	XUM 877	MD2RA361	1-3-1957	28-7-1971	b	
878	XUM 878	MD2RA362	1-3-1957	28-7-1971	b	
879	XUM 879	MD2RA363	1-3-1957	29-10-1971	e	
880	XUM 880	MD2RA364	1-3-1957	22-10-1971	e	
881	XUM 881	MD2RA365	1-3-1957	30-6-1971	b	
882	XUM 882	MD2RA366	1-3-1957	30-6-1971	b	
883	XUM 883	MD2RA367	1-3-1957	28-7-1971	e	
884	XUM 884	MD2RA368	24-3-1957	30-9-1971	f	
885	XUM 885	MD2RA369	1-3-1957	28-6-1971	b	
886	XUM 886	MD2RA370	1-3-1957	19-7-1971	b	
887	XUM 887	MD2RA371	24-3-1957	11-3-1971	a	
888	XUM 888	MD2RA372	1-3-1957	5-10-1971	e	
889	XUM 889	MD2RA373	24-3-1957	28-7-1971	a	
890	XUM 890	MD2RA374	1-3-1957	28-9-1971	e	
891	XUM 891	MD2RA375	24-3-1957	29-10-1971	e	
892	XUM 892	MD2RA376	1-3-1957	29-7-1971	b	
893	XUM 893	MD2RA377	24-3-1957	26-10-1971	e	
894	XUM 894	MD2RA378	1-3-1957	22-9-1971	e	

a   840-6, 848, 849, 851-9, 862, 872, 874, 887, 889 to Paul Sykes, Blackerhill, near Barnsley, 8-1971 for scrap.
b   847, 860-1, 863-871, 875-8, 881-2, 885-6, 892 to Auto Spares, Bingley, 9 and 10-1971 for scrap.
c   850 sold to Fisher & Ford, Carlton, for scrap. 5-1971.
d   873 to Hartwood Finance Ltd., Barnsley, 9-1970. Scrapped by Dovedale Commercials, Barnsley.
e   879-80, 883, 888, 890-1, 893-4 to Paul Sykes dealer and breaker, Blackerhill, Barnsley, 6/7-1972 for scrap.
f   884 to Paul Sykes, dealer and breaker, Blackerhill, Barnsley, 10-1972 for scrap.

1957

Daimler CVG6 chassis. Gardner 6LW 8·4 litre engine.
Weymann H33/27R metal body, 7ft.6in. wide x 27ft.0in long bodies, tin front.

Cost £4,888 15s.0d. each.
Unladen weight 6 tons 17 cwt 3 qrs.

No.	Regn. No.	Chassis No.	In Service	Withdrawn	Disposal	Notes
552	YNW 552	19005	29-9-1957	26-8-1971	a	
553	YNW 553	19006	30-9-1957	10-9-1971	a	
554	YNW 554	19007	30-9-1957	30-9-1971	b	
555	YNW 555	19008	29-9-1957	30-9-1971	b	
556	YNW 556	19009	30-9-1957	30-9-1971	b	
557	YNW 557	19010	29-9-1957	30-9-1971	b	
558	YNW 558	19011	29-9-1957	30-9-1971	b	
559	YNW 559	19012	30-9-1957	30-9-1971	b	
560	YNW 560	19013	30-9-1957	30-9-1971	b	
561	YNW 561	19014	29-9-1957	30-3-1972	a	
562	YNW 562	19015	30-9-1957	20-10-1971	a	
563	YNW 563	19016	30-9-1957	1-7-1971	c	
564	YNW 564	19017	30-9-1957	30-3-1972	a	
565	YNW 565	19018	30-9-1957	9-3-1971	d	
566	YNW 566	19019	30-9-1957	28-4-1972	b	
567	YNW 567	19020	29-9-1957	9-11-1971	a	
568	YNW 568	19021	30-9-1957	9-7-1971	c	
569	YNW 569	19022	29-9-1957	4-6-1971	c	
570	YNW 570	19023	29-9-1957	28-3-1972	a	
571	YNW 571	19024	4-9-1957	14-7-1971	c	

a   552-3, 561-2, 564, 567 and 570 to Paul Sykes, dealer and breaker, Blackerhill, Barnsley, 6/7-1972 for scrap.
b   554-560, 566 to Paul Sykes, dealer and breaker, Blackerhill, Barnsley, 10-1972 for scrap, then 555, 556 and 559 to R. Askin, Barnsley. 11-1972, also for scrap.
c   563, 568-9, 571 to Paul Sykes, dealer and breaker, Blackerhill near Barnsley, 9-1971 for scrap.
d   565 to Paul Sykes, dealer and breaker, Blackerhill near Barnsley, 8-1971 for scrap.

1958

A.E.C. Regent V chassis, AV 470 7·7 litre six cylinder engine, two-pedal monocontrol, air brakes. Cost £4,650 14s.0d. each
Charles H.Roe Ltd. H33/29R 8ft.0in. wide x 27ft.0in. long bodies, exposed radiator.   Unladen weight 7 tons 4 cwt 0 qrs.

No.	Regn. No.	Chassis No.	In Service	Withdrawn	Disposal	Notes
895	1895 NW	MD2RA509	10-5-1958	30-4-1973	a	
896	1896 NW	MD2RA510	10-5-1958	27-4-1973	a	
897	1897 NW	MD2RA511	1-5-1958	23-12-1971	b	
898	1898 NW	MD2RA512	2-6-1958	10-8-1972	c	
899	1899 NW	MD2RA513	2-6-1958	4-11-1972	c	
900	1900 NW	MD2RA514	1-7-1958	21-11-1972	c	
901	1901 NW	MD2RA515	2-6-1958	31-10-1972	c	
902	1902 NW	MD2RA516	1-7-1958	22-5-1973	a	
903	1903 NW	MD2RA517	1-7-1958	24-5-1973	a	
904	1904 NW	MD2RA518	2-6-1958	27-2-1973	a	
905	1905 NW	MD2RA519	2-6-1958	29-7-1972	a	
906	1906 NW	MD2RA520	2-6-1958	27-2-1973	a	Fluorescent lights to indicators 9-64
907	1907 NW	MD2RA521	1-7-1958	10-11-1972	c	
908	1908 NW	MD2RA522	1-7-1958	16-4-1973	a	
909	1909 NW	MD2RA523	1-7-1958	29-11-1973	d	

a   895-6, 902-6 and 908 to W.North, (P.V.) Ltd. dealers, Sherburn-in-Elmet in 11-1973 for scrap.
b   897 to Paul Sykes, dealer and breaker, Blackerhill, Barnsley 7-1972 for scrap.
c   898-901 and 907 to Auto Spares, Bingley, 4-1973 for scrap.
d   909, withdrawn from service, passed to the WYPTE on 1-4-1974. Retained for possible preservation, but stored outside and vandalised. Reported sold to R. Taylor, Stockport, 3-1981, but later sold at Central Motor Auctions, Rothwell, 25-2-1982. Believed sold to owner in Manchester area.

1958-59

Leyland PD3/5, 0·600 engine, pneumocyclic gearbox, air brakes.   Cost £5,276 15s,5d. each, (capital account)
Charles H. Roe Ltd. H39/32R 8ft.0in. wide x 30ft.0in. long bodies, composite construction, exposed radiator.
Unladen weight 8 tons 2 cwt 1 qr.

No.	Regn. No.	Chassis No.	In Service	Withdrawn	Disposal	Notes
221	5221 NW	581944	9-11-1958	19-2-1973	a	Commercial Motor Show Bus 1958.
222	5222 NW	581998	28-3-1959	19-3-1973	a	
223	5223 NW	581999	28-3-1959	28-9-1973	b	
224	5224 NW	582000	28-3-1959	6-11-1972	c	
225	5225 NW	582001	29-3-1959	30-6-1973	a	
226	5226 NW	582002	29-3-1959	12-9-1973	b	Learner 6 from 25-10 to 9-11-73,i
227	5227 NW	582051	1-4-1959	19-2-1973	a	
228	5228 NW	582052	28-3-1959	31-7-1973	d	Learner 6 from 13-11-1973.
229	5229 NW	582053	28-3-1959	13-7-1973	e	
230	5230 NW	582054	30-3-1959	26-9-1973	f	Learner 7 from 23-10 to 6-11-73, i
231	5231 NW	582055	30-3-1959	24-7-1974	g	To WYPTE 1-4-1974

No.	Regn. No.	Chassis No.	In Service	Withdrawn	Disposal	Notes
232	5232 NW	582073	28-3-1959	4-10-1974	b	To WYPTE 1-4-1974
233	5233 NW	582074	28-3-1959	10-8-1972	h	
234	5234 NW	582099	28-3-1959	16-5-1974	j	To WYPTE 1-4-1974
235	5235 NW	582100	1-4-1959	19-4-1973	a	
236	5236 NW	582101	28-3-1959	6-8-1975	e	To WYPTE 1-4-1974
237	5237 NW	582115	28-3-1959	11-10-1974	b	To WYPTE 1-4-1974
238	5238 NW	582116	30-3-1959	28-9-1973	j	
239	5239 NW	582117	31-3-1959	28-7-1973	d	Learner 7 from 8-11-1973
240	5240 NW	582118	29-3-1959	28-9-1973	k	
241	5241 NW	582523	28-3-1959	29-9-1973	k	
242	5242 NW	582221	31-3-1959	18-5-1973	a	
243	5243 NW	582251	28-3-1959	28-9-1973	e	
244	5244 NW	582252	28-3-1959	8-8-1973	a	
245	5245 NW	582253	1-4-1959	15-2-1973	a	
246	5246 NW	582306	1-4-1959	28-7-1973	a	
247	5247 NW	582307	28-3-1959	26-11-1973	b	
248	5248 NW	582309	30-3-1959	19-11-1973	k	
249	5249 NW	582316	28-3-1959	8-9-1973	f	E600 engine fitted
250	5250 NW	582317	28-3-1959	13-12-1974	l	
251	5251 NW	582318	28-3-1959	26-11-1973	f	
252	5252 NW	582463	28-3-1959	14-9-1972	c	
253	5253 NW	582464	28-3-1959	15-11-1973	k	
254	5254 NW	582470	28-3-1959	16-8-1973	m	
255	5255 NW	582481	28-3-1959	17-9-1973	k	
256	5256 NW	582482	29-3-1959	23-11-1973	k	
257	5257 NW	582308	1-4-1959	25-6-1973	k	
258	5258 NW	582522	29-3-1959	29-12-1973	f	
259	5259 NW	582524	29-3-1959	14-2-1973	a	
260	5260 NW	582639	29-3-1959	21-2-1975	g	To WYPTE 1-4-1974
261	5261 NW	582658	29-3-1959	28-12-1973	m	
262	5262 NW	582659	29-3-1959	19-12-1973	f	
263	5263 NW	582663	29-3-1959	18-1-1974	f	
264	5264 NW	582664	28-3-1959	29-12-1973	j	
265	5265 NW	582665	28-3-1959	26-6-1973	a	
266	5266 NW	582704	27-3-1959	19-12-1973	j	
267	5267 NW	582976	29-3-1959	31-12-1975	n	To WYPTE 1-4-1974
268	5268 NW	582977	29-3-1959	1-9-1972	c	
269	5269 NW	582978	1-4-1959	9-9-1975	o	To WYPTE 1-4-1974
270	5270 NW	582979	1-4-1959	18-1-1974	p	Tree lopper from 4-2-1975
271	5271 NW	583078	29-3-1959	25-1-1974	f	
272	5272 NW	583079	30-3-1959	8-6-1973	a	
273	5273 NW	583080	29-3-1959	12-11-1973	k	
274	5274 NW	583085	1-4-1959	28-12-1973	e	
275	5275 NW	583086	29-3-1959	23-10-1973	k	
276	5276 NW	583251	29-3-1959	18-1-1974	f	
277	5277 NW	583252	1-4-1959	18-1-1974	j	
278	5278 NW	583253	28-3-1959	22-8-1975	o	To WYPTE 1-4-1974
279	5279 NW	583254	1-4-1959	31-12-1975	n	To WYPTE 1-4-1974
280	5280 NW	583255	29-3-1959	30-12-1975	q	To WYPTE 1-4-1974
281	5281 NW	583294	28-3-1959	31-12-1975	n	To WYPTE 1-4-1974
282	5282 NW	583295	30-3-1959	14-11-1975	q	To WYPTE 1-4-1974
283	5283 NW	583296	29-3-1959	31-12-1975	q	To WYPTE 1-4-1974
284	5284 NW	583297	29-3-1959	2-7-1975	r	To WYPTE 1-4-1974
285	5285 NW	583298	1-4-1959	31-12-1975	q	To WYPTE 1-4-1974
286	5286 NW	583302	29-3-1959	31-12-1975	q	To WYPTE 1-4-1974
287	5287 NW	583303	29-3-1959	20-7-1972	c	
288	5288 NW	583304	29-3-1959	23-12-1975	q	To WYPTE 1-4-1974
289	5289 NW	583305	29-3-1959	3-12-1975	q	To WYPTE 1-4-1974
290	5290 NW	583306	1-4-1959	30-12-1975	q	To WYPTE 1-4-1974
291	5291 NW	583320	29-3-1959	3-8-1972	h	Withdrawn after accident.

All buses of this type were altered from H39/32R to H38/32R from August to October 1960.

Learner buses 6 (ex-228) and 7 (ex-239) passed to the West Yorkshire Passenger Transport Executive on 1-4-1974.
The following buses were in stock, but withdrawn on 1-4-1974: 223, 226, 229, 230, 238, 243, 247, 248, 250, 251, 254, 258, 261-264, 266, 270, 271, 274, 276, 277.

a   221, 222, 225, 227, 235, 242, 244-246, 259, 265 and 272 to W.North (P.V) Ltd. dealers, Sherburn-in-Elmet, 11-1973.

b   223, 226 (withdrawn by Driving School 10-12-1973). 232, 237, 247 to D.Rollinson, breaker, Barnsley, 5-1975 for scrap

c   224, 252, 268, 287 to Paul Sykes, dealer and breaker, Blackerhill, Barnsley, 4-1973 for scrap.

d   228 and 239 to WYPTE 1-4-1974. Withdrawn as Learners 1-1978. Both purchased for preservation. 228 to Crowther, Leeds by 9-1982. To A. Blackman, Halifax, 1-2005. 239 to A. Bell, Leeds, 8-1981, to Rollinson, Carlton, for scrap 4-1987.

e   229, 236, 243, 274 to Jones, Barnsley, 11-1975 for scrap. 229, 236 and 274 subsequently broken up by Carlton Metals, Barnsley.

f   230 (last used by Driving School 4-12-1973), 248, 251, 258, 262, 263, 271 and 276 to D. Rollinson, breaker 12-1974.

g   231 and 260 to D. Rollinson, breaker, Barnsley, 8-1975 for scrap.

h   233 and 291 to Auto Spares Ltd., BIngley, in 10-1972 for scrap.

j   234, 238, 264, 266 and 277 to Hartwood Exporters, Barnsley, 10-1974 for scrap.

k   240, 241, 249, 253, 255-257, 273 and 275 sold to Hartwood Finance Ltd., Barnsley, 3-1-1974.

l   250 to F.Smith, breaker, Rotherham Road, Barnsley, for scrap 1-1975.

m   254 and 261 to Hartwood Exporters Ltd., Barnsley, 5-1975, 254 broken up by D, Rollinson, Barnsley, 5-1975.

n   267, 279 and 281 to D. Rollinson, breaker, Barnsley, 4-1976.

o   269 and 278 to Dunscroft Commercials, Dunscroft, near Doncaster, 3-1976.

p   270 to WYPTE 1-4-1974. Withdrawn as tree lopper 4-1980. Purchased by Crowther, Leeds, 11-1982 for spares for 228.

q   280, 282, 283, 285, 286, 288-290 to Lister, dealer, Bolton, 3-1976, 280 later to Mile Cross Transport Collection 3-1976 for preservation then to Walker, Huddersfield c 7-1982. Then to D.H.Crowther, High Wycombe by 12-1988, then Black Prince Buses Ltd. (B.Crowther) Morley. 3-2001. 282 to Jameson, breaker, Dunscroft,   3-1976.
283 to Student's International Services Ltd. Paris House, Wilbury Villas, Hove, East Sussex, 23-3-1976, then to T. Wigley, breaker, Carlton, 6-1979. 285, 289 and 290 to Crawford, Neilston, Scotland. 3-1976. Entered service 5-1976. 290 to Jackson, Beith 4- 1976, then to Crawford, Neilston, 5-1977, to Lister, dealer, Bolton, 7-1979 then C.F.Booth, breaker, Rotherham, 7-1979.   289 to Sunningdale, Thornliebank, Glasgow 9-1976 then to Crawford, Neilston 3-1977. 288 to Gorman, Dunoon, by 6-1976, then to Ribble Vehicle Preservation Group 2-1977 for spares. 286 to J. Sykes, Carlton, c 3-1976.

r   284 to O.K. Motor Services, Bishop Auckland 3-1976. Resold to the Tyne and Wear PTE 4-1976 as Tyne & Wear 415. To Barraclough, breaker, Carlton, 10-1976.

1959

Daimler CVG6LX/30   Gardner 6LX 10·45 litre engine, Daimatic transmission (two pedal control).   Cost £5,318 each.
Charles H. Roe Ltd. H39/32R 8ft.0in. wide x 30ft.0in. long composite bodies, concealed radiator.
Unladen weight 8 tons 4 cwt 1 qr.

No.	Regn. No.	Chassis No.	In Service	Withdrawn	Disposal	Notes		
502	7502 UA	30045	2-10-1959	19-12-1975	a	Renumbered 702	18-11-1972	
503	7503 UA	30046	10-10-1959	30-12-1975	b	,,	703	,,
504	7504 UA	30047	1-11-1959	23-8-1974	c	,,	704	,,
505	7505 UA	30048	1-11-1959	30-12-1975	d	,,	705	,,
506	7506 UA	30049	1-11-1959	29-7-1976	e	,,	706	,,
507	7507 UA	30050	1-11-1959	8-10-1976	f	,,	707	,,
508	7508 UA	30051	7-11-1959	8-10-1976	f	,,	708	,,
509	7509 UA	30052	7-11-1959	15-10-1976	f	,,	709	,,
510	7510 UA	30053	1-11-1959	8-11-1975	g	,,	710	,,
511	7511 UA	30054	1-11-1959	30-12-1976	h	,,	711	,,
512	7512 UA	30055	7-11-1959	30-12-1976	j	,,	712	,,
513	7513 UA	30056	7-11-1959	30-12-1976	k	,,	713	,,
514	7514 UA	30057	7-11-1959	31-12-1976	l	,,	714	,,
515	7515 UA	30058	7-11-1959	19-7-1976	e	,,	715	,,
516	7516 UA	30059	7-11-1959	12-11-1975	m	,,	716	,,
517	7517 UA	30060	7-11-1959	15-7-1975	n	,,	717	,,
518	7518 UA	30061	7-11-1959	13-9-1974	o	,,	718	,,
519	7519 UA	30062	7-11-1959	11-11-1974	p	,,	719	,,
520	7520 UA	30063	7-11-1959	12-11-1974	p	,,	720	,,
521	7521 UA	30064	7-11-1959	12-11-1974	p	,,	721	,,
522	7522 UA	30065	7-11-1959	11-11-1974	p	,,	722	,,
523	7523 UA	30066	7-11-1959	3-12-1974	q	,,	723	,,
524	7524 UA	30067	7-11-1959	3-12-1974	q	,,	724	,,
525	7525 UA	30068	7-11-1959	11-1-1975	r	,,	725	,,
526	7526 UA	30069	7-11-1959	15-9-1975	g	,,	726	,,
527	7527 UA	30070	7-11-1959	21-8-1975	s	,,	727	,,
528	7528 UA	30071	7-11-1959	2-8-1974	o	,,	728	,,
529	7529 UA	30072	7-11-1959	27-9-1975	t	,,	729	,,
530	7530 UA	30073	7-11-1959	18-9-1975	u	,,	730	,,
531	7531 UA	30074	7-11-1959	18-9-1975	u	,,	731	,,

All buses of this series were altered from H39/32R to H38/32R August and September 1960.
702-731 passed to the West Yorkshire Passenger Transport Executive on 1-4-1974.
719-722 were transferred to the Bradford District of the WYPTE 13 to 15-11-1974. 719 and 721 withdrawn 26-9-1975, 720 and 722 withdrawn 30-8-1975.
723 and 724 were transferred to the Calderdale District of the WYPTE 6-12-1974. Both withdrawn 19-9-1975.

a   702 to Calderdale for spares 19-3-1976, then F. & S. Vehicle Dismantlers, (Cooper), Barnsley. 6-1976.

b   703 to Carlton Metals, Carlton, Barnsley 6-1976 for scrap.

c   704 to F. Smith, breaker, Rotherham Road, Barnsley, 1-1975.

d   705 to F. & S. Vehicle Dismantlers, (Cooper), Barnsley, 6-1976 for scrap.

e   706 and 715 to Carlton Metals, breakers, Carlton, Barnsley 2-1977 for scrap.

f   707-709 to Hartwood Exports, Barnsley, 5-1977. 708 and 709 to Dickinson & Sheppey, Monk Bretton, by 10-1977.

g   710 and 726 to D. Rollinson, breaker, Barnsley, 6-1976 for scrap.

h   711 Learner bus 5 from 1-3-1977. To Bradford District 12-1978. To Kirklees District c 6-1979 and renumbered A23. Withdrawn by 5-1981 and to P.V.S. Carlton, 5-1981.

j   712 presented to the Lille Transport Museum, France, 4-1977. Left Leeds for Lille 13-4-1977.

k   713 Learner bus 3 from 1-2-1977. Wdn 9-1978. Sold by auction on 21-12-1978 at Central Motor Auctions, Leeds.

l   714 sold to 514 Preservation Group (M. Foster, M. King and A. Wilson) of Leeds, 24-8-1981. Wilson sole ownership from 1-1988. To Keighley Bus Museum Trust 1-2002.

m 716 to D. Rollinson, breaker, Barnsley, 4-1976, then to E. Bough, breaker, Cundy Cross, Barnsley 6-1976.
n 717 to Dennis Bros. Ltd. Guildford, for experimental use with new type of chassis and engine 8-1975 by London Transport. Painted orange and white and operated on trial by Leicester City Transport, 1-1976, South Yorkshire PTE 4-1976, Leicester 10-1976, Derby 3-1977, Returned to Dennis Bros. 26-10-1977 then to Dundee until 12-11-1977 , then to Aberdeen. To Leicester 1-1978, engine and gear box used for spares, remainder of vehicle to F.Berry, scrap dealer, Leicester. 3-1978 and scrapped 4-1978.
o 718 and 728 to D, Rollinson, breaker, Carlton, near Barnsley, breaker, 12-1974, for scrap.
p 719-722 to Paul Sykes, Barnsley, 12-1975 for scrap.
q 723 and 724 to Carlton Metals, Barnsley, breaker, 1-1976 for scrap.
r 725 to D, Rollinson, breaker, Barnsley, 5-1975 for scrap.
s 727 to Carlton Metals, Barnsley, breaker 2-1976 for scrap.
t 729 to Carlton Metals, Barnsley, 3-1976 for scrap.
u 730 and 731 to D, Rollinson, breaker, Barnsley, 1-1976 for scrap.

1959

A.E.C. Reliance AH 470 7·75 litre engine, monocontrol.   Cost £4,626 18s.0d. each. (revenue account).
Charles H. Roe Ltd. B34+24C metal body.   Unladen weight 5 tons 15 cwt 1 qr.

No.	Regn. No.	Chassis No.	In Service	Withdrawn	Disposal	Notes
37	8737 UA	2MU2RA2585	1-11-1959	31-3-1968	a	
38	8738 UA	2MU2RA2586	1-11-1959	25-4-1968	a	

a To Ford and Fisher, breakers, Barnsley, 6-6-1969 (37) and 7-6-1969 (38), broken up 7-1969.

1960

A.E.C. Regent V, AV 590 9·6 litre engine,   monocontrol.   Cost £5,133 14s.0d. each, (capital account).
M.C.C.W. Orion H39/32R body. 8ft.0in. wide x 30ft.0in. long. Exposed radiator.   Unladen weight 7 tons 14 cwt 1 qr.

No.	Regn. No.	Chassis No.	In Service	Withdrawn	Disposal	Notes
910	3910 UB	2D2RA731	1-5-1960	31-3-1975	a	
911	3911 UB	2D2RA732	1-5-1960	9-10-1974	b	
912	3912 UB	2D2RA733	1-6-1960	22-4-1975	c	
913	3913 UB	2D2RA734	1-6-1960	11-11-1974	d	
914	3914 UB	2D2RA735	1-5-1960	22-11-1974	d	
915	3915 UB	2D2RA736	1-5-1960	8-4-1975	e	
916	3916 UB	2D2RA737	1-6-1960	22-4-1975	f	
917	3917 UB	2D2RA738	1-6-1960	8-4-1975	a	
918	3918 UB	2D2RA739	1-5-1960	24-3-1975	a	
919	3919 UB	2D2RA740	1-6-1960	22-4-1975	e	
920	3920 UB	2D2RA741	1-5-1960	20-11-1974	b	
921	3921 UB	2D2RA742	1-5-1960	11-3-1975	e	
922	3922 UB	2D2RA743	1-5-1960	25-3-1975	a	A
923	3923 UB	2D2RA744	1-6-1960	22-10-1974	g	

All buses of this series were altered from H39/32R to H38/32R August and September 1960.
A 922 loaned to Aberdeen Corporation from 19-7-1960 to 31-7-1960.
   910-923 passed to the West Yorkshire Passenger Transport Executive on 1-4-1974.
   917 transferred to Bradford District of the WYPTE 2-11-1974 to 12-11-1974.
a 910, 917-8, 922 to Jones, Barnsley, 8-1975 for scrap.
b 911 and 920 to Hartwood Exporters Ltd., Barnsley, 5-1975 for scrap.
c 912 to Wolds Gliding Club as a mobile winch 27-7-1975. Sold to gypsies 4-1986. Last noted at Cawood, Selby. 5-1986.
d 913, 914 to Auto Spares (Bingley) 5-1975 for scrap. 914 derelict until 1984 then to T. Wigley, breaker, Carlton, for scrap.
e 915, 919 and 921 to D.Rollinson, breaker, Carlton, near Barnsley, 7-1975 for scrap.
f 916 sold to Mersey and Calder Bus Preservation Group, Halifax, David Heap, for preservation, removed 12-10-1975. To J.E. Foster, Cowling, near Keighley for continued preservation 7-1986. Later to Mick Berry. Currently operational.
g 923 to D, Rollinson, breaker, Carlton, near Barnsley, 12-1974 for scrap.

1962

Daimler CVG6LX/30 Gardner 6LX 10·45 litre engine, Daimatic transmission, two pedal control. Cost £6,382 19s.0d. each
Charles H. Roe Ltd. H39/31F body. 8ft.0in. wide x 30ft.0in. long. Concealed radiator.   Unladen weight 8 tons 9 cwt 0 qr.

No.	Regn. No.	Chassis No.	In Service	Withdrawn	Disposal	Notes
572	572 CNW	30141	27-5-1962	8-8-1977	a	Renumbered 872 1-12-1973
573	573 CNW	30142	28-5-1962	30-1-1978	b	Renumbered 873 1-12-1973
574	574 CNW	30143	27-5-1962	29-11-1977	c	Renumbered 874 1-12-1973
575	575 CNW	30144	27-5-1962	21-4-1978	d	Renumbered 875 1-12-1973
576	576 CNW	30145	28-5-1962	24-1-1978	b	Renumbered 876 1-12-1973

572-576 were advertised for sale in 1966, but were not sold.   872-876 passed to the WYPTE on 1-4-1974.
872 and 873 transferred to the Kirklees District of the WYPTE 30-5-1974, given Nos. 4202-3. Reverted to old numbers 12-1974. To Calderdale District 10-12-1975. 873 to Bradford District 26-8-1976.
874-876 transferred to the Kirklees District of the WYPTE 21-6-1974, given Nos. 4204-6. Reverted to old Nos. 12-1974.
875 to Calderdale District 10-11-1975 and 874 and 876 ditto 29-11-1975. 874-876 to Bradford District 9-1977.
a 872 (ex-572) withdrawn 8-8-1977, then painted orange and used as mobile exhibition unit for the West Yorkshire Metropolitan County Council from 16-1-1978. Ownership transferred to WYCC Recreation and Arts Department at Ludlam Street, Bradford 5-1984. To Rexquote, Norton, Fitzwarren. 9-1998. Current condition unknown.
b 873 (ex-573) withdrawn 30-1-1978, and 876 (ex-576), withdrawn 24-1-1978, sold by auction at Central Motor Auctions 21-12-1978 for scrap. Broken up 1-1979.
c 874 (ex-574) withdrawn 29-11-1977, then painted orange and used as mobile exhibition unit for the West Yorkshire

Metropolitan County Council from 16-1-1978 to 7-1978, then repainted Verona green and buttermilk with red band
Becoming a Metro Show Bus, repainted blue with coloured stripes 8-1980. Ownership transferred to WYCC
Recreation and Arts Dept. at Ludlam Street, Bradford, in 5-1984. Repainted in dark green with yellow lettering.
Restored to Leeds condition at Ludlam Street by the West Yorkshire Transport Museum in 1986. Then to D.H.
Crowther, High Wycombe 3-1992. To M. King 11-2001 and to W. McClintock 9-2004. Stored to north east of Leeds.

d   875 (ex-575) withdrawn 21-4-1978. Sold by auction at Central Motor Auctions, Rothwell, on 22-3-1979 to Swift
Exports, Thurgoland. Engine believed exported. Remains to a Barnsley breaker.

1962

Daimler CVG6LX/30 Gardner 6LX 10·45 litre engine. Daimatic transmission, two pedal control. Cost £5,951 19s.0d. each.
Charles H. Roe Ltd. H39/31R body. 8ft.0in. wide x 30ft.0in. long. Concealed radiator.   Unladen weight 8 tons 5 cwt 1qr.

No.	Regn. No.	Chassis No.	In Service	Withdrawn	Disposal	Notes
577	577 CNW	30136	1-8-1962	30-5-1974	a	Renumbered 877 1-12-1973
578	578 CNW	30137	1-8-1962	30-5-1974	b	Renumbered 878 1-12-1973
579	579 CNW	30138	1-8-1962	30-5-1974	c	Renumbered 879 1-12-1973
580	580 CNW	30139	1-8-1962	10-5-1974	d	Renumbered 880 1-12-1973
581	581 CNW	30140	1-8-1962	30-5-1974	e	Renumbered 881 1-12-1973

877-881 passed to the West Yorkshire Passenger Transport Executive on 1-4-1974.
a   877 to F. Smith, breaker, Rotherham Road, Barnsley, 1-1975 for scrap.
b   878 to D. Rollinson, breaker, Barnsley, 10-1975 for scrap.
c   879 to D. Rollinson, breaker, Barnsley, 5-1975 for scrap.
d   880 to Auto Spares, Bingley, 10-1974 for scrap.
e   881 to Auto Spares (Bingley) Ltd. 9-1975 for scrap.

1962

A.E.C. Regent V   AV 590 9·6 litre engine, monocontrol.   Cost £5,629 7s.2d. each.
Charles H. Roe Ltd. H49/31R body. 8ft.0in. wide x 30ft. long. Concealed radiator.   Unladen weight 8 tons 3 cwt 1 qr.

No.	Regn. No.	Chassis No.	In Service	Withdrawn	Disposal	Notes
924	924 CUG	2D2RA1132	1-10-1962	13-8-1974	a	
925	925 CUG	2D2RA1133	1-10-1962	23-8-1974	b	
926	926 CUG	2D2RA1134	2-9-1962	29-5-1974	c	
927	927 CUG	2D2RA1135	2-9-1962	31-5-1974	c	
928	928 CUG	2D2RA1136	1-10-1962	15-3-1974	c	
929	929 CUG	2D2RA1137	2-9-1962	30-5-1974	c	
930	930 CUG	2D2RA1138	2-9-1962	22-2-1974	c	
931	931 CUG	2D2RA1139	2-9-1962	30-5-1974	c	
932	932 CUG	2D2RA1140	2-9-1962	15-5-1974	c	
933	933 CUG	2D2RA1141	1-10-1962	31-10-1973	d	

924-932 passed to the West Yorkshire Passenger Transport Executive on 1-4-1974.
a   924 to Auto Spares (Bingley) 5-1975 for scrap. Derelict for 9 years and then to T. Wigley, Carlton, 5-1984 for scrap.
b   925 to Hartwood Exporters, Ltd. Barnsley, 5-1975, for scrap.
c   926-932 to Auto Spares Bingley, 10-1974 for scrap.
d   933 to Hartwood Finance, Barnsley, 3-1974 for scrap.

1962

A.E.C. Reliance.   AH 470 7·75 litre engine.   monocontrol.   Cost £5,319 2s.2d, each.
Charles H. Roe Ltd. B41D composite body. 8ft. 2 1/2in. wide x 30ft. 8in. long.   Unladen weight 6 tons 8 cwt 1 qr.

No.	Regn. No.	Chassis No.	In Service	Withdrawn	Disposal	Notes
39	839 CUM	2MU2RA4105	2-12-1962	18-12-1970	a	A
40	840 CUM	2MU2RA4106	2-12-1962	31-12-1970	a	
41	841 CUM	2MU2RA4107	2-12-1962	31-12-1970	a	
42	842 CUM	2MU2RA4108	2-12-1962	29-12-1970	a	
43	843 CUM	2MU2RA4109	2-12-1962	31-12-1970	a	B

A   39 on trial at Wolverhampton during October 1962.
B   43 exhibited at Commercial Motor Show, Earls Court, London, 21 to 29–9-1962.
a   39-43 to P.Sykes, dealer, Blackerhill, near Barnsley, 19-7-1971. Subsequently all to T.D. Alexander, Arbroath, 8-1971.
    42 withdrawn c 2-1973 and cannibalised for spare parts. Then to Dunsmore, dealer and breaker, Larkhall 4-1977. 43
    also to Dunsmore 4-1977. No information on other vehicles.

1962

Leyland PD3A/2, 0·600 engine, pneumocyclic gear box, air brakes.   Cost £6,486 10s.0d. each.
Weymann H39/31R body. 8ft.0in. wide x 30ft.0in long, 'fibreglass front'.   Unladen weight 7 tons 16 cwt 3 qrs.

No.	Regn. No.	Chassis No.	In Service	Withdrawn	Disposal	Notes
311	311 DUA	621182	1-11-1962	17-10-1974	a	To Halifax Learner fleet 20-2-1975
312	312 DUA	621183	19-10-1962	5-9-1975	b	
313	313 DUA	621184	1-11-1962	11-10-1974	c	
314	314 DUA	621185	19-10-1962	14-2-1975	d	
315	315 DUA	621186	1-11-1962	11-10-1974	b	
316	316 DUA	621187	1-11-1962	25-11-1974	e	Learner 14 from 9-12-1974
317	317 DUA	621188	1-11-1962	17-10-1974	f	Learner 15 from 9-12-1974
318	318 DUA	621189	1-11-1962	11-10-1974	e	Learner 16 from 2-12-1974
319	319 DUA	621190	19-10-1962	17-10-1974	g	To Halifax Learner fleet 4-12-1974
320	320 DUA	621191	1-11-1962	17-10-1974	h	To Halifax Learner fleet 5-12-1974

311-320 had Weymann body numbers M169, M162, M167, M163, M166, M168, M170, M165, M164, M171 respectively.

311-320 passed to the West Yorkshire Passenger Transport Executive on 1-4-1974.

311 withdrawn as a Learner bus 30-9-1975. 316-318 were renumbered 14-16 from 18-10-1975. 319 withdrawn as a Learner bus 28-11-1975.

312 to Bradford District of the WYPTE 23-5-1975, returned to Leeds 8-1975.

a 311 to W. North, dealer, Sherburn-in-Elmet c 1-76 for scrap.

b 312 and 315 to Jones, Barnsley, 11-1975 for scrap.

c 313 to Hartwood Exporters Ltd., Barnsley, 5-1975 for scrap.

d 314 to Auto Spares (Bingley) Ltd. 9-1975 for scrap.

e Learner 14 (ex-316) and 16 (ex-318) withdrawn 9-1978. Sold by auction at Central Motor Auctions, Rothwell on 21-12-1978. 14 to G. Jones (Carlton Metals), Carlton. 16 to K. Askin, breaker, Barnsley.

f Learner 15 (ex-317) withdrawn 21-6-1978 and auctioned for scrap at Central Motor Auctions, Rothwell on 21-12-1978. to K. Askin, breaker, Barnsley.

g 319 to Lister, dealer, Bolton, 3-1976 then to Ensign, dealer, Hornchurch, Essex, then to Hillside Autos, breaker, Great Yeldham, Essex, 4-1976.

h 320 involved in an accident at Mytholmroyd 6-1-1975 and withdrawn and then to Auto Spares (Bingley) Ltd. 4-1975 for scrap.

1963

Daimler CVG6LX Gardner 6LX 10·45 litre engine. Daimatic transmission, two pedal control.　　Cost £6,066 each.
Charles H, Roe H39/31R body 8ft.0in. wide x 30ft.0in. long. Concealed radiator.　　Unladen weight 8 tons 5 cwt 1 qr.

No.	Regn. No.	Chassis No.	In Service	Withdrawn	Disposal	Notes
582	582 FUM	30218	1-10-1963	27-6-1975	a	Renumbered 882 1-12-1973
583	583 FUM	30219	23-9-1963	30-6-1975	b	Renumbered 883 1-12-1973
584	584 FUM	30220	2-9-1963	30-6-1975	c	Renumbered 884 1-12-1973
585	585 FUM	30221	16-9-1963	30-6-1975	c	Renumbered 885 1-12-1973
586	586 FUM	30222	2-9-1963	11-6-1975	d	Renumbered 886 1-12-1973
587	587 FUM	30223	23-9-1963	30-6-1975	e	Renumbered 887 1-12-1973
588	588 FUM	30224	23-9-1963	20-6-1975	e	Renumbered 888 1-12-1973
589	589 FUM	30225	16-9-1963	30-6-1975	c	Renumbered 889 1-12-1973
590	590 FUM	30226	16-9-1963	30-6-1975	c	Renumbered 890 1-12-1973
591	591 FUM	30227	4-10-1963	30-6-1975	c	Renumbered 891 1-12-1973
592	592 FUM	30228	23-9-1963	30-6-1975	f	Renumbered 892 1-12-1973
593	593 FUM	30229	16-9-1963	30-6-1975	c	Renumbered 893 1-12-1973
594	594 FUM	30230	16-9-1963	29-8-1975	g	Renumbered 894 1-12-1973
595	595 FUM	30231	16-9-1963	31-8-1975	h	Renumbered 895 1-12-1973
596	596 FUM	30232	1-10-1963	31-8-1975	h	Renumbered 896 1-12-1973

882-896 passed to the West Yorkshire Passenger Transport Executive on 1-4-1974.

894-896 transferred to the Calderdale District of the WYPTE 17-1-1975, then 894 to Bradford District 3-2-1975, withdrawn 29-8-1975. 895 and 896 withdrawn by Calderdale 31-8-1975 and cannibalised for spares. 892 cannibalised for spare parts 12-1975.

a 882 sold to Carlton Metals, Barnsley, 1-1976 for scrap.

b 883 to D. Rollinson, breaker, Barnsley 6-1976 for scrap.

c 884, 885, 889-891 and 893 to D.Rollinson, breaker, Barnsley, 4-1976 for scrap.

d 886 to D, Rollinson, breaker, Barnsley, 11-1975 for scrap.

e 887 and 888 to D.Rollinson, Barnsley, 1-1976 for scrap.

f 892 to Jones, breaker, Barnsley, 3-1976 for scrap.

g 894 to Paul Sykes, Barnsley, 12-1975 for scrap.

h 895 and 896 to Carlton Metals, breaker, Carlton, Barnsley, 1-1976 for scrap.

1963

Leyland PD3A/2, 0·600 engine, pneumocyclic gear box, air brakes.　　Cost £5,970 each.
Weymann H39/31R body, 8ft.0in. wide x 30ft.0in. long, fibreglass front.　　Unladen weight 7 tons 17 cwt 3 qrs.

No.	Regn. No.	Chassis No.	In Service	Withdrawn	Disposal	Notes
321	321 GNW	L00220	10-10-1963	4-3-1975	a	
322	322 GNW	L00221	10-10-1963	5-9-1975	b	
323	323 GNW	L00222	11-10-1963	5-9-1975	b	
324	324 GNW	L00223	8-10-1963	1-5-1975	b	
325	325 GNW	L00224	9-1963	29-4-1975	b	
326	326 GNW	L00225	11-10-1963	5-9-1975	b	
327	327 GNW	L00226	8-10-1963	3-12-1974	c	
328	328 GNW	L00718	10-10-1963	11-8-1975	b	
329	329 GNW	L00719	9-10-1963	5-9-1975	d	
330	330 GNW	L00720	16-10-1963	29-8-1975	e	

321-330 passed to the West Yorkshire Passenger Transport Executive on 1-4-1974.

322, 323, 326, 328 and 329 transferred to Bradford District 23-5-1975, All last used in Bradford 11-8-1975 and returned to Leeds for service. 328 was not used in Leeds.

a 321 to D. Rollinson, Barnsley, 8-1975 for scrap.

b 322-326, 328 to Carlton Metals, Barnsley, 11-1975 for scrap.

c 327 to Hartwood Exporters Ltd. Barnsley, 5-1975 for scrap.

d 329 to D, Rollinson, breaker, Barnsley, 10-1975 for scrap.

e 330 sold to O.K. Motor Services, Bishop Auckland, Co. Durham, 12-1975 for spares. Body scrapped 12-1975, chassis 10-1976.

1963

A.E.C. Regent V   AV 590 9·6 litre engine, monocontrol.   Cost £5,752 10s.0d. each.
Charles H. Roe Ltd. H39/31R body 8ft.0in. wide x 30ft.0in. long. Concealed radiator.   Unladen weight 8 tons 4 cwt 1qr.

No.	Regn. No.	Chassis No.	In Service	Withdrawn	Disposal	Notes
934	934 GUA	2D2RA1319	12-11-1963	30-6-1975	a	
935	935 GUA	2D2RA1320	14-11-1963	26-9-1975	b	
936	936 GUA	2D2RA1321	8-10-1963	30-6-1975	a	
937	937 GUA	2D2RA1322	24-10-1963	26-9-1975	c	Tyne & Wear PTE 409 5-4-1976
938	938 GUA	2D2RA1323	24-10-1963	30-6-1975	d	
939	939 GUA	2D2RA1324	22-11-1963	31-10-1975	e	
940	940 GUA	2D2RA1325	23-10-1963	25-9-1975	f	
941	941 GUA	2D2RA1326	21-11-1963	28-10-1975	e	
942	942 GUA	2D2RA1327	20-11-1963	31-10-1975	g	
943	943 GUA	2D2RA1328	12-11-1963	30-10-1975	e	
944	944 GUA	2D2RA1329	24-10-1963	29-8-1975	c	Tyne & Wear PTE 410 5-4-1976
945	945 GUA	2D2RA1330	14-11-1963	12-2-1975	d	
946	946 GUA	2D2RA1331	23-10-1963	26-9-1975	c	Tyne & Wear PTE 411 8-4-1976
947	947 GUA	2D2RA1332	24-11-1963	30-10-1975	e	
948	948 GUA	2D2RA1333	21-11-1963	31-10-1975	h	

934-948 passed to the West Yorkshire Passenger Transport Executive on 1-4-1974.

a   934 and 936 to D. Rollinson, breaker, Barnsley, 10-1975 for scrap.

b   935 to Dunscroft Commercials, Dunscroft, near Doncaster, 2-1976.

c   937, 944 and 946 to O.K. Motor Services, Durham 12-1975, then resold to Tyne and Wear PTE 4-1976, 944 to North's, Sherburn-in-Elmet 7-1977.

d   945 to Carlton Metals, Barnsley, 8-1975 for scrap. 938 also to Carlton Metals 10-1975.

e   939, 941, 943, and 947 to Carlton Metals, breaker, Barnsley, 4-1976.

f   940 to R. Askin, Barnsley, 12-1975 for scrap.

g   942 to Paul Sykes, Barnsley, 5-1976, for scrap.

h   948 to Carlton Metals, breaker, Barnsley, 3-1976 for scrap.

1964

A.E.C.Regent V AV 590 9·6 litre engine, monocontrol.   Cost £5,927 each.
Charles H. Roe Ltd. H39/31R body 8ft.0in. wide x 30ft.0in. long. Concealed radiator.   Unladen weight 8 tons 4 cwt 0 qrs.

No.	Regn. No.	Chassis No.	In Service	Withdrawn	Disposal	Notes
949	949 JUB	2D2RA1576	9-7-1964	31-10-1975	a	
950	950 JUB	2D2RA1577	17-7-1964	29-8-1975	b	Tyne & Wear PTE 412 5-4-1976
951	951 JUB	2D2RA1578	9-7-1964	28-11-1975	c	
952	952 JUB	2D2RA1579	1-7-1964	29-8-1975	b	Tyne & Wear PTE 413 5-4-1976
953	953 JUB	2D2RA1580	1-7-1964	18-11-1975	c	
954	954 JUB	2D2RA1581	7-7-1964	15-10-1975	d	
955	955 JUB	2D2RA1582	1-7-1964	31-12-1975	c	
956	956 JUB	2D2RA1583	3-7-1964	16-10-1975	e	
957	957 JUB	2D2RA1584	1-7-1964	27-8-1975	e	
958	958 JUB	2D2RA1585	1-7-1964	15-10-1975	b	Tyne & Wear PTE 414 6-4-1976
959	959 JUB	2D2RA1586	2-7-1964	24-6-1975	e	
960	960 JUB	2D2RA1587	2-7-1964	31-12-1975	f	
961	961 JUB	2D2RA1588	13-7-1964	28-11-1975	c	
962	962 JUB	2D2RA1589	15-7-1964	28-11-1975	c	
963	963 JUB	2D2RA1590	3-7-1964	24-10-1975	c	

949-963 passed to the West Yorkshire Passenger Transport Ex>cuitive on 1-4-1974.

a   949 to Carlton Metals, breaker, Barnsley, 4-1976 for scrap.

b   950, 952, 958 sold to O.K. Motor Services, Durham, 12-1975, then resold to Tyne and Wear PTE 4-1976. 950 to North's, Sherburn-in-Elmet 7-1977. 952 to S .Milner of the Lincolnshire Vintage Vehicle Society for preservation 5-1977. Located at the Society's Museum in Lincoln.

c   951, 953, 955, 961-3 to D. Rollinson, breaker, Barnsley, 6-1976.

d   954 to D. Rollinson, breaker, Barnsley, 1-1976.

e   956, 957 and 959 to R. Askin, breaker, Barnsley, 12-1975.

f   960 to Paul Sykes, dealer, 5-1976.

1964

A.E.C.Reliance   AH 470 7·75 litre engine, monocontrol.   Cost £5,600 each.
Charles H. Roe Ltd. B41D composite body. 8ft. 2¹/₂in. wide x 30ft. 8in. long.   Unladen weight 6 tons 8 cwt 1 qr.

No.	Regn. No.	Chassis No.	In Service	Withdrawn	Disposal	Notes
44	44 KUA	2MU2RA5500	7-8-1964	31-12-1970	a	
45	45 KUA	2MU2RA5501	1-8-1964	31-12-1970	a	
46	46 KUA	2MU2RA5502	18-8-1964	24-12-1970	a	
47	47 KUA	2MU2RA5503	5-8-1964	31-12-1970	a	

a   44 and 45 to Aberdeen Corporation Transport Department 30-6-1971, 46 and 47 ditto 7-7-1971. Retained same fleet numbers in Aberdeen. All withdrawn by 10-1976. then to Dunsmore, dealer, Larkhall 11-1976, then 44, 45 and 47 to Wilson, Carnwath, 11-1976 for further use. 45 to Dunsmore. Larkhall, dealer, 11-1984.

1964

Daimler Fleetline CRG6LX, Gardner 6LX 10·45 litre engine. Daimatic transmission, two pedal control. Cost £6,840 each.
Charles H. Roe Ltd. H41/29F all metal body, 8ft.0in. wide x 30ft.0in. long. Unladen weight 9 tons 1 cwt 0 qrs.(101)
8 tons 19 cwt 2 qrs. (102-110).

No.	Regn. No.	Chassis No.	In Service	Withdrawn	Disposal	Notes
101	101 LNW	60769	13-12-1964	1-1980	a	A, B, To one man 24-2-1971.
102	102 LNW	60770	2-12-1964	9-1-1981	a	To one man 12-1973
103	103 LNW	60771	1-12-1964	13-10-1980	a	To one man 1-1974
104	104 LNW	60772	1-12-1964	9-1-1981	a	To one man 10-1973
105	105 LNW	60773	1-12-1964	30-9-1982	a	To one man 10-1973
106	106 LNW	60774	7-12-1964	30-7-1980	b	To one man 11-1973
107	107 LNW	60775	7-12-1964	30-10-1980	c	To one man 10-1973
108	108 LNW	60776	7-12-1964	15-8-1980	d	To one man 2-1974
109	109 LNW	60777	8-12-1964	20-11-1976	e	To one man 1-1974
110	110 LNW	60778	7-12-1964	30-10-1980	c	To one man 3-1974

101-110 passed to the West Yorkshire Passenger Transport Executive 1-4-1974.

A 101 exhibited at the Commercial Motor Show, Earls Court, London, 25-9-1964 to 3 -10-1964. Wrap round windscreen.
B 101 fitted with three sliding ventilators to alternate windows on each side 7 and 8-1967. 101 was experimentally converted for one-man operation in 2-1971, The remainder of this class were similarly converted and fitted with short wave radio equipment from 10-1973 to 3-1974. 101-110 passed to the WYPTE on 1-4-1974.   101-108 and 110 were subsequently repainted in WYPTE livery.

a 101 and 102 transferred to Calderdale District 9-6-1978, 103-5 ditto 15-6-1978. 101 withdrawn 1-1980, sold at Central Motor Auctions, Rothwell, 22-5-1980 to T. Wigley, Carlton, for scrap. 102 and 104 withdrawn 9-1-1981. 102 to J. Sykes, breaker, Carlton. 104 to C.F. Booth Ltd., Rotherham, 3-1981. 103 withdrawn 13-10-1980. No known disposal. 105 withdrawn 30-9-1982 and sold at Central Motor Auctions, Rothwell, on 24-2-1983 to D. Rollinson, Carlton, for scrap.
b 106 sold at Central Motor Auctions, Rothwell, 25-9-1980 to G. Jones (Carlton Metals), Carlton, for scrap.
c 107 and 110 sold at Central Motor Auctions, Rothwell, 18-12-1980 to P.V.S., dealer, Carlton, for scrap.
d 108 to D. Rollinson, Carlton, 12-1980 for scrap.   e 109 to J.S.N. Sefton, Barnsley, 8-1977 for scrap.

1964

Daimler CVG6LX/30 Gardner 6LX 10·45 litre engine. Daimatic transmission, two pedal control.   Cost £6,181 each.
Charles H. Roe Ltd. H39/31R body 8ft.0in. wide x 30 ft.0in. long.   Unladen weight 8 tons 7cwt 1 qr.

No.	Regn. No.	Chassis No.	In Service	Withdrawn	Disposal	Notes
111	111 LNW	30259	2-11-1964	31-12-1975	a	
112	112 LNW	30260	5-11-1964	30-12-1975	a	
113	113 LNW	30261	2-11-1964	31-12-1975	a	
114	114 LNW	30262	2-11-1964	31-12-1975	a	
115	115 LNW	30263	2-11-1964	31-12-1975	a	

111-115 passed to the West Yorkshire Passenger Transport Executive on 1-4-1974.

a 111-115 to J. Sykes, breaker, Barnsley, 6-1976.

1965

A.E.C. Reliance   AH 470 7·75 litre engine. monocontrol.   Cost £5,885.
Charles H Roe Ltd. C37F body. 8fft.0in. wide x 30ft.6in long.   Unladen weight 6 tons 7 cwt 0 qrs.

No.	Regn. No.	Chassis No.	In Service	Withdrawn	Disposal	Notes
10	ANW 710C	2MU2RA5504	10-3-1965	24-11-1973	a	

a 10 sold to W.North (P.V.) Ltd. dealers, Sherburn-in-Elmet, 11-1973. To Hudson, Cottingham, near Hull, 4-1974, then to Halford, later Astons, Kempsey, East Midlands, 1-1975. Purchased by D.H. Crowther of High Wycombe for preservation 18-2-1984. Sold when Crowther went into liquidation. Current location unknown.

1965

Leyland Atlantean PDR1/1 Mk.II, 0·680 engine, pneumocyclic gear box, air brakes.   Cost £6,698 6s.8d. each.
Weymann H41/29F bodies. 8ft.0in. wide x 30ft.0in. long.   Unladen weight 8 tons 12 cwt 3 qrs.

No.	Regn. No.	Chassis No.	In Service	Withdrawn	Disposal	Notes
331	CUB 331C	L20375	9-7-1965	2-4-1981	a	To one man 4-1974
332	CUB 332C	L20376	15-7-1965	30-10-1980	b	To one man 4-1974
333	CUB 333C	L20391	7-7-1965	30-10-1980	b	To one man 4-1974
334	CUB 334C	L20392	7-7-1965	19-9-1979	c	To one man 9-1974
335	CUB 335C	L20393	14-7-1965	30-10-1980	b	To one man 4-1974
336	CUB 336C	L20460	12-7-1965	30-10-1980	b	To one man 4-1974
337	CUB 337C	L20461	10-7-1965	30-10-1980	d	To one man 9-1974
338	CUB 338C	L20462	6-8-1965	30-10-1980	b	To one man 5-1974
339	CUB 339C	L20511	5-7-1965	8-1-1981	e	To one man 5-1974
340	CUB 340C	L20510	7-10-1966	13-4-1978	f	A, To one man 6-1973

This batch of buses was originally to be registered 331-340 JUG, but had to be re-registered owing to the long delay in their delivery caused by strikes at the Weymann factory.
331-339 had Weymann body numbers M1509/11/14/13/16/15/12/17/10 respectively.
A 340 did not enter service until 10-1966. It had a body started by Weymann in mid-1965, but was not completed by the time its Addlestone factory closed down. It was eventually completed by Metropolitan-Cammell at Birmingham. It was really a "one-off" and differed considerably in design, both inside and out, to 331-339 and was exhibited at the Commercial Motor Show. It had been allocated Weymann body number M1518. Its unladen weight was 8 tons 15 cwt 1 qr.
331-340 passed to the West Yorkshire Passenger Transport Executive 1-4-1974.

a 331 purchased by J. Proctor, Leeds, for preservation, 7-1981. Operational and currently stored in the Leeds area.
b 332. 333, 335, 336, 338 sold at Central Motor Auctions, Rothwell, 18-12-1980. 332 to J. Sykes, Carlton, for scrap.
c 334 lost its roof in accident 19-9-1979. Converted into tree lopper 5-1980, new unladen weight 8320 kg. To PVS, Carlton, 9-1983 for scrap via Central Motor Auctions, Rothwell.
d 337 sold at Central Motor Auctions, Rothwell, 26-2-1981.
e 339 to K. Askin, Barnsley, 5-1981 for scrap.
f 340 sold by auction by Central Motor Auctions, Rothwell, 21-12-1978 for scrap to K.Askin, breaker, Barnsley.

1965

A.E.C. Regent V   AV 590 9·6 litre engine, four speed semi-automatic gear box.   Cost £6,373 1s.5d. each.
Charles H. Roe Ltd. H39/31R body 8ft.0in. wide x 30ft.0in. long. Concealed radiator.   Unladen weight 8 tons 5 cwt 3 qrs.

No.	Regn. No.	Chassis No.	In Service	Withdrawn	Disposal	Notes
964	DUM 964C	2D2RA1656	21-12-1965	31-12-1975	a	
965	DUM 965C	2D2RA1657	6-12-1965	16-7-1976	b	
966	DUM 966C	2D2RA1662	13-12-1965	31-12-1975	c	
967	DUM 967C	2D2RA1665	6-12-1965	9-9-1976	b	
968	DUM 968C	2D2RA1666	16-12-1965	31-12-1975	c	
969	DUM 969C	2D2RA1667	8-12-1965	31-12-1975	c	
970	DUM 970C	2D2RA1668	8-12-1965	31-12-1975	c	
971	DUM 971C	2D2RA1673	14-12-1965	6-10-1976	d	
972	DUM 972C	2D2RA1674	3-12-1965	31-12-1975	e	
973	DUM 973C	2D2RA1675	4-12-1965	28-11-1975	f	

964-973 passed to the West Yorkshire Passenger Transport Executive 1-4-1974.
a 964 to D. Rollinson, breaker, Barnsley 6-1976 for scrap.
b 965 and 967 to J.S.N. Sefton, breaker, Barnsley, 2-1977.
c 966, 968-970 to D,Rollinson, breaker, Barnsley, 6-1976 for scrap. 970 to E. Bough, breaker, Barnsley, 6-1976.
d 971 to Hartwood Exports, Barnsley, 5-1977 for scrap.
e 972 to Paul Sykes, dealer, Barnsley 5-1976 for scrap.
f 973 to Lister, dealer, Bolton, 3-1976, then to A1 Services, Ardrossan 5-1976. Not used, scrapped c 2-1977.

1966

A.E.C.Regent V   AV 590 9·6 litre engine, four speed semi-automatic gear box.   Cost £6,373 1s.5d. each.
Charles H. Roe Ltd. H39/31R body 8ft.0in. wide x 30ft.0in. long. Concealed radiator.   Unladen weight 8 tons 5 cwt 3 qrs.

No.	Regn. No.	Chassis No.	In Service	Withdrawn	Disposal	Notes
974	ENW 974D	2D2RA1658	1-1-1966	29-9-1976	a	
975	ENW 975D	2D2RA1659	7-1-1966	31-10-1975	b	
976	ENW 976D	2D2RA1660	5-1-1966	27-10-1976	c	
977	ENW 977D	2D2RA1661	2-1-1966	24-5-1976	a	
978	ENW 978D	2D2RA1663	1-1-1966	31-12-1975	d	
979	ENW 979D	2D2RA1664	1-1-1966	30-12-1975	d	
980	ENW 980D	2D2RA1669	1-1-1966	20-12-1975	b	
981	ENW 981D	2D2RA1670	1-1-1966	31-12-1975	e	
982	ENW 982D	2D2RA1671	8-1-1966	31-12-1975	d	
983	ENW 983D	2D2RA1672	6-1-1966	20-12-1975	d	

974-983 passed to the West Yorkshire Passenger Transport Executive 1-4-1974.
a 974 and 977 to J.S.N. Sefton, breaker, Barnsley, 2-1977.
b 975 and 980 to Lister, dealer, Bolton, 3-1976. 980 to A.A. Motor Services, (Dodds), Ayr, 4-1976. 980 sold for preservation 5-1979 to D.H. Gray of Lincoln. To Leeds Regent Preservation Group 8-1988 and then Keighley Bus Museum Trust 4-1999.
c 976 to Hartwood Exports Barnsley, 5-1977 then to Dickinson & Sheppey, breakers, Monk Bretton 6-1977.
d 978, 979, 982, 983 to D. Rollinson, breaker, Barnsley 6-1976 for scrap.
e 981 to Paul Sykes, dealer, Barnsley, 5-1976 for scrap.

1966

Daimler Fleetline CRG6LX. Gardner 6LX 10·45 litre engine, semi-automatic transmission.   Cost £7,210 11s.5d. each.
Charles H. Roe Ltd. H41/29F bodies, 8ft.0in. wide x 30ft.0in. long.

No.	Regn. No.	Chassis No.	In Service	Withdrawn	Disposal	Notes
116	FUB 116	61426	1-5-1966	15-4-1978	a	To one man 5-1973 A
117	FUB 117	61427	11-5-1966	28-5-1976	b	To one man 5-1973
118	FUB 118	61428	23-5-1966	14-6-1976	b	To one man 4-1973
119	FUB 119	61429	17-5-1966	31-3-1978	c	To one man 2-1973 B
120	FUB 120	61430	19-5-1966	16-6-1976	b	To one man 3-1973
121	FUB 121	61431	4-5-1966	15-6-1976	b	To one man 5-1973
122	FUB 122	61432	20-5-1966	15-6-1976	b	To one man 5-1973
123	FUB 123	61433	11-5-1966	16-6-1976	b	To one man 3-1973
124	FUB 124	61434	6-5-1966	16-6-1976	b	To one man 6-1973
125	FUB 125	61435	16-5-1966	4-6-1976	b	To one man 2-1973
126	FUB 126	61436	1-5-1966	11-6-1976	b	To one man 5-1973
127	FUB 127	61437	2-5-1966	14-4-1978	d	To one man 7-1973 C
128	FUB 128	61438	11-5-1966	16-6-1976	e	To one man 3-1973
129	FUB 129	61439	1-5-1966	9-8-1976	e	To one man 7-1973
130	FUB 130	61440	1-5-1966	10-6-1976	e	To one man 8-1973

116-130 were converted for one man operation and fitted with short wave radio equipment from 2 to 8-1973.

116-130 passed to the West Yorkshire Passenger Transport Executive 1-4-1974.

116-7, 119, 121-2. 124, 127 and 129 were subsequently repainted in WYPTE livery.

A 116 Learner bus 17 from 8-1978.

B 119 Learner bus 18 from 10-7-1978, withdrawn by 4-1985.

C 127 Learner bus 19 from 10-1978.

a 17 (ex-116) delicensed from 4-7-1983. No known disposal.

b 117-8, 120-6 to J.S.N. Sefton, Barnsley 8-1977 for scrap. Broken up by various local breakers.

c 18 (ex-119) to PVS, Carlton, breakers, 4-1985.

d 19 (ex-127) withdrawn 1984? No known disposal or withdrawal date.

e 128-130 sold by auction at Central Motor Auctions, Rothwell, on 21-12-1978 for scrap. 128 and 129 to K.Askin, breaker, Barnsley. 130 to D. Rollinson, breaker, Carlton. Scrapped 5-1979.

1966

A.E.C. Swift AH 505 8·2 litre engine,   Cost £6,458 10s.0d.
Charles H. Roe Ltd. B48D body, 8ft. 2 1/2in. wide x 36ft. 0in. long.   Unladen weight 6 tons 14 cwt 0 qrs.

No.	Regn. No.	Chassis No.	In Service	Withdrawn	Disposal	Notes
51	GUM 451D	MP2R053	14-10-1966	20-9-1978	a	

This was the first rear-engine single decker in the fleet and was exhibited at the Commercial Motor Show, Earls Court, 23-9-1966 to 1-10-1966. It was demonstrated in Blackpool on 26 January 1967.

51 passed to the West Yorkshire Passenger Transport Executive 1-4-1974. Renumbered 1251 12-4-1974.

a 1251 sold by auction at Central Motor Auctions, Rothwell, on 21-12-1978 to Kennedy's Film Services, Morley, then to some members of the Leeds Regent Preservation Group and R. Wardroper, Dewsbury, 10-1984. Eventually considered to be in too bad a condition to restore and was sold for scrap to J.Sykes, Carlton, 4-1995.

1966

Daimler Fleetline CRG6LX   Gardner 6LX 10·45 litre engine, semi-automatic transmission.   Cost £7,490 6s.3d.
Charles H. Roe Ltd. H45/33F body, 8ft. 2 1/2in. wide x 33ft. 0in. long.   Unladen weight 9 tons 12 cwt 2 qrs.

No.	Regn. No.	Chassis No.	In Service	Withdrawn	Disposal	Notes
131	HNW 131D	61979	28-11-1966	13-9-1977	a	To one-man 11-1972

131 was exhibited at the Commercial Motor Show, Earl's Court, London, from 23-9-1966 to 21-10-1966. It was the first bus of its type in Leeds.   131 passed to the West Yorkshire Passenger Transport Executive on 1-4-1974.

a Learner bus 20 from 8-1978. To Bradford District 22-2-1979. Earmarked for preservation by the West Yorkshire PTE in 10-1983. To WYCC Recreation and Arts Dept. 6-1984 for West Yorkshire Transport Museum. Restored at Thornbury Works 1984-5. To Transperience, Low Moor, Bradford 7-1995. To Keighley Bus Museum Trust 9-1998.

1966-7

Leyland Atlantean PDR1/1 Mk.II, 0·680 engine, pneumocyclic gear box, air brakes.   Cost £7,143 2s.5d. each.
M.C.C.W. H41/29F bodies, 8ft.0in. wide x 30ft.0in. long.   Unladen weight 8 tons 13 cwt 0 qrs.

No.	Regn. No.	Chassis No.	In Service	Withdrawn	Disposal	Notes
341	HUA 341D	L62758	20-12-1966	14-11-1978	a	to one-man 2-1973
342	HUA 342D	L62759	6-1-1967	14-11-1978	a	to one-man 2-1973
343	HUA 343D	L62939	22-12-1966	24-10-1978	b	to one-man 2-1973
344	HUA 344D	L62868	2-1-1967	30-11-1978	c	to one-man 2-1973
345	HUA 345D	L63225	2-1-1967	14-11-1978	d	to one-man 2-1973
346	HUA 346D	L62940	11-1-1967	19-7-1978	e	to one-man 3-1973
347	HUA 347D	L63044	3-1-1967	7-8-1978	f	to one-man 8-1973
348	HUA 348D	L63045	12-1-1967	7-8-1978	c	to one-man 8-1973
349	HUA 349D	L63227	2-1-1967	12-4-1978	g, c	to one-man 9-1973
350	HUA 350D	L63226	2-1-1967	1-6-1978	e	to one-man 9-1973
351	HUA 351D	L63341	2-1-1967	26-6-1980	g	to one-man 9-1973
352	HUA 352D	L63043	2-1-1967	15-4-1978	g	to one-man 10-1973
353	HUA 353D	L63342	4-1-1967	6-3-1978	g	to one-man 10-1973
354	HUA 354D	L63496	7-1-1967	8-8-1978	f	to one-man 10-1973
355	HUA 355D	L63495	13-1-1967	8-8-1978	b	A, to one-man 10-1973

341-355 were originally ordered from Weymann and the series was allocated body numbers M1878-92.

A 355 in service 8-7-1968 with fully automatic transmission by Self Changing Gears, Coventry. Removed 7-1970.
341-355 converted for one-man operation and fitted with radio equipment 1973.
341-355 passed to the West Yorkshire Passenger Transport Executive on 1-4-1974.
9349 (ex-342) passed to Yorkshire Rider Ltd. 26-10-1986.

a 341 Learner 20 from 5-1979 to Bradford District. Renumbered 14 in 5-1979. Sold by Central Motor Auctions, Rothwell, on 12-7-1984. 342 Learner 15 from 4-1979 to Leeds District, then Kirklees District 19-8-1980. Renumbered A15 then H349 in 5-1985 and 9349 1-12-1985. Withdrawn 9-1987. Sold at British Motor Auctions, Brighouse, 6-7-1988.

b 343 and 355 sold by auction at Central Motor Auctions, Rothwell, on 22-2-1979. 343 to P.V.S. (Barnsley) Ltd. Cudworth. 355 to K. Askin. breaker, Barnsley.

c 344 and 348 sold at Central Motor Auctions. Rothwell, 24-1-1982. 348 to Thornton & Lloyd, Barnsley 2-1982.

d 345 Learner 16 from 3-1979 to Leeds District. Delicensed by 4-1981. To Thornbury Works, Bradford, for training purposes. Sold by Central Motor Auctions 12-7-1984 to D. Rollinson, Carlton, for scrap.

e 346 and 350 sold at Central Motor Auctions, Rothwell, 18-12-1980.

f 347 and 354 sold at Central Motor Auctions, Rothwell, on 24-4-1980. 347 to T. Wigley, Carlton for scrap. 354 to Wombwell Diesels Co. Wombwell. then to D.Rollinson, Carlton. 5-1980.

g 349, 351-3 transferred to Bradford District 23-5-1978. 349 withdrawn 18-12-1978 and sold at Central Motor Auctions, Rothwell, 24-1-1982. 351 transferred back to Leeds 27-3-1980, 352 withdrawn 30-11-1978. 351-2 sold at Central Motor Auctions, Rothwell, 25-9-1980. 351 to Wombwell Diesels Co. then to J. Hughes, dealer, Cleckheaton, by 5-1981 then to

Central Motor Auctions, Rothwell, on 28-10-1982 to Wombwell Diesels Co. again. 353 withdrawn 14-6-1979. 353 sold at Central Motor Auctions on 23-8-1979 to Whiting Bros. Purston, near Pontefract, then to North, Sherburn-in-Elmet, 9-1979.

1967

A.E.C. Swift   AH 505 8·2 litre engine   Cost £6,458 10s.0d. each.
Charles H. Roe Ltd. B48D body, 8ft. 2 1/2in. wide x 36ft. 0in. long.   Unladen weight 6 tons 14 cwt 0 qrs.

No.	Regn. No.	Chassis No.	In Service	Withdrawn	Disposal	Notes
52	JNW 952E	MP2R054	1-4-1967	12-1-1978	a	
53	JNW 953E	MP2R055	1-4-1967	30-1-1979	b	
54	JNW 954E	MP2R056	1-4-1967	28-12-1977	c	
55	JNW 955E	MP2R057	7-4-1967	3-1-1978	c	
56	JNW 956E	MP2R058	3-4-1967	14-11-1977	a	
57	JNW 957E	MP2R059	7-4-1967	10-3-1978	c	
58	JNW 958E	MP2R060	3-4-1967	28-12-1977	c	
59	JNW 959E	MP2R061	3-4-1967	3-4-1978	c	
60	JNW 960E	MP2R062	6-4-1967	9-2-1978	c	

52 to 60 passed to the West Yorkshire Passenger Transport Executive on 1-4-1974. Renumbered 1252-1260 12-4-1974.
a 1252 and 1256 to J.S.N. Sefton, breaker, Barnsley 10-1978 for scrap.
b 1253 sold by auction at Central Motor Auctions, Rothwell, on 26-4-1979 to T. Wigley, breaker, Carlton, for scrap.
c 1254, 1255, 1257-1260 to C.F. Booth Ltd. Rotherham, 10-1978 for scrap.

1967

Daimler Fleetline CRG6LX   Gardner 6LX 10·45 litre engine, semi-automatic transmission.   Cost £7,490 6s.3d. each.
Charles H. Roe Ltd. H45/33F bodies 8ft. 2 1/2in. wide x 33ft.0in. long.   Unladen weight 9 tons 12 cwt 2 qrs.

No.	Regn. No.	Chassis No.	In Service	Withdrawn	Disposal	Notes
132	LUA 132F	61980	9-9-1967	27-5-1978	a	To one-man 11-1972
133	LUA 133F	61981	2-10-1967	25-5-1978	b	To one-man 12-1972
134	LUA 134F	61982	12-10-1867	27-5-1978	a	To one-man 12-1972
135	LUA 135F	61983	25-9-1967	27-5-1978	c	To one-man 1-1973
136	LUA 136F	61984	2-10-1967	12-4-1978	d	To one-man 3-1973
137	LUA 137F	61985	28-9-1967	1-6-1978	e	To one-man 4-1973
138	LUA 138F	61986	29-9-1967	15-4-1978	f	To one-man 10-1972
139	LUA 139F	61987	2-10-1967	1-6-1978	g	To one-man 10-1972
140	LUA 140F	61988	4-10-1967	15-4-1978	h	To one-man 10-1972
141	LUA 141F	61989	3-10-1967	2-6-1978	j	To one-man 11-1972
142	LUA 142F	61990	2-10-1967	2-6-1978	k	To one-man 12-1972
143	LUA 143F	61991	6-10-1967	2-6-1978	l	To one-man 10-1972
144	LUA 144F	61992	11-10-1867	8-6-1978	m	To one-man 1973
145	LUA 145F	61993	16-10-1967	26-5-1978	n	To one-man 12-1972

132 to 145 were all converted for one-man operation from 10-1972 to 4-1973 and fitted with radio equipment. All had front entrances only. All were transferred to the Learner fleet between 8-1978 and 3-1979.
132-145 passed to the West Yorkshire Passenger Transport Executive on 1-4-1974.
9344 (ex-135), 9357 (ex-137), 9354 (ex-144) to Yorkshire Rider Ltd. 26-10-1986.
132-134 to learner fleet 29-5-1978, 132 Learner 21 to Leeds, 133 Learner A22 from 2-1979 to Kirklees, 134 Learner 23 from 3-1979 to Leeds. 135 to Learner fleet 1-6-1978, as 24 from 10-1978 to Calderdale, renumbered T4, then H344 1-1985, then 9344 from 1-12-1985. 136 Learner 25 from 9-1978 to Leeds, to Bradford 3-9-1982. 137 and 139 to Learner fleet 20-6-1978. 137 Learner 26 from 6-1979 to Leeds, renumbered 9357 1-12-1985. 139 Learner 28 from 10-1978 to Bradford, 138 Learner 27 and 140 Learner 29 1978. 141-3 to Learner fleet 5-6-1978, 144 ditto 9-6-1978. 141 Learner 30 from 11-1978 to Bradford. 142 L'ner 31 from 1-1979, to Leeds, renumbered 9353 1-12-1985. 143 L'ner 32 from 10-1978 to Bradford, 144 L'ner 33 from 3-1979 to Leeds, renumbered 9354 1-12-1985. 145 L'ner A13 from 10-1978 to Kirklees.
a 21 (ex-132) and 23 (ex-134) delicensed 4-1981. Sold by Central Motor Auctions, 24-11-1983 to Thornton, Carlton.
b A22 (ex-133) withdrawn 1984. No known breaker.
c 9344 (ex-135) withdrawn 12-1986. Sold at British Motor Auctions, Brighouse, 6-7-1988 to Parton & Allen, Carlton.
d 25 (ex-136) withdrawn 1-1985. To J. Sykes, Carlton, 2-1987.
e 9357 (ex-137) partially converted into tree lopper 1988. Withdrawn 31-3-1989. Sold 10-9-1990.
f 27 (ex-138) delicensed from 4-7-1983 No known breaker.
g 28 (ex-139) withdrawn 28-2-1981, to T. Wigley, Carlton, 4-1985 for scrap.
h 29 (ex-140) withdrawn by 8-1985, to Rollinson, Carlton, 2-1987, for scrap.
j 30 (ex-141) sold at Central Motor Auctions, Rothwell, 14-6-1984 to Rollinson, Carlton, for scrap.
k 9353 (ex-142) withdrawn 8-1986. To unknown breaker.
l 32 (ex-143) sold by Central Motor Auctions, Rothwell, 12-6-1984. To Rollinson Carlton. 6-1984.
m 9354 (ex-144) withdrawn 20-6-1988. Sold at British Motor Auctions, Brighouse, 6-7-1988 to unknown breaker.
n A13 (ex-145) withdrawn by 4-1985, to PVS, Carlton, 4-1985 for scrap.

1968

A.E.C. Swift   AH 505 8·2 litre engine   Cost £6,852 4s. 8d. each.
Charles H. Roe Ltd. B48D bodies. 8ft. 2 1/2in. wide x 36ft.0in. long.   Unladen weight 7 tons 1 cwt 0 qrs.

No.	Regn. No.	Chassis No.	In Service	Withdrawn	Disposal	Notes
76	MUG 476F	MP2R129	2-3-1968	20-6-1980	a	
77	MUG 477F	MP2R130	3-3-1968	14-4-1980	a	
78	MUG 478F	MP2R131	3-3-1968	21-3-1980	b	
79	MUG 479F	MP2R132	4-3-1968	9-1-1979	c	
80	MUG 480F	MP2R133	4-3-1968	30-4-1980	a	

No.	Regn. No.	Chassis No.	In Service	Withdrawn	Disposal	Notes
81	MUG 481F	MP2R143	5-1968	6- 5-1979	c	
82	MUG 482F	MP2R135	4-3-1968	24-3-1979	c	
83	MUG 483F	MP2R136	3-3-1968	20-3-1979	c	
84	MUG 484F	MP2R137	2-3-1968	26-2-1979	d	Cannibalised for spares 5-1979
85	MUG 485F	MP2R138	3-3-1968	8-2-1980	e	

76-85 passed to the West Yorkshire Passenger Transport Executive on 1-4-1974. Renumbered 1276-1285 12-4-1974.

a   1276-7 and 1280 sold at Central Motor Auctions, Rothwell on 23-7-1980. 1276-7 to T. Wigley, Carlton, for scrap. 1280 to Kilton Coronets Jazz Band, Worksop. Resold by 9-1981 to Parton & Allen, Carlton, for scrap.

b   1278 sold at Central Motor Auctions, Rothwell, 18-12-1978 to P.V.S. (Laverick), Carlton , for scrap.

c   1279, 1281-3 sold at Central Motor Auctions, Rothwell on 20-12-1979. 1279 to Barraclough. Shafton. 1281 to Whitting Biggin, Beighton, Sheffield, then to T. Wigley, Carlton. 1282 and 1283 to T. Wigley, Carlton, for scrap.

d   1284 sold at Central Motor Auctions, Rothwell, on 28-6-1979 to A. Barraclough, Carlton, for scrap.

e   1285 to Kennedy's Film Services, Morley, by 12-1980, withdrawn accident damage and then to members of the Leeds Regent Preservation Group and R. Wardroper, Dewsbury, 7-1985 for spare parts for 1251. To J.Sykes, Carlton, 4-1995.

1968

A.E.C. Swift   AH 505 8·2 litre engine.   Cost £6,762 1s.3d each.
M.C.W. B48D bodies, 8ft. 2 1/2in. wide x 36ft.0in. long.   Unladen weight 7 tons 11 cwt 3 qrs.

No.	Regn. No.	Chassis No.	In Service	Withdrawn	Disposal	Notes
61	MNW 161F	MP2R108	23-3-1968	2-8-1979	a	
62	MNW 162F	MP2R109	27-3-1968	21-8-1979	a	
63	MNW 163F	MP2R110	25-3-1968	21-8-1979	a	
64	MNW 164F	MP2R111	27-3-1968	27-2-1980	b	
65	MNW 165F	MP2R112	25-3-1968	10-7-1979	c	
66	MNW 166F	MP2R113	31-3-1968	27-2-1980	b	
67	MNW 167F	MP2R114	1-4-1968	19-10-1979	d	Withdrawn after accident.
68	MNW 168F	MP2R115	1-4-1968	30-7-1979	c	
69	MNW 169F	MP2R116	2-4-1968	1-2-1980	b	
70	MNW 170F	MP2R117	6-4-1968	17-3-1980	e	
71	MNW 171F	MP2R118	6-4-1968	21-3-1980	e	
72	MNW 172F	MP2R119	9-4-1968	10-5-1979	f	
73	MNW 173F	MP2R120	10-4-1968	18-3-1980	e	
74	MNW 174F	MP2R121	12-4-1968	26-3-1980	e	
75	MNW 175F	MP2R122	12-4-1968	28-3-1980	e	

These buses were not fitted with limited stop signs.

61-75 passed to the West Yorkshire Passenger Transport Executive on 1-4-1974. Renumbered 1261-1275 12-4-1974.

a   1261-3 sold at Central Motor Auctions, Rothwell, 25-10-1979 to D. Rollinson, Carlton, then 1261 to T. Wigley, breaker, Carlton, 1262 to K. Askin, Barnsley, 1263 to Barraclough, Shafton and then to P.V.S. (Barnsley) Ltd. Carlton, all for scrap.

b   1264, 1266 and 1269 sold at Central Motor Auctions, Rothwell, 24-4-1980.

c   1265 1268 sold at Central Motor Auctions, Rothwell, 23-8-1979. 1265 to T. Wigley, Carlton, then to R. Askin. Barnsley. 1268 to Whiting Bros, Purston, near Pontefract.

d   1267 sold at Central Motor Auctions, Rothwell, 28-2-1980 to R. Askin, breaker, Barnsley.

e   1270-1, 1273-5 sold at Central Motor Auctions, Rothwell, 22-5-1980. 1273-5 to Wombwell Diesels Ltd. for scrap.

f   1272 on loan to Kitson College of Engineering, Leeds, from 8-1979 to 6-1983. To Wombwell Diesels Ltd. 7-1985.

1968

A.E.C. Swift.   AH 505 8·2 litre engine.   Cost £6,762 1s.3d, each.
M.C.W. B48D bodies. 8ft. 2 1/2in. wide x 36ft.0in. long.   Unladen weight 7 tons 11cwt 3qrs.

No.	Regn. No.	Chassis No.	In Service	Withdrawn	Disposal	Notes
86	MUB 186F	MP2R134	5-5-1968	22-2-1980	a	
87	MUB 187F	MP2R139	2-5-1968	5-3-1980	a	
88	MUB 188F	MP2R140	8-5-1968	11-2-1980	a	
89	MUB 189F	MP2R141	15-5-1968	13-4-1979	b	
90	MUB 190F	MP2R142	13-5-1968	28-2-1980	a	
91	MUB 191F	MP2R220	11-5-1968	7-1-1980	c	
92	MUB 192F	MP2R221	8-5-1968	26-2-1980	a	
93	MUB 193F	MP2R222	2-5-1968	29-2-1980	a	
94	MUB 194F	MP2R223	7-5-1968	25-3-1980	d	
95	MUB 195F	MP2R224	5-5-1968	19-12-1979	e	
96	MUB 196F	MP2R225	2-5-1968	17-10-1979	f	
97	MUB 197F	MP2R226	6-5-1968	16-1-1980	c	
98	MUB 198F	MP2R227	5-5-1968	11-1-1980	c	
99	MUB 199F	MP2R228	2-5-1968	12-5-1979	f	
100	MUG 100F	MP2R229	15-5-1968	17-5-1979	f	

These buses were not fitted with limited stop signs.

86-100 passed to the West Yorkshire Passenger Transport Executive on 1-4-1974. Renumbered 1286-1300 12-4-1974.

a   1286-8, 1290, 1292-3 sold at Central Motor Auctions, Rothwell, 22-5-1980. 1286, 1288 and 1292 to Wombwell Diesels Ltd. 1287 to B. & D. Commercial Spares, Carlton.

b   1289 sold at Central Motor Auctions, Rothwell 23-8-1979 to T. Wigley, Carlton, for scrap.

c   1291, 1297-8 sold at Central Motor Auctions on 24-4-1980. To unknown breaker.

d   1294 sold at Central Motor Auctions, Rothwell, 20-7-1980 to T. Wigley, Carlton, for scrap.

e   1295 sold at Central Motor Auctions, Rothwell, 28-2-1980. To unknown breaker.

f   1296, 1299 and 1300 sold at Central Motor Auctions, Rothwell, on 20-12-1979, all to T. Wigley, Carlton, for scrap.

1968

Leyland Atlantean PDR2.1 0·680 engine, pneumocyclic gears, air brakes.   Cost £8,096 13s.7d. each.
Park Royal H45/33F bodies, 8ft 2¹/2in. wide x 33 ft.0in. long.   Unladen weight 9 tons 6 cwt 1 qr.

No.	Regn. No.	Chassis No.	In Service	Withdrawn	Disposal	Notes
356	PNW 356G	801860	2-9-1968	28-5-1981	a	Body No.55989
357	PNW 357G	801861	2-9-1968	22-5-1981	b	,, ,, 55985
358	PNW 358G	801910	3-9-1968	24-4-1981	c	,, ,, 55986
359	PNW 359G	801911	3-9-1968	29-5-1981	c	,, ,, 55987
360	PNW 360G	801912	3-9-1960	27-5-1981	d	,, ,, 55988
361	PNW 361G	801913	2-9-1968	21-5-1981	e	,, ,, 55990
362	PNW 362G	801945	3-9-1968	29-5-1981	f	,, ,, 55991
363	PNW 363G	801946	3-9-1968	5-5-1981	g	,, ,, 55992
364	PNW 364G	802069	2-9-1968	27-5-1981	a	,, ,, 55993
365	PNW 365G	802070	2-9-1968	28-5-1981	d	,, ,, 55994
366	PNW 366G	802085	2-9-1968	27-5-1981	e	,, ,, 55995
367	PNW 367G	802086	2-9-1968	27-5-1981	d	,, ,, 55996
368	PNW 368G	802170	2-9-1968	28-5-1981	c	,, ,, 55997
369	PNW 369G	802171	3-9-1968	30-7-1980	h	,, ,, 55998
370	PNW 370G	802172	3-9-1968	30-7-1980	h	,, ,, 55999
371	PNW 371G	802173	1-9-1968	1-12-1979	j	,, ,, 56000
372	PNW 372G	802174	1-9-1968	27-5-1981	c	,, ,, 56001
373	PNW 373G	802225	1-9-1968	28-5-1981	k	,, ,, 56002
374	PNW 374G	802226	1-9-1968	27-5-1981	l	,, ,, 56003
375	PNW 375G	802317	1-9-1968	28-5-1981	m	,, ,, 56004
376	PNW 376G	802318	1-9-1968	28-5-1981	f	,, ,, 56005
377	PNW 377G	802319	1-9-1968	28-5-1981	n	,, ,, 56006
378	PNW 378G	802357	1-9-1968	7-5-1981	m	,, ,, 56007
379	PNW 379G	802358	1-9-1968	28-5-1981	c	,, ,, 56008
380	PNW 380G	802424	1-9-1968	29-4-1981	c	,, ,, 56009
381	PNW 381G	802425	1-9-1968	28-5-1981	a	,, ,, 56010
382	PNW 382G	802438	3-9-1968	28-5-1981	e	,, ,, 56011
383	PNW 383G	802439	11-9-1968	28-5-1981	m	,, ,, 56012
384	PNW 384G	802629	11-9-1968	28-5-1981	f	,, ,, 56013
385	PNW 385G	802630	3-10-1968	28-5-1981	o	,, ,, 56014

These buses were fitted with limited stop signs and had front entrances only. All the buses of this series were converted for one-man operation and fitted with radio equipment between 5-1972 and 10-1972.

356-385 passed to the West Yorkshire Passenger Transport Executive on 1-4-1974.

a 356, 364 and 381 to unknown breakers 5-1981.

b 357 sold at Central Motor Auctions, Rothwell, 27-5-1982 to D. Rollinson, Carlton, for scrap.

c 358-9, 368, 372, 379 and 380 sold at Central Motor Auctions, Rothwell, 28-10-1982. 358 to D. Rollinson, breaker, Carlton. 379 to Jones (Carlton Metals).

d 360, 365 and 367 sold at Central Motor Auctions, Rothwell, 22-7-1982 to D. Rollinson, Carlton, for scrap.

e 361, 366 and 382 to T. Wigley, Carlton, 1-1982. 366 to Jones, dealer, Carlton, 2-1982.

f 362, 376 and 384 to T. Wigley, Carlton, for scrap.

g 363 transferred to Bradford District 3-9-1978. Returned to Leeds early 1980 and entered service 4-1980. To Rollinson, Carlton, by 10-1983 for scrap.

h 369 and 370 sold at Central Motor Auctions, Rothwell, 25-9-1980. 369 to Wombwell Diesels Ltd., 370 to J. Sykes, Carlton, for scrap.

j 371 in accident 1-12-1979 sold at Central Motor Auctions, Rothwell, 28-8-1980 to T. Wigley, Carlton, for scrap.

k 373 on loan to Kirklees District 9-1-1981 to 9-3-1981. Sold at Central Motor Auctions, Rothwell, 24-11-1983.

l 374 sold at Central Motor Auctions, Rothwell, 24-11-1983 to Thornton, Cundy Cross, Barnsley.

m 375, 378 and 383 sold at Central Motor Auctions, Rothwell, 24-1-1982. 375 and 378 to J.Whiting, Carlton, 383 to T. Wigley, Carlton then to Parton & Allen, Carlton, for scrap.

n 377 sold at Central Motor Auctions, Rothwell, 22-12-1983 to Meynell, Carlton, for scrap.

o 385 to Thornton, Carlton, by 12-1983 for scrap.

1968

Daimler Fleetline CRG6LX Gardner 6LX engine, semi-automatic transmission.   Cost £9,238 2s.3d. each.
Charles H. Roe Ltd. H45/33D bodies. 8ft. 2 ¹/2in. wide x 33ft.0in. long.   Unladen weight.

No.	Regn. No.	Chassis No.	In Service	Withdrawn	Disposal	Notes
146	PUB 146G	61994	24-11-1968	27-5-1981	a	
147	PUB 147G	61995	24-11-1968	28-5-1981	a	
148	PUB 148G	61996	24-11-1968	30-7-1980	b	
149	PUB 149G	61997	24-11-1968	28-5-1981	c	
150	PUB 150G	61998	24-11-1968	30-7-1980	b	
151	PUB 151G	61999	24-11-1968	28-5-1981	d	
152	PUB 152G	62000	24-11-1968	19-4-1980	e	
153	PUB 153G	62001	24-11-1968	10-7-1980	b	
154	PUB 154G	62002	24-11-1968	30-9-1980	f	
155	PUB 155G	62003	6-12-1968	18-9-1980	f	

146-155 were the last new buses to be fitted with limited stop signs.

146-155 passed to the West Yorkshire Passenger Transport Executive on 1-4-1974.

a 146 and 147 to Thornton, Cundy Cross, Barnsley, 12-1983, for scrap.

b 148, 150, 153 sold at Central Motor Auctions, Rothwell, 25-9-1980. 148 and 150 to T. Wigley, Carlton, for scrap.

c 149 sold at Central Motor Auctions, Rothwell, 24-11-1983 to unknown breaker.
d 151 to Thornton, Cundy Cross, Barnsley, by 9-1983 for scrap.
e 152 sold at Central Motor Auctions, Rothwell, 28-8-1980 to T. Wigley, Carlton, for scrap.
f 154 and 155 to D. Rollinson, Carlton, 12-1980, for scrap.
1968.

Daimler Fleetline CRG6LXB Gardner 6LXB 10·45 litre engine, Daimatic automatic transmission.   Cost £9,587 2s.3d. each.
Charles H. Roe Ltd. H45/33D bodies. 8ft. 2 1/2in. wide x 33ft. 0in. long.   Unladen weight 9 tons 19 cwt 2 qrs.

No.	Regn. No.	Chassis No.	In Service	Withdrawn	Disposal	Notes
156	PUB 156G	62004	24-11-1968	30-7-1981	a	A
157	PUB 157G	62005	24-11-1968	30-9-1980	b	
158	PUB 158G	62006	24-11-1968	30-7-1981	c	A
159	PUB 159G	62007	24-11-1968	30-7-1981	c	B
160	PUB 160G	62008	24-11-1968	29-9-1980	b	

156-160 had fully automatic transmission with power assisted steering, and were the first buses in Leeds to be fitted with the new Gardner 6LXB engine. They were not fitted with limited stop signs.
A 156 and 158 were exhibited at the Commercial Motor Show, Earl's Court, from 20 to 28-9-1968.
B 159 went to Lille, France, from 8-10-1968 to 23-10-1968 for a British Shopping Week.
    156-160 passed to the West Yorkshire Passenger Transport Executive on 1-4-1974.
a 156 to T. Wigley, Carlton, by 10-1983 for scrap.
b 157 and 160 to Whiting Bros. Carlton, 12-1980 then 157 to T. Wigley, Carlton, for scrap.
c 158-9 sold at Central Motor Auctions 28-7-1983. 158 to PVS Carlton, 159 to Lloyd, Cundy Cross, Barnsley.

1969

A.E.C. Swift. AH 691 11·3 litre engine with C.A.V. automatic transmission.   Cost £7,742 10s.2d. each.
Park Royal B48D bodies 8ft. 2 1/2in. wide x 36ft. 0in. long.   Unladen weight 7 tons 13 cwt 0 qrs.

No.	Regn. No.	Chassis No.	In Service	Withdrawn	Disposal	Notes
1001	SUB 401G	5P2R673	6-7-1969	31-7-1981	a	Body No. 56493
1002	SUB 402G	5P2R674	7-7-1969	30-11-1982	b	,, ,, 56494
1003	SUB 403G	5P2R675	6-7-1969	31-7-1981	c	,, ,, 56495
1004	SUB 404G	5P2R676	9-7-1969	19-5-1983	d	,, ,, 56496
1005	SUB 405G	5P2R677	6-7-1969	26-7-1983	e	,, ,, 56497
1006	SUB 406G	5P2R678	6-7-1969	19-1-1984	f	,, ,, 56498
1007	SUB 407G	5P2R679	6-7-1969	30-9-1980	g	,, ,, 56499
1008	SUB 408G	5P2R680	7-7-1969	31-1-1984	h	,, ,, 56500
1009	SUB 409G	5P2R681	6-7-1969	31-1-1984	h	,, ,, 56501
1010	SUB 410G	5P2R682	6-7-1969	26-1-1983	a	,, ,, 56502
1011	SUB 411G	5P2R683	15-7-1969	31-7-1981	a	,, ,, 56503
1012	SUB 412G	5P2R684	6-7-1969	20-11-1982	j	,, ,, 56504
1013	SUB 413G	5P2R685	16-7-1969	6-5-1980	k	,, ,, 56505
1014	SUB 414G	5P2R686	9-7-1969	18-6-1980	k	,, ,, 56506
1015	SUB 415G	5P2R687	6-7-1969	26-7-1983	l	,, ,, 56507
1016	SUB 416G	5P2R688	9-7-1969	30-9-1980	m	,, ,, 56508
1017	SUB 417G	5P2R689	11-7-1969	4-1-1984	f	,, ,, 56509
1018	SUB 418G	5P2R690	14-7-1969	18-5-1981	a	,, ,, 56510
1019	SUB 419G	5P2R691	14-7-1969	25-9-1980	m	,, ,, 56511
1020	SUB 420G	5P2R692	10-7-1969	30-9-1980	m	,, ,, 56512
1021	SUB 421G	5P2R693	17-7-1969	24-2-1983	n	,, ,, 56513
1022	SUB 422G	5P2R694	17-7-1969	30-9-1980	m	,, ,, 56514
1023	SUB 423G	5P2R695	14-7-1969	30-10-1980	o	,, ,, 56515
1024	SUB 424G	5P2R696	19-7-1969	1-8-1983	a	,, ,, 56516
1025	SUB 425G	5P2R697	23-7-1969	5-7-1980	p	,, ,, 56523
1026	SUB 426G	5P2R698	22-7-1969	30-9-1980	m	,, ,, 56517
1027	SUB 427G	5P2R699	16-7-1969	29-5-1980	p	,, ,, 56518
1028	SUB 428G	5P2R700	23-7-1969	27-11-1980	r	,, ,, 56519
1029	SUB 429G	5P2R701	18-7-1969	25-2-1983	s	,, ,, 56521
1030	SUB 430G	5P2R702	25-7-1969	27-11-1980	r	,, ,, 56520
1031	SUB 431G	5P2R703	28-7-1969	30-1-1981	m	,, ,, 56522
1032	SUB 432G	5P2R704	28-7-1969	28-1-1981	t	,, ,, 56524
1033	SUB 433G	5P2R705	28-7-1969	30-1-1981	t	,, ,, 56525
1034	SUB 434G	5P2R706	24-7-1969	30-1-1981	u	,, ,, 56526
1035	SUB 435G	5P2R707	28-7-1969	24-9-1980	m	,, ,, 56529
1036	SUB 436G	5P2R708	27-7-1969	25-2-1983	n	,, ,, 56527
1037	SUB 437G	5P2R709	28-7-1969	10-7-1980	p	,, ,, 56528
1038	SUB 438G	5P2R710	28-7-1969	30-1-1981	v	,, ,, 56530
1039	SUB 439G	5P2R711	11-8-1969	28-11-1980	v	,, ,, 56533
1040	SUB 440G	5P2R712	8-8-1969	28-11-1980	r	,, ,, 56531
1041	SUB 441G	5P2R713	11-8-1969	30-1-1981	m	,, ,, 56532
1042	SUB 442G	5P2R714	20-8-1969	28-11-1980	r	,, ,, 56534
1043	SUB 443G	5P2R715	22-8-1969	28-1-1981	t	,, ,, 56535
1044	SUB 444G	5P2R716	28-8-1969	28-11-1980	r	,, ,, 56537
1045	SUB 445G	5P2R717	4-9-1969	30-7-1980	v	,, ,, 56536
1046	SUB 446G	5P2R718	4-9-1969	4-8-1980	w	,, ,, 56538

No.	Regn. No.	Chassis No.	In Service	Withdrawn	Disposal	Notes		
1047	SUB 447G	5P2R719	12-9-1969	30-9-1980	x	,,	,,	56539
1048	SUB 448G	5P2R720	4-11-1969	30-1-1981	m	,,	,,	56540
1049	SUB 449G	5P2R721	6-11-1969	23-1-1981	m	,,	,,	56541
1050	SUB 450G	5P2R722	20-11-1969	28-5-1981	y	,,	,,	56542

1001-1050 passed to the West Yorkshire Passenger Transport Executive on 1-4-1974.

a   1001, 1010-11, 1018 and 1024 to unknown breakers.

b   1002 sold at Central Motor Auctions, Rothwell, 24-2-1983 to T. Wigley, breaker, Carlton.

c   1003 sold at Central Motor Auctions, Rothwell, 28-10-1982.

d   1004 to Kennedy's Film Services, Morley. C 10-1983. To Morris, breaker, Carlton, by 6-1989.

e   1005 sold to Wolds Gliding Club, Pocklington, 8-1983. Sold for scrap 8-1992.

f   1006 and 1017 sold at Central Motor Auctions, Rothwell 23-2-1984. 1006 to PVS, Carlton. 1017 to Thornton, Barnsley.

g   1007 to K. Askin, Barnsley 12-1980.

h   1008-9 sold at Central Motor Auctions, Rothwell, 12-4-1984.

j   1012 sold at Central Motor Auctions, Rothwell, 28-4-1983.

k   1013-14 sold at Central Motor Auctions, Rothwell, 27-11-1980. 1014 to T. Wigley, Carlton, for scrap.

l   1015 sold 10-1983 to Jubb, breaker, Drighlington.

m   1016, 1019-20, 1022, 1026, 1031, 1035, 1041, 1048-9 to K. Askin, Barnsley, 3-1981. 1016, 1022, 1031 and 1049 to Jones (Carlton Metals), in 1-1982, 10-1981, 9-1981 and 5-1981 respectively. 1041 and 1048 to J. Sykes, Carlton, 5-1981.

n   1021 and 1036 to PVS, Carlton, 9-1983, for scrap.

o   1023 sold at Central Motor Auctions, Rothwell, 18-12-1980 to T. Wigley, Carlton, for scrap.

p   1025, 1027, 1037 sold at Central Motor Auctions, Rothwell, 25-9-1980. 1025 and 1037 to T. Wigley, Carlton. 1027 to Wombwell Diesels Ltd. by 12-1980, all for scrap.

r   1028, 1030, 1040, 1042, 1044 sold at Central Motor Auctions, Rothwell, 26-2-1981. 1028 to T. Wigley, Carlton. 1030 to J. Sykes, Carlton, 1042 to K. Askin, Barnsley, then Jones (Carlton Metals) for scrap.

s   1029 sold at Central Motor Auctions, Rothwell, 28-7-1983 to T. Goodwin, Carlton, then to Jones (Carlton Metals).

t   1032-3, 1043 to J. Sykes, Carlton. 3-1981, for scrap.

u   1034 to Transport and General Workers Union for use on publicity and recruitment duties, 3-1981, then to Kennedy Film   Services, Morley, 5-1987. To Morris, breaker, Carlton, 6-1989.

v   1038-9 and 1045 sold at Central Motor Auctions, Rothwell, 25-6-1981. 1038 to PVS, Carlton, for scrap.

w   1046 to P.V.S. (Laverick), Carlton, 12-1980, for scrap.

x   1047 to T. Wigley, Carlton, 12-1980, for scrap.

y   1050 sold at Central Motor Auctions, Rothwell, 24-1-1982 to Thornton & Lloyd, Cundy Cross, Barnsley.

1969

Daimler Fleetline CRG6LXB Gardner 6LXB 10·75 litre engine, Daimatic transmission.   Cost £9,106 2s.6d. each.
Charles H. Roe Ltd. H45/33D bodies. 8ft. 2 1/2in. wide x 33ft. 0in. long.   Unladen weight 9 tons 19 cwt 2 qrs.

No.	Regn. No.	Chassis No.	In Service	Withdrawn	Disposal	Notes
161	UNW 161H	63483	17-9-1969	30-7-1981	a	
162	UNW 162H	63484	1-10-1969	31-3-1981	b	
163	UNW 163H	63485	1-10-1969	31-3-1981	b	
164	UNW 164H	63486	15-9-1969	30-11-1981	c	
165	UNW 165H	63487	1-10-1969	18-8-1981	d	
166	UNW 166H	63488	13-10-1969	22-10-1981	e	
167	UNW 167H	63489	2-10-1969	15-9-1979	f	Withdrawn due to fire damage
168	UNW 168H	63490	3-11-1969	5-1-1983	g	
169	UNW 169H	63491	7-11-1969	30-9-1981	h	
170	UNW 170H	63492	3-11-1969	30-1-1981	j	
171	UNW 171H	63493	1-10-1969	16-4-1981	d	
172	UNW 172H	63494	14-10-1969	10-2-1982	k	
173	UNW 173H	63495	7-9-1969	7-7-1982	c	
174	UNW 174H	63496	1-10-1969	15-10-1980	l	
175	UNW 175H	63497	29-10-1969	25-9-1981	k	
176	UNW 176H	63498	3-10-1969	27-4-1981	c	
177	UNW 177H	63499	30-10-1969	31-3-1982	m	
178	UNW 178H	63500	11-9-1969	30-10-1980	l	
179	UNW 179H	63501	14-9-1969	30-6-1983	n	
180	UNW 180H	63502	10-9-1969	22-1-1981	j	

Unlike 155-160, this series of buses had semi-automatic transmission.

161-180 passed to the West Yorkshire Passenger Transport Executive on 1-4-1974.

a   161 to J. Sykes, Carlton, 1-1982 for scrap.

b   162 and 163 to Kirklees, withdrawn 31-3-1981 by Kirklees. Sold at Central Motor Auctions, Rothwell, 28-4-1983. 162 to PVS Carlton, 163 to T. Wigley, breaker, Carlton.

c   164, 173 and 176 to D, Rollinson, Carlton, 8-1982.

d   165 and 171 to unknown breaker 1981.

e   166 to T. Rollinson, Carlton, by 3-1982.

f   167 cannibalised for spares then to unknown breaker 1980.

g   168 sold at Central Motor Auctions 28-7-1983 to PVS, Carlton, then to Jones (Carlton Metals) for scrap.

h   169 sold at Central Motor Auctions, Rothwell, 24-11-1983.

j   170 and 180 sold to C.F. Booth, Rotherham, 3-1981.

k   172 and 175 sold at Central Motor Auctions, Rothwell, 27-5-1982. 172 to Parton & Allen, dealers, Carlton,

l   174 and 178 sold at Central Motor Auctions, Rothwell, 18-12-1980. 178 to T. Wigley, breaker, Carlton.

m   177 sold at Central Motor Auctions, Rothwell, 28-10-1982 to T. Wigley, breaker, Carlton.

n   179 to T. Wigley, Carlton, by 10-1983 for scrap.

1970

Leyland Atlantean PDR2.1 0·680 engine, pneumocyclic gears, air brakes.　　　　　Cost £8,704 19s.0d. each.
Charles H. Roe Ltd./ Park Royal H45/33D bodies 8ft. 2 ¹/2in. wide x 33ft.0in. long.　　Unladen weight 9 tons 13 cwt 3 qrs.

No.	Regn. No.	Chassis No.	In Service	Withdrawn	Disposal	Notes
386	UNW 386H	901599	13-2-1970	24-4-1981	a	
387	UNW 387H	901600	18-2-1970	29-6-1981	a	
388	UNW 388H	901601	20-2-1970	30-11-1981	b	
389	UNW 389H	901658	29-1-1970	29-6-1981	b	
390	UNW 390H	901659	6-2-1970	30-11-1981	c	
391	UNW 391H	901774	12-2-1970	29-6-1981	c	
392	UNW 392H	901775	6-2-1970	29-6-1981	a	
393	UNW 393H	901776	21-1-1970	4-1-1981	d	Withdrawn after accident
394	UNW 394H	901777	30-1-1970	31-3-1982	c	
395	UNW 395H	901778	26-1-1970	31-3-1982	c	
396	UNW 396H	901892	28-1-1970	30-7-1981	c	
397	UNW 397H	901893	19-1-1970	30-7-1981	c	
398	UNW 398H	901894	14-2-1970	23-4-1981	a	
399	UNW 399H	901895	2-2-1970	30-7-1981	c	
400	UNW 400H	901948	11-1-1970	7-11-1980	e	A
401	UNW 401H	902093	14-1-1970	31-10-1980		A, B
402	UNW 402H	902094	6-1-1970	31-10-1980		A, B
403	UNW 403H	902095	13-1-1970	17-10-1980		A, B
404	UNW 404H	902096	19-1-1970	23-10-1980		A, B
405	UNW 405H	902097	1-1-1970	26-6-1981	c	A

386-405 were the first Leylands to be delivered with front entrance/centre exit bodies.
386-405 passed to the West Yorkshire Passenger Transport Executive on 1-4-1974.

A　400-405 had spring brakes in place of the normal hand brakes.

B　401-4 sold to Ipswich Borough Transport 19-11-1980 becoming 41-44. Withdrawn 7-1985, 2-1983, 2-1986 and 4-1986 respectively. 41 and 44 then to I.T.T. Training Services Ltd., Mendlesham, Suffolk, 8-1985 and 7-1986 resp. 42 to Mills, dealer, Holesley, 12-1983 and 43 to Ipswich Co-op Silver Spinners by 4-1987. Renamed Ipswich Silver Spinners 1993, then De Vere Show Corps, Earls Colne, 10-1994, Roberts, Cromer 4-1997, then to Danny Chaband, France, 9-1999, for use as a mobile showroom. Then to La Femme du Buisson (dance and theatre group), Noisiel, Mame-La-Vallee (near Euro Disney).

a　386-7, 392 and 398 sold at Central Motor Auctions, Rothwell, 24-1-1982. 387 to Thornton & Lloyd, Cundy Cross, Barnsley. 392 to Smith, Sacriston, Co. Durham, 3-1982 to PVS, Carlton by 10-1984. 398 to T.Wigley, Carlton, 2-1982.

b　388 sold at Central Motor Auctions, Rothwell, 27-5-1982 and 389 ditto on 25-2-1982.

c　390-1, 394-7, 399 and 405 sold at Central Motor Auctions, Rothwell, 22-7-1982. 390 to D, Rollinson, Carlton, 391 and 396 to Whiting, dealer, Carlton, 394-5 and 405 to T.Wigley, Carlton, for scrap. 397 and 399 to Parton & Allen, Carlton.

d　393 sold at Central Motor Auctions, Rothwell, 25-6-1981 to unknown breaker.

e　400 sold at Central Motor Auctions, Rothwell, 26-2-1981.

1970

Daimler Fleetline SRG6LXB-36, Gardner 6LXB engine, semi-automatic transmission.　　Cost £8,100 4s.0d. each.
Park Royal B48D bodies 8ft. 2 ¹/2in. wide x 36ft. 0in. long.　　　　Unladen weight 8 tons 12 cwt 0 qrs.

No.	Regn. No.	Chassis No.	In Service	Withdrawn	Disposal	Notes
1201	UNW 201H	63370	16-1-1970	28-5-1981	a	Body No. 56465
1202	UNW 202H	63371	16-1-1970	29-3-1983	b	Body No. 56466
1203	UNW 203H	63372	2-2-1970	19-5-1981	a	Body No. 56467
1204	UNW 204H	63373	15-1-1970	19-12-1980	c	Body No. 56464
1205	UNW 205H	63374	2-2-1970	27-5-1981	d	Body No. 56468
1206	UNW 206H	63375	2-2-1970	28-5-1981	d	Body No. 56469
1207	UNW 207H	63376	2-2-1970	15-4-1982	e	Body No. 56470
1208	UNW 208H	63377	2-2-1970	31-8-1983	f	Body No. 56471
1209	UNW 209H	63378	3-2-1970	28-5-1981	g	Body No. 56472
1210	UNW 210H	63379	2-2-1970	26-9-1984	g	Body No. 56473
1211	UNW 211H	63380	2-2-1970	24-6-1981	d	Body No. 56474
1212	UNW 212H	63381	2-2-1970	20-5-1981	e	Body No. 56475
1213	UNW 213H	63382	3-2-1970	12-5-1981	a	Body No. 56476
1214	UNW 214H	63383	2-2-1970	28-5-1981	b	Body No. 56477
1215	UNW 215H	63384	2-2-1970	2-3-1983	h	Body No. 56478
1216	UNW 216H	63385	1-3-1970	30-1-1984	j	Body No. 56479
1217	UNW 217H	63386	17-1-1970	27-5-1981	k	Body No. 56463
1218	UNW 218H	63387	1-3-1970	28-5-1981	d	Body No. 56480
1219	UNW 219H	63388	1-3-1970	22-5-1981	a	Body No. 56481
1220	UNW 220H	63389	1-3-1970	28-5-1981	g	Body No. 56482
1221	UNW 221H	63390	1-3-1970	30-12-1982	l	Body No. 56483
1222	UNW 222H	63391	2-3-1970	30-12-1982	m	Body No. 56484
1223	UNW 223H	63392	4-3-1970	28-5-1981	b	Body No. 56485
1224	UNW 224H	63393	2-3-1970	16-4-1981	d	Body No. 56486
1225	UNW 225H	63394	18-3-1970	27-1-1984	n	Body No. 56487
1226	UNW 226H	63395	1-3-1970	27-5-1981	d	Body No. 56488
1227	UNW 227H	63396	4-3-1970	27-5-1981	d	Body No. 56489

No.	Regn. No.	Chassis No.	In Service	Withdrawn	Disposal	Notes
1228	UNW 228H	63397	2-3-1970	11-5-1981	d	Body No. 56490
1229	UNW 229H	63398	2-3-1970	28-5-1981	d	Body No. 56491
1230	UNW 230H	63399	1-3-1970	11-12-1982	o	Body No. 56492

1201-1230 passed to the West Yorkshire Passenger Transport Executive on 1-4-1974.

a 1201, 1203, 1213 and 1219 to D. Rollinson, Carlton, 1-1982 for scrap.

b 1202, 1214 and 1223 sold at Central Motor Auctions, Rothwell, 24-11-1983. 1202 and 1223 to Thornton, Barnsley.

c 1204 to K. Askin, Barnsley, 3-1981, for scrap.

d 1205-6, 1211, 1218, 1224, 1226-9 sold at Central Motor Auctions, Rothwell, 24-1-1982. 1205, 1211, and 1224 to
   A. Barraclough, Carlton. 1206 and 1228 to P.V.S., Carlton. 1226 to PVS. Carlton, then to Whiting, Carlton, later in
   2-1982.

e 1207 and 1212 sold Central Motor Auctions, Rothwell, 28-10-1982, 1207 to Carlton Metals, 1212 to PVS., Carlton.

f 1208 with PVS, Carlton, by 4-1986, for scrap.

g 1209-10 and 1220 to unknown breakers.

h 1215 to T. Wigley, Carlton, by 10-1983 for scrap.

j 1216 sold at Central Motor Auctions, Rothwell, 12-4-1984 to Wombwell Diesels Co. for scrap.

k 1217 to PVS, Carlton, by 10-1983, for scrap.

l 1221 to T.Wigley, Carlton, by 12-1983 for scrap.

m 1222 to Rollinson, Carlton, by 10-1983 for scrap.

n 1225 to West Midlands P.T.E. on behalf Rotary Clubs. 13-2-1984. Overhauled and sent to Tanzania for use by the
   Buguniri School for the Deaf, sponsored by Dar Es Salaam North Rotary Club.

o 1230 sold at Central Motor Auctions, Rothwell, 28-7-1983 to PVS. Carlton, breakers.

1970

Daimler Fleetline CRG6LXB   Gardner 6LXB 10·75 litre engine, Daimatic transmission.   Cost £10,901 2s.6d. each.

Charles H. Roe Ltd. H45/33D bodies. 8ft. 2 1/2in. wide x 33ft. 0in. long.   Unladen weight 9 tons 19 cwt 2 qrs.

No.	Regn. No.	Chassis No.	In Service	Withdrawn	Disposal	Notes
181	UNW 181H	63503	11-3-1970	29-9-1981	a	
182	UNW 182H	63504	10-4-1970	22-11-1981	b	
183	UNW 183H	63505	14-4-1970	12-11-1982	c	
184	UNW 184H	63506	12-5-1970	28-6-1984	d	
185	UNW 185H	63507	1-4-1970	30-1-1984	e	
186	UNW 186H	63508	1-4-1970	30-11-1981	f	
187	UNW 187H	63509	5-4-1970	31-1-1984	g	
188	UNW 188H	63510	18-3-1970	20-6-1984	d	
189	UNW 189H	63511	2-5-1970	26-7-1983	a	
190	UNW 190H	63512	12-5-1970	31-1-1984	g	
191	UNW 191H	63513	1-4-1970	4-11-1983	h	
192	UNW 192H	63514	1-4-1970	30-11-1981	f	
193	UNW 193H	63515	11-4-1970	9-9-1981	b	
194	UNW 194H	63516	1-4-1970	22-2-1983	j	
195	UNW 195H	63517	12-3-1970	28-6-1984	a	
196	UNW 196H	63518	9-3-1970	14-6-1984	d	
197	UNW 197H	63519	17-3-1970	14-3-1983	j	
198	UNW 198H	63520	1-4-1970	28-2-1983	k	
199	UNW 199H	63521	1-4-1970	25-2-1983	m	
200	UNW 200H	63522	1-4-1970	10-1-1984	h	

181-200 passed to the West Yorkshire Passenger Transport Executive 1-4-1974.

a 181, 189 and 195 to unknown breakers.

b 182 and 193 sold at Central Motor Auctions, Rothwell, 28-10-1982. 182 to T. Wigley, breaker, Carlton.

c 183 sold at Central Motor Auctions 28-4-1983 to PVS. Carlton, for scrap.

d 184, 188 and 196 to Rollinson, Carlton, by 6-1985 for scrap.

e 185 to Hardwick, breaker, Carlton, 6-1985.

f 186 and 192 sold at Central Motor Auctions, Rothwell, 27-5-1982 to Parton & Allen, dealers, Carlton, then to T.
   Goodwin, Carlton, by 6-1982. 192 then to Whiting Bros., Carlton.

g 187 and 190 sold at Central Motor Auctions 12-4-1984 to W. North (P.V.) Ltd. Sherburn-in-Elmet, 190 then to Parton &
   Allen, Carlton, 9-1984, then to Sefton, Carlton, by 10-1984 and scrapped.

h 191 and 200 sold at Central Motor Auctions, Rothwell, 23-2-1984. 191 to Thornton, Barnsley, 200 to Meynell, Carlton.

j 194 and 197 sold at Central Motor Auctions 28-7-1983, to T. Wigley, Carlton, breakers.

m 198 sold at Central Motor Auctions, Rothwell, 24-11-1983 to Rollinson, Carlton, for scrap.

n 199 to Thornton, Cundy Cross, Barnsley, 9-1983 for scrap.

1970

Leyland Atlantean PDR2.1 0·680 engine, fully automatic transmission, air brakes.   Cost £ 9,680 19s.4d. each.

Charles H. Roe Ltd. H45/33D bodies 8ft. 2 1/2in. wide x 33ft.0in. long.   Unladen weight 9 tons 11 cwt 0 qrs

No.	Regn. No.	Chassis No.	In Service	Withdrawn	Disposal	Notes
406	UNW 406H	7000274	26-7-1970	25-3-1983	a	
407	UNW 407H	7000275	1-7-1970	24-2-1983	b	
408	UNW 408H	7000387	26-7-1970	15-4-1983	a	
409	UNW 409H	7000388	1-7-1970	29-4-1983	a	
410	UNW 410H	7000427	29-7-1970	12-5-1983	a	
411	UNW 411H	7000428	27-7-1970	18-1-1984	c	
412	UNW 412H	7000494	1-7-1970	11-2-1983	a	

No.	Regn. No.	Chassis No.	In Service	Withdrawn	Disposal	Notes
413	UNW 413H	7000495	27-7-1970	30-3-1984	d	
414	UNW 414H	7000588	1-7-1970	29-3-1983	e	
415	UNW 415H	7000589	27-7-1970	31-12-1982	f	A
416	UNW 416H	7000905	1-7-1970	31-8-1984	g	
417	UNW 417H	7000906	26-7-1970	5-7-1983	b	
418	UNW 418H	7001226	1-7-1970	2-2-1984	h	
419	UNW 419H	7001227	27-7-1970	21-8-1984	g	
420	UNW 420H	7001278	26-7-1970	31-12-1982	j	
421	UNW 421H	7001279	1-7-1970	30-3-1984	k	
422	UNW 422H	7001482	1-7-1970	9-2-1984	h	
423	UNW 423H	7001483	1-7-1970	29-3-1984	b	
424	UNW 424H	7001503	2-7-1970	31-12-1982	j	
425	UNW 425H	7002813	1-7-1970	26-6-1983	l	

A 415 in Huddersfield Commercial Vehicle Parade 26-7-1970.

   406-425 passed to the West Yorkshire Passenger Transport Executive on 1-4-1974.

a 406, 408-410 and 412 sold at Central Motor Auctions, Rothwell, 2-7-1983. 406 and 408-410 to T. Wigley, breaker, Carlton. 412 to PVS, Carlton for scrap.

b 407, 417 and 423 to unknown breakers.

c 411 sold at Central Motor Auctions, Rothwell, 23-2-1984 to T. Wigley, Carlton, for scrap.

d 413 to Hardwick, breaker, Carlton, 6-1985.

e 414 to Thornton, Cundy Cross, Barnsley, 9-1983, for scrap.

f 415 sold at Central Motor Auctions, Rothwell, 24-11-1983.

g 416 and 419 to Cranes and Commercials Exports Ltd, Western Docks, Southampton, then shipped to Australia, in 12-1984.

h 418 and 422 sold at Central Motor Auctions. Rothwell, 12-4-1984. 418 to Rollinson, Carlton.

j 420 and 424 sold at Central Motor Auctions, Rothwell, 28-4-1983.

k 421 to Wombwell Diesels Co. Ltd. 6-1985.

l 425 to Morris dealer, Carlton, 10-1983, then to T. Goodwin, Carlton. 11-1983.

1970

Leyland Atlantean PDR2.1 0·680 engine, fully automatic transmission, air brakes.   Cost £10,854 7s.9d. each.

Charles H. Roe Ltd. H45/33D bodies 8ft. 2 1/2in. wide x 33ft.0in. long.   Unladen weight 9 tons 11 cwt 0 qrs.

No.	Regn. No.	Chassis No.	In Service	Withdrawn	Disposal	Notes
426	XUM 426J	7002813	6-10-1970	31-1-1984	a	
427	XUM 427J	7002840	19-9-1970	31-8-1984	b	Learner H350 from 1-1985. A
428	XUM 428J	7002841	19-10-1970	14-1-1983	c	B
429	XUM 429J	7003049	19-9-1970	28-3-1984	d	
430	XUM 430J	7003050	3-10-1970	17-9-1981	e	Withdrawn after accident.
431	XUM 431J	7003062	20-9-1970	31-1-1984	a	
432	XUM 432J	7003063	21-9-1970	30-4-1984	f	
433	XUM 433J	7003064	3-10-1970	11-5-1984	d	
434	XUM 434J	7003139	3-10-1970	5-1-1987	g	
435	XUM 435J	7003140	3-10-1970	21-12-1983	h	Withdrawn after accident.
436	XUM 436J	7003051	7-11-1970	30-11-1983	h	
437	XUM 437J	7003141	11-11-1970	25-10-1982	j	
438	XUM 438J	7003239	16-11-1970	29-6-1984	k	
439	XUM 439J	7003240	11-11-1970	30-11-1982	l	
440	XUM 440J	7003241	6-11-1970	12-11-1982	l	
441	XUM 441J	7003487	16-11-1970	31-12-1982	l	
442	XUM 442J	7003488	17-11-1970	29-10-1982	j	
443	XUM 443J	7004109	1-1-1971	29-10-1982	j	
444	XUM 444J	7004210	1-1-1971	31-12-1982	l	
445	XUM 445J	7004411	1-1-1971	28-1-1983	c	

A H350 (ex-427) renumbered 9350 1-12-1985.

B 428 displayed at Earls Court, London, from 18 to 26-9-1970.

   426-445 passed to the West Yorkshire Passenger Transport Executive on 1-4-1974.

   9350 (ex-427) and 434 to Yorkshire Rider Ltd. 26-10-1986.

a 426 and 431 sold by Central Motor Auctions, Rothwell, 12-4-1984.

b H350 (ex-427) later 9350, withdrawn 20-4-1989. Sold 10-9-1990.

c 428 and 445 sold at Central Motor Auctions, Rothwell, 28-7-1983. 428 to T. Wigley, breaker, Carlton.

d 429 and 433 to unknown breakers.

e 430 sold at Central Motor Auctions, Rothwell, 24-1-1982 to A. Barraclough, Carlton.

f 432 sold by Central Motor Auctions, Rothwell, 12-7-1984 to unknown breaker.

g 434 cannibalised for spares then to PVS, Carlton, 2-1988 for scrap.

h 435 and 436 sold at Central Motor Auctions, Rothwell, 23-2-1984. 435 to Thornton, Cundy Cross, Barnsley. 436 to D Rollinson, Carlton. Both scrapped.

j 437, 442-3 sold at Central Motor Auctions 24-2-1983. 437 and 442 to T. Wigley, breaker, Carlton.

k 438 to T. Wigley, Carlton, 2-1985 for scrap.

l 439-441, and 444 sold at Central Motor Auctions, Rothwell, 28-4-1983. 439, 441 and 444 to A, Barraclough, breaker, Carlton. 440 to T. Wigley, then to A. Barraclough, breaker, Carlton.

1970

Mercedes Benz L406D/35R minibuses   Cost £3,195 each.
Deansgate B13F bodies (9 standing) by Williams Motor Co. (Manchester) Ltd. Unladen weight 2 tons 13 cwt 1 qr. (30),
2 tons 12 cwt 1 qr. (31 and 32), 2 tons 12 cwt 0 qrs, (33-35).

No.	Regn. No.	Chassis No.	In Service	Withdrawn	Disposal	Notes
30	YUA 530J	048290	30-11-1970	5-8-1976	a	A
31	YUA 531J	049263	23-11-1970	5-8-1976	b	
32	YUA 532J	048746	30-11-1970	5-8-1976	b	
33	YUA 533J	048782	30-11-1970	23-8-1976	c, b	
34	YUA 534J	049101	30-11-1970	5-8-1976	b	
35	YUA 535J	049349	23-12-1970	5-4-1974	b	

A   30 exhibited at the Commercial Motor Show, Earl's Court, London, from 18 to 26-9-1970.
    30-35 passed to the West Yorkshire Passenger Transport Executive on 1-4-1974.
a   30 transferred by WYPTE to Hansons, Huddersfield, 1-8-1975, back to Leeds 11-1975 then to service fleet 8-1976.
    It was kept in Sovereign Street Yard, little used, and sold by auction at Central Motor Auctions, Rothwell, on 22-2-1979
    to L. Allen, Galley Fields Trading Estate, Abingdon. Exported to Sri Lanka in 5-1979. No further information.
b   31-35 to Paul Sykes, dealer, Barnsley, 3-1977, all broken up 7-1977.
c   33 on loan to West Riding Automobile Co. Ltd. 23-8-1976 to 8-11-1976 then withdrawn and returned to Leeds.

1971

Leyland Atlantean PDR2.1 0·680 engine, fully automatic transmission, air brakes.   Cost £11,897·32p each.
Charles H. Roe Ltd. H45/33D bodies 8ft. 2 1/2in. wide x 33ft.0in. long.   Unladen weight 9 tons 11 cwt 0 qrs.

No.	Regn. No.	Chassis No.	In Service	Withdrawn	Disposal	Notes
446	ANW 446J	7004110	1-2-1971	31-12-1982	a	
447	ANW 447J	7004111	5-1-1971	20-11-1982	b	
448	ANW 448J	7004277	1-2-1971	12-11-1982	b	
449	ANW 449J	7004278	1-2-1971	31-8-1984	b	
450	ANW 450J	7004412	1-2-1971	31-8-1984	c	
451	ANW 451J	7004413	1-2-1971	31-8-1984	c	
452	ANW 452J	7004573	1-2-1971	13-11-1982	a	
453	ANW 453J	7004574	1-2-1971	10-2-1983	d	
454	ANW 454J	7004575	1-2-1971	30-1-1984	e	
455	ANW 455J	7004670	13-1-1971	29-9-1982	f	
456	ANW 456J	7004671	1-3-1971	31-12-1982	g	
457	ANW 457J	7004672	5-3-1971	19-5-1982	h	
458	ANW 458J	7100163	13-3-1971	19-1-1983	j	
459	ANW 459J	7100012	1-3-1971	8-3-1983	k	
460	ANW 460J	7100013	1-3-1971	14-1-1983	l	
461	ANW 461J	7100014	10-3-1971	19-3-1983	m	
462	ANW 462J	7100110	1-3-1971	31-8-1984	c	
463	ANW 463J	7100111	1-3-1971	21-1-1983	l	
464	ANW 464J	7100112	1-3-1971	17-8-1984	c	
465	ANW 465J	7100164	1-3-1971	6-3-1987	n	

    446 to 465 passed to the West Yorkshire Passenger Transport Executive 1-4-1974.
    465 to Yorkshire Rider Ltd. 26-10-1986.
a   446 and 452 sold at Central Motor Auctions, Rothwell, 28-4-1983.   452 to A. Barraclough, breaker, Carlton.
b   447-9 to unknown breakers.
c   450-1, 462 and 464 to Cranes and Commercials Exports Ltd. Western Docks, Southampton, for export to Australia,
    11-1984. 451 and 462 shipped to Australia 12-1984. 450 ditto 1-1985.
d   453 to PVS, Carlton 9-1983 for scrap.
e   454 sold at Central Motor Auctions, Rothwell, 12-4-1984.
f   455 sold at Central Motor Auctions, Rothwell, 24-2-1983 to T. Wigley, breaker, Carlton.
g   456 to Morris, dealer, Carlton, then to T.Goodwin, Carlton, 8-1983.
h   457 sold at Central Motor Auctions, Rothwell, 28-10-1982 to T. Thornton, Cundy Cross, Barnsley.
j   458 to Lloyd, Cundy Cross, Barnsley, 9-1983.
k   459 noted at Central Motor Auctions, Rothwell, 12-1990.
l   460 and 463 sold at Central Motor Auctions, Rothwell, 28-7-1983. 460 to T. Wigley, Carlton. 463 to PVS, Carlton.
m   461 to Morris, Carlton, for scrap.
n   465 to Ensign, dealer, Purfleet. 9-1987, then to PVS, Carlton, 5-1988, for scrap.

1971

A.E.C. Swift   AH 691 11·3 litre engine fully automatic transmission.   Cost £9,034·68p each.
Charles H. Roe Ltd. B48D bodies. 8ft. 2 1/2in. wide x 36 ft.0in. long.   Unladen weight 7 tons 17cwt 1 qr.

No.	Regn. No.	Chassis No.	In Service	Withdrawn	Disposal	Notes
1051	AUB 151J	5P2R946	2-6-1971	17-1-1983	a	
1052	AUB 152J	5P2R947	2-6-1971	29-8-1984	b	
1053	AUB 153J	5P2R948	1-7-1971	31-8-1984	c	
1054	AUB 154J	5P2R949	1-7-1971	7-2-1984	d	
1055	AUB 155J	5P2R950	2-6-1971	31-8-1984	e	
1056	AUB 156J	5P2R951	2-6-1971	29-6-1984	b	
1057	AUB 157J	5P2R952	12-7-1971	6-4-1984	f	
1058	AUB 158J	5P2R953	1-7-1971	31-8-1984	e	
1059	AUB 159J	5P2R954	9-7-1971	31-8-1984	e	

No.	Regn. No.	Chassis No.	In Service	Withdrawn	Disposal	Notes
1060	AUB 160J	5P2R955	1-7-1971	27-9-1984	e	
1061	AUB 161J	5P2R956	8-7-1971	28-9-1984	e	
1062	AUB 162J	5P2R957	2-6-1971	31-8-1984	e	
1063	AUB 163J	5P2R958	2-6-1971	14-9-1984	e	
1064	AUB 164J	5P2R959	2-6-1971	28-9-1984	e	
1065	AUB 165J	5P2R960	7-6-1971	26-9-1984	e	
1066	AUB 166J	5P2R961	1-7-1961	31-8-1984	e	
1067	AUB 167J	5P2R962	3-7-1971	7-7-1984	g	
1068	AUB 168J	5P2R963	1-7-1971	20-12-1984	h	
1069	AUB 169J	5P2R964	23-7-1971	31-8-1984	j	
1070	AUB 170J	5P2R965	9-7-1971	22-2-1985	k	

1051 to 1070 passed to the West Yorkshire Passenger Transport Executive on 1-4-1974.

a   1051 sold at Central Motor Auctions, Rothwell, 28-7-1983 to Jones (Carlton Metals), Carlton, for scrap.

b   1052 and 1056 to unknown breaker 1984.

c   1053 sold to Kennedy's Film Services, Morley, 10-1984. To Morris, breaker, Carlton, by 6-1989.

d   1054 sold at Central Motor Auctions, Rothwell, 12-4-1984 to Rollinson, Carlton, for scrap.

e   1055, 1058-1066 to Cranes and Commercials Exports Ltd. Western Docks, Southampton, for export to Australia. 11-84.

f   1057 sold at Central Motor Auctions, Rothwell, 12-7-1984.

g   1067 to D.C. Morris Commercials, Monk Bretton. 2-1985.

h   1068 to Rollinson, breaker, Carlton, by 5-1986.

j   1069 to Royds School, Oulton, 11-1984. Repainted in blue and cream livery, then to J. Sykes, Carlton, by 2-1986.

k   1070 the last Leeds A.E.C. ,to Ouse Gliding Club, Rufforth, 4-1985. Derelict at Ebor Trucks, Acaster Malbis, 2001.

1971

Leyland Atlantean PDR2.1 0·680 engine, fully automatic transmission, air brakes.   Cost £11,521·60p each.
Charles H. Roe Ltd. H45/33D bodies 8ft. 2 ¹/2in. wide x 33ft.0in. long.   Unladen weight 9 tons 14 cwt 1 qr.

No.	Regn. No.	Chassis No.	In Service	Withdrawn	Disposal	Notes
466	DUA 466K	7101725	20-10-1971	31-12-1982	a	
467	DUA 467K	7101863	2-10-1971	16-4-1988	b	
468	DUA 468K	7101864	1-10-1971	23-9-1988	c	
469	DUA 469K	7101865	1-10-1971	26-10-1982	a	
470	DUA 470K	7102021	1-10-1971	31-3-1988	b	
471	DUA 471K	7102022	1-10-1971	5-9-1988	d	
472	DUA 472K	7102023	1-10-1971	31-10-1987	b	
473	DUA 473K	7102308	1-10-1971	5-9-1988	e	
474	DUA 474K	7102309	18-10-1971	24-12-1987	b	
475	DUA 475K	7102310	1-10-1971	31-10-1987	b	
476	DUA 476K	7102400	6-9-1971	21-5-1988	f	
477	DUA 477K	7102401	18-10-1971	31-8-1984	g	
478	DUA 478K	7102402	13-10-1971	2-11-1988	c	
479	DUA 479K	7102465	7-10-1971	31-8-1984	g	
480	DUA 480K	7102679	1-10-1971	30-10-1987	b	
481	DUA 481K	7102680	25-10-1971	26-10-1987	b	
482	DUA 482K	7102681	6-9-1971	17-6-1988	f	
483	DUA 483K	7102781	3-9-1971	3-12-1987	b	
484	DUA 484K	7102782	6-9-1971	19-2-1988	b	
485	DUA 485K	7102783	6-9-1971	4-10-1988	c	
486	DUA 486K	7102924	1-10-1971	27-1-1988	b	
487	DUA 487K	7102925	12-10-1971	30-10-1987	b	
488	DUA 488K	7102926	6-9-1971	11-7-1988	c	
489	DUA 489K	7103196	1-10-1971	31-1-1984	h	
490	DUA 490K	7103197	6-10-1971	31-10-1987	b	
491	DUA 491K	7103198	2-10-1971	24-12-1987	b	
492	DUA 492K	7103199	1-10-1971	24-12-1987	b	
493	DUA 493K	7103200	1-10-1971	31-10-1987	b	
494	DUA 494K	7103201	12-10-1971	31-8-1984	j	
495	DUA 495K	7103202	12-10-1971	31-8-1984	k	

466-495 passed to the West Yorkshire Passenger Transport Executive on 1-4-1974.

467-468, 470-476, 478, 480-488, 490-493 to Yorkshire Rider Ltd. 26-10-1986.

a   466 sold by Central Motor Auctions, Rothwell, 28-7-1983 to PVS Carlton, breakers. 469 ditto to T. Wigley 24-2-1983.

b   467, 470, 472, 474, 475, 480-1, 483-4, 486-7, 490-3 sold at British Car Auctions, Brighouse, 27-4-1988. 467, 470, 474, 480, 481, 483, 490 and 492 to PVS, Carlton, for scrap. 472, 475, 486-7, and 493 to T. Wigley, Carlton, for scrap.

c   468, 478, 485, 488 sold at British Car Auctions, Brighouse, 23-11-1988. 478 to PVS, Carlton, for scrap. 485 and 488 to T. Wigley, Carlton, for scrap.

d   471 converted by Yorkshire Rider into mobile lounge for National Express, Birmingham, for use at Victoria Coach Station, London. Delivered 18-1-1989. To Riggott, Brierley, by 3-1993 then to T. Wigley, Carlton, by 12-4-1994 for scrap.

e   473 sold to Yorkshire Evening Post, Leeds, 1-1989 as a promotional vehicle. Extant 2007.

f   476 and 482 sold at British Car Auctions, Brighouse, 6-7-1988. 482 to T. Goodwin, Carlton, for scrap.

g   477 and 479 to Cranes and Commercial Exports Ltd. Western Docks, Southampton, for export to Australia, 1-1985. Shipped 2-1985.

h   489 sold at Central Motor Auctions, Rothwell, 12-4-1984.

j   494 to Ripley, breaker, Carlton, by 6-1986.

k   495 sold to Merseyside Health Authority as mobile instructional unit 13-10-1984.

1972-3

Daimler Fleetline CRL6-33, Leyland 0·680 engine   spring parking brake,   Cost £12,931·72p each.
Charles H. Roe H45/33D bodies   8ft. 2 1/2in. wide x 33ft.0in. long.   Unladen weight 10 tons 0 cwt 1qr.

No.	Regn. No.	Chassis No.	In Service	Withdrawn	Disposal	Notes
751	JUM 201L	65563	16-9-1972	19-2-1985	a	Renumbered 201 3-1974
752	JUM 202L	65564	19-9-1972	31-8-1984	b	Renumbered 202 3-1974
753	JUM 203L	65565	27-9-1972	25-3-1985	c	Renumbered 203 3-1974
754	JUM 204L	65566	28-9-1972	27-2-1985	c	Renumbered 204 3-1974
755	JUM 205L	65567	22-12-1972	6-6-1985	d	Renumbered 205 3-1974
756	JUM 206L	65568	8-12-1972	15-8-1985	e	Renumbered 206 3-1974
757	JUM 207L	65569	9-1-1973	31-8-1984	f	Renumbered 207 3-1974
758	JUM 208L	65570	8-12-1972	31-8-1984	g	Renumbered 208 3-1974
759	JUM 209L	65571	10-10-1972	12-2-1985	h	Renumbered 209 3-1974
760	JUM 210L	65572	3-10-1972	31-8-1984	j	Renumbered 210 3-1974
761	JUM 211L	65573	1-11-1972	15-1-1985	k	A Renumbered 211 3-1974
762	JUM 212L	65574	28-9-1972	20-8-1984	b	Renumbered 212 3-1974
763	JUM 213L	65575	20-10-1972	27-2-1985	d	Renumbered 213 3-1974
764	JUM 214L	65576	29-9-1972	31-8-1984	l	Renumbered 214 3-1974
765	JUM 215L	65577	21-12-1972	2-2-1985	a	Renumbered 215 3-1974
766	JUM 216L	65578	19-12-1972	31-12-1983	m	Renumbered 216 3-1974
767	JUM 217L	65579	4-1-1973	27-2-1985	n	Renumbered 217 3-1974
768	JUM 218L	65580	23-10-1972	22-8-1984	g	Renumbered 218 3-1974
769	JUM 219L	65581	20-10-1972	14-1-1985	a	Renumbered 219 3-1974
770	JUM 220L	65582	11-10-1972	26-2-1985	j	Renumbered 220 3-1974
771	JUM 221L	65583	8-12-1972	20-8-1984	j	Renumbered 221 3-1974
772	JUM 222L	65584	8-1-1973	12-10-1984	b	Renumbered 222 3-1974
773	JUM 223L	65585	2-1-1973	14-11-1984	o	Renumbered 223 3-1974
774	JUM 224L	65586	19-12-1972	27-2-1985	l	Renumbered 224 3-1974
775	JUM 225L	65587	6-10-1972	16-1-1985	j	Renumbered 225 3-1974
776	JUM 226L	65588	16-10-1972	3-10-1984	j	Renumbered 226 3-1974
777	JUM 227L	65589	28-12-1972	13-3-1985	a	Renumbered 227 3-1974
778	JUM 228L	65590	21-12-1972	8-1-1985	p	Renumbered 228 3-1974
779	JUM 229L	65591	8-1-1973	27-2-1985	q	Renumbered 229 3-1974
780	JUM 230L	65592	19-12-1972	19-6-1985	d	Renumbered 230 3-1974

A 761 exhibited at the Commercial Motor Show, Earl's Court, London, 22 to 30-9-1972.
  201-230 passed to the West Yorkshire Passenger Transport Executive on 1-4-1974.
a 201, 215, 219 and 227 to PVS Ltd. Carlton, 7-1985, all for scrap.
b 202, 212 and 222 after withdrawal destroyed by fire at Torre Road Garage 16-11-1984. Cut up on site by Askin, of Barnsley, between 26-11-1984 and 4-12-1984.
c 203 and 204 to Rollinson, Carlton, by 9-1985 and 2-1987 respectively for scrap.
d 205, 213 and 230 to Ripley, Carlton, 10-1985 for scrap.
e 206 to PVS, Carlton, 9-1986 for scrap.
f 207 to Ripley, Carlton, by 6-1985 for scrap.
g 208 and 218 sold to Merseyside Health Authority for use as mobile instructional units 13-10-1984.
h 209 converted into a playbus in Halifax 6-1986.
j 210, 220, 221, 225 and 226 to unknown breakers.
k 211 to Hartwood Exports Ltd., Barnsley. 7-1985.
l 214 and 224 to Merseyside, 214 to South Sefton Health Authority 4-1985. 224 to Merseyside Area Health Authority 3-1985, then to Dumbarton District Council 2-1990 as a mobile health promotion unit.
m 216 withdrawn following fire damage. Scrapped by WYPTE at Middleton Garage 10-1984.
n 217 later operated by S.J.J. Consultants (an Employment Training Organisation) by 7-1990.
o 223 to PVS, Carlton, 6-1985 for scrap.
p 228 to Wombwell Diesels Co. Ltd. 7-1985 for scrap.
q 229 sold at British Car Auctions, Brighouse, 15-3-1989.

1973

Leyland Atlantean AN68.2R 0·680 engine, air brakes.   Cost £12,271·65p each (495-515). £13,071·65p each (516-530).
Charles H. Roe Ltd. H45/33D bodies 8ft. 2 1/2in. wide x 33ft.0in. long.   Unladen weight 9 tons 17 cwt 3 qrs.

No.	Regn. No.	Chassis No.	In Service	Withdrawn	Disposal	Notes
496	JUG 496L	7201864	25-1-1973	6-4-1988	a	
497	JUG 497L	7201865	25-1-1973	21-5-1988	b	A 9-1987
498	JUG 498L	7201866	2-2-1973	30-3-1990	c	A 1987
499	JUG 499L	7201867	26-1-1973	21-5-1988	b	
500	JUG 500L	7201980	19-1-1973	21-5-1988	b	
501	JUG 501L	7201981	16-2-1973	21-12-1989	d	A 12-1988
502	JUG 502L	7201982	19-1-1973	31-3-1988	a	
503	JUG 503L	7201983	6-2-1973	30-3-1990	d	A 9-1989
504	JUG 504L	7202089	22-2-1973	26-3-1990	e	A 6-1989
505	JUG 505L	7202090	6-2-1973	21-5-1988	b	
506	JUG 506L	7202091	8-2-1973	30-3-1990	d	
507	JUG 507L	7202092	6-2-1973	30-3-1990	d	A 8-1989
508	JUG 508L	7202195	19-1-1973	12-5-1988	b	
509	JUG 509L	7202196	20-2-1973	25-6-1991	f	A 11-1988

No.	Regn. No.	Chassis No.	In Service	Withdrawn	Disposal	Notes
510	JUG 510L	7202197	13-2-1973	1-3-1990	g	A 3-1989
511	JUG 511L	7202198	22-2-1973	15-12-1992	d	A 8-1988
512	JUG 512L	7202989	2-2-1973	14-7-1988	h	To Learner bus 9373 11-4-1989
513	JUG 513L	7203037	13-2-1973	21-5-1988	j	To Learner bus 9369 12-9-1988
514	JUG 514L	7203038	2-2-1973	30-3-1990	k	A 2-1989
515	JUG 515L	7203039	2-2-1973	17-5-1990	d	A 7-1988
516	JUG 516L	7300221	30-4-1973	21-10-1988	l	To Learner bus 9375 27-4-1989
517	JUG 517L	7300222	3-5-1973	21-5-1988	m	To Learner bus 9370 23-9-1988.
518	JUG 518L	7300223	9-5-1973	15-11-1985	n	
519	JUG 519L	7300224	16-4-1973	15-11-1988	o	
520	JUG 520L	7300225	9-4-1973	15-10-1988	p	A 2-1987
521	JUG 521L	7300226	17-4-1973	28-11-1988	d	
522	JUG 522L	7300227	8-5-1973	21-5-1988	b	
523	JUG 523L	7300228	20-4-1973	21-3-1986	q	
524	JUG 524L	7300229	27-4-1973	20-9-1988	r	
525	JUG 525L	7300230	17-4-1973	26-2-1988	a	
526	JUG 526L	7300440	16-5-1973	18-2-1986	s	
527	JUG 527L	7300441	21-4-1973	31-1-1990	t	A 2-1989
528	JUG 528L	7300442	12-4-1973	28-10-1987	a	
529	JUG 529L	7300443	25-4-1973	31-10-1987	a	
530	JUG 530L	7300444	4-5-1973	31-10-1987	a	

496-530 passed to the West Yorkshire Passenger Transport Executive on 1-4-1974.
496-517, 519-522, 524-525, 527-530 to Yorkshire Rider Ltd. 26-10-1986.

A   Subsequently repainted in Yorkshire Rider livery.

a   496, 502, 525, 528-530 sold at British Car Auctions, Brighouse, 27-4-1988.   496, 529 and 530 to T. Wigley, Carlton, for scrap.   525, to PVS, Carlton, for scrap. 528 to W. North (P.V.) Ltd., Sherburn-in-Elmet, then to PVS, Carlton. 7-1988.

b   497, 499, 500, 505, 508, 522 sold at British Car Auctions, Brighouse 6-7-1988. 497, 500 and 508 to PVS, Carlton , for scrap. 505 and 522 to T. Wigley, Carlton, for scrap.

c   498 sold through A.D.T. Auctions, Belle Vue, Manchester, 22-5-1990 to W. North Ltd. Sherburn-in-Elmet, for scrap.

d   501 to PVS, Carlton, 9-2-1990. 503, 506-7, 12-4-1990. 511, 3-1993. 515, 5-1991. 521, 18-10-1989 all for scrap.

e   504 sold 2-4-1990 to Rushton, Barnsley, then to W. North, Sherburn-in-Emet 4-1990, then to PVS, Carlton, for scrap.

f   509 sold by auction in Sovereign Street Yard, Leeds, 4-7-1991 to PVS, Carlton, for scrap.

g   510 sold 26-3-1990 to Rushton, Barnsley and then to W. North, Sherburn-in-Elmet 4-1990, for scrap.

h   9373 (ex-512) withdrawn from Learner fleet 5-6-1993. To PVS, Carlton, 2-6-1993 for scrap.

j   9369 (ex-513) withdrawn 31-1-1991.

k   514 sold 22-5-1990 through A.D.T. Auctions, Belle Vue, Manchester, to Black Prince Coaches, Morley, Leeds.

l   9375 (ex-516) withdrawn from Learner use 25-6-1993.

m   9370 (ex-517) to PVS. Carlton, 1-1993 for scrap.

n   518 to unknown breaker 1986.

o   519 sold at British Car Auctions, Brighouse, 15-3-1989 to PVS, Carlton, for scrap.

p   520 donated to the National Playbus Association 28-6-1989 to Tyburn Road Works of West Midlands Travel, Birmingham, for conversion into playbus. Homebase Horticultural Therapy bus, Beech Hill, 9-1990.

q   523 to T. Wigley, Carlton, 9-1986 for scrap.

r   524 sold through British Car Auctions, Brighouse, 11-1988 to W,North, (P.V.) Ltd. Sherburn-in-Elmet by 2-1989 then to PVS, Carlton,4-1989 for scrap.

s   526 sold 9-1986 for conversion into playbus.

t   527 to Yorkshire Rider Apprentice Training School, Ludlam Street Garage, Bradford. Then to Kitson College, Leeds, 10-1990 (on loan for training purposes). To PVS, Carlton, 1-1993 for scrap.

1973

Leyland Leopard PSU3B.4 coach.   0·680 engine, pneumocyclic gears, air brakes.   Cost £10,490·85p each.
Plaxton Elite Express III bodies C49F.   Unladen weight 8 tons 14 cwt 3 qrs.

No.	Regn. No.	Chassis No.	In Service	Withdrawn	Disposal	Notes
20	MUG 520L	7300040	4-7-1973	18-7-1975		Body No. 733589
21	MUG 521L	7300041	23-7-1973	18-7-1975		Body No. 733590
22	MUG 522L	7300077	28-7-1973	20-7-1975		Body No. 733591

20-22 passed to the West Yorkshire Passenger Transport Executive on 1-4-1974. Renumbered 60-62 respectively 30-4-
Transferred by the WYPTE to Hansons, Huddersfield, 19 and 21-7-1975, then to Calderdale and back to Hansons
60, 12-1975, 62, 15-2-1976, 61 1-3-1976. Renumbered 119, 117 and 118 respectively 5-1977 and transferred to
Baddeley Bros. Ltd. 119 and 118 to Wooliscroft, Darley Dale, in 2-1984 and numbered 79 and 80 respectively. 79 to
Hulley, Baslow, 7-1988. 80 withdrawn and passed to Burman, Minworth, near Birmingham 1986. 117 to Clarke, Barnsley,
by 5-1986.

1973

Leyland Atlantean AN68.2R   0·680 engine, pneumocyclic gears, air brakes.   Cost £13,071·65p each.
Charles H. Roe Ltd. H45/33D bodies, 8ft. 2 1/2in. wide x 33 ft.0in. long.   Unladen weight 9 tons 17 cwt 3 qrs.

No.	Regn. No.	Chassis No.	In Service	Withdrawn	Disposal	Notes
531	PUM 531M	7302290	24-9-1973	12-10-1987	a	
532	PUM 532M	7302291	4-9-1973	18-4-1988	a	A 11-1987
533	PUM 533M	7302292	4-9-1973	24-2-1986	b	
534	PUM 534M	7302293	21-9-1973	23-5-1990	c	A 9-1989
535	PUM 535M	7302294	7-9-1973	21-5-1988	d	A 12-1986

No.	Regn. No.	Chassis No.	In Service	Withdrawn	Disposal	Notes
536	PUM 536M	7302295	11-9-1973	14-11-1986	e	
537	PUM 537M	7302385	5-9-1973	30-3-1990	f	A 2-1989
538	PUM 538M	7302386	7-9-1973	10-5-1988	d	
539	PUM 539M	7302387	17-9-1973	8-8-1988	g	A 3-1987
540	PUM 540M	7302388	13-9-1973	14-11-1986	h	
541	PUM 541M	7302389	13-9-1973	20-6-1988	d	
542	PUM 542M	7302390	19-10-1973	14-11-1986	j	
543	PUM 543M	7302391	2-10-1973	14-11-1986	j	
544	PUM 544M	7302392	1-10-1973	21-5-1988	d	
545	PUM 545M	7302393	29-9-1973	25-2-1988	k	
546	PUM 546M	7302532	24-9-1973	6-7-1988	l	
547	PUM 547M	7302533	1-10-1973	20-5-1988	d	
548	PUM 548M	7302534	4-10-1973	6-9-1984	m	Destroyed by fire at Headingley
549	PUM 549M	7302673	4-10-1973	16-1-1987	n	
550	PUM 550M	7302674	10-10-1973	26-10-1987	a	
551	PUM 551M	7303585	17-10-1973	30-3-1990	f	A 2-1989
552	PUM 552M	7303586	8-10-1973	4-3-1988	a	A 6-1987
553	PUM 553M	7303587	15-10-1973	26-2-1990	o	A 2-1989
554	PUM 554M	7303924	11-10-1973	10-1986	j	
555	PUM 555M	7303925	11-10-1973	21-11-1988	p	To Learner bus 9376 8-6-1989

531-555 passed to the West Yorkshire Passenger Transport Executive on 1-4-1974.

531-532, 534-547, 549-555 to Yorkshire Rider Ltd. 26-10-1986.

A Subsequently repainted in Yorkshire Rider livery.

a 531-2, 550, and 552 sold at British Car Auctions, Brighouse, 27-4-1988. 531, 550 and 552 to T. Wigley, Carlton, for scrap. 532 to PVS, Carlton for scrap.

b 533 to D, Rollinson, breaker, Carlton, 10-1986.

c 534 sold 14-8-1990 to W.North, (PV) Ltd. Sherburn-in-Elmet, for scrap.

d 535, 538, 541, 544 and 547 sold at British Motor Auctions, Brighouse, 6-7-1988. 535, 538 to PVS, Carlton, 541, 544 and 547 to T. Wigley, Carlton, for scrap.

e 536 converted into a show bus for Yorkshire Rider Ltd. and re-registered YR 3939 5-1987, first used 14-6-1987. Sold to Leeds City Council 3-1990.

f 537 and 551 sold 12-4-1990 to PVS Ltd. Carlton, for scrap.

g 539 sold through British Car Auctions , Brighouse, 11-1988 to W. North, Sherburn-in-Elmet by 2-1989, then to PVS, Carlton, 4-1989 for scrap.

h 540 to Yorkshire Rider Apprentice Training School, Ludlam Street Garage, Bradford, then to PVS, Carlton, 7-8-1991.

j 542-3 and 554 to Ensign, dealer, Purfleet, 9-1987. 542-3 to Blackhorse Bus, London SE6, 9-1988. Returned to Ensign 4-1989. 542 to Purnell, Harold Hill, 6-1989 then to Ward, Arlesford by 4-1992. 554 to Mac, Roydon, Herts, 3-1988. Withdrawn 11-1989.

k 545 after stripping for spares, to PVS, Carlton, 3-1988 for scrap.

l 546 sold through British Car Auctions, Brighouse, 11-1988, to W. North, Sherburn-in-Elmet by 11-1989 for scrap.

m Remains of 548 scrapped by WYPTE at Bramley Garage 9-1984.

n 549 used by Yorkshire Rider Engineering Dept. for test purposes. 2-1987. To British Car Auctions, Brighouse 11-1988 then to PVS, Carlton, for scrap.

o 553 sold through A.D.T. Auctions, Manchester, 22-5-1990 to unknown breaker.

p 9376 (ex-555) withdrawn as Learner 12-7-1993. Last ex-L.C.T. vehicle to be used. To PVS, Carlton, 7-1993 for scrap.

1973-4

Leyland Atlantean AN68.2R 0·680 engine, pneumocyclic gears, air brakes. Cost £16,205·63p each.
Charles H. Roe Ltd. H45/33D bodies, 8ft. 2 1/2in. wide x 33 ft.0in. long.

No.	Regn. No.	Chassis No.	In Service	Withdrawn	Disposal	Notes
556	SUG 556M	7303190	13-2-1974	7-2-1990	a	A 12-1988
557	SUG 557M	7303192	9-1-1974	2-2-1990	b	A 1-1987
558	SUG 558M	7303193	22-1-1974	13-4-1988	c	
559	SUG 559M	7303194	12-12-1973	27-11-1990	d	A 3-1989
560	SUG 560M	7303352	2-1-1974	19-12-1988	e	To Learner bus 9377 8-6-1989
561	SUG 561M	7304186	16-1-1974	20-12-1991	f	A 9-1988
562	SUG 562M	7304303	1-1-1974	28-11-1991	d	A 9-1989
563	SUG 563M	7304304	2-1-1974	28-7-1988	d	
564	SUG 564M	7304305	20-12-1973	27-10-1987	c	
565	SUG 565M	7304572	21-12-1973	21-5-1988	g	
566	SUG 566M	7304573	11-12-1973	7-6-1988	g	
567	SUG 567M	7304574	10-1-1974	5-3-1991	h	A 10-1988
568	SUG 568M	7304807	16-1-1974	1-6-1991	j	A 1-1989
569	SUG 569M	7304808	24-1-1974	9-3-1990	k	A 9-1989
570	SUG 570M	7304809	13-2-1974	13-2-1991	l	A 10-1988
571	SUG 571M	7304810	5-2-1974	19-2-1991	m	A 2-1989
572	SUG 572M	7305071	14-12-1973	26-3-1991	n	A 8-1989
573	SUG 573M	7305072	31-1-1974	28-3-1988	c	
574	SUG 574M	7305257	30-1-1974	10-10-1991	o	A 1-1989
575	SUG 575M	7305258	5-2-1974	19-2-1993	k	A 6-1987
576	SUG 576M	7303191	5-4-1974	17-1-1992	p	A 12-1988
577	SUG 577M	7303195	25-3-1974	20-12-1987	c	
578	SUG 578M	7303351	16-4-1974	19-2-1991	q	A 12-1988

No.	Regn. No.	Chassis No.	In Service	Withdrawn	Disposal	Notes
579	SUG 579M	7305259	15-3-1974	7-2-1991	q	A 4-1989
580	SUG 580M	7400246	25-3-1974	31-3-1993	r	A 10-1988
581	SUG 581M	7400247	7-6-1974	18-3-1992	s	Delivered in WYPTE livery. A 8-89
582	SUG 582M	7400248	18-3-1974	6-3-1991	h	A 1-1989
583	SUG 583M	7400249	5-4-1974	11-12-1992	k	A 3-1989
584	SUG 584M	7400493	15-3-1974	31-5-1991	t	A 9-1988
585	SUG 585M	7400494	2-4-1974	31-5-1991	d	A 2-1989
586	SUG 586M	7400495	29-4-1974	10-7-1992	d	Delivered in WYPTE livery A 9-89
587	SUG 587M	7400496	7-5-1974	31-3-1993	k	Delivered in WYPTE livery A 7-89
588	SUG 588M	7400497	23-4-1974	26-3-1993	u	Delivered in WYPTE livery A 9-89
589	SUG 589M	7400664	26-4-1974	31-3-1993	k	Delivered in WYPTE livery A 9-88
590	SUG 590M	7400665	16-4-1974	31-3-1993	v	A 3-1989
591	SUG 591M	7400950	29-3-1974	3-2-1993	w	A 1-1991
592	SUG 592M	7400951	3-5-1974	23-1-1993	k	Delivered in WYPTE livery A 7-89
593	SUG 593M	7401134	10-5-1974	30-11-1992	k	Delivered in WYPTE livery B, A,
594	SUG 594M	7401135	17-5-1974	31-5-1991	x	Delivered in WYPTE livery A 7-88
595	SUG 595M	7401290	17-5-1974	31-5-1991	x	Delivered in WYPTE livery A 7-88

A Subsequently repainted in Yorkshire Rider livery.

B   593 to Northampton for demonstration 13 to 17-5-1974.
556-595 to West Yorkshire Passenger Transport Executive 1-4-1974.
556-595 passed to Yorkshire Rider Ltd. 28-10-1986.

a 556 sold 22-5-1990 through A.D.T. Auctions, Belle Vue, Manchester, to Wombwell Diesels Co. Wombwell Diesels yard closed 3-1994 and 556 then passed to T. Wigley, Carlton, for scrap.

b 557 sold 1-3-1990 to Yorkshire Electricity Board, Leeds, for conversion to a mobile display unit. Then to Humberside County Council Youth Service by 4-1994 and numbered 79904. Believed to be scrapped.

c 558, 564, 573 and 577 sold at British Car Auctions, Brighouse, 27-4-1988. 564 and 573 to PVS, Carlton, for scrap. 577 to T. Wigley, Carlton, for scrap.

d 559 to PVS, Carlton 17-12-1990. 562 1-1993. 563 30-10-1989. 585 9-10-1991. 586 1-1993 all for scrap.

e 9377 (ex-560) withdrawn from Learner fleet 18-12-1991. To Wolds Gliding Club, Pocklington, 4-1992. Purchased by J. Fairchild and W. McClintoch 11-2004 for spares in restoration of 591.

f   561 sold 17-3-1992, chassis to Hylton Castle, East Bolden, near Sunderland 9-1992 for rebodying as a single decker with East Lancs B46F body. In service 12-1992 re-registered HIL 4349. Later to Jones, Llanfaethlu, Anglesey, 6-2002?.

g   565 and 566 sold at British Car Auctions, Brighouse, 6-7-1988. 565 to T. Wigley, Carlton and 566 to PVS, Carlton.

h   567 and 582 sold 29-3-1991 to unknown breakers.

j   568 sold at A.D.S. Auctions, Belle Vue, Manchester, 28-6-1991.

k   569 sold 3-4-1990 to PVS Ltd. Carlton, 575 16-4-1993. 583 and 592 2-1993. 587 and 589 21-5-1993. 593 3-1993 all for scrap.

l   570 loaned to Greenwich Borough Council 15 to 23-3-1991 and decorated as a Pakistani Festival Bus. Sold to PVS, Carlton, 21-5-1992 for scrap.

m 571 sold by auction in Sovereign Street Yard, Leeds, 4-7-1991 to PVS, Carlton then to Monetgrange, Nottingham, 6-1991. To PVS, Carlton, by 24-1-1994 for scrap.

n   572 donated 28-3-1991 to "Leisurefree", a charity. To Epstein, Whitefield, 3-1991.

o   574 sold 27-7-1992 to Pennine Blue, Dukinfield. To D. Entwhistle, Calverley, Leeds, for preservation, 10-1994. Later scrapped.

p   576 to Wallace Arnold Coaches Ltd. Leeds 2-1992 as a mobile office at South Mimms Coach Interchange.

q   578, 579 sold on 3-4-1991 to unknown breakers.

r   580 to W. North, Sherburn-in-Elmet, 25-3-1994. Then to Jones, Oakley, 8-1994.

s   581 sold 3-4-1992 to unknown breaker.

t   584 sold to W.North Ltd. , Sherburn-in-Elmet, 17-3-1992.

u   588 sold 6-8-1993 to Eureka Children's Museum, Halifax.

v   590 sold 6-5-1993.

w   591 sold to J. Paxton, West Yorkshire Youth Association, Kettlethorpe, Wakefield. 2-1993. Acquired by J. Fairchild and W. McClintoch 9-2004 for preservation. Stored to the north east of Leeds.

x   594 and 595 sold 17-8-1992. 594 to W. North, Sherburn-in-Elmet.. 595 to PVS, Carlton. Chassis to Hylton Castle, East Bolden, near Sunderland 9-1992 for rebodying as a single decker with East Lancs B46F body. In service 12-1992 re-registered HIL 4346. To Southern National 10-1998. Later to Foster of Martlesham 5-2000.

1974

Leyland National 1151/1R/0401, Leyland O·510 engine, 5 speed gear box by Self Changing Gears Ltd. Cost £13,403·50p.
Leyland National B52F body 11·3 metres long.

No.	Regn. No.	Chassis No.	In Service	Withdrawn	Disposal	Notes
1301	SUA 301M	01031	19-2-1974	9-10-1986	a	A

A 1301 was delivered with standard Leyland National seating. It was painted in NBC poppy red livery and was given a Leeds registration and completely reseated in new WYPTE style before entering service, becoming B48F.
1301 passed to the West Yorkshire Passenger Transport Executive on 1-4-1974.
1301 transferred to the Calderdale District of the WYPTE 23-10-1974. Returned to Leeds District 12-1975. Then to Kirklees District. Fitted for wheel chair access 7-1983 and painted in a special livery of Verona green with wide red centre band. Withdrawn 9-10-1986.

a sold to Oldham Community Transport 2-1987 and reseated to B42D. To Ebor Trucks, Acaster Malbis, York, for storage. Then to D.S. Services, Menston. Current location believed to be the Channel Islands.

DEMONSTRATION BUSES 1952 TO 1974

1952

Sentinel (Shrewsbury) Ltd. STC6 six cylinder underfloor engine 120 b.h.p., five speed gear box, air brakes.
Beadle B44F body 30ft.0in. long x 8ft.0in. wide. New in 1951.

No.	Regn. No.	Chassis No.	In Service	Withdrawn	Disposal
----	HAW 578	6/44/91	3-1952	3-1952	Later with R. Boyes & Son. Rothley, Leics.

1952

Daimler Freeline single deck bus with under floor engine 125 h.p.   Livery dark blue and cream.
Duple body B30D plus 30 standing. 30ft. long x 8ft. wide. New in 1951.   Unladen weight 7 tons 12 cwt 0 qr.

No.	Regn. No.	Chassis No.	In Service	Withdrawn	Disposal
----	LRW 377	25001	6-1952	7-1952	Later with Samuel Ledgard, Leeds.

1953

Leyland Tiger Cub PSUC1/1 350 engine, constant mesh gear box, air brakes.   Livery red and cream.
M.C.W. "Hermes" B44F lightweight body 8ft. wide x 30 ft. long. New in 1952.   Unladen weight 5 tons 7cwt 1qr.

No.	Regn. No.	Chassis No.	In Service	Withdrawn	Disposal	Notes
----	RTB 49	515177	20-7-1953	1-8-1953	a	

a Demonstrated nationwide throughout 1953 and 1954 before being sold to Rawtenstall Corporation (57) in 1955.

1954

Daimler CVG6   Gardner six cylinder 8·4 litre engine.   Livery maroon and cream without lining.
Northern Counties metal-framed lightweight H33/28R body. New in 1954.   Unladen weight 6 tons 18 cwt 2 qrs.

No.	Regn. No.	Chassis No.	In Service	Withdrawn	Disposal	Notes
----	PHP 220	18337	24-8-1954	14-9-1954	a	Body No. 4841.

a Demonstrated to several undertakings in 1954-6. Purchased by Burwell & District Motor Services, Burwell, 3-1956.

1958

A.E.C. Bridgemaster A.E.C. AV 590 9·6 litre engine. air suspension.   Livery red and white with maroon roof.
Crossley H41/31R body 30ft/ long x 8ft. wide. New in 1957.   Unladen weight 7 tons 16 cwt 0 qr.

No.	Regn. No.	Chassis No.	In Service	Withdrawn	Disposal	Notes
----	76 MME	B3RA004	18-6-1958	29-6-1958	a	

a Demonstrated nationwide prior to sale to Barton Transport (805).

1958

Daimler CVG6LX-30 Gardner 6LX 10·45 litres engine. Daimatic automatic transmission,   Livery red and white.
Willowbrook H41/33R body 30ft. long x 8ft. wide. New in 1958.

No.	Regn. No.	Chassis No.	In Service	Withdrawn	Disposal	Notes
----	VKV 99	30001	1-8-1958	18-9-1958	a	

a Demonstrated at the Commercial Motor Show, at Earls Court, 26-9-1958 to 4-10-1958. To many other operators
   and then to McGill, Barrhead, near Glasgow, by 8-1961.

1959

Leyland Atlantean PDR1/1 0·600 engine, pneumocyclic gears, air brakes.
M.C.C.W. H44/34F body. 30 ft long x 8ft. wide. New in 1959.

No.	Regn. No.	Chassis No.	In Service	Withdrawn	Disposal	Notes
----	398 JTB	582861	2-9-1959	3-9-1959	a	

a Not used in passenger service in Leeds. Demonstrated for three years then sold to Scout of Preston (No.2) in 1961.
   To Ribble when Scout was taken over.

1961

Daimler CRD6 Fleetline   Daimler CD6 8·6 litre engine Daimatic transmission. Livery: Birmingham dark blue and cream.
M.C.C.W. LD44/33FD body. New in 1960.

No.	Regn. No.	Chassis No.	In Service	Withdrawn	Disposal	Notes
----	7000 HP	60000	5-1961	5-1961	a	

a This was the prototype Daimler Fleetline and was in Leeds for a fortnight in early May 1961. It was exhibited at the
   1960 Commercial Motor Show. It did not operate in passenger service in Leeds.

1962

Albion Lowlander LR1   Leyland 0·600 engine pneumocyclic gears, air brakes.   Livery: Western S.M.T. red and cream.
Alexander H41/31F body 30 ft. long x 8ft. wide.

No.	Regn. No.	Chassis No.	In Service	Withdrawn	Disposal	Notes
	none		31-1-1962	1-2-1962	a	

a This was the prototype Albion Lowlander designed by Albion in conjunction with Leyland. It was exhibited at the
   Scottish Motor Show held in 11-1961. It was not used in passenger service in Leeds.

1963

Dennis Loline III   Aldershot & District Traction Co. No. 465. New in 1962.
Alexander body. H68F.

No.	Regn. No.	Chassis No.	In Service	Withdrawn	Disposal	Notes
465	465 EOT	1103L3AAA1	27-5-1963	27-5-1963	a	

A This bus was not used in passenger service in Leeds. It paid a brief visit to Kirkstall Road Works.

Leyland Atlantean demonstrator SGD 669 in Sovereign Street Yard on 4 September 1963. *J.B.Parkin.*

Seddon Midibus Demonstrator PBU 951M pictured at the New Woodhouse Lane Car Park on 11 December 1973. *J.B.Parkin.*

1963

Leyland Atlantean PDR1/1 M. II 0·600 engine.   Livery yellow/orange and cream.
Alexander H44/34F body.

No.	Regn. No.	Chassis No.	In Service	Withdrawn	Disposal	Notes
LA91	SGD 669	623350	28-8-1963	5-9-1963	a	

a   This bus was formerly Glasgow Corporation Transport LA51, new in January 1963, but in June 1963 was repurchased by Leyland Motors Ltd. as a demonstrator. It did not run in passenger service in Leeds and left for Sunderland on 5–9-1963. It visited Paris and was sold to Fishwicks of Leyland in early 1965.

1965

Leyland PD3A/3   0·600 engine, synchromesh gears, vacuum brakes. Voith Divabus 200S automatic transmission.
Alexander 67 seat lowbridge body with rear entrance 30ft.0in. long x 8ft.0in. wide., fibreglass front. New in 1961.

No.	Regn. No.	Chassis No.	In Service	Withdrawn	Disposal	Notes
1682	RCS 380	610314	2-1965	2-1965	a	

a   This bus was Western S.M.T. 1682 new in 1961. It had recently been fitted with Voith transmission. It did not run in passenger service in Leeds.

1965

A.E.C. Swift   AH 505 8·2 litre engine.   Livery red and cream.
Willowbrook B53F body 36ft.0in. long x 8ft. 2 1 2in. wide.   Unladen weight 7 tons 7cwt 1qr.

No.	Regn. No.	Chassis No.	In Service	Withdrawn	Disposal	Notes
----	FGW 498C	MP2R001	13-12-1965	18-12-1965	a	

a   This bus was the prototype Swift and was not used in passenger service in Leeds.

1972

Morrison Electricar, battery-operated electric minibus. Leyland Redline 900FG chassis adapted by Crompton Leyland Electricars. Lead-acid traction type batteries 110 cells (220 volts) 376Ah capacity at 5 hour rate. 24 h.p. motor. Willowbrook B9F all-metal frame body with 17 standing. 22ft.0in. long x 8ft.1 1/2in. wide x 9ft.6in. high. Type P190/110NP26.
Unladen weight 7·75 tons. Livery deep yellow with pale grey/white panel below windscreen.

No.	Regn. No.	Chassis No.	In Service	Withdrawn	Disposal	Notes
----	CWO 516K	403975	10-4-1972	27-7-1972		

After trials in Leeds, the Electricar went to Sheffield for three months and then to West Midlands PTE.   Returned to its owners, the Department of Trade and Industry.

1973

Seddon Midibus   Gardner 6 HLXB 10·45 litre engine.   Livery blue and yellow.
Seddon Motors Ltd. Seddon Pennine VII B25F body (built 11-1973)   Unladen weight 4740 kg.

No.	Regn. No.	Chassis No.	In Service	Withdrawn	Disposal	Notes
	PBU 951M	54685	10-12-1973	20-12-1973	Body No. 1286	

Prior to entering service in Leeds, this bus had been exhibited at the Scottish Motor Show, held in November 1973 at the Kelvin Hall, Glasgow. It was the first bus to be fitted with a horizontally mounted Gardner 6LXB engine. After the Leeds visit, the bus went to Halifax for trials.

Sentinel Demonstrator HAW 578 was photographed at Whingate Junction in March 1952.   It was running on the 45 Harehills to Wortley service. *W.D.Wilson/L.T.H.S.*

Leyland Tiger Cub demonstrator RTB 49 emerges from Upper Wortley Road at Whingate Junction on 29 July 1953. It is on the Harehills to Wortley service. *W.D.Wilson/ L.T.H.S.*

Daimler CVG6LX/30 VKV 99 in Otley Road at Shaw Lane in August 1958. It is working on the Lawnswood to Beeston service. *W.D.Wilson/L.T.H.S.*

Chamberlain car 35 was one of the three Chamberlains with pivotal trucks that were painted in a special blue livery in November 1950. The other cars were 69 and 133. No. 35 is on the spur in City Square and the photograph was taken on 4 July 1953. *Author.*

In 1950 Chamberlain car 16 was one of the trams painted in an experimental all over red livery with straw coloured lining, black beadings and brown indicators. It was photographed in Briggate on 31 March 1954 and was bound for Kirkstall Abbey. The Kirkstall Abbey route closed on 3 April and 16 was withdrawn on the previous day. *Author.*

Vehicle Liveries 1953 to 1974

Tramcar Liveries

The numerous tramcar liveries were discussed in Volumes 1 to 3 and from 1953 to 1959 there was little change.

Repainting of the Chamberlain cars ceased in June 1953, but in July 1955, seven, 60, 74, 76, 84, 93, 124 and 139 appeared in service, repainted. They were in the usual B.E.T. red unlined livery, but the sole bars were repainted red instead of black, and the gutters were also red in place of black. The black beadings were reduced in number and the colour of the trucks was dark brown.

In regard to the Horsfield cars, the unlined red and white livery adopted in 1952 was retained until the end of the tramway system. A slight variation occurred in March 1954 when the gutters formerly black, were repainted red. Similar alterations were made to the Felthams from the same time. The gutters were red instead of black and the beadings under the lower saloon windows became red in place of black.

Tramcar repainting ceased in February 1958, the last Horsfield to be repainted being 186 (30-1-58) and the last Feltham 532 (1-3-58). After that only part repainting and touching up was carried out. Painting of car interiors ceased in June 1957, car 187 (21-6-57) being the last.

Chamberlain car 147 in the unlined red and white livery was rather scruffy when this view was taken at Lawnswood on 8 July 1955. *Author.*

Chamberlain 76 was one of the trams repainted in 1955 in a simpler red and white livery. The gold gill sans numerals did not show up too well on the red background. It was photographed when newly repainted at Whingate terminus on 13 August 1955. *Author.*

THE FELTHAMS 501-590 LIVERY AND PAINTING DETAILS

No.	First repaint	Second repaint	Third repaint	Fourth repaint	No.	First repaint	Second repaint
501	10-1949 A	17-8-1953 H	17-3-1955 J	27-3-1957 JP	551	1-10-1951 E	5-11-1954 J
502	10-9-1950 B,C	20-12-1953 H	1-5-1955 J	5-3-1957 JP	552	21-10-1951 E	17-12-1954 J
503	25-9-1950 D	1-11-1953 H	7-4-1955 J	--------------	553	4-11-1951 E	19-12-1954 J
504	24-10-1950 C	10-1-1954 H	23-1-1956 J	--------------	554	30-11-1951 E	11-11-1954 J
505	22-10-1950 C	17-1-1954 H	12-6-1955 J	21-3-1957 JP	555	11-11-1951 E	5-12-1954 J
506	5-11-1950 E	1-2-1954 H	4-2-1956 J	30-3-1957 JP	556	2-12-1951 E	11-1954 J
507	11-1950 C	--------------	--------------	--------------		30-5-1957 JP	--------------
508	17-12-1950 E	21-3-1954 J	25-2-1956 J	--------------	557	25-11-1951 E	7-12-1954 J
509	3-12-1950 F	28-3-1954 J	15-2-1956 J	15-2-1958 JP		6-6-1957 JP	--------------
510	18-11-1950 E	7-3-1954 J	1-3-1956 J	7-2-1958 JP	558	2-12-1951 E	24-12-1954 J
511	11-1950 E	14-3-1954 J	7-3-1956 J	--------------	559	16-12-1951 E	28-2-1954 J
512	7-1-1951 E	6-1953 H	7-3-1955 J	7-3-1957 JP	560	12-1-1952 E	7-1-1955 J
513	10-12-1950 E	6-12-1953 H	8-5-1955 J	5-4-1957 JP	561	31-1-1952 E	1-1-1955 J
514	31-12-1950 E	3-4-1954 J	20-5-1956 J	--------------	562	23-12-1951 E	19-1-1955 J
515	7-1-1951 E	11-4-1954 J	14-6-1956 J	--------------	563	31-1-1952 E	--------------
516	24-12-1950 E	12-12-1953 H	15-5-1955 J	--------------	564	2-1-1952 E	--------------
517	7-1-1951 E	24-2-1954 H	24-6-1956 J	--------------	565	1-3-1952 E	--------------
518	11-2-1951 E	25-4-1954 J	9-3-1957 JP	--------------	566	1-2-1952 E	--------------
519	27-1-1951 E	4-4-1953 H	24-3-1955 J	--------------	567	3-1955 J	--------------
520	21-1-1951 E	18-4-1954 J	--------------	--------------	568	14-3-1956 J	16-11-1957 JP
521	9-9-1951 E	12-11-1953 H	24-4-1955 J	1-3-1957 JP	569	22-6-1955 J	5-7-1957 JP
522	7-2-1951 E	7-2-1954 H	3-4-1957 JP	--------------	570	31-1-1952 E	--------------
523	9-9-1951 E	22-9-1954 J	17-10-1956 J	--------------	571	--------------	--------------
524	11-2-1951 E	1-5-1954 J	15-5-1956 J	15-12-1957 JP	572	--------------	--------------
525	11-2-1951 G	10-5-1954 J	1-7-1956 J	15-2-1958 JP	573	27-3-1956 J	--------------
526	10-2-1951 E	15-4-1954 J	14-7-1956 J	--------------	574	4-5-1956 J	30-11-1957 JP
527	11-3-1951 E	20-5-1954 J	7-1956 J	--------------	575	--------------	--------------
528	19-3-1951 E	27-5-1954 J	16-3-1957 JP	--------------	576	--------------	--------------
529	25-3-1951 E	11-7-1954 J	1-8-1956 J	6-12-1957 JP	577	--------------	--------------
530	19-3-1951 E	4-6-1954 J	21-7-1956 J	--------------	578	--------------	--------------
531	21-4-1951 G	7-6-1954 J	8-1956 J	22-12-1957 JP	579	30-1-1952 E	16-1-1955
532	7-4-1951 E	1-3-1954 J	8-1956 J	1-3-1958 JP	580	1-1952 E	--------------
533	8-4-1951 E	17-6-1954 J	--------------	--------------	581	23-1-1952 E	7-2-1955
534	15-4-1951 E	27-6-1954 J	1-10-1956 J	--------------	582	10-6-1956 J	24-11-1957 JP
535	29-4-1951 E	18-7-1954 J	4-9-1956 J	--------------	583	31-2-1952 E	19-2-1955 J
536	6-1951 E	22-8-1954 J	11-10-1956 J	--------------	584	--------------	--------------
537	6-5-1951 E	1-10-1953 H	17-4-1955 J	--------------	585	6-1956 J	--------------
538	6-5-1951 G	24-7-1954 J	7-9-1956 J	--------------	586	31-12-1951 E	1-3-1955 J
539	13-5-1951 E	1-8-1954 J	--------------	--------------	587	20-5-1955 J	14-6-1957 J
540	27-5-1951 E	10-8-1954 J	17-4-1957 J	--------------	588	30-1-1952 E	1-4-1955 J
541	3-6-1951 E	17-8-1954 J	--------------	--------------	589	27-2-1952 E	27-6-1957 JP
542	6-1951 E	1-9-1954 J	15-9-1956 J	--------------	590	5-1952 E	6-3-1955 J
543	6-1951 E	5-9-1954 J	--------------	--------------			
544	7-1951 E	12-9-1954 J	--------------	--------------			
545	7-1951 E	19-9-1954 J	--------------	--------------			
546	29-7-1951 E	1-10-1954 J	21-9-1956 J	--------------			
547	22-7-1951 E	10-10-1954 J	11-4-1957 JP	--------------			
548	22-7-1951 E	12-12-1953 H	22-5-1955 J	--------------			
549	29-7-1951 E	24-10-1954 J	--------------	--------------			
550	22-7-1951 E	30-10-1954 J	--------------	--------------			

Liveries

A. London Transport type livery, red and off white window frames, black beadings and bogies, gilt Gill Sans numerals, no lining. Car 2099 (501) only.

B   B.E.T. red livery with window frames in olive green, Brunswick black beadings, gutters, bogies and grey roof, gilt Gill Sans numerals, no lining. Car 502 only for a few days, but not in service.

C   B.E.T. red livery, narrow white band below upper saloon windows and broad white area above those of lower saloon, gilt Gill Sans numerals, Brunswick black beadings, gutters and bogies, grey roof, straw lining on dashes and lower panelling. Cars 502, 504, 505 and 507 only.

D   B.E.T. red livery, overall red with Brunswick black beadings, gutters and bogies, grey roof, gilt Gill Sans Numerals, straw lining on dashes and lower panelling, one straw line below upper saloon windows. Car 503 only.

E   B.E.T. red livery, similar livery to Livery C, but with the addition of broad white band on the upper part of the dash. The band was lined in red with gilt Gill Sans numerals. From about November 1950 bogies were painted reddish brown instead of black, but complete details have not been recorded. Cars repainted after 533 had dark blue and later black Gill Sans numerals. From April-June 1951 all Felthams in this livery had their gilt numerals painted dark blue, later black. Most cars as table above.

F   B.E.T. red livery, similar to Livery E, but the window frames were painted white instead of red., and there was no upper saloon white band, Brunswick black bogies. Car 509 only.

G   Post Office red livery, but the same in all other respects to Livery E. Cars 525, 531 and 538 only.

H   B.E.T. red livery of the same style as Livery E, but with no lining, black beadings and gutters retained, grey roof, reddish brown bogies and bumpers. Many cars as table above.
J   B.E.T. red livery of the same style as Livery H, but red gutters, red instead of black over lower saloon windows. All subsequent Feltham repaints were in this livery.
JP As livery J but partial repaint, generally exterior of car only.
    From March to July 1958 cars were part repainted or patched, usually lower saloons only. This applied to cars 502, 504, 506, 512, 526, 538, 546, 556, and 573. After July 1958 only touching up of the paintwork was carried out.

501 was at first painted in London Transport livery, but in August 1953 was repainted in an unlined red and white livery (style H).   It is seen here at the Railway Viaduct in Kirkstall Road on 16 January 1954.   The viaduct still exists, but all the property on this photograph has since disappeared.   Compare with the photograph on page 1279 taken at the same location eleven years later. *Author.*

In March 1958 No. 532 became the last Feltham to receive a partial repaint.   It is in Kirkgate on the final day of tramway operation, 7 November 1959.   The tram pole with overhead feeder was the last in Leeds to have an ornamental cast iron base of the type used from 1897-1914. It was removed in May 1999 and its fate is unknown. *Author.*

In September 1950 Feltham 503 was painted in an experimental livery of red with straw coloured lining and black beadings. It is on the Burley Mills siding and the date is 9 May 1953. *Author.*

In January 1952 Feltham 563 was painted in the then "standard" red and white lined livery. It retained this livery throughout its brief sojourn in Leeds. No. 563 was photographed at Halton terminus on 19 August 1955 and on the right hand side is the Irwin Arms, closed about November 2003 and demolished in May 2006. In October of that year a start was made on the construction of a supermarket on the site. *Author.*

1948-built car 276 was newly repainted when this view was taken on 2 July 1955. A push chair is being loaded on to the driver's platform at Roundhay Park.   The line of trams on the kerbside third track await passengers as 2 July was Children's Day. *Author.*

The paintwork on ex-London HR/2 car 278 and the adjacent Felthams, was in very good condition when this view was taken in Low Fields Road scrap yard on 12 October 1957. *Author.*

Motor Bus Liveries

From the introduction of the green livery for buses in 1950 the livery had been in two shades, mid-Brunswick green and chrome green. In 1952 it was replaced by a revised livery.

The standard livery became mid-Brunswick green, dark Brunswick green and Leeds Lincoln Green (also sometimes referred to as Nile green). The bulk of the body of the bus was painted in mid-Brunswick green and was relieved by a light green band (Lincoln green) above the lower saloon windows. The bottom panels were painted in the slightly darker shade of dark Brunswick green. The two Brunswick greens met immediately below the bottom deck window line and the shade change was barely distinguishable, except on newly repainted buses. From June 1952 to 1956 this was the standard livery for Leeds City Transport buses.

A number of buses continued to be repainted in the pre-June 1950 Dominion blue and light grey drab blue livery. These were the buses used on the British Electricity Authority Works service until October 1955. The buses involved were 264 (14-6-54), 271 (22-6-54) 272, 280 (6-54) and they are discussed further on page 914 of Volume 3.

The various buses exhibited at the Commercial Motor Show held annually at Earls Court were painted in the three shades of green livery, but all had in addition gold leaf lining. 800 (later renumbered 678), the 1953 show bus, is mentioned in Volume 3 and like earlier show buses had three gold lines. The following Show buses were in a similar livery, 730 (1-10-54), (which also had different style numerals) and 839 (9-56). Single deckers 29-36 when new in 1954-5 had gold lining. The next Show bus 221 (10-58) and A.E.C. Reliance single deckers 37 and 38 when new in November 1959 also had gold lining.

From January 1955 the painting of the fleet number over the fuel cap became a standard feature on all L.C.T. buses. Until May 1956 buses carried a washing plant height-group number painted on the front. After this date it was omitted.

The delivery of the series of A.E.C. Regent V, 760- 839, in 1956 saw the appearance of a new style of external fleet numeral. The numerals were of a simpler plain thin Gill Sans style in gilt, edged in black. There were small numerals on the front of the bus and larger numerals at the rear. The earlier numerals had been more ornamental, being in gold, blocked in pale blue and white with a black shadow. This was a relic of the blue livery days. Beginning with Leyland PD1 319 (25-9-56), some subsequent bus repaints had the new style numerals until supplies of the original transfers ran out. The last bus to appear with the old numerals was 678 (16-1-57). The old style disappeared by December 1959, The Leyland PS1 single deckers, 27 and 28, were the last buses to run with the old style numerals.

At the same time that 319 received the new numerals 320 (26-9-56), appeared in two shades of green only. The whole of the areas previously in the two Brunswick green shades were now painted in one dark green, this colour being referred to as permanent green. The light green band was retained around the centre cant rail. From 1956 the livery adopted by 320 became the standard.

During the last week of June in 1961 an exhibition was held at the Leeds College of Art in which students submitted new ideas for transport in Leeds. There were designs for uniforms, bus shelters, insignia and a proposal that the bus livery be changed to orange and grey. None of the suggestions were taken up by the Transport Committee.

In August 1961 a number of A.E.C. Leyland and Crossley appeared with their radiators repainted bright light green in place of black. Previously the only bus with a green radiator was Show bus 221 - the radiator was later repainted black!

In September 1961 a livery variation occurred when Daimler CVG6 536 (6-9-61) was repainted. It was still in the permanent green and Lincoln green livery but the lighter Lincoln green shade was extended from the normal centre band to the lower saloon window surrounds. The appearance of the vehicle was considerably lightened by the variation. 536 also had black wings in place of the normal green ones on this type of bus. 536 was a "one off" at first, buses continuing to be painted in the earlier style of livery for six weeks. 548 (19-10-61) then appeared in the new style, but with green wings. However, a few buses, 479, 678 and 762, received black wings. After a month 12 buses had been repainted in the new livery, but the colour scheme then reverted to the old style. The last bus to be repainted in the old style was A.E.C. Regent III 464, (27-11-61) after which all buses appeared in the new livery.

With repaints beginning with 731 (14-2-62), a new style was adopted for the General Manager's name and the Transport Department's address. In place of the gold script transfer, a new transfer with capital letters about one inch high was adopted. The letters were in gold.

In October 1963 most of the Daimler CVG6 (532-541), at Sovereign Street Garage had their green mudguards painted black. Newly repainted buses at this time had a different style of fleet number over the offside fuel filler; lettering to used ticket boxes, emergency door and seating capacity transfer on the rear were also of a new type. All were in gold with black edgings.

In late February 1964 two withdrawn buses, 420 and 425, (LUA 420 and 425) were repainted in experimental liveries. The liveries had been designed by a firm of Architects, Building Design Partnership, who had also been commissioned to design new stopping places and Transport Department stationery.

The buses were lined up inside Sovereign Street Garage, along with Daimler 561, repainted in the normal livery. On 16 March 1964 the three buses were inspected by members of the Transport Committee and returned to Kirkstall Road Works the following day. The two liveries were as follows:

420 – This bus was painted in the existing livery of permanent green, but the Lincoln green centre band and lower saloon windows were altered. The centre band was primrose, as also were the nearside window surrounds, but on the offside, the window surrounds were light grey. The rear and front window surrounds were also primrose. The normal coat of arms and insignia were positioned on the offside, but the nearside had a new style emblem with a very small coat of arms to the left of the letters "L.C.T.", the whole being enclosed in a rectangle.

425 – This bus was in a very pale grey livery (almost white) with the centre band, lower saloon window surrounds and Roe waist rail all painted in a rather dark khaki green colour. Both sides of the bus were painted identically, and each had another new style emblem, consisting of a coat of arms (very small) surrounded by "Leeds City Transport" in a circle.

The Transport Committee decided that there would be no change in the bus livery, but the bus stopping places and stationery designs were accepted.

The new bus stop signs appeared in February and March 1968 and were more readable than the older type. They had a dark green background with yellow lettering. The old signs had quickly faded and had had a light green background with white lettering.

In common with the usual practice with new single deck buses, Nos. 39-47 received the permanent green and Lincoln green livery with gold lining.

The Commercial Motor Show of September/October 1964 saw a new L.C.T. bus livery. A Daimler Fleetline, 101, the first to appear in Leeds, was exhibited. It was painted in a revised livery of permanent green and Lincoln green. The upper saloon windows were in Lincoln green similar to the windows of the lower saloon. As was customary with Show models, simple gold lining was applied. This gave the vehicle a very smart appearance.

During the latter part of 1964 and early 1965 the remaining buses still in the old style livery with a single Lincoln green band, had the band repainted and the Lincoln green extended over the lower saloon window pillars. The last bus to run in the old style livery was 450, last seen in service on 5 March 1965.

In February 1965 a new A.E.C. Reliance coach was delivered to the Transport Department. Numbered 10 it was in a new style livery. There was a light green roof, cream window surrounds and lower panels, with a central dark green band immediately below the windows. The City coat of arms was positioned on the centre side panels, the title "Leeds City Transport" being on the dark green band beneath the forward side windows. There were chrome strips lined in red dividing the different colours. The only external numeral was on the flap over the fuel tank filler cap.

In July 1965 the first of a batch of Leyland Atlanteans was delivered. Painting details were similar to the Fleetlines, but the centre Lincoln green band was considerably wider. At the front, small numerals were provided immediately below the offside windscreen.

The second batch of Daimler Fleetlines, 116-130, differed in livery details to the earlier series 101-110. The entrance doors were painted entirely in permanent green, whereas, 101-110 had the top half painted in Lincoln green.

Commercial Motor Show buses, Daimler Fleetline 131 and A.E.C Swift 51 (both 9-66) were painted in the standard livery with the addition of gold lining.

The delivery of a new A.E.C. Swift (61) with an M.C.W. body in March 1968 saw a modification in livery for this type of bus. The Lincoln green colour around the window surrounds was extended downwards giving a greater amount of relief to the permanent green. The usual insignia was replaced by "LEEDS CITY TRANSPORT" in gold, set on two lines to the right of the coat of arms. Both the insignia and coat of arms were positioned at the front by the door just below window level, instead of in the centre of the panel as normal.

At the Commercial Motor Show in September 1968, two Leeds City Transport Daimler Fleetline buses 156 and 158 were exhibited. They were finished in the permanent green and light green livery, but the colours were reversed. The predominant colour was the paler light green - slightly different to Lincoln green and called Apple green - with a permanent green centre band, lower saloon windows and a broad band below the windows. The new style insignia was incorporated on both the nearside and offside of the bus. In addition the roof was painted in permanent green. The front fleet numbers were positioned above the windscreen and below the destination indicators. The rear numerals were on the engine compartment. After the Show the front fleet numbers were relocated to a new position on the nearside of the bus on the panel to the right of the front entrance doors. The rest of the series was delivered with the numbers in this position.

On 30 October 1968, Daimler Fleetline 160 and A.E.C. Swift 77, painted in the reversed colour scheme, were inspected by Transport Department officials. The roofs were painted in permanent green, but the centre portion, only visible from above, was silver.

Thomas Lord, the Transport General Manager, recommended that all one-man operated buses be repainted in the new reversed livery. His advice was approved by the Transport Committee. Alderman Turnbull, Chairman, said that the new livery was "much neater and attractive and would make the front-entrance buses easier to recognise." The city coat of arms near the front of the bus instead of in the centre, was in a "less Victorian setting," he said.

After October 1968 all repaints of one-man buses, both single and double deck, were in the reversed colour scheme. Repaints in November 1968 included 39, 331, 341-344, 102 and 116-124, all in the new livery. 331 had large front numerals positioned below the offside windscreen on the dark green section. These showed up better than those on the other new repaints, which had smaller gold transfers on the light green. On the new repaints the "LEEDS CITY TRANSPORT" lettering was smaller than on the M.C.W.-bodied A.E.C. Swifts on which the style was introduced. On the latter the lettering was soon replaced by the new type.

Repaints of the older buses in December 1968, 799-820, were in the older green livery, but from 802 onwards, the new style of coat of arms and insignia were used. In 1968 an old established practice, believed to have started in 1902 by Manager, J.B.Hamilton, was discontinued. This was the painting of a repaint date on the vehicle, which had appeared on the trams and buses. 802 (3-12-68) was the last bus to receive an exterior paint date and 524 the last an interior date.

In January 1969, Daimler Fleetline 131, the 1966 Show bus, was repainted in the new reversed livery. It was the last double decker to have gold lining.

During 1969, to help repainting, beading was fixed on the lower panels on certain of the Atlanteans and Fleetlines between the light green and dark green sections. Leyland Atlanteans 356-361, repainted in June 1969, had their unladen weight, seating capacity and legal ownership painted in black, in place of gold, on the light green. Gold did not stand out on the light green and was difficult to see. Fleet numerals continued to appear in gold irrespective of whether they were positioned on the light or dark green. In August 1969 various trials were made to make the numerals more visible. Leyland Atlanteans 371-377 and 379 were repainted during that month and from 373 upwards, the gold transfers were positioned higher so that they were on the dark green band below the windscreen, while at the rear 373 and 374 had them on the normal position on the engine compartment, but they had a small dark green panel as a background. 376, 377 and 379 plus single deckers 45, 76 and 78, repainted at the same time, had black numerals at the rear. Soon afterwards a number of buses already painted in the new reversed livery had their numerals painted black at both front and rear and this then became the standard.

A.E.C. Swifts 1001-1038, delivered in 1969, were in the reversed green livery but all had silver roofs.

In October 1969, newly delivered Daimler Fleetline double deckers 146-160 and A.E.C. Swift 1047, were fitted with holders for a new type of sign approximately 2ft.0in long by 6in. deep. They were positioned at the bottom of the windscreen on the nearside and held up to three boards. Two boards were produced which read:

Yellow lettering on a black background "Limited Stop".

On the reverse, yellow lettering on a blue background, reading "Sightseeing". The other board had black lettering on a yellow background, reading "pay as you enter please". On the reverse, yellow lettering on a green background, reading "Fastaway".

In January 1970 a start was made on repainting the last of the Leyland Atlanteans in the old permanent green and Lincoln green livery into the reversed colour scheme. 383-385, repainted in early February 1970, were the last rear engined double deckers to run in the old style livery. A.E.C. Swifts 59, 85 and 60, in that order, were the last of the Roe-bodied single deckers in the old livery. They were also repainted in February 1970 and were the last buses in the fleet to carry gold lining, the feature for a number of years of Earls Court Commercial Motor Show exhibits and newly built Roe-bodied single deckers. There were still a

A.E.C. Regent V 800 in the final livery that was adopted for the older type of buses. It was photographed at Pudsey on 4 June 1972. It was on a 'Leeds & District Transport News' private tour. *W.D.Wilson/L.T.H.S.*

In February 1964 A.E.C. Regent III 420 was repainted in an experimental livery of green and cream. It was also one of the buses sold to Halifax Corporation in July 1964 and it retained its experimental livery. It is seen on a 'Leeds & District Transport News' tour in Halifax with 441 in the standard L.C.T. livery in the background. The date is 9 May 1965. *Author.*

In February 1964 A.E.C. Regent III 425 was also repainted in an experimental pale grey livery with dark khaki green windows. This livery was impractical and would very quickly have looked dirty and, with that of 420 opposite, was rejected by the Transport Committee. The bus was sold to a group of Leeds University students for a continental tour, which never materialised. No. 425 was photographed at Bodington Hall, Lawnswood, on 19 July 1964. *H.Heyworth.*

In February and March 1973 Mercedes Benz minibuses 30 and 32 were painted in a new livery of cream with a relief band of green. The name "LEEDS" was added and the livery was referred to as buttermilk and emerald green. This livery was a precursor to the livery eventually adopted by the West Yorkshire Passenger Transport Executive for its vehicles. No. 32 was photographed in New Market Street on 24 July 1974. *W.D.Wilson/L.T.H.S.*

number of A.E.C. Swifts in the old style livery. These were the M.C.W.- bodied Swifts 61-75 and 86-100. Until 1971 many of these had been repainted in the old livery and it was thought that this was to remain the standard for these particular buses. However, this was to change for, in March 1971 90 and 92, appeared in the reversed green livery. In February the following year, with the repainting of 99, there were no single deckers left in the old green colour scheme.

The six Mercedes Benz minibuses ordered for the new City Centre car park services were painted in a new style livery. They were painted in ivory with a dark green band of what appeared to be a different shade - containing more yellow than the standard permanent green. The colour scheme was approved by the Transport Committee on 27 March 1970.

In February 1971 new Leyland Atlanteans, 446-455, had a slightly different style of fleet numeral at the rear.

The experimental battery electric minibus, (CWO 516K), which ran in Leeds from April to July 1972, was painted in an overall orange yellow livery with a pale grey front panel below the windscreen. The name of the Department of Trade and Industry appeared on the side of the bus together with Leeds City Transport legal ownership.

Following repaints in April and May 1973, buses of the 116-130, 131-145 and 356-385 series received silver roof tops, similar to the dual-doorway Fleetlines and Atlanteans.

In February and March 1973 two of the Mercedes Benz minibuses, 30 and 32, were repainted and appeared in a new style livery. The livery was cream with a relief band round the centre painted green. The name "LEEDS" was also added in the new green, which was similar to the malachite green of Southern Railway engines. It was a mid-green, quite different from the greens normally used on Leeds buses. The livery was officially referred to as buttermilk and emerald green. 32 entered service in the new livery on 19 February 1973 and was followed by the other minibuses over the following four months. This was also to be the livery of the new coaches delivered in July and August 1973. The new Leyland Leopard coaches, 20-22, were painted overall in buttermilk relieved by a band of emerald green below the windows.

The emerald green and buttermilk livery was the precursor of the livery, which was to be adopted as standard by the West Yorkshire Passenger Transport Executive, due to take over operation of the Leeds buses from 1 April 1974.

Although strictly outside the remit of this volume the experimental liveries for the Leeds W.Y.P.T.E. buses are now discussed as several were prepared by L.C.T.

In September 1973 A.E.C. Swift 1065 was experimentally repainted on the front and nearside only in the buttermilk and emerald green livery. The latter colour was where the permanent green was painted in the then standard livery. The buttermilk replaced the Lincoln green shade. The startling part of the experiment was the painting of the entrance doors in yellow and the exit doors in red. The wheel centres were also red.

New Leyland Atlanteans, 556-595, delivered in late 1973 and early 1974, had red painted wheel centres. In early 1974 buses of all types running from Bramley and Middleton Garages appeared with similar red wheel centres.

In October 1973 two more buses were repainted in the experimental buttermilk livery. They were Mercedes Benz mininbus 30 which had its emerald green band replaced with a band of darker green, with an additional strip of green at the bottom of the panels, and Leyland Atlantean 447. The latter had the bottom half of the lower panels, plus the roof and upper saloon window surrounds painted green in the same shade as 30. The shade was very similar to the green used on West Riding buses until this time. On the front panel below the windscreen, the buttermilk was carried down lower than on the side panels, going to a level just

below the headlights and side light/trafficator units. The front exit doors were yellow, centre exit doors red and the wheel centres were also red.

The livery of 1065 was modified to conform with that of 447. The green on 1065 was now restricted to the lower and front panels in the same style as 447 and the roof was painted green. The window surrounds remained in buttermilk.

On 8 November 1973 1065 and 447 were presented for inspection to the press. They were intended to test public reaction to the new bus colours of the Leeds Division of the West Yorkshire Passenger Transport Executive. The colours were officially referred to as buttermilk and transport green.

Arnold Stone, Deputy General Manager, said the livery would be gradually introduced as buses were repainted. Buses in the other districts would have the basic buttermilk background, but, said Stone, "will be blue in the case of Bradford, orange for Halifax and red for Huddersfield. These were the main colours in these areas." Both vehicles carried standard L.C.T. gold numerals but there was a new WY logo in silver with the words "METRO LEEDS" on the sides. The letters of the logo "WY" were arranged in an eight-sided pattern, the base of the Y's extending into the base of the design, which was intended to resemble a Yorkshire rose.

"The reason we have chosen Leeds Metro is that obviously West Yorkshire Passenger Transport Executive will not fit easily on a side of a bus. Leeds Metro or Metropolitan will indicate the Leeds district and the WY symbol, West Yorkshire," said Stone.

The new legal owner of the buses was painted in small capital letters on the sides of the vehicles.

The interiors of both 447 and 1065 were redecorated and new upholstery fitted. Details of these alterations are felt to be part of the story of the W.Y.P.T.E. and are not discussed here.

Both buses entered service on Monday, 12 November 1973, in their new colour schemes.

In mid-January 1974, after inspecting buses painted in the proposed different liveries for the other districts, the W.Y.P.T.E. decided that all buses in the new authority would be painted in the Leeds green and buttermilk scheme. Local emblems were to be carried by the buses and denote to which district it belonged.

The new Leyland National, 1301, (SUA 301M), delivered to the Leeds Transport undertaking in National Bus Company poppy red, was repainted in the new experimental P.T.E. livery and in a similar style to 1065. The Metro insignia was, however, outlined in dark brown, which made it stand out much more than on 447 and 1065.

Mercedes minibus 30 experimentally repainted in October 1973, had not entered service in its new colour scheme. It was modified, the whole of the bus being in buttermilk with a transport green skirt and roof. It was first used in this new livery on 28 January 1974. It had also been reseated with two and one seating in place of the former perimeter seating.

On 1 April 1974 the new livery for the P.T.E. was officially launched at a Press Conference held at the Mercury Motor Inn, Garforth Bridge. Examples of seven buses or coaches and one service van were displayed, all painted in the new colours. The colours chosen were Verona green (the new name for emerald green) and buttermilk, the same as initially used on 1065, the Leyland Leopard coaches, 20-22, and Mercedes Benz minibuses 30, and 32-35.

The livery style consisted of a wide skirt panel and roof, and also the upper saloon window surrounds on double deckers, painted Verona green. The remainder of the bus was buttermilk with the exception of a Verona green band above the windscreen, finished with white lining on the green. This band and lining continued round the side of the bus and dropped to a level with the bottom of the lower saloon windows to the right of the front door (nearside) or behind the cab (offside). On single deckers, this band merged with the green roof, but the white lining was carried round the front above the windscreen. The painting style was modified slightly on the various buses in the new livery in order to suit particular designs. Doors were painted green and the idea of yellow and red doors was abandoned. Wheel centres were red.

Buses of all districts were painted in an identical livery, the Metro symbol and lettering being in white. Fleet numbers were black where positioned on the buttermilk but white when on the Verona green. Leeds vehicles displayed at Garforth Bridge were buses 22, 30, 447, 1301 and Leeds service van LUG 766L.

Shortly before this time a British Standard range of colours, B.S.4800, was produced. This enabled exact shades to be produced by paint manufacturers, regardless of the name given by the individual manufacturer to the shade. The two colours, buttermilk and Verona green, were part of this new colour range, buttermilk being B.S. 10 C 31 and Verona green B.S. 14 E 53. The older L.C.T. colours,

permanent green and Lincoln green, did not form part of the B.S. 4800 range and hence did not receive B.S. numbers.

Other Metro liveries also used B.S.4800 colours. The brown livery used by coaches and minibuses was buttermilk 10 C 31, brown 06 C 39, fleet names orange 06 D 43 and lower red band 04 E 53. The Metro coach livery was 10 C 31 and 04 E 53.

Of the last batch of Leyland Atlanteans delivered to the Leeds City Transport undertaking, 576-580, 582-585, 590 and 591 all arrived in full Leeds City Transport livery. 581, 586-589, 592-595 were delivered in the new PTE delivery.

Daimler Fleetline 132 is believed to have been the last repaint in the full L.C.T. light green livery, while Leyland PD3/5 234, was the last repaint in the old style dark green livery. Both were repainted in March 1974.

One type of livery that the Leeds Transport Committee was always opposed to, was an overall advertising livery. In January 1973 a Bradford Corporation bus appeared in Leeds with an overall advertisement. The Committee asked Bradford not to run the bus within the Leeds City boundary.

The successor to L.C.T., the W.Y.P.T.E., later, was not as particular in regard to advertising liveries. After five or six years of takeover, advertising liveries were to be seen on buses in Leeds.

Leyland Atlantean 482 in the reversed green livery pictured at Halton Moor on 18 May 1976. *Author.*

Car 359 as decorated for Leeds University Charity Rag Week in June 1954. During the week it spent nearly all its time parked on the spur in City Square. This photograph was taken on 25 June. This was the last occasion on which a Leeds tram was decorated for Rag Week. *Author.*

Car 359 as decorated for the National Savings Drive in March 1955. The car made its final journey as a decorated car on 12 March and this photograph was taken at Meanwood terminus on its last day in use. *Author.*

Decorated Trams and Buses 1954 to 1974

21 to 25 June 1954. University Rag Week.

Tram 359, painted in yellow and silver by art students, was decorated for Rag Week. It spent nearly all of its time parked on the City Square spur. There had been trams decorated for Rag Week in 1950, 1952 and 1953 and the 1954 car was the last.

21 to 26 June 1954. Leeds Trades Council.

On 15 February 1954 the Transport Committee agreed to hire an "obsolescent omnibus" to the Leeds Trades Council on payment of a fee of £5. It was used for the distribution of literature. A.E.C. Regent 76, a learner bus, was selected. It was decorated with suitable slogans and for the first three days was parked in front of the Town Hall and later in the car park adjoining the Central Bus Station.

2 to 9 October 1954 Safety First Week.

A.E.C. Regent 274, suitably labelled, toured the city in connection with Safety First Week.

7 to 12 March 1955 National Savings Drive.

Tram 359, repainted and redecorated for the National Savings Drive, toured all the tram routes. All the exterior decorative lighting was removed and the car now carried its fleet number over the driver's window,

This was the last occasion on which 359 was used as a decorated vehicle.

A.E.C.Regent 263 toured the city decorated to assist the National Savings Drive. The bus ran on trade plates.

15 to 20 September 1958. Trade Union Recruitment Week.

1934 vintage A.E.C. Regent 139 was loaned to the Leeds Trades Council for Trade Union Recruitment Week. Several seats were removed from the lower saloon and tables were fitted. Loud speaker equipment was placed inside the upper saloon, with the loud speaker sticking out of the emergency door. The vehicle was adorned with posters and ran on trade plates. It was parked in three locations: outside the Town Hall, Millgarth Street Car Park and Eastgate Car Park.

28 September 1958. Safety First Tram.

Horsfield car 247 was used as a Safety First tram at Temple Newsam in connection with the Leeds Accident Prevention Committee's Veteran Car Rally. It preceded a service car and arrived as a special car at Temple Newsam terminus at 1.45 p.m. It left there again at 5.05 p.m. It was adorned with Safety First posters and photographs of road accidents.

7 November 1959. Final Tramcar Procession.

Two Horsfield cars were decorated for the formal closure of the Leeds tramways, 160 and 178. The cars were withdrawn from passenger service on 17 and 5 October respectively and suitably modified and decorated in Swinegate Depot. The two cars had four rows of coloured electric lights fitted around the exterior of the car, these being located around the gutter, below the upper saloon windows, and both above and below the lower

In March 1955 the "globe" end of 359 was adorned with a National Savings flag. The location is Meanwood terminus and date 12 March 1955. *Author.*

A.E.C. Regent 76 was modestly decorated with paper notices by the Leeds Trades Council for a recruitment drive in June 1954. No. 76 was parked outside the Town Hall when this photograph was taken on 25 June. *Author.*

A.E.C. Regent 263 ascending Kirkstall Hill on 9 March 1955. The bus ran on trade plates and was adorned for National Savings Week. *W.D.Wilson/L.T.H.S.*

A.E.C. Regent 139 was loaned to the Leeds Trades Council for a recruitment drive in September 1958. It was photographed on the Millgarth Street car park on 16 September. The Leeds Police Headquarters were later built on this site. In the 1950's and 60's Leeds Corporation had a large hoarding indicating the number of accidents that occurred on the roads and in the home. Part of it can be seen on the right hand side.
W.D.Wilson/L.T.H.S.

On Sunday, 28 September 1958 Horsfield car 247 was parked at Temple Newsam terminus adorned with paper safety posters. It was used in connection with the Leeds Accident Prevention Committee's Veteran Car Rally.
D. Tate.

saloon windows. On the upper side panels were the words "LEEDS CITY TRAMWAYS", while ones bearing the dates "1894 – 1959" were positioned on the lower side panels. The letters "L.C.T." were displayed on the destination boxes. Both cars were identical and did not carry fleet numbers.

Before being altered, on 5 October 1959, 178 was driven to Cross Gates and measured for clearances. The guttering at the track side of the concrete tram shelters at Harehills Lane and Sutton Approach had to be removed to allow the necessary space for the trams to pass. Some stop signs were also bent back to allow sufficient clearance.

The two cars went out a day or two prior to the procession to test clearances at the various shelters. They were used to carry the Lord Mayor, Lady Mayoress. Transport Committee and other members of the City Council and their guests. 160 led the final procession of ten trams and 178, the last tram to leave Cross Gates - the official last tram - was in the rear. Further details of the procession can be found in Chapter 75.

19 to 24 March 1962. Premium Bond Week.

Pre-war A.E.C. Regent 106 was decorated for Premium Bond week. The lower panels and the upper saloon advertisement panels carried paper adverts for premium bonds and four strips of electric light bulbs were positioned round the bus. The lower saloon and other parts of the bus where the green livery showed were repainted. For most periods of the day, someone was in the lower saloon selling premium bonds. The bus was parked on Millgarth Street Car Park or outside the Town Hall at various times during the week. It also toured the suburbs, both by day and night.

14 July 1962 Children's Day Procession.

In addition to the usual single deck buses - in 1962 37 and 38 - A.E.C. Regent 106 was used for the procession. It was painted as a road safety vehicle with posters and slogans. The procession started from the Town Hall for Roundhay Park, but 106 dropped out at Oakwood, owing to overhanging tree branches in the Park. It returned to Torre Road Garage.

13 July 1963 Children's Day Procession.

A.E.C. Regent 106 was again used in the procession. 1963 was the last year in which Children's Day was celebrated in Leeds. The special day had first appeared in 1920 and, apart from the war years, had been a very popular annual event. It was organised by a dwindling number of school teachers, working on a voluntary basis, and involved a large amount of effort. Poor weather on 13 July and a substantial financial loss marked the end of the event.

30 April to 7 May 1966 National Savings Week.

To mark the 50th anniversary of the National Savings Movement, A.E.C. Regent 106 (not used since July 1963) came out of retirement and toured the city and suburbs. Over the lunchtime period it was to be seen in the Millgarth Street Car Park. The bus had National Savings posters and was illuminated during the evenings.

24 to 28 April 1967 Trade Union Week.

A.E.C. Regent III 467 was used as a recruiting vehicle during Trade Union Week. Posters were fixed to the outside of the bus, which was used to tour factories and works in the city. It was also parked on different car parks in the central area at various times.

This was the last occasion on which a vehicle of the Transport Department was decorated for a special occasion. It marked an end to a practice started 65 years earlier in 1902, when a tram was specially decorated and illuminated to celebrate the end of the Boer War.

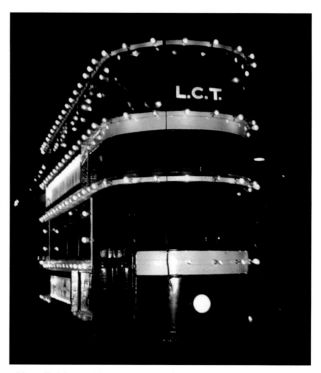

Horsfield car 178 was one of the two cars decorated and illuminated for the final procession on 7 November 1959. It was photographed in Swinegate Depot before the start of the procession. *L.T.H.S.*

A.E.C. Regent 106 at Iveson Approach, Ireland Wood, on 24 March 1962 decorated for Premium Bond Week.
W.D. Wilson/ L.T.H.S.

For the 50th anniversary of the National Savings Movement, A.E.C. Regent 106 was decorated and spent much of its time parked in Millgarth Street Car Park. It was pictured on 5 May 1966. *J.B. Parkin.*

On 5 October 1959 Horsfield 178 was driven to Cross Gates terminus to test clearances at the various shelters etc. The foreman at Swinegate Depot, Jim Wade, is crouching in front of the car. *H. Heyworth.*

Horsfield car 160 was the last tram to Temple Newsam and led the final procession back to Swinegate Depot. It was illuminated and is pictured at Temple Newsam terminus on 7 November 1959. *Author.*

Leeds City Transport Special Services 1953 to 1974

Introduction

There were special bus services in Leeds to serve certain hospitals, works, sports grounds and schools. There were also night bus services. In the case of some works and schools there were sometimes up to six different routes serving the same premises. Some schools services were subject to fairly frequent alteration. Although the precise routes of most of the special services are known, for space reasons they are not generally included in the text, but are shown on the maps.

Hospital Services

In 1953 there were three services specifically used for visitors to the hospitals in Leeds. There was one to Meanwood Park Colony - renamed Meanwood Park Hospital in the late 1940's. Buses had run to the Colony from 1933 and had been discontinued on the outbreak of war. There was also a special bus to the hospital at Menston, but the principal service was that to the Ida and Cookridge Hospitals. These two adjacent hospitals dealt mainly with cancer patients. In 1953 this bus service was new and had only been in operation a few months.

100   Meanwood Park Hospital

Meanwood Park Hospital was a mental hospital situated in Tongue Lane, Meanwood. On 21 March 1947 a service from the Central Bus Station had been reintroduced to the hospital. With the introduction of route numbers for all special services in March 1963, this route was allocated the number 100. From 4 May 1969 buses were rerouted via the new one-way scheme at Sheepscar, The service was still in operation on the takeover of the Leeds City Transport undertaking by the West Yorkshire Passenger Transport Executive on 1 April 1974.

Menston Hospital

Menston was also a mental hospital. There was a special bus, which had started on 4 February 1948 from the Central Bus Station to the hospital, about ten miles from Leeds. The bus followed the route taken by the service 71 Guiseley buses. With the abandonment of this bus service on 30 April 1955, the Menston Hospital service was taken over by the West Yorkshire Road Car Company.

101   Ida and Cookridge Hospitals

The bus service to the adjacent Ida and Cookridge Hospitals ran on visiting days and had commenced on 3 December 1952. It followed the route of the 33 Cookridge buses to the Ring Road and then ran via Spen Lane and Iveson Drive. From 29 October 1962 daily journeys were introduced for evening visiting to the Ida Hospital, but two months later, on 7 January 1963, the evening journeys on Saturdays and Sundays were withdrawn. In March 1963, the service was allocated the number 101. From 30 September 1973 the route was extended from the Ireland Wood Estate into the hospital grounds and was still operating on 1 April 1974.

The bus park at Roundhay with buses on the Roundhay Park Special service 103. Leyland PD3/5 252 is about to return to Leeds. The occasion was August Bank Holiday Monday, 3 August 1964, the last occasion on which service 103 operated. *Author.*

A.E.C. Regent III 616 on hospital service 101 in Iveson Drive, Ireland Wood Estate, on 29 April 1966. *Author.*

140   Killingbeck Hospital
On 18 November 1964 a new service was introduced between the Central Bus Station and Killingbeck Hospital. Following the closure of New York Road on 11 November 1969, the route from the Woodpecker to the Bus Station was diverted. Still in operation on 1 April 1974.

St. James' Hospital
As part of the 42 Harehills-Lower Wortley bus service, four buses in the afternoon and three in the evening short worked from City Square to the Hospital.

Sports Services
There had been sports services in Leeds from pre-war days. Special trams and buses had run to the Elland Road and Headingley Football Grounds and there was also the special evening tram service to the Greyhound Racing track in Elland Road. There were also special services to Roundhay Park on sports and gala days.

102   Football Specials
Following a gap of six years owing to the war, the special trams and buses to the Elland Road and Headingley grounds had been reinstated on 5 January 1946. Both services had run from Infirmary Street, and there was also a short-lived service, which had operated from Holbeck Railway Station to Elland Road in early 1952. From the abandonment of the Sovereign Street - Elland Road special trams in 1955 and 1957, two bus services operated to the Elland Road Football Ground, the one from Infirmary Street and another from Sovereign Street (Concordia Street), replacing the trams. In March 1963 both services were given the number 102.

The special buses to the Headingley Rugby Football and Cricket Ground, which ran to Infirmary Street mainly via the 76 bus route, were not given a number, and were duplicates on service 76.

On 28 September 1963 a new service was introduced between Bramley Town End and Elland Road. and three weeks later (on 19 October 1963), another between the Middleton Arms and Elland Road. Both services displayed 102.

From 5 April 1965 the service was rerouted due to the introduction of a one-way system in the city centre. There were further minor reroutings in August 1965 and January 1966. From 4 December 1966 the service was again altered as a result of the introduction of a one-way traffic system in the Gelderd Road, Spence Lane and Wellington Road area.

The buses starting from Infirmary Street loaded in Bond Street, but in June 1967 the section of this road from Park Row to Infirmary Street was permanently closed to make way for a new comprehensive development scheme. From the start of the 1967 football season - 12 August 1967 - buses loaded in Park Row. From 12 January 1969 the service was rerouted owing to the introduction of Phase 1 of the South Leeds gyratory system and from 2 September 1972 was partially operated by one-man operated buses. In operation 1 April 1974.

Dog Racing Specials
From 2 June 1954, buses replaced trams for traffic to and from meetings at Leeds Greyhound Stadium, Elland Road. Whereas there had been special trams, the buses were incorporated in the normal service buses operating along Elland Road, these being supplemented at race meeting times.

103   Roundhay Park Specials
From the earliest days of the trams there had been special cars to Roundhay Park during holiday periods, Children's Day, and the various galas, tattoos and sporting events that were held at the park. From the 1930's buses had supplemented the trams and in 1937 a parking space for about 20 buses had been opened. Roundhay Park was a very busy place during holiday periods, but this fell off rapidly after 1963 when the annual Children's Day was discontinued. In March 1963 the Roundhay Park Specials were given the route number 103. The service last operated at August Bank Holiday Monday, 3 August 1964. Buses had run from Vicar Lane to the Park, but, owing, it was reported, to the introduction of a

one-way system in the city centre, they had to be discontinued. In 1967 the number 103 was given to a new Works service.

174   New Hunslet Rugby Football Ground

From Sunday 26 August 1973 two football special services were introduced to serve the new ground of the Hunslet Rugby League Football Club at the Elland Road Greyhound Stadium.   One service started from Moor Road (junction with Belle Isle Road) and the other from Dewsbury Road (Waincliffe Drive) to the ground.

Works Services

In 1953 there were three Works bus services in operation, the long established Troydale service, a relatively new service to Barnbow and the Yorkshire Copper Works services.

103   Brown Lane Trading Estate

From 4 September 1967 a new service, numbered 103, was introduced from Vicar Lane to the Brown Lane Trading Estate. This number had formerly been used by the Roundhay Park Specials. Three return journeys daily were operated and the route was still in operation on 1 April 1974.

104   Yorkshire Copper Works

The biggest of the special works services was that to the Yorkshire Copper Works at Stourton. In 1953 there were routes from the Central Bus Station, Middleton "Circus", Wellington Road, and Torre Road Depot, York Road. There were also services worked by other local operators such as the West Riding Automobile Company. About 1961 a Bus Station was opened at the Works and over 10,000 passengers a week were using the buses. A minor alteration occurred from 8 April 1956 when the Central Bus Station-Copper Works specials were rerouted on outward journeys through the city centre. From 8 April 1953 there had been a fare increase on the buses, but otherwise in 1963 the services were unchanged. In March of that year the four services were given the number 104. . From 4 December 1966 the service from Wellington Road was rerouted as a result of the introduction of the one-way traffic system in the Gelderd Road, Spence Lane and Wellington Road area. On 30 April 1967 the service was altered and on 16 March 1969 was rerouted on the introduction of the South Accommodation/Hunslet Road one-way system. On 7 May 1972 a rerouting took place on the service from the Central Bus Station. The various services were still in operation on 1 April 1974.

105   Royal Ordnance Factory, Barnbow

During the war there had been special bus services to Barnbow, but these seem to have been discontinued at the end of the war. Special buses were reintroduced on 5 May 1952 and a bus park was opened at the end of Austhorpe Road near the Factory on 23 February 1953. In 1953 there were three services to Barnbow: from the Central Bus Station, Oakwood, and the Wykebeck Arms, Halton. From 3 May 1954 revised fares and "limited stop" conditions were introduced and a new service was introduced from Barnbow and the Barwick Road/York Road junction in Seacroft Village. From 19 March 1955 the Service from Halton was extended via Selby Road to Halton Dial.

The opening of a new bus station in Rockingham Street in 1954 resulted in the introduction, from 13 April 1955, of a bus to Barnbow. The bus station was short lived and hence also the special service. It ceased to operate on 31 December 1960. From 27 August 1956, the route from Seacroft village was withdrawn and was replaced by a new service from Seacroft (Boggart Hill Drive) to Barnbow. In 1963 the various Barnbow services were given the route number 105 and all were still in operation on 1 April 1974.

106   Troydale Mills

The Troydale Mills services were long established. They had been started in 1926 and had run throughout the war. One of the services started from Hyde Park and the other ran from Carr Manor, Moortown, via the city centre. These special buses had been incorporated into bus services 49 and 32 respectively.   In March 1963 both were given their own route

The new Bus Station at the Yorkshire Copper Works soon after it was opened about 1961.   L.C.T. buses discernible are, from the left, 922, 556, 568, 431 and 649. There are also a number of West Riding buses. Skelton Grange Power Station on the left was built from 1948 to 1962 and demolished in 1995 and 1996. *L.T.H.S.*

Leyland PD2/14 307 in Tong Road on 21 August 1968. It is proceeding towards Bramley Town End on the Elland Road - Bramley Town End Football service 102. *W.D.Wilson/L.T.H.S.*

The "Paddy train" which served Waterloo Main Colliery. The engine is an 0-6-0 saddle tank "Antwerp" and is pictured running alongside Pontefract Lane half way along the line between East End Park and Waterloo Main Colliery.   On the top of the hills in the background is Temple Newsam Park.   The date is 20 August 1959, four days before the passenger service ceased. *J.B.Parkin.*

number 106. From 4 December 1966 the service was rerouted consequent upon the introduction of a one-way traffic system in the Gelderd Road/Spence Lane/Wellington Road area. From 6 March 1967 the Moortown-Troydale Mills service was withdrawn, but the Hyde Park-Troydale Mills service was still in operation on 1 April 1974.

107   Waterloo Main Colliery

Until 1959 the Waterloo Main Colliery, off Pontefract Lane, Temple Newsam, was served by a "Paddy train" consisting of an 0-6-0 saddle tank engine and two elderly bogie coaches. The railway remained open for coal traffic, but after Monday, 24 August 1959, was not used by passengers. It was replaced by a special bus service from the Bridgefield Hotel, East End Park, to the Colliery. The route was about three and a half miles long and four journeys per day were operated in each direction on weekdays and one on Saturdays. The fare was 5d. The duties were worked from Torre Road No.2 Garage and in 1963 the service was given route number 107. The Colliery, the last coal mine to be worked in Leeds, closed in November 1968, but a skeleton staff was retained for a few months. The last coal carrying steam train ran from Waterloo Main to Neville Hill sidings on 23 November 1968. Apart from privately operated trains, it was also the last steam locomotive to run in Leeds. The bus service finally ceased operation on 11 February 1969. This was one of the more interesting of the special services as it took Leeds buses into an area in which they had not previously been seen. In the colliery yard there was very little room to reverse, buses having to turn by reversing between the narrow concrete supports holding up part of the coal staithes.

107   Rose Forgrove Works, Seacroft, to Morley

On 14 April 1969 a new service was started from Morley, Fountain Inn, to the Works via a very circuitous route between the two points. The through fare was 1s.6d. From 16 August 1971 the section between Morley and Dewsbury Road via Middleton was withdrawn, but the rest of the route was extant in 1974.

108 and 109   Weir Foundries Ltd, Pontefract Lane

On Pontefract Lane was the works of Weir Foundries Ltd. Beginning on 12 June 1961, a bus service was introduced from the Central Bus Station to the newly constructed factory. On Mondays to Fridays one daily journey was made in each direction and the fare was 4d. The journey time was eight minutes and the buses were provided from Torre Road No.2 Garage. The service was to be an experiment for eight weeks, but proved successful and two services via slightly different routes were reintroduced on 19 March 1962. In 1963 the two services were allocated the numbers 108 and 109. From 16 March 1969 the 108 service was rerouted on the introduction of the South Accommodation Road/Hunslet Road one-way system. From 5 November 1971 route 109 via Black Bull Street was discontinued. Service 108 continued to operate between the Bus Station and Weir Foundries via East Street. On 6 December 1971 a new service 109 was introduced between the Rex Cinema, Beeston and Weir Foundries. On 10 January 1972, a service was started from Dewsbury Road to the Weir Foundries. The 109 service was renumbered 108, and all routes to Weir Foundries now showed this number, in line with school practice.

109   Westland Trading Estate

From 1 October 1973 an experimental service was commenced from Vicar Lane to the Estate, terminating at the works of R.F. Winder Ltd. It was withdrawn on 1 March 1974 owing to lack of support.

Knostrop Sewage Works

On 7 November 1961 a new works service was introduced between Torre Road Garage and Knostrop Sewage Works. On Mondays to Fridays one daily journey was made in each direction. The journey time was 15 minutes. The service was not given a route number in 1963 as it had been discontinued by this date.

137   Skelton Grange Power Station

As discussed in Volume 3, there had been a Corporation bus service to Skelton Grange Power Station during its construction period. Services had begun on 1 March 1949 using elderly buses loaned to the British Electricity Authority by the Transport Department. B.E.A. purchased ten buses from Leeds and in October 1953 began to run its own bus service. Buses purchased were pre-war A.E.C. Regents 220, 260-262, 275, 278, 281, 283, 285 and 288. They were numbered 1-10 respectively by B.E.A. (later the Central Electricity Authority). With the exception of 262 (B.E.A. No.4), taken out of service in 1955, all of the buses ran until January 1958, They were then replaced by nine of the 1939-40 "HUM" A.E.C. Regents: 107, 109, 110, 113, 119, 121, 122, 123, and 125, which became, respectively, 5, 1, 2, 4, 9, 3, 6, 7, and 8 in the C.E.G.B. fleet. The "HUM's" were all withdrawn on 6 February 1963 and broken up a few months later. This marked the end of the C.E.A.'s efforts to run its own buses.

The construction work on Skelton Grange Power Station had taken a very long time. It was started in October 1948 and completed fourteen years later - in October 1962. The old buses had been used for the building workers and after October were used to convey maintenance workers to the site. The vehicles had been kept in Torre Road Depot Yard and were maintained by the Transport Department. The employees at the Power Station required better buses and on 7 February three Corporation Works services were introduced on a contract basis: from Swinegate, from Leeds Parish Church and from Torre Road Garage to the Power Station.

In addition some buses ran to and from Swinegate via the Parish Church route. For the first month the new services did not have a route number, but in March 1963 all were given the number 137.

From 10 February 1964 the city terminal points were transferred from Swinegate and the Parish Church to the Central Bus Station, Platform E, stand 2. On 16 March 1969 the service was rerouted on the introduction of the South Accommodation Road/Hunslet Road one-way system and again rerouted on 7 May 1972 from Bridge End by way of Meadow Lane, Great Wilson Street and Hunslet Lane to Hunslet Road. In operation 1 April 1974.

148   Wholesale Markets

From June 1965 to October 1966 a new wholesale fish, fruit and vegetable market was constructed off Pontefract Lane. The scheme included an abattoir and meat market. Trading began on 10 October and from the 17th, service 148 was established between Eastgate and the new market. The old abattoir in York Street was closed and later demolished in June 1969. Buses ran in connection with the main times of opening and closing of the various branches of the market, making nine journeys daily outward and seven inward. Unlike the other special services, the Markets service was advertised in the local L.C.T. timetable. From 19 January 1969 the service became one-man operated. Following the closure of New York Road on 11 November 1969, the route was diverted in a similar manner to Hospital service 140. The service was discontinued on 6 June 1970 and incorporated into a revised 63 service.

A.E.C. Regent III 700 on the approach road to Waterloo Main Colliery on 1 October 1967. The colliery closed in November 1968 and was the last coal mine to be worked in Leeds. *Author.*

149 Montague Burton Ltd

On 31 March 1968 a service was opened from Kippax to Montague Burton's Clothing Factory in Hudson Road, Leeds. This had formerly been worked by the Kippax & District Motor Company. A similar service from Garforth to Montague Burton's was taken over from the same day. Both services were numbered 149. Following co-ordination of services between Leeds City Transport and the West Riding Automobile Company in the Kippax and Garforth areas, the last Leeds vehicles worked the service on 5 March 1971. From then on West Riding took over the duties.

162 Sandleas Trading Estate, Manston

From 7 October 1968 a service was opened between the Central Bus Station and the Estate. Following the closure of New York Road on 11 November 1969, the service was rerouted in a similar manner to Hospital service 140. From 6 September 1971 the service was renumbered 170. This was in order to avoid confusion with West Riding route 162 (Leeds to Castleford), as both services used York Road on their route to the city. Latterly there was a private service from Cookridge Street to Chorley & Pickersgills' on the Sandleas Estate, which had displayed 162. From 27 September 1971 these buses showed 171. Service 170 was still in operation on 1 April 1974.

171 Sandleas Trading Estate, Manston

From 3 January 1972, the former private hire service to Chorley & Pickersgill Works, officially became service 171, running from Cookridge Street to the Sandleas Trading Estate.

177 Elida Gibbs Works, Whinmoor

From 19 November 1973 a new service was introduced from Chapeltown to the Works and it was still in operation on 1 April 1974.

279 Pudsey Show Ground

On 12 July 1969 a special service was operated from Pudsey Bus Station to Calverley in connection with Pudsey Show. It was given the route number 279. The service operated on one day every year until 10 July 1976. The following July it was renumbered P48.

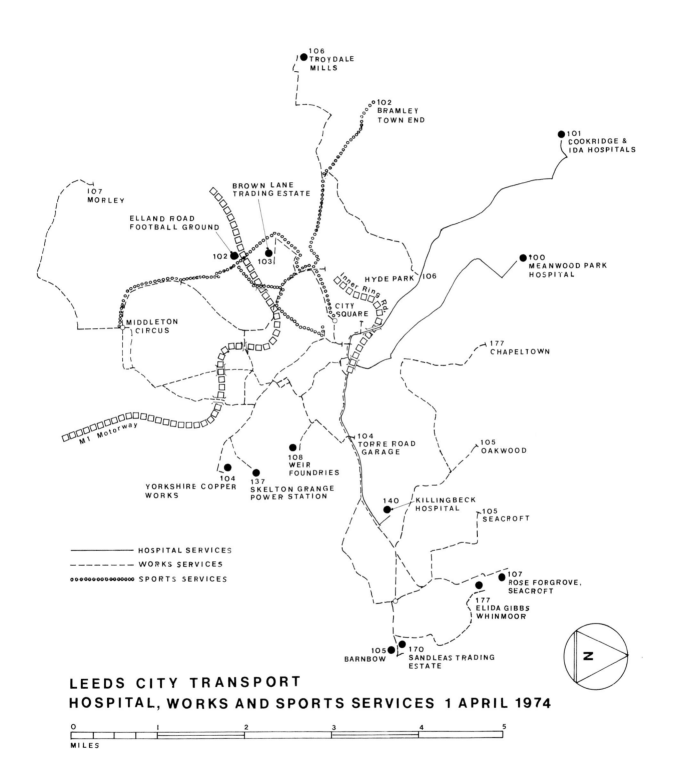

LEEDS CITY TRANSPORT

HOSPITAL, WORKS AND SPORTS SERVICES 1 APRIL 1974

1573

Leyland Atlantean 388 on special service 279 to Pudsey Show. The location is Pudsey Bus Station and date 11 July 1970. *J.B.Parkin.*

School Services

The origins of the school bus in Leeds are discussed in Volume 3 and, by 1953, there were several services in operation. From then on the story was one of continual expansion and modification, serving existing or new schools. For clarity the L.T.H.S. thought that the simplest way was to list the services introduced, withdrawn or modified during the period covered by this volume. As with the Hospital and Works services etc, although most of the routes and modifications are known, for space reasons details are not indicated, but are shown on the accompanying map. As will be seen below, the services became so numerous that in 1963 route numbers were adopted. This made things easier for both the staff and Department generally. In addition to the routes listed there were a large number of private hire school services. Individual fares were not charged to passengers and routes were subject to frequent change. They are not listed.

School Bus Services in operation prior to 1953

Note: These lists may not be complete as some school bus services were not included in the L.C.T. official records.

Allerton High School, King Lane to Oakwood
The school was officially opened on 28 March 1939 and a bus service started at the beginning of the summer term from Oakwood to the School. This service was operated throughout the war and was still in operation in 1953. Became service 110 in 1963.

Talbot Road Council School   St. Edmund's Church to Roman Avenue via the School
This service in a slightly different form had operated pre-war but had been discontinued in September 1939. On 26 January 1948 a new service from St, Edmund's Church, Roundhay, to the School was instituted. The service was later extended via the 36 bus route to Vicar Lane. It was still in operation in 1953.

Bentley Lane Council School, Meanwood
There had been a special bus service to Bentley Lane Council School from the Carr Manor Estate, from 1937 to the outbreak of war. This had been done by supplementing the 43 bus service (Eastgate-Carr Manor). In February 1947 a service from Shaw Lane, Headingley, via Bentley Lane Council School, Meanwood Road, to Allerton High School, was introduced. The service was discontinued in September 1956 when a service was opened from Leeds Girl's High School to Allerton High School by-passing Bentley Lane School by about 300 yards.

Leeds Girl's High School and Leeds Modern School
Service started 27 January 1947 from Leeds Girl's High School to the Leeds Modern School at the Ring Road, West Park, and was extended to the traffic island at Broadway, Horsforth. It was still in operation in 1953.

Roundhay High School to Selby Road
By February 1948 a service had been introduced from Selby Road to the School   The service was short lived.

West Leeds High School, Whingate, to Shaw Lane and Rodley
By February 1948 a service had been opened from Shaw Lane, Headingley, to the School. On 22 October 1950 a service from Rodley to the School, was opened. Became service 114 in 1963.

St. Anthony's School, Beeston, to Cottingley
From 6 December 1948 a service was opened from Cottingley to the School, rerouted through Cottingley Estate from 13 July 1952. Became service 120 in 1963.

Coldcotes School to Seacroft
From 6 December 1948 a service was opened from Seacroft to the School. Became service 117 in 1963.

West Park Senior Modern School, Spen Lane, to Cookridge and Ireland Wood

On 9 September 1952 services were opened from both Cookridge and Ireland Wood bus termini to the new School. Became service 121 in 1963.

Potternewton School for Crippled Children

About September 1952 a service was introduced from Headingley Garage to the School. The service was short lived.

School Bus Services introduced or modified 1953 to 1963

St. Anne's R.C. School to Stainbeck Avenue

About November 1954 a service was introduced from Stainbeck Avenue to the school. From 26 January 1959 the journeys were varied to include the Boy's School in Mount Preston Street. By 1963 the service had been discontinued.

Wykebeck C.P. School to Seacroft

From 10 January 1955 a service was introduced from the 67 terminus at Seacroft to the school. From 8 October 1956 this service was extended on certain journeys from Boggart Hill Drive to Monkswood Gate and from North Parkway to Bailey's Lane. A further alteration took place from 8 September 1959 when the journeys to and from Bailey's Lane were withdrawn. A revised route was introduced for buses operating to and from Monkswood Gate. In July 1961 the service was withdrawn.

Iveson House C.P. School to Tinshill and Headingley Garage

On 17 October 1955 a service was introduced from Tinshill to the School via the 30 and 33 bus routes. From 11 April 1956 the service was extended from the Tinshill Estate to Wood Nook Drive. Reroutings on 11 February 1957, 25 November 1957, 10 November 1958 and 29 March 1959. By 1963 a service was also operated from Headingley Garage. Became service 125 in 1963.

Hough Side Secondary School to Whingate Junction

On 11 April 1956 a service was introduced from Whingate Junction to the School. Became service 132 in 1963.

Leeds Girl's High School to Allerton High School

On 21 September 1956, a service was introduced from Leeds Girl's High School to Allerton High School. On 12 January 1960, the School Specials were extended to start from Leeds Girl's Junior School, Ford House, in Buckingham Road, off Headingley Lane. There was a minor rerouting from 8 October 1962. Became service 112 in 1963.

Allerton High School to Oakwood and Shaw Lane

From 30 April 1957, the service from Oakwood to the school originally introduced in 1939, was shortened by over a mile being rerouted from Harrogate Road via Street Lane West to King Lane instead of Harrogate Road and King Lane. From 24 June 1957 these buses also picked up children for Allerton Grange School. From 12 October 1959 one daily journey was extended from Allerton High School to Alwoodley Lane End in the afternoon. On 8 October 1962 there was a minor rerouting of the Shaw Lane service. Became service 110 in 1963,

Swarcliffe and Saville Green

From 10 September 1957 a school bus service between Swarcliffe and Saville Green was discontinued. When this service started is not known.

Seacroft Grange School to Boggart Hill Drive

From 10 September 1957 a service was introduced from Boggart Hill Drive to the School. The service was discontinued at the end of the summer term in July 1958.

St. Anthony's R.C. School, Beeston, and Beeston C.P. School to Cottingley Estate

From 6 October 1958 the service was extended from the Cottingley Estate to Dewsbury Road bus terminus for pupils attending Parkside C.S. School. From 30 November 1959 it was extended on the afternoon journey only to the Fountain Inn, Morley. A morning journey was introduced from Beeston to a School at Cottingley. Became service 120 in 1963.

West Leeds High School to Rodley and Shaw Lane

From 30 January 1959 the School specials from Rodley and Shaw Lane were extended to the new West Leeds High School for Girls in Congress Mount. From 26 October 1960 the service from Shaw Lane was rerouted. Became service 114 in 1963.

Parklands High School to Halton

From 8 September 1959 a service was introduced from the Irwin Arms, Halton, to the School. From 14 September 1959 the route was revised. Became service 130 in 1963.

Cow Close C.S. School, Farnley, to Amen Corner, Kirkstall

From 21 September 1959 a service was introduced from Amen Corner, Kirkstall, (Wyther Park Estate) to Cow Close C.S. School at Old Farnley. Became service 133 in 1963.

Leeds Grammar School to Moortown and Roundhay Park

From 5 October 1959 the service was extended from Moortown to Roundhay Park. It is not known when the service to Moortown originally started. Became service 113 in 1963.

Our Lady C.P. School, Weetwood Court, Headingley, to Tinshill

From 2 November 1959 service introduced from Tinshill to the School. On 6 September 1960 a further service was started from the School to Green Road, Meanwood, Became service 127 in 1963.

Beckett's Park C.P. School to Moor Grange

On 28 March 1960 a service was introduced from Old Oak Lawn to the School. From 27 February 1961 the service was extended from Old Oak Lawn to Latchmere Crest. Became service 135 in 1963.

Highfield C.P. School, Shadwell

From 17 October 1960 two journeys daily (on weekdays) extended on service 37 from the Shadwell terminus at Gateland Avenue to Strickland Avenue. Later incorporated into service 37.

West Park C.S. School to Cookridge, Tinshill and Infirmary Street

From 10 January 1961 a service was introduced between the School and Cookridge and on 23 January 1961 a service from the School to Tinshill. From November 1954 some children attending Ireland Wood School were allowed to travel from Cookridge on the West Park bus. On 17 September 1962 a service was introduced between the School and Infirmary Street. Became service 121 in 1963.

Lawnswood Girl's High School

On 23 February 1961 new services were introduced between the School and Cookridge and from the adjacent Leeds Modern School to Tinshill. Became service 123 in 1963.

Ireland Wood C.P. School to Tinshill
From 11 April 1961 a service was introduced between the School and Tinshill. Became service 126 in 1963.

Talbot Road C.P. School to Vicar Lane
From 17 September 1961 the service between Vicar Lane and Moortown was incorporated in the new 31 route.

St. Thomas Aquinas R.C. Grammar School and St. John Bosco R.C. School to various places
From 5 September 1961 five services were introduced to the two adjacent schools: From Sheepscar Street South, near Appleyard's Garage, from the Gaumont Cinema, Cookridge Street; from the Shaftesbury Cinema, York Road; from Infirmary Street; and from the Stainbeck Avenue stop in Stonegate Road, Meanwood. From 14 January 1963 an additional service was introduced from the two schools to Tinshill. All services numbered 116 in 1963.

Holy Family R.C. School, Armley, to New Farnley
From 5 September 1961 a service was introduced from New Farnley to the School. From 4 December 1961 the service was rerouted and on 12 September 1962 the service was extended to the Parish Hall, Green Lane. Became service 119 in 1963.

Fir Tree C.P. School to Meanwood
From 5 September 1961 a service from Meanwood terminus to the School was introduced. Became service 118 in 1963.

Matthew Murray Comprehensive School Brown Lane, Holbeck, to Balm Road, Beeston, and Middleton
On 12 September 1961 two services were introduced to the new school, one from Balm Road and the other from Beeston. From 26 October 1961 a new service from the school to Thorpe Lane, Middleton, opened. Both numbered 128 in 1963.

James Graham College to Lawns House, Farnley
On 2 October 1961 a service was introduced from Lawns House, Farnley to the College. It was short lived.

Gott's Park C. of E. School to Wortley
From 29 November 1961 service was istarted from Oldfield Lane, Wortley, to Amen Corner, Kirkstall. Became service 134 in 1963.

Ireland Wood C.P. School to Tinshill and Cookridge
From 1 May 1962 two services were introduced from the school to Tinshill and Cookridge. Became service 126 in 1963.

Sacred Heart R.C. School, Argie Avenue, to Hyde Park or Headingley
On 7 May 1962 a service started between the School and Hyde Park and on 21 May the same year, another service was opened to the number 7 bus terminus near Headingley Station. On 4 September 1962 the service was rerouted and extended to Spen Lane. Became service 129 in 1963.

St. Mary's R.C. School and Blackman Lane
From 4 September 1962 a service was introduced between Blackman Lane (Woodhouse Lane Junction) and the School. It was withdrawn on 6 November 1962.

Moor Grange C.S. School and Tinshill
From 26 November 1962 a service started between the School and Tinshill. Became service 122 in 1963.

Leeds Girl's High School and Leeds Modern School to Bradford Road
From 3 December 1962 the service was extended from Horsforth via Broadway and the Ring Road. School journeys became incorporated in the number 9 Ring Road service.

Abbey Grange C. of E. School to Tinshill
From 5 December 1962 new service was from the school in Butcher Hill, to Tinshill. Became service 136 in 1963.

The special school services were becoming very complicated and in March 1963 the various services were allocated route numbers. There were 27 services at the time and these were given the following numbers:

110 **Allerton High School** to Oakwood and Shaw Lane.
111 **Allerton Grange School** to Alwoodley. Allerton High School to the School.
112 **Leeds Girl's High School** to Allerton High School.
113 **Leeds Grammar School** to Moortown and Roundhay.
114 **West Leeds High Schools** to Rodley and Shaw Lane to the Schools.
115 **Christ the King R.C. School.** Hyde Park to Pudsey (formerly operated as part of Service 9).
116 **St.Thomas Aquinas, and St.John's Boscoe R.C. Schools** to various places.
117 **Coldcotes County Primary School** to Seacroft.
118 **Fir Tree C.P. School** to Meanwood.
119 **Holy Family R.C. School** to New Farnley.
120 **St.Anthony's R.C. School, Beeston** to Morley, and Cottingley.
121 **West Park C.S. School** to Cookridge and Tinshill.
122 **Moor Grange C.S. School** and Tinshill.
123 **Lawnswood Girl's High School** to Cookridge.
124 **Leeds Modern School** to Tinshill.
125 **Iveson House County Primary School, Tinshill Road,** to Headingley Garage.
126 **Ireland Wood C.P School** to Tinshill and Cookridge.
127 **Our Lady R.C. School** to Meanwood and Tinshill.
128 **Matthew Murray School** to Beeston, Hunslet and Middleton.
129 **Sacred Heart R.C. School** to Hyde Park or Spen Lane.
130 **Parklands High School, Seacroft,** to the Irwin Arms. Halton.
131 **City Square** to Moortown via Gledhow. Served several schools. (formerly operated as part of Service 31).
132 **Hough Side Secondary School** to Whingate.
133 **Cow Close C.S. School, Old Farnley,** to Amen Corner, Kirkstall.
134 **Gott's Park School** to Wortley.
135 **Beckett's Park C.P. School** to Moor Grange.
136 **Abbey Grange C. of E. School** to Tinshill.

As a general rule all services operating from several points to the same school carried the same service number.
Service 135 was a new service.

New or Modified School Services March 1963 to April 1974

110 Allerton High School

From 26 November 1966 the evening journey was extended to start from St. Paul's R.C. School instead of Allerton High School. From 4 May 1969 the service was rerouted via the new Sheepscar one-way scheme. In operation 1 April 1974.

111 Allerton Grange High School

From 7 September 1965 and 19 January 1968 the service between the School and Allerton High School was rerouted. From 4 January 1971 new services from Alwoodley Gates and from Shadwell to the School were opened. From 8 October 1973 services rerouted. In operation 1 April 1974.

112 Leeds Girl's High School

Service unchanged from 1963 to 1 April 1974.

113 Leeds Grammar School

Service unchanged from 1963 to 1 April 1974.

114 West Leeds High School

Service unchanged from 1963 to 1 April 1974

115 Christ the King R.C. School

From 8 June 1964 a new service was introduced between Intake and the School. In operation 1 April 1974.

116 St. Thomas Aquinas and St. John Bosco R.C. Schools

From 25 May 1964 a new service was introduced between Whitkirk and the two schools. From 31 January 1966 the evening journey was withdrawn. On 4 May 1969 the Sheepscar Street South service was rerouted via the new Sheepscar one-way scheme. In operation 1 April 1974.

117 Coldcotes C.P. School

From 5 January 1965 service introduced from Roundhay Park Swimming Pool to the School. From 1 November 1965 the service was rerouted. From 16 November 1967 the School to Seacroft service was extended from Seacroft to the Seacroft Town Centre. From 4 September 1972 school was renamed Dorset Primary School and altered to start at Oakwood. In operation 1 April 1974.

118 Fir Tree C.P. School

Service unchanged from 1963 to 1 April 1974.

119 Holy Family R.C. School to New Farnley

From 23 June 1971 a minor rerouting took place. In May 1972 rerouted due to closure of Main Road, Armley. From 19 June 1972 and September 1972 rerouted again. In operation 1 April 1974.

120 Beeston C.P. School

Service unchanged from 1963 to 1 April 1974.

121 West Park C.S. School

From 6 December 1971, service from City Square to School introduced. In operation 1 April 1974.

122 Moor Grange C.S. School

From 13 December 1965, new service introduced between the School and Cookridge. From 6 December 1971, service from City Square to School commenced. (formerly part of 74 service). In operation 1 April 1974.

123 Lawnswood Girl's High School

From 5 January 1965 service introduced from School to Tinshill. From 24 April 1968 rerouting. From 6 December 1971, service from City Square to School commenced. From 4 September 1972, combined with service 124.

123 Braimwood School

From 4 September 1972 service introduced between the School and Whinmoor. In operation 1 April 1974.

124 Leeds Modern School

On 27 September 1971 a service was commenced between Alwoodley and the School. From 4 September 1972 incorporated service 123. The adjacent Girl's High School was incorporated into the Modern School and the two schools were renamed Lawnswood School. Services from the School were now to Tinshill, Cookridge and Alwoodley with a new service to Chapeltown. From 30 April 1973 starting points were modified. In operation 1 April 1974.

125 Iveson House C.P. School

From 4 October 1965 a new service was introduced between Woodside Tavern, Horsforth, and the School. From 8 January 1968 the service was rerouted from Tinshill Road. From 12 November 1971 the service was withdrawn. From 4 September 1972 a new service, also numbered 125, from Kirkstall to the School, was introduced. From 4 September 1973 service extended to Tinshill Middle School. Three separate routes to school. In operation 1 April 1974.

126 Ireland Wood C.P. School

Service unchanged from 1963 to 1 April 1974.

127 Our Lady R.C. School

From 25 October 1965 the service was extended to Tinshill Road Top. From 15 January 1968 the service was rerouted. From 9 September 1968 the service between Meanwood and the School was amended providing certain journeys to Stonegate Road Circus. From 7 April 1971 the service from Tinshill to the School was withdrawn. School to Meanwood service still in operation 1 April 1974.

128 Matthew Murray School (later Matthew Murray High School)

From 30 October 1963 a new school service was introduced from Cottingley to the School. From 29 November 1965 the service was extended to Middleton Road, Belle Isle. From 19 June 1967 an additional service was introduced between the school and Dewsbury Road. From 5 February 1973, extended from Middleton Road to top of Belle Isle Road. In operation 1 April 1974.

129 Sacred Heart R.C. School

Service unchanged from 1963 to 1 April 1974.

130 Parklands High School, Seacroft

From 20 September 1965 the service was extended from Irwin Arms, Halton, to Wykebeck Arms, Selby Road. In operation on 1 April 1974.

131 Moortown-Vicar Lane

From 16 November 1973 the service was withdrawn.

131 Seacroft New Primary School

From 7 March 1974 service commenced from the old Seacroft Primary School at Seacroft Green to the replacement school. In operation 1 April 1974.

A.E.C. Regent III 739 on service 113 has just left Leeds Grammar School and is rounding the corner from Moorland Road into Hyde Park Road. It is bound for Moortown and the date is 17 June 1970. *W.D.Wilson/L.T.H.S.*

132   Houghside Secondary School
From 6 May 1963, service rerouted. Withdrawn July 1963.

132   St. Nicholas School, Gipton
From 4 November 1963 a journey was run in the morning from the Corn Exchange to the School. From 12 September 1972, service extended to Lupton Avenue. In operation 1 April 1974.

133   Cow Close C.S. School, Old Farnley
From 9 December 1963 rerouted between Whingate Junction and Old Farnley. In operation 1 April 1974.

134   Gotts Park C. of E. School
From 23 October 1970 the service between the School and Oldfield Lane, Wortley, was withdrawn.

134   Temple Moor School, Halton
From 4 January 1971 a new service was opened from Seacroft to the School. From 12 January 1972, service rerouted due to new underpass under York Road from Whinmoor Way to Stanks Drive. In operation on 1 April 1974.

135   Beckett's Park C.P. School
From 26 July 1970 the terminal point at Moor Grange was altered. From 4 September 1972 extended to serve Bennett Road and St. Chad's School. After a few days, on 12 September, reverted to original route. In operation 1 April 1974.

136   Abbey Grange C. of E. School
From 28 October 1971 the service was extended from Tinshill to Cookridge. In operation on 1 April 1974.

138   St. Mary's R.C. School
From 10 September 1963, new services were introduced from Seacroft, (North Parkway), or Swarcliffe to the School. From 9 September 1964 morning journeys from both termini were withdrawn. From 5 October 1964 afternoon journeys also withdrawn.

138   Clapgate C.P. School
From 5 January 1965 a new service was introduced between Belle Isle (Southcroft Gate) and the School. From 1 November 1965 the service was extended to the Middleton Arms. From 7 February 1966 and 21 April 1969, the service was rerouted. From 4 September 1973, altered to start at Middleton (Acre Square) instead of Middleton Arms. In operation on 1 April 1974.

139   St. Benedict's R.C. School
From 1 February 1965 a new service was introduced between Hyde Park and the School and another from Wellington Road. From 17 October 1966 the Hyde Park service was rerouted on journeys from the School. In operation 1 April 1974.

141   Cross Green C.S. School
From 5 January 1965 a service was introduced from Whitkirk Church to the new school and on 8 June 1970 a service was instituted from Compton Road. From 28 October 1971 a service introduced from Halton Moor. In operation 1 April 1974.

142   St. Paul's R.C. School
From 11 January 1965 a service was introduced between Oakwood and the School. In operation 1 April 1974.

143   Beechwood C.P. School
From 11 January 1965 service introduced between Swarcliffe and the School. From 7 September 1965 extended to a new terminus at Stanks Drive and rerouted via a newly constructed portion of the Ring Road from Seacroft to Barwick Road. On 21 December 1966 service withdrawn.

143   John Smeaton School
From 8 September 1969 this route number became occupied again when two services were opened to the new John Smeaton School in Barwick Road. They were one-man operated and one service ran from the Wykebeck Arms, Selby Road, and another from Whitkirk Church. One-man operated double deck buses were introduced on the route from 7 September 1970. From 18 September 1972 a new service was started from Austhorpe to the School. From 5 October 1972 a new service was introduced from Harehills to the School. In operation 1 April 1974.

144   Stainbeck C.S. School
From 7 September 1965 a new school service was introduced between Cranmer Bank, Moortown, and the School. In operation 1 April 1974.

145   St. Joseph's R.C. School and St. Francis' R.C. School
From 4 October 1965 a new school service was introduced between the Middleton Arms and St.Joseph's R.C. School. From 6 September 1966 service was extended from the School to St. Francis' R.C. School. From 16 February 1967 the service between the Middleton Arms and St. Francis' R.C. School was rerouted via Hunslet Road owing to closure of part of Jack Lane. From 7 October 1968 ran direct from the Middleton Arms to St. Francis R.C. School, not picking up at St.Joseph's R.C.School. From 27 January 1972, minor rerouting. In operation 1 April 1974.

146   St. Charles' R.C. School to Cross Green C.S. School
From 6 September 1966 a new service was introduced between East End Park (Cross Green C.S. School) and the School. From 31 March 1969 rerouted. From 6 October 1969 the service was withdrawn and replaced by a new service from Osmondthorpe to the School. From 9 December 1971, terminal arrangements altered. In operation 1 April 1974.

147   Kirkstall C.S. School
From 6 September 1966 a service was introduced between Hawksworth and the School. On 28 October 1968 the service was withdrawn.

147   Holy Rosary R.C. School
From 1 April 1971 this number was allocated to a service from the School in Leopold Street, Chapeltown Road, to the Holy Rosary Church, Carlton Street. The service had formerly operated on a private hire basis.   From 6 September 1971 a new service was commenced from Woodhouse Square to the School. On 2 November 1971 the School was renamed St.Dominic's R.C. School and the service number for the Woodhouse Square section was altered to 157.

A.E.C. Regent V 963 on service 133 on 23 June 1975.   It is at the major landmark on the Cookridge bus route, the Post Office Tower in Otley Old Road at Tinshill.   Built on the highest point in Leeds, 649 feet above sea level, in 1965 and 1966, it was commissioned in 1967.   Over the years the equipment on the tower has been modified and extended.   In 1989-90 a fire station (opened 27 April 1990 by Councillor Conlan) was built on the field adjacent to the bus and the base of the tower is currently obscured. *W.D.Wilson/L.T.H.S.*

148 Roundhay School

As early as March 1968 Roundhay High School had requested the Transport Committee to provide school services, but these had been refused. Following a further request in September 1970, two services were commenced from Roundhay School on 11 January 1971 using the former route number of the Wholesale Markets service. One route was from the School to Allerton High School, Alwoodley, and the other ran to Stainbeck Lane, Chapeltown, via Moortown to the School. In operation 1 April 1974.

149 Alwoodley C.P. School

From 7 September 1966 a new service was introduced between Meanwood and the School. On 9 September 1966, after only three days operation it was withdrawn owing to lack of support.

149 Garforth Comprehensive School

From 8 March 1971 buses working between Ledston Luck and the School were given this number. Previously the service had been operated as part of route 85. In operation 1 April 1974.

150 Acres Hall Avenue and Troydale to Pudsey Town Hall. Served several schools.

From 1 April 1968 a new school service was introduced from Acres Hall Avenue and Troydale to Pudsey Town Hall. After July 1968 service incorporated into the 81 bus service, following a rearrangement of bus services in the Troydale area.

150 Bruntcliffe High School

From 9 September 1968 a new service was established between the School and Elland Road, (Cottingley Drive). In operation 1 April 1974.

NOTE: On 16 October 1967 Leeds City Transport Department took over the operation of the School services formerly worked by the Exors. of Samuel Ledgard Ltd. from Armley Garage in Leeds. Most of the schools concerned had a large number of handicapped and E.S.N. (educationally sub-normal) children and coaches had been used. Services taken over were as follows:

Route No.	Service
150	Horsforth (Broadway) to **Armley Lodge**
150	Whitehall Road (Cattle Market) to **Armley Lodge**
151	Hyde Park to **Cardinal Square**
151	Holbeck (Spence Lane) to **Cardinal Square**
152	Meanwood (Meanwood Hotel) to **Cottingley C.P. School**
153	Harehills (Clock Cinema) to **East End Park**
153	Halton Moor (Neville Road) to **East End Park**
153	Moortown (Cranmer Road) to **East End Park**
154	Beeston (Broadway, Dewsbury Road), to **Elmete Hall**
154	Chapeltown (Sholebroke Mount) to **Elmete Hall**
155	Kirkstall (Star and Garter), to **Grafton**
156	Farnley (Ring Road, Tong Road), to **John Jamieson**, withdrawn 25 October 1967
156	Halton Moor (Ullswater Crescent) to **John Jamieson**, withdrawn 3 November 1967
156	Hyde Park (Delph Lane) to **John Jamieson**, withdrawn 3 November 1967
156	Seacroft (Kentmere Avenue) to **John Jamieson**, withdrawn 3 November 1967
157	Leeds (Duke Street) to **Roundhay Lodge**
157	Roundahay (Bentcliffe Drive) to **Roundhay Lodge**
157	Harehills (Bayswater Road) to **Roundhay Lodge**, withdrawn 2 November 1967
158	Seacroft (North Parkway) to **St. Bernadette's**
158	Seacroft (Hansby Gate) to **St. Bernadette's**
159	Rouindhay (Bentcliffe Drive) to **Wykebeck C.P. School**

In agreement with the Leeds Education Department most of these services were sub-contracted to other operators on a private hire basis. Fares were not charged and children were picked up as near as possible to their homes. The routes were therefore subject to frequent changes. Wallace Arnold Tours Ltd. was one of the main beneficiaries. Five services were soon withdrawn and transferred to private operators and others incorporated into existing services. From 1 July 1968, routes 151 to 158 in a radically altered form, became:

151 Cowper Street C.P. School

Existing private hire service given route number. From Cowper Street C.P. School to Harehills C.P., Roundhay Road C.P., Chapeltown C.P., Meanwood Road C.P., and Lovell Road C.P. From 10 September 1973 service rerouted from Earl Cowper School to Meanwood Road School, Lovell Park Primary School, Woodhouse Street, and Brudenell School. Service ceased 11 January 1974 and replaced by new service 151 from Earl Cowper School - Lovell Park Primary School - Meanwood Road School. From 28 January 1974 rerouted. In operation 1 April 1974.

152 Brownhill C.P. School - Beckett Street C.P.School – Cowper Street C.P. School

A new school service was introduced between Brownhill School and Cowper Street C.P. School via Beckett Street School. From 5 July 1971 a route alteration took place. From 28 November 1973 service extended from Lincoln Green School to Ebor Gardens School. From 6 January 1974 reverted to former route from Earl Cowper School to Lincoln Green School. In operation 1 April 1974.

153 Cowper Street C.P. School to Keplar School and Lovell Road C.P. School

Existing private hire service given route number. From 4 September 1972 Cowper Street School renamed Earl Cowper School. From 9 October 1972 altered to run from Keplar School to Grange Avenue. From 7 January 1974 rerouted. In operation 1 April 1974.

154 Lovell Road C.P. School to Roundhay Road C.P. School

Existing private hire service given route number. Route from Lovell Road C.P.School to Meanwood Road C.P., Chapeltown C.P., Cowper Street C.P., Harehills C.P. and Roundhay Road C.P. Schools. From 4 September 1972 service rerouted. After operation on 7 September 1973 withdrawn following introduction of revised 151 service on 10th.

155 Burley C. of E. School to Lovell Road C.P. School

Existing private hire service given route number. From 18 September 1970 service withdrawn.

156   Lovell Road C.P. School to Cowper Street C.P. School

Existing private hire service given route number. From 22 November 1971 and 9 April 1973 minor rerouting. Later rerouted again. In operation 1 April 1974.

157   Kepler C.P. School - Lovell Road C.P. School – Cowper Street C.P. School

Existing private hire service given route number.

157   St. Dominic's R.C. School to Woodhouse Square (see service 147)

From 2 November 1971 service from renamed school (St.Dominic's) in Leopold Street to Holy Rosary Church introduced.

158   Lovell Road C.P. School to Headingley Cricket Ground

Existing private hire service given route number. From Lovell Road C.P.School–Headingley Cricket Ground. From 18 September 1970 the service was withdrawn.

158   Colton C.P. School

From 8 March 1971 this number was allocated to buses running between the School and the 14 terminus at Halton. The buses had formerly operated as Duplicates on part of the 41 service on a private hire basis. In operation 1 April 1974.

159   St. Anne's R.C. School

From 3 November 1965 a new school service was introduced between Blackman Lane and the School. From 8 November 1965 the service was rerouted. On 9 September 1968 a service numbered 159 and extended to Stainbeck Avenue. The service was operated on a private hire basis until 1 April 1971. In operation 1 April 1974.

160   Cobden C.P. School

From 12 September 1967 a private hire service was introduced from New Farnley to the School. On 9 September 1968 it was given service number 160. From 20 January 1969 the service was extended from the School to Farnley C.P. School. From 4 September 1972 rerouted. In operation 1 April 1974.

161   Kirkstall C.S. School

Former private hire service from Spencer Place to school given route number on 9 September 1968. Rerouted 4 November 1968.

161   Blenheim C.P. School

From 13 September 1971, new service opened from Woodhouse Square to the School. Withdrawn 19 November 1971.

161   Middlethorne School

From 4 September 1972 services from Alwoodley and Moortown to School introduced. In operation 1 April 1974.

161   Ryecroft School

Service started 4 September 1972 from New Farnley to Cow Close School and Ryecroft School. From 29 October 1973 section of route within the Cow Close Estate was withdrawn. In operation 1 April 1974.

162   St. Joseph's R.C. School

This was a part replacement of service 145. From 7 October 1968 a service was introduced between the School and the Middleton Arms via Balm Road. There was also a service from Belle Isle Circus to the School. From 17 May 1971 a route alteration. From 18 September 1972 Middleton Arms and Belle Isle services combined. In operation 1 April 1974.

164   Foxwood School, Seacroft

From 6 January 1970 two services were commenced to this school. One ran from Stanks (Kelmscott Green) and the other from Swarcliffe (Stanks Drive) to the School. Both services ceased 20 December 1972 and, from 3 January 1973, combined into new service from Stanks via Swarcliffe to School. From 23 November 1973 service discontinued.

164   Brudenell School to Woodhouse Primary School and Quarry Mount School

Following the closure of Brudenell School for repairs, from 14 January 1974 three new services were introduced all numbered 164. Brudenell School – Woodhouse Primary School; Brudenell School to Quarry Mount School; Woodhouse Primary School – Quarry Mount School – Brudenell School. In operation on 1 April 1974.

165   Bramley St. Peter's C.of E. School to Green Lane School

From 9 September 1970 a new service was opened from the School to Green Lane School, Wortley. Withdrawn 4 September 1972 (last ran end of summer term 1972).

165   Iveson House School Annex

From 4 September 1973 two new services were introduced from Rodley and Half Mile Lane to the School. From 17 September 1973 services renumbered 176.

165   Holt Park School

From 3 January 1973 a new service was introduced from Five Lane Ends, Eccup, to the School. From 4 September 1973 extended at Holt Park end to Ireland Wood School. In operation on 1 April 1974.

166   Cross Gates School

From 4 September 1972 a new service was introduced between Halton Moor and the School. From 1 October 1973 service rerouted. In operation on 1 April 1974.

167   Oak Tree Middle School

From 4 September 1973 a new service was introduced from Seacoft to the School. In operation 1 April 1974,

168   Morris Silman School

From 4 September 1973 a new service from Chapeltown to the School was introduced. In operation 1 April 1974.

169   Seacroft Park School to Moor Allerton School

From 4 September 1973 service introduced between Moor Allerton School and the School. From 1 October 1973 service rerouted. In operation 1 April 1974.

172   Armley Park School

From 4 September 1973 service introduced between Whingate Road School and the School. In operation 1 April 1974.

173   Priesthorpe School

From 4 September 1973 service introduced from Rodley to the School. In operation on 1 April 1974.

175   Thornhill School

From 17 September 1973 new service introduced from Wortley to the School. In operation 1 April 1974.

176   Iveson House School annex

Formerly service 165 from 17 September 1973, numbered 176. In operation 1 April 1974.

178   St. Kevin's R.C. Secondary School

From 19 November 1973 a service from Burmantofts and back to City Square commenced. In operation 1 April 1974.

After April 1974 under the West Yorkshire Passenger Transport Executive the School services continued to increase and change. In September 1976 all the school services and other special services were renumbered and given an "L" prefix.

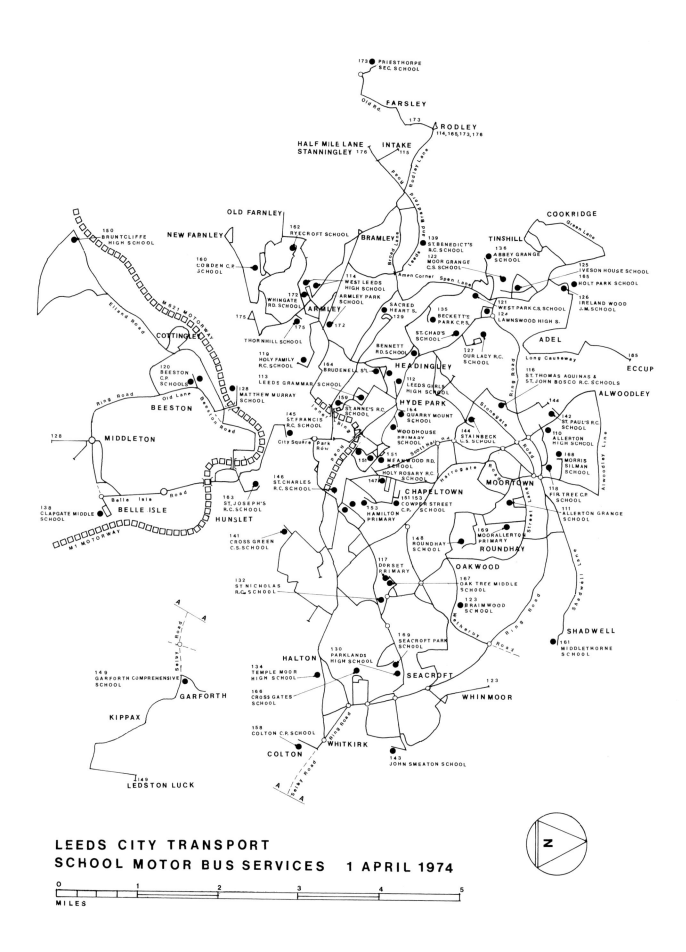

LEEDS CITY TRANSPORT
SCHOOL MOTOR BUS SERVICES   1 APRIL 1974

MILES

Leyland PD2/11 208 on service 134, the Gotts Park C. of E. School service, pictured in Wortley Road.
W.D.Wilson/L.T.H.S.

Night Bus Services 1946 to 1974

On 27 October 1946 night bus services were reintroduced after the war. Route numbers were allocated in October 1968 and were first used on 13 July 1969. They and subsequent alterations and extensions were as follows:

Infirmary Street to MOORTOWN (Allerton High School) via Chapeltown, later service 302

Reintroduced 27-10-1946. Stand removed from Infirmary Street to City Square (Boar Lane) and rerouted in city centre 30-4-1967. Allocated route number **302**. In operation 1 April 1974.

Infirmary Street to ROUNDHAY via Harehills, later service 310

Reintroduced 27-10-1946. Stand removed from Infirmary Street to City Square (Boar Lane) and rerouted in city centre 30-4-1967. Allocated route number **310**. In operation 1 April 1974.

Infirmary Street to MIDDLETON, Middleton Arms, via Dewsbury Road, later service 312

Reintroduced 27-10-1946. Extended via Middleton Park Avenue to **THORPE LANE**, 15-8-1948. Stand removed from Infirmary Street to City Square 2-5-1965. Some journeys diverted to run to Middleton Garage from 13-11-1966. Allocated route number **312**. In operation 1 April 1974.

Infirmary Street to HALTON (Green Lane), via York Road, later service 314

Reintroduced 27-10-1946. Extended to **WHITKIRK** 30-3-1947. Stand moved from Infirmary Street to City Square 22-2-1958. Extended via Ring Road, Halton, to Whitkirk 39 terminus at Selby Road on Saturday nights 27-1-1962. Rerouted in city centre 30-4-1967. Allocated route number **314**. In operation 1 April 1974.

Infirmary Street to GIPTON, via Compton Road, later service 316

Reintroduced 27-10-1946. Extended to **SEACROFT** 1-6-1952. Extended from Ironwood View to North Parkway/Kentmere Avenue junction, 13-5-1956. Stand moved from Infirmary Street to City Square 22-2-1958. Later back to Infirmary Street. Buses rerouted in city centre 30-4-1967 and stand changed to City Square. . Allocated route number 311, but number changed to **316**. In operation 1 April 1974.

Infirmary Street to BELLE ISLE, via Hunslet Road, later service 321

Reintroduced 27-10-1946. Rerouted from 25-4-1949. Stand removed from Infirmary Street to City Square 2-5-1965. All journeys extended to Middleton Garage 13-11-1966. Allocated route number **321**. In operation 1 April 1974.

Infirmary Street to KIRKSTALL, via Kirkstall Road, later service 324

Reintroduced 27-10-1946. Extended to Fleece Hotel, **HORSFORTH**, on certain journeys 1-5-1955. Kirkstall terminus extended from Star and Garter to Abbey Walk 24-9-1956. Stand removed from Infirmary Street to City Square. Allocated route number 325, but changed to **324**. In operation 1 April 1974.

Infirmary Street to CROSS GATES, via York Road, later service 325

Reintroduced 27-10-1946. Stand removed from Infirmary Street to City Square by 1960. Rerouted in city centre 30-4-1967. Allocated route number **324**. Extended to **SWARCLIFFE** (Stanks Drive), 13-7-1969 and route number changed to **325**. In operation 1 April 1974.

Infirmary Street to LOWER WORTLEY, via Wellington Road, later service 332

Reintroduced 27-10-1946. Stand moved from Infirmary Street to City Square 8-3-1958. Certain journeys extended to Butterbowl Hotel from 26-2-1967. Allocated route number **342**. Extended via Branch Road to SWINNOW, and renumbered **332** 13-7-1969. In operation 1 April 1974.

Infirmary Street to HEADINGLEY and WEST PARK, later service 336

Reintroduced 27-10-1946. Extended via Otley Road to the Ring Road 21-11-1948. Extended to **IRELAND WOOD** via Otley Old Road, 8-7-1950. Extended from Ireland Wood to **TINSHILL** on Friday and Saturday nights, 5-6-1959. Stand moved from Infirmary Street to City Square 30-4-1967. Allocated route number **330** for Ireland Wood section and **336**, for Tinshill section. **336** used for whole route from 13-7-1969. In operation 1 April 1974.

Infirmary Street to Half Mile Lane, STANNINGLEY, via Stanningley Road, later service 365

Reintroduced 27-10-1946. Stand moved from Infirmary Street to City Square 24-3-1958. Extended from Half Mile Lane to **PUDSEY**, Market Place, 25-1-1959. Allocated route number **365**. In operation 1 April 1974.

Infirmary Street to EAST END PARK

Reintroduced 27-10-1946. Withdrawn 30-3-1947.

Infirmary Street to ELLAND ROAD

Reintroduced 27-10-1946. Withdrawn 30-3-1947.

Infirmary Street to GUISELEY, White Cross, via Kirkstall Road

New service introduced 30-3-1947. Withdrawn 30-4-1955.

Infirmary Street to MORLEY (Fountain Inn), via Beeston Road, later services 352 and 353

New service introduced 30-3-1947. Stand removed from Infirmary Street to City Square 30-4-1967. Allocated route number 352 via Beeston. Returned as **353** via Elland Road. In operation 1 April 1974.

Infirmary Street to WHINGATE, via Wellington Road, later service 315

New service introduced 30-3-1947. Stand moved from Infirmary Street to City Square 8-3-1958. Extended to **BRAMLEY** on last journey 22-7-1956. Allocated route number **316**, but number changed to 315. In operation 1 April 1974.

Infirmary Street to HEADINGLEY (Shaw Lane), CHAPELTOWN and WHITKIRK, later service 339

New service introduced by 8-1947. Stand moved from Infirmary Street to City Square 30-4-1967. Allocated route number **344**. City terminus changed to Westgate (opposite Yorkshire Post building) from 5-10-1970. Service renumbered **339** 5-12-1971. From 31 January 1972 the service curtailed from Whitkirk to **HALTON** (Irwin Arms). In operation 1 April 1974.

Infirmary Street to Park Gates, BEESTON, via Beeston Road

New service introduced by 7-9-1947. Short lived service. Beeston served by Morley buses from 1-8-1950. Beeston service incorporated into Morley service 6-1964.

Infirmary Street to MEANWOOD, via Meanwood Road

New service introduced late 1948 . Saturday night only service. Stand removed from Infirmary Street to City Square (Boar Lane) and rerouted in city centre 30-4-1967. Allocated route number **308**, but the number was not used as the service was withdrawn on 13-7-1969.

Infirmary Street to SEACROFT (Monkswood Gate) via Harehills, later service 367

New service introduced 20-8-1956. Stand moved from Infirmary Street to City Square 22-2-1958. Rerouted in city centre 30-4-1967 and stand moved to City Square. Allocated route number **367**. In operation 1 April 1974.

Astoria Ball Room, HAREHILLS, to WHITKIRK

New service introduced 25-3-1961 via Roundhay Road and the 38 bus route on Saturdays nights only, after dances. This service was short lived.

On 13-7-1969 the Night Bus Services were converted to one-man operation using single-deck buses.
From 5-12-1971 all staff buses were numbered in the Night Bus series. Ordinary passengers could be carried on all these duties with the exception of services 373 and 377. The numbers allocated were as follows:

306	Torre Road Garage – Cross Gates – Halton – Torre Road Garage.
311	Torre Road Garage – City Square.
317	Seacroft Garage – Cross Gates – Gipton – Torre Road Garage.
318	Middleton Garage – Sovereign Street Garage.
326	Seacroft Garage – Cross Gates – Swarcliffe – Seacroft Garage.
327	Torre Road Garage – Gipton – Cross Gates – Swarcliffe – Seacroft Garage.
344	Torre Road Garage – Harehills – Stainbeck Road – Headingley Garage.
345	Seacroft Garage – Harehills – Gipton – Seacroft Garage.
346	Middleton Garage – Dewsbury Road – Hunslet – Belle Isle – Middleton Garage.
350	Headingley Garage – Hyde Park _ Headingley Garage.
361	Torre Road Garage – Sovereign Street Garage.
373	Bramley Garage – Bramley area – Bramley Garage.
377	Bramley Garage – Bramley area – Bramley Garage.

Leeds City Transport Timetables and Maps

TIMETABLES

1930 to 1939

Before the War, the timetables were of a similar style. At first printed quarterly and then monthly and finally at two monthly intervals, the timetable changed colour for each issue. It was comprehensive and gave details of all the tram and bus services, routes, fares, the Parcels Department with rates, postal boxes on tramcars and buses, etc.

In regard to tramcars the times of the first and last trams was given with the average service on the various routes. The service varied from every four minutes on most routes to ten minutes on the less busy. The Temple Newsam route had a 30 minutes service. Full details of the bus timetables were given with the routes, fares and stages. The centre pages consisted of a tram and bus route map, but after the end of 1937 this ceased to be included. The timetable was free of charge and available from conductors, depots, or at the Swinegate Head Office.

1940 to 1946

The timetables issued during the War were of a slightly larger format. They were issued quarterly and the colour of the paper cover was changed with each issue. There was no map and the contents were restricted to the details of the first and last tramcars, service frequency, and the bus timetables. There were no details of the routes covered by the buses. There was a generalised advertisement for the parcels service.

The same style of cover was used after the war, but the timetable was now issued bi-monthly. The tramways timetable was more detailed and after October 1946 details of the Night Service buses were included. Throughout this period the timetable was free of charge. All timetables issued from 1930 to 1946 were printed by Jowett & Sowry Ltd. of Leeds.

1947 to 1960

In 1947 a two-colour (later three-colour) cover was introduced of a "modern" design typical of the period. The contents were, however, the same as the timetables issued in 1945 and 1946. This cover design was used until March 1960, but in the meantime there had been some alterations and additions. Beginning with the August 1951 issue, a charge of 3d. was made for the timetable. From November 1957 fare tables for both the tram and bus routes were included. All the timetables from 1947 to 6 July 1957 were printed by Jowett & Sowry Ltd. This firm also printed the traffic notices used by the Department. From the issue dated 7 July 1957 to March 1960, G.W. Belton Ltd. of Scarborough were the printers.

1960 to 1964

From the issue of 27 March 1960 the cover was modified. It was of a much simpler design with a beige background and lettering of a different colour for each issue. G.W. Belton Ltd. was the printer of the new style timetable until 27 April 1963 when W.A. Smith of Leeds took over the printing for three years. 7,500 copies of each issue were printed.

1964 to 1974

A radical improvement to the timetable was made in June 1964. The covers were of a much stiffer card in two shades of green and included a photograph of a bus. A different photograph was provided for each issue. The contents were, however, similar to those introduced in November 1957, but the night buses were presented in a more detailed form. From July 1965 instead of the heading "LEEDS CITY TRANSPORT" at the head of the timetable a new style "L C T" logo was incorporated. The lettering of the logo was at first in light green and from October 1965, in white. This cover design persisted until the takeover by the West Yorkshire Passenger Transport Executive on 1 April 1974. The final issue showed an illustration of one of the original Roundhay Park electric tramcars of 1891.

In April 1965 the Transport Committee received a request from the Municipal Passenger Transport Association asking local authorities to consider introducing the 24-hour clock for bus services and timetables. The Transport Committee rejected this proposal, Alderman Rafferty said that they would wait until some uniformity emerged among passenger transport operators. This occurred the following year for May 1966 saw a big change in the contents of the timetable. The number of pages was increased from 104 to 176 and it was laid out in accordance with a new standard. It was easier to read and more detailed than the earlier timetables. The now almost universal 24-hour clock notation appeared for the first time. The basic contents were, however, the same. From July 1966 the cost was increased to 4d.

The timetable was becoming more costly to produce and from the April-June 1968 issue the price was increased to 6d. With decimalisation in February 1971 the price was rounded up to 3p and it remained at this level for the remainder of the existence of the Leeds City Transport undertaking. By September 1971 the timetable had increased in size to over 200 pages and from this month was increased further to 226 pages by the inclusion of four services operated by the West Riding Automobile Company: the No.1 service from Leeds to Selby and Goole, 162/163 Leeds - Garforth – Kippax and Castleford and the 166 Leeds – Garforth – Sherburn – South Milford.

In place of a list of routes at the front of the timetable, from the November 1971 to January 1972 issue, a fairly comprehensive index was included which listed the principal places and streets in the city together with the bus routes which served them. By then the timetable resembled a small booklet and became too thick for staples. These were omitted from the May to July 1972 and subsequent issues.

W.A. Smith of Leeds were the printers of the timetable until 30 April 1966 when G.W. Belton took over the printing of the new, but more expensive timetable. As before, 7,500 copies were printed of each bi-monthly issue, but by 1971 this number had been increased to 11,000. Belton retained the printing contract until the demise of the Leeds Transport undertaking in April 1974 and for a year or so afterwards.

POST 1974

From the takeover by the West Yorkshire PTE the timetable was expanded to about 450 pages and included the National Bus Company services operated by the West Riding, Yorkshire Woollen District and West Yorkshire Road Car Companies. The cost was increased to 5p. Alas the Leeds District timetable did not last long in this form. It was costly to produce – about £1,120 per issue - and when Belton's contract expired in August 1975, that was the last. There were a series of large format Leeds District timetables issued in May 1976, November 1976, and June 1977. They had about 550 pages and cost 15p a copy. They were followed by similar timetables in February and July 1979 costing 20p and another in September 1980 costing 35p. The last timetables to

The front of the timetable that was issued from 1930 to 1939.   The colour of the front differed from month to month. Size 102mm x 137mm (4in x 5³/₈ in.)

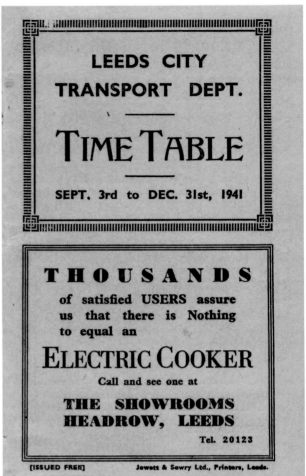

The front of the quarterly timetable issued from 1940 to 1946.   The colour differed from month to month. Size 105mm x 165mm (4¹/₈ in. x 6¹/₂in.)
In the column opposite is the front of the timetable issued from 1947 to 1960.   From the August 1951 issue a charge of 3d. was made for the timetable. Size 105 mm x 163mm (4¹/₈in x 6³/₈ in.).

appear which listed all the bus routes in Leeds were in January to October 1986 when three small format, 650 page, timetables were produced costing 50p each. There was a similar timetable in May 1987, but generally after 1986 separate timetables were issued by METRO for individual bus routes free of charge.

MAPS

There had been route maps included in the timetables until 1937, but this practice was then discontinued. In 1961 a separate bus route map was produced at a cost of 1s.0d. It was in three colours, the routes being in black, destinations red and black and parks and open spaces in green. Special bus services were not shown. On the reverse of the map the services were listed and there was also an index showing principal locations on the map. For the most part the maps were accurate. There were 12 editions and whereas the first five were hand drawn some mechanical aids were used in the production of editions 6 to 12. There was a two years gap between the printing of the fifth and sixth editions, but the sixth was improved. It was printed in the same three colours. Routes were black as before, termini and important buildings were in red and open park areas green. There was also the list of services and index on the back.   The cover was of a different style and incorporated the new LCT logo. The price was still 1s.0d.   With the eighth edition the price increased to 1s.3d. and the ninth to 1s.6d.   The ninth edition was quickly out of date, but was on sale until early 1969. Lists of alterations since publication were included with the map. The tenth edition cost 2s.0d. and the eleventh and twelfth editions 12p each. All issues were printed by E.J. Arnold & Son Ltd. Leeds, 5,000 copies being printed of each issue. Costing £270 16s. 8d. to print the first edition, the twelfth edition cost £841-50p to produce. With bus route alterations the maps were not accurate for very long. The 12 editions were as follows:

Edition	Published	Accurate from:
1st	June 1961	26-2-1961 to 24-6-1961
2nd	September 1961	17-9-1961 to 3-12-1961
3rd	January 1962	28-1-1962 to 1-9-1962
4th	October 1962	28-10-1962 to 27-4-1963
5th	December 1963	24-11-1963 to 1-2-1964
6th	March 1966	1-1966 to 30-4-1966
7th	September 1966	25-9-1966 to 12-11-1966
8th	February 1967	26-2-1967 to 29-7-1967
9th	June 1968	30-6-1968 to 25-7-1968
10th	January 1970	19-1-1970 to 15-3-1970
11th	May 1971	3-5-1971 to 20-7-1971
12th	January 1973	8-1-1973 to 30-3-1973

LEEDS CITY TRANSPORT

LEEDS CITY TRANSPORT
TIMETABLE
9 MAY 1965 TO 3 JULY 1965
PRICE 3d.

The front cover of the timetable issued from June 1964 to April 1974. The colours remained the same, but the photograph was altered for every issue. From the 4 July 1965 issue the timetable was headed with the LCT logo. This issue, the last of the earlier type, shows coach 10 on the front cover. Size 108mm x 160mm (4 1/4in. x 6 3/8in.)

The front of the timetable that was issued from March 1960 to 1964. The beige colour was present on all the issues, but the lettering colour varied every quarter. Size 102mm x 169mm (4 in. x 6 5/8in.)

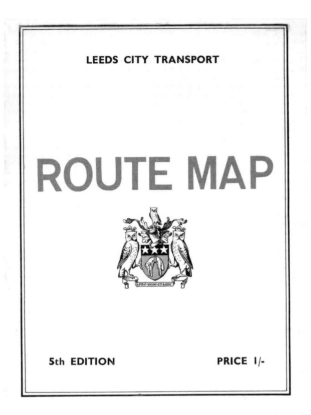

LEEDS CITY TRANSPORT

TIMETABLE

4 JULY 1965 TO 4 SEPTEMBER 1965

PRICE 3d.

LEEDS CITY TRANSPORT

ROUTE MAP

5th EDITION   PRICE 1/-

The cover used after 4 July 1965 showed the LCT logo at the top.   On this issue there is a photograph of a Leyland PD2 ascending Rodley Lane.

The front of the 5th edition of the Leeds City Transport route map issued in December 1963. The printing was in black with the words "ROUTE MAP" in red. Size 140mm x 184mm. (5½in. x 7³/₁₆in.)

Leyland PD2/11 214 in Eccup Lane at Adel Bridge, Adel. Eccup Lane was a road not used by service buses. The date is 2 August 1955 and the bus is on a "See Your City" tour. *W.D. Wilson/ L.T.H.S.*

"See Your City Tours" 1928 to 1974

There had been special tours of Leeds by bus as early as 1928. During Leeds Civic Week from 22 to 28 September of that year there were two different tours.

Tour 1 ran on Monday, Tuesday and Wednesday, 24, 25 and 26 September and comprised a drive through Temple Newsam Park, the new sewage works to the south east of the city, Middleton and new roads and housing schemes to the south west, passing Kirkstall Abbey and returning via Hawksworth Wood Estate, West Park and Headingley Lane.

Tour 2 ran on Wednesday, Thursday and Friday, 26, 27 and 28 September and included Headingley, Weetwood, Moortown, Meanwood Housing Estate, the "new and picturesque" Gledhow Valley Road, Scott Hall Road, Ring Road Shadwell, Wetherby Road, Oakwood, and Cross Gates Housing Estate.

Each tour was about 28 miles long and tickets were 1s.0d. per tour purchased a day in advance from the tramway offices. Tour routes were as follows:

1928 Tour 1.

From Town Hall, via New York Road, York Road, Selby Road and Temple Newsam Road to Temple Newsam, through Park and past the Mansion to Pontefract Lane, Thorpe Stapleton, to Hunslet, then via Pepper Road and Middleton Road to Middleton Housing Estate, Middleton Park Road, Ring Road, Dewsbury Road, Old Lane and Wesley Street, to Elland Road. Then to the Ring Road, crossing Gelderd Road and Whitehall Road. Then along Hrenconner Lane past the Greenthorpe Housing Estate, crossing Stanningley Road, Cockshott Lane, past Wyther Housing Estate to Kirkstall Bridge, then via Abbey Road, Hawksworth Road, and Butcher Hill to Hawksworth Wood Housing Estate. Return via Spen Lane, West Park and Headingley to the Town Hall.

1928 Tour 2.

From Town Hall via Headingley Lane, Otley Road to West Park, passing Filter Beds. Then along Ring Road to Smithy Mills Lane and Ring Road to Moortown, Stonegate Road, Monk Bridge Road, and Shaw Lane into Grove Lane, across Meanwood Road and up Stainbeck Road through the Meanwood Housing Estate, to Harrogate Road at King Lane Junction. Then along the new Gledhow Valley Road, to Roundhay Road, Barrack Road, Buslingthorpe Lane and Scott Hall Road to Moortown. Then via Sand Hill Lane and Shadwell Lane to a "fine" section of the Ring Road to Wetherby Road, Oakwood, Oakwood Lane past Easterly Road and Hollin Park Housing Estate, Foundry Lane, York Road, Cross Gates Lane, Cross Gates Road. Return via York Road, New York Road, Briggate and The Headrow to the Town Hall.

It was another nine years before city bus tours reappeared. These were on the occasion of the Coronation of King George VI. Three tours ran on Sundays 9 to 23 May 1937 at a fare of 1s.0d. for adults and 6d. for children.

1937 Tour 1.

City Square, Park Row, Cookridge Street, Woodhouse Lane, Headingley Lane, Otley Road, Weetwood Lane, Smithy Mills Lane, Ring Road, Harrogate Road, Sand Hill Lane, Shadwell Lane, Ring Road, Wetherby Road, Easterly Road, Oakwood Lane, Foundry Lane, Cross Gates Road, Station Road, Hollyshaw Lane, Green Lane, Cross Green Lane, Chapel Street, Selby Road, York Road, Ivy Street, East Park Parade, Cross Green Lane,

Pre-war A.E.C. Regent 269 (GUA 794) at King Lane on a "See Your City Tour" on 2 August 1955.
W.D.Wilson/L.T.H.S.

A.E.C. Regent V 781 at Five Lane Ends, Adel, about 1965. The bus is turning from King Lane into Eccup Lane on a "See Your City Tour". This was a popular place for photographs. *Leeds City Transport.*

A.E.C. Swift 58 at the Temple Newsam lodge gates at the end of Colton Road. It had travelled from Whitkirk and was photographed on a Temple Newsam tour on 12 August 1968. *J.B.Parkin.*

Green Lane, East Street, Kirkgate, Call Lane, Duncan Street and Boar Lane to City Square.

1937 Tour 2.

City Square, Boar Lane, Duncan Street, Call Lane, New York Street, York Street, York Road, Selby Road, Ring Road, Hollyshaw Lane, Station Road, Cross Gates Road, Foundry Lane, Oakwood Lane, Easterly Road, Roundhay Road, Gledhow Valley Road, Stainbeck Road, Grove Lane, Shaw Lane, Otley Road, Horsforth Lane, Spen Lane, Butcher Hill, Lea Farm Road, Hawkswood Crescent, "Circus", Broadway. Vesper Road, Spen Lane, Morris Lane, Kirkstall Hill, Burley Road, Park Lane, East Parade and Infirmary Street to City Square.

1937 Tour 3.

City Square, Bishopgate Street, Neville Street, Great Wilson Street, Hunslet Lane, Hunslet Road, Low Road, New Pepper Road, Pepper Road, Middleton Road, Middleton Park Road, Beeston Park Road, Dewsbury Road, Ring Road to Tong Road, Whingate, Hill Top Road, Green Hill Road, Henconner Lane, Town Street (Bramley) Broad Lane, Newlay Lane, Leeds and Bradford Road, Bridge Road, Kirkstall Lane, Morris Lane, Spen Lane, Vesper Road, Broadway, "Circus", Hawkswood Crescent, Lea Farm Road, Butcher Hill, Spen Lane, Horsforth Lane, Otley Road, Headingley Lane, Woodhouse Lane, Cookridge Street and Park Row to City Square.

There were also three special bus tours of the city held on Sunday afternoons in July and August of 1938 and June to August 1939. Fares were as the 1937 tours. Buses started from Infirmary Street and each tour was approximately 20 miles. Brief details of the tours were given and appear to have been identical to the three tours of 1937.

At Whitsuntide and on Sundays in June to August 1939 two tours were operated. Both tours appear to have been identical to Tours 1 and 2 of 1937.

The war period and 1940's were a period of severe austerity throughout the country as a whole. There was rationing of many commodities and it was not until 1950 that the Transport Department considered the reintroduction of summer bus tours of the city. Tours began at Whitsuntide 1950 and were held annually on the dates shown and indicated in the tables below, Most departures were from the Central Bus Station and usually in the afternoon between 2.00 p.m. and 4.30 p.m.

1950 Two City Tours (1st post war).

Whit Monday and Tuesday 29-30 May 1950 and Bank Holiday Monday and Tuesday 7-8 August 1950.

There were two 30 mile tours from the Central Bus Station. Although the complete routes are not known they included visits to Gipton Estate, Seacroft, Roundhay Park, Moortown, Alwoodley, Adel Church, Hawksworth, Sandford, Cottingley, Middleton and Belle Isle. Fares were 1s.3d. adult, 9d. child. The tours were successful and over the two days in May 17,000 passengers were carried and 60 double deck buses were used.

The tours from 1951 to 1957 followed a similar pattern to those of 1950 and included tours of the various Corporation housing estates. They were intended primarily for Leeds citizens. A new tour was introduced in 1958 and in 1963 the tours were expanded.

1951 City Tour.

Whit Monday and Tuesday 14-15 May. Route and fares as 1950

1952 City Tour.

Whit Monday and Tuesday 2-3 June. Route and fares as 1950.

1953 City Tour New Tour (2nd post war).

6-7 April, 25, 26 May, 2 June. Tour started at Platform F at the Central Bus Station but route is not known. The tour on Coronation Day (2 June) was stated to be "interesting, colourful and picturesque." Fares 2s.0d. adult, 1s.0d. child.

City Tour.

7-8 June, 2-3 August. Route and fares as 1953.

1955 City Tour.

12 April, 30-31 May, 1-2 August. Route and fares as 1953.

1956 City Tour. New Tour (3rd post war).

3 April, 21-22 May, 6-7 August. Route not known. Fares as 1953.

1957 City Tour.

10-11 June, 5-6 August. Route as 1956. Fares as 1953.

1958 City Tour. New Tour (4th post war).

26-27 May, 4-5 August. Route: Central Bus Station, York Road, Selby Road, Ring Road, Station Road, Cross Gates Road, Ring Road, Seacroft, Wetherby Road, Oakwood, 45 bus route to King Lane, Moortown Ring Road, Weetwood Lane, Otley Road to city, Westgate roundabout, Westgate, Wellington Street, City Square, then to Middleton and Belle Isle and back to Bus Station. Fares as 1953.

1959 City Tour.

18-19 May, 3-4 August. Route as 1958. Fares as 1953.

1960 City Tour.

6-7 June, 1-5 August, 8-12 August. Route as 1958. Fares as 1953.

1961 City Tour. New Tour (5th post war).

22-23 May, 7-8 August. From 7 August a revised tour was introduced. The route from the Central Bus Station was via Eastgate, New York Road, Burmantofts Street, Beckett Street, Stanley Road, Compton Road, Foundry Approach, Coldcotes Circus, Coldcotes Drive, Wykebeck Valley Road, South Parkway Approach, Kentmere Avenue, North Parkway, Ramshead Drive, Ring Road, Shadwell Lane, Harrogate Road, Street Lane West, Stonegate Road Circus, King Lane, Five Lane Ends, Eccup Lane, Church Lane, Otley Road, Ring Road, Spen Lane, Queenswood Drive, Kirkstall Lane, Otley Road, Headingley Lane, Woodhouse Lane, Fenton Street, Calverley Street, East Parade, Infirmary Street, City Square, Wellington Street, Westgate, The Headrow, and Eastgate to the Central Bus Station. Fares as 1953.

1962 City Tour.

23-24 April, 11-12 June, 6-7 August. Route as 1961. Fares as 1953.

1963 City Tour.

15,16 April, Route as 1961. Fares as 1953.

1963 City Tour. New Tour (6th post war).

From Whit Monday, 3 June 1963, there was a major reorganisation of the tour buses. The idea was to attract visitors from outside the city. A new City Tour route was operated and two new Wednesday afternoon Sightseeing tours were instituted. Both the Wednesday tours were about 25 miles in length.

On 3-4 June, and 5-6 August, (both Bank Holidays) the City Tour ran via a new route: From Central Bus Station via Eastgate, Vicar Lane, New Market Street, Call Lane. Bridge End, Meadow Lane, Meadow Road, Elland Road, Holbeck Moor, Domestic Street, Gelderd Road, Ring Road (Wortley), Whitehall Road, New Farnley, Back Lane, Tong Road, Hall Lane, Butt Lane, Ring Road, Swinnow Lane, Stanningley Road, Town Street, Bradford Road, Ring Road to Moortown, then Harrogate Road, Stainbeck Road, Scott Hall Road, Sheepscar Street North and South, Regent Street and St. Peter's Street to the Bus Station. Fares as1953 i.e. 2s.0d. adult, 1s.0d. child.

On Bank Holiday Monday, 5 August, the tour was altered to start in St. Peter's Street outside the Bus Station.

1963 Tour 1 Adel Church and Kirkstall Abbey.

Wednesday afternoons, 5 June to 25 September. Route from Central Bus Station via the 35 service route, to Alwoodley Lane End, then via King Lane, to Five Lane Ends, Eccup Lane, Church Lane to Adel Church, Otley Road, Ring Road, Spen Lane, Abbey Walk, Kirkstall Abbey, number 4 service route, Vicar Lane and Eastgate to the Bus Station. There was a 20 minutes stop at Adel

Church where the Rector, Canon Simpson, described the history of the Church. 1¼ hours was spent at Kirkstall Abbey. Fares 2s.0d. adult, 1s.0d. child.

1963 Tour 2 Roundhay Park and Temple Newsam.

Wednesday afternoons, 5 June to 25 September. Route from Central Bus Station via Eastgate, Regent Street, Roundhay Road, Princes' Avenue, Mansion Lane, through Roundhay Park and then via Wetherby Road, Ring Road, Coal Road, York Road, Cross Gates Lane, Station Road, Hollyshaw Lane, Colton Road, and through the Park to Temple Newsam bus terminus, then via the 22 service route to the Bus Station. There was a stop of 25 minutes at the Lakeside Café in Roundhay Park and a 1½ hours stay at Temple Newsam.

Fares 2s.0d. adult, 1s.0d. child.

1964 City Tour.

30-31 March, 17-18 May, 3-4 August (all Bank Holidays). Route and fares as 1963.

1964 Tour 1 Adel Church and Kirkstall Abbey.

Each Tuesday and Thursday afternoon from 2 June to 17 September. Route and fares as 1963.

1964 Tour 2 Roundhay Park and Temple Newsam.

Each Monday, Wednesday and Friday afternoon from 1 June to 18 September. Stay at Roundhay Park amended to Canal Gardens from 1964. Route and fares as 1963.

1965 City Tour, New Tour (7th post war).

19, 20 April, 7-8 June, 2-3 August. From St. Peter's Street via Eastgate, Vicar Lane, New Market Street, Call Lane, Bridge End, Meadow Lane, Dewsbury Road, Moor Road, Belle Isle Road, Ring Road, Dewsbury Road, Ring Road (Beeston), Branch Road, Lower Wortley Road, Upper Wortley Road, Tong Road, Carr Crofts, Town Street (Armley), Branch Road, Canal Road, Willow Road, Burley Road, Kirkstall Hill, Kirkstall Lane, North Lane, Otley Road, Shaw Lane, Monkbridge Road, Stonegate Road, King Lane, Ring Road to Cross Gates Road, York Road, New York Road and Eastgate to St. Peter's Street. Fares as 1963.

1965 Tour 1 Adel Church and Kirkstall Abbey.

From Thursday 10 June and each Tuesday and Thursday afternoon until 16 September. Route and fares as 1963. Inward route altered owing to one-way scheme of 4 January 1965. Buses now ran from Boar Lane via Briggate and The Headrow to Eastgate.

1965 Tour 2 Roundhay Park and Temple Newsam.

From Wednesday 9 June and each Monday, Wednesday and Friday until 17 September. Route and fares as 1963.

To demonstrate the "good neighbourliness" between Leeds and Bradford, it was intended to run Leeds buses to Bolling Hall, Bowling Park and Lister Park in Bradford. Bradford buses were to run to Roundhay Park, Temple Newsam, Adel and Kirkstall Abbey. Although planned to run from 9 June to 17 September 1965, the Bradford tours did not start until the following year.

1966 City Tour.

29 and 30 August. Route as 1965, Fares as 1963.

Tour 1 Adel Church and Kirkstall Abbey.

Each Tuesday and Thursday from 2 June to 15 September (except Tuesday 30 August). In conjunction with Bradford Corporation on Wednesdays 15 June, 13 July, 10 August and 7 September. Route and fares as 1963. Bradford Corporation operated buses from Petergate, Bradford, to the Central Bus Station and then over the Leeds route.

1966 Tour 2 Roundhay Park and Temple Newsam.

Each Monday and Friday from 3 June to 16 September (except Monday 29 August). In conjunction with Bradford Corporation on Wednesdays 1 June, 29 June, 27 July and 24 August. Route and fares as 1963. Bradford Corporation operated buses from Petergate, Bradford, to the Central Bus Station and then over the Leeds route.

1966 Tour 3 Bolling Hall and Bowling Park.

Wednesday afternoons 8 June, 6 July, 3 August and 31 August. Duration 3 hours. Fare adult 4s.0d. child 2s.0d.

Operated in conjunction with Bradford Transport Department. Central Bus Station to Petergate, Bradford, via the 72 service route, then over the Bradford City Transport tour route to Bolling Hall and Bowling Park.

1966 Tour 4 Lister Park and Cartwright Hall.

Wednesday afternoons 22 June, 20 July, 17 August, 14 September. Duration 3 hours. Fare adult 4s.0d. child 2s.0d. Operated in conjunction with Bradford Transport Department. Central Bus Station to Petergate, Bradford, via the 72 service route, then over the Bradford City Transport tour route to Lister Park and Cartwright Hall.

1967 City Tour, New Tour (8th post war).

27, 28 March, 21, 22 May, 28 and 29 August. From St. Peter's Street via Eastgate Circus, St. Peter's Street, Duke Street, East Street, Cross Green Lane, Pontefract Lane, The Avenue, Bullerthorpe Lane, Selby Road, Ring Road (Halton), Station Road, Austhorpe Road, Pendas Way, Barwick Road, Stanks Lane South, Stanks Drive, Swarcliffe Avenue, Swarcliffe Drive, Barwick Road, York Road, North Parkway, Seacroft Avenue, Seacroft Crescent, Brooklands Avenue, Bailey's Lane, North Parkway, Kentmere Avenue, Boggart Hill Drive, Easterly Road, Wetherby Road, Roundhay Road, Gledhow Valley Road, King Lane, Eccup Lane, Church Lane, Farrar Lane, Otley Road, Headingley Lane, Woodhouse Lane, New Woodhouse Lane, Inner Ring Road, Westgate, The Headrow and Eastgate to St.Peter's Street. Fares as 1963.

1967 Tour 1 Adel Church and Kirkstall Abbey.

Mondays 3 July to 31 August, In conjunction with Bradford Corporation on Wednesdays 12, 26 July, 9, 23 August. Route and fares as 1963.

1967 Tour 2 Roundhay Park and Temple Newsam.

Tuesdays and Fridays 4 July to 1 September, In conjunction with Bradford Corporation Wednesdays 5, 19 July, 2, 16, 30 August. Route and fares as 1963.

1967 Tour 3 Bolling Hall and Bowling Park.

Wednesday 12 and 26 July, 9 and 23 August. Route and fares as 1966.

1967 Tour 4 Lister Park and Cartwright Hall.

Wednesdays 5, 19 July, 2, 16, 30 August. Route and fares as 1966.

1968 City Tour.

3-4 June. Route as 1967. Fares adult 2s.6d. child 1s.3d.

1968 Tour 1 Adel Church and Kirkstall Abbey.

Tuesdays and Fridays 2 July to 30 August. In conjunction with Bradford Corporation on Wednesdays 10, 24, July, 7, 21 August. Route as 1963. Fares adult 2s. 6d. child 1s.3d.

1968 Tour 2 Roundhay Park and Temple Newsam.

Mondays and Thursdays 1 July to 29 August. In conjunction with Bradford Corporation Wednesdays 3, 17, 31 July, 14, 28 August. Route as 1963. Fares adult 2s.6d. child 1s.3d.

1968 Tour 3 Bolling Hall and Bowling Park.

Wednesdays 10, 24 July, 7, 21 August. Route as 1966. Fares adult 4s.6d. child 2s.3d.

1968 Tour 4 Lister Park and Cartwright Hall.

Wednesdays 3. 17. 31 July, 14, 28 August. Route as 1966, Fares adult 4s.6d. child 2s.3d.

1969 City Tour. New Tour (9th post war).

7-8 April, 26-27 May. St. Peter's Street, Eastgate, Vicar Lane, then service 10 route to Middleton Arms, followed by 9 Ring Road route to Bradford Road, then via Bradford Road, Woodhall Lane and Woodhall Road to Calverley, A657, to Ring Road, Rodley, Broadway, Low Lane, Butcher Hill, Spen Lane, joining 50 service route at Morris Lane then to Eastgate and Bus Station. Fares adult 3s.0d. child 1s.6d.

1969 Tour 1 City Tour.

As a substitute for a planned Thruscross and Washburn Valley tour originally planned for 1969, this tour was altered on Monday afternoons from 30 June to 1 September. Route as the Easter and Whitsuntide tours

1946-built Semi-utility Daimler 85 on a "See Your City Tour" on 6 August 1956. The bus was photographed in Church Lane, Adel. *L.T.H.S.*

A.E.C. Regent III 489 pictured at Oakwood on a "See Your City Tour" in June 1960. *L.T.H.S.*

except that instead of running into the city direct from Broadway (Horsforth) the bus continued around the Ring Road as far as Seacroft, and then to the Bus Station via York Road, Marsh Lane, York Street and Duke Street. Fares adult 3s.0d. child 1s.6d.

1969 Tour 2 Adel Church and Kirkstall Abbey.

Tour renumbered 2. Tuesday afternoons from 1 July to 26 August. In conjunction with Bradford Corporation 9, 23 July, 6, 20 August and 3 September. Route as 1963. Fares adult 3s.0d. child 1s.6d.

1969 Tour 3 Bolling Hall and Bowling Park.

9, 23 July, 6. 20 August, 3 September. Route as 1966. Fares adult 5s.0d. child 2s.6d.

1969 Tour 4 Lister Park and Cartwright Hall.

2, 16, 30 July, 13, 27 August. Route as 1966. Fares adult 5s.0d. child 2s.6d.

1969 Tour 5 Roundhay Park and Temple Newsam.

Tour renumbered 5. Thursday afternoons from 3 July to 4 September. In conjunction with Bradford Corporation on Wednesdays 2, 16, 30 July, 13, 27 August. Route as 1963 except inward route altered due to closure of New York Road. (from 11 November 1968). Now via Marsh Lane, York Street and Duke Street to Central Bus Station. Fares adult 3s.0d. child 1s. 6d.

1969 Tour 6 Middleton Park and Farnley Park.

Friday afternoons from 4 July to 5 September. New tour from Central Bus Station via Eastgate, Vicar Lane, service 10 route to Middleton Park Road, St, Philip's Avenue, to Middleton Park. Then via Town Street, Sharp Lane, Middleton Park Road, Ring Road (Beeston Park), Dewsbury Road, Ring Road (Churwell), Ring Road (Beeston), Ring Road (Lower Wortley), Whincover Drive, Butterbowl Drive, Cross Lane to Farnley Park. Return to Bus Station via Hall Lane, Tong Road, Ring Road (Lower Wortley), Gelderd Road, Smithfield Street, Whitehall Road, Gelderd Road, Spence Lane, Whitehall Road, Thirsk Row, Wellington Street, City Square, Boar Lane, Briggate, The Headrow, Eastgate and St. Peter's Street. Fares adult 3s.0d. child 1s.6d.

1969 Tour 7 Lotherton Hall.

7 August, daily to 30 September. In 1967 this hall was given to the City of Leeds and was opened to the public from 7 August 1969. The bus was operated "on hire" in conjunction with the West Yorkshire Road Car Company Ltd. The toute from the Central Bus Station was via Eastgate, New York Road, York Road, Barwick Road, and unclassified roads to Aberford, Great North Road and unclassified roads to Lotherton Hall, where there was a two-hour stay. The return was via an unclassified road to Hook Moor, A642, to Garforth and Garforth Bridge, Selby Road, York Road and the reverse road to the Bus Station. Fare adult 4s.0d. child 2s.0d., which included entry to the Hall.

1970 City Tour.

Easter Monday, 30 March, 25, 26 May, 31 August. Route and fares as 1969.

1970 Tour 1 Thruscross and Washburn Valley.

Mondays 29 June, 6, 13, 20, 27 July, 3, 10. 17 and 24 August. New tour taking the place of the Tour 1 of 1969. Leaving Central Bus Station at 12.30 p.m. route was via Eastgate, The Headrow, Albion Street, Woodhouse Lane, Headingley Lane, Otley Road A660 to Dyneley Arms, A658 to Pool, B6161 to Leathley and Beckwithshaw, A59 Skipton Road, Meagill Lane, and unclassified road to Throscross Reservoir. Halt of 1¹/₂ hours then via unclassified road, Meagill Lane, A59, B6451 to Otley, A660 to Bramhope and Lawnswood, Otley Road, Headingley Lane, Woodhouse Lane, The Headrow, Eastgate, and St, Peter's Street to the Bus Station. The tour was worked by arrangement with the West Yorkshire Road Car Company using "on hire" facilities.

Fares 8s.0d. adult, 4s.0d. child.

1970 Tour 2 Roundhay Park and Temple Newsam.

Renumbered as Tour 2. Tuesdays 30 June to 25 August. In conjunction with Bradford Corporation 1, 15, 29 July, 12 and 26 August. Route and fares as 1969.

1970 Tour 3 Bolling Hall and Bowling Park.

Wednesdays 8, 22 July, 5, 19 August, 2 September. Route as 1966. Fares as 1969.

1970 Tour 4 Lister Park and Cartwright Hall.

Wednesdays 1, 15, 29 July, 12, 26 August. Route as 1966. Fares as 1969.

1970 Tour 5 Adel Church and Kirkstall Abbey.

Tour renumbered 5. Thursdays 2 July to 3 September. In conjunction with Bradford Corporation 8, 22 July, 5, 19 August, 2 September. Route as 1963. Fares as 1969.

1970 Tour 6 Farnley Park and Middleton Park.

Fridays 3 July to 4 September. New route from Central Bus Station via Eastgate, Vicar Lane, New Market Street, Duncan Street, Boar Lane, City Square, Aire Street, Whitehall Road, Spence Lane, Wortley Lane, Gelderd Road, Ring Road (Lower Wortley), Whincover Drive, Butterbowl Drive, and Cross Lane to Farnley Park. Then via Hall Lane, Tong Road, Ring Road, Dewsbury Road, Ring Road (Beeston Park), Middleton Park Road, St, Philip's Avenue, to Town Street, with a stay at Middleton Park. Then via Town Street, Belle Isle Road, Balm Road, Church Street, Waterloo Road, Hunslet Road, Bridge End, Briggate, The Headrow, Eastgate and St. Peter's Street to Central Bus Station. Fares as 1969. Last ran 4 September 1970.

1970 Tour 7 Lotherton Hall.

27-31 March, Sundays 5 April to 25 October. IDaily from 24 May to 27 September and also on Thursday evenings in August. Outward route altered following closure of New York Road from 3 May 1970. Route from Bus Station now via Eastgate Circus, St, Peter's Street, Duke Street, York Street, and Marsh Lane to York Road. Fares as 1969.

During 1970 all Tour Services were operated by one-man buses, displaying "SIGHTSEEING" and the appropriate tour number.

1971 City Tour.

Easter Monday 12 April, 30, 31 May, 29, 30 August. Route as 1969. Fare 20p.

1971 Tour 1 Thruscross and Washburn Valley.

Mondays, Wednesdays and Thursdays between 28 June and 3 September. Route as 1970. Fare 40p. On Mondays and Fridays it was worked by LCT buses, on Wednesdays by West Yorkshire vehicles.

1971 Tour 2 Adel Church and Kirkstall Abbey.

Tour renumbered 2. Tuesdays 29 June to 24 August. In conjunction with Bradford Corporation on 7, 21 July, 4, 18 August, 1 September. Route as 1963. Fare 20p.

1971 Tour 3 Bolling Hall and Bowling Park.

Wednesdays, 7, 21 July, 4, 18 August, 1 September. Route as 1966. Fare 25p.

1971 Tour 4 Lister Park and Cartwright Hall.

Wednesdays 30 June, 14, 28 July, 11, 25 August. Route as 1966. Fare 25p.

1971 Tour 5 Roundhay Park and Temple Newsam.

Renumbered as Tour 5. Thursdays 1 July to 2 September. In conjunction with Bradford Corporation 14, 28 July, 11, 25 August. Route as 1969. Fare 20p.

1971 Tour 6 Lotherton Hall.

9-12 April, Sundays only and then daily 23 May to 26 September, then Sundays only during October. Route as 1970. Fare 25p.

1972 City Tour.

Spring Bank Holiday, 30 May 1972. Route as 1969, but altered outward from Bridge End by way of Meadow Lane and Hunslet Lane to Hunslet Road. Fares as 1971. Last ran 30 May 1972.

1972 City Tour. New Tour (10th post war).

In 1972, beginning on Easter Monday, 3 April, and on Whit Monday a special South Leeds Motorway Tour was operated. The route from St.Peter's Street was via Duke Street, York Street, Marsh Lane, York Road, Ivy Street, East Park Parade, Pontefract Lane, Easy Road, South Accommodation Road, Hunslet Road, Low Road, Thwaite Gate, Wakefield Road, M1 Motorway, M62 Motorway, A62 Huddersfield Road, Church Street (Gildersome), Scott Green, Gildersome Lane, Back Lane, Tong Road, Hall Lane, Butt Lane, Ring Road (Farnley), Ring Road (Wortley), Gelderd Road, Smithfield Street, Whitehall Road, Gelderd Road, Spence Lane, Wellington Road, Wellington Street, Westgate, Inner Ring Road, Marsh Lane, York Street and Duke Street to St. Peter's Street.

Altered on Bank Holiday Monday, 28 August 1972 from Pontefract Lane via Cross Green Lane, Knowsthorpe Crescent to South Accommodation Road. When the route above was started, the railway bridge in Knowsthorpe Crescent was closed and buses had been diverted via Easy Road.

1972 Tour 1 Thruscross and Washburn Valley.

Mondays, Wednesdays and Fridays between 26 June and 1 September. Route as 1970. Fare as 1971.

1972 Tour 2 Adel Church and Kirkstall Abbey.

Each Tuesday from 27 June to 29 August, In conjunction wity Bradford Corporation on 2 and 16 August. Route as 1963. Fares as 1971.

1972 Tour 3 Bolling Hall and Bowling Park.

5, 19 July, 2, 16, 30 August. Route as 1966. Fare as 1971.

1972 Tour 4 Lister Park and Cartwright Hall.

28 June, 12, 26 July, 9, 23 August. Route as 1966. Fare as 1971.

Tour 5 Roundhay Park and Temple Newsam.

Thursdays 29 June to 31 August. In conjunction with Bradford Corporation on 26 July, and 9 August. Route as 1969. Fare as 1971. This tour did not operate after 31 August 1972.

1972 Tour 6 Lotherton Hall.

From Easter Sunday, 2 April, and each Sunday until 29 October. Also daily from 21 May to 24 September. Route as 1970. Fare as 1971.

1973 Motorway Tour.

The Bank Holiday Monday Motorway tours continued in 1973. At Easter, instead of going through the East End Park area, they ran from St.Peter's Street via The Headrow, Westgate roundabout and then the full length of the Inner Ring Road to York Road, Ivy Street to Hunslet Road, then Hunslet Lane, Great Wilson Street, Meadow Lane and Dewsbury Road to join the M1 at its starting point. Buses then returned via the former route, but omitted the return section along the Inner Ring Road.

1973 City Tour, New Tour.

Easter Monday, 23 April 1973. From St. Peter's Street via Eastgate, The Headrow, Westgate, Inner Ring Road, York Road, Ivy Street, East Park Parade, Pontefract Lane, Cross Green Lane, Knowsthorpe Crescent, South Accommodation Road, Hunslet Road, Hunslet Lane, Great Wilson Street, Meadow Lane, Dewsbury Road, then M1 Motorway to Lofthouse intersection, and as original route above to Wellington Street, City Square, Boar Lane, Briggate, The Headrow, Eastgate, and St. Peter's Street.

1973 Tour 1 Thruscross and Washburn Valley.

Mondays, Wednesdays and Fridays between 25 June and 31 August. Route as 1970. Fare as 1971.

1973 Tour 2 Adel Church and Kirkstall Abbey.

Each Tuesday from 26 June to 28 August. Route as 1963. Fare as 1971.

1973 Tour 3 Bolling Hall and Bowling Park.

Wednesdays 4, 18 July, 1 15, 29 August. Route as 1966. Fare as 1971.

1973 Tour 4 Lister Park and Cartwright Hall.

Wednesdays, 27 June, 11, 25 July, 8. 22 August. Route as 1966. Fare as 1971.

1973 Tour 5 Bus and Canal Tour.

New tour although it was operated on an experimental basis on two occasions on 17 and 22 August 1972. Operated on Thursdays 5 July, 2, 16, 23, 30 August, leaving the Central Bus Station at 1.30 p.m. It consisted of a bus ride to Rodley, followed by a canal trip from Rodley to Saltaire, then a return bus ride to Leeds., the whole outing lasting $3^{3/4}$ hours. Fare 75p adult, 50p child.

1973 Tour 6 Lotherton Hall.

Easter Sunday, 22 April, and every Sunday until 28 October. Also daily from 27 May to 23 September. Route as 1970. Fare as 1971.

1973 River, Road and Rail Tour.

Sundays 29 July, 5 and 12 August. This tour was based on one organised by the Middleton Railway Trust on 7 and 8 April 1973 using the same route. Route from Canal Wharf via Water Lane, Great Wilson Street, Meadow Lane, Dewsbury Road, and Tunstall Road to Middleton Railway (train ride). Then by South East Leeds Motorway to Stourton, then Wakefield Road to Knostrop, (Boat to Canal Wharf). The tour also operated in reverse starting with the boat trip.

The Roundhay Park and Temple Newsam tours were omitted in the 1973 season, as were the Wednesday trips on the two Bradford, Adel Church and Kirkstall Abbey tours.

Until 1963 the sightseeing tours were normally operated by double deck buses, but in 1963 and 1964 were largely worked by one-man single deckers, 39-43. From 1965 to 1973 one-man single deckers, supplemented by one-man double deckers were used.

The West Yorkshire Passenger Transport Executive continued the operation of the summer sightseeing tours including some new ones for a short period. The last City Tour ran on 2 September 1974 and the Adel Church and Kirkstall Abbey tour was withdrawn on 29 August 1975. The other tours lasted until 1977.

Ex-Bullock & Sons HL 5774, a Daimler CP6 of 1933 vintage was the oldest bus in the Farsley fleet at the Wallace Arnold takeover in October 1952. It was photographed on 4 January 1953, after withdrawal, at Pratt Bros. Garage, Harrogate, situated on the A61 Harrogate-Ripon Road about 100 yards on the Ripon side of the junction with the Skipton Road. The bus was still in the Farsley Omnibus Company livery of red with a cream waist band black wings and beads. There was also a straw coloured line at the top of the waist panel. *Author.*

Farsley Omnibus Company 11 (LUB 547) at Stanningley on 4 October 1952. Built in 1948 it was a Daimler CVD6 and one of the four Farsley buses taken over by Wallace Arnold. Behind is a Bradford Corporation A.E.C. Regent III 31 (FKY 31). Numbers 11 and 12 were painted in a "streamlined" livery of red and cream with red wings and waist band. They had high back seats and were often used on private hire and "express" trips. *Author.*

Farsley Omnibus Company and Kippax & District Motor Company Fleets

FARSLEY OMNIBUS COMPANY LTD. FLEET LIST PRIOR TO 1-10-1952.

In November 1924 E. & W. Lawson, garage proprietors of Bramley, started a bus service from Rodley to Stanningley. There were four buses. In April 1927 Maurice Greenwood and his wife took over the service and named the undertaking the Farsley Omnibus Company. Unfortunately details of the vehicles in the Farsley fleet are not complete prior to the takeover by Wallace Arnold Ltd. Any additional information would be welcome by the L.T.H.S.

No.	Regn. No.	Type	Chassis No.	Body	Body Type	In Service	Disposal	Notes
	??	Ex-E. & W.Lawson			B14	1924?	?	
	??	Ex-E. & W.Lawson			B14	1924?	?	
	??	Ex-E. & W.Lawson			B14	1924?	?	
	??	Ex-E. & W,Lawson			B14	1924?	?	
	UM 9230	Commer 2P	6509		B24	10-1927	Wdn 9-1936	
	UA 7687	Commer 5P	27007		B20F	4-1929	Wdn 6-1938	
	UB 7343	Commer 6TK	28275		B20F	7-1931	Wdn 1939	a
	UG 9687	Commer Centurion	56045		B20F	5-1934	Wdn 1944	b
	MV 3065	Bedford WLB			B20F	?	?	
	HE 4163	Gilford				?	?	
	UP 7895	Leyland TS4	2396		C30	?	?	c
	HL 4742	Daimler CF6	7384	Taylor's	B32F	10-1936	Wdn c 1948?	d
	HL 4743	Daimler CF6		Taylor's	B32F	10-1936	Wdn c 1948?	d
	HL 5774	Daimler CP6	8088	Roe	B32R	3-1937	Wdn 9-1952	e
10	GNW 776	Daimler COG5	8376	Roe	B36F	6-1938	Wdn 9-1952	f
	HNW 156	Commer PLNF5	87006	Waveney	C26F	3-1939	Wdn 1948	g
	JUA 642	Bedford OWB	10718	Roe	B32F	11-1942	Wdn 5-1952	
	JUA 643	Bedford OWB		Roe	B32F	11-1942	Wdn 8-1949	h
	JUA 738	Bedford OWB	13549	Roe	B32F	4-1943	Wdn 9-1952	j
	JUB 536	Daimler CP6	8067	Burlingham	B34F	1945	Wdn 9-1952	k
7	ADU 469	Daimler COG5	8102	Roe	B35F	1946	Wdn 9-1952	l
8	KUB 695	Daimler CVD6	13275	Roe	B35F	3-1947	To W.A.	m
9	LUB 546	Daimler CVD6	14106	Roe	B35F	3-1948	To W.A.	m
11	LUB 547	Daimler CVD6	14107	Roe	B35F	3-1948	To W.A.	m
12	LUB 548	Daimler CVD6	14108	Roe	B35F	3-1948	To W.A.	m
6	HL 6368	Leyland LT5A	4360	Roe	B32F	1949	Wdn 9-1952	n

NOTES

a   UB 7343 scrapped by Grace & Sutcliffe Ltd. Keighley 8-1939.

b   UG 7687 to W.H. Martin, Barnby-on-the-Moor, by 9-1944, J.R.Mellors, Barton-on-Humber, 4-1946, then E, Scott, Goole, 8-1947, for caravan.

c   UP 7895 new to Charlton, Hebburn, 7-1933 and acquired by United (LT90), 3-1936. Then to Farsley.

d   HL 4742-3 were coaches with sliding roofs, curtains and roof luggage racks, new to Bullock & Sons in 5-1930. The bodies were built by Taylor's of Barnsley and they had fleet numbers 112 and 113. Withdrawn in 1936 and sold for £200 each to the Farsley Company. The price included a roof alteration from sliding to fixed, repainting and lettering a the making of a sliding door for 113. They were collected from the B. & S. Featherstone Garage on 1-10-1936 (113) and 2-10-1936 (112).

e   HL 5774 was a sun saloon coach new to Bullock & Sons in 5-1933 and had fleet number 153. Withdrawn by B. & S. 2-1937 and sold to Farsley Omnibus Company for £725. It was collected by the Daimler Company for M. Greenwood on 3 March 1937. To P.M.Morrell, dealer, Leeds, 10-1952. At Pratt's Garage, Harrogate, 4-1-1953.

f   GNW 776 (10) to P.M.Morrell, dealer, Leeds, 10-1952, then to Greenhow & Sons, Darfield, from 12-1952 to 7-1954.

g   HNW 156 to unknown owner 7-1948, Last owner, Foster, Taunton.

h   JUA 643 withdrawn 8-1949 and then to Sykes Appleton Roebuck, 12-1949.

j   JUA 738 to P.M.Morrell, dealer, Leeds 10-1952, then to W.King & Sons, Islington, later to Comberhill Motors, Wakefield, 8-1954 and A.M.C.C. dealers, London E11.

k   This bus was thought to be new to Bullock & Sons in 5-1933 (154) registered HL 5775. However, according to John Lambert, HL 5775 was an A.E.C. Regal with a 32-seat Roe body. It was taken over by the military authorities, Northern Command, York, along with several other B. & S. buses in 8-1940. JUB 536 was rebodied by Burtlingham in 3-1945, but its origin is unknown. To P.M. Morrell, Leeds 10-1952 then to R.Clough, Keighley.

l   ADU 469 was new in 1934 as a demonstrator and came to Farsley via South Wales Transport. To P.M.Morrell, Leeds 10-1952 then to Bagley's Bottle Works, Ferrybridge.

m   KUB 695, LUB 546, 547 and 548 passed to Wallace Arnold 1-10-1952. All ended their days working for this Company at Sayner Road Garage, Leeds. KUB 695 and LUB 548 from Farsley to Leeds Garage 12-1956. LUB 546-7 from Farsley to Leeds Garage 2-1958. KUB 695 and LUB 546 Leeds Garage to Farsley 7-1958. LUB 548 fitted with a second hand Burlingham C33F body in 1957 and later sold to S. Hughes, dealer, then Beehive, Doncaster. KUB 695 sold to Ezra Laycock, Barnoldswick, (No.59) in 1961 and by 7-1962 to Archibald Jackson, contractor, Garforth. LUB 546 withdrawn late 1959 and broken up at Sayner Road Garage 2-1960. LUB 547 withdrawn late 1959 and sold 1-1960 to R. Cheseborough of Allerton Bywater, near Castleford, as a mobile shop.

n   HL 6368 was ex-West Riding 377 new 1-8-1934, sold to P.M.Morrell of Leeds 25-1-1949, then to Farsley Company 1949. To Morrell again 10-1952.

FARSLEY OMNIBUS COMPANY LTD. FLEET LIST POST 1-10-1952 to 30-3-1968

This fleet list includes the vehicles that were added by Wallace Arnold Ltd. It does not include the many Wallace Arnold coaches that were used on hire from time to time, some running for long periods. . Fleet numbers had been allocated latterly by the Farsley Company to some buses, but these were discontinued when Wallace Arnold took over.

Regn. No.	Type	Chassis No.	Body	Body Type	In Service	Disposal	Notes
DUB 926	Leyland Titan TD4c	11124	Roe	H31/25R	8-5-1954	Wdn 31-12-1956	o
MUM 458	Daimler CVD6	13688	Roe	H33/28R	5-2-1956	Wdn 30-3-1968	p
MUM 460	Daimler CVD6	13691	Roe	H33/28R	2-1856	To Kippax 3-1967	p
MUM 461	Daimler CVD6	16327	Roe	H33/28R	5-2-1956	To Kippax 3-1958	p
AUM 404	A.E.C. Regent	06613234	M.C.C.W	H30/26R	10-1956	Wdn 31-12-1956	q
MUB 433	Daimler CVD6	17256	Roe	H33/28R	1-1-1957	Wdn 30-3-1968	r
MUM 459	Daimler CVD6	15150	Roe	H33/28R	1-1-1957	Wdn 30-3-1968	r
KUM 849	Daimler CVD6	13800	Roe	H33/28R	28-5-1957	Wdn 28-3-1968	s
ARN 185	Leyland PD1/1	460501	Burlingham	H30/26R	6-1960	Sold 6-1963	t
WUM 49	Leyland PSCU1/2	564807	Burlingham	DP41F	10-1961	Wdn 11-1965	u
909 EUM	Leyland PD3A/1	629346	Roe	H41/32R	5-1963	Wdn 2-1967	v
833 KUA	Leyland PSU3/2R	L06259	Plaxton	DP51F	10-1964	Wdn 29-3-1968	w
9207 NW	A.E.C. Reliance	2MU3RA 2368	Plaxton Panorama	C41F	10-1965	Wdn 29-3-1968	x
GWX 824	Leyland PD2/1	481222	Leyland	H30/26R	11-1965	To Kippax 11-66	y
HNW 366D	Leyland PD3A/2	L60225	Roe	H41/32R	1-11-1966	Wdn 29-3-1968	z
9206 NW	A.E.C. Reliance	2MU3RA 2367	Plaxton Panorama	C39F	18-2-1967	Wdn 29-3-1968	aa
327 NMP	Demonstrator A.E.C. Reliance		Park Royal		5-1962	Then to Kippax	ab
LYY 827D	Demonstrator A.E.C. Swift	MP2R011	Marshall	B48D	7-1967		ac

NOTES

o   DUB 926 was originally Leeds C.T. 72, new in 1936 and withdrawn on 31-12-1948. It was sold to Wallace Arnold Tours Ltd. on 7-1-1950 and in 1952 passed to Hardwicks Services, Snainton, Scarborough, a subsidiary company of Wallace Arnold. Painted in a brown and cream livery it passed to Farsley 5-1954.

p MUM 458, 460 and 461 were Wallace Arnold coaches with Wilks & Meade's bodies. New in 1949 they were withdrawn in August 1955 and the chassis sent to Charles H. Roe of Cross Gates to be fitted with new double deck H33/25R bodies. MUM 461 was transferred to the Kippax and District fleet by 11-3-1958. MUM 460 to Kippax 3-1967. MUM 458 to Stanley Hughes, dealer, 5-4-1968.

q ANW 404 was originally Leeds C.T. 161, new in 7-1935 and withdrawn in 9-1949. Sold to Wallace Arnold 12-1949 and used for contract work and then passed to Hardwick's Scarborough, where it was painted buff and brown. Returned to Leeds, painted red and cream in 8-1955. Used on school contract work from Wallace Arnold's, Royston Depot until October 1956. Then to Farsley. After withdrawal on 31-12-1956, sold to M. Ratcliffe, Hull.

r New in 1949 MUB 433 and MUM 459 were formerly single deck Wallace Arnold coaches and were fitted with new double deck bodies by Charles H. Roe Ltd. In 1956. Both to Stanley Hughes, dealer, 5-4-1968.

s New in 1947 KUM 849 was formerly a single deck Wallace Arnold Coach. It was painted in Farsley Omnibus Company livery, but at first was on loan to the Kippax and District Motor Company. Transferred to Farsley by 5-1957. The chassis originally had a Wilks & Meade coach body, this being replaced in 11-1952 by a Burlingham 33 seat body ex-NUA 783. To Stanley Hughes, dealer, 5-4-1968.

t ARN 185 new to Ribble Motor Services 2451 in 1946. To Kippax and District 1-1959. To Farsley (Pudsey Garage) as spare bus 6-1960. Sold for scrap 6-1963.

u WUM 49 was a Leyland Tiger Cub with Burlingham "Seagull" body ex-Wallace Arnold coach fleet and was with Farsley from 10-1961. It was fitted with bus type seats from a Rotherham trolley bus and the seating was increased to 43. Withdrawn and sold to Phillipson, Goldthorpe in 11-1965.

v 909 EUM transferred to Hardwicks Scarborough 17-2-1967.

w 833 KUA was a Leyland Leopard with a Plaxton "Highway" body, number 642388 and was painted in an all red livery. It was purchased for use on the Monday-Friday service between Pudsey and Tinshill. A single deck bus had to be used owing to a weight restriction on the railway bridge at Horsforth Station. On Saturdays and Sundays it was used on excursion or private hire work usually from Bradford. From 18-2-1967 used on one-man operation. To Wallace Arnold coach fleet 1-4-1968.

x New in 1959, 9207 NW was ex-Wallace Arnold coach fleet with Plaxton Panorama body. Converted to C38F for one-man operation in 2-1967. From 18-2-1967 certain journeys in Farsley were one-man operated. To Wallace Arnold coach fleet 1-4-1968.

y GWX 824 was with Kippax and District from 1948. Transferred on loan to Farsley 11-1965 and returned to Kippax 11-1966.

z HNW 366D to Hardwicks, Scarborough 1-4-1968.

aa New in 1959, 9206 NW was transferred from Hardwicks, Scarborough in 2-1967 after being converted to C39F for one-man work. From 18-2-1967 used for one-man operation. To Wallace Arnold coach fleet 1-4-1968.

ab Demonstrator 327 NMP had a 54-seat Park Royal body built to the new maximum dimensions of 36ft. long x 8ft. 2^{1}/2in. wide. It was in a maroon livery and ran from 29 to 31 May 1962. It was then transferred to Kippax and District for trials, but returned to Farsley during the week commencing Monday 25 June 1962. It was for one-man operation.

ac Demonstrator LYY 627D was on loan for a fortnight at the beginning of July 1967, It was in a livery of light green with dark green window surrounds.

Leyland Titan TD4c, ex-Leeds City Transport 72 (DUB 926), dated from 1936 and was sold to Wallace Arnold Tours in 1950 and went to Hardwick Services at Scarborough. It ran for the Farsley Omnibus Company from 1954 to 1956. Newly painted it was photographed at Pudsey on 5 June 1954. *W.D.Wilson/L.T.H.S.*

Ex-Leeds City Transport 161, (AUM 404), an A.E.C. Regent of 1935 vintage, had an all-metal body by M.C.C.W. It was sold to Wallace Arnold Tours in December 1949 and ran for the Farsley Omnibus Company for two months at the end of 1956. It is seen here on Wallace Arnold Elland Road Football Special duties at Low Fields Road on 10 April 1950. Behind is one of J. Foster's Bedford coaches, (CWU 602), also a Football Special. A Chamberlain tram with E.M.B. Pivotal truck, in the Matterface royal blue livery, is on the Football siding. *W.D.Wilson/L.T.H.S.*

KIPPAX AND DISTRICT MOTOR COMPANY LTD. FLEET LIST 1925 to 1-6-1956

In October 1925 the Kippax & District Motor Company, owned by the Watson family, started a bus service from New York Road, Leeds, to Kippax and Ledston Luck Colliery. Of the original Kippax fleet, details are known of the complete range of fleet numbers from 1 to 16 (with the exception of 13 which was not used). The fleet numbers of 1-3 have not been confirmed, but have been arrived at by deduction. No details are known of two Karrier vehicles, which are believed to have been owned at the beginning of the Company's history.

No.	Regn. No.	Type	Chassis No.	Body	Body Type	In Service	Disposal	Notes
(1)	WU 3399	Karrier CL	20966		B23	1925	Wdn ?	
(2)	WU 7393	Leyland PLSC	45216		B32	1926	Wdn 1936	
(3)	WU 9011	Leyland PLSC	45387		B31	1926	Wdn by 1-1937	
4	WW 2566	Leyland PLSC	45951		B31	1927	Wdn by 3-1938	
5	WW 6657	Leyland PLSC	47082		B35	1928	Wdn 1942	
6	WX 3126	Leyland TS1	60730	Leyland	B30F	1930	Wdn 1950	
7	YG 2465	A,E,C, Regal	6621450	Duple	C32	1933		a
8	AWT 128	Leyland TD4	6183	Leyland	H30/26R	1935	Wdn 1953	b
9	BWR 98	Leyland TD4	10641	Leyland	H28/26R	1936	To W.A. 1956.	c
10	BYG 147	A.E.C. Regal	06622186	Roe	B32F	1937	To W.A. 1956	d
11	YG 2465	A,E,C, Regal	6621450	Roe	B32F	1937	Ex-7 To W.A.1956	d
12	EWU 247	Daimler CWA6	11527	Roe	H30/26R	1944		e
14	GWX 823	Leyland PD2/1	481223	Leyland	H30/26R	1948	Wdn 2-1967	e
15	GWX 824	Leyland PD2/1	481222	Leyland	H30/26R	1948	Wdn 13-4-1967	f
16	EWU 247	Daimler CWA6	11527	Roe	H31/25R	1953	Wdn 25-9-1966	e

NOTES

a   YG 2465 rebodied by Roe 1937 and renumbered 11.

b   AWT 128 withdrawn in 1953 and dismantled.

c   BWR 98 withdrawn 31-12-1958 and sold to North, dealer, Leeds, 1-1959, in part exchange for ARN 185. Roof removed at Stourton yard by 8-1959. and remainder subsequently broken up by Higgs, Monk Bretton.

d   YG 2465, new in 1933, rebodied by Roe 1937 and renumbered 11. BYG 147 and YG 2465 reported as sold to Ratcliffe, a showman in 12-1956.

e   EWU 247 had a war-time Roe H56R Utility body when built in 1944. Rebodied by Roe in 1953 and renumbered 16. To Dysons Motor Auctions, Low Fields Road, Leeds 11, in 10-1966.

f   GWX 824 at Farsley from 11-1965 to 11-1966. GWX 823 and 824 sold to unknown breaker in 1967.

KIPPAX AND DISTRICT MOTOR SERVICES LTD. FLEET LIST 1-6-1956 to 30-3-1968

This fleet list includes the vehicles that were added by Wallace Arnold Ltd. It does not include the many Wallace Arnold coaches that were used on hire from time to time, some running for long periods. Wallace Arnold did not use fleet numbers.

Regn. No.	Type	Chassis No.	Body	Body Type	In Service	Disposal	Notes
ASD 121	Daimler CWA6	11322	Massey	H30/26R	6-1956	Wdn 31-10-1956	g
LNW 869	Daimler CVD6	13796	Roe	H33/28R	13-1-1957	Wdn 29-3-1968	h
MUM 461	Daimler CVD6	16327	Roe	H33/28R	11-3-1958	Wdn 30-3-1968	j
ARN 185	Leyland PD1/1	460501	Burlingham	H30/26R	1-1-1959	To Farsley 6-1960	k
6237 UB	Leyland PD3/1	592862	Roe	H41/32R	1-6-1960	Wdn 30-3-1968	l
556 DUA	Leyland PD3A/1	613210	Roe	H41/32R	13-10-1962	Wdn 30-3-1968	m
DUG 166C	Leyland PD3A/1	L41705	Roe	H41/32R	5-11-1965	Wdn 28-3-1968	l
DUG 167C	Leyland PD3A/1	L41706	Roe	H41/32R	5-11-1965	Wdn 30-3-1968	l
MUM 460	Daimler CVD6	13691	Roe	H33/28R	3-1967	Wdn 29-3-1968	n
SUA 296	Leyland PD2/12	540028	Leyland	H30/26R	10-5-1967	Wdn 30-3-1968	o
327 NMP	Demonstrator A.E.C. Reliance		Park Royal	B54F	6-1962		p
KTD 551C	Demonstrator Leyland PDR1/1	L23296	Park Royal	H41/33F	6-1965		q

NOTES

g   ASD 121 was ex-Western S.M.T. KR245, new in 1943. It remained in Western Livery and was soon withdrawn on 31-10-1956 and sold to Stanley Hughes, dealer, Gildersome, who resold it to Blamires, breaker, Bradford, 4-1958.

h   LNW 869 was new in 1948 and had a Wilks and Meade coach body. In 1952 a Burlingham coach body was fitted from coach NUA 752. A third body was fitted by Roe in 1956 and it was the first Kippax and District bus to have a rear indicator. To S.Hughes, dealer 4-1968.

j   MUM 461 was transferred from the Farsley Omnibus Company fleet in 3-1958. To S.Hughes, dealer 4-1968.

k   ARN 185 was new in 1946 and was formerly Ribble Motor Services No. 2451 and was purchased via North's, dealers, Leeds, in 1958. To Farsley as spare bus 6-1960 after arrival of 6237 UB.

l   6237 UB and DUG 167C to S.Hughes, dealer 4-1968. DUG 166C to S.Hughes 5-4-1968.

m   556 DUA was the first bus in the fleet to have folding doors to the platform. To S.Hughes, dealer, 4-1968.

n   MUM 460 was transferred from the Farsley Omnibus Company in 3-1967. To S,Hughes, dealer 4-1968.

o   SUA 296 was new in 1954 and was transferred from Hardwick's, Scarborough on 17–2-1967. To S.Hughes 4-1968.

p   After use at Farsley (see Farsley Omnibus Company list) 327 NMP ran on the Kippax services from 1 to 4-6-1962,

q   KTD 551C was a Leyland Atlantean painted in a white livery with blue bands and roof. In use from 7 to 21–6-1965.

Kippax and District Motor Company A.E.C. Regal 10 (BYG 147) at the Central Bus Station on 16 April 1955.
J.B. Parkin.

ASD 121 was ex-Western S.M.T. KR245, new in 1943 and the first bus to be supplied by Wallace Arnold to the Kippax fleet in 1956. It was in SMT livery and lasted a few months only. *J.B.Parkin.*

Kippax and District Leyland PD3A/1 DUG 166C emerging from Chapel Street, Halton, into Selby Road at the Halton Institute. The date is 29 May 1966. *J.B.Parkin.*

Leyland PD2/12 SUA 296 ran for Kippax and District in 1967-8. It is pictured at the railway bridge in Ninelands Lane, Garforth, on 9 March 1968. The bridge no longer exists and carried the former Garforth-Castleford railway line, closed to passengers on 22 January 1951. *J.B.Parkin.*

Leeds Motor Bus Destination Indicators

With information supplied by D.J.Macken, J.B.Parkin and A.K.Terry

Destination Indicators pre-1937

Unfortunately details of the destination displays, which appeared on the first buses do not seem to have been recorded and the only information is from the few photographs available. The screens simply stated the destination. With the delivery of Karrier bus 53 in 1927, some buses were fitted with a second box above the destination indicator. This could have served as a number box and in one or two photographs numbers were shown, but apparently only for illustrative purposes. The second box was occupied by the insignia "L.C.T.", in yellow on blue glass.

There were complaints about the poor bus destination screens and, from 12 March 1935, many screens were supplemented by painted boards clipped to the bus sides. Sometimes a rectangular tablet was fastened to the front of the vehicle.

Double deckers, 40 and 53, and single deckers 54-90 had the second box, but the box was omitted on double deckers, 91-113. Vane Morland reintroduced the insignia box with the A.E.C. Regals of 1932 and the feature was continued upon all subsequent new buses until the introduction of the large destination box in 1936. Exceptions to this arrangement were the experimental streamlined double deckers, 200 and 201, which had their own special boxes.

Post-1937 Destination Indicators

On 1 July 1937 route numbers were introduced on all buses. A new destination box was required and this was in two parts consisting of an upper destination screen and a lower combined number and route screen.

The L.C.T. insignia box was omitted on new buses from the "DUB" Leyland Titans (66-75) onwards. By the end of 1938 most of the older buses had been fitted with the new destination arrangement.

As with earlier destination screens, the indicators were turned by the conductor externally by him climbing up on to the front of the bus.

All buses supplied from the Leyland Titans in 1936 had large rear destination indicators. The double deckers had the new two part screens similar to those on the front and the Leyland Tiger TS8 single deckers, (19-26), a single line display with a separate small number box at the right hand side.

Buses that were delivered in the immediate post war era, the 'Utility' Daimlers, Crossley 27 (later 701) and the Leyland PD1 had front indicators only. However. the "JUG" and "LUA" A.E.C. Regent III (401-449 and 600) had in addition to the front indicators, a single line indicator above the platform doorway. Buses with the same arrangement were the Daimler CVD6 (522-531), and Crossley 702-721. Beginning with A.E.C Regent III, 450-475, the side destinations were omitted and replaced with a full rear two screen destination display, similar to the buses supplied from 1937. Rear destination indicators were fitted to all new buses from 1949, throughout the 1950's and until 1968. Single deckers 27-38 had side destination indicators in addition to the front indicators.

The early two-blind screens were complex with many variations and alterations and complete details will probably never be known. Thanks to the late Donald Macken details of some pre-war screens have been recorded. Examples of the upper destination screens are included in Tables 1

A.E.C. Regent III 475 in Templar Place on 20 July 1963 during diversions due to the reconstruction of the Central Bus Station. It has the post-1937 style of destination indicator layout. *Author.*

and 2, but, although dating from the same period, they are widely different. There were also many differences in the lower route/number screens. Some are included in Table 8.

Alterations were usually made by adding new names on to the ends of the screens. Sometimes old names were deleted, but often not, and the whole system became very haphazard.

By 1953 a "standard" destination order had been devised, various routes being grouped together. This order, with alterations and additions was to be maintained for the next ten years or so.

In June 1956 A.E.C. Regents, 785-790, 794-6 and 805 entered service fitted with new destination and route/number screens. From then on bus destination screens or blinds were split into two groups for purposes of printings. "No.2 blind" covered routes operating from Torre Road and the new Seacroft Garage, and the No. 1 or "Universal" blind, all the other garages as a group. No.2 blinds were initially fitted to the new buses and also to A,E.C. Regents 450-479. The vehicles carried a number "2' in white, on a card with a red background, which was placed in a holder on the front of the bus.

Both types of blind carried some names common to each An examination of the No.2 blinds showed that obsolete destinations, OSMONDTHORPE, GUISELEY and RAWDON had been removed. The destinations on the top screen only related to the route/numbers on the lower. There were additional special names: BARNBOW, COPPER WORKS, PRIVATE and ROUNDHAY and extra names CROSSFLATTS, MIDDLETON, BELLE ISLE and IRELAND WOOD for use on the night services.

By April 1959 buses fitted with No.2 blinds were recorded as 221-291, 455-486, 552-571, 600. 626-648, 700-721, When buses moved between garages the screens were usually exchanged from one type to the other.

Screens were either of "Kelbus" or "Norco" manufacture. Kelbus were at Willow Lane, Lancaster, and Norco screens were made by T. Norbury & Co. Ltd. The two types of screen are illustrated, the lettering of the Norco screen was slightly more bold than the Kelbus.

Kelbus and Norco blinds (or screens) side by side. The earlier Kelbus screen is on the left and dates from November 1953. The Norco screen is "brand new" and has never been in a bus. It was one of the last batch of the old type screens delivered in 1968. The lettering on the Norco screens was slightly bolder than the Kelbus and the space between the destinations was narrower. *Author.*

The arrival of the new front entrance Daimlers, 572-576, in May 1962 marked the end of the No.1 and 2 screens and the introduction of a new style of destination layout. In place of a destination screen situated over a combined "via" and number screen, the new layout consisted of a three-digit number screen over a destination blind, thus doing away with all the "via" names. The number screens consisted of rolls numbered from 0 to 9, the third of which had the letters "CIRC." positioned diagonally, following the number 9. This layout gave a coverage of numbers from 1 to 999 with provision for numbering the existing circular services, 2, 3, 12, and 57-64 inclusive.

The destinations had a new feature in that all were arranged in alphabetical order on the screen. The only name, which appeared twice was CENTRAL BUS STATION, not only in its correct alphabetical position, but also after YORK ROAD. New names added were HOSPITAL SPECIAL, SCHOOL SPECIAL, SOUTH ACCOMMODATION ROAD, and WORKS SPECIAL.

Names omitted from the new blinds were WILLOW ROAD, COPPER WORKS, CIRCULAR, ROCKINGHAM STREET, WORTLEY-NEW INN, HUDSON ROAD, OSMONDTHORPE, BARNBOW, ALLERTON HIGH SCHOOL and HOSPITAL.

Services to the Yorkshire Copper Works and Barnbow were covered by WORKS SPECIAL. Buses to Allerton High School now showed SCHOOL SPECIAL. Similarly all Hospital services displayed HOSPITAL SPECIAL.

It was interesting that on the new screens two obsolete destinations were included. COMPTON ROAD was still shown as the terminus of the 50 and 77 services although they had been extended to the Fairway Hotel, Coldcotes, years before. NORTH LANE was shown as the terminus of

service 7 although it operated to Headingley Station, about half a mile past North Lane.

The new screens were larger than the older screens being 38in. wide as against 34in. Side destination screens had been only 29in. in width. Lettering was 4in. high.

New Leyland PD3A/2 buses, 311-320, introduced in October 1962, were fitted with the new alphabetical screens, although the three-digit number blinds were positioned below the destination - unlike 572-6. All other new buses delivered around this time, 39-43, 577-581 and 924-933 had the same arrangement as 311-320.

In January 1963 the 'Leeds & District Transport News' listed the various types of screens then in use:

No.1 type (Universal): 27, 29-38, 201-220, 301-310, 340-399, 431-500, 532-541, 601-619, 626-645, 649-663, 668-675, 730-782. 805-854 and 863-894.

No.2 type (Torre Road & Seacroft Garages only): 221-291, 401-413, 415-430, 502-531, 542-571, 600, 620-625, 646-648, 664-667. 676-678, 700, 714-717, 720, 783-804, 855-862, and 895-923.

Three-digit number screens: 39-43, 311-320, 572-581 and 924-933.

In March 1963 a start was made on fitting new alphabetical destination screens to all the older buses in the fleet. Instead of three separate digital screens there was one number screen only. The number was placed in the centre of the former "via" blind position and a black metal mask was fitted around it. The new number blinds, which were extremely long, showed numbers from 1 to 77, even though some of these numbers were not in use. Tramway practice was revived with displays of 2 CIRCULAR, 3 CIRCULAR and 12 CIRCULAR as well as the ordinary displays of 2. 3 and 12. Works, hospital and school services were catered for with the numbers 100-138 inclusive.

The top destination screens were similar to those fitted to the 1962 deliveries, but the new screens were narrower. As a result several names were abbreviated e.g. SEACROFT MONKSWOOD, SEACROFT SOUTH P'WAY, SEACROFT NORTH P'WAY, and S.ACCOMMODATION RD in place of SEACROFT MONKSWOOD GATE, SEACROFT SOUTH PARKWAY, SEACROFT NORTH PARKWAY and SOUTH ACCOMMODATION ROAD. The Morley destinations were shortened to MORLEY-FOUNTAIN, MORLEY-PROSPECT, MORLEY-FOUNTAIN ST, and MORLEY-TINGLEY. CIRCULAR also appeared on the new blinds.

The first bus to appear with the new displays was Daimler CVG6LX, 503, delivered from Kirkstall Road Works to Torre Road Garage on 22 March 1963. By October 1963 all buses of this type had been fitted with the new displays. On Saturday afternoon, 30 March, 507 was used as an Elland Road football special and was the first bus to be noted displaying the number 102, the correct route number for this special service.

Older buses were fitted with the new screens spasmodically and in no particular order. The first of the Leyland PD3/5's, 245, appeared in April 1963, but it was not until July 1964 that the whole of this series had been converted. By this date all of the 30ft. long buses in the fleet had been changed.

By September 1964 all the A.E.C. Regent V buses had been fitted with the new screens.

In November 1963 the Transport Department re-named the three different types of destination screens. New buses with three-digit number blinds or converted from the old type, were now said to have "Universal" blinds. The older blinds, originally called Universal or No. 1, were officially No.1 blinds and the No.2 type, used by Torre Road and Seacroft Garages, continued to be referred to as the No. 2 blind.

The Daimler CVG6LX, 502-531, were the first of the older buses to be fitted with the new style destination screens. 518 is seen here at Kirkstall Forge on 14 October 1967. *Author.*

The fitting of new Universal blinds to older buses ceased at the end of 1964. Certain buses never received the new blinds. These included the Leyland PD2 340-399, and A.E.C. Regent III, 401-500, except for 452-457, fitted with new screens in October 1963. The older single deck buses, 29-38, also never received the new blinds.

By January 1965 all the buses running from Torre Road and Seacroft Garages with No.2 blinds had had them replaced. An exception was A.E.C. Regent III, 439, which was the last bus to run with No.2 blinds. It was withdrawn on 26 February 1965.

452-457 were taken out of service in December 1965 and to replace them, in January 1966, 472-477 were fitted with Universal blinds.

September 1968 saw the withdrawal of the last of the buses to run with the old No.1 type blinds: 476, 481 and 498 on the 30th of the month. The last PD2 394, and 396-8 had been taken out of service on 29 August and a few months earlier the last of the single deckers, 37 and 38, had been withdrawn. These two buses had also been the last in the fleet to have side destination indicators.

When new, A.E.C. Swift single deckers 51-60 and 76-85 had been fitted with rear destination indicators. In September and October 1969 the indicators were panelled over on the outside and the internal winding gear was removed.

In connection with the new 402 service opened on 15 March 1971 from the Central Bus Station to the New Leeds Playhouse a board headed "TO LEEDS PLAYHOUSE" was carried.

After a very short period of extinction, side blinds were reintroduced in November 1968 - on Daimler Fleetlines 146-155, Leyland Atlanteans 386-405 and A.E.C. Swifts 1001-1050. The destinations, which showed both route number and destination, were positioned on the nearside adjacent to the entrance and within easy reach of the driver. The new side displays consisted of a standard 38in. wide destination screen to the left of a smaller three-track digital route number indicator. The numbers were 5in. in height. In addition CIRC (on a diagonal) also appeared. There were no rear destination indicators on these buses. The increasing adoption of one-man operation rendered rear destinations impractical. The last buses to appear with this feature were Leyland Atlanteans 356-385 - from August to October 1968.

To make things easier for the drivers of double deck buses newly converted for one-man operation, the indicator gears were substantially altered or replaced to enable both destination and digital number screens to be altered from the driver's compartment. There had been access doors in the upper saloon to enable the blinds to be turned by the conductor. These were now locked in position, and the digital track mechanisms from the old rear indicators, fitted at the front.

The 1972 Earls Court Show model, 761, was equipped with a new type of selector which operated both the front and side number screens simultaneously. The destination gear was also power-operated from a simple three-position switch (forward – off – reverse). Leyland Atlantean 450 was also fitted with automatic destination equipment. On 450, the number blinds were selected simultaneously in both boxes by the use of three control knobs. The destination blind, however, was controlled manually.

The electrically-operated destination gear on 761 can not have been satisfactory for on 16 July 1973 the bus was in service with the experimental equipment removed and normal manual destination gears were fitted. 450 also had its electrical gear removed at the same time. At the close of this volume all the destination screens were manually operated and had been supplied by either T. Norbury & Co. Ltd. (Norco) or the Kelbus Company.

Daimler CVG6LX 526 with the new type alphabetical destination screen rolled out. The 40 feet long screen appears to be of Norco manufacture. The date is 15 May 1964. *L.T.H.S.*

TABLE 1   LEEDS CITY TRANSPORT   EXAMPLE OF BUS DESTINATION SCREEN   PRE-1939

Details of a pre-war top destination blind, post July 1937, with later insertions, recorded by D.J.Macken on 4 February 1950. Numbers are for reference only. All destinations were centralised and justified on the screen.

NO.	DESTINATION	NO.	DESTINATION	NO.	DESTINATION
1	NEW FARNLEY	27	KIRKSTALL	53	CIRCULAR
2	COOKRIDGE	28	GREENTHORPE EST.	54	DIB LANE
3	GLEDHOW	29	STANNINGLEY	55	FOUNDRY LANE
4	SEACROFT	30	WHINGATE	56	OAKWOOD LANE
5	GIPTON	31	WORTLEY	57	LOWER WORTLEY
6	EASTGATE	32	BRAMLEY TOWN END	58	HAREHILLS
7	RODLEY	33	WELLINGTON ROAD	59	LEEDS
8	BRAMLEY BROAD LANE	34	MIDDLETON	60	OTLEY
9	LEEDS BUS STATION	35	BEESTON	61	BURLEY
10	STAINBECK LANE	36	HOLBECK MOOR	62	GUISELEY
11	KING LANE JUNCTION	37	COTTINGLEY	63	RAWDON
12	ALWOODLEY	38	TROYDALE	64	LEEDS BUS STATION
13	SHADWELL	39	PUDSEY	65	BRADFORD
14	MEANWOOD	40	OLD FARNLEY	66	BECKETTS PARK
15	CARR MANOR	41	WILLOW ROAD	67	NORTH LANE
16	MOORTOWN	42	HYDE PARK	68	CITY SQUARE
17	OAKWOOD	43	EASTGATE	69	BELLE ISLE
18	VICAR LANE	44	HORSFORTH	70	PRIVATE
19	HALTON	45	HAWKSWORTH ESTATE	71	ELLAND ROAD
20	STANKS	46	SANDFORD ESTATE	72	ROUNDHAY
21	COLTON	47	TINGLEY	73	HEADINGLEY
22	WHITKIRK	48	MORLEY FOUNTAIN STREET	74	CROSS GATES
23	HALTON MOOR	49	BRUNTCLIFFE	75	EAST END PARK
24	OSMONDTHORPE	50	MORLEY (FOUNTAIN INN)	76	WEST PARK
25	YORK ROAD	51	MORLEY (PROSPECT HOTEL)	77	ARMLEY
26	ROUNDHAY ROAD	52	CHURWELL DYE WORKS	78	COPPER WORKS

TABLE 2   LEEDS CITY TRANSPORT   EXAMPLE OF BUS DESTINATION SCREEN   PRE-1939

Details of a pre-war top destination blind, post July 1937, with later insertions, recorded by D.J.Macken in 1950. Numbers are for reference only. All destinations were centralised and justified on the screen.

NO.	DESTINATION	NO.	DESTINATION	NO.	DESTINATION
1	LONG CAUSEWAY	30	MEANWOOD	59	CIRCULAR
2	NEW FARNLEY	31	CARR MANOR	60	DIB LANE
3	CATTLE MARKET	32	OSMONDTHORPE	61	FOUNDRY LANE
4	HOUGH END	33	YORK ROAD	62	OAKWOOD LANE
5	TROYDALE	34	ROUNDHAY ROAD	63	PRIVATE
6	PUDSEY	35	KIRKSTALL	64	BURLEY
7	ROUNDHAY	36	STANNINGLEY	65	OTLEY
8	CITY SQUARE	37	WHINGATE	66	GUISELEY
9	LEYSHOLME EST.	38	WORTLEY	67	RAWDON
10	IRELAND WOOD	39	HAREHILLS RD.	68	HORSFORTH (FLEECE INN)
11	COOKRIDGE	40	BRAMLEY TOWN END	69	LEEDS
12	ALWOODLEY	41	WOODHOUSE HILL	70	LOWER WORTLEY
13	MEANWOOD PARK COLONY	42	WELLINGTON ROAD	71	HAREHILLS
14	GLEDHOW	43	MIDDLETON	72	EASTGATE
15	SEACROFT	44	WATERLOO ROAD	73	BRADFORD
16	EASTGATE	45	BEESTON	74	COTTINGLEY
17	RODLEY	46	OLD FARNLEY	75	HOLBECK MOOR
18	BROAD LANE BRAMLEY	47	WILLOW ROAD	76	BECKETTS PARK
19	LEEDS BUS STATION	48	HYDE PARK	77	NORTH LANE
20	STAINBECK LANE	49	EASTGATE	78	CITY SQUARE
21	KING LANE JUNCTION	50	HORSFORTH	79	SANDFORD ESTATE
22	SHADWELL	51	HAWKSWORTH ESTATE	80	ELLAND ROAD
23	MOORTOWN	52	TINGLEY	81	GIPTON
24	OAKWOOD	53	BRUNTCLIFFE	82	CROSS GATES
25	VICAR LANE	54	FOUNTAIN ST (MORLEY)	83	EAST END PARK
26	HALTON	55	"FOUNTAIN" MORLEY	84	WEST PARK
27	STANKS	56	"PROSPECT" MORLEY	85	HEADINGLEY
28	COLTON	57	DYE WORKS CHURWELL		
29	WHITKIRK	58	FOOTBALL GROUND		

NOTES

A number of post-1937 destinations are not shown on either of the blinds in Tables 1 and 2. These included GOLDEN ACRE PARK (service discontinued September 1938), YEADON, HEADINGLEY STATION, HEADINGLEY MOUNT, CROWN WORTLEY and NURSERY LANE, which were no longer terminal points, and MENSTON HOSPITAL which by 1950 showed PRIVATE on the blinds.

Some obsolete destinations still appeared although services had been altered or discontinued. These included OTLEY, BURLEY, CATTLE MARKET and HOUGH END.

TABLE 3 LEEDS CITY TRANSPORT   EXAMPLE OF BUS DESTINATION SCREEN   NOVEMBER 1953

Numbers are for reference only   In indicates a later insert. All destinations were centralised and justified on the screen.

NO.	DESTINATION	NO.	DESTINATION	NO.	DESTINATION
1	In TEMPLENEWSAM	35	RAWDON	69	MORLEY FOUNTAIN INN
2	In PRIMLEY PARK	36	GUISELEY	70	MORLEY FOUNTAIN STREET
3	ARMLEY	37	SEACROFT	71	MORLEY TINGLEY MILL
4	LONG CAUSEWAY	38	GIPTON	72	BRUNTCLIFFE
5	NEW FARNLEY	39	IRELAND WOOD	73	BRADFORD
6	COOKRIDGE	40	LEYSHOLME ESTATE	74	CROSSGATES
7	STAINBECK LANE	41	LEEDS CITY SQUARE	75	WEST PARK
8	KING LANE CIRCUS	42	ELLAND ROAD	76	COPPER WORKS
9	ALWOODLEY	43	HOLBECK MOOR	77	CIRCULAR
10	MOORTOWN	44	COTTINGLEY	78	PRIVATE
11	GLEDHOW	45	BECKETTS PARK	79	LEEDS BUS STATION
12	SHADWELL	46	TROYDALE	80	HALF MILE LANE
13	LEEDS BUS STATION	47	WORTLEY	81	In TINSHILL
14	WHITKIRK	48	MEANWOOD	82	In BURLEY MILLS
15	HALTON	49	HAREHILLS	83	In COMPTON ROAD
16	COLTON	50	LOWER WORTLEY	84	In LEEDS ROCKINGHAM ST.
17	STANKS	51	EASTGATE	85	In SWARCLIFFE
18	CARR MANOR	52	ROUNDHAY ROAD	86	In INTAKE
19	PUDSEY	53	OAKWOOD	87	In WORTLEY – NEW INN
20	OLD FARNLEY	54	EAST END PARK	88	In HUDSON ROAD
21	WHINGATE	55	HALTON MOOR	89	In LEEDS – CORN EXCHANGE
22	WILLOW ROAD	56	OSMONDTHORPE	90	In SWINEGATE
23	HYDE PARK	57	YORK ROAD	91	In WHINGATE JUNCTION
24	VICAR LANE	58	HEADINGLEY	92	In GIPTON
25	ROUNDHAY	59	KIRKSTALL	93	In SEACROFT NORTH PARKWAY
26	HAWKSWORTH	60	STANNINGLEY	94	In SEACROFT SOUTH PARKWAY
27	HORSFORTH	61	GREENTHORPE	95	In SEACROFT IRONWOOD VIEW
28	SANDFORD	62	BEESTON	96	In CITY SQUIARE
29	In BRAMLEY (BROAD LANE)	63	MIDDLETON	97	In SEACROFT GARAGE
30	RODLEY	64	BELLE ISLE	98	In TORRE ROAD GARAGE
31	LEEDS BUS STATION	65	WELLINGTON ROAD	99	In KIRKSTALL FORGE
32	NORTH LANE	66	In BRAMLEY TOWN END	100	In HUNSLET
33	DIB LANE	67	LEEDS	101	In SWINNOW
34	FOUNDRY LANE	68	MORLEY PROSPECT HOTEL		

NOTES

This is a Kelbus screen. In the case of destinations 13, 31,41, 68, 69, 70, 71, 93, 94 and 95 the last two words of the destination were positioned one over the other. All destinations were centralised and justified on the 34 in. wide screen.

TABLE 4 LEEDS CITY TRANSPORT   EXAMPLE OF BUS DESTINATION SCREEN   1968

Numbers are for reference only   In indicates a later insert. All destinations were centralised and justified on the screen.

NO.	DESTINATION	NO.	DESTINATION	NO.	DESTINATION
1	BRACKENWOOD	29	PUDSEY	56	ROUNDHAY ROAD
2	RING ROAD	30	OLD FARNLEY	57	OAKWOOD
3	TEMPLE NEWSAM	31	WHINGATE	58	EAST END PARK
4	LAWNSWOOD	32	HYDE PARK	59	HALTON MOOR
5	WEST PARK	33	VICAR LANE	60	YORK ROAD
6	HEADINGLEY	34	ROUNDHAY	61	HEADINGLEY
7	CITY SQUARE	35	HAWKSWORTH	62	KIRKSTALL
8	CORN EXCHANGE	36	HORSFORTH	63	STANNINGLEY
9	SWINEGATE	37	SANDFORD	64	GREENTHORPE
10	CROSS FLATTS PARK	38	BRAMLEY BROAD LANE	65	MIDDLETON
11	BEESTON	39	RODLEY	66	MOOR GRANGE
12	PRIMLEY PARK	40	OAKWOOD HOTEL	67	BELLE ISLE
13	ARMLEY	41	DIB LANE	68	WELLINGTON ROAD
14	LONG CAUSEWAY	42	FOUNDRY LANE	69	BRAMLEY TOWN END
15	NEW FARNLEY	43	SEACROFT	70	LEEDS
16	COOKRIDGE		MONKSWOOD GATE	71	MORLEY PROSPECT HOTEL
17	STAINBECK LANE	44	IRELAND WOOD	72	MORLEY FOUNTAIN INN
18	KING LANE CIRCUS	45	LEYSHOLME ESTATE	73	MORLEY FOUNTAIN STREET
19	ALWOODLEY	46	ELLAND ROAD	74	MORLEY TINGLEY MILL
20	MOORTOWN	47	HOLBECK MOOR	75	BRUNTCLIFFE
21	GLEDHOW	48	COTTINGLEY	76	BRADFORD
22	SHADWELL	49	BECKETT'S PARK	77	CROSS GATES
23	CENTRAL BUS STATION	50	TROYDALE	78	CENTRAL BUS STATION
24	WHITKIRK	51	WORTLEY	79	HALF MILE LANE
25	HALTON	52	MEANWOOD	80	TINSHILL
26	COLTON	53	HAREHILLS	81	KIRKSTALL FORGE
27	STANKS	54	LOWER WORTLEY	82	BURLEY MILLS
28	CARR MANOR	55	EASTGATE	83	COMPTON ROAD

84	SWARCLIFFE	92	CITY SQUARE	100	COPPER WORKS
85	INTAKE	93	NORTH LANE	101	BARNBOW
86	WHINGATE JUNCTION	94	HUNSLET	102	SEACROFT GARAGE
87	GIPTON	95	BRIGGATE	103	TORRE ROAD GARAGE
88	SEACROFT COAL ROAD	96	DEWSBURY ROAD	104	CIRCULAR
89	SEACROFT NORTH PARKWAY	97	CHAPELTOWN	105	PRIVATE
90	SEACROFT SOUTH PARKWAY	98	ALLERTON HIGH SCHOOL	106	In SWINNOW
91	SEACROFT IRONWOOD VIEW	99	HOSPITAL		

NOTES

This is a Norco screen. In the case of destinations 38, 43, 69, 71, 72, 73, 74, 88, 89. 90 and 91, the last two words of the destination were positioned one over the other. All destinations were centralised and justified on the screen. SWINNOW was added by L.C.T. after the main screen had been printed. There was a white space at the beginning and ends of screens. The screens were 34in. wide with lettering 4in. high.

TABLE 5 DESTINATIONS ADDED OR DELETED FROM THE EARLIER TYPE SCREENS 1953 TO 1966

New A.E.C. Regents of the 730-754 series were fitted with new destination screens and second hand route and number blinds in July 1954. The new screens included the destinations LEEDS-CORN EXCHANGE and BARNBOW and all the names as listed.

Older destination screens had the following order of names inserted at the end:

LEEDS BUS STATION; HALF MILE LANE; TINSHILL; BURLEY MILLS; COMPTON ROAD; LEEDS-ROCKINGHAM ST.; SWARCLIFFE, INTAKE and WORTLEY–NEW INN.

TINSHILL, BURLEY MILLS and COMPTON ROAD had been added at the ends of some destination screens in December 1953. HALF MILE LANE had been inserted on other screens in August 1953. Except for TINSHILL, these destinations were added in connection with tramway replacement. Some screens had LEEDS-MERRION ST. instead of LEEDS-ROCKINGHAM ST., but there is no record of the Merrion Street destination being displayed.

LEEDS-CORN EXCHANGE and SWINEGATE were added at the ends of some front and side screens in July 1955. The same destinations plus CROSS FLATTS PARK and BEESTON were added to the tops of some screens about October 1955. These destinations were all added in connection with tramway replacement.

LAWNSWOOD, WEST PARK, HEADINGLEY and LEEDS-CITY SQUARE were inserted at the top of destination screens in January 1956 in readiness for tramway replacement.

Added to the ends of the screens of several Leyland PD2 buses running from Bramley and Torre Road Garages were WHINGATE JUNCTION, GIPTON, SEACROFT NORTH , SEACROFT SOUTH SEACROFT IRONWOOD and PARKWAY PARKWAY VIEW CITY SQUARE. Many of these destinations were required for tramway replacements.

In June 1956 a number of new destinations were added including SEACROFT MONKSWOOD. This was a future terminus of GATE route 67, the destination SEACROFT becoming redundant. OAKWOOD HOTEL was added for use by duplicate vehicles on the 67 (Seacroft) and 68 (Foundry Lane) services. OAKWOOD was retained for use by buses short-working on service 38 (Moortown-Whitkirk). CHAPELTOWN, BRIGGATE, CRESCENT and DEWSBURY ROAD were tramway replacement destinations. ALLERTON HIGH SCHOOL, HOSPITAL, SEACROFT GARAGE and TORRE ROAD GARAGE were new "special" destinations.

In May 1957 KIRKSTALL FORGE was added to the No.1 destination screens to several buses and the following month to a new printing of the No.2 screens (by Kelbus) included this destination. CITY SQUARE and CORN EXCHANGE replaced LEEDS-CITY SQUARE and LEEDS-CORN EXCHANGE.

In December 1958 buses with No.2 blinds appeared with altered screens. The destination CRESCENT was replaced by CROSS FLATTS PARK. This insertion supplemented CROSS FLATTS PARK, which was already on the top end of the screen for short workings on route 1 (Lawnswood-Beeston). The names MIDDLETON and BELLE ISLE were also inserted at the lower end, supplementing similar destinations printed at the top of the screen.

In March 1959, in connection with tramway replacement, the destination HUNSLET was added to the No. 1 blinds of A.E.C. Regent III buses operating from Hunslet and Headingley Garages.

In October 1959, Leyland PD2/1 buses 340-359, allocated to Bramley Garage, were fitted with new No. 1 blinds, which differed from the normal blinds in several displays as follows:

WILLOW ROAD was omitted. MONKSWOOD GATE, TEMPLE NEWSAM, CROSS GATES, LEEDS BUS STATION (in place of CENTRAL BUS STATION) were added. The printing of LEEDS-CITY SQUARE, LEEDS-CORN EXCHANGE, LEEDS-ROCKINGHAM STREET and BRAMLEY TOWN END reverted to the earlier style. The name MONKSWOOD GATE replaced SEACROFT, which was omitted from these screens. TEMPLE NEWSAM was also added to the No. 2 blinds at this period.

In October 1960 RING ROAD was added to the destination screens of some buses to be used in connection with the new 9 service.

In November 1960 SEACROFT COAL ROAD was added to the No.2 blinds in readiness for an extension of service 16.

In March 1961 BRACKENWOOD was added to the No.1 type blinds in connection with an alteration of the 31 route. In May the destination was added to the No.2 blinds.

In June 1963 SWINNOW was added to certain screens allocated to Seacroft and Bramley Garages. This was in preparation for the proposed extension of Service 11 from Greenthorpe to Swinnow.

In May 1966 RAYNVILLE was added to the screens of the remaining Leyland PD2/1's of the 380-399 series in order that they could work on new service 40 from Bramley Depot.

TABLE 6 LEEDS CITY TRANSPORT EXAMPLE OF ALPHABETICAL BUS DESTINATION SCREEN 1963

Numbers are for reference only. All destinations were centralised and justified on the screen

NO.	DESTINATION	NO.	DESTINATION	NO.	DESTINATION
1	ALWOODLEY	37	HAREHILLS	73	RING ROAD
2	ARMLEY	38	HAWKSWORTH	74	RODLEY
3	BECKETTS PARK	39	HEADINGLEY	75	ROUNDHAY
4	BEESTON	40	HOLBECK MOOR	76	ROUNDHAY ROAD
5	BELLE ISLE	41	HORSFORTH	77	SANDFORD
6	BRACKENWOOD	42	HOSPITAL SPECIAL	78	SEACROFT TOWN CENTRE
7	BRADFORD	43	HUNSLET	79	SEACROFT COAL ROAD
8	BRAMLEY – BROAD LANE	44	HYDE PARK	80	SEACROFT L.C.T. GARAGE
9	BRAMLEY – TOWN END	45	INTAKE	81	SEACROFT – IRONWOOD V.
10	BRIGGATE	46	IRELAND WOOD	82	SEACROFT- MONKSWOOD
11	BRUNTCLIFFE	47	KING LANE CIRCUS	83	SEACROFT-NORTH P'WAY
12	BURLEY MILLS	48	KIRKSTALL	84	SEACROFT-SOUTH P'WAY
13	CARR MANOR	49	KIRKSTALL FORGE	85	SCHOOL SPECIAL
14	CENTRAL BUS STATION	50	LAWNSWOOD	86	SHADWELL
15	CHAPELTOWN	51	LEEDS	87	S.ACCOMMODATION RD.
16	CIRCULAR	52	LEYSHOLME ESTATE	88	STAINBECK LANE
17	CITY SQUARE	53	LONG CAUSEWAY	89	STANKS
18	COLTON	54	LOWER WORTLEY	90	STANNINGLEY
19	COMPTON ROAD	55	MEANWOOD	91	SWARCLIFFE
20	COOKRIDGE	56	MIDDLETON LCT GARAGE	92	SWINEGATE
21	CORN EXCHANGE	57	MIDDLETON	93	SWINNOW
22	COTTINGLEY	58	MOOR GRANGE	94	TEMPLE NEWSAM
23	CROSS FLATTS PARK	59	MOORTOWN	95	TINSHILL
24	CROSS GATES	60	MORLEY-FOUNTAIN	96	TORRE ROAD GARAGE
25	DEWSBURY ROAD	61	MORLEY-FOUNTAIN ST.	97	VICAR LANE
26	DIB LANE	62	MORLEY-PROSPECT	98	WELLINGTON ROAD
27	EAST END PARK	63	MORLEY-TINGLEY	99	WEST PARK
28	EASTGATE	64	NEW FARNLEY	100	WETHERBY ROAD
29	ELLAND ROAD	65	NORTH LANE	101	WHINGATE
30	FOUNDRY LANE	66	OAKWOOD	102	WHINGATE JUNCTION
31	GIPTON	67	OAKWOOD HOTEL	103	WHINMOOR
32	GLEDHOW	68	OLD FARNLEY	104	WHITKIRK
33	GREENTHORPE	69	PRIMLEY PARK	105	WORKS SPECIAL
34	HALF MILE LANE	70	PRIVATE	106	WORTLEY
35	HALTON	71	PUDSEY	107	YORK ROAD
36	HALTON MOOR	72	RAYNVILLE	108	CENTRAL BUS STATION

NOTES

These screens were of the type fitted to older vehicles in place of earlier screens. They were usually manufactured by Norco. There was a white space at the beginning and ends of screens.

TABLE 7 DESTINATIONS ADDED OR DELETED FROM THE ALPHABETICAL SCREENS 1963 TO 1974

In June 1963 SWINNOW was added to the screens.

In October 1965 six new destination names were added to the screens of many vehicles. Of these new names, only one was a replacement of an existing display, i.e. SEACROFT GARAGE. The six new names were:

MIDDLETON L.C.T. GARAGE   RAYNVILLE,   SEACROFT L.C.T. GARAGE   SEACROFT TOWN CENTRE   WETHERBY ROAD and WHINMOOR.

The new displays were for various service alterations due to take place in the near future. Services 11,15,16 and 45 were to be extended to the new Town Centre at Seacroft, while RAYNVILLE was for a new service on the western side of the city. WETHERBY ROAD was for a short working on Service 9, (Ring Road), while WHINMOOR was for a service into a new housing estate.

In connection with the takeover of the former Ledgard services, in October 1967 CALVERLEY and TROYDALE were added to the screens in their alphabetical position.

Route number 78 was added to the new screens in October 1967. The first buses to be so equipped were the smaller A.E.C. Regent V buses from 825 upwards allocated to Torre Road No.1 garage.

In March 1968 KING LANE, GARFORTH, KIPPAX and LEDSTON LUCK were added in their alphabetical position on certain blinds. KING LANE was for use on service 45 in place of CARR MANOR. The other destinations were for use on the former Kippax and District routes.

In April 1968 FARSLEY was added to the screens of certain buses in connection with the takeover of services from the Farsley Omnibus Company.

HORSFORTH FLEECE HOTEL & HORSFORTH OLD BALL INN were added to screens in October 1968 in connection with the linking of service 26 (Leeds-Horsforth) through to Swarcliffe.

In January 1969 BRADFORD ROAD was added to the destination screens of the single deck and certain double deck buses for use on service 9 (Ring Road).

In July 1969 three names were added to the destination blinds fitted to the A.E.C. Swifts numbered from 1001 upwards. These were: AUSTHORPE, BRAMLEY L.C.T. GARAGE   and SEACROFT LIMEWOOD APPROACH.

Names deleted from blinds in September 1969 were CARR MANOR, OAKWOOD HOTEL, SOUTH ACCOMMODATION ROAD and WHINGATE. In addition MORLEY–GLEN ESTATE and SEACROFT COAL ROAD were modified.

In June 1970 CROSS GREEN and SIGHTSEEING were added to the destination screens of the single deck buses. The former was to be the terminus of a new service 63 and the latter for the sightseeing tours operated by the Department.

In February 1971 SWILLINGTON was added to the screens. This was in preparation for a joint service with the West Riding Automobile Company.

In April 1972 the name HOLT PARK was added to the screens of buses allocated to Torre Road Garage. This was in preparation for the extension of service 1 from Lawnswood to the new estate.

In March 1973 the destination CAR PARK SERVICE was added to the screens of some of the A.E.C. Swift single deckers allocated to Sovereign Street Garage. These were for use on service 403 when the Swifts replaced the Mercedes Benz minibuses operating on the route from the Woodhouse Lane multi-storey car park to the city centre.

TABLE 8 LEEDS CITY TRANSPORT   TYPICAL BUS ROUTE/NUMBER SCREEN 1953

There were many variations at various times and those indicated are typical only. All screens were 34in. wide.

Destination	No.	Destination	No.	Destination	No.
White Space		HUNSLET HOLBECK ARMLEY	46	BRAMLEY STANNINGLEY	65
YORK ROAD OSMONDTHORPE	28	WHITEHALL ROAD RING ROAD	47	WELLINGTON ROAD OLDFIELD LANE	66
HOLBECK MOOR DOMESTIC STREET	29	MIDDLETON PARK RD. OLD LANE	48	HAREHILLS EASTERLY ROAD	67
RAYNVILLE ROAD BRAMLEY	30	ARMLEY WHINGATE JCTN.	49	HAREHILLS EASTERLY ROAD	68
CITY SQUARE WHITEHALL ROAD	31	BURLEY ROAD MORRIS LANE	50	SCOTT HALL ROAD KING LANE	69
WHITEHALL ROAD SWINNOW	32	BURLEY ROAD MORRIS LANE	51	SCOTT HALL ROAD KING LANE	70
HEADINGLEY OTLEY OLD ROAD	33	ELLAND ROAD CHURWELL	52	KIRKSTALL HORSFORTH RAWDON	71
SCOTT HALL ROAD HARROGATE ROAD KING LANE	34	ELLAND ROAD CHURWELL	53	BRAMLEY STANNINGLEY LAISTERDYKE	72
SCOTT HALL ROAD KING LANE HARROGATE ROAD	35	STANNINGLEY RD. BRAMLEY	54	HEADINGLEY WEETWOOD	73
HAREHILLS OAKWOOD	36	DEWSBURY ROAD MORLEY	55	BURLEY ROAD CITY SQUARE JACK LANE	74
SCOTT HALL ROAD MOORTOWN	37	UNIVERSITY ROAD VICTORIA ROAD	56	BURLEY ROAD CARDIGAN ROAD	75
OAKWOOD FOUNDRY LANE	38	BELLE VUE ROAD WOODHOUSE STREET	57	BURLEY ROAD CARDIGAN ROAD	76
YORK ROAD HALTON	39	BELLE VUE ROAD WOODHOUSE STREET	58	BURLEY ROAD KIRKSTALL	77
HALTON CROSS GATES	40	WOODHOUSE STREET BELLE VUE ROAD	59	BECKETT STREET COLDCOTES	78
HALTON WHITKIRK	41	WOODHOUSE STREET MOUNT PRESTON	60	BECKETT STREET COLDCOTES	79
BECKETT STREET CITY SQUARE WELLINGTON ROAD	42	EAST END PARK HUDSON ROAD BLACKMAN LANE	61	SPECIAL	
SCOTT HALL ROAD MEANWOOD	43	BLACKMAN LANE HUDSON ROAD EAST END PARK	62	DUPLICATE	
CHAPEL TOWN HEADINGLEY KIRKSTALL	44	YORK ROAD S.ACCOMMODATION RD. HUNSLET ROAD	63	White Space	
MEANWOOD HEADINGLEY KIRKSTALL	45	HUNSLET ROAD S. ACCOMMODATION RD. YORK ROAD	64		

TABLE 9 SUBSEQUENT ALTERATIONS TO ROUTE/NUMBER SCREENS FROM 1953 TO 1961

ALL SCREENS WERE 34 IN. WIDE

KIRKSTALL HEADINGLEY — 73

Route 30 discontinued, new 73 service. Greenthorpe-Long Causeway, from 22 March 1953.

ARMLEY ROAD STANNINGLEY RD. — 14

Replacement of tram service 14 from Corn Exchange-Half Mile Lane. Addition to screen in use from 4 October 1953.

HEADINGLEY WEST PARK — 30

Route/number blind introduced 10 January 1954 for new bus route to Ireland Wood.

COMPTON ROAD HEADROW KIRKSTALL ROAD — 4

Replacement of tram services 4 and 10. Addition to top of screen in use from 4 April 1954.

INTAKE BURLEY ROAD KIRKSTALL — 23

SWARCLIFFE YORK ROAD CROSSGATES — 24

YORK ROAD CROSSGATES — 40

New routes 23 intake and 24 Swarcliffe opened 19 September 1954 showed above displays. From same date, route 40 Stanks display modified.

COMPTON ROAD COLDCOTES — 78

COMPTON ROAD COLDCOTES — 79

[blank] — 11

Route indication for 78 and 79 services from 11 March 1955. 11 blank shown for Gipton tram route conversion.

SHEEPSCAR CORN EXCHANGE MEADOW LANE — 8

HOLBECK MOOR BEESTON — 29

HAREHILLS CORN EXCHANGE WHITEHALL ROAD — 31

SHEEPSCAR CORN EXCHANGE ELLAND ROAD — 52

SHEEPSCAR CORN EXCHANGE ELLAND ROAD — 53

The conversion of tram routes 6 and 8 to bus operation on 25 June 1955 resulted in many route changes. Bus routes 36 and 48 were discontinued, 29, 31, 52 and 53 extended and a new route 8 opened with the corresponding.

MEADOW LANE — 5

From 18 November 1955 the 5 Beeston tram service was discontinued, and buses displayed the above. MEADOW ROAD replaced MEADOW LANE on some screens in January 1956.

WOODHOUSE LANE CITY SQUARE MEADOW ROAD — 1

The abandonment of tram service 1 on 3 March 1956 resulted in the appearance of the above bus display. From June 1956 new screens showed HYDE PARK, CITY SQUARE and MEADOW ROAD.

YORK ROAD CITY SQUARE WELLINGTON ROAD — 11

COMPTON ROAD CITY SQUARE WELLINGTON ROAD — 15

COMPTON ROAD CITY SQUARE WELLINGTON ROAD — 16

BECKETT STREET CITY SQUARE WELLINGTON ROAD — 66

From 21 July 1956 routes 78 and 79 were withdrawn. 11 was a route extension and replacement for the blank 11. 15 and 16, were for buses replacing trams on the Tong Road services. 66 was a more accurate route description.

HEADINGLEY WEST PARK — 36

New service introduced 12 August 1956 from Rockingham Street Bus Station to Tinshill.

MEANWOOD CITY SQUARE SWINNOW — 32

From 7 July 1957 services 32 and 43 were discontinued and replaced by a new 32 service from Carr Manor to Pudsey.

CHAPEL TOWN ROAD CORN EXCHANGE MEADOW LANE — 2

Display for replacement of the 2 and 9 tram services Moortown-Dewsbury Road from 29 September 1957.

YORK ROAD CITY SQUARE STANNINGLEY ROAD — 54

From 29 December 1957 services 28 and 54 were discontinued and a new service, Rodley-Halton Moor started.

MEADOW LANE LEEDS BRIDGE CHAPELTOWN ROAD — 2

Altered from 10 December 1958 on buses with No.2 screens.

MEADOW LANE BRIGGATE CHAPEL TOWN ROAD — 2 CIRC

ROUNDHAY ROAD BRIGGATE BELLE ISLE — 3

BELLE ISLE BRIGGATE ROUNDHAY ROAD — 3 CIRC

ROUNDHAY ROAD BRIGGATE HUNSLET ROAD — 6

MEADOW LANE DEWSBURY ROAD — 12

MEADOW LANE **DEWSBURY ROAD**	**12** **CIRC**

Rearrangement of bus routes following replacement of tram routes 3, 12, 26 and 27 from 29 March 1959.

BURLEY ROAD **CITY SQUARE** **HUNSLET ROAD**	**7**

Replacement of Hunslet tram service from 19th April 1959 by new bus service from Hunslet-North Lane, Headingley.

YORK ROAD **CITY SQUARE** **KIRKSTALL ROAD**	**4**

YORK ROAD **CITY SQUARE** **STANNINGLEY ROAD**	**14**

YORK ROAD **HALTON**	**22**

STONEY ROCK LANE **HEADROW** **BURLEY ROAD**	**50**

STONEY ROCK LANE **HEADROW** **BURLEY ROAD**	**77**

Rearrangement of routes following the final tramway abandonment on 7 November 1959. Route 51 abandoned. 22 was replacement of tram route 22 to Tempe Newsam. Other were extensions/alterations to existing services.

WOODHOUSE LANE **VICTORIA ROAD**	**56**

Added to destination screens. April 1960 for pending closure of University Road. University Road finally closed to buses on 16 February 1962.

HORSFORTH **WEST PARK** **MOORTOWN**	**9**

Display for new Ring Road service introduced 30 October 1960.

HEADINGLEY **WEST PARK**	**33**

Revised display on new destination screens fitted to certain A.E.C. Regents of the "MUG" "NNW" and "WUA" series of buses in November 1961. Last modification to old screens.

TABLE 10
SPECIAL SCREENS
A.E.C. Reliance Coach 10
The new A.E.C. Reliance coach, No.10 (ANW 710C), in 1965 had its own special blind and it displayed the following:

White space
CITY TOUR
LEEDS CITY TRANSPORT
SIGHTSEEING TOUR No.1
SIGHTSEEING TOUR No.2
SIGHTSEEING TOUR No.3
SIGHTSEEING TOUR No.4
SIGHTSEEING TOUR No.5
SIGHTSEEING TOUR No.6
White space

Mercedes Benz Minibuses
Destination blinds on the Mercedes Benz minbuses, 30-35, displayed.

White space
CENTRAL BUS STATION
CITY STATION
HOSPITAL SPECIAL
NIGHT SERVICE
PRIVATE
SCHOOL SPECIAL
401 SHOPPERS SERVICE
SIGHTSEEING
WORKS SPECIAL
White space

The opening of the 403 service from Woodhouse Lane Car Park to the city centre on Monday, 4 October 1971, resulted in **403 CAR PARK SERVICE** being added to the blinds of these buses.

From 9 September 1972 the minibuses ceased to run through the shopping area and the 401 SHOPPERS SERVICE destination became redundant. Instead buses displayed 401 CITY STATION or 401 CENTRAL BUS STATION as appropriate.

LEYLAND LEOPARDS
The new Leyland Leopard coaches, 20-22, introduced in the summer of 1973, had digital three-track number indicators, each blind carrying the numbers 0 – 9, along with the letters C, I and R. Destinations on the blind were:

PRIVATE
FASTAWAY
ON HIRE
SIGHTSEEING
ON TOUR
LOTHERTON HALL
THRUSCROSS

Leyland National 1301
1301 appeared in February 1974 and it was found that the normal 38in. wide destinations would not fit. A special 31in. wide blind was provided. The blind was unusual in that it was very short and covered the names required for working from Sovereign Street Garage only. The destinations were as follows:

white space
CITY SQUARE
CROSS CREEN
ELLAND ROAD
FASTAWAY
GARFORTH
HEADINGLEY
HOLBECK MOOR
KIPPAX
LEEDS
PRIVATE
SCHOOL SPECIAL
TOUR
VICAR LANE
WORKS SPECIAL
white space

TABLE 11 THREE TRACK DIGITAL NUMBER BLINDS

0	0	0
1	1	1
2	2	2
3	3	3
4	4	4
5	5	5
6	6	6
7	7	7
8	8	8
9	9	9

Although steam powered barges are not strictly within the remit of the Leeds Transport Historical Society, the writer could not resist including this superb atmospheric view of Leeds Bridge. On the bridge can be seen two open top B.T/H. trams of the 133-182 series built in 1899. The factory chimney is adjacent to the site of what was later to become the Tramways Department Sovereign Street Permanent Way Yard. The date of the photograph – about 1904. *W. & T.Gaines/L.T.H.S.*

Addenda to Volumes 1 to 3

Many readers have kindly written with comments about the three volumes published by the Leeds Transport Historical Society. This has applied particularly to Volume 3, which is within the living memory of some readers. The Society is very grateful to those who have been kindly pointed out any errors and provided additional information. Some photographs, new to the L.T.H.S., have also been generously provided and some of these are reproduced.

VOLUME 1

Page 5 "Woodpecker" coach and Headingley omnibus.

Information supplied by the Far Headingley Village Society, and further research by the L.T.H.S. has found that in addition to James Sykes' "Woodpecker", Wortley, Bramley and Pudsey coach, in 1818, a daily service was also provided by an "accommodation coach" from Leeds to other surrounding villages. It is the earliest known attempt to run a local passenger transport service in Leeds. The stage coach was operated by a William Aveson, who ran daily services from the White Cross Inn, Leeds, to and from Chapel Allerton, Potternewton and Kirkstall. His coach began running on Monday, 18 May 1818, the 'Leeds Intelligencer' commenting that the "fashionable villages adjacent to Leeds, it seems, are about to have a regular daily stage at stated hours, quite on the London plan." The service was not, however, successful and after three months ceased operation, Aveson stating that his coach would operate "as orders may suit". This appears to have been his only attempt to run a local transport service in Leeds. Aveson was not new to coaching and in 1817 had run a coach from the White Cross Inn to London via Sheffield, in opposition to other coaches. This coach was called the "Royal Alexander", but was short lived and may have been the vehicle that was used in Leeds.

Aveson had started as a waiter at the Bull and Mouth Hotel in Briggate and took over as landlord at the White Cross (opposite the Hotel in Briggate) in April 1813.

Sykes' "Woodpecker" coach, also introduced in 1818, was similarly short lived. There were some wealthy residents in the villages served, but not enough it appears to support a regular coach service. Stage coach travel was expensive and beyond the means of the average citizen who thought nothing of a two to five miles walk from his village home to Leeds.

On 18 July 1838, a month after the institution of John Wood's omnibus from Leeds to Headingley, he appeared at the Court House, Leeds, prosecuted for forcibly throwing a difficult customer off his bus. The customer, a merchant named C.S. Jackson objected to the seat he considered his own, being occupied by someone else. Wood was supported by many passengers and won his case. Thus was established the rule in bus travel – first come, first served.

Pages 1 to 5 Early cars and buses.

A 'Directory of Stage Coach Services, 1836' has been found. It was compiled by an Alan Bates and published in New York in 1969. Written in long hand it lists all the stage coach services in England in 1836. It is interesting that Mr. Bates has found some records of H.M. Commissioners for the Affairs of Stamps and Taxes, which licensed the stage coaches and early buses. These are supposed to have been destroyed by fire in the 1870's, but it appears that copies of some of the documents exist in the U.S.A. He lists the local services in Leeds. The number shown is the licence plate that was fixed to the coach and the other numbers represent the seating capacity of the vehicle. For

example, 8429 (4-8), referring to E. Boynes' stage coach, which ran from Leeds to Yeadon, the 8429 was the licence number of the coach, 4 represented the number of inside passengers and 8 the maximum number of outside passengers that could be carried. The 1836 list is as follows:

Leeds and Bramley   4 miles.
J. Shires, 8397 (5-4), two return journeys Tuesday and Saturday.
Leeds and Guiseley 9 miles.
J. Smith, 8399 (6- -), one return journey Tuesday and Saturday.
Leeds and Kirkstall 2¹/₂ miles,
J. Dawkes. 8395 (6- -), four return journeys Tuesday, five return journeys Saturday.
R. Johnson. 8392 (6- -), four return journeys Tuesday, six return journeys Saturday.
Leeds and Railway Depot 1 mile.
J. Atkinson & Co. 8432 (12 - -) three return journeys Monday to Saturday, one return journey on Sunday.
Leeds and Thorp Arch 12 miles.
W. Adkin, 8398 (6-3) one return journey Tuesday, Thursday and Saturday.
Leeds and Yeadon 8 miles.
E. Boyne, 8429 (4-8) one return journey Tuesday and Saturday.

The Directory does not distinguish between stage coaches, cars and buses, but it would appear that the Guiseley and Kirkstall vehicles were six-seat cars and Atkinson's Railway bus had 12 seats. The other vehicles seem to have been conventional stage coaches. There is no mention of Isaac Morley's stage coach to Bramley or the cars which John Cockhill ran to Kirkstall. It seems that Robert Johnson was running cars to Kirkstall as early as

Thanks to Dr. Andrew Turton, great great grandson of William Turton, Chairman of the Leeds Tramways Company, we are able to include a portrait of Turton at the height of his success. Turton was born in Leeds on 2 January 1825 and died aged 76 on 6 August 1900.
Dr. A. Turton.

1836 and may have been the first operator on this route. In 1830 he was listed in Parson and Whites' Directory as having "gigs and horses" at Green Parrot Yard, Mill Hill, Leeds. By 1843 Johnson's vehicle was referred to as a bus.

From 1830-1839 Edward Boyne ran a seasonal stage coach service from Leeds to Ilkley on a new turnpike road which ran from Kirkstall via Horsforth, Rawdon, Yeadon and Guiseley to Otley. The Kirkstall-Otley turnpike road had opened in January 1828. The Leeds-Yeadon coach, which ran for an unknown period appears to have been a short working of this service.

The L.T.H.S. has rechecked the 'Leeds Mercury', 'Leeds Intelligencer' and local directories for the period and can find no mention of Messrs. Shires, Smith, or Dawkes.

Although Bates' Directory lists all the coaches, (by licence number - not name), which ran from Leeds, it makes no reference to the summer seasonal coaches, which ran to such places as Scarborough, Bridlington, Whitby, Redcar, Ilkley etc.

Pages 91-102 Roundhay Electric Tramway.

An article appeared in The Electrical Engineer' for 6 November 1891 and described the opening of the tramway. It gives little additional information, but states that the engineer in charge of the Generating Station was a J.W.Watkins and J.J.McMahon was the assistant superintendent of the line and foreman linesman. Many

dignatories were present at the opening of the line and it is interesting that William Turton, the Chairman of the Leeds Tramways Company, was not present.

Page 206 Tramcar renumbering.

A photograph of Starbuck single deck horse car 12 in rebuilt form has been found. The photograph was taken about October 1899 at the Oak Inn, Headingley, shortly before electrification. It shows that not all the cars scheduled to be renumbered in March 1897 had received their new numbers by 1899. Car 12 was to have been renumbered 80.

VOLUME 2

Page 283 Photograph of car 276.

John G. Kaye of Epsom, Surrey, has an original of this photograph and states that it was taken by W. Taylor, a local Bramley photographer. Mr. Taylor took a similar view of the same car, 276, in Town Street at Bramley Town End.

Page 366-70 Ryknield Buses.

Geoff Lumb has done extensive research into the 'Commercial Motor' and 'Motor Traction' for the years 1905-6. These throw a different and more favourable light on the Ryknield buses than recorded in the local Leeds press and City Council records.

At first known as the Ryknield Engine Co. Ltd. in

Most photographs taken of trams at the Roundhay, Horse Shoe Corner terminus, later known as Oakwood, are close ups. This interesting view shows the background. Wetherby Road is on the left and the road leading up the hill is Horse Shoe Lane. The building on the right behind the trees is the Roundhay Post Office. It is currently an estate agent's office. Local directories show that Horse Shoe Lane was renamed Oakwood Lane in 1895-7 and at the same time a street of houses known as Oakwood Avenue was built. The developer named his property after a nearby house called "Oakwood". This house was occupied by the Hudson family who owned a considerable amount of land in the area. "Horse Shoe Corner" was probably considered "down market" and it appears that the district was renamed from these tiny beginnings. It seems it took some time for the name "Oakwood" to be generally accepted for, from about 1902, Leeds Corporation trams showed "GLEDHOW LANE" on their destination indicators followed by "OAKWOOD" at a later date. The house originally known as "Oakwood" still exists, but is currently "Sabourn Court", a nursing home. This photograph of the Roundhay Electric car was taken about 1894. *L.T.H.S.*

Thanks to L.N. Ball and Brian Pickup for sending this superb photograph.   A man with a begging bowl stands in hope as a fully laden Milnes horse tram drawn by three horses and a trace horse struggle up Woodhouse Lane. The setting is Blenheim Chapel (currently offices) at Blackman Lane and the date is about 1898.   A tramcar of this type (number 107) is at present being restored by the Leeds Transport Historical Society.
L.N.Ball / L.T.H.S.

December 1905 it went into voluntary liquidation and the business was taken over by a new company called the Ryknield Motor Company of Burton-on-Trent.

The 'Commercial Motor" reported that tests on the first Ryknield bus were completed on Wednesday 19 October 1905 and the bus was dispatched to Leeds on 14 November, The second bus completed its tests at Burton on 14 December 1905 and was sent to Leeds on 20 January 1906. This latter date is rather later than indicated in other contemporary accounts.

…."its climbing capacity was shown on some hills of 1 in 10, which it negotiated with the greatest ease. The engine gives out 35 h.p. at 850 revolutions per minute, the cylinders are cast separately and a special feature is made of the accessibility of both the inlet and exhaust valves, The patent spring drive seems particularly efficient, and its shock absorbing qualities were noticeable when stopping or starting the chassis."

'Commercial Motor', 21 December 1905.

'Motor Traction' published an article on the buses. It described the Ryknield bus as a "handsome, well-proportioned vehicle, having accommodation for fourteen inside and twenty four out, excluding the 'box' seat.

…."The interior is very effectively designed, the oak woodwork with maple panels and roof having a light and

artistic appearance. The semi-spiral stairway, which gives easy access to the roof, is an improvement on the stairways found on many buses.   The battery for supplying illuminating power to the five 5 c.p. incandescent lamps which light the interior and the one 5 c.p. electric lamp fixed on the roof, together with the headlamps, is placed at the rear end of the under carriage, its 16 cells being sufficient for supplying the eight 30-volt lamps for 12 hours."

Motor Traction, 15 February 1906, page 146.

It was stated that the transmission drive was by internal spur gearing direct to the rear road wheels, the driving pinions being mounted on the end of a differential shaft, carried on the triangular underframe. The LCT engineer in charge of the buses was a Mr. Ellison who had previously been a foreman for Ryknield in its erecting and fitting shops.

'Motor Traction" quoting the 'Armley & Wortley News', of 27 April 1906, described a journey on the new route from Lower Wortley to Farnley Moor Top in which a journey with a full complement of 38 passengers was achieved in 14 minutes. There was a glowing report of a ride up Reservoir Hill from Headingley to West Park with 60 passengers. Reference was made to the Aster vehicle U 325, which was said to have a 30 cwt chassis, a 12 h.p. two cylinder Aster engine and travelled 9 miles per gallon of fuel. Transmission was of the Panhard type and the vehicle had 20 seats.

On 9 August 1906 Ryknield tested a new 40 h.p. double deck bus in Leeds. It was built for the Silsden Motor Bus Company Ltd. and ran from the Queen's Hotel in City Square via Boar Lane, Briggate, North Street, Chapeltown Road, Harehills Avenue, Roundhay Road, North Street and Vicar Lane back to the Hotel. The bus also made a trip to Otley and several of the passengers "expressed themselves surprised and delighted with the running of the vehicle."

Dougill's Enginering Ltd. of Great George Street, Leeds, complained about Ellison's association with Ryknield and on the invitation of Farnley residents, on 29 September 1906 ran a charabanc with 23 passengers from Lower Wortley to Farnley in 12 minutes. It passed the Corporation bus broken down on the way.

Page 507 Burrows' service.

R. Wills of Barnsley confirms that Burrows' buses were of course extended to Rawmarsh via Wentworth and Greaseborough and not Wentbridge.

Page 586 Model of Car 232.

W. Mark Lloyd of Liverpool has found the patent for the top cover on car 232. It was to the design of W. Yates and was registered as patent number 22,682 at the Patents Office on 26 September 1904. It appears in the Abridgments Register for Class 118 (Railway and Tramway Vehicles). William Yates & Son were painters and paper hangers at 45 Burmantofts Street, Leeds.

Page 699 Tramways staff outing.

Jamie Guest confirms that the photograph is taken in Settle Market Place.

Page 707 1d. Park and 3½d. Workmen's Return.

The letters DEHLN at the top of these tickets are "day" letters. The ticket was valid on one day only and the conductor punched the relevant letter.

20,682 Yates, W. Sept. 26

Tramcars; bodies; covers for exposed seats; windows; ventilating. - The upper-deck seats of a tramcar are enclosed by a fixed arched framework A provided with end domes B, the openings in the roof being fitted with revolving shutters C. The side openings are fitted with adjustable plane windows D and curved windows E which are balanced and hung on guide-rollers. Suitable ventilators may be placed in or over the side windows and in the top of the cover.

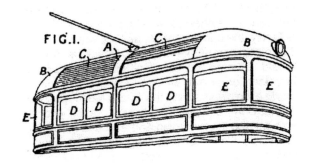

The patent for Yates' top cover 1904.

This picture postcard shows Brush car 31 in Headingley Lane about 1903. The tram pole on the right has a white painted section, which indicates that it was used as a tram stop. Vitreous enamel stop signs were introduced in 1905. The photograph also shows that in 1903-4 there was a crossover in this part of Headingley Lane. The cyclist is using the smoothest part of the road – the space between the tram rails.   *H.Graham Glen, Wortley.*

This fine view of B.T-H car 175 was sent to the L.T.H.S. by David Bates of Rangiora, New Zealand. It shows his grandfather, Frank Thornton, - later a Chief Inspector - standing alongside the car. The location is Headingley terminus and the date about 1904. Frank Thornton joined the Tramways Department in 1898 working on the steam trams. He retired in 1945. *D.Bates.*

VOLUME 3

Page 756 Museum Terrace loop.

Eric Bryan states that the photograph is taken at Granville Place, the "penny stage" a few streets nearer to the city centre than Museum Terrace.

Page 761 Illustration of car 400.

It should have been noted in the caption to the illustration that Darby's Advertising Agency Ltd. were the advertising contractors for the Leeds Tramways and Transport Department from 1 January 1925 to 1 January 1970. Car 400 was one of the most distinctive of the Leeds trams and according to notes made by the late Phillip R. Brown it had the Darby's advertisement from 1925 until the middle 'thirties. From 1927, Dick,Kerr car 232 displayed the advertisement until the car was withdrawn in 1930. The late Donald Wilson recalled the Horsfield car of the same number, 232, having the overall advertisement throughout the 'thirties. Chamberlain car 119 had one side panel displaying the same advertisement in the late 1920s. From 1897 to the end of 1924 the advertising contractor had been James W. Courtenay Ltd.

Page 772 Morley bus stop.

John Kaye correctly points out that the Morley bus stop in Duncan Street remained in this position until 25 June 1955 when the Meanwood and Elland Road tram service was converted to bus operation.

Page 786 Photograph of car 116.

The photograph of car 116 in Boar Lane was taken on 24 November 1936.

Page 813 Photograph of car 193.

Several readers have correctly pointed out that the photograph of 193 is taken at the Wykebeck Arms, Halton Hill, not at Middleton. The photograph was taken on 3 September 1947 when a party of Dutch people visited Leeds. Their trip was organised by Bertrand Mather, and 193, newly repainted, took the visitors from Sovereign Street to Kirkstall Road Works and then to Temple Newsam. The party later rode on a Middleton bogie to Middleton.

Pages 835 and 923. Rebbla and Biddell.

Brian Render points out that the correct spelling of the surnames of these two gentlemen was Rebla and Bedell. Mr. Bedell was Chief Draughtsman at the Swinegate Head Office and Brian's boss from 1943 to 1946 when Bedell moved to Huddersfield. Rebla died in 1955.

Page 848. Photograph of car 272.

Many readers have pointed out that 272 is, of course, leaving West Park for Lawnswood.

Page 858 Photograph of bus 125

Henry Heyworth points out that the photograph of Dennis Lance 125 is taken in Queenswood Drive and the driver is the late Laurie Houghton, who was latterly at Torre Road Garage.

This postcard dating from about May 1905, shows ex-trailer car 129 at Meanwood terminus. The Beckett's Arms on the left was removed in 1938 to make way for a new public house of the same name. (see page 1414 which shows the replacement building). Of the five ex-trailers, 128-132, photographs of all have been found in open top condition and running on the Meanwood-Elland Road service. It must be assumed that these cars were "regulars" on this route during the first decade of the 20th century. *Phototype Company.*

Leeds-built car 362 in Chapeltown Road about 1925. The spur into Harehills Avenue, used by cars short working to Reginald Terrace, is in the right foreground. *Holmes, Chapeltown.*

Thanks to detailed notes on tramway rolling stock made by the late Philip Brown in the 1920's this photograph can be dated almost to the day.   The clue is the paper notice on the dash which is advertising the cricket Test Match at Headingley, which was held from 12 to 14 July 1924. The match was between England and South Africa and England won.   The location is Street Lane at Moortown Corner and passengers are boarding Leeds-built car 116. *W. Taylor, Moortown.*

Page 864 Photograph of bus crash, Armley.

David Watson of Armley points out that the photograph of Guy Arab 37 is taken in Stocks Hill, Armley, (between Wesley Road and Chapel Lane) at the premises of Mosley and Richmond, printers.

Page 868 Maudslay 10.

Location is Donisthorpe Street Depot Yard.

Page 888 Torre Road Depot.

The photograph of buses outside Torre Road Depot was taken on 26 April 1937.

Page 892 Lord Ashfield.

Lord Ashcroft should read Lord Ashfield.

Page 893 Caption for illustration of bus 49 etc.

John Kaye points out that Putney and Ponders End were two separate garages several miles apart. Ponders End is correctly named Enfield Garage from which garage route 107 ran. Putney is in south west London and had no connection with route 107. It is assumed that the bus was transferred between the two garages.

Page 901 Learner bus 44.

Henry Heyworth states that the bus is not undergoing a tilt test. It is probably being lowered into an overturned position to practice recovery using the then newly acquired A.E.C. Matador MUB 647. Note the coverings on the floor and wooden beams below the upper saloon windows.

Page 908 Leeds buses on loan to London.

John Kaye also points out that in the P.S.V. Circle publication L50 it is stated that the Leeds Regents were returned in late June and early July 1950. There is also photographic evidence showing some of them working the

Morden Station-Epsom Race Course Special service, which operated on Derby Day, 7 June 1950. In London, from November 1949 to July 1950, they were worked from Bromley depot on routes 61 and 138. It is not known where they were garaged from September to November 1949.

Page 912 Bus 644.

Henry Heyworth points out that bus 644 is passing what was the gardener's cottage on the Newton Green Hall Estate. His late mother, Florence Tingle, sister of Harry Tingle, driver of bus 27 on the enthusiast's tour pictured on page 907, was born in the cottage.

Page 923 S.G. Baldwin

Mr. Baldwin was the Foreman at Torre Road Depot in 1942.

Page 933 Note AB Car 348.

The lower saloon of car 348, (in very poor condition) was still in Dudley Hill Railway Station Yard in use as a hen hut in April 1967. The other lower saloon bodies had disappeared by this date.

Pages 961 to 975 Middleton bogies and Lance Corporals.

John D. Markham of Stockport has been researching tramcar regenerative control and has made some interesting comments.

Car 255 was initially fitted with four motor equipment, comprising four MV109CZ motors and two OK42B camshaft type direct controllers. It was demonstrated to the press and entered service in this form. The MV109CZ motor was an MV109Z rewound with compound fields for regeneration. Whilst mechanically similar, armature and field windings were different. CZ machines had a fourth interpole. MV109Z motors were used on the second batch of London HR/2 cars, 101-159 which did not have trolleys, and were the axle hung version of the MV109 motors used on the first batch of HR/2s, 1853-1903.

John was interested in the re-motoring of 255 in 1952 (see pages 966 and 968). He does not think that the car could have been fitted with G.E.C. WT28MS motors as these were designed for two motor equipments, not four, and were unlikely to fit in 255's bogies. According to Metropolitan Vickers data sheets which John has, the four MV109GZ motors ordered by Leeds in 1951 were specifically for a "prototype single deck car" i.e. car 601.

He offered an intriguing alternative possibility. As Victor Matterface, the tramway rolling stock engineer, was ex-London Transport he would be aware that some of the HR/2's were fitted with MV109Z series motors with axle suspension. John thinks it "perfectly feasible" that the four MV109CZ regenerative motors from 255 were removed, dispatched to London, and "surreptitiously" exchanged for four good series wound MV109Z's taken from an HR/2 car destined for scrap. The copper value would be 34 lbs in London's favour. It could well explain Matterface's reluctance to reveal what type of motors were fitted to 255 in its latter days. Such an exchange could have been through an "Old Boy" network and not documented. The return transport to and from Leeds would be at Leeds' expense, but would probably cost less than re-working the regenerative motors to become series machines.

John states that after conversion the resistance notching for 255 was different to the other Middleton bogie cars - a hand written note on a print of the original schematic diagram says this - and suggests a motor characteristic different to that of the G.E.C. motors on the main batch of Middleton bogie cars.

Page 973 Reseating of cars 272-274.

Eric T. Smith recalls that Mr. Matterface told him that the replacement seats on cars 272-274 were purchased second hand from Bradford Corporation. This is also confirmed in a note, which appeared in the 'Modern Tramway' in April 1949, describing the reseating of car 273.

Pages 976 and 977. Car 104/275.

Eric Smith points out that this car had a small step from the platform into the lower saloon. The step was painted white. It was said that passengers on the 14 route were used to this feature and that this was the reason 275 continued to be used on this route after the tram was transferred to Swinegate Depot in 1948. The step was later removed by the substitution of a gentle slope from the platform. Car 276 had a similar slope from the platform to the saloon.

A contradiction has occurred in the notes on the livery of this car. On its 1-2-1948 repaint it is stated to be without lining whereas the photograph on page 978 shows it with lining. Other later photographs show the lining missing and it assumed that this was removed when the car was re-varnished in May 1949.

Page 984 Caption Barnet.

Barnett should of course read Barnet.

Page 1008. Illustration of car 446.

Colin Wright of Halifax says that the "not known" gentleman, second from the left is the late Maurice Peck who lived near Pudsey Lane End in the 1950s. This, however, is disputed by Stanley King, who knew Maurice personally. Just visible, standing inside the car at the bottom of the staircase, is the late Bob Parr. The 14 years old boys looking out of the window in the upper saloon

Chamberlain car 109 at Cardigan Road terminus about 1928. It is showing the early (1926-9) route number 6 BALM ROAD. *Lilywhite Ltd.*

No. 583, (London 2160), was one of the three Felthams in Leeds which did not have a panel added with ventilation slots for the resistances to left of the lower saloon windows. Compare with the photograph of car 531 on page 1029 of Volume 3. Car 583 is seen here at Halton on 17 February 1955. *Author.*

have been identified. In the middle is Eric T. Smith of the L.T.H.S. and underneath Robert W. Phizackerley who later went to work for British Railways.

Page 1018 Car 473.

Henry Heyworth states that the driver of 473 when it fell into the pit at Swinegate Depot was the late Walter Dunderdale. "The idiot got sacked for re-selling used tickets."

Page 1022 Ex-Hull car 463.

The late Bob Mack photographed this tram in Wellington Street on Friday, 5 August 1949. The car was burned on the following Monday and the 5th must therefore have been 463's last day in service. Ex-Hull cars very rarely ran on Sundays and on Saturdays were used mainly on special duties – football specials etc.

Pages 1025 to 1037 The Felthams.

Colin Withey of Croydon, Surrey, has done research into the Felthams in London and makes a number of interesting points.

In London, seating was provided for 22 passengers only in the lower saloon. In Leeds the seating capacity was increased to 28 by allowing people to sit on the upholstered tops of each of the two sand boxes. For safety reasons this was not permitted in London.

The last Feltham constructed, entered service in June 1931.

In 1947 the L.P.T.B. discontinued the use of the front exit door except for driver use and emergencies. In Leeds it was used for perambulators and large items of luggage. In 1948 the L.T.E. fitted quick air release valves after requests from the Telford Avenue depot staff. An interesting point made by Mr. Withey is that in 1933 to 1934 there were problems with over heating of the resistances and Victor Matterface, (later the Leeds Tramways Rolling Stock Engineer), arranged for a duct to be provided with an external grille positioned on the wide panel at the left hand side of the lower saloon windows. The grille had five slots. Five trams, 2082, 2137, 2160, 2162 and 2163 did not have the grille. Of these, three, 2082 (Leeds 504), 2137 (Leeds 559) and 2160 (Leeds 583), came to Leeds. An illustration is shown of car 583 with the grille omitted. The drawing on page 1037, copied from original L.P.T.B. drawings, shows the grille on the wrong side of the panel. The "Corgi" models of these cars, presumably taken from the same drawings, also have the grille on the wrong side!

On page 1036 describing the liveries, Mr. Withey states that 2099, painted in Livery A, was in London Transport red and cream. Off white referred to the Underground livery. In Leeds the lower saloon panel with ventilation grille (see above) was painted grey whereas in London it was cream. In Leeds the roof was grey; in London Feltham roofs were painted black and there were other minor differences.

It should be noted that 509 (see below), which at first had white window frames in Leeds, also had the grille panel painted grey.

With regard to Livery J it should have read that the beading *under* the lower saloon windows was painted red instead of black. See the photograph of car 529 on page 1033 which is newly repainted in Livery J. Compare with 503 on page 1032 which is in Livery H.

Pages 1029 and 1140. Car 509.

Eric Smith recalls that on one of his visits to Kirkstall Road Works, Mr. Matterface told him that car 2078 (Leeds 509) had been recently repainted in London and that it was intended to simply repaint in red the side panel bearing the London Transport insignia and paint a white band on the dashes. This would account for the odd livery of the car.

Page 1038 507 accident at Oakwood.

Several readers have pointed out that the person talking to Mr. Matterface is an inspector. Looking at the camera is the tram driver, Basil Norris, who, with the conductor, was dismissed after the accident.

Page 1061 Parcels Van.

The photograph of Leonard Bowman with the parcels van was taken in March 1941.

Page 1106 Night Bus Tickets 1937.

John Kaye states that he has one of the special machines that were used to print the night bus tickets. He believes that there were 12 machines altogether of which his bears the number 7. He says that the machine carries on its left hand side the legend "Siemens Brothers London - AUTOWAYBIL - Patent applied for". On the top face of the machine are windows for "Class", "Stage", "Fare", "Tickets" and "Receipts" together with a sliding control for Journey In/Out direction and a cancellor for return tickets. A black knob, on the end of a rotating arm, on the right hand side sets the fare and issues the ticket whilst also on the right are controls to set the class and fare stage, the latter having a flat to indicate when the stage is set correctly since one complete rotation indexes the stage number by one. Also on the right, is a knob with felt pad attached to enable re-inking of the chamber feeding the printing plate. The printing plate has provision for the insertion of a small plate giving the service number of the bus, The date e.g. 22JA,

or 22 January, was set by means of three rotating dials within the printing plate. These were probably adjusted by traffic staff before the machine was issued to the conductor. Access was gained through a hinged cover which was also used to retain the roll of blank paper.

The machine was fitted on a back plate with a leather backing and was housed in a metal box (8 in. wide x 6 in. deep x 7 1/2 in. high) with brackets to retain the machine. There was a hinged lid and space for spare ticket rolls in the box. The machine weighed about 3 lbs and machine and box just under 7 lbs. It also acted as an early adding machine as the receipts were counted in 1/2d. units.

The ticket produced was the same width as a "T.I.M." ticket (1 1/2 in.) and just under 3 1/2 in. long.

Pages 1124-1127 A.E.C. Regent engines.

Phillip Groves of East Sussex has been researching pre-war A.E.C. Regents built between 1936 and 1942. He states that the Leeds CNW, DUB, FNW, GUA and HUM registered batches all had preselector gear boxes, but the engine types were a bit varied in the buses as built new. The CNW had the A171N 7·58 litre engine. (Coventry used to call this engine the "Light 6" in Daimler COA6's). The DUB all had A171 engines, A171F in some, A171N in others and A171R in the remainder. The A171N and A171R were described as having "Comet" cylinder heads. The FNW had the A171RB engine with a Comet 3" head which was probably the smoothest of all the indirect injection six-cylinder engines produced by A.E.C. and made its debut in 1937. The GUA had the version referred to as A171XB. Finally the HUM had the direct injection A173T unit, which A.E.C. had introduced quietly in 1936 and announced as a standard in early 1939. Many A171 engines were converted to the A173 type from 1939 onwards; Coventry for example converted all its A171 to A173 between 1939 and 1947 and Nottingham carried out a big programme during the same period.

Thanks to John Kaye for forwarding this view of pre-war A.E.C. Regent 172 (AUM 415) in London in 1949.
J.Kaye.

At the request of Harold Pullan and others interior views of Middleton bogies are included. This view shows the upper saloon of car 269 on 9 August 1956. *A.D.Packer.*

The interior of the lower saloon of Middleton bogie 268 photographed on 27 September 1956.
M.J.O'Connor/National Tramway Museum.

At the request of a number of readers we have included a few additional views of tramcars in the blue livery including this, the only known colour photograph of an ex-Manchester Pilcher car in the 1948 Matterface light blue livery. It had white window frames and silver roof.   The colour scheme looked smart when the tram was newly repainted, but soon, as in this photograph, looked shabby.   No. 285 is at Hunslet terminus and the date is 2 August 1952. *Author.*

A line of Chamberlain cars, in various blue and red liveries, on the Low Fields Road Football siding on 11 April 1953. 45 was one of the few cars with E.M.B. Pivotal trucks to receive single blind destination indicators. *Author.*

Chamberlain car 13 on its E.M.B. Pivotal truck was never repainted in the red livery. It was still in the pre-1948 princess blue livery when scrapped. The location is Low Fields Road Permanent Way Yard and the date 20 June 1953. Both 13 and 41, behind, were burned on 24 June. *Author.*

Pages 1144 to 1148 and 1152. Liveries.

A close examination of many photographs has shown that all cars in the lined out Matterface liveries of 1948 to 1952 appear to have had cavetto corners to the lining. Ovolo corners ceased in June 1948. See page 1166 for a detail of the cavetto corners (car 397) and page 1101 (car 32) for the ovolo corners.

Page 1157 Pre-war buses in green livery.

Omitted in error from the list of pre-war buses repainted in green were the TS8, 19-26, and bus 290.

Page 1178 and 1179 Destinations etc.

Eric Smith points out that cars running from 5 BEESTON to 3 HAREHILLS showed VIA CORN EXCHANGE.

Page 1183 Upper Wortley Road Tramway.

A photograph has been found that shows that when trams ran to Upper Wortley Road in the 1901-1903 period they showed OLDFIELD LANE on the destination indicator.

Page 1184 Caption to upper illustration.

The trailer attached to engine number 13 was built by the Milnes Company, not the Ashbury Company.

As a tribute to the late Donald Wilson we have included some of his fine black and white tramway photographs taken in the 1940's. Donald took this view of ex-Hull car 452 on the Easterly Road spur, Harehills, on 12 June 1946. It is the only known photograph of this particular tram. *W.D.Wilson/L.T.H.S.*

Donald Wilson took some excellent views of open balcony car 309 on its tour of the city on 8 May 1949. This photograph was taken in New Market Street with Horsfield car 188 bound for Elland Road. The driver and conductor of 188 are admiring 309, which looked splendid in its 1912 livery. *W.D.Wilson/L.T.H.S.*

This view of Leeds built Chamberlain car 444 was taken at Whingate Junction on 14 March 1945 just before the end of World War II. The car has the war time white band on the dash and headlamp masks. *W.D.Wilson/L.T.H.S.*

Photographs of Middleton bogie 262 in its pre-1948 condition are not common. This view was taken on a dull day at Middleton terminus on 24 February 1946. The car is in need of an urgent repaint. *W.D.Wilson/L.T.H.S.*

The first illustration in this Volume was a view of one of the most numerous trams in the Leeds fleet, a Chamberlain car, and the last illustration is also a Chamberlain. No. 75 is in the royal blue livery of 1949-50 and is loading in Call Lane at the Corn Exchange on 1 May 1953. *Author.*